Designing Publi

The third edition of this highly regarded book provides a concise and accessible introduction to the principles and elements of policy design in contemporary governance. It examines in detail the range of substantive and procedural policy instruments that together comprise the toolbox from which governments choose tools to resolve policy problems and the principles and practices that lead to their use.

Guiding readers through the study of the many different kinds of instruments used by governments in carrying out their tasks, adapting to, and altering, their environments, this book:

- Considers the principles and practices behind the selection and use of specific types of instruments in contemporary government and arrangements of policy tools, especially procedural tools and policy portfolios.
- Evaluates in detail the merits, demerits, and rationales for the use of specific organization, regulatory, financial, and information-based tools and the trends visible in their use.
- Examines key issues, such as policy success and failure, and the role of design in it; policy volatility and risk management through policy design; how behavioural research can contribute to better policy designs; and the 'micro' calibrations of policies and their importance in designs and outcomes.
- Addresses the issues not only surrounding individual tools but also concerning the evolution and development of instrument mixes, their relationship to policy styles, and the challenges involved in their (re)design, as well as the distinction between design and 'non-design'.

Providing a comprehensive overview of this essential component of modern governance and featuring helpful definitions of key concepts and further reading, this book is essential reading for all students of public policy, administration, and management.

Michael Howlett is Burnaby Mountain Professor and Canada Research Chair (Tier 1) in the Department of Political Science at Simon Fraser University specializing in public policy analysis, political economy, and resource and environmental policy.

Routledge Textbooks in Policy Studies

This series provides high-quality textbooks and teaching materials for upper-level courses on all aspects of public policy as well as policy analysis, design, practice and evaluation. Each text is authored or edited by a leading scholar in the field and aims both to survey established areas and present the latest thinking on emerging topics.

Designing Public Policies

Principles and Instruments

Third Edition

Michael Howlett

Routledge
Taylor & Francis Group

LONDON AND NEW YORK

Designed cover image: Erfun Ghodoosi/Unsplash

First published 2024
by Routledge
4 Park Square, Milton Park, Abingdon, Oxon OX14 4RN

and by Routledge
605 Third Avenue, New York, NY 10158

Routledge is an imprint of the Taylor & Francis Group, an informa business

British Library Cataloguing-in-Publication Data
A catalogue record for this book is available from the British Library

Library of Congress Cataloging-in-Publication Data
Names: Howlett, Michael, author.
Title: Designing public policies : principles and instruments /
    Michael Howlett.
Description: 3rd edition. | Abingdon, Oxon ; New York, NY : Routledge,
    2024. | Includes bibliographical references and index. | Summary:
    "Providing a comprehensive overview of this essential component of
    modern governance and featuring helpful definitions of key concepts and
    further reading, this book is essential reading for all students of public
    policy, administration and management"—Provided by publisher.
Identifiers: LCCN 2023030779 (print) | LCCN 2023030780 (ebook) |
    ISBN 9781032380902 (hardback) | ISBN 9781003343431 (ebook)
Subjects: LCSH: Policy sciences. | Political planning.
Classification: LCC JF1525.P6 H69 2024 (print) | LCC JF1525.P6 (ebook) |
    DDC 320.6—dc23/eng/20230815
LC record available at https://lccn.loc.gov/2023030779
LC ebook record available at https://lccn.loc.gov/2023030780

ISBN: 978-1-032-38090-2 (hbk)
ISBN: 978-1-032-38086-5 (pbk)
ISBN: 978-1-003-34343-1 (ebk)

DOI: 10.4324/9781003343431

Typeset in Sabon
by Apex CoVantage, LLC

The first and most elementary principle of this science is that a committee is organic rather than mechanical in its nature; it is not a structure but a plant. It takes root and grows, it flowers, wilts, and dies, scattering the seed from which other committees will bloom in their turn. Only those who bear this principle in mind can make real headway in understanding the structure and history of modern government.

C. Northcote Parkinson
Parkinson's *Law or the Pursuit of Progress* (1957)

Contents

Figures

Tables

Preface

This book introduces students to the principles and elements of policy design in contemporary governance. It does so through the detailed study of the instruments used by governments in carrying out their tasks in adapting to and altering their environments and of the processes in government which lead to tool selection and enactment. These tools form the basic foundations or structures upon which all policies and programmes rest. An essential component of modern governance, the range of substantive and procedural policy instruments together comprises the toolbox from which governments select specific tools expected to resolve particular kinds of policy problems. The book begins with a discussion of several aspects of instrument use in contemporary government linked to factors such as the rise of globalization and the increasingly networked nature of modern society. It then moves on to consider the principles behind the selection and use of specific types of instruments in the process of policy formulation. The merits, demerits, and rationales for the use of specific organization, regulatory, financial, and information-based tools and the trends visible in their use are set out in separate sections of the book along with the problems faced in their use and design due to factors such as uncertainty, non-compliance, and maliciousness. Finally, by way of conclusion, the issue of how best to design policy programmes is addressed alongside a discussion of the future research agenda of studies of policy design.

Acknowledgements

The book could not have been written without the pioneering work of the many, many scholars who individually and collectively have spent a great deal of time and effort developing the empirical cases and carefully building the many frameworks and models used throughout the text. Many colleagues have also more directly helped contribute to the ideas, models, and concepts found in the book. They include M. Ramesh, Richard Simeon, Ishani Mukherjee, G. Bruce Doern, Luc Bernier, Giliberto Capano, Jeremy Rayner, Ben Cashore, Scott Fritzen, Adam Wellstead, Pearl Eliadis, Rejean Landry, Tony Zito, Margaret Hill, Azad Singh Bali, Evert Lindquist, Anthony Perl, Wu Xun, JJ Woo, Jale Tosun, Allan McConnell, Jenny Lewis, Lester Salamon, Mark Considine, Mike Mintrom, Guy Peters, Pablo del Rio, Andrea Migone, Brian Head, Kent Weaver, Moshe Maor, Robert Hoppe, Martijn van der Steen, Laurent Dobuzinskis, Andy Jordan, Achim Kemmerling, Namrata Chindarkar, Josh Newman, Sreeja Nair, Peter May, Daniel Béland, Claire Dunlop, Eric Montpetit, Ed Araral, Don Low, Caner Bakir, Anka Kekez, Jae Moon, Hans de Bruijn, Mark Considine, Christine Rothmayr-Allison, Frederic Varone, Ciqi Mei, Arno Simons, Jan-Peter Voss, Meng Hsuan Chou, Jonathan Craft, Nina Belyaeva, Dmitry Zatysev, Adam Graycar, Arnost Vesely, Thurid Hustedt, Marleen Brans, Iris Geva-May, Darryl Jarvis, Adam Wellstead, Tim LeGrand, Kidjie Saguin, Ishani Mukherjee, Araz Taeihagh, Altaf Virani, Nihit Goyal, Kerem Coban, Ching Leong, Caner Bakir, and the participants in a variety of workshops and students in many classes held in North America, Europe, Asia, and Australia over the years where papers on aspects of policy design and instrument choice were delivered and critiqued. A special debt is owed to Rebecca Raglon for her patience, support, and encouragement. Thank you all for your ideas and inspiration.

Part I

INTRODUCTION: POLICY DESIGN AND GOVERNANCE IN THE MODERN STATE

Chapter 1

Understanding the role of policy design in contemporary policy-making

Transforming policy ambitions into practice is a complex process. Historically, many attempts of policy-makers to address policy problems and maintain political order have failed due to efforts which have not adequately incorporated this complexity into policy formulation, leading to poor decisions and difficult or ineffective implementation (Howlett 2012; Cohn 2004). These experiences have led to a greater awareness of the various obstacles that can present themselves to effective policy designs and have gradually fuelled better understandings of the unique characteristics of policy processes and the design spaces in which policy formulation efforts are embedded (Peters et al. 2018; Siddiki 2020).

Policy design is itself a complex subject, however. It is not synonymous with *policy-making* but rather is one type of such activity that entails the conscious and deliberate effort to define policy aims and map them instrumentally to policy tools expected to achieve those goals (Majone 1975; May 2003; Gilabert and Lawford-Smith 2012). In this sense, policy design signifies a particular type of policy formulation that involves activities such as collecting knowledge about policy instrument content and use and the impact such instrument use has upon policy target behaviour and policy outcomes. It involves analyzing its relevance, and creating and implementing policy alternatives meant to attain specific policy goals and aspirations (Weaver 2009b, 2010a; Bobrow and Dryzek 1987; Bobrow 2006; Montpetit 2003c).

In Davis Bobrow's (2006) apt phrase, policy design is 'ubiquitous, necessary and difficult' but surprisingly little studied and understood (Junginger 2013). Until recently, it received some treatment in the existing policy literature, but not as much, or in as much detail, as many other subjects in the field (May 1981, 1991, 2003; Weimer 1992a, 1992b; Bobrow 2006). Within the policy sciences, it has appeared as part of studies of policy implementation

DOI: 10.4324/9781003343431-2

3

and policy instruments (May 2003), of those into policy ideas and policy formulation (Linder and Peters 1990c, 1990d; James and Jorgensen 2009), and has been a large, if typically implicit, part of the study of governance and 'meta-governance' (Meuleman 2009, 2010b). More recently, it has been linked to efforts at 'co-design' and the emergence of policy labs specifically aimed at improving public service delivery and outcomes and to the application of the tenets and processes of 'design-thinking' – borrowed from the design sciences and product development – to policy-making (Bason 2014; Blomkamp 2018). In all these cases, however, this has typically been done without the benefit of clear and systematic analysis of how policies and governance arrangements fit together and without systematic attention being paid to such basic elements as the definition of key terms, the question of agency, the nature of policy tools or levers and the mechanisms which make them 'work', or the articulation of standard concepts and principles needed to denote, and create, superior policy designs and design processes.

The academic inquiry of policy design – that is, self-consciously dealing with both policy processes and substance under an instrumental rubric – has undergone several bouts of attention and subsequent decline. It emerged and flourished briefly throughout the 1970s and 1980s (e.g. see Salamon 1981, 1989, 2002c), although studies of policy designs had been undertaken since at least the 1950s (Tinbergen 1952; Dahl and Lindblom 1953; Kirschen et al. 1964). It then declined again until re-emerging in the first decade of the new millenium.

The origins of policy design studies in the sense used in this book, in fact, can be traced to the very roots of the policy sciences, which espoused the overall idea of achieving better outcomes through the organized application of knowledge to policy-making, especially, but not limited to, formulation and the improved crafting and evaluation of policy alternatives (Wildavsky 1979; May 2003; Mintrom 2007).

Most early studies focused on policy tools and had a strong focus on improving policy implementation outcomes and processes, paying less attention to the development of policy options and the formulation issues which are the hallmark of current policy studies within a design orientation (Hood 1986c; Hood and Margetts 2007). In the Lasswellian foundations of the policy sciences, for example, a distinction between processes of formulation and implementation was drawn in order to emphasize the significance of policy instruments and features of instrument choice to both activities, but mainly the latter (Lasswell 1954).

Of course, not all past work on policy design restricted itself to only considerations of policy formulation and implementation. Larger issues about feedback processes from instrument choices to the politics of policy formation, as well as work on network governance (see Lascoumes and Le Galès 2007; de Bruijn and ten Heuvelhof 1997), examined many broader design issues linked to agenda-setting and decision-making, among others, such as how design issues emerged in policy deliberations, how choices were made among alternatives, and how the results of such efforts could be monitored and evaluated.

These activities all remain part of contemporary policy design studies, and are the subjects of the latter's concern for detailing the nuances involved in understanding and activating mechanisms to meet policy goals. And they also form the background in which the many considerations which exist around ensuring the political as well as technical feasibility and acceptability of policy design choices and selections are included in design deliberations.

For the first generation of policy design studies that arose in this work, the historical and institutional contexts within which these activities took place were considered to significantly affect both the content and activities of design and designing (Torgerson 1985, 1990; Clemens and Cook 1999). Changes in designs were thus often understood as resulting from broader changes to the existing fabric of policy institutions within which existing policy designs and design activity were embedded. In this way of thinking, as policy conditions altered and evolved, so would the considerations for the arrangements of policy means considered by policy actors engaged in formulation activity to be feasible or realistic. These actors, in turn, were thought to be themselves impacted by evolving ideas and logics of appropriateness which promoted particular designs congruent with dominant and relatively long-lasting sets of ideas, or 'paradigms', which set out common understandings of the nature and roots of policy problems and their likely means of redress (March and Olsen 2004; Goldmann 2005; Howlett 2011; Hogan and Howlett 2015).

This 'reactive' orientation toward formulation propagated a critique of early efforts toward 'design thinking' on the part of many policy and organization studies scholars. They emphasized the highly contingent processes of formulation followed in many instances and the limits – from limited time available for research or deliberation to concerns about the electoral or legislative and other concerns of political actors – which they argued often prevented the kinds of careful analysis of knowledge and the practices of informed deliberation needed for effective policy design activity (Cohen et al. 1979; Dryzek 1983; Kingdon 1984). Some scholars, for example, were sceptical as to whether, given these dynamics, policy could ever actually be designed in the calm and detached ways that other scholars suggested should and could occur (Lindblom 1959; Dryzek and Ripley 1988; Linder and Peters 1990a; deLeon 1988).

This is a view still held by some (Eijlander 2005; Franchino and Hoyland 2009). It harkens back to post-WWII criticisms of overly ambitious planning efforts in many countries and sectors (Lindblom 1959; Simon 1957) which led to reflections on the nature of the bounded rationality of political actors and the tendencies of policy-makers to trend toward incrementalism or only marginal adjustments of existing policies (see Baumgartner and Jones 1991, 2002a; Howlett and Migone 2011).

This critique suggests that at best only a very limited ambit exists to the extent to which policy design is possible and promotes the view that many, if not most, policy efforts occur in a 'non-design' direction. That is, one in which the formulation process is highly contingent on current events, highly partisan, and conflict-riddled and subject to unpredictable time, bargaining, and other negotiative dynamics rather than calm identification and utilization of knowledge in the public interest (Howlett and Mukherjee 2014, 2018).

Many other observers, however, have challenged what they feel is an overemphasis in this critique on unpredictable contextuality and the significance and appearance of less than rational behaviour on the part of policy-makers in the pursuit of their goals. Following the lead of Linder and Peters in a series of articles published in the late 1980s and early 1990s, a revitalized discipline argued that despite these concerns, designs could still be formulated as 'ideal-types', that is, of arrangements of policy elements more or less independent of temporal contexts, and thus could be prepared in advance of particular problems emerging on legislative and executive agendas. They argued such activity was common among such groups as think tanks and academics, as well as government ministries, which then adapted these 'ideal' designs to circumstances as needed when the opportunity arose. In this view, they argued, policies could be designed in much the same manner as buildings in which plans are often developed in the abstract and then adapted to fit building sites, the financial constraints on owners, building codes and zoning rules, to name only a few of the contextual realities of the construction industry (Linder and Peters 1984, 1988, 1990b, 1991; Schön 1988, 1992).

This approach allows policy designs to be differentiated in theory from the overall processes of policy-making and in practice from specific activities around policy formulation and implementation which might undermine or fail to reflect a 'design orientation'. And it facilitated the development of a such an orientation (Schön 1988, 1992) within the policy sciences as well as a proliferation of possible alternative designs and options.

Of course, it is immediately clear from even brief anecdotal observation, let alone the many comments on policy-making in the popular media and elsewhere, that both designed and non-designed policies exist and that some policies are well-designed while others poorly so. That is, in many instances of policy-making, prominent political or personal interests are featured, where whatever 'designs' are put in place are much less than evidence-driven or ideal efforts serving the public interest. This includes a variety of contexts in which policy formulators or decision-makers engage in not very well thought out trade-offs or logrolling between different values or resource uses, often in response to concerns about legislative expediency and timetables, which often result in *ad hoc* and loosely cobbled-together policy elements and instruments which can only vaguely be considered a design. And it also in many cases features less-than-ideal efforts on 'the dark side' of policy-making, involving activities such as such as corruption or maliciousness, where policies are designed for more nefarious ends than public value (Howlett 2022; Howlett and Leong 2022b).

Both these latter processes and situations can be called *non-design* ones, for lack of a better term. They are situations in which policy formulation is driven neither by instrumental knowledge-driven problem-solving nor often even by any effort to deal with pressing socio-political concerns. Rather, policies can emerge, for example, when policy-makers engage in venal or corrupt behaviour in which personal gain from a decision may trump other evaluative and decision-making criteria. Policy measures that serve symbolic, rather than practical, technical, or political, purposes, for example, are often produced in such situations and are often poorly integrated and flimsily constructed (Williams et al. 2020); the hallmark of 'non-design' outcomes and instrument choices (Howlett and Mukherjee 2017).

This logic contrasting policy design and non-design now dominates current thinking on policy design and designs. In the contemporary literature, policies are now treated as complex entities – policy mixes – composed of multiple elements, some of which may have emerged in a largely *ad hoc* way, while others may have been formulated with more care given to evidence and logics of causes and effects.

Accepting this reality, current studies in the field now focus both upon improving the logic and effectiveness of designs themselves and also upon better understanding the processes of policy advice and formulation which lead to both the adoption and subsequent alteration of certain kinds of designs rather than others (van der Heijden 2011; Thelen 2003; Howlett 2014a, 2004b; Craft and Howlett 2012; Howlett et al. 2015, Howlett and Lejano 2013; Jordan et al. 2013). The expectation in the field is that the superiority of the designs over the non-designs in terms of effectiveness – being able to generate popular support and actually fix or resolve public problems – means the general trend over time is for the advance of designed elements over non-design ones. This can occur either in the initial stages of policy adoption or over time as packages of policy tools are refined and altered in a process sometimes referred to as '*policy patching*' (Howlett and Mukherjee 2017a), removing some of their ineffective or contradictory or sub-optimal parts and enhancing the ability of the package as a whole to meet government aims in a relatively efficient manner. All of these subjects are addressed in the chapters which follow.

Foundational concepts: the tools orientation in policy studies

In the field of policy studies, work on policy design is inextricably linked to the subject of policy tools. This has been the case historically and in contemporary policy studies, and the study of policy 'design' remains closely associated with the analysis of the policy instruments which comprise a design (May 2003). Their implementation and the study of the effect of policy advice and ideas on tool selection in the process of policy formation remain key focii of studies of policy designs (and non-designs) (Linder and Peters 1990a, 1990c; Howlett et al. 2009).

Policies in this view are understood as having a *substantive* element that comprises the technical arrangements of alternatives that can potentially resolve the policy problem at hand – and a *procedural* component that entails all the processes and activities necessary to coordinate the activities of policy actors in charge of formulating, making decisions, and administering those alternatives (Howlett 2011).

These two aspects of policies have not always received equal treatment from students of the subject, however. Policy design studies in the 1980s, for example, shifted from the study of the procedures and practices of 'designing' to the study of the substance of 'designs' themselves, with a specific focus on better understanding how individual implementation-related policy tools and instruments, such as taxes and subsidies or regulation and public ownership, operated in theory and practice and lost or ignored their focus on policy processes (Sterner 2003; Woodside 1986; Mayntz 1983).

This 'substantive' orientation nevertheless marked the beginning of modern studies of policy tools and sparked interest in a range of related subjects over the next several decades, with policy scholars turning their attention to the description and classification of alternative instruments and the factors which conditioned their effective use and deployment (Mayntz 1979; O'Toole 2000; Goggin et al. 1990). This included their role in the study of implementation failures, the conditions of policy success, and the linkages connecting the two (McConnell 2010).

At this time, some scholars, like Bardach (1980) and Salamon (1981), went so far as to argue that the orthodox definition of *policy* in terms of efforts to resolve 'issues' or 'problems' originally made by foundational scholars like Lasswell at the outset of the policy studies movement (Mintrom 2007) was misguided and that *policy* should instead be, and have been, defined in terms of the 'tools' used to give policies effect. They advocated shifting the focus of policy studies away from the analysis of the impact of ideas, actors, and institutions on policy-making and instead squarely oriented toward the study of the design and operation of policy tools in both theory and practice (Howlett 2000c).

These students of public policy-making were joined in this effort by economists and legal scholars who already worked on the content and quality of policy outputs and tool choices in areas such as fiscal and monetary policy-making and on the role played by tools such as law, regulation, and legislation affecting policy content and outcomes (Stokey and Zeckhauser 1978; Bobrow and Dryzek 1987; Keyes 1996). Studies in management and administration sought to better explore the linkages between politics, administration, and implementation in the effort to better understand trends in policy tool choices and their patterns of use, such as movements at the time of governments away from regulation toward de-regulation or from the creation of public enterprises to their privatization (Lowi 1966, 1972, 1985; Trebilcock and Hartle 1982; Howlett and Ramesh 1993). New trends, such as advances in thinking around governance or the relationships existing between governments and their publics advocated the enhanced use of network management and non-governmental tools in areas such as environmental regulation, among others, and generated much interest in the field (Peters and Pierre 1998).

By the early 1980s, the tools literature had incorporated the insights of these efforts to constitute a distinct policy design orientation and began to emerge as a body of literature in its own right (Salamon 1981). Students of policy tools consequently embarked upon theory building and testing, developing more and better typologies of policy instruments in order to aid the conceptualization of the instruments available to governments, seeking to better specify tool similarities and differences, and attempting to provide a greater understanding of the motivations and reasons underlying their use in practice as well as in theory (Salamon 1981; Tupper and Doern 1981; Hood 1986c; Bressers and Honigh 1986; Bressers and Klok 1988; Trebilcock and Hartle 1982).

This literature sparked interest in a range of related subject areas from policy history to regulatory studies, and other scholarly work during this period served to further elucidate the nature and use of specific kinds of policy instruments tools. This included study of the origins and types of 'command-and-control', and of the emergence of other kinds of regulations and financial inducements, such as tax incentives and tax expenditures (Landry et al. 1998; Tupper and Doern 1981; Hood 1986c; Vedung 1998; Howlett 1991).

In general, it was believed that a greater understanding of implementation instruments and the reasons underlying instrument choice would benefit policy-making both as a practice and as a theoretical body of knowledge, contributing to better policy designs and more positive policy outcomes (Woodside 1986; Linder and Peters 1984; Mayntz 1983). Studies and practices at that time in new areas of government activity, such as pollution prevention, for example, benefited from advances in the systematic study of policy instruments which influenced the design and creation of new market-based tools, such as pollution credits and emissions trading systems, which joined the older state-based, standard-setting kinds of regulation then typically deployed in these and other fields (Hippes 1988; Trebilcock and Prichard 1983).

While most work focused on tool design, constructivist and behavioural perspectives were also brought to bear on the formulation processes involved in policy designing, most prominently in Schneider and Ingram's (1990a, 1990b, 1994) studies of the impact of policy-maker conceptions of policy target motivations and behaviour on policy tool choices. These studies highlighted the manner in which policy-maker and public opinions and views of the behaviour and worthiness of specific sections of the public affected the range and type of services social groups were provided and how they were treated in their provision. This work provided a deeper understanding of the social and behavioural factors underpinning the use and consideration of specific kinds of policy designs in practice. Subsequent contributions by these authors as well as others working in a similar vein further advanced the study of the behavioural aspects of design *processes* as a needed complement to studies of the substantive components of policy designs (Ingram and Schneider 1990; Schneider and Ingram 1997; Mondou and Montpetit 2010; Timmermans et al. 1998; Hood 2007a).

In a very important development in the late 1990s, some scholars began to progress from the study of single tools and design choices to the analysis of the design and operation of more complex multi-tool 'policy mixes' (Grabosky 1994; Gunningham et al. 1998; Howlett 2004b). This work on the origins, nature, and content of policy portfolios further advanced the understanding of the theory and practice of policy designs. It more closely approximated the situation of design-in-practice encountered by policy-makers on the ground who rarely faced situations which featured dichotomous choices between single instruments or instrument types.

The contemporary design orientation in the policy sciences: policy design as a field of study

The contemporary design orientation in policy studies has built on this work. It calls for the continued broadening of thinking about policy design beyond individual policy tool choices, examining combinations of substantive and procedural instruments and their interactions in complex policy mixes (Bali et al. 2022). It also involves the study of both substantive policy tools directed at altering the behaviour of targeted groups and individuals as well as procedural tools, such as interest group funding or freedom of information legislation directed at altering the nature of policy processes themselves (Bali et al. 2021). So in doing, it continued expanding design studies well beyond implementation while continuing to focus more detailed study into the actual formulation processes involved in tool and design choices as these occur and evolve over time (Linder and Peters 1990d; Schneider and Ingram 1997; Considine 2012).

These studies have obvious theoretical and practical consequences for making and understanding public policies (Braathen and Croci 2005; Braathen 2007a; Grant 2010; Skodvin et al. 2010). Environmental and energy policy-making, for example (Jordan et al. 2013), have both featured the continued development and application of 'design thinking' around areas such as emissions trading systems and sustainability transitions and led to the development of new approaches to questions surrounding key contemporary issues, such as climate change (van Buuren et al. 2020).

As work on the substantive aspects of policy designs has continued, work on the procedural components has also moved forward. That is, equally importantly as a field of study, rather than be confined within the technical and capacity restrictions of their policy area, policy designers are now urged to 'be familiar not only with the technical aspects of the menu of instruments before them, but also with the nature of the governance and policy contexts in which they are working' (Howlett 2013) and how those contexts affect policy design choices, and vice versa.

As May (2003: 226) has argued, this involves treating design not simply as a technical activity of finding the best design but as a process involving channelling the energies of disparate actors toward agreement in working toward similar goals and as a field of study in its own right. That is, one which views policy design as a field of inquiry centred on the observation of activity conducted by a number of policy actors in the hope of improving policy-making and policy outcomes through the accurate anticipation of the consequences of government actions (Tinbergen 1958, 1967; Schön 1992).

While somewhat similar to other fields of study, such as planning and strategic management, policy design is less technocratic in nature than these other efforts at 'scientific' government and administration (Forester 1989; Voss et al. 2009). However, it, too, is oriented toward avoiding many of the inefficiencies and inadequacies apparent in other, less-knowledge-informed ways of formulating policy, such as pure political bargaining, ad hocism, or trial and error decision-making (Bobrow 2006).

This kind of *design-centred* policy inquiry is situated firmly in the 'rational' tradition of policy studies, one aimed at improving policy outcomes through the application of policy-relevant and policy-specific knowledge to policy-making processes. More specifically, it involves an effort at crafting alternative possible courses of action intended to address social, political, economic, and other kinds of policy problems based on experience with, and knowledge of, the kinds of policy tools available to governments in their effort to resolve problems (Cahill and Overman 1990; Bobrow 2006; Peters 2018).

In general, though, it is less comprehensive than planning in developing specific possible alternative courses of action rather than fully detailed 'plans', and acknowledges the uncertainty of the future and the contingent nature of policy outcomes (Voss et al. 2009). It is more open than other fields like strategic management to the idea that there are alternative sources of knowledge and design criteria than those residing in, or proposed by, experts (Fischer and Forester 1987; May 1991).

Of course, as noted earlier, many policy scholars interested in policy-making have argued for decades that in many instances, processes of policy formulation are governed less by concerns about the efficiency and effectiveness of state action than by political, religious, ideological, and self-interested considerations. However, proponents of policy design argue the policies which emerge from these processes commonly lack evidence and rigour and often fail to address the root causes of problems. The design orientation thus urges policy-makers to think more systematically and analytically about their situations, options, and alternatives before acting and to marshal as much evidence and knowledge as possible about the policy aim, target behaviour, and policy tools proposed to be deployed before taking action (Bobrow and Dryzek 1987; Bobrow 2006).

Of course, policy outputs may not always be problem-centred, although even partisan, electoral, or legislative *politics-centred* policy formulation can retain a design component, in the instrumental sense of the term, when its purpose is to deliberately choose instruments and design programmes which advance the interest of powerful stakeholders rather than to solve policy problems (Colebatch 2018; Turnbull 2017). This is something that occurs very often in 'clientelistic' regimes, for example, where a major criterion for tool selection and programme design is the delivery of benefits to supporters of current incumbents (Manor 2013; Gans-Morse et al. 2014). But whether it is problem- or politics-centred, design-oriented policy-making differs from other kinds in that it involves the deliberate and conscious attempt to define policy goals and connect them to instruments or tools expected to realize those objectives in a logical and informed way.

Policy design, in this sense, can thus be seen as a specific form of policy formulation based on the gathering and application of knowledge of the effects of policy tool use on policy targets to the development and implementation of policies aimed at the attainment of desired policy ambitions (Weaver 2009a, 2010b; Bobrow and Dryzek 1987; Bobrow 2006; Montpetit 2003b). In a time when policy-makers are often tasked with developing innovative solutions to increasingly complex policy problems, the need for intelligent design of policies and a better understanding of the policy formulation processes they involve has never been greater.

This design orientation toward formulating policies begins with the analysis of the abilities of different kinds of policy tools and resources to trigger behavioural and other mechanisms among target groups in order to affect policy outputs and achieve desired outcomes (Hood 1986c). This instrumental or mechanistic knowledge is contextual in the sense that understandings of how the use of specific kinds of instruments affects outcomes, such as levels of target group compliance. And it includes consideration of many constraints on tool use originating in the limits of existing knowledge, prevailing governance structures, government and other policy actor capacities, and other similar and related arrangements. These considerations may preclude certain options and favour others thought to be more feasible. Combined with the institutional and actor arrangements and legacies of past policy efforts, these activities and constraints may combine over time to create a *policy style* or favoured mode of operation in many sectors and governments, a subject addressed later in this volume.

In general, however, a means–ends or 'instrumental' understanding of policy formulation permeates the policy design orientation (Tribe 1972; Colebatch 1998, 2018). Although acknowledging that policy-making does not always necessarily lend itself to or result in purely instrumental thinking about policy issues, this instrumental orientation is significant in policy design studies. This is because policy formulators operating in accordance with its strictures are expected to base their actions on analyses which are logical and knowledge- and experience-based rather than, for example, from purely political calculations or bargaining or other forms of satisficing behaviour, religious or ideological presuppositions or beliefs (Sidney 2007; Bendor et al. 2009).

Of course, as mentioned earlier, and as bears much repeating, this does not preclude recognition and acceptance of the fact that some policy decisions and formulation processes are in fact made in a much more contingent and less-rational fashion in which 'design' considerations may be more or less absent (Sager and Rielle 2013). However, the extent to which considerations such as political gain or blame avoidance, policy emotions, and symbolic needs or manoeuvres outweigh instrumental considerations in a given instance of policy formulation is an empirical question whose answer varies widely. But in general, it is desired by adherents of policy design that the number of non-designed policies be as minimal as possible and that such considerations should surrender pride of place in policy deliberations to more instrumental, evidence-driven ones (Hood 2010).

Conceptually, such an instrument-oriented and instrumental policy design process begins with an assessment of the abilities of different policy tools or levers to affect policy outputs and outcomes and of the availability of the kinds of resources required to allow them to operate as intended (Hood 1986c; Salamon 2002c). As Linder and Peters (1991) noted, this kind of activity is a 'spatial' one in that possible and feasible design choices exist within a defined policy 'space'. That is, it is

> a systematic activity composed of a series of choices. . . . Design solutions, then, will correspond to a set of possible locations in a design space. . . . This construction emphasizes not only the potential for generating new mixtures of conventional solutions, but also the importance of giving careful attention to tradeoffs among design criteria when considering instrument choices.
>
> (130)

Instrument knowledge is always contextual in the sense that tool deployment involves a relationship between the use of governing resources and the effects they have on some policy actors in a given policy context, while those contexts can change along with the motivations of those actors which makes them susceptible to government manipulation, or not. That is, unlike the situation with a hammer and a nail where the effect of the impact of the hammer is normally quite certain and the nail cannot alter its shape or move out of the way, in a policy-making situation, it is never certain exactly how policy targets will respond to the appearance of a government tool.

Policy design, then, requires a special understanding of how the use of specific kinds of instruments affects target group behaviour and compliance with government aims (Weaver 2009 2009a, 2009b, 2014 2015), and this is also a subject explored in depth later in the book. This is much the same as in the case of other design activities in areas such as product design, where how a user or purchaser will interact with a product is largely unknown at the outset of the design process but is an essential part of that process and selection of, for example, a particular kind of user interface (Redström 2006).

Aside from this substantive concern, the field of policy design studies also includes process concerns and requires knowledge and consideration of the many constraints on tool use which originate in the limits of existing knowledge, prevailing governance structures, and other arrangements and behaviours which may preclude consideration of certain options and promote others whether or not they might be considered as optimal or sub-optimal (Howlett 2009a, 2011). Some tools, for example, may be prohibited in certain circumstances, such as the use of subliminal advertisements to encourage people to stop smoking, or restricted by custom or preference, such as jailing homeless or indigent populations, while the unknown causes of many problems, such as illegal drug use, can preclude the devising of effective solutions to them.

Design thus requires both analytical and evidentiary capacity on the part of the government as well as the intention to exercise it in the face of uncertainty and ambiguity concerning the future. These knowledge issues are also addressed in the book, along with their implications for what makes an effective design over time, or what makes a design 'robust' or 'resilient' in the face of change.

The general goal of policy designs: policy effectiveness

As this brief overview has shown, past studies have helped clarify the role of historical processes, policy capacities, and design intentions in affecting policy formulation processes and, more recently, in understanding how the bundling of multiple policy elements together to meet policy goals can be better understood and accomplished. This literature and its implications are set out in subsequent chapters.

But while some aspects of studies of policy design are new, it bears repeating that policy studies have always been interested in analyzing and improving the sets of policy tools adopted by governments to correct policy problems and in better understanding and improving processes of policy analysis and policy formulation in order to do so. While this work on policy tools has progressed, however, the discussion of what general *goals* policy designs should serve remains disjointed (Petek et al. 2021, 2022; Moore 1994).

Many scholars interested in this subject have focused on general goals like efficiency or the attainment of the greatest possible benefit at the least possible cost, or justice and equity, or environmental sustainability, as key aims of policy-makers and policy designs. However, the central goal of policy designs and policy design studies has typically been 'effectiveness' (Peters et al. 2018; Mukherjee and Bali 2019).

Effectiveness serves as the basic goal of any design and is what ultimately is expected to set a designed policy above and beyond a non-designed one as the latter is expected to be less effective given its weaker ability to marshal and utilize knowledge in arriving at policy decisions and choices. It is effectiveness upon which are built other goals, such as efficiency or equity, which can be seen as alterations or additions to the initial goal, since efficiency without effectiveness is impossible and ineffective equity or environmental measures are also not desirable goals (Peters et al. 2018).

In general, contemporary design scholars argue that feasible and realizable alternatives will be generated through better policy formulation and design processes. They are confident that such alternatives will emerge triumphant in deliberations and conflicts involved in decisions to adopt certain tools and not others when effective processes are in place to encourage design and discourage non-design formulation activity.

Policy effectiveness in this sense is a multi-level phenomenon in which process, design, and outcomes are expected to be linked closely together (see Figure 1.1).

As Figure 1.1 shows, the overall supposition of design studies in this field is thus that a good process of policy design is one in which there is an expectation that a superior process of policy formulation ('designing') will lead to a superior set of policy instruments and components being proposed ('design'), which will, in turn, result in a superior outcome than would some other kind of policy or formulation process. These other kinds of processes – such as pure legislative bargaining or logrolling – are expected to result in an inferior mix of policy tools and elements which, by definition, will typically generate inferior results than would those arrived at through a better, more evidence-informed process.

That is, using 'effectiveness' as a criterion in judging a policy design infers that the essence of policy design resides in the articulation of policy options logically expected to meet government goals and that those designs which do this best are the most desirable (Majone 1976; Linder and Peters 1984; May 2003; Bobrow 2006). This involves the systematic effort to analyze

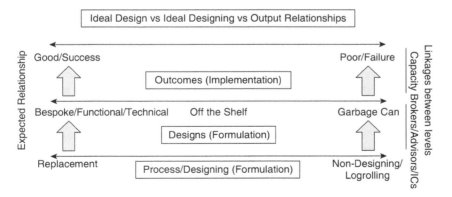

Figure 1.1 Policy effectiveness as the relationship between process, design, and outcome.

the impacts of policy instruments on policy targets, as well as the application of this knowledge to the creation and realization of policies that can reasonably be expected to attain anticipated policy outcomes (Weaver 2009a, 2009b; Bobrow and Dryzek 1987; Sidney 2007; Gilabert and Lawford-Smith 2012). Studies in these areas are a feature of contemporary policy design work, and their content and lessons are set out in the book.

The general conundrum of policy design: uncertainty

Effectiveness is an elusive goal, however, and is not simple to achieve. This is due to both the many uncertainties policy-makers face in designing policies which successfully reach goals not only in the present but also into the future, and to the propensity or possibility not only that mistakes can be made but also that policies might ensue instead from non-design processes.

Problems have different orders of complexity, and as Becker and Brownson (1964) and others have pointed out, even at a relatively simple level, when a problem is well-known and knowledge is available on a subject. Even in such situations policy-makers may not be aware of that knowledge and thus undertake decision-making on the basis of uniformed ignorance rather than informed awareness. This situation and goal become even more complex and elusive when knowledge of a subject or phenomenon is completely lacking or disputed, such as occurred with issues such as the emergence of AIDS in the early 1980s, climate change in the 1990s, and the COVID-19 global disease pandemic in 2020.

The view, although pervasive in some quarters of the policy sciences, however, that it is always possible to develop an effective and efficient policy is not backed up by a great deal of empirical evidence (deLeon 1999a; Hargrove 1975). Policy-making in situations characterized by malfeasance and corruption, where policy processes and instrument decisions are severely compromised by partisan, group, and self-interest, or situations of poverty and under-development, where the resources needed for effective policies and policy-making are lacking, often lead to compromised design or non-design processes and policy failures.

However, even when policy processes are less corrupt and resources are available, effective policy designs often do not occur and do not automatically result in effective policy outcomes, even with well-intentioned and well-resourced governments. While having many possible causes, many of the problems encountered in these circumstances stem from *uncertainty* (Jarvis 2011b; Morgan and Henrion 1990).

Uncertainty about outcomes and future and contemporary behaviour and circumstances is in fact the central conundrum of policy design. It has serious implications not only for policy success and failure but also for the kinds of designs and design problems that can emerge in a given situation.

Knowledge uncertainty: wicked and tame problems

As the Nobel Prize–winning student of public administration Herbert Simon (1973) pointed out many years ago, social and organizational problems come in different shapes and forms, and the methods and means by which societies deal with them vary in terms of the extent of available knowledge and the ability and desire of decision-makers to incorporate that knowledge into their thinking.

Some problems are 'well-structured' in the sense that their causes and effects and the means to deal with them are well-known. Others are ill-structured in the sense that knowledge of problems and solutions is unknown or unrealized and the level of uncertainty in which they are grappled is much higher. This was the basis for the distinction made in the 1970s by Rittel and Weber between 'wicked' and 'tame' problems (see Table 1.1).

These analyses acknowledge that there is much more ambiguity in scenario forecasts and projections and thus many more difficulties encountered in policy design, for example, when critical data are lacking or non-existent than when they are readily available. It is much more difficult to assign probability distributions to possible future scenarios with any confidence, for example, when key data is lacking (McInerney et al. 2012; Lempert et al. 2002; Walker et al. 2010; Jarvis 2011a).

Historically, students of 'wicked' and 'tame' policy problems such as Churchman (1967) and Rittel and Webber (1973) thought about uncertainty in this sense (Simon 1973; Head and Alford 2015). Allowing for a greater

Table 1.1 Tame and wicked problems

		Nature of knowledge of the problem	
		Known/well-defined and understood	Unknown/ill-defined
Nature of knowledge of the solution	Known/well-defined and understood	Well-structured ('tame problem') (e.g. automobile traffic control/street racing)	Ill-structured problem (e.g. tobacco control/addiction)
	Unknown/ill-defined	Ill-structured solution (e.g. homelessness)	Poorly structured ('wicked problem') (e.g. climate change)

range in estimates and efforts, as well as building-in results monitoring and learning activities, such as mid-term and first-year policy reviews, are common techniques for dealing with such issues and the high levels of uncertainty they entail. However, more complex design challenges exist when both the level of 'objective' knowledge of problems as well as the relative nature of decision-makers' knowledge of that 'fact-base' are taken into account, or if there is little agreement on the choice of variables to be included in models (Walker et al. 2001, 2010; Kwakkel et al. 2010) (see Table 1.2).

That is, uncertainties can relate to 'the quality of the knowledge base' or the degree of agreement upon or the absolute size of the evidentiary support for models, or the 'value-ladenness' of policy choices, which includes different actor perspectives on the worth and value of the knowledge and information being utilized for decision-making (Mathijssen et al. 2007). Understanding the nature of these different types and levels of uncertainty in general and their risks and consequences in specific policy-making instances is central to policy designing (Schrader et al. 1993; Leung et al. 2015; Bond et al. 2015).

Thus, for example, in utilizing policy instruments, policy-makers face at least five different types of uncertainty (see Figure 1.2). This includes

Table 1.2 Policy-maker's knowledge and comprehension matrix

		Nature of existing knowledge of a phenomenon	
		Aspects of the problem and possible solutions are known	Aspects are unknown
Nature of decision-makers' awareness of existing knowledge of a phenomenon	Aware	Known–known: key policy actors are aware of the known aspects of a phenomenon (INFORMED AWARENESS)	Known–unknown: key policy actors are aware that certain aspects of the phenomenon are unknown (PRUDENT AWARENESS)
	Ignorant	Unknown–known: key policy actors are unaware of known aspects of a phenomenon (UNINFORMED IGNORANCE)	Unknown–unknown: key policy actors are unaware that certain aspects of the phenomenon are unknown (IMPRUDENT IGNORANCE)

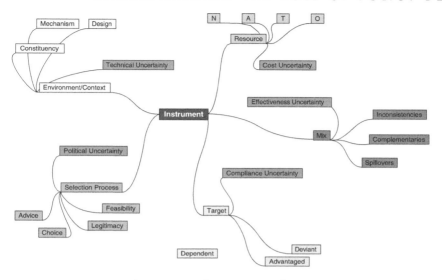

Figure 1.2 Five types of uncertainty designers must face.

'technical' uncertainty, about whether or not a specific tool or mix of tools will perform as expected; 'resource' or cost uncertainty, or whether or not a government possesses adequate and plentifully available resources or capacities to implement a policy effectively; 'compliance' uncertainty, or whether or not policy targets will comply with government wishes and to what extent; 'political' uncertainty over whether a design will be adopted as intended or amended or otherwise interfered with; and 'effectiveness' uncertainty, or whether or not the elements in a policy mix will work together toward a common aim or work at cross-purposes toward each other.

Design uncertainty: policy under- and over-design

Two of the most common problems which result from uncertainty for policy designs and designing have to do with the propensity for policy under and over-design, that is, underestimating or under-reacting to problems (under-design) or, on the other hand, over-estimating a problem and over-reacting to it (over-design).

That is, most policy design theory operates under the assumption that governments will attempt to act as effective and efficient policy-makers, or at least wish to do so as a normative goal, if not one always achieved in practice. This often assumes government policy efforts can be 'perfectly calibrated' to seamlessly lead to the minimum appropriate amount of effort being used to maximize the solution to a policy problem. The essence of much policy analysis, modelling, and advice is thus to provide templates for action appropriate or 'proportionate' to the objective characteristics and severity of policy problems.

Table 1.3 Cases of disproportional policy reaction and design

Nature of policy response	Nature of policy design problem	
	Simple	Large/complex
Simple	Proportionate design (e.g. automobile speeding)	Under-design (e.g. climate change)
Large/complex	Over-design(e.g. national security)	Proportionate design (e.g. air traffic regulation)

That is, standard policy theory assumes that government policy efforts can be calibrated to address the fundamental issue at stake with exactly the appropriate amount of effort and resources. However, much empirical evidence and day-to-day observation of policy-making effort and results suggests a more complex pattern of policy response in which few efforts are at least immediately well-calibrated to the problem at hand and that many either systematically under- or over-react to a problem, often oscillating between these two states over time in a sometimes vicious cycle.

As Table 1.3 shows, well-calibrated designs may occur when effort and problem match. But there is always the possibility of 'disproportionate' responses when policy reactions over- or under-'shoot' the severity of the problem or otherwise do not adequately match its nature (Maor 2012b, 2014a; Jones et al. 2014; Maor 2014b; Howlett and Kemmerling 2017).

This can sometimes occur intentionally when, for example, a government wishes to display its commitment to the resolution of a problem, like national security or crime prevention, and overspends on the army or police, or in the opposite direction, when it ignores opposition party demands to spend in areas its supporters consider low priority, regardless of the actual severity of the concern (Maor 2014b; Jones et al. 2014). In this sense, both under- and over-design can be thought of as 'designed'. However, it can also occur unintentionally, when knowledge of the real nature of a problem is unknown or when decision-makers are over- or under-confident in the knowledge they have. These dynamics and their design implications are discussed in more detail in Chapter 14.

Conclusion: policy design as instrumental knowledge mobilization in an uncertain world

As the review of the existing policy design literature contained in this book shows, experience from a variety of sectors and jurisdictions has alluded to different aspects of what constitutes effectiveness and refers to this criterion in identifying and setting out *best practices* towards selecting instruments and managing uncertainty in the activity of policy design. But discussion of this latter topic is largely scattered over a large body of policy studies, presenting some difficulties in drawing precise lessons about what 'effectiveness' means in compiling and co-ordinating the many aspects of a design, ranging from abstract policy goals and instrument logics that inform the policy design environment to the more specific mechanics of policy programmes and toolkits that help to better match particular policy objectives to individual tool settings (Howlett 2009).

Designing public policies in the sense set out earlier is also a difficult task in practice for many reasons, including lack of resources, the existence of corrupt or inefficient bureaucracies and other policy actors, crises, the presence of powerful veto players among both state and societal actors, vague goal definition and poor implementation, evaluation, and other policy practices, among others. These lead to high levels on uncertainty in policy responses and outcomes. The modern policy studies movement began with the observation that public policy-making not only commonly results from the interactions of policy-makers in the exercise of power rather than knowledge but also with the recognition that even when it does not, this does not always guarantee effective policies or the attainment of desired results (Arts and van Tatenhove 2004; Lasswell 1958; Stone 1988).

Despite these concerns, or, rather precisely because these risks exist, modern policy design studies were founded on the idea that accumulating and utilizing knowledge of the effects and impacts of a relatively well-known set of policy means developed over many years of state-building experience can help marshal and utilize governing resources in a more effective way and, in so doing, help devise methods to accomplish policy outcomes which enhance public value (Lerner and Lasswell 1951; Howlett and Mukherjee 2014; Moore 1995). This is the design orientation that drives the field of policy design studies.

This is in keeping with the motivational impulses of the modern policy studies movement which began with the recognition that public policy-making results from the interactions of policy-makers in the exercise of power, legitimate or otherwise (Lasswell 1958; Arts and van Tatenhove 2004; Stone 1988) but also with the observation that while some of policy-making efforts may be arbitrary or capricious, many can be considered good faith efforts to achieve a public purpose.

Of course, policy goals can be wide-ranging and often pose no small amount of difficulty and complexity in both definition and diagnosis, with the implication that the formulation of solutions that are likely to succeed in addressing them necessitates systematic consideration of the impact and feasibility of the kinds of policy means or instruments expected to achieve them (Parsons 1995, 2001). Most policy studies thus urge concerted and intentional efforts on the part of governments to act instrumentally in policy design, that is, to achieve a particular policy goal or end through the use of well-known sets of policy means (Lerner and Lasswell 1951). Thus, early work depicted policy design as a specific kind of policy-making in which knowledge of the policy impacts of specific policy tools was combined with the practical capacity of governments to identify and implement as closely as possible the most suitable technical means in the effort to achieve a specific policy aim.

This activity was often expected to occur *ex ante* and independently of other considerations, such as political or personal gain, which might also affect formulation processes. But this 'design' activity was later recognized as requiring a situation where there was support for policy analysis and design work on the part of policy-makers and also low policy 'lock-in' on existing policy and programme arrangements. Such favourable design circumstances have to be coupled with the presence of a high level of capacity and expertise on the part of policy analysts if knowledge is to be mobilized effectively so that policy instruments can be effectively and efficiently matched to policy goals and targets (Howlett 2009a; Dunlop 2009a; Radaelli and Dunlop 2013; Howlett and Rayner 2015).

When all such conditions are present in an optimal design 'space', purposive design activity is thought to be possible and preferable to other forms of policy formulation, much as is urged in the current era by efforts to enhance knowledge mobilization through the promotion of 'evidence-based policy-making' (Bhatta 2002; Locke 2009). When they are not, it is thought that less technical and more overtly political forms of policy-making and the propensity for over- and under-design and less-effective or ineffective policy outcomes are more likely to ensue (Davies 2004; Moseley and Tierney 2004; Howlett 2009b).

The fervent wish of proponents of the design orientation both in the past and now is to reduce the latter instances to as few as possible by promoting the kinds of orientations and dedication of resources required for the former, in the belief that better policy process can produce better-designed policies more likely to solve pressing problems and correct social ills (Bobrow 2006; Azuela and Barroso 2012).

Plan of the book

This book introduces students to the principles and elements of policy design in contemporary governance outlined earlier. It does so through the detailed study of the implementation instruments used by governments in carrying out their tasks and adapting to and altering their environments which form the basic foundations or structures upon which policies and programmes rest. An essential component of modern governance, the range of substantive and procedural policy instruments together comprises the toolbox from which governments select specific tools expected to resolve policy problems and any erstwhile policy designer must be familiar with them in all their nuances and variations.

The book begins with the discussion of several aspects of design processes in contemporary government and then moves on to consider the logic of policy design and the principles behind the selection and use of specific types of instruments in the process of policy formulation. It then discusses in more detail when this occurs in policy-making and who makes these kinds of decisions. The merits, demerits, and rationales for the use of specific organization, regulatory, financial, and information-based tools and the trends visible in their use are then set out.

This is followed by a discussion of what it is that makes a design a good one and what are some of the dangers that must be avoided if a good design is to be achieved.

Readings

Bason, C. and S. Andrea. (2014). 'Public Design in Global Perspective: Empirical Trends'. In C. Bason (ed.), *Design for Policy*. Burlington, VT: Gower, 23–40.

Bobrow, D. (2006). 'Policy Design: Ubiquitous, Necessary and Difficult'. In B. G. Peters and J. Pierre (eds.), *Handbook of Public Policy*. London: Sage, 75–96.

Churchman, C. W. (1967). 'Wicked Problems'. *Management Science 14*, no. 4: B141–B142.

Clarke, A. and J. Craft. (2019). 'The Twin Faces of Public Sector Design'. *Governance 32*: 5–21.

Colebatch, H. K. (2018). 'The Idea of Policy Design: Intention, Process, Outcome, Meaning and Validity'. *Public Policy and Administration* (18 May): 365–383.

Dryzek, J. S. and B. Ripley. (1988). 'The Ambitions of Policy Design'. *Policy Studies Review 7*, no. 4: 705–719.

Hansson, S. O. (1996). 'Decision Making Under Great Uncertainty'. *Philosophy of the Social Sciences 26*, no. 3 (1 September): 369–386.

Hermus, M. and A. van Buuren. (2017). 'Applying Design Methodology in Public Administration: A State of the Art Based upon a Systematic Literature Review'. Presented at the ICPP, Singapore.

Howlett, M. (2014). 'Policy Design: What, Who, How and Why?' In H. Charlotte, L. Pierre and L. G. Patrick (eds.), *L'instrumentation et ses effets*. Paris: Presses de Sciences Po, 281–315.

Howlett, M. and R. P. Lejano. (2013). 'Tales from the Crypt: The Rise and Fall (and Re-Birth?) of Policy Design Studies'. *Administration & Society 45*, no. 3: 356–380.

Howlett, M. and J. Tosun. (2018). 'Policy Styles: A New Approach'. In M. Howlett and J. Tosun (eds.), *Policy Styles and Policy-Making*. Lonodn: Routledge.

Levin, K., B. Cashore, S. Bernstein and G. Auld. (2012). 'Overcoming the Tragedy of Super Wicked Problems: Constraining Our Future Selves to Ameliorate Global Climate Change'. *Policy Sciences 45*, no. 2 (23 May): 123–152.

Linder, S. H. and B. G. Peters. (1984). 'From Social Theory to Policy Design'. *Journal of Public Policy 4*, no. 3: 237–259.

Maor, M. (2017). 'The Implications of the Emerging Disproportionate Policy Perspective for the New Policy Design Studies'. *Policy Sciences 50*, no. 3 (September): 383–398.

Mintrom, M. and J. Luetjens. (2016). 'Design Thinking in Policymaking Processes: Opportunities and Challenges'. *Australian Journal of Public Administration 75*, no. *3* (1 September): 391–402.

Petek, A., B. Zgurić, M. Šinko, K. Petković, M. Munta, M. Kovačić, A. Kekez and N. Baketa. (2022). 'From Hierarchy to Continuum: Classifying the Technical Dimension of Policy Goals'. *Policy Sciences 55*, no. 4 (December 2022): 715–736.

Ralph, P. and Y. Wand. (2013). 'A Proposal for a Formal Definition of the Design Concept'. *Annual Review of Policy Design 1*, no. *1* (6 September): 1–35.

Rittel, H. W. J. and M. M. Webber. (1973). 'Dilemmas in a General Theory of Planning'. *Policy Sciences 4*: 155–169.

Schön, D. A. (1992). 'Designing as Reflective Conversation with the Materials of a Design Situation'. *Knowledge-Based Systems 5*, no. *1* (March): 3–14.

Simon, H. A. (1973). 'The Structure of Ill Structured Problems'. *Artificial Intelligence 4*, no. *3–4* (Winter): 181–201.

Chapter 2

Policy design in the contemporary era

Beyond globalization and governance

As we have seen, policy design studies in the sense set out in Chapter 1 deal with the vagaries of policy formulation by analytically separating two dimensions of the design experience: on the one hand, the exploration of the procedural aspects of design ('designing') – the specific types of policy formulation activities which lead to design rather than some other form of policy generation – and the substantive ('design') – that is, the substance or content of the design itself. This is the policy-relevant articulation of the well-known distinction in design studies generally between 'design-as-verb' – in this case, the process of 'policy formulation' – and 'design-as-noun' – in the policy realm, the mix of policy tools and instruments put into place (Hillier et al. 1972; Hillier and Leaman 1974; Gero 1990).

Although popular in the 1970s and 1980s, this orientation within policy studies declined after 1990. This was largely due to the emergence of a competitive research agenda in the policy sciences which shifted attention toward events occurring at the international and meta-societal levels of analysis, which were often seen by proponents to dictate domestic policy tool choices and push them in a certain direction, making their detailed analysis unnecessary or redundant (Howlett 2011; Howlett and Lejano 2013; Jordan et al. 2013). This orientation was reflected in the late 1990s and early 2000s in a substantial shift in scholarly attention toward the impact on tool selection of the more 'meta' level of policy institutions, sparked by the emergence of *globalization* and its preference for market-based tools as well as the start of '*governance*' studies undertaken in Europe and elsewhere which emphasized the role of non-state actors – especially networks – in policy-making (Howlett and Lejano 2013).

DOI: 10.4324/9781003343431-3

These emergent globalization and governance literatures often implied that instrument choices were more or less preordained by meta-level changes in the relationships existing between states, markets, and civil society organizations which favoured the latter two, therefore reducing the significance and the need for sophisticated and lengthy analysis of the activities of the former (Rhodes 1996; Kooiman 2000).

At best, this 'globalization and governance turn' perpetuated a polarity in discussions between, for example, instruments of the 'market' and the 'state' or dichotomous governance styles, such as 'hierarchies' and 'markets', which coloured many design debates of the era (Howlett 2004b, 2011; Koch 2013). Studies influenced by these literatures often promoted the use of particular types of tools – mainly market- and network-based ones – which were well suited to, respectively, dealing with global production chains and activities which transcended national state activities and enhancing subnational civil society linkages and service delivery mechanisms. In many cases, however, the use of these kinds of tools was suggested regardless of context and with little regard for the appropriateness of their selection or consideration of how well they might interact with other pre-existing tools and policy arrangements (Howlett and Lejano 2013).

Difficulties with both the formulation and implementation of policy proposals based on such conceptions led to a spate of studies in the first decade of the new millennium which chronicled their misuse (see e.g. Jarvis 2011a; Ramesh and Howlett 2006; Ramesh and Fritzen 2009) and re-asserted the centrality of the role of government in policy formulation and implementation (Capano 2011; Koch 2013). This latter work emphasized the continuing importance and need for the use of other types of tools in policy-making and better understandings of the formulation and implementation processes surrounding them, and led to a resurgence in studies of policy design.

The changing context of policy design studies: the globalization and governance turns of the 1990s

Globalization involves the extensification and intensification – 'stretching and deepening', in the words of Held et al. (1999) – of cross-border interactions. While much of this process comprises trade and economic interactions, it also includes events and activities in the cultural, political, military, and ideational realms as well as in policy-making more generally.

There is a broad agreement among many popular commentators that this kind of globalization during the last decades of the twentieth century fundamentally altered many aspects of contemporary governance and policy designs. As a result of trade treaties and other globalization arrangement, many states' governance practices were altered as the use of certain tools, like industrial subsidies and tariff protection, to name only two, was greatly constrained (Cerny 1996; Reinicke 1998). That is, as globalization proceeded, states' options in some realms in terms of the policy instruments available to them in order to realize their ends changed, and they were no longer able to manage many public policy-making processes and outcomes as they had in past eras.

Similarly, many commentators also argued, either separately or in conjunction with the globalization thesis, that state practices also changed during this period as societies were transformed internally by improved information and communication technologies, allowing ever more complex networks of interorganizational actors to emerge in civil society (Mayntz 1993; Castells 1996). This increased 'networkization' of society meant that many functions and activities traditionally undertaken exclusively by governments now increasingly involved ever-larger varieties of non-governmental actors, themselves involved in increasingly complex relationships with other societal, and state, actors (Foster and Plowden 1996). This second movement toward the development of networked societies further complicated policy-making and accentuated the constraints globalization imposed upon the capabilities of domestic states, again altering their design choices and alternatives in many sectors of life (Dobuzinskis 1987; Lehmbruch 1991).

As networkization increased, it was argued, both formulation and implementation practices became more participatory and consultative, and these developments led to the accentuation of what might be called 'the governance turn' in the policy sciences (Alshuwaikhat and Nkwenti 2002; Arellano-Gault and Vera-Cortes 2005). A trend apparent in many sectors dealing with, for example, social or health policy combined with changes occasioned by globalization over this same time period in the economic sphere to alter many governments' preferences for the use of particular kinds of policy tools. This involved a shift towards those tools which emphasized or accentuated the role of private and non-governmental actors in the achievement of public ends. During this period, for example, many public enterprises in transportation and other industries were privatized, and previously government-provided services in many areas such as health, housing, and social services were contracted out to non-governmental organizations (NGOs). In addition, in many sectors, other activities, such as regulatory ones, shifted from 'enforcement' to 'compliance' or more persuasive regimes and tax incentives substituted for earlier systems of cash-based subsidies and grants. Many countries placed an increasing emphasis on public information and other similar types of campaigns in areas such as consumer protection and public health, often replacing or supplementing more coercive or organizational forms of government activity with this more educational activity (Woodside 1983; Hawkins and Thomas 1989; Hood 1991; Howlett and Ramesh 1993; Weiss and Tschirhart 1994; Doern and Wilks 1998).

While the evidence of some changes in how governments function in the contemporary era due to these developments is undeniable and will be discussed in depth in subsequent chapters, the scope, significance, and causes of these changes remain contentious. Especially contentious is the belief that the changes in formulation and implementation practices which occurred were triggered solely by these changes in the domestic and international spheres and that domestic governments had no choice in their policy designs but to accommodate these transformations and continue to work toward the reduction of a state presence in the economy and society as these dual processes continued to unfold and intensify (Levi-Faur 2009; O'Toole and Meier 2010).

The effects of globalization and internationalization on policy design

In order to assess the actual effects and impact of such large-scale political economic and technological changes on state behaviour, including policy tool and design preferences, it is necessary to first acknowledge that serious gaps exist in our understanding of the workings and characteristics of globalization and its policy consequences (Hay 2006). Contrary to what is commonly believed and often advocated, for example, in our global era, the domestic state remains far from overwhelmed and lacking autonomous decision-making capacity (Weiss 2003; Braithwaite 2008), and the source of many of the changes in the patterns of policy-making and instrument choice found in contemporary society described earlier very often lay in developments in the domestic rather than the international arena. And even when domestic states were driven by international developments, they did not just react to changes in their international environments in an automatic way but were very much involved in the design and implementation of policies expected to achieve their ends in the new environment (Lynn 1980; Vogel 2001).

This was amply displayed during the COVID-19 pandemic, for example, where domestic states took the lead role in combating the coronavirus and did so in many different and sometimes idiosyncratic ways (Capano et al. 2020). Policies there were linked to, for example, demographic changes, shifts in life expectancies and lifestyles, organizational and administrative capacities, partisan ideologies, and leadership personalities, as had also been the case in other spheres of life in earlier decades (Scott et al. 2004; Levi-Faur 2009).

To the extent that global factors have had an impact on domestic policy designs and governance practices, it is often through what can be termed more 'indirect' and 'opportunity' effects spilling over from trade and other activities, rather than from the 'direct' effects that are cited in arguing that state behaviour changed in reaction to these developments (Howlett and Ramesh 2006).

That is, the direct effects of globalization on domestic state instrument choice have often been limited to specific sectors and activities, such as banking and finance, industrial policy, and other areas covered by treaties and international agreements. Indirect effects have been more common despite their less formal nature. These typically consist of 'spill-over' effects from better communications and increased opportunities for interaction as well as increased learning and lesson drawing which occurred as a side effect of globalization.

One of the spill-over effects of increasing integration of international markets, for example, is manifested in governments' reluctance to resort to new taxes or establish new public enterprises, lest they send the 'wrong' signals to financial markets and discourage investment. While governments still can, and do, employ an extensive array of command-and-control tools to direct private sector behaviour, they must now anticipate possible adverse commercial reactions from the use of these kinds of tools and prepare to deal with them. Deregulation and privatization measures, for example, are widely reported in the international media and help build the international pro-business reputation of governments undertaking them. Hence, a side effect of globalization is that governments may resort to increased use of information provision as a means to advertise a market-friendly outlook and a favourable disposition toward foreign direct investment. If these measures succeed in attracting foreign investment, the success is cited as a reason for further deregulation and privatization and for further use of state advertising to promote it, although alternative mechanisms and methods often remain possible and in effect.

Globalization also increases opportunities for cross-sectoral and cross-national interaction among policy practitioners and commentators. Policy-makers not only have instant access to information available on the internet but also routinely gather with their foreign counterparts at countless governmental and non-governmental meetings at various levels of seniority that are held on the entire gamut of policy subjects from the performance of the global economy to cyber regulation.

These meetings are key forums for policy-makers and administrators, NGOs, and others to learn from each other's experiences and to better appreciate the technical, economic, and political potential and limitations of different policy tools. Other countries' experiences often form the starting point for governments embarking on domestic policy reforms, and this kind of policy learning, emulation, or transfer plays a critical role in efforts to reform the policy instruments used to implement public policies (Huber 1991; Bennett and Howlett 1992; Hall 1993; Dolowitz and Marsh 2000; Stone 2000).

Thus, for example, many countries emulated the use of pollution trading rights in other areas of the environment and society after its perceived success in controlling the use of ozone-depleting chlorofluorocarbons (CFCs) in the 1987 Montreal Protocol (Parson and Fisher-Vanden 1999). But this is an indirect rather than direct effect of globalization. Meseguer (2003) and Simmons and Elkins (2004), for instance, list learning and emulation as the key factors underlying the spread of privatization and liberalization, rather than trade treaties or other more coercive and mandatory diktats. Meseguer in particular found little evidence that international pressures played any significant role in most domestic state adjustments.

But here again, as with more direct effects, it must be recognized that policy learning and emulation are processes which are also constrained by existing domestic political and institutional factors. Domestic political opposition to the adoption of measures that have successfully worked elsewhere, for example, is commonplace, often forcing policy-makers to compromise in their use in new situations. The imperatives of path dependency domestically – the tendency for old choices to become entrenched and institutionalized, such as a decision to sell off oil and gas rights or auction telecommunications spectrum which is not easily reversed – also often make it difficult to adopt a new policy instrument that is substantially different from current practice (March and Olsen 1989; Pierson 2000).

In other words, while there is little doubt that economic, diplomatic, military, and aid-related relations among nations help and have helped shape many choices of existing policies and policy tools, these impacts and effects can easily be over-exaggerated. It is well-known, for example, that many countries are aggressive in pressuring other countries to weaken regulations or preferential tax or subsidy treatments that restrict international firms' business activities, and global and regional multilateral agreements are the most direct ways by which extra-territorial factors can shape the choice of policy instruments.

But these efforts exist only in very few sectors and often have large areas of exclusion even when they are present. Trade and investment deals, such as the World Trade Organization (WTO) agreements, and various free trade agreements, for instance, often specify in great detail the measures that governments can or cannot adopt vis-à-vis domestic and international producers. However powerful these treaties are, they only prohibit the use of a small number of very specific instruments, such as tariffs and quotas, to assist domestic producers, and even then, they often contain many exceptions to those bans for purposes of national security or to protect vulnerable sectors, like agriculture, from international competition. The use of subsidies of various kinds specifically intended to assist domestic producers, for example, is often restricted by countervailing duty clauses and other similar measures that allow other countries to punish these subsides by adding their own retaliatory tariffs, but activities in the cultural, military, health, and agricultural realms are often excluded from these measures. And in the case of bilateral treaties, often sensitive but very local industries, such as trucking or pharmaceutical production, may also be excluded.

More general political agreements, whether formal or informal, can have a constraining direct effect on the choice of policies and policy tools. The European Union is an extreme case of the formal transfer of decision-making authority to a supra-national centre, for example, which often severely limits what national governments in Europe can do and what kinds of instruments they can employ to affect their decisions (Kassim and Le Galès 2010). However, even here the restrictions on national governments' abilities to employ regulatory and fiscal tools on their own are often less significant than assumed (Halpern 2010). And even when they are restricted, national governments are often able to craft their own specific solutions to ongoing policy problems with little regard to EU policy through mechanisms such as 'subsidiarity' or the 'open method of coordination', which allow local states to determine and design their own policy responses to EU-level initiatives (Meuleman 2010b; Heidbreder 2011; Lierse 2010; Tholoniat 2010).

Thus, while there is no doubt that the evolution of international treaties and arrangements is an important development, in many sectors and areas of government activity, they impose only very minimal or no constraints on the choice of policy tools utilized by governments in their policy designs – nowhere near those alleged by both proponents and opponents of globalization-led pro-market reform efforts (Palan and Abbott 1996; Clark 1998; Weiss 1999; Bernhagen 2003). There are few international agreements that specifically require governments to privatize or deregulate, for example, and the developments which occurred in sectors which have experienced the deepest deregulation and privatization in recent decades – financial, telecommunications, and air transportation services – predate many current treaties.

Hence, to date, the actual impact of globalization on domestic state policy designs and designing activity has been, outside of several well-known sectors and events, much less than often alleged. The direct international constraints on policy designs typically cited by proponents of the globalization, for example, have largely been confined to cross-border economic exchanges and do not cover much of what domestic governments do and how they do it. Traditional command-and-control instruments of governance, such as regulation by government or independent regulatory commissions, state-owned enterprises, and direct taxation and subsidization, are far from antithetical to globalization, as is evident in their continued and at times even increasing use in policy designs in a variety of national and sectoral settings (Jayasuriya 2001, 2004; Vogel and Kagan 2002; Jordana and Levi-Faur 2004a; Ramesh and Howlett 2006).

Changing network effects: the 'government to governance' hypothesis

The situation is much similar in the case of any ostensible shifts toward new forms of governance, that is, bringing states and civil society actors together in new ways. The need, noted earlier, to shift toward the greater use of network management tools and activities put forward by adherents of the argument that states have moved 'from government to governance' as a result of changes in technology and society and the way in which government interacts with them, is also lacking a great deal of empirical evidence (Howlett et al. 2009; Schout et al. 2010).

While it is clear that the development of modern information and communications technologies have had a serious impact on the way in which individuals and organizations interact and organize themselves in contemporary societies, it is not clear that these developments have had an equally direct effect in altering most traditional government practices and policy designs (Hood 2006; Hood and Margetts 2007).

That is, as is well-known, 'governing' is what governments do: controlling the allocation of resources among social actors; providing a set of rules and operating a set of institutions setting out 'who gets what, where, when, and how' in society; while at the same time managing the symbolic resources that are the basis of political legitimacy (Lasswell 1958). Governing involves the establishment of a basic set of relationships between governments and their citizens, which can vary from highly structured and controlled to arrangements that are monitored only loosely and informally, if at all.

In its broadest sense, 'governance' is a term used to describe a specific *mode* of coordination exercised by state actors in their interactions with societal actors and organizations (de Bruijn and ten Heuvelhof 1995; Kooiman 1993, 2000; Rhodes 1996; Klijn and Koppenjan 2000c). It is about establishing, promoting, and supporting a specific type of relationship between governmental and non-governmental actors in the governing process, in which the two sets of actors sometimes act in more equitable ways than exist in a state-led hierarchical relationship.

In modern democratic capitalist societies, this means governments involve and manage relationships with businesses and civil society organizations in the creation of public value and the delivery of goods and services to citizens (Hall and Soskice 2001; Williamson 1996b). As Steurer (2013) suggested, these three basic sets of governance actors can be portrayed as interacting within a set of interrelated spheres of activity generating at least four ideal-type governance arrangements at their intersections: *market governance*, between governments and businesses; *civil society governance*, between governments and non-governmental actors; *private governance*, between market and civil society actors; and *network governance*, between all three.

Typical management activities related to collaborative or network modes of governance are those which affect network creation, recognition, capacity-building, and content creation or alteration. Robert Agranoff (Agranoff and McGuire 1999), for example, observed that in a typical 'network management' situation, 'the primary activities of . . . [a] manager involve selecting appropriate actors and resources, shaping the operating context of the network and developing ways to cope with strategic and operational complexity' (21).

However, the logic of governance is more extensive than often suggested, since different combinations of government, civil society, and businesses exist, and within each combination, different sets of actors have different core roles and strengths. As observers such as Knill and Lehmkuhl have noted, governance arrangements feature different relative strengths of the public and private actors involved (Knill and Lehmkuhl 2002; Jordan et al. 2005) and vary according to whether these relationships are expressed in formal or informal terms (Treib et al. 2007; Kritzinger and Pulzl 2008).

Possible variations in governance types and outcomes and the possibility of distinct sectoral variations make the situation more complex than what might first be surmised (van Kersbergen and van Waarden 2004; Meuleman 2009; Harrop 1992; Cerny 1993; Pontusson 1995; Daugbjerg 1998; Haas 2004; Zielonka 2007).

The nature of regulatory activity, for example, focuses on the formal or informal nature of the legal instruments deployed in policy implementation. 'Hard' law is thus typically conceived as synonymous with formal, state-centric, command-and-control types of regulation that impose generally applicable obligations onto target groups of actors, articulated with a relatively high degree of precision and directly enforceable through the courts. In contrast, 'soft' law represents a weakening (or softening) along these key metrics of obligation, precision, and enforceability (Tollefson 2004; Tollefson et al. 2008).

When variations on the strength of each actor in a governance relationship are included, the types of governance arrangements or 'modes' stretch to at least a dozen types, as shown in Figure 2.1.

Considine and his colleagues investigated these many different kinds of possible arrangements and linkages and identified four common governance arrangements found in modern liberal-democratic states. The mechanisms in Figure 2.1 involving the dominance of hierarchy (cells 1 and 2) can be seen to essentially involve a legal mode of governance, while those featured by the dominance of market mechanisms (cells 3 and 4) form market modes of governance. Trilateral arrangements in which hierarchy dominates (cells 5 and 6), strongly or weakly, are best described as corporatist mode of governance. Trilateral mechanisms in which network or market dominates and the government plays a secondary role (cells 7, 8, 9, and 10) constitute different forms of network governance. Finally, private modes of governance

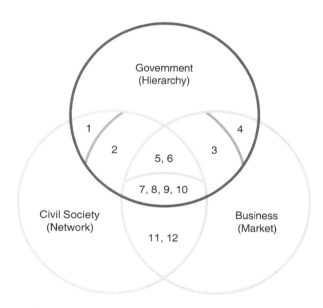

Figure 2.1 Modes of governance, including variation by lead actor.

33

involve market and network mechanisms (cells 11 and 12), with the government playing only a peripheral (albeit essential) role (see Table 2.1).

Table 2.1 Modes of governance (empirical content)

Mode of governance	Central focus of govern-ance activity	Form of state control of relation-ships	Overall governance aim	Prime service delivery mechanism	Key proce-dural tool for policy imple-mentation
Legal gov-ernance	Legality – promotion of law and order in social relationships	Legislation, law, and administra-tion	Legitimacy – voluntary compliance	Rights – property, civil, and human	Courts and litigation
Corporate gover-nance	Manage-ment – of major organized social actors	Plans	Controlled and bal-anced rates of socio-economic development	Targets – operational objectives, subsidies, and grants	Special-ized and privileged advisory committees
Market gover-nance	Competition – promotion of small- and medium-sized enterprises	Contracts and regulations	Resource/ cost efficiency and control	Regulatory boards and prices – controlling for externali-ties, supply, and demand	Tribunals and commissions
Network gover-nance	Relation-ships – promotion of inter-actor organiza-tional activity	Collabora-tion	Co-optation of dissent and self-organization of social actors	Networks of governmental and non-governmental organizations	Network brokerage activities

Source: Modified from Considine, 2001 and English and Skillen 2005.

Many early proponents of the idea of increased 'networkization' simply expected governance arrangements to shift evenly across many different policy sectors and activities away from the sets of formal institutions, coercive power relations, and substantive regulatory tools found in hierarchical systems, toward more informal institutions, non-coercive relationships of power, and a marked preference for procedural instruments and soft law in more plurilateral systems (Dunsire 1993b; Kooiman 1993).

As Capano (2011) and Capano et al. (2015) described it, however, governance comes in many different varieties and modes. The existence of several possible alternative types or 'modes' of governance existing simultaneously at the sectoral level suggests a more complex picture of governance arrangements, instrument choices, and policy designs than the one-to-one national-level, multi-sectoral shift toward the use of more participatory and less 'command and control' tools often proposed by adherents of the 'government to governance' thesis (Koppenjan and Klijn 2004; Barnett et al. 2009; Esmark 2009; Hysing 2009; Edelenbos et al. 2010; Hardiman and Scott 2010; Schout et al. 2010).

A new design research agenda beyond globalization and governance

It is only recently that policy design has re-emerged as a distinct field of inquiry as the merits of the older tools orientation were re-discovered following the failure in many jurisdictions of globalization and governance predictions to come to pass and the realization that many trends in these directions had been exaggerated or over-estimated (Tollefson et al. 2012; Hay and Smith 2010; Jarvis 2011a).

This 'new' policy design orientation is different from its predecessor, however. Like the former, it continues to advocate for the construction and analysis of ideal arrangements of policy components that can then be adapted to meet the bounds of a particular context in order to result in expected outcomes (Hood 2007a; Hood and Margetts 2007). Unlike it or that inspired by globalization and governance logics, however, it focuses on the articulation of design involving multiple tools, not single ones, and without a preferred set of tools or policy design specified *a priori*.

Dealing with policy mixes

One way in which the new design orientation differs from earlier pre-globalization and governance thinking is that it now focuses on bundles or portfolios of tools rather than single choices. Current studies seek to better describe the nature of these mixes and to help understand the interactive effects which occur when multiple tools are used over time (Doremus 2003; Howlett 2014a; Howlett et al. 2014; Jordan et al. 2011, 2012). Significantly, it is especially concerned with interactive effects which occur when multiple tools are used in policy packages operating in complex multi-policy, multi-actor, and multi-level design contexts expected to address multiple goals and objectives (Howlett 2014a; Howlett and Lejano 2013; Howlett et al. 2014). The design and construction of portfolios capable of operating in such contexts are a key feature of contemporary design studies and practices in the post-globalization and post-governance period (del Río and Howlett 2013).

These studies also delve more deeply than before into the behavioural characteristics of designers (Considine 2012) and into the location and activities of different kinds of advisors, experts, and the public involved in policy formulation activities (Craft and Howlett 2012; Bason 2014) and how their activities and advice affect policy designs and designing, a subject which is explored in later chapters.

Dealing with policy dynamics

Current policy design studies are especially interested in the different means and patterns through which policy mixes evolve over time (van der Heijden 2011; Thelen 2003, 2004; Kay 2007; Feindt 2012).

This important research area in the new policy design studies deals with better understanding the temporal processes through which designs and design spaces are created and evolve. Where the old design orientation often assumed a constrained yet blank slate available to policy designers, newer design thinking is rooted more in an empirical experience that has generally shown policy designers having to work in spaces with already-established policy mixes and significant policy legacies. Mixes may emerge over long stretches of time as a result of earlier policy decisions. As a result, even when the initial logic of these decisions matching policy tool and target may have been clear, through multiple layering processes they can gradually degenerate over time (van der Heijden 2011; Bode 2006; Howlett and Rayner 1995; Orren and Skowronek 1998; Rayner et al. 2001; Torenvlied and Akkerman 2004; Hacker 2005).

In understanding this temporality of policy-making, current design studies draw heavily on the work of historical and sociological neo-institutionalists (for example, Thelen 2003, 2004), who noted how macro-institutional arrangements have often been less the product of calculated planning than the result of processes of incremental modifications or reformulations such as 'layering' or 'drift' (Kay 2007; van der Heijden 2011), in which successive reforms are 'patched' into or on top of existing arrangements. In the new design orientation, these processes are seen as also applying equally to policy-making.

Optimizing the choice of instruments in such mixes requires an additional level of knowledge of instrument–goal interactions and consideration of the long- and short-term processes of policy change which affect them. That is, in addition to questions relating to the integration of policy tools and understanding the nature of the design spaces, the evolution and history of policy mixes are also of concern to the most recent generation of design thinkers. Scholars in the new design orientation, for example, are concerned with how the effectiveness of 'unintended' policy mixes, created and limited by historical legacies, can be hampered due to internal inconsistencies, whereas other policy instrument groupings can be more successful in creating an internally supportive and more effective combination (Howlett and Rayner 2007; Grabosky 1994; Gunningham et al. 1998; del Río 2010).

While the old orientation tended to suggest that design could only occur in spaces where policy packages could be designed *en bloc* and *de novo*, the new orientation recognizes that most design circumstances involve building on foundations created in another era and working within sub-optimal or 'second-best' design spaces which preclude the creation of entirely new policy packages. This contextual 'lock in' impacts the formulation process by restricting a government's ability to evaluate alternatives and plan or design in a wholly open-ended manner (Howlett 2009a; Oliphant and Howlett 2010; Williams 2012).

In such situations, 'designers often attempt to patch or restructure existing policy elements rather than propose alternatives *de novo* although the situation may require the latter' (Howlett 2013; see also Gunningham and Sinclair 1999a; Thelen 2003, 2004; Eliadis et al. 2005). Contemporary policy design scholars are very interested in such processes and how policy formulators, such as software designers, issue 'patches' to correct flaws in existing mixes or allow them to better adapt to changing circumstances (Rayner 2013; Howlett 2013; Howlett and Rayner 2013). And they are also interested in related subjects, such as how policy experiments can help reveal the possibilities of re-design (Hoffman 2011) or how building temporal properties into tool mixes – sometimes refered to as 'adaptive policy-making' (Swanson et al. 2010) – can make designs more flexible or resistant to shifting conditions (Walker et al. 2010; Haasnoot et al. 2013). These and other related subjects are discussed in greater length in subsequent chapters.

Dealing with 'new' policy tools: co-production, co-design, social media, and nudges

A third contemporary research area concerns the analysis and inclusion in designs of several new, or at least apparently new, policy tools into the basic vocabulary or toolbox at the disposal of policy-makers and policy designers (Hood and Margetts 2007). Most notable in the present era are concerns for the design and operation of collaborative tools and platforms, such as crowdsourcing, co-production, and social media use, as well as behavioural tools, such as the use of defaults and other tools derived from the insights of recent research in behavioural economics, such as 'nudges' (Thaler and Sunstein 2009).

The former set of tools includes the use of social media platforms (Taeihagh 2017; Liu 2017) to organize both the delivery of services – 'co-production' (Pestoff 2006; Pestoff et al. 2006) – and to influence the

POLICY DESIGN IN THE CONTEMPORARY ERA

design process – 'co-design' (Blomkamp 2018). The latter includes a variety of tools designed to affect the automatic cognitive system in humans and 'nudge' them toward behaviours in their 'best interests' (Thaler and Sunstein 2009; Thaler et al. 2010).

The use of tools in the first category to promote collaboration and co-production is a growing area which links closely with governance thinking around the increased networkization of society but has received surprisingly little detailed treatment in the policy instruments literature to date. It concerns recent trends toward the increased promotion of collaboration and the co-production of many public services, a predominant feature of initiatives such as the new public governance (NPG) approach to public management, which focuses upon the increased use of non-state actors and organizations to provide 'policy-like' outputs and activities. These range from using disability and elderly support organizations to provide services to these groups ('co-production') as well as other activities, such as the use of non-governmental 'stewardship' councils to provide a basic framework of regulation ('co-management'), as occurs with groups such as the Forest Stewardship Council with respect to logging activities, the Marine Stewardship Council with respect to the fisheries, and many others (Ansell and Gash 2017; Cashore 2002; Cashore et al. 2003).

Notwithstanding some arguments which continue to be made about the inevitability of moves in this direction, many proponents of enhanced collaboration between state and societal actors claim 'collaborative governance' combines the best of both government and market-based arrangements by bringing together public and private actors in a policy sector in a constructive and inexpensive way to provide valuable services to society (Koffijberg et al. 2012; Rhodes 1997). Many key sectors from health to education and others already feature elements of either or both hierarchical approaches, such as regulation, bureaucratic oversight and service delivery, as well as market- and network-based non-hierarchical approaches, such as co-pays and exchanges, voluntary organizations, and increasingly, co-production (Brandsen and Pestoff 2006; Pestoff 2006; Pestoff et al. 2006, 2012). This is true of most educational systems, for example, where extensive unpaid work by parents is encouraged, and in the health and medical sector in collaborative arrangements between, usually, public hospitals and private clinics and surgeries (Brandsen and Pestoff 2006; Tenbensel 2005).

Some of these tools also can be used to develop a more 'bottom-up', citizen-centred type of policy design sometimes referred to as 'co-design' (Blomkamp 2018; Bason 2014). This is an extension of older practices around public participation and collaborative governance, in which an effort is made to enhance the 'wisdom of crowds' and citizen knowledge in the policy formulation and design process.

Although often promoted as one-size-fits-all solutions to many policies and governance challenges, any general preference for collaboration has little evidence supporting it (see Adger and Jordan 2009; Howlett et al. 2009;

Hysing 2009; Kjær 2004; Van Kersbergen and Van Waarden 2004; Tunzelmann 2010). And unfortunately, poor definitions and poor theorization plague many accounts of collaboration in which otherwise-dissimilar governance efforts are often clumped under the same rubric and their nuances and differences ignored.

Thus, in practice, many 'collaborative' governance arrangements (Ansell and Gash 2008) are often prescribed without knowing exactly what they are and under what conditions they are likely to succeed or fail (Howlett and Ramesh 2016a, 2016b). The use and abuse of such arrangements require better analysis.

A second set of tools which has received a great deal of attention of late is comprised of those often relatively small-scale efforts at behavioural modifications premised on the notion of 'nudges' (Thaler and Sunstein 2009). The idea of utilizing this kind of behaviour-altering device has gained much traction within policy-making circles in recent times (see Center d'analyse stratégique 2011; Dolan and Galizzi 2014).

Nudges are geared toward using what has been termed 'system 1' thinking, which is the less-cognitive, more automatic or reflexive mode of thinking, compared to the more conscious 'system 2' mode (Kahneman 2013a), and to trigger desirable changes in individual behaviour, such as reducing speeding or promoting organ donations through system 1 'prompts'. Most of these are tools that attempt to alter public and individual behaviour through information provision, although with a decidedly less conscious or rational bent than in previous work (John 2013).

Sunstein (2014) identifies ten important nudge types which have been used or experimented with by governments in recent years in areas from pension reform to public hygiene. They include (1) default rules; (2) simplification; (3) use of social norms; (4) increases in ease and convenience; (5) disclosure; (6) warnings, graphic, or otherwise; (7) pre-commitment strategies; (8) reminders; (9) eliciting implementation intentions; and (10) informing people of the nature and consequences of their own past choices. These are discussed in more detail in later chapters.

Despite the rising popularity and promotion of the 'nudge' approach by new behavioural insight units in many governments (Strassheim 2021), however, the utilization of these kinds of tool also has its share of detractors. For instance, in some treatments of such tools, behavioural modification is expected to follow from government cues unthinkingly, although many of the tools listed earlier, such as disclosure and reminders, also require some aspects of 'system 2' or conscious thinking and cognition if they are to be effective.

Similarly, the role of trust and credibility of the information sent and received is also often underestimated. According to proponents of the nudge approach, for example, it is desirable and possible for public institutions to influence behaviour, such as making it more difficult to access junk food by removing it from sight, while they must also respect freedom of choice in what Thaler and Sunstein term a pattern of 'libertarian paternalism' (Sunstein and Thaler 2003; Thaler and Sunstein 2009). The paternalism which underlies the urge to deploy nudges (Sunstein 2015), however, may well undermine these efforts at persuasion by leading to a general distrust of government intentions (Wilkinson 2013; Mols et al. 2015; Galizzi 2014; Momsen and Stoerk 2014).

Critics also argue that in seeking to exploit and improve imperfections in human judgment, nudging is a manipulative technique, and thus the concept of 'liberty' on which it hinges precludes it from being empowering in any substantive sense and thus restricts it, at best, to marginal changes to existing practices (Goodwin 2012; Mills 2013; Wilkinson 2013; Sunstein 2015a; Coons and Weber 2014). Nudges have also been criticized for not being effective in changing deeply ingrained behaviour due to their overemphasis on individual preferences and their reliance on an atomistic approach to social structure (Goodwin 2012). The processes through which nudges enter into policy debates have also been called into question both in terms of the ostensibly privileged position enjoyed by nudge units in government dedicated to their spread (Feitsma 2018) and in terms of the general lack of familiarity of many analysts and others with the basic concepts involved in their design and implementation (Bandsma et al. 2021).

Dealing with the 'dark side': better analysis of policy risk through better understanding policy-maker and policy-taker behaviour

A fourth area of interest in contemporary design and instrument studies is 'policy volatility' or better assessing policy risks and the conditions under which policies succeed and fail.

Effective risk management in government needs to address both the external and internal sources of volatility. While the former risks from crises and emergencies and other events have received a great deal of treatment in recent years, culminating in the many works on policy-making during the COVID pandemic (Boin et al. 2021), the latter kind have not generally received as much attention as they deserve in policy studies.

That is, not all risks are exogenous to the policy process, and while most studies of policy risk management examine only the impact of 'external' risks, such as the impact of climate change, extreme weather events, or financial calamities, on policy outcomes and choices, there is a large second area of concern which also exists.

These 'internal risks' are those related to the adverse or malicious behaviour of policy-makers or to 'policy-takers' evading or otherwise undermining government initiatives mentioned earlier (Howlett 2020; Leong and Howlett 2022b). They originate in the oft-observed situations where policy-makers are driven by malicious or venal motivations rather than socially beneficial or disinterested ones or where the behaviour policy targets or 'policy-takers' have proclivities and tendencies toward activities such as gaming, free-rider-ship, and rent-seeking, which similarly undermine the notion of purely virtu-ous utilitarian or other-regarding behaviour (Howlett 2022).

Ignoring these risks does a disservice to both policy design and policy studies by failing to address a significant area that contributes to many policy failures and continuing policy problems. Internal risks, as well as external ones, must be curbed if policies are to achieve their aims, and policy design plays an important but little-studied role in this effort (Hoppe 2017; Feld-man 2018). This can be achieved through the use of tools which, singly or in combination, are less 'volatile' or combine together in positive rather than negative or counterproductive ways. And it can be aided by ensuring that instead of being rigid and stiff, policies are agile and flexible. Ensuring some level of accountability, including risk management processes and evaluations designed into a policy from the outset, is key in this area.

External risks stemming from causes such as wars, famines, pandemics, and other kinds of crises, and what can be done about them in policy designs, are generally well studied and understood (Boin et al. 2005; Boin and 't Hart 2010). These kinds of risks are the subject of most current risk management regimes, both in the public and private sector, which monitor and observe the external environment for signs of financial and other threats to supply chains, product lines, legal liability, and other dynamics that can affect profit-ability and shareholder value (e.g. FATF 2021; Human Rights Watch 2021; Pandemic Prevention Institute 2021).

This is less the case for internal risk factors, although some, such as fraud, malfeasance, dishonesty, and other actions on the part of public officials or general public, are addressed in other fields, such as audits and accountancy practice, performance reviews and hiring, and other kinds of personnel and corporate compliance 'best' practices which are the subject of public manage-ment and organization studies. Neither of these literatures, however, is tied very well to that on public policy or policy design, being a feature instead of studies of public and business management and administration.

But both internal and external risks are aspects of policy-making which can contribute to instability and the unpredictability of policy outcomes, ultimately often contributing to policy failure (Leong and Howlett 2022a). Incorporating instruments in policy designs that come with high risk of fail-ure, and failing to hedge or offset those risks, often leads to unstable policy results. When these risks are clearly understood and mitigation measures adopted in policy designs, however, better outcomes are more likely (Howlett 2020).

Dealing with such risks requires hard choices to be made both in policy formulation and implementation. There is therefore a need to 'design in' correctives, such as stricter accountability mechanisms, verification, and monitoring plans right at the outset to ensure these are locked in and left in place while a programme or policy matures (Plaček et al. 2018; Vine and

Sathaye 1999). As many governments have come to realize recently, without better risk management it is difficult to offset policy risks. That is, there is just as much of a need to better assess and address the internal risks of failure right at the outset when a policy is first considered as there is with the more familiar 'external' risks (Falco 2017; Taylor et al. 2019).

In response, in practice, many governments have begun to create guidelines and agencies to systematically anticipate and mitigate these kinds of risks. But this process has been very uneven and varies by jurisdiction.

Conclusion: moving forward in policy design studies

The recognition of the continued vitality of the state in a globalized environment, along with the existence of multiple modern sectoral modes of governance, suggests a more subtle and nuanced account of policy design trends and influences is required than is typically found in the discussions about instrument use and policy design which have flowed from studies of globalization and network governance. Embedding the discussion of policy design in the Procrustean bed of globalization and network theory is not a useful way to advance thinking on the subject.

Better understanding contemporary policy design rather requires an effort to develop more nuanced understandings of the policy formulation and implementation activities of governments than is provided by adhering to either or both of the 'globalization' and 'government to governance' hypotheses.

The future research agenda for scholars in the new design orientation thus includes many important and sometimes neglected subjects. As set out earlier, four of the subjects of current interest include outlining principles of design quality in complex, multi-tiered mixes and understanding design spaces, their evolution, and the evaluation of different kinds of design processes associated with them, dealing with 'new' or innovative policy tools, such as co-production or behavioural nudges, and effectively designing for policy risk of all types, especially the less well-studied and understood 'internal' ones.

Fortunately, other scholarship on policy design and policy instrument choice has offered pathways to a better understanding of these aspects of instrument selection and policy design by grounding knowledge more carefully in empirical studies and in more nuanced and sophisticated analyses of policy-making practices and activities (Bressers and O'Toole 1998; de Bruijn and Hufen 1998; Van Nispen and Ringeling 1998).

This more detailed and systematic understanding of the kinds of policy choices open to governments and of their ability to choose specific combinations of policy tools in their efforts to create and manage public policy-making is needed to advance our understanding of policy design and is discussed in Part II (Ingraham 1987).

Readings

Bason, C. and A. Schneider. (2014). 'Public Design in Global Perspective: Empirical Trends'. In C. Bason (ed.), *Design for Policy* (new edn). Farnham, UK; Burlington, VT: Gower, 23–40.

Blomkamp, E. (2018). 'The Promise of Co-Design for Public Policy'. *Australian Journal of Public Administration* 77 (forthcoming). Accessed 31 October 2018.

Bovaird, T. (2007). 'Beyond Engagement and Participation: User and Community Coproduction of Public Services'. *Public Administration Review* 67, no. 5: 846–860.

Brandsen, T. and M. Honingh. (2016). 'Distinguishing Different Types of Coproduction: A Conceptual Analysis Based on the Classical Definitions'. *Public Administration Review* 76, no. 3: 427–435.

Cerny, P. G. (1996). 'International Finance and the Erosion of State Policy Capacity'. In P. Gummett (ed.), *Globalization and Public Policy*. Cheltenham, UK: Edward Elgar, 83–104.

De Bruijn, J. A. and E. F. ten Heuvelhof. (1995). 'Policy Networks and Governance'. In D. L. Weimer (ed.), *Institutional Design*. Boston, MA: Kluwer Academic Publishers, 161–179.

Hobson, J. and M. Ramesh. (2002). 'Globalisation Makes of States What States Make of It: Between Agency and Structure in the State/Globalisation Debate'. *New Political Economy* 7, no. 1: 5–22.

Howlett, M. (2014). 'From the "Old" to the "New" Policy Design: Design Thinking Beyond Markets and Collaborative Governance'. *Policy Sciences* 47, no. 3: 187–207.

Howlett, M. (2020). 'Challenges in applying design thinking to public policy: Dealing with the varieties of policy formulation and their vicissitudes'. *Policy & Politics* 48, no. 1: 49–65.

Howlett, M. (2022). 'Avoiding a Panglossian Policy Science: The Need to Deal with the Darkside of Policy-Maker and Policy-Taker Behaviour'. *Public Integrity* 24, no. 3 (4 May): 306–318.

Howlett, M. and R. Lejano. (2013). 'Tales from the Crypt: The Rise and Fall (and Re-Birth?) of Policy Design Studies'. *Administration & Society* 45, no. 3: 356–380.

Howlett, M. and M. Ramesh. (2006). 'Globalization and the Choice of Governing Instruments: The Direct, Indirect and Opportunity Effects of Internationalization'. *International Public Management Journal* 9, no. 2: 175–194.

John, P. (2013). 'All Tools Are Informational Now: How Information and Persuasion Define the Tools of Government'. *Policy & Politics* 41, no. 4 (1 October): 605–620.

Johnson, E. J., S. B. Shu, B. G. C. Dellaert, C. Fox, D. G. Goldstein, G. Häubl, R. P. Larrick, J. W. Payne, E. Peters, D. Schkade and B. Wansink. (2012). 'Beyond Nudges: Tools of a Choice Architecture'. *Marketing Letters* 23, no. 2 (June): 487–504.

Kahneman, D. (2013). *Thinking, Fast and Slow* (1st edn). New York: Farrar, Straus & Giroux.

Kooiman, J. (1993). 'Governance and Governability: Using Complexity, Dynamics and Diversity'. In J. Kooiman (ed.), *Modern Governance*. London: Sage, 35–50.

Liu, H. K. (2017). 'Crowdsourcing Government: Lessons from Multiple Disciplines'. *Public Administration Review 77*, no. 5: 656–667.

Milward, H. B. and K. G. Provan. (2000). 'Governing the Hollow State'. *Journal of Public Administration Research and Theory 10*, no. 2: 359–380.

Rhodes, R. A. W. (1996). 'The New Governance: Governing Without Government'. *Political Studies 44*: 652–667.

Schubert, C. (2017). 'Green Nudges: Do They Work? Are They Ethical?' *Ecological Economics 132*, no. *Supplement* C (1 February): 329–342.

Taeihagh, A. (2017). 'Crowdsourcing: A New Tool for Policy-Making?' *Policy Sciences 50*, no. 4 (1 December): 629–647.

Treib, O., H. Bahr and G. Falkner. (2007). 'Modes of Governance: Towards a Conceptual Clarification'. *Journal of European Public Policy 14*, no. 1: 1–20.

Van Kersbergen, K. and F. Van Waarden. (2004). ' "Governance" as a Bridge Between Disciplines: Cross-Disciplinary Inspiration Regarding Shifts in Governance and Problems of Governability, Accountability and Legitimacy'. *European Journal of Political Research 43*: 143–171.

Weiss, L. (1998). *The Myth of the Powerless State: Governing the Economy in a Global Era*. Cambridge: Polity Press.

Weiss, L. (2005). 'The State-Augmenting Effects of Globalisation'. *New Political Economy 10*, no. 3: 345–353.

Part II

SYSTEMATICALLY STUDYING POLICY DESIGN

What is policy design? Key definitions and concepts in the study of policy design

Providing a better, more nuanced understanding of policy design and the factors which influence it is the goal of this book. In attaining that goal, it is helpful to go back a step and provide several definitions of key concepts commonly used in the study of policy design.

What is public policy?

The first term which requires definition is 'public policy'. The most concise formal definition of a public policy was set out by Thomas Dye in his early and best-selling text on the subject, where he defined *policy* simply as 'what government chooses to do or not to do' (Dye 1972). This is a useful definition insofar as it underscores the notions that policies are conscious choices and not accidents or accidental occurrences; that they result from government decisions and not those of other actors in society, such as private companies or other non-governmental organizations; and that so-called 'negative decisions' – that is, decisions to consciously avoid changing the status quo – are just as much public policies as the more commonly understood 'positive decisions', which do, in fact, alter some aspect of current circumstances.

This definition, however, is not all that helpful from a design perspective because it does not reveal anything about the *processes* through which policies are made, or the *substantive content* of government decisions and the different elements which go into making them up. In addressing these two issues, a second definition put forward almost two decades before Dye's by one of the earliest proponents of the modern policy sciences, the University of Chicago political psychologist Harold Lasswell, is quite helpful. Lasswell, like Dye, also

DOI: 10.4324/9781003343431-5

defined *public policies* as government decisions but noted that they were composed of two interrelated elements: *policy goals* and *policy means* operating at different levels of abstraction (Lasswell 1958). *Policy goals* in this sense are the basic aims and expectations governments have in deciding to pursue (or not) some course of action, while *policy means* are the techniques they use to attain those goals (Walsh 1994). Both these elements can be focused on a range of activities, from abstract principles associated with governance arrangements to much more concrete administrative programme specifications.

In terms of *content*, this suggests that policies are composed of a number of analytically distinct elements, with some policies focused on attaining concrete outputs while others focus on less-tangible normative and cognitive aspects of policy-making. However, the situation is much more complex than might first appear. A typical substantive policy, for example, involves some very abstract general 'aims' or goals, such as, in the cases of criminal justice or education policy, attaining a just society or a prosperous one, along with a set of less abstract 'objectives' actually expected to achieve those aims, such as, in the examples provided earlier, reducing crime or providing better educational opportunities to members of the public. Further, those objectives themselves must be concretized in a set of specific targets or measures which allow policy resources to be directed toward goal attainment, such as reducing specific types of crimes to specific levels within specified periods of time or increasing post-secondary educational attendance by some percentage within a set period of time (Cashore and Howlett 2007; Stavins 2008; Howlett and Cashore 2009; Howlett et al. 2023).

Similarly, the means or techniques for achieving these goals also exist on several levels. These run from highly abstract preferences for specific forms of policy implementation, such as a preference for the use of market, government, or non-profit forms of organization to implement policy goals in areas such as healthcare or crime prevention, to the more concrete level of the use of specific governing tools or mechanisms, such as regulation, information campaigns, public enterprises, or government subsidies, to alter actor behaviour in order to promote or increase wellness or prevent crime. And this extends further to the most specific level of deciding or determining exactly how those tools should be 'calibrated' in order to achieve policy targets. This latter activity, to continue the examples, might include providing a specific number of additional police on the streets within a specified period of time or a specific level of subsidy to non-profit groups to provide additional hospital beds or other types of health services, again within a set period of time (Howlett 2005, 2009a; Stavins 2008).

Policies are thus complex entities composed of different kinds of policy goals and means arranged in several layers, ranging from the most general level of a relatively abstract governance mode to the level of a regime of policy tools and objective and, finally, to the level of specific programme settings (Cashore and Howlett 2006, 2007; Howlett and Cashore 2009). The principal 'components' of public policies involved in any policy design, following this logic, are set out in Table 3.1.

Table 3.1 Components of public policies involved in policy design

		Policy level		
		Governance mode: high-level abstraction	Policy regime: programme-level operationalization	Programme settings specific on-the-ground measures
Policy component	Policy goals	General abstract policy aims: the most general macro-level statement of government aims and ambitions in a specific policy area	Operationalizable policy objectives: the specific meso-level areas that policies are expected to address in order to achieve policy aims	Specific policy targets: the specific, on-the-ground aims of efforts to achieve objectives and aims
	Policy means	General policy implementation preferences: the long-term preferences of government in terms of the types of organizational devices to be used in addressing policy aims	Policy tool choices: the specific types of governing instruments to be used to address programme-level objectives	Specific policy tool calibrations: the specific 'settings' of policy tools required to implement policy programmes

Source: Adapted from Howlett and Cashore (2009).

In terms of policy-making *processes*, Lasswell (1956) also discussed this subject in a useful way. He did so by using one of the historically most popular models for analyzing public policy-making, which has been to think of it as a set of interrelated stages through which policy issues and deliberations flow in a more or less sequential fashion from 'inputs' (problems) to 'outputs' (policies). The resulting sequence of stages is expected to be repeated as times and circumstances change, leading to what has often been referred to as the 'policy cycle' (Jann and Wegrich 2007; Howlett et al. 2009).

This idea of a policy cycle is straightforward but has received somewhat different treatment in the hands of different authors. In his own work, for example, Lasswell (1971) divided the policy process into seven stages, which, in his view, described not only how public policies were actually made but also how they should be made: (1) intelligence, (2) promotion, (3) prescription, (4) invocation, (5) application, (6) termination, and (7) appraisal (see also Weible et al. 2022). In this construct, the policy process began with intelligence-gathering, that is, the collection, processing, and dissemination of information for those who participate in decision-making. It then moved to the promotion of particular options by those involved in making the decision. In the third stage, the decision-makers prescribed a course of action. In the fourth stage, the prescribed course of action was invoked alongside a set of sanctions to penalize those who fail to comply with these prescriptions. The policy was then applied by the courts and the bureaucracy and ran its course until it was terminated or cancelled. Finally, the results of the policy were appraised or evaluated against the original aims and goals.

In this view, standard in the policy sciences, policy-making is viewed not as primarily a random, ritualistic, or symbolic form of state activity but as a conscious attempt to match the means of policy implementation to formulated policy goals. While there is no doubt that some aspects of policy-making can be heavily symbolic and ritualized (Edelman 1964, 1971), from a design perspective, these are not the defining characteristics of policy-making, which is typically viewed as a much more pragmatic activity: that is, one intended to effectively alter practices on-the-ground in a more or less conscious or deliberate way through the efficient use of available governing resources or the creation of new ones. That is, policy-making is viewed as an *instrumental* problem-solving activity, one in which various governing resources are marshalled behind a set of techniques which could at least potentially or theoretically achieve the aims, objectives, and goals of policy-makers.

Lasswell's original formulation provided the basis for many other later models of the policy process which each contained slightly different interpretations of the names, number, and order of stages in the cycle but used the same logic to describe them, that of 'applied problem solving' (Lyden et al. 1968; Simmons et al. 1974; Brewer 1974; Anderson 1983; Brewer and de Leon 1983; Jones 1984; deLeon 1999b; Hill and Hupe 2006). This logic is ultimately what gives the 'standard' cycle model its form (Howlett et al. 2019).

The basic stages in applied problem-solving and their corresponding stages in the policy process are depicted in Figure 3.1.

In this 'standard' model, *agenda-setting* refers to the process by which problems come to the attention of governments; *policy formulation* refers to how policy options are formulated within government; *decision-making* is the process by which governments adopt a particular course of action or non-action; *policy implementation* relates to how governments put policies into effect; and *policy evaluation* refers to the processes by which the results of policies are monitored by both state and societal actors, the outcome of which may be reconceptualization of policy problems and solutions.

The idea of a policy process or cycle has often been used to view policy-making in essentially pragmatic terms, as the embodiment of efforts to improve the human condition through harnessing reason to guide human

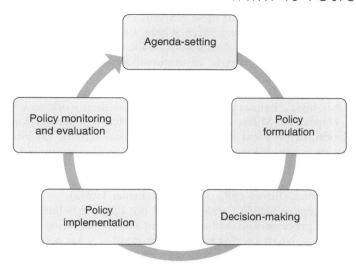

Figure 3.1 The five stages of the policy cycle and their relationship to applied problem-solving.

activities, in this case, in the process of governing (Hawkesworth 1992). In this view, policy means or instruments are often viewed mainly as *technical* mechanisms used to attain policy goals and as existing only in the stages of policy formulation – when policy means are proposed – and policy implementation – when they are put into effect.

However, a process model can also be used to describe policy-making as a much more overtly social or political process in which actors compete with each other in order to define problems and attain their goals or collectively 'puzzle' through toward the solution to an issue (Howlett et al. 2009; Wu et al. 2010). In this view, policy instruments are thought of as much less technical than political in nature and are typically viewed as extending to activities located in all stages of the policy process, including not just policy formulation and implementation but also agenda-setting, decision-making, and policy evaluation (Howlett 2022a).

What is a policy style?

In describing long-term patterns in policy-making or what happens after many iterations of a policy cycle, policy studies typically draw on the notion of 'policy regimes' or long-term arrangements which include a common set of policy ideas (policy paradigm), a long-lasting governance arrangement (policy mix), a common or typical policy process (policy style), and a more or less fixed set of policy actors (policy subsystem or policy monopoly).

Together, it is argued that these elements combine to ensure policy outputs typically will remain very much within a range of options compatible with the pillars of the regime. In his work on social policy, for example, Gosta Esping-Andersen found 'specific institutional arrangements' to have been adopted by societies in the pursuit of work and welfare. He argued that 'a given organization of state – economy relations is associated with a particular social policy logic' (Rein et al. 1987). Similarly, in their work on US policy-making, Harris and Milkis (1989: 25) argued that regimes developed as a 'constellation' of (1) ideas justifying governmental activity, (2) institutions that structure policy-making, and (3) a set of policies. Eisner similarly defined a regime as a 'historically specific configuration of policies and institutions which establishes certain broad goals that transcend the problems' specific to particular sectors, (Eisner 1993: xv; see also Eisner 1994a).

The concept of a *policy style* is useful not only for helping to describe typical policy processes and deliberations but also for capturing an important aspect of policy dynamics, that is, as a description of what policies look like and how they are developed thanks to the relatively enduring nature of policy regime elements (Larsen et al. 2006). Numerous case studies over the several decades have highlighted the manner in which ideological and institutional factors insulate policy-making from pressures for change. Pierson's (2000) work on path dependence and policy lock-in, for example, illustrated these dynamics.

As early as the mid-1970s, it was apparent to many observers that actors in the policy processes, as Simmons et al. (1974: 461) put it, tended to 'take on, over a period of time, a distinctive style which affect . . . policy decisions, that is, they develop tradition and history which constrains and refines their actions and concerns'.

The general idea of polities developing a characteristic way of doing things, or a style of governing or ruling, of course, is not new. It has clear links to the foundational studies of bureaucracy and bureaucratization developed by Weber and others in the late nineteenth and early twentieth centuries (Weber 1978; Eisenstadt 1963). And it was also a major part of the first wave of comparative administrative studies carried out after the Second World War which focused on the identification and elaboration of national administrative cultures (Waldo 1948; Barker 1944).

The concept of such styles re-emerged in the late 1990s in the works of, among others, Héritier et al. (1996), Knill (1998, 1999), Bekke et al. (1993, 1996a, 1996b, 2000), and Bekke (1999), scholars interested in the difficulties encountered in the countries of the European Union (EU) in adopting and implementing EU-wide administrative initiatives as the Union unfolded. This scholarship suggested the critical importance of the concept of national administrative styles in understanding the role played by existing national-level administrative systems in affecting public policy processes and outcomes, including impeding efforts to reshape the administration itself through the EU process.

The first modern studies of policy styles argued that public policy outcomes varied directly according to the nature of the political system found in each country (Peters et al. 1978). Although some empirical evidence of substantial differences in *outcomes* was uncovered in empirical tests of this hypothesis (Castles 1998; Obinger and Wagschal 2001), it was soon suggested that the concept could be fruitfully applied not only to outcomes but also to the policy processes followed in a particular country and to the kinds of tools governments preferred to use in implementing their wishes. Richardson and his colleagues, for example, looked at the similarities and differences that existed among the countries of Western Europe in terms of their propensity to take *anticipatory or reactive* decisions and, in either case, whether they tended to do so in a *top-down state-driven or bottom-up societally driven* fashion. On this basis, it was argued that each country or group of countries could be said to have its own pattern of policy-making or 'style', which characterized its policy processes and the resulting policy decisions (Richardson et al. 1982).

Although not inclusive of all aspects of a regime, the manner in which policy deliberations take place and the kinds of instruments chosen to implement policies can be said to constitute a policy style. This style is exercised within the constraints imposed by institutional arrangements, which shape its contours, such as political and electoral conventions and institutions, as well as within a policy paradigm that shapes its content (Hogan and Howlett 2015). The style helps determine the typical range and type of alternatives and final policy outputs which occur as policy issues are processed within a regime.

Policy styles are sturdy because they are intimately linked with governance contexts and institutional arrangements (Howlett 2002c). National policy systems, for example, can be seen as the offshoots of larger national governance and administrative traditions or cultures (Dwivedi and Gow 1999; Bevir and Rhodes 2001), such as parliamentary or republican forms of government and federal or unitary states. This leads to different concentrations of power in the central institutions of government, degrees of openness, and access to information and patterns of reliance on certain kinds of governing instruments rather than others. Civil service organizations have rules and structures affecting policy and administrative behaviour, such as the constitutional order establishing and empowering administrators and affecting patterns and methods of recruiting civil servants and how they interact with each other and the public, which make their deployment by governments more or less difficult and often inflexible (Bekke et al. 1993).

As such, a policy style is a useful concept for describing and explaining the long-term patterns found in policy processes and in the substance of policy-making. The general idea is that policy-making tends to develop in such a way that the same actors, institutions, instruments, and governing ideas tend to dominate policy-making for extended periods of time, infusing a policy sector with both a consistent content and a set of typical policy processes or procedures and actors, heavily influencing preferred policy designs and design thinking and practice in the jurisdiction concerned (Knill 1998; Tosun and Lang 2017; Kuks 2004; de Vries 2005).

What is policy design?

As we have seen in Chapter 1 and Chapter 2, within the policy sciences, 'design' has been linked both to policy instruments and implementation (May 2003) and to the impact of policy ideas and advice on policy formulation (Linder and Peters 1990a). It is usually thought to involve the deliberate and conscious attempt to define policy goals and connect them in an instrumental or logical fashion to the instruments or tools expected to realize those objectives (Gilabert and Lawford-Smith 2012; Majone 1975; May 2003). *Policy design*, in this sense, was defined earlier as

> a specific form of policy formulation based on the gathering of knowledge about the effects of policy tool use on policy targets and the application of that knowledge to the development and implementation of policies aimed at the attainment of specifically desired public policy outcomes and ambitions.

This design activity occurs mainly at the policy formulation stage of the policy process but is not synonymous with that stage. Rather, it represents one way in which sets of ideas about policy-making and possible policy outcomes can be combined (Goggin 1987).

In this sense, paralleling the situation with policies themselves, policy designs can be seen to contain both a substantive component – a set of alternative arrangements thought potentially capable of resolving or addressing some aspect of a policy problem, one or more of which is ultimately put into practice – as well as a procedural component – a set of activities related to securing some level of agreement among those charged with formulating, deciding upon, and administering that alternative (Howlett 2011).

Design thus overlaps and straddles both policy formulation, decision-making, and policy implementation and involves actors, ideas, and interests active at each of these stages of the policy process (Howlett et al. 2009). However, it also posits a very specific form of interaction among these elements, driven by knowledge and evidence of alternatives' merits and demerits in achieving policy goals rather than by other processes such as bargaining or electioneering among key policy actors (Bobrow 2006; Bobrow and Dryzek 1987; Montpetit 2003a; Weaver 2009a, 2010b).

The idea of policy design is inextricably linked with the idea of improving government actions through the conscious and systematic consideration during policy formulation of the likely outcomes of policy implementation activities. This is a concern both for non-governmental actors concerned with bearing the costs of government failures and incompetence, as well as for governmental ones who may be tasked with carrying out impossible duties and meeting unrealistic expectations.

As discussed earlier, regardless of regime and issue type and regardless of the specific weight given by governments to different substantive and procedural aims, all governments commonly wish to have their goals effectively achieved and usually wish to do so in an efficient way, that is, with a minimum of effort and cost, so as to preserve their scarce resources for other tasks where they may be needed (Weimer 1993). All governments, of whatever stripe, are interested in applying knowledge and experience about policy issues in such a way as to ensure the more or less efficient and effective realization of their aims, even if those aims – like re-election or the elimination of opponents or self-enrichment – are not particularly laudable or beneficial to the public at large (deLeon 1999a; Potoski 2002).

Goal attainment efforts involve governments of all types and persuasions in processes of more or less conscious and rational efforts at design (Dryzek 1983). It also allows us to define policy designing as the effort

> to more or less systematically develop efficient and effective policies through the application of knowledge about policy means gained from experience and reason to the development and adoption of courses of action that are likely to succeed in attaining their desired goals or aims within specific policy contexts.
>
> (Bobrow and Dryzek 1987; Bobrow 2006; Montpetit 2008)

As discussed in the introductory chapter to this book, in their many works on the subject in the late 1980s and early 1990s, Stephen H. Linder and B. Guy Peters argued that policy designs could be considered in the abstract since, at least in theory, the actual process followed in public policy decision-making, and the actual conditions in which a tool would be deployed could, in an analytical sense, be divorced from a design. That is, in the same way that while in practice an architectural concept can not be divorced from its engineering manifestation, this can occur in the abstract when, for example, the idea for a Romanesque public building or a 'temple' bank is suggested.

Policy designs in this sense, they argued, can be thought of as 'ideal types', that is, as ideal configurations of sets of policy elements which can reasonably be expected, within a specific contextual setting, to deliver a specific outcome. Whether or not all the aspects of a design are realizable in a specific contextual configuration in practice, in their view, can be thought of as more or less incidental to the design, in the same way that a building budget may not allow as grandiose a plan for a bank or headquarters or public building to be realized as was originally proposed. As Linder and Peters (1988) argued:

> Design then, is not synonymous with instrumental reasoning but certainly relies greatly on that form of reasoning. Moreover, the invention or fashioning of policy options is not designing itself and may not even call

on any design. While somewhat at odds with conventional (mis)usage, our treatment focuses attention on the conceptual underpinnings of policy rather than its content, on the antecedent intellectual scheme rather than the manifest arrangement of elements. As a result, the study of design is properly 'meta-oriented' and, therefore, one step removed from the study of policy and policy-making.

(Linder and Peters 1988: 744)

In this view, conceptually, a policy design process begins with knowledge of the abilities of different kinds of policy tools to affect policy outputs and outcomes and of the kinds of resources required to allow those tools to operate as intended (Hood 1986c; Salamon 2002c).

This instrumental knowledge is contextual in the sense that it requires an understanding of the source of policy tool effects and of how the use of different kinds of instruments affects target group behaviour and compliance with government aims in specific ways in specific circumstances. And it also includes knowledge and consideration of the many possible constraints on tool effectiveness originating in the limits of existing knowledge, prevailing governance structures, and other arrangements and behaviours which may preclude consideration of certain options and promote others whether appropriate to the context or not (Howlett 2009a, 2011). Much like building construction, then, policy design is a process which requires propitious circumstances including high levels of both analytical skills and evidentiary capacity as well as the intention to exercise those skills and capacity in the development and realization of a design (Howlett 2009a).

Such a means–ends understanding of policy-making permeates the policy design orientation, but as noted earlier, of course, is only one possible orientation or set of practices which can be followed in policy formulation and result in policy outputs (Colebatch 1998; Tribe 1972; Howlett and Mukherjee 2017). In the design case, policy formulators are expected as much as possible to base their analyses on logic, knowledge, and experience rather than, for example, purely political calculations or forms of satisficing behaviour which also can generate policy alternatives (Bendor et al. 2009; Sidney 2007).

Policy design studies deal with alternative forms of policy formulation by separating out two dimensions of the design experience: on the one hand, the procedural aspects of design – the specific types of policy formulation activities which lead to design – and, on the other, the substantive components – that is, the substance or content of an ideal type of design in terms of the configuration of instruments and instrument settings of which it is composed. The idea is that even when policy processes are less rational or knowledge-driven and more political or interest-driven, the design of an ideal type of policy, conceptually at least, can be divorced from the processes and circumstances involved in its enactment.

Thus, regardless of the nature of the actual formulation process which exists in a specific policy-making context, it is still possible to consider in the abstract and promote policy alternatives 'in-themselves' as ideal-type artifacts. These can then be developed and studied in preparation for their application in actual decision-making circumstances which might or might not be propitious to their adoption either in 'pure' form or with adjustments or amendments needed to meet conditions on the ground.

Again, as Linder and Peters (1990b) argued, such an ideal-typical

> design orientation to analysis can illuminate the variety of means implicit in policy alternatives, questioning the choice of instruments and their aptness in particular contexts. The central role it assigns means in policy performance may also be a normative vantage point for appraising design implications of other analytical approaches. More important, such an orientation can be a counterweight to the design biases implicit in other approaches and potentially redefine the fashioning of policy proposals.
>
> (304)

This is the bread-and-butter of policy design work undertaken by think tanks, policy institutes, policy schools, and many academics who develop and propose alternatives to existing policy arrangements, often quite far in advance of when an issue will actually appear on a government agenda, and thus are able to propose well-developed alternatives when the opportunity arises. That is, they develop new or revised solutions to potential or existing problems, solutions which are argued to be more likely to better achieve government or societal goals and/or to do so more effectively than present practices or considered alternatives.

Although often focused exclusively on means, policy design activity also extends to policy goals themselves, since goal articulation inevitably involves considerations of feasibility, or what is practical or possible to achieve in given conjunctures or circumstances (Huitt 1968; Majone 1975; Ingraham 1987). Even when the goals pursued are not laudable, such as personal enrichment or military adventurism, or when the knowledge or the means utilized is less than scientific, such as religious or ideologically inspired dogma or implementation preferences, and even when these efforts are much more *ad hoc* and much less systematic than might be desired, as long as a desire for effective resource use in goal attainment guides policy-making, it will involve some effort at design. However, this does not mean that all designs are equal or equally likely to generate similar results.

Rather, policy designs differ not only in the types of means chosen and the nature of the goals they pursue but also in the quality of the logical or empirical relations postulated to exist between policy components. Possible solutions to problems may be incorrect or ignored, means may be mis-specified or poorly executed, and/or problems and solutions poorly or mismatched. And as discussed in earlier chapters, such errors may be endemic or unavoidable if only a poor state of knowledge exists concerning both problems and solutions and the processes in place expected to match them together (Cohen et al. 1979; Dryzek 1983; Eijlander 2005; Franchino and Hoyland 2009; Kingdon 1984; Sager and Rielle 2013).

As was discussed in Chapter 1, this includes a variety of contexts in which formulators or decision-makers, for example, may engage in interest-driven trade-offs or logrolling between different values or resource uses or, more extremely, might engage in venal or corrupt behaviour in which personal gain from a decision may over-ride other evaluative criteria. These 'non-design' situations are well-known in political science but have not been well studied in the policy sciences, and the extent to which considerations such as political gain or blame avoidance calculations outweigh instrumental factors in policy formulation is a key question in contemporary policy design studies (Hood 2010; Hinterleitner 2020, 2018; Hansson 2018).

It is also important to note, again, that policy-making and, especially, policy tool selection are a highly constrained process. In this regard, the exact processes by which policy decisions are taken in different governments and contexts vary greatly by jurisdiction and sector and reflect the great differences and nuances that exist between different forms of government – from military regimes to liberal democracies – and within each type. These differences affect what kinds of factors are taken into account in decision-making and what kinds of policy tools are *prefered* (Howlett and Tosun 2018, 2021a).

And of course, the particular configuration of issues, actors, and problems which various governments, of whatever type, face in particular areas or sectors of activity – be it health or education policy, industrial policy, transportation or energy policy, social policy, or many others (Ingraham 1987; Howlett et al. 2009) – at specific points in time, also vary. In some circumstances, such as crises, for example, policy decisions are often required quickly, precluding extensive public participation or completion of new studies, and choices are much more likely to be more highly contingent and driven by situational logics and opportunism than at other times, when more careful deliberation and assessment are possible (Boin et al. 2005; Boin and 't Hart 2022; Tosun and Howlett 2021).

It is also typically the case, as noted above, that the development of programme-level objectives and means choices takes place within a larger governance context in which sets of institutions, actors, and practices are 'pre-defined' and make up the 'environment' within which policy-making takes place, affecting key aspects of policy deliberations and design choices. Some of the key elements which comprise a policy, notably, abstract policy aims and general implementation processes, for example, are often pre-defined at this 'meta' level of policy-making. Hence, as we have seen, a legal mode of governance may contain a preference for the use of laws, while a market mode of governance may involve a preference for a light regulatory touch and the extended use of financial tools, such as favourable tax treatment and subsidies.

Choices of programme-level tools and targets are constrained by these existing governance modes and preferences while, similarly, an existing policy regime logic is affected by the kinds of governing resources and capacities a government, and non-governmental actors, can muster (Skodvin et al. 2010).

Thus, for example, an existing preference to combat homelessness through public provision of rental accommodation rather than private family housing construction affects the choices of meso-level programme objectives and similarly constrains the establishment of micro-level targets (Petek et al. 2021).

This multi-level, nested, and often pre-given nature of the policy components that go into a policy design must be taken into account in any effort to design or plan policy outcomes (Howlett 2009). Better designs are more effective at doing this, generating policy processes and outcomes which are more consistent with their policy regime and governance environments.

What is a policy instrument?

The policy alternatives which policy designers create are composed of different sets or combinations of the policy elements described earlier are set out in more detail in Chapters 9–12. As Linder and Peters noted, policy instruments are especially significant in policy designs and designing as they are the techniques or means through which states can attempt to attain their goals. These tools are the subject of deliberation and activity at all stages of the policy process and affect both the agenda-setting and policy formulation processes as well as decision-making, policy implementation, and evaluation (Howlett 2005; Howlett, Ramesh and Perl 2009; Howlett 2022a).

Other terms have been developed in the field of policy studies to describe the same phenomenon, such as 'governing instruments', 'government instruments', 'policy levers', 'policy tools', and the 'tools of government', and while these sometimes are used to refer to different mechanisms and calibrations of policy means, they are more often used synonymously.

These tools have a special place in the consideration and study of policy design because, taken together, they comprise the contents of the toolbox from which governments must choose in building or creating any public policy. As we have seen, policy design studies elevates the analysis and practice of such policy instrument choices – typically but not exclusively those linked to policy implementation – to a central focus of inquiry, making their understanding and analysis a key design concern (Salamon 1981; Linder and Peters 1990a). Instrument choice, from this perspective, in a sense, *is* public policy-making, and understanding and analyzing potential instrument choices involved in implementation activity *is* policy design. One role of a textbook in policy design is thus assisting 'in constructing an inventory of potential public capabilities and resources that might be pertinent in any problem-solving situation' (Anderson 1975: 122), and this is one of the main goals of this book.

In this effort, as Hood (1986c) argued, although there are many policy tools, they can usefully be classified into a relatively small number of basic kinds, depending on the kind of 'governing resource' they deploy – in Hood's scheme, these being nodality (or information), authority, treasure, and organization, or NATO (see Table 3.2 for examples of the kinds of tools found in each category) (Margetts and John 2023).

Table 3.2 A resource-based taxonomy of procedural and substantive policy instruments

| | | Governing resource | | | |
		Nodality or information	Authority	Treasure	Organization
Purpose of tool	Substantive	Public information campaign	Independent regulatory agencies	Subsidies and grants	Public enterprises
	Procedural	Official secrets acts	Administrative advisory committees	Interest group funding	Government organizations

Note: Cells provide examples of instruments in each category.

Source: Howlett, M. (2000c)

While much attention has been paid to the use of these tools and resources in policy implementation, it is important to note that policy instruments exist at *all* stages of the policy process – with specific tools such as stakeholder consultations and government reviews intricately linked to agenda-setting activities, ones like legislative rules and norms linked to decision-making behaviour and outcomes, and others linked to policy evaluation, such as the use of ex-post, or after-the-fact, cost–benefit analyses (see Figure 3.2).

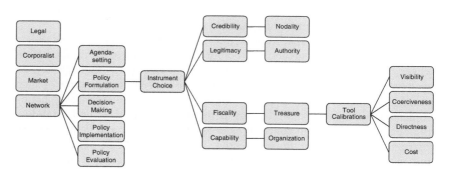

Figure 3.2 An example of the range of policy instruments by governance mode and stage of the policy cycle.

Policy tools are, in a sense, 'multi-purpose' and often 'substitutable' since, for example, regulation can appear in the implementation activities of several governance modes, while some tools, such as impact assessments, can also appear within several stages of the cycle, from agenda-setting to decision-making and policy evaluation. And what can be achieved by (involuntary) regulation, for example, can sometimes be achieved through (voluntary) subsidies.

However, many, instruments are not 100 percent substitutable. Voluntary subsidies, for example, even if set very high, may not be able to attain as high a level of compliance with government wishes as regulation backed up by the force of law and the threat of jail sentences for non-compliance. Similarly, providing a financial subsidy to encourage members of the public to undertake some activity may often prove more effective than just asking them to do the same thing – such as purchase electric vehicles or install solar panels and heat pumps in the effort to reduce greenhouse gases.

Moreover, a regulation appearing within the implementation phase of a network mode of governance which mandates information disclosure, for example, serves a different purpose than a regulation found in a market mode which limits a firm to ownership of only a specific percentage of an industry. Similarly, consultations which take place in the agenda-setting stage of the policy process have a different purpose and effect than those which take place after a decision has been made. While the general terminology may be similar, pains must be taken to distinguish these tools and activities in order to avoid confusion and errant efforts at instrument selection in policy design.

What is an implementation tool?

Policy instruments appear in all stages of the policy process, and those affecting the agenda-setting, decision-making, and evaluation stages of the policy process are very significant and important in public management (Wu et al. 2010; Howlett 2022a). However, most policy designs deal with the formulation of plans for implementation, and thus, the key sets of policy instruments of concern to most design studies are those linked to policy implementation in the first instance and to policy formulation in the second.

In the first category are examples of many well-known governing tools, such as public enterprises and regulatory agencies, which are expected to alter or affect the delivery of goods and services to the public and government (Salamon 2002c). In the second, are instruments such as procedures for public participation which are put into place in order to alter and affect aspect(s) of the nature of policy deliberations and the consideration and assessment of alternatives (Turnpenny et al. 2009).

The role played by instruments in policy implementation is one of the central foci of many of the chapters of this book, while the nature of formulation activity is the subject of many others. It is the presence and configuration of implementation tools, and that of their possible calibrations, however, which constitute a policy alternative and provide the substance or content of design deliberations occurring at the formulation stage of policy-making. Understanding implementation tools is thus key to policy design, although not its exclusive focus. These implementation instruments are government actions which affect either the content or processes of policy implementation, that is, which alter the way goods and services are delivered to the public or the manner in which such implementation processes take place (Howlett 2000c).

As Linder and Peters (1984) noted, it is critical for policy scientists and policy designers alike to understand this basic vocabulary of design:

> Whether the problem is an architectural, mechanical, or administrative one, the logic of design is fundamentally similar. The idea is to fashion an instrument that will work in a desired manner. In the context of policy problems, design involves both a systematic process for generating basic strategies and a framework for comparing them. Examining problems from a design perspective offers a more productive way of organizing our thinking and analytical efforts.
>
> (253)

That is, as is the case with tools in general, some implementation instruments alter the actual substance of the kinds of day-to-day production, distribution, and consumption activity carried out in society, while others focus more upon altering political or policy behaviour in the process of the articulation of implementation goals and means. *Substantive* implementation instruments are those used to directly affect the production, distribution, and consumption of goods and services in society, while *procedural* implementation instruments accomplish the second purpose (Ostrom 1986; Howlett 2000c, 2005; Lang 2022).

This distinction is apparent in common definitions of governing instruments, although its significance is sometimes over-looked. Vedung, for example, usefully defined policy instruments used in implementation activities as 'the set of techniques by which governmental authorities wield their power in attempting to ensure support and effect social change' (Vedung 1997a). This definition can be seen to include both 'substantive' tools, those Hood (1986c) defined as attempting to 'effect or detect' change in the socio-economic system, as well as those 'procedural' tools designed to 'ensure support' for government actions.

Substantive instruments are expected to alter some aspect(s) of the production, distribution, and delivery of goods and services in society. This is a large field of action since it extends not only to goods and services provided or affected by markets but also well beyond them, to state or public provision and regulation, as well as to those goods and services typically provided by the family, community, non-profit, and voluntary means, often with neither a firm market nor state basis (Salamon 1989; 2002a).

These goods and services are broadly conceived to include both mundane goods and services, such as school lunches, to crude vices, such as gambling or illicit drug use, to more common individual virtues, such as charitable giving or volunteer work with the physically challenged, and include the attainment of sublime collective goals, such as peace and security, sustainability, happiness, and well-being.

Substantive implementation instruments can affect many aspects of production, distribution, and consumption of goods and services. Production effects, for example, include determining or influencing:

1. Who produces a good or service – for example, via licencing, bureaucracy/procurement, or subsidies for new start-ups.
2. The types of goods and services produced – for example, through bans or limits or encouragement.
3. The quantity of goods or services provided – for example, via subsidies or quotas.
4. The quality of goods or services produced – for example, via product standards, warranties.
5. Methods of production – for example, via environmental standards or subsidies for modernization.
6. Conditions of production – for example, via health and safety standards, employment standards acts, minimum wage laws, and inspections.
7. The organization of production – for example, via unionization rules, antitrust or anti-combines legislation, securities legislation, or tax laws.

Consumption and distribution effects are also manifold. Some examples of these are:

1. Prices of goods and services – such as regulated taxi fares or wartime rationing.
2. Actual distribution of produced goods and services – affecting the location and types of schools or hospitals, forest tenures, or leases.
3. Level of consumer demand for specific goods – for example, through information release, nutritional and dangerous goods labelling (cigarettes), export and import taxes, and bans and similar activities.
4. Level of consumer demand in general – via interest rate, monetary, and fiscal policy.

Procedurally oriented implementation tools, on the other hand, affect production, consumption, and distribution processes only indirectly, if at all. Rather, they instead affect the behaviour of actors involved in policy implementation. That is, policy actors are arrayed in various kinds of policy communities, and just as tools can alter or affect the actions of citizens in the productive realm, so too can tools affect and alter aspects of policy-making behaviour (Knoke 1987, 1993).

Procedural implementation tools are an important part of government activities aimed at altering policy interaction within policy subsystems, but as Klijn et al. (1995) put it, they typically 'structure . . . the game without determining its outcome' (441). That is, these behavioural modifications affect the manner in which implementation unfolds, but without predetermining the results of substantive implementation activities.

These tools and their effects are not as well studied or understood as are substantive instruments, although several procedural techniques, such as the use of specialized investigatory commissions and government reorganizations, are quite old and well-used and have been the objects of study in fields such as public administration, public management, and organizational behaviour for some time (Woodley 2008; Schneider and Sidney 2009). Just like their substantive counterparts, they are a key part of policy designs and policy design activity (Bali et al. 2021).

Some of the kinds of implementation-related activities that can be affected by the use of procedural tools (Klijn et al. 1995; Goldsmith and Eggers 2004; Klijn and Koppenjan 2006) include:

1. Changing actor policy positions
2. Setting down, defining, or refining actor positions
3. Adding actors to policy networks
4. Changing access rules for actors to governments and networks
5. Influencing network formation
6. Promoting network self-regulation
7. Modifying system-level policy parameters (e.g. levels of market reliance)
8. Changing evaluative criteria for assessing policy outcomes, success, and failure
9. Influencing the pay-off structure for policy actors
10. Influencing professional and other codes of conduct affecting policy actor behaviour
11. Regulating inter-actor policy conflict
12. Changing policy actors' interaction procedures
13. Certifying or sanctioning certain types of policy-relevant behaviour
14. Changing supervisory relations between actors

As was discussed in Chapters 1 and 2 earlier, policy designs typically contain 'bundles' or 'mixes' of tools, and this includes mixes of both procedural and substantive implementation tools (Howlett 2000c, 2002c).

The nature of these policy portfolios is an important subject in policy designs and one to which we will return in subsequent chapters.

What isn't policy design?

As we have seen in earlier chapters, public policies are the result of efforts made by governments to alter aspects of behaviour – both that of their own agents and of society at large – in order to carry out some end or purpose. They are comprised of complex arrangements of policy goals and policy means matched through some decision-making process, and these policy-making efforts can be more or less systematic in attempting to match ends and means in a logical fashion or can result from much less systematic and rational processes.

Dimensions of policy design and non-design, including processes and outcomes, have often been viewed as existing along a spectrum from the more ordered (designed) to the disordered (non-designed). While the ordered end of the spectrum is well studied and theorized, there is little useful analytical language to describe the less-ordered end of the spectrum. Metaphors like 'muddles' (Lindblom 1959), 'messes' (Roe 2016), 'garbage cans' (Cohen et al. 1972), and 'anthills' (Czarniavswka 2009) exist but fail to capture the level of nuance required for a deeper analysis of 'non-design'.

These notions do, however, carry the sense that policy decisions can be careful and deliberate in attempting to best resolve a problem or can be highly contingent and driven by situational logics. The academic inquiry of policy design – that is, self-consciously dealing with both policy processes and substance under a knowledge-driven, instrumental rubric – emerged and flourished throughout the 1970s and 1980s in studies trying to clarify what a design process involved and when it was likely to occur (see e.g. Salamon 1981, 1989, 2002c). These also addressed many examples of poor designs and instances in which design considerations and intent were wholly lacking. Decisions stemming from bargaining or opportunism, for example, can be distinguished from those which result from careful analysis and assessment.

'Policy design' also implies a knowledge-based process in which the choice of means or mechanisms through which policy goals are given effect follows a logical process of inference from known or learned relationships between means and outcomes. This includes both designs in which means are selected in accordance with experience and knowledge and those in which principles and relationships may be incorrectly or only partially articulated or understood. However, it does not extend to other kinds of processes in which logical and evidence-informed analysis of alternate goals and means and instrumental choices of designs may be wholly lacking.

With respect to these latter instances of *non-design*, it bears repeating that the modern policy studies movement did begin with the clear recognition that public policy-making was not a purely technical exercise in matching means and ends but rather results from the interactions of policy-makers in the exercise of power, legitimate or otherwise (Arts and van Tatenhove 2004; Lasswell 1958; Stone 1988). This is an analysis which allows and expects not all choices to be made through careful, well-informed, and public-spirited deliberation.

Although some of these latter cases were noted to be simply arbitrary or capricious, most were viewed as representing a design failure rather than a lack of a design intention. That is, many studies of policy processes and outcomes underscored the concerted efforts of governments to intentionally act in an instrumental way, that is, to attempt to achieve a particular policy goal or end through the use of a relatively well-known set of policy means developed over many years of state-building experience (Lerner and Lasswell 1951). But as previously discussed, it was not always the case that the processes followed or their timelines allowed systematic review and evidence collection which would permit the analysis of multiple possible alternative courses of action (Parsons 1995, 2001).

This highlights that favourable design circumstances require not only the presence of high-quality information on the range and impacts of policy alternatives but also the presence of a favourable design environment: one in which there is a high level of technical capacity and expertise on the part of policy analysts and the time and desire to use it so that best available knowledge can be mobilized in order for policy instruments to be effectively and efficiently matched to policy goals and targets (Dunlop 2009a; Howlett 2009a, 2009d, 2010; Radaelli and Dunlop 2013).

The subject of what makes for a favourable 'design space' has been discussed earlier and is also considered in more detail in other parts of the book. Table 3.3, however, presents a schematic illustrating how two different aspects of policy-making – a design intention and the capacity to carry it out – create different policy formulation spaces which enable very different policy design processes. This sets out a number of different formulation processes lying between the intention and ability to undertake purposive, instrumental policy design and the intention to meet more political goals, coupled with the presence of significant policy resource constraints or tool lock-in affects.

This last phenomenon was recognized early on in studies of policy design: that not only 'spatial' but also 'temporal' aspects of policy formulation contexts, such as policy legacies or prior commitments, and issues, such as fast- and slow-moving crises, or the working of electoral, budgetary, and other kinds of temporal cycles (Howlett and Goetz 2014) affect how policy-makers actually formulate and consider alternatives.

Where there is a relatively high policy 'lock-in' on existing tool arrangements, for example, this can preclude adoption of potentially superior alternatives (Howlett and Rayner 2013). And as mentioned earlier, a rapidly spreading crisis – such as COVID-19 – could, for example, accelerate consideration of certain options, put the brakes on others, or allow deliberation of radically new alternatives (Hogan et al. 2022; Capano et al. 2022).

Table 3.3 Types of policy formulation spaces: situating design and non-design processes

		Level of government knowledge and other constraints	
		High	Low
Government formulation intention	**More instrumental**	Capable policy design space Relatively unconstrained formulation via design possible	Poor policy design space Only partially informed or restricted design possible
	Less instrumental	Capable political non-design space Relatively unconstrained non-design processes possible	Poor political non-design space Only poorly informed non-design possible

When propitious conditions are present, purposive design activity resulting in good alternative generation and assessment is thought to be possible (Bhatta 2002; Locke 2009; Nutley et al. 2007). When conditions are not ripe, on the other hand, either poor designs would ensue from the mobilization of only incomplete knowledge and information, even with the best government intent, or leading to less evidentiary and more interest-driven policy-making when that intent is missing (Davies 2004; Howlett 2009b; Moseley and Tierney 2004).

The extent to which either situation exists in contemporary policy-making is contested. It is often claimed, for example, that non-designed policy assemblages are increasingly common amidst a growing complexity in the nature of policy problems, their often more rapid onset, their multiple inter-linkages and the ensuing problems which occur in efforts to address them. Indeed, many scholars increasingly see policy change as a contested, negotiated, and constructed phenomenon shaped by a diverse mix of actors, ideas, institutions, and contiguous subsystems, what is sometimes described as a 'polycrisis' (Lawrence et al. 2023; von Homeyer et al. 2021).

And some contemporary studies of problems in areas such as climate change do show that instances of non-design appear to be more frequent as sectoral boundaries and process routines no longer condition how policy-makers and publics think about complex policy problems (Hartley et al. 2019; Head 2019; Nair and Howlett 2017a; Peters and Tarpey 2019). These studies suggest that non-designed assemblages, or what has been termed the emergence of 'policy nexuses' or loosely inter-locked set-up problems transcending old sectoral boundaries – such as sustainability or climate change – can lead to variety of phenomena, including increases in malfeasance, accident, unproductive or incomplete negotiation of conflicting interests, poor knowledge mobilization, and generally poor policy designs and outcomes (Boas et al. 2016; Liu et al. 2018; Stein and Jaspersen 2019).

Such circumstances, processes and practices can indeed frustrate the efforts of many policy-makers and analysts to devise feasible policy alternatives (Head 2010; Howlett 2020; Howlett and Mukherjee 2014), and introduce instability and disruption into what design-based theories would posit should be a more rational and logical policy process.

Even if they are not preferred, these non-designed decisions and arrangements are important to understand not only because they might be increasing in frequency but also because, once in place, they too may be very difficult to remove or amend, resulting in long-term sub-optimal policy lock-in. That is, it is often assumed that policies which emerge through non-design processes will terminate in evolutionary dead ends or failures. However, empirical observation shows that such assemblages can endure over considerable lengths of time. Many such mixes form complex and durable systems that emerge from processes in which components are often woven together opportunistically or accidentally but nevertheless prove quite durable.

Understanding all of these processes and the spaces in which they occur is a requisite of policy design studies, and the impact on policy formulation of tradition, policy styles, and path dependencies (Howlett and Tosun 2018; Enkler et al. 2017; Haydu 2010) should not be ignored or discounted. These factors often fill gaps left by the absence of formal design, intent, and rationality and must be included in any discussion of policy design, its drivers, and its determinants.

Different conceptions of policy design activity

As Clarke and Craft (2019) have argued, several variants of 'policy design thinking' now compete in the policy studies literature, all purporting to be empirical descriptions of actual design behaviour and often also constituting normative positions concerning what mode of designing is capable of generating the 'best' policy outcomes.

These modalities of policy design range from the classic expert-driven technocratic paradigm espoused by early students of policy processes to more recent proposals for citizen-driven participatory co-design efforts (Blomkamp 2018), with what has been termed by Colebatch (2018) as 'authoritative instrumentalism' sitting somewhere between these two poles (Turnbull 2017).

These approaches differ in their designation of the nature of the designers themselves, emphasizing the significance of state or societal actors, and on the extent to which they include both technical and political criteria in design work and considerations. 'Authoritative instrumentalism' occupies a sweet spot at the centre of these continua and, as such, represents the comfortable middle of policy design thinking.

Technocratic planning

The first type of policy design, lying at the extreme of a state-based technical approach, was a feature of some of the early work and expectations of the policy sciences movement (Mintrom 2007) but in the western world was more common in the field of urban planning and others like it in the United States in the 1960s and 1970s. This is the world of the neutral, technical, and expert 'planner' said to constitute the realm of policy analysis in the United States and elsewhere in the 'first generation' of such policy professionals (Radin 1997, 1992, 2000).

In this way of thinking, a new generation of 'policy analysts' – professionals trained in data analysis and evidence-based policy-making – would develop and assess policy alternatives before presenting them to decision-makers, who would then choose from among these pre-packaged options (Meltsner 1975, 1976, 1979, 1980).

Of course, this ambition was never achieved in practice, with much analytical work disappearing into the bureaucratic and bureau-political void (Shulock 1999), and many policy analysts were deployed for lower-level fire-fighting and public relations or ministerial support roles rather than assuming their expected positions at the commanding heights of the policy process (Page and Jenkins 2005; Howlett and Wellstead 2011; Connaughton 2010).

This idea of neutral technocratic state officials driving policy-making was also heavily criticized at a normative level as an undesirable blockage in democratic policy-making, privileging officials over people and leading to rule by experts (Fischer 1990; Esterling 2004). This critique ranged from detailed studies of how experts dominated policy advisory panels (Rowe et al. 2013; Schreffler 2013) to wholesale critiques of the evils of technocracy (Brint 1990; Hendriks 2009; DeMenno 2017).

Co-design and the co-production of policy design

A second approach to this subject is more recent and can be seen to be the polar opposite of the technical planner model. This is the vision of policy design as a bottom-up, societally driven process of policy development which is contained in efforts to promote co-design as a mode of participatory design activity (Blomkamp 2018). Bason and Schneider (2014), for example, have pointed to the growth of many policy labs in universities and governments over the past five to six years as evidence of this movement occurring on a worldwide basis, although, as Clarke and Craft (2019) have pointed out, this conflates many different kinds of policy labs, including many behavioural or nudge labs (Strassheim et al. 2016), which are typically very top-down, state-driven technical design institutions. Nevertheless, it is undeniable that much effort has been put into understanding, developing, and promoting co-design as a method of problem-solving and policy design over the past several years (Lee 2008; Parsons et al. 2016), generating a very different view of policy design from orthodox policy studies models and which will be discussed in more detail in subsequent chapters.

Co-design efforts are expected to correct for the undemocratic aspects of more technocratic, expert-led processes and, by expanding the range of interests and knowledge sources available for policy-making, to simultaneously enhance output legitimacy and policy effectiveness through the 'co-production' of policy design. As has been pointed out many times, however, these efforts often contain a somewhat-naïve view of a depoliticized and conflict-free design process whereby 'thinking outside the box' leads to the development, and unproblematic adoption, of new policy ideas and directions. In practice, many such processes either fail to produce a consensus or produce utopian plans which cannot be adopted by the powers that be (Binder and Brandt 2008; Clarke and Craft 2019; Colebatch 2018).

Political pluralism and (non)design

This third view of policy formulation processes almost completely lacks the emphasis on knowledge found in the previous two types and instead is more closely related to thinking around how policy is made through the exercise of power in government.

In this view, decisions are taken by authorized government agents – be they politicians, officials, legislatures, or cabinets – and the key criteria for such decisions are often not efficiency or effectiveness in the solution of policy problems but rather a much more political calculus of achieving electoral, legislative, or partisan advantage (Scott 1969; Shore et al. 2011; Bacchi 2014).

This kind of analysis places great emphasis on the workings of interest group pluralism and the impact on decision-making of activities such as lobbying (Klüver 2013), the personal ambitions and preferences of leaders and decision-makers for re-election or promotion and advancement (Thompson 1994), and the presence of decision-making behaviour such as logrolling and other forms of legislative activity (Dahm and Glazer 2015). It is argued that it is these kinds of activities rather than knowledge-based 'design' in any recognizable sense, per se, which lead to the adoption of policies.

Although often clearly associated with the operating principles and practices of representative democracy, this form of policy-making can also be applied to many authoritarian states and is generally lambasted within the policy design community for its irrational – meaning, unsystematic and non-knowledge-based – approach to 'resolving' policy problems (Saward 1992).

That is, it is an approach often associated with non-designs rather than design activity of the kind discussed here. Nevertheless, it is clear that it is a common phenomenon often identified in studies of knowledge utilization, or rather its lack or its very selective use, in government policy decisions (Newig et al. 2015; Rimkutė and Haverland 2015; Shaw et al. 2015).

Anarchistic or Garbage-Can (non)design

Policy design can be used as a neutral term to describe a policy mix of whatever type, although as set out earlier, it is more commonly used only to describe policy packages which emerge from an adoption process in which tools are compiled and put into action with a rational intent, logical order, marshalling of evidence. It is expected to emerge from productive interactions among actors – in other words, with knowledge of policy problems applied to carefully constructing and deploying solutions in the expectation of ameliorating some problematic governance situation (Colebatch 2018).

Despite the allure of such conceptualizations, however, it is apparent to even casual observers of policy-making dynamics that such processes are often absent from policy-making and that policy 'designs' exist which show little evidence of 'classical' design characteristics, such as an internal logic and consistency of effort, and instead can result from pluralist processes of the type described above or from the accumulation of policies where each layer has been driven by the government's reacting to often poorly articulated public demands. This is the case, for example, with the creation of fuel or food subsidies in many countries often created in the wake of public protests and quickly engendering them again if and when any government attempts to remove the subsidy.

That is, while it remains empirically demonstrable that instrument mixes exist in some problem area, they often materialize through much less deterministic technical or political processes than conventionally assumed and are less formal in nature than 'classical' or co-design theory would anticipate. In contrast to 'formal' policy design, these kinds of policy processes lack even a minimum role for knowledge of the techniques of legislative bargaining and complex problem-solving required of more pluralist processes (Howlett and Mukherjee 2014, 2017b).

As critics of excessive formalism in policy design are wont to point out, shifting macro-conditions, local contextual idiosyncrasies, and cross-sectoral dynamics, among other factors, commonly impede efforts to rationalize policy problems and calibrate effective solutions (Hartley and Howlett 2021). Time is often limited, knowledge even more so, and contestation and conflict can pervade policy deliberations and decision-making to the extent that 'deliberation' in any meaningful sense of the term does not occur.

These kinds of processes have been described as 'garbage can' ones, in so far as alternatives are mooted and rejected until finally, often, one is pulled from the trashbin and put into action when time runs out (Kingdon 1984; Cohen et al. 1972). In the modern era, some 'designs' that emerge from media- or crowd-based processes have a similar characteristic (Wazny 2017).

Authoritative instrumentalism

A fifth approach to design is the one described in most detail in this book. It is a top-down one, in which state actors play a central role in selecting the policy tools which combine to create designs, but in which it is acknowledged that while they are self-interested actors, they also do not have *carte blanche* to do whatever they please. Similarly, while they typically need to take public sentiments into consideration they are not driven by them. Rather, they are seen as operating within a set of constraints that affect their 'degrees of freedom' or room to vary existing routines and procedures (Howlett 2019). This approach has been dubbed 'authoritative instrumentalism' by Colebatch (2018).

In this view, design choices emerge from and must generally be congruent with the governance modes or styles practiced in particular jurisdictions and sectors (Howlett 2009). 'Goodness of fit' between tool and context is thus seen as a key concern in contemporary policy design considerations and can be seen to occur at several different levels (Brandl 1988). That is, different orientations toward state activity require different capabilities on the part of state and societal actors, and since different governance modes or styles rely on these to greater or lesser degrees, policy designs, it is argued, must take into account both the desired governance context and the actual resources available to a governmental or non-governmental actor in carrying out its appointed role.

71

Thus, for example, planning and 'steering' involve direct coordination of key actors by governments requires a high level of government policy capacity to identify and utilize a wide range of policy tools in a successful policy 'mix' or 'arrangement' which may or may not exist (Arts et al. 2006).

Work on 'policy styles' and administrative traditions (Knill 1998) has identified common patterns and motifs in the construction of typical policy designs in different jurisdictions reflecting capacities (Howlett and Tosun 2019, 2021), which are said to lead to preferences for particular kinds of tools. This makes choices about their design and adoption simpler than would otherwise be the case and limits the extent to which any group or interest can dominate a design process. The issue here often is the leeway that policy designers have in developing new designs, given existing historical arrangements, path dependencies, policy legacies, and lock-in effects.

As Christensen et al. (2002) note, 'these factors place constraints on and create opportunities for purposeful choice, deliberate instrumental actions, and intentional efforts taken by political and administrative leaders to launch administrative reforms through administrative design' (p. 158). In this view determining how much room to manoeuvre or the degrees of freedom designers have to be creative (Considine 2012) or, to put it another way, to what degree they are 'context bound' in time and space is key for contemporary design studies in this approach.

Reconciling these models: a taxonomy of design modalities

As the earlier discussion has shown, these views of policy design differ in a number of important ways, especially with respect to who is the designer and their orientation toward knowledge, experts, and the public. The general orientation and approach in all cases is well situated in what has sometimes been termed 'design thinking' (Mintrom and Luetjens 2016) and highlights differences in how design is conceived and analyzed in different fields from sociology to political science, planning and policy studies.

Four of the variants, for example, can be placed in the cells of a simple matrix highlighting the location of designers inside or outside the state and whether designers are experts or non-experts (Table 3.4).

This allows us to arrange these four types into a two-dimensional space (Figure 3.3).

Both depictions, however, beg the question of where to place the fifth type: authoritative instrumentalism. Rather than fall into one of the archetypal locations, it can be seen to occupy a 'sweet spot' right at the centre of the design modality space (see Figure 3.4). That is, it includes both state and societal actors in policy advisory systems (Craft and Howlett 2013) and combines both technical and political concerns in its assessments of

Table 3.4 Design types, by location and orientation of agents

| | | Location | |
		State	Society
	Experts/ technical	State planning	Co-design
Orientation/ agents	**Public/ participatory/ political non- experts**	Political or pluralistic 'non-design'	Anarchistic or crowd-based 'design'

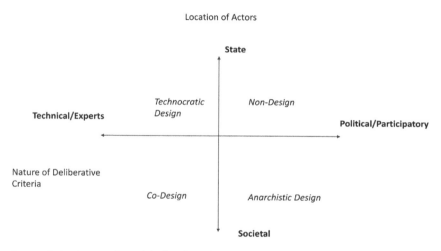

Figure 3.3 A spatial model of policy design modalities.

factors such as 'goodness of fit' and 'degrees of freedom' (Howlett and Rayner 2013a).

This, of course, helps explain its popularity as a model or framework of policy design. Although sometimes referred to by adherents of other modes of policy design in pejorative terms as a debased form of technical planning, it differs in many regards from the old state planning model and in fact covers much of the same ground as the other three models. It differs mainly in its lack of emphasis on a single exclusive actor or interest, and its insistence on the need for knowledge-driven policy processes, facets of this approach which its adherents find to both be a better fit with empirical reality than any of the other modes and to deliver better, that is, more effective outcomes in the face of uncertainty.

Location of Actors

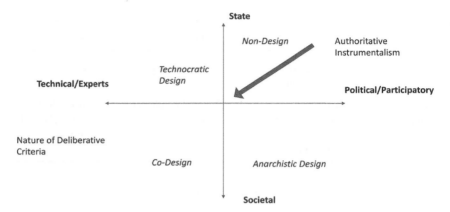

Figure 3.4 Authoritative instrumentalism as the sweet spot of policy design modes.

Conclusion: the re-emergence of policy design as an active field of study

After a two-decade hiatus, the reinvigoration of a 'design' orientation toward policy-making is now well underway (Howlett and Lejano 2013). As this chapter has laid out, there are some differences between present-day and past efforts to develop policy formulation in a design direction, leading to the distinction sometimes made between the 'old' and the 'new' policy design (Howlett 2014; Howlett et al. 2015), and there are several different processes through which observers have found, or suggest, policy designing and non-designing occur.

Differences between the 'old' and 'new' design work in the policy sciences include the tendency of the 'old' design work to focus its attention on fairly simple situations in which single or a small number of tools were deployed to meet a fairly limited number of goals, often by a single government, while the 'new' policy design focuses attention on more complex mixes or bundles of tools, often with extensive multi-agency or governmental links and often pursuing a wide range of not necessarily coherent goals (Howlett and Rayner 2007; Howlett and del Rio 2015; Rogge & Reichardt 2016; Flanagan et al. 2011).

This newer approach to studying and analyzing public policy has antecedents in early work in the policy sciences on policy tools and instruments and the theoretical work of Simon (1971; see also Barzelay and Thompson 2010) and Lasswell (1970) and is built on top of its insights. It is thoroughly immersed in detailed work and criticism throughout the 1980s and 1990s by authors such as Dryzek (1983; Dryzek and Ripley 1988), Bobrow (2006; Bobrow and Dryzek 1987), and above all, Linder and Peters (1987, 1989, 1990a, 1990b, 1990c, 1991), who coined many key concepts from design spaces to policy tools.

In general, one can say that this approach is concerned with policy formulation (Howlett and Mukherjee 2014, 2017a, 2017b) and advocates a specific kind of thinking about, and process of, formulation in which a more or less systematic effort is made by some policy actors to marshal evidence and logic in trying to match available policy tools to the effective achievement of policy goals (Peters et al. 2018; Howlett and Mukherjee 2018).

This is not the only way that policies can emerge or can be formulated, however, and policy design in this sense can be contrasted with other types of formulation which are more top-down or bottom-up and sometimes lack any kind of systematic rationality altogether. These other methods of policy formulation in which concerns for policy effectiveness and evidence take a back seat to other considerations in formulating policy alternatives, from purely electoral considerations to those of personal enrichment or legislative bargaining, among others, are important subjects but not discussed as much in detail in this book as are the tenets and attributes of authoritative instrumentalism.

Rather, the book emphasizes this latter approach to policy design, one concerned with understanding not only why different forms of formulation occur but, especially, also articulating modes of conduct or 'best practices' among practitioners in marshalling evidence and best, or at least better, matching tools to targets and to the job at hand (Howlett 2017, 2018; McGann et al. 2018).

Readings

Alexander, D., J. M. Lewis and M. Considine. (2014). 'How Governments Think: Skills, Expertise, and Experience in Public Policy Making'. In D. Alexander, J. M. Lewis and M. Considine (eds.), *Making Public Policy Decisions: Expertise, Skills and Experience*. London: Routledge, 44–65.

Bason, C. and A. Schneider. (2014). 'Public Design in Global Perspective; Empirical Trends'. In C. Bason (ed.), *Design for Policy*. London: Gower Pub Co., 23–40.

Binder, T. and E. Brandt. (2008). 'The Design Lab as Platform in Participatory Design Research'. *CoDesign*, 4, no. 2: 115–129.

Blomkamp, E. (2018). 'The Promise of Co-Design for Public Policy'. *Australian Journal of Public Administration*, 77, no. 4: 729–743.

Bobrow, D. (2006). 'Policy Design: Ubiquitous, Necessary and Difficult'. In B. G. Peters and J. Pierre (eds.), *Handbook of Public Policy*. Beverley Hills: Sage, 75–96.

Brint, S. (1990). 'Rethinking the Policy Influence of Experts: From General Characterizations to Analysis of Variation'. *Sociological Forum 5*, no. 3, 361–385.

Clarke, A. and J. Craft. (2019). 'The Twin Faces of Public Sector Design'. *Governance 32*, 5–21.

Colebatch, H. K. (2018). 'The Idea of Policy Design: Intention, Process, Outcome, Meaning and Validity'. *Public Policy and Administration 33*, no. 4: 365–383.

Considine, M. (2012). 'Thinking Outside the Box? Applying Design Theory to Public Policy'. *Politics & Policy 40*, no. 4: 704–724.

Dryzek, J. S. and B. Ripley. (1988). 'The Ambitions of Policy Design'. *Policy Studies Review 7*, no. 4: 705–719.

Fischer, F. (1990). *Technocracy and the Politics of Expertise*. Beverly Hills: Sage.

Howlett, M. (1991). 'Policy Instruments, Policy Styles and Policy Implementation'. *Policy Studies Journal 19*, no. 2: 1–21.

Howlett, M. (2004). 'Administrative Styles and the Limits of Administrative Reform: A Neo-Institutional Analysis of Administrative Culture'. *Canadian Public Administration 46*, no. 4: 471–494.

Howlett, M. and I. Mukherjee. (2014). 'Policy Design and Non-Design: Towards a Spectrum of Policy Formulation Types'. *Politics and Governance 2*, no. 2: 57–71.

Howlett, M. and J. Tosun. (2018). 'Empirical Insights on National Policy Styles and Political Regimes'. In M. Howlett and J. Tosun (eds.), *Policy Styles and Policy-Making*. New York: Routledge, 377–396.

Lasswell, H. D. (1970). 'The Emerging Conception of the Policy Sciences'. *Policy Sciences 1*, 3–14.

Linder, S. H. and B. G. Peters. (1990a). 'Policy Formulation and the Challenge of Conscious Design'. *Evaluation and Program Planning 13*, 303–311.

Meltsner, A. J. (1980). 'Creating a Policy Analysis Profession'. In S. S. Nagel (ed.), *Improving Policy Analysis*. Beverly Hills: Sage, 235–249.

Mintrom, M. and J. Luetjens. (2016). 'Design Thinking in Policymaking Processes: Opportunities and Challenges'. *Australian Journal of Public Administration 75*, no. 3: 391–402.

Richardson, J., G. Gustafsson and G. Jordan. (1982). 'The Concept of Policy Style'. In J. J. Richardson (ed.), *Policy Styles in Western Europe*. London: George Allen & Unwin, 1–16.

Rimkutė, D. and M. Haverland. (2015). 'How Does the European Commission Use Scientific Expertise? Results from a Survey of Scientific Members of the Commission's Expert Committees'. *Comparative European Politics 13*, no. 4: 430–449.

Rowe, S., N. Alexander, C. M. Weaver, J. T. Dwyer, C. Drew, R. S. Applebaum, S. Atkinson, F. M. Clydesdale, E. Hentges, N. A. Higley and M. E. Westring. (2013). 'How Experts Are Chosen to Inform Public Policy: Can the Process Be Improved?' *Health Policy 112*, no. 3, 172–178.

Simon, H. A. (1971). 'Style in Design'. In *Proceedings of the 2nd Annual Conference of the Environmental Design Research Association*. Carnegie Mellon University Press, 1–10.

Thompson, C. R. (1994). 'The Cabinet Member as Policy Entrepreneur'. *Administration Society 25*, no. 4, 395–409.

Van Buuren, A., J. M. Lewis, B. G. Peters and W. Voorberg. (2020). 'Improving Public Policy and Administration: Exploring the Potential of Design'. *Policy & Politics 48*, no. 1, 3–19.

Chapter 4

What do policy designs and policy design processes look like?

As the previous chapters discuss, transforming policy ambitions into practice is a difficult process. Formulation efforts can be done well or poorly, can reflect some wholesale or partial effort to match knowledge about policy goals and means in a sophisticated way linked to improving outcomes, or can be driven by personal interests, crowd dynamics, or legislative and partisan bargains which militate against detailed and rigorous analysis. While this helps us understand the process of designing a policy, exactly what a design looks like, however, is unclear.

Several common ways in which policy designs have emerged and evolved over time have been identified in the literature, however, which help us understand why policy designs look the way they do. These processes include 'replacement', 're-calibration', 'patching', 'stretching', and 'layering' and address the manner in which policy elements are configured in a policy mix. Each of these processes is discussed in turn next.

'Replacement': a relatively rare event

Fairly rapid policy change in which many elements of policy are created or altered significantly 'at one go' is one model of policy change identified in the policy studies literature. This kind of design process and intent is sometimes referred to as 'replacement', in which existing tools, targets, governance arrangements, and other policy elements are replaced all at once or over a very limited time span.

The idea of such replacement is one which often underlies the aspirations of policy designs and designers, critics, and promoters of alternate perspectives and approaches to resolving public problems. Rapid and substantive policy change, for example, is implicitly associated with a desire to put into

DOI: 10.4324/9781003343431-6

place completely new tools and objectives, to 'think outside the box' and develop and implement innovative solution to problems.

However, this is most definitely easier said than done and full 'replacement' of one policy by another completely different one is very rare in the real world. Such innovation requires not only a very high degree of cognitive and evaluative rationality on the part of policy-makers and formulators in understanding how past efforts failed but also a situation favourable to dramatic policy reform (Hogan and Howlett 2015). Nevertheless, there is a distinct tendency on the part of many critics of existing policies and promoters of new ones to talk about 'design' in a manner which associates the nature and scope of design as *necessarily* wide-ranging and transformative, taking some existing policy and reforming it completely, rather than, as is much more common in practice, the mechanics of simply amending or reforming it (Streeck and Thelen 2005; Thelen 2003; Mahoney and Thelen 2010).

Examples of the creation of entirely new policy 'packages' or course do exist in some areas, from welfare policy to high-technology ones such as recent efforts to create regulatory regimes for Artificial Intelligence (AI). However, often the opportunities to create such entirely new packages exist only historically, reflecting times before which there was no previous history of a policy response to a perceived policy problem. Once some action has been taken, this opportunity often disappears for extended periods of time as efforts are made to operate the new regime. For example, the United States (US) Clean Air Act (CAA) (first enacted in 1970) was the first major federal air pollution legislation in the United States and established the very first national benchmark for many products such as ambient sulphur dioxide ($SO_{2)}$ (Libecap 2005; Schmalensee et al. 1998). While there may have been precedents in other areas, most environmental regulation emerged fairly quickly over a short period of time and has since been modified, rather than fully replaced. Rather than being described as 'replacement', such modifiications are sometimes referred to as 'packages' of reforms, since they may not actually 'replace' policies from an earlier era.

For these reasons, examples of new policy designs, be they 'replacements' or 'packages', are understandably few. Most policy initiatives deal with already-created policies and do so in situations in which the possibilities for innovation are limited by historical legacies. Instead, reforms and revisions (re-designs) typically attempt to address and correct problems which may have surfaced in how an existing policy is or is not effectively achieving its intended aim. In many, cases this involves adding or otherwise modifying the policy tools at work or in other cases, new goals may be added to an existing policy mix, and reforms are intended to modify or add new tools to help achieve those new goals.

A view only toward packaging and replacement, therefore, conflates design with 'planning' and similar kinds of large-scale and rapid policy reform efforts and undermines analysis of other design processes which have more limited scope and range, but which occur more frequently, and which arguably have a greater overall effect on policy than wholesale re-design or novel policy creation (Carstensen 2011).

Re-calibrating policy: a neglected area of study

On the other end of the spectrum, some policy design processes change only the details or technical components of policies, such as their calibrations or 'settings', for example, the amount of a fine or subsidy. In such circumstances, other aspects of an existing design may be left in place, and changes restricted to, for example, expanding or contracting to whom the policy is directed – such as when the threshold for an income tax credit is raised or lowered in order to allow more taxpayers to qualify or to reduce their number, or when a new regulation simply adds a new substance to a list of banned chemicals.

The significance of such detailed changes is often over-looked or dismissed (Sewerin et al. 2022). Many studies commonly conceive alterations in policy paradigms and governance styles or preferences to be the primary drivers of policy change (Hall 1993), for example. Only changes in these macro policy elements, rather than those at the meso- and especially the micro-level, are said to drive 'fundamental' policy change. Although occasionally the impact of changes in policy components at micro-levels is sometimes acknowledged, they are often dismissed as secondary and in general they remain both under-investigated and under-theorized (Cashore and Howlett 2007; Sewerin et al. 2022).

This is clear, for example, in Peter Hall's (1993) pathbreaking effort in the early 1990s to disaggregate public policies into three different components and investigate their role in policy change. Hall's work was pathbreaking in challenging the then-dominant view in policy scholarship that tended to conflate all the elements of a 'policy' into a single dependent variable (Heclo 1974; Rose 1976; Hofferbert 1974; Howlett et al. 2020) but in focusing on the significance of ideational change in the shift of the UK from Keynesianism to monetarism in the Thatcher era downplayed the significance of changes in policy calibrations and specifications for overall policy dynamics.

For Hall, changes which affected the 'calibrations' of policy instruments, such as tightening specifications for face masks or varying the amount of subsidy for hospitals during a pandemic, were said to be merely 'first-order' changes. These occur within existing institutional and instrument confines, and their impact on the overall policy was said to be minimal. 'Second-order' changes involved alterations to the dominant types of policy instruments utilized within an existing policy regime, such as switching from a public enterprise to regulated private firm to provide some good or service. These changes were said to be more significant than first-order ones but still lack significance. 'Third-order' changes in governance ideas and cognitive constructs, on the other hand, were said to involve shifts in overall policy goals and drive forward significant 'replacement' type processes. Such a change in a health sector, for example, could involve a shift away from government support for access to healthcare as a right for all to support only for essential healthcare for those who fall below a certain income threshold, or vice versa, and Hall gave priority to such changes in overarching sets of policy ideas in explaining significant policy changes. These sets of ideas were said to allow minor adjustments to occur at the meso- and micro-level while retaining the same basic shape or content of a policy over the short, medium, or long term, until such time as the dominant set of ideas or 'paradigm' itself changed.

Subsequent work by Cashore and Howlett (2007; Howlett and Cashore 2007, 2009) developed a more comprehensive model of policy components based on this threefold logic. In this revised model, policy elements (see Figure 4.1) can be seen to include both policy aims and means at three different levels of specificity: the high 'macro' level of abstract policy goals and means; the mid-level 'meso' policy objectives and policy instruments; and the 'micro' level of policy settings and calibrations, thus encompassing Hall's original three types while adding three more policy components.

While Hall (1989b, 1990) mainly examined policy interactions at the level of macro policy goals, meso policy tools, and micro-calibrations, Cashore and Howlett argued that this over-looked significant policy activities surrounding policy objectives, policy goal settings or specifications, and instrument choices and calibrations, which could also influence significant degrees and patterns of change.

Changes to policy calibrations and specifications still remain very much the 'missing link' in existing studies of policy composition and dynamics. These changes have tended to be either dismissed as epi-phenomenal, and their basic nature and contours ignored, or just assumed to fall into line as

		Policy Content		
		High-Level Abstraction	*Programme-Level Operationalization*	*Specific, On-the-Ground Measures*
Policy Focus	*Policy Ends or Aims*	HIGH-LEVEL POLICY GOALS What General Types of Ideas Govern Policy Development?	PROGRAMME - LEVEL POLICY OBJECTIVES What Does Policy Formally Aim to Address?	OPERATIONAL SPECIFICATIONS or POLICY GOAL TARGETS What are the Specific On-the-ground Requirements of Policy
	Policy Means or Tools	GOVERNING INSTRUMENT LOGIC What General Norms Guide Implementation Preferences?	POLICY TOOL CHOICES What Specific Types of Instruments are Utilized?	CALIBRATIONS OF POLICY TOOLS What are the Specific Ways in Which the Instrument is used?

Figure 4.1 A modified taxonomy of policy components following Hall. (*Note*: Shaded area corresponds to the three elements originally identified by Hall [1993]).

Source: Modified from Cashore and Howlett (2007).

larger-scale policy change occurs in the realm of ideas and governance relationships (Daugbjerg and Bazza 2022).

Some literature on this level of policy components does exist, however, which can help identify and characterize changes in policy at this level and aid in the development of better policy designs (Grohmann and Feindt 2023; Howlett et al. 2023). In particular, this subject has been examined in passing by luminaries such as the Nobel Prize Winner Elinor Ostrom (2009), Stephen Linder and Guy Peters (1989), and Lester Salamon (2002), among others, and their insights can help construct a useful model of the nature and content of policy specifications and calibrations and their impact on policy development and dynamics.

As Ostrom noted in her 2009 Nobel Prize lecture, for example, the creation of effective government institutions, including regulations and other kinds of policy tools, requires the specification of many different kinds of 'rules' governing who is included and excluded in its purview, who benefits from it, who can change it, and so on. Translated into the policy realm, this means specifying to whom a programme applies and to whom it does not, who will implement the programme and change it once it is in place, and precisely what it is that different actors affected by and implementing the programme are expected to do (see Table 4.1).

Table 4.1 Ostrom's seven sets of foundational rules for collective action

Attribute of programme	Nature of specification	Ostrom meaning	Policy relevance	Example in use
Clarification of programme aims	Scope rules	Specifying the outcomes that actors are expected to affect	Designation of expected programme outcomes	Aim to provide assistance to recent mothers
Coverage	Boundary rules	Specification of which actors to be included in a policy	Clarify targeting	Aim for a programme for mothers with infants less than 2 years old
Designation of eligibility	Position rules	Specifying a set of positions and how many actors may hold each one	Establishing the features a target must meet to qualify for a programme	Target national citizens and permanent residents

(Continued)

Table 4.1 (Continued)

Attribute of programme	Nature of specification	Ostrom meaning	Policy relevance	Example in use
Criteria for selection	Choice rules	Specifying which actions are assigned to a specific actor holding a position	Establishing what an individual target must do to qualify	Aim to provide a subsidy for each child through the local school district
Transmission of goals and aims	Information rules	Specifying the channels of communication among actors and what information they must, may, or must not share	Establishing how programme administrators and targets are to communicate	Aim to integrate the system with the vital statistics bureau and annual reporting
Benefit goals	Pay-off rules	Specifying how benefits and costs are to be distributed to actors in positions	Specifying expected activities to be incentivized or disincentivized	Aim to provide 90 percent of funding to targets and 10 percent for administration
Administrative goals	Aggregation rules	If needed, rules specifying how decisions are made by actors	Establish decision structures	Aim to create a self-governing, parent-consultative board to advise on the programme

Source: Ostrom, 2009.

Many of these kinds of rules, in effect, specify policy 'goals' in the sense that they are aspirational statements about what aims a programme is expected to achieve at the operational level, while others are calibrations of policy tools in the sense that they determine or affect how an institution or tool will actually operate in practice. In a similar vein, Schaffrin et al. (2014) put forward a different scheme in which, more inductively, six dimensions of calibrations and settings found in a large-scale transnational survey of climate policies were highlighted, including their level integration, their scope, the targets targeted, and the provisions related to budgets, implementation, and monitoring.

Studies such as these are useful in helping to identify some parameters of policy instrument calibrations and policy target specifications, filling in the missing gap concerning the micro-components of public policies and policy designs. That is, they suggest that goal specifications provide answers to the 'what, who, when' questions which surround policy actions, while calibrations provide the answers to the 'how' questions, that is, how these specified goals are to be achieved on the ground.

As Petek et al. (2021) suggest in their appraisal of policy goals and objectives, goal or target specifications may be single or multiple but, in either case, must address what is the expected outcome of a policy on the ground, often in the form of an indicator (for example, that the incidence of violent crime will be reduced by 15 percent), who is the target or 'object' of government action (in the previous example, violent criminals), and over what time frame the goal is expected to be achieved (see Table 4.2). Of course, in some cases, some of these elements may not be specified, and in others, they may be implied (for example, 'over the term in office' of a government). And they may be mis-specified, for example, using the wrong indicator or an infeasible one. However, in order for a goal to be implemented, these criteria need to be specified.

Table 4.2 Policy goal specification parameters

Attribute of goal	Nature of specification	Parameters	Examples in use
Expected outcome ('What the policy will actually do')	Indicator	Increase or decrease	Reduce health insurance fraud by 15 percent
Target or object of action ('Who will be affected by it')	Social actor	More or less precise	Reduce health insurance fraud by closely auditing providers' billing
Time frame ('When this will occur')	Time period	Short or long	Achieve the expected outcome over five years

Calibrations, on the other hand, are more complex. Linder and Peters, in their pathbreaking 1989 study of policy tools, for example, described eight 'attributes of instruments', which can be thought of as representing the range of possible choices that can be made in tool design. These were complexity of operation, level of public visibility, adaptability across uses, level of intrusiveness, relative costliness, reliance on markets, chances of failure, and precision of targeting (Linder and Peters 1989: 56).

Some of these, such as 'reliance on market' or 'chances of failure', are considerations affecting tool choice rather than calibrations, and in later work, Peters (2000a) also added some additional attributes – replicating in part the ideas of Salamon (2002), who highlighted the difference between tools in terms of only four aspects: 'automaticity' (or the degree to which a tool is 'self-administering') while clarifying the concepts of 'intrusiveness' ('enforcement or persuasion') and adding 'directedness' (the extent to which 'the entity authorizing, financing, or inaugurating a collective activity is involved in carrying it out'). Taken together with Ostrom's insights, these authors highlight six key characteristics of policy tools that can be manipulated and designed.

These include:

1. How the goal is to be achieved (precise mode of delivery/automaticity)?
2. How public is it (visibility/need for collaboration)?
3. How coercive is it for targets and non-targets (intrusiveness/precision)?
4. How resource-intensive is it (complexity of operation and resources)?
5. Who will carry it out (directness)? and
6. How is the effort evaluated and monitored (stringency of accountability)?

Examples of the nature of the design elements that flow from these questions are depicted in Table 4.3).

Table 4.3 Policy instrument calibration

Attribute of instrument	Nature of calibration	Examples in use
Precise mode of delivery ('How the goal is to be achieved')	Level of precision (includes 'automaticity')	Provide or tighten licensing requirements for therapists
Publicness ('How the public will be involved')	Level of societal participation (includes 'visibility')	Consult with therapists and citizens' group on their regulation
Intrusiveness ('How this will affect targeted groups or individuals')	Level of coercion	Provide tougher penalties for unlicensed therapists
Resource-intensiveness ('How much this will cost')	Level of financial and personnel resources (includes 'complexity of operation')	Increase funding and hire more staff to administer licences

Attribute of instrument	Nature of calibration	Examples in use
Administering agency ('Who will carry this out')	Number of agencies with responsibility (includes 'directedness')	Create a new agency or designate an existing agency to coordinate different medical services
Monitoring and auditing ('How administrators will be held accountable')	Stringency of accountability	Tighten monitoring and identification of unlicensed therapists

As with goal specifications, the precise content of these choices is constrained and/or facilitated by the other more macro and meso aspects of policy, including current knowledge and thinking in the field, as well as the configuration of actors and institutions in the existing system, combined with the nature of tool preferences and objectives of a government and society. But in general, it is these elements of policy which are at the cutting edge of a policy when it is implemented and hence are a key subject for policy designs.

Patching and packaging, stretching, and layering as common design processes

While early formulation and design thinking tended to suggest that the creation of instruments could only occur in spaces where new policy packages could be designed entirely *de novo*, or 'from scratch' – that is, through 'packaging' or 'replacement' – it is now widely recognized that in most circumstances, policy formulation involves building on the foundations created in another era and working with the constraints they pose in the designation and alteration of key existing policy elements. That means dealing mainly with alterations in instruments and objectives, and tool calibrations and target specifications, rather than paradigmatic ideas or governance arrangements which are more difficult to alter and generally more long-lasting.

Students of policy formulation and policy design are thus very interested, as mentioned earlier, in how policy formulators, like software designers, rather than design new packages of policy elements to replace existing ones, rather often issue 'patches' to existing arrangements in order to correct perceived flaws in existing mixes or allow them to adapt to changing circumstances (Howlett 2013; Howlett and Rayner 2014).

This is more accurate in describing actual design processes on the ground. It also recognizes the very practical concern that although other policy element groupings might theoretically be more successful in creating an internally supportive combination, it may be very difficult to accomplish or even propose such changes as a policy, once in place, tends to develop a constituency who will oppose its alteration. This is the case, to give only one example, with the beneficiaries of fuel subsidies in many countries who are prone to rioting if and when such subsides are eliminated (Grabosk 1994; Gunningham et al. 1998; Hou and Brewer 2010; Howlett 2004b; Howlett and Rayner 2007; del Río 2010; Barnett and Shore 2009; Blonz et al. 2008; Buckman and Diesendorf 2010; Roch et al. 2010). The contextual 'lock-in' that occurs once a design is in place impacts the formulation process by restricting a government's ability to propose and evaluate many possible alternatives and thus to plan or design in a purely optimal manner (Howlett 2009a; Oliphant and Howlett 2010; Williams 2012).

Layering is a typical result of successive patching processes where (re) design alters only some aspects of a pre-existing arrangement. Originally developed in the neo-institutional sociological literature (see Béland 2007; Béland and Hacker 2004; Hacker 2004b; Stead and Meijers 2004; Thelen 2004) in order to explain the pattern through which social and political institutions have evolved over long periods of time, 'layering' connotes a process in which new elements are simply added to an existing regime, often without abandoning previous ones ('de-layering'), so that polices accrete in a palimpsest-like fashion (Carter 2012). It is the most common design outcome and one which focuses attention on policy tools and their calibrations as well as the more micro and meso aspects of policy goals and objectives.

This kind of patching can easily lead to internal contradictions emerging between tools and goals within policy mixes (Hacker 2004a), and mixes of policy elements can emerge over long stretches of time as a result of successive layering decisions which are not necessarily logical or rational in any objective sense of the term.

An example of such unplanned incongruence within a policy mix caused by layering can again be found in the US Clean Air Act (Ackerman 1981; Greenstone 2001; among others). The 1977 amendments to the Act created a 'new source bias', as all new coal-powered plants were required to install scrubbers even if they used low-sulphur coal. This rule undermined the comparative advantage of 'cleaner' coal, as the amendments raised the cost of shifting to new, less-polluting plants and extended the economic lives of older, more polluting plants that did not have to shoulder the added cost of scrubbers (Libecap 2005). This is only one small example of a general situation where the initial logic of a decision which matched policy tools and targets may have been clear enough but where, through multiple layering processes, a policy can gradually transform into an incongruent mix that contains various incompatibilities, tending to frustrate the achievement of original or new policy goals (Bode 2006; Hacker 2004c; Howlett and Rayner 1995; Orren and Skowronek 1998; Rayner et al. 2001; Torenvlied and Akkerman 2004; van der Heijden 2011).

Distinguishing between different types of layering allows us to further separate and identify different kinds of design and non-design processes from each other. One such design process is '*smart layering*' or '*smart patching*', where a new layer is formulated in an effort to overcome specific anomalies or problems identified with an earlier mix (Howlett and Rayner 2013).

An example of a poor patching process, on the other hand, is policy '*stretching*' (Feindt and Flynn 2009). This is where, operating over periods of decades or more, elements of a mix are simply extended to cover areas they were not intended to at the outset. Stretching often involves calibration or specification changes and is problematic when multiple small changes in the mixture of policy elements over time create a situation where the elements fail to be mutually supportive, incorporating contradictory goals or instruments. These new combinations can create perverse incentives that frustrate initial policy goals, often setting the stage for further rounds of tinkering and layering that may make them worse (Feindt and Flynn 2009).

Stretching is problematic as a design process since the addition of new goals or objectives increases the risk of incoherence, while the introduction of policy instruments through poor patching, for example, when a market orientation is introduced into an instrument set that has been based on a regulatory approach (Howlett and Rayner 2007), is also problematic. Using the case of British food policy, Feindt and Flynn (2009), for example, describe a situation of institutional stretching where 'concerns about food supply and high productivity were overlaid with policies addressing food safety, the environment, quality foods, obesity and climate change' (386) resulting in poor outcomes.

Both stretching and poor patching efforts can create a particular form of '*tense layering*' (Kay 2007) which occurs when repeated bouts of layering lead to incoherence among the goals and inconsistency with respect to the instruments and settings used in a policy area. Inconsistencies arise where means work at cross-purposes, 'providing simultaneous incentives and disincentives towards the attainment of stated goals' (Kern and Howlett 2009: 6). And incongruence occurs when an otherwise-consistent mix of instruments fails to support the goals.

Revisiting the spectrum of policy design and non-design

Layering and patching thus have two sides. On the one hand, stretching or poor patching can exacerbate tensions between regime elements. However, patching can also have a positive side and help ameliorate or reduce tensions through 'smart' layering. Stretching and poor patching are thus design practices which exist at the break point between design and non-design activities of government. Processes such as patching and stretching fall between the 'pure' design ('replacement') and 'pure' non-design ends of the spectrum of design processes suggested in Figure 4.2.

As Figure 4.2 shows, policy design efforts move from highly intentional and instrumental replacement ones to those which are more partial and less

Figure 4.2 A spectrum of design processes.

intentional, such as 'smart' patching, and, ultimately, to those which involve poor design, such as 'stretching' and poor layering. In cases such as these, tense layering introduces progressively more severe inconsistencies and incongruencies and tensions between layers, and policy-making and formulation may begin to take on an increasingly difficult complexion as the original logic and causality of a mix recedes into dim memory.

Non-design occurs when partisan and ideological, religious, or other criteria cloud, crowd out, or replace even the most modest instrumental design intentionality. Non-design mechanisms, as highlighted earlier, include activities such as alternative generation by bargaining or logrolling, through corruption or co-optation efforts or through other faith-based or pure electoral calculations which are not instrumental in the same knowledge-based sense as design efforts. In such contexts, the ability of policy goals to be met or the ability of means to achieve them are often of secondary concern to other concerns, such as ideological purity or the need to retain or augment legislative or electoral support, secure bribes or other similar behaviour.

What makes a good policy process: evidence-based policy-making and policy design

While a good policy design may be one in which the component parts work together to resolve social and political problems, what makes a good design *process*? Many efforts have been undertaken by reformers in governments over the past half century in order to enhance the efficiency and effectiveness of public policy-making and while some are crude ('sweep out the deadwood', 'throw out the bums') most typically try to do so through by applying a systematic evaluative rationality to policy problems in the form of a policy re-design (Mintrom 2007). In these efforts, it is expected that through a process of theoretically informed empirical analysis, governments can better learn from experience and both avoid repeating the errors of the past as well as better apply new techniques to the resolution of old and new problems (Sanderson 2002b; May 1992). This same logic is applied to policy patches as well as to policy packages.

What is often refered to as 'evidence-based' or 'evidence-informed' policy-making represents a process-related goal of such policy reform efforts and, in its most recent incarnation, can be seen as an effort to reform or re-structure policy processes in such a way as to minimize non- and poor designs and incidences by prioritizing evidentiary-based analytical and decision-making criteria over non-evidence based ones such as 'faith-based', ideological or overtly partisan policy-making. This is done in the expectation that superior policies and results will emerge from evidence-based processes than from non-evidence-based ones (Nutley et al. 2007; Pawson 2006; Sanderson 2006).

Exactly what constitutes 'evidence-based policy-making' and whether analytical efforts in this regard actually result in better or improved policies, however, are subjects which remain contentious in the literature on the subject (Boaz et al. 2008; Jackson 2007; Packwood 2002; Pawson 2002). A spate of studies, for example, has questioned the value of a renewed emphasis on the collection and analysis of large amounts of data in all policy-making circumstances (Tenbensel 2004). Among the concerns raised about an increased emphasis purely on data as evidence in contemporary policy-making are:

- That such evidence is only one type of knowledge involved in policy-making and is not necessarily able to overcome other factors relevant to policy-making quality such as constitutional divisions of powers or jurisdictions which can arbitrarily assign locations and responsibilities for particular issue areas to specific levels or institutions of government and thus diminish the rationality level of policy-making by so doing (Davies 2004; Radin and Boase 2000; Young et al. 2002).
- That data collection and analytical techniques employed in its gathering and analysis by specially trained policy technicians may not be necessarily superior to the experiential judgments of politicians and other key policy decision-makers (Jackson 2007; Majone 1989).
- That the kinds of 'high-quality' and universally acknowledged evidence initially proposed when 'evidence-based policy-making' first entered the lexicon of policy analysts in the healthcare field – especially the 'systematic review' of clinical findings – often have no analogues in many policy sectors where generating evidence using the 'gold standard' of random clinical trial methodologies may not be possible (Innvaer et al. 2002; Pawson et al. 2005).
- That an increased emphasis on evidence-based policy-making can stretch the analytical resources of participating organizations, be they governmental or non-governmental, to the breaking point (Hammersley 2005). That is, government efforts in this area may have adverse consequences both for themselves in terms of requiring greater expenditures on analytical activities at the expense of operational ones as well as for many non-governmental policy actors, such as small-scale NGOs whose analytical resources may be non-existent and who may also be forced to divert financial, personnel, and other scarce resources from implementation activities to policy-making in order to meet increased government requests for more and better data on the merits and demerits of their proposed policy solutions and programme (Laforest and Orsini 2005).

That is, if evidence-based policy-making is to be achieved, policy actors require the ability to collect and aggregate information in order to effectively develop medium- and long-term projections and proposals for and evaluations of future government activities. Any increased emphasis on the use of evidence in policy-making requires that policy actors, and especially governmental ones, have the analytical capability required to collect appropriate data and utilize it effectively in the course of policy-making activities (Howlett 2009).

Riddell (1998) summarized the requisites of *policy analytical capacity* as lying in

> a recognized requirement or demand for research; a supply of qualified researchers; ready availability of quality data; policies and procedures to facilitate productive interactions with other researchers; and a culture in which openness is encouraged and risk taking is acceptable.

Organizations both inside and outside of governments require a significant and non-trivial level of human, financial, network, and knowledge resources enabling them to perform the tasks associated with managing and implementing an evidence-based policy process. Without this, they might only marshal these resources in particular areas, resulting in a 'lumpy' set of departmental or agency competences in which some agencies are able to plan and prioritize over the long-term while others focus on shorter-term issues. Or, if inadequate resources are evenly distributed, may result only in agencies being able to react to short- or medium-term political, economic, or other challenges and imperatives occurring in their policy environments (Voyer 2007).

Nevertheless, one criterion for a 'good' policy design process remains its use of accurate information and data, and processes which do so can easily be distinguished from those that do not.

What is a superior mix of tools: coherence, consistency, and congruence in policy designs

As noted in Chapters 2 and 3, a greater emphasis on tool mixes and on the processes that effectively create complex policy tool bundles has been a feature of policy design research over the last decade (Hood 2007a; Howlett 2011). These studies have increased awareness of the many dilemmas that can appear in the path of effective policy tool or 'toolkit' designs and realities (Peters and Pierre 1998; Klijn and Koppenjan 2000c; Doremus 2003; Sterner 2002).

Policy mixes in this sense are combinations of policy instruments that are expected to achieve particular policy objectives and which are generally seen as more efficient and effective than single-instrument uses (Gunningham et al. 1998). However, not all tools work well with others, and designing an effective mix is not simply a matter of piling instruments together in a kind of bundle or jumble.

Some instruments may work well with others by nature – as is the case with 'self-regulation' set within a regulatory compliance framework (Gibson 1999; Grabosky 1994; Trebilcock et al. 1979) – while other combinations may not, such as, notably, independently developed subsidies and regulation aimed at the same policy goal.

Constructing a superior policy design, then, is largely a matter of designing a policy mix with compatible and reinforcing tools capable of achieving government goals in an efficient and effective way.

Some aspects of superior mixes are well-known and easily observable, while others are less well-known or under-investigated.

Good policy designs, for example, are expected to feature few contradictions and display an integrated effort to match policy tools and goals (Buckman and Diesendorf 2010; Roch et al. 2010; Barnett and Shore 2009; Blonz et al. 2008; del Río 2010). Works on 'smart regulation' by Gunningham et al. (1998), for example, led scholars to focus on how instruments within a policy mix or 'portfolio' can effectively complement each other or conversely, have fewer conflicts, providing a template for more sophisticated policy designs in which complementarities are maximized and conflicts avoided (Buckman and Diesendorf 2010; Roch et al. 2010; Barnett and Shore 2009; Blonz et al. 2008; del Río 2010).

These concerns, such as how to make the most of policy synergies while curtailing contradictions in the formulation of new policy packages, for example, have been a major continuing topic of investigation within the new design orientation (Hou and Brewer 2010; Kiss et al. 2012; Lecuyer and Quirion 2013). They join other major concerns of those working in contemporary policy design studies such as, as noted earlier, whether reform of combinations of different policy instruments, which have evolved independently and incrementally, can accomplish complex policy goals as effectively as more deliberately customized portfolios (Howlett 2014b). And they join another major topic of current research concerning how some combinations of tools may be designed to promote resiliency and adaptiveness in the face of internal and external challenges (Braathen and Croci 2005; Braathen 2007b; Swanson et al. 2010; Walker et al. 2010).

This latter concern has added the dimension of *robustness* to older concerns for the *coherence, consistency,* and *congruence* of policy means and goals established to judge superior policy designs and will be discussed in a later section (Chapter 14) of the book devoted to that subject.

Conclusion: better designs through better knowledge of policy instrument attributes and interactions

The recent policy design literature has engaged in lengthy discussions about how best to effectively integrate policy mixes so that multiple instruments are arranged together in complex but effective portfolios of policy goals and means, often with an additional multi-level governance component (Gunningham et al. 1998; Doremus 2003; Briassoulis 2005a; Howlett 2011; Yi and Feiock 2012; Peters et al. 2005; Jordan et al. 2011, 2012; del Río and Howlett 2013; Trien et al. 2023).

This discussion has tried to clarify and fill out the space between 'design' and 'non-design' in the spectrum of policy formulation activities and has drawn from other fields and literatures to add terms and the notions such as 'replacement', 'layering', and 'stretching', and others derived from works on the historical sociology of institutional development to help better understand policy-making and policy designs.

Effectively optimizing the choice of instruments in such mixes requires both knowledge of instrument–goal interactions and consideration of how mixes evolve over the long run and requires an understanding of both long- and short-term processes of policy change and how the various elements which make up a policy contribute to such dynamics. The components of any policy mixes include policy goals and policy means at various levels of generality and design, and instrument selection in these contexts is 'all about constrained efforts to match goals and expectations both within and across categories of policy elements' (Kern and Howlett 2009; Cashore and Howlett 2007; Howlett 2009a, 2009d: 74).

How precisely this can best be achieved in practise is a subject taken up in detail in the chapters to follow.

Readings

Boaz, A., L. Grayson, R. Levitt and W. Solesbury. (2008). 'Does Evidence-Based Policy Work? Learning from the UK Experience'. *Evidence & Policy 4*, no. 2: 233–253.

Hartley, K. and M. Howlett. (2021). 'Policy Assemblages and Policy Resilience: Lessons for Non-Design from Evolutionary Governance Theory'. *Politics and Governance 9*, no. 2 (25 June): 451–459.

Hill, M. and P. Hupe. (2002). *Implementing Public Policy: Governance in Theory and Practice*. London: Sage.

Howlett, M. (2000). 'Managing the "Hollow State": Procedural Policy Instruments and Modern Governance'. *Canadian Public Administration 43*, no. 4: 412–431.

Howlett, M. (2005). 'What Is a Policy Instrument? Policy Tools, Policy Mixes and Policy Implementation Styles'. In P. Eliadis, M. Hill and M. Howlett (eds.), *Designing Government: From Instruments to Governance*. Montreal, QC: McGill-Queen's University Press, 31–50.

Howlett, M. (2009). 'Governance Modes, Policy Regimes and Operational Plans: A Multi-Level Nested Model of Policy Instrument Choice and Policy Design'. *Policy Sciences 42*, no. 1: 73–89.

Howlett, M. and I. Mukherjee. (2014). 'Policy Design and Non-Design: Towards a Spectrum of Policy Formulation Types'. *Politics and Governance 2*, no. 2 (13 November): 57–71.

Howlett, M. and J. Rayner. (2013). 'Patching vs Packaging in Policy Formulation: Assessing Policy Portfolio Design'. *Politics and Governance 1*, no. 2: 170–182.

Lasswell, H. D. (1956). *The Decision Process: Seven Categories of Functional Analysis*. College Park, MD: University of Maryland Press.

Linder, S. H. and B. G. Peters. (1990a). 'The Design of Instruments for Public Policy'. In S. S. Nagel (ed.), *Policy Theory and Policy Evaluation: Concepts, Knowledge, Causes, and Norms*. New York: Greenwood Press, 103–119.

Linder, S. H. and B. G. Peters. (1991). 'The Logic of Public Policy Design: Linking Policy Actors and Plausible Instrument'. *Knowledge in Society* 4: 125–151.

Nutley, S. M., I. Walter and H. T. O. Davies. (2007). *Using Evidence: How Research Can Inform Public Services*. Bristol, UK: Policy Press.

Parsons, W. (2004). 'Not Just Steering but Weaving: Relevant Knowledge and the Craft of Building Policy Capacity and Coherence'. *Australian Journal of Public Administration 63*, no. *1*: 43–57.

Peters, B. G., P. Ravinet, M. Howlett, G. Capano, I. Mukherjee and M. H. Chou. (2018). *Designing for Policy Effectiveness: Defining and Understanding a Concept*. Elements Series. Cambridge: Cambridge University Press.

Radaelli, C. M. (1995). 'The Role of Knowledge in the Policy Process'. *Journal of European Public Policy 2*, no. *2*: 159–183.

Trein, Philipp, Manuel Fischer, Martino Maggetti and Francesco Sarti. (2023). 'Empirical Research on Policy Integration: A Review and New Directions'. *Policy Sciences 56*, no. *1* (1 March): 29–48.

Weimer, D. L. (1993). 'The Current State of Design Craft: Borrowing, Tinkering, and Problem Solving'. *Public Administration Review 53*, no. 2 (April): 110–120.

Wu, X., M. Ramesh, M. Howlett and S. A. Fritzen. (2017). *The Public Policy Primer: Managing the Policy Process* (2nd edn). New York: Routledge.

Chapter 5

Why policy design? Tools, behavioural mechanisms, and the need for policy design

Policy sectors – such as health policy, energy policy, transport policy, and many others – constitute distinct policy regimes consisting of the current collectively accepted definition of an issue, the current relevant policies (laws, regulations, fiscal instruments, government programmes, and relationships), and the actors and institutions (both inside and outside government) actively engaged in implementing and modifying them (Harris and Milkis 1989; Eisner 1994a, 1994b).

These regimes are often viewed as examples of a general class of stable, 'homeostatic' systems whose elements, once put in place, are self-adjusting or self-equilibrating in routine circumstances and often thought of as changing only under the pressure of external shocks or 'jolts' which introduce new extraneous elements into the system, throwing them out of equilibrium (Aminzade 1992). This notion of the exogenous nature of policy changes focuses analytical attention on the various types of external crises which could provoke changes in policy goals and objectives and instruments or their settings, an approach to understanding policy dynamics which is common in comparative policy studies (Wilsford 1994).

However, the empirical purchase of the metaphor of contemporary policy-making as the workings of a homeostatic system has increasingly come to be challenged in the policy sciences. Contemporary thinking now tends to favour more adaptive constructs in which it is assumed that policy actors not only react to external changes but can also affect their own environments and, as a result, can endogenously induce significant policy change through the policy designs they adopt and the designing processes they undertake (Daneke 1992; Buckley 1968; Smith 2000). In other words, policies are not always purely reactive or subordinate features of large-scale socio-economic forces but rather themselves can engender important social change processes.

DOI: 10.4324/9781003343431-7

This reconceptualization has led to a greater interest in policy design in general and more specifically to greater efforts to measure, chronicle, and account for the precise social and psychological mechanisms which are activated in policy designs and to better understand how policy instruments activate them and affect the behaviour of policy 'targets'.

Many of these mechanisms operate at the level of individual or group behaviour and include phenomena such as the propensity of individuals to search for advantage or normative harmony, status, and prestige or to make utility-based calculations of costs and benefits, risks and gains, as well as aspects of group behaviour, such as rent or influence-seeking, which often lie behind the formation and actions of interest groups and other kinds of collective actors (Olson 1965).

There is also a third class of such mechanisms, ones in which policy network relationships alter as new nodes and links are added to policy subsystems. These structural adaptation mechanisms can be triggered by government policy interventions which introduce new actors and ideas into policy structures, often through the deployment of 'procedural' policy tools which trigger this activity (Howlett 2000c; Lang 2019). These can precipitate and re-shape specific types of policy behaviour on the part of network members through their impact upon the nodes and links of policy subsystems, the nature of policy deliberations and discourses, and ultimately, policy outputs (Lang 2019).

Policy designs are calibrated arrangements of tools which use government resources to trigger these mechanisms in order to alter target behaviour. This, of course, is typically done intentionally and in the expectation that the triggered behaviour will promote government aims and ambitions. However, this is not always the case, as tools and targets may be mismatched or unexpected or unintended behaviours triggered by the deployment of a policy tool or mix.

Each of these basic types of mechanisms is set out in the following along with the general logic of the expected relationships existing between policy tools and target behaviour in each.

What do policy designs do? Uncertain target behaviour and the need for persuasive designs

In 1955, Herbert Simon developed the concept of 'bounded rationality' to highlight the great distance existing between theories of human choice processes and the administrative theory of the time which often ignored cognitive and other limits in knowledge and information involved in proposals for administrative and policy action (Simon 1955, 1957). Close to 70 years later, public policy studies still confront the criticisms formulated by Simon concerning the nature of human rationality and the assumptions commonly made about it by scholars and practitioners of public administration and public policy (Barile et al. 2015; Steg et al. 2014). Disentangling theory and reality with respect to policy behaviour remains a key subject of interest to policy studies in general (Leong and Howlett 2020b) and to policy design studies in particular (Leong and Howlett 2022a).

Recently, however, under the influence of findings in behavioural economics, public policy studies have gradually showed an increasing willingness to recognize the nature and extent of the limitations of often-implicit conceptions of rational behaviour among policy-makers and policy-takers. They have begun to apply concepts and lessons derived from this body of work to both the study of policy-maker behaviour and to that of policy targets or 'policy-takers' in order to better understand and improve both policy designs and outcomes (Tversky and Kahneman 1974; Howlett et al. 2020).

More work still needs to be done in both these areas, but studies and practices inspired by Thaler and Sunstein in particular, captured in the notion of 'nudges' (Sunstein 2014; Thaler and Sunstein 2009) described in earlier chapters and detailed in Chapter 12, have begun to provide insights important to the basic foundations of policy implementation and design studies (Lehner et al. 2015; Rathi and Chunekar 2015; Kersh 2015; Matthies et al. 2016).

In the design context, much of this work is oriented toward the articulation and successful implementation in the policy world of what has been termed 'persuasive design' (McCalley et al. 2006; Redström 2006) or 'design with intent' (Lockton et al. 2016). This is the effort to design an item, from a hand razor or washing machine to a public information campaign or subsidy, in such a way that the user or recipient of the good or service finds it easy to use and 'naturally' complies with its requirements and aspects. This same logic can be applied to policy designs which, it is argued, should make compliance simple and costfree to intended targets.

As we have seen in earlier chapters, however, compliance, and the reasons why it occurs or not, is a complex subject in itself. However, it has often been treated in a unidimensional way in the policy design literature, necessitating a re-thinking of the subject. This has begun to occur in recent years and has engendered some new terminology and approaches, such as the development and design of 'compliance regimes' (Weaver 2014) which policy design scholars are now embracing (Olejniczak et al. 2020). The elements of the older standard 'compliance-deterrence' model, and its limitations, are set out in the following section.

Orthodox assumptions about human behaviour in the policy sciences: the standard compliance-deterrence model

The aim of most public policy is to invoke behavioural change in the 'targets' of government efforts through deployment of governing resources in the adoption of substantive and procedural policy tools (Anderson 1977; Baldwin 1985). Desired changes can be large or small, and the behaviour expected to change can be rapid or gradual. But in all cases, some changes in behaviour in a direction congruent with government aims is expected to result from the mobilization and utilization of state resources.

This expenditure of governing resources is typically done in order to secure better adherence of target populations with government aims and ambitions, be it the deployment of police to enhance public safety and security by deterring crime or in the use of public funds to encourage people to exercize and thus enhance public health and social welfare.

Of course, if perfect compliance with governments' aims existed automatically, there would be little need to undertake additional state activity beyond information provision regarding state aims in order to attain a policy goal. Thus, why a high level of compliance is not always forthcoming is a key question in the policy sciences and one which has often been examined in policy work, but often in a very cursory fashion and under the burden of many, mainly economistic, assumptions about the motivations of policy targets. Neverthless, recently, more behaviourally inclined economic studies have engendered their own criticisms of those assumptions for being unrealistic in many compliance circumstances (John et al. 2009; Oliver 2015; Goodwin 2012; Hausman and Welch 2010), and have begun to shed much-needed light on this hitherto under-investigated aspect of policy formulation and implementation (Weaver 2014, 2015).

This behavioural 'turn' (Leong and Howlett 2022a) is in contrast to the utilitarian basis of thinking about public policy compliance and policy implementation which has been pervasive in the policy sciences since the very founding of the discipline (Tribe 1972; Banfield 1977). Traditionally, compliance theory in economics and elsewhere has been based on the notion of incentives and disincentives; that is, the concept of rewards for compliant behaviour and 'deterrence' of non-compliant populations and individuals (Kaine et al. 2010). This is based in turn on the idea that narrow self-interest and calculable utility in enhancing pleasure and avoiding pain ('hedonics') are the primary motivators of compliance behaviour on the part of policy actors (Kaine et al. 2010; Stover and Brown 1975), with governments enhancing pain (disincentives) and pleasure (incentives) in efforts to deter specific kinds of activity and encourage others.

This latter approach to the subject continues to influence even more nuanced recent thinking about tool use which has otherwise led to the questioning of many traditional utilitarian concepts and assumptions, such as the assumption that individuals have perfect information and reciprocal risk and benefit valuations in determining the best course of action for them to follow (Stover and Brown 1975; Oliver 2015; Legett 2014; Room 2013a; John et al. 2009). Current work on 'nudges', for example, which focus on the deployment of policy tools based on insights into less conscious biases which human possess – like overweighting risks and underestimating benefits – disputes the idea of 'perfect rationality' among policy targets, although it still often accepts uncritically most of the hedonic assumptions of classic utilitarian thinking: that 'subjects' are motivated to promote pleasure and avoid pain and do so in an essentially calculating 'cost–benefit' fashion when confronted by the choice of whether or not to comply with government wishes and orders.

In practice, the older standard compliance-deterrence model meant compliance of policy targets with government intentions was often, and often still is, viewed as a problem equated with the adoption of carrots and sticks or 'incentives and disincentives' designed to secure a certain level of obedience with government aims. That is, for example, the idea that governments expect legitimate taxes to be paid and tax rules obeyed, and establish a system of penalties and fines to punish non-compliance in such a way as to 'deter' unwanted and illegitimate tax evasion (Doern and Phidd 1983).

As suggested earlier, however, the behavioural situation is more complex than a purely utilitarian perspective would have it. Even the most basic activities of governance, such as paying taxes and obeying rules, involve not just individual hedonic calculations about possible fines and punishments but also considerations on the part of targets of the legality and normative 'appropriateness' or legitimacy of government activity, including their right to levy and collect taxes in the first place (March and Olsen 1989). Moreover, different kinds of target groups and individuals exist – such as different types of employees who pay their taxes and report their incomes in different ways – and these need to be monitored and treated differently by governments in terms of expectations of the nature of their compliant or non-compliant behaviour. Scofflaws should not be treated the same as well-intentioned but poorly informed or underprivileged citizens, for example, in punishing tax avoiders (McLeod et al. 2015). And of course, governments have more tools at their disposal than just authority- and treasure-based ones in encouraging or discouraging target population behaviour and thus have a larger range of options with respect to promoting compliance beyond simple coercion or lack of it, including those linked to education and persuasion (Hawkins and Thomas 1989; Hood 1986c).

The compliance situation in particular is made difficult by the fact that different targets have not only different resources and capabilities when it comes to determining whether or not they will comply but also sometimes deep-rooted cultural and societal reasons motivating how and to what extent they will or will not comply (Weaver 2009b). These attitudes can be quite complex and rooted in historical and culturally specific views of government intentions and the moral and other aspects of compliant and non-compliant behaviour influenced by deeply held religious or ideological beliefs (Wan et al. 2014, 2015). These can include, for example, considerations of the legitimacy and illegitimacy of government actors and actions not just in specific fields, such as constitutional, religious, or privacy-related ones where they might be expected, but often involve differences in ethnic-, gender-, or class-based concerns and attitudes toward state activity and intentions (Cialdini and Goldstein 2004; Beetham 1991; Weber 1978; Hofmann et al. 2014).

Whether a policy action triggers behaviour linked to 'affiliation' or 'conformity' with government wishes or results in non-compliance or even a 'boomerang' effects (encouraging the action it is aimed at discouraging or vice versa) is critical knowledge required for effective policy design (Cialdini and Goldstein 2004; Cialdini et al. 2006) but is not well understood. Hence, for example, Kallgren et al. (2000) and de Groot and Schuitema (2012) note that norm compliance can be affected even by the type of 'message' sent urging compliance and its negative or positive nature and the way it has been framed, as well as by other factors linked to the character of the underlying norm itself, for example, whether or not certain behaviours are considered socially acceptable (see also Schultz 2007).

This variation in target motivation and compliance behaviour makes policy design a much more challenging activity than that surmised from a simple, hedonic utilitarian perspective or even from the more complex, behavioural economics inspired 'rules' of the semi-rational economic calculations which lie behind nudges (Knetsch 2011; Koh 2011). Better and more accurate knowledge of these drivers and motivations among target populations is essential if effective policy designs are to be developed and succeed.

Better understanding the behaviour of policy-takers: 'policy targets' and compliance issues

Policy targets come in all shapes and flavours, from individuals with certain kinds of characteristics to organizations and groups of various shapes and sizes, histories, backgrounds, and memberships. The preferences of such targets are always an issue (Lichtenstein and Slovic 2006; Unsworth and Fielding 2014) and cannot simply be assumed away through the use of policy models based on unproven or implicit assumptions about the nature of relevant policy target behaviour and compliance (Meier and Morgan 1982).

That is, in all but the simplest situations, governments are faced with complex compliance environments in which they encounter not just one but multiple actors and groups as 'targets'. Hence, for example, healthcare clients and citizens facing obesity challenges may be young or old, share some ethnic or racial characteristics, be segmented by gender and in other ways, and come into a policy situation with a range of understandings and knowledge of obesity science and views about exercise, food, and its preparation and intake.

As Weaver (2009a, 2009b, 2014) has pointed out, this typically generates a spectrum of potential compliers and non-compliers ranging from uninformed and unwilling ones to voluntary or willing compliers, and in proposing policies, governments need to know which and how many specific kinds of actors fall into which group (Braithwaite 2003). What works with one group may not work with another, and thus, it is not unusual for a range of governing resources and tools to have to be deployed in order to deal with complex, 'target-rich' environments, resulting in many of the complex, multi-tool policy mixes described in previous chapters.

In such circumstances, governments must determine (a) what exactly is a 'target', that is, whom a policy is aimed toward; (b) whether or not a target is likely to comply with government actions and intentions; (c) whether any such compliance is reluctant or freely given; and (d) how 'resistance' can be overcome and compliance encouraged (Scholz 1991). These considerations are important aspects of policy formulation and heavily influence policy designs and policy tool choices.

As Table 5.1 shows, estimations and diagnoses about likely compliance behaviour are closely linked to the abilities of specific kinds of governing instruments involved in the coercive and persuasive actions of governments (Hawkins and Thomas 1989).

Table 5.1 Nature of compliance of policy targets

| | | Likelihood of compliance | |
		High	Low
Willingness to comply	High	Model subjects: require little coercion, education, or persuasion	Reluctant subjects: require education and persuasion
	Low	Resistant subjects: require incentives to comply	Combative subjects: require a high level of coercion and monitoring to compel compliance

Source: Modelled after Scholz, J. T. (1991).

Thus, how governments perceive targets and classify individual groups within them is a critical aspect of policy design.

But as Schneider and Ingram (1993, 1997, 2005) have repeatedly pointed out, there are some limits to the ability and desire of governments to discern the true nature of these relationships. Social and political constructions of target populations are often stereotypes about particular groups of people that have been created by politics, culture, socialization, history, media, literature, religion, and the like, and the expected behaviour of policy targets is often framed by government agencies and policy-makers using the dual aspects of 'positive' or 'negative' stereotypes and whether they are powerful or weak actors in society (Schneider and Ingram 1993, 1997, 2005).

Positive constructions include images such as 'deserving', 'intelligent', 'honest', and 'public-spirited', for example, while negative constructions include images such as 'undeserving', 'stupid', 'dishonest', and 'selfish' (see Table 5.2). And exactly what kinds of tools are deployed in policy mixes and how they are calibrated can depend a great deal on these kinds of assumptions and presuppositions.

Table 5.2 Perceptions of policy targets after Schneider and Ingram (1993)

| | | Conception of social role | |
		Positive	Negative
Conception of power	Strong/powerful	Advantaged: subsidies and incentives	Adversaries: regulation and controls
	Weak/vulnerable	Dependents: moral suasion and exhortation	Deviants: coercion and punishments, disincentives

Source: Modelled after Schneider, and Ingram. (1993).

That is, in practice, the types of designs used to address problems involving target groups vary directly according to their categorization, with positively viewed targets receiving benefits and negatively viewed ones 'burdened' by costs. More coercive measures, Schneider and Ingram argued, are often used against groups perceived as 'deviants' rather than against other groups who might actually be more resistant to government initiatives, while tools such as subsidies and other kinds of payments might be most effective if used in dealing with 'dependents' but are often given instead to advantaged groups (Schneider and Ingram 1993: 337).

Of course, while there is no denying that targets are politically and socially constructed, there is also a significant 'objective' linkage between target group types and compliance behaviour that reinforces expectations governments have about compliance. That is, advantaged groups are usually expected to comply or have similar interests or share government aspirations in general more than do deviants, and this is often the case. It is also true that dependents are often able to evade controls in the same way as do adversary groups (Pierce et al. 2014).

This discussion highlights the significant linkages which exist between both perceptions of target behaviour and actual target behaviour for policy tool design and government tool use. Accurately determining the nature of compliance requires research and clarity on the part of government and the avoidance of stereotypes and simple estimations of target group attitudes and power. Several techniques, such as the use of policy 'pilots' or test cases and the use of policy experiments, discussed later, can be very important and useful in helping to provide the more accurate information on target behaviour needed to inform the design of effective policies.

The logic of policy design: policy change as behavioural change

The utilitarian viewpoint behind much thinking about policy design has only been seriously challenged in the policy sciences in relatively few instances where it has been undeniably apparent that target behaviour is motivated by considerations other than utility. This is the case, for example, when logics of appropriateness clearly dominate over those of calculation in displays of patriotism or religiously inspired altruistic or resistant activity, such as donating to charities or objecting to war or in the case of drug abuse, where individual health considerations and interests are often ignored by users (March and Olsen 1989, 2004; Tyler 1990, 2013). In the negative case, behaviour that is clearly self-destructive, such as drug, alcohol, or smoking addiction, is especially difficult to explain or correct using a purely utilitarian framework (Vimpani 2005; McGoldrick and Boonn 2010).

Despite the relative lack of challenges to orthodox thinking about behaviour in the policy sciences, however, empirically, such a position has become increasingly difficult to hold. Consideration and plans for 'nudging' and other aspects of behavioural psychology and economics which focus on semi-conscious cues and suggestions, for example, have undermined the utilitarian paradigm in the discipline. And the new focus in many contemporary policy studies on the deployment of policy tools, such as co-production or faith-based public service delivery, which rely more on the existence of altruistic behaviour, has done the same (Alford 1998; Hula et al. 2007; Kissane 2007; Zehavi 2008).

So too, although to a lesser extent, has work done on areas affected by 'social marketing' (Pykett et al. 2014) which explicitly rely on group norms in order to be effective. This is the case, for example, pertaining to the use of information-based tools or moral suasion to try to convince citizens to do their duty and refrain from, for instance, littering (Grasmick et al. 1991; John 2013), or to 'do the right thing', in giving up their seats on public transportation to pregnant women, the disabled, the elderly, and others less fortunate than themselves (Stanbury and Fulton 1984; Bardach 1989a; Torgler 2004; Corner and Randall 2011).

Such approaches have been especially significant in some jurisdictions in recent years, often displacing the deployment of regulation and financial incentives (Chatterton and Wilson 2014). Together, these have undermined confidence in the ability of utilitarian models to capture the critical aspects of the target behaviour responsible for participation in and compliance with many government schemes and intentions and prompted many questions and new research efforts (DiMento 1989; Kahneman 1994; Jones et al. 2011). Despite this, however, many analyses still introduce utilitarian assumptions 'through the back door' by linking policy success or failure to issues such as 'inability' or 'incapacity' of targets to comply, which can reintroduce the idea of utilitarianism, albeit in modified form (capability issues preventing a more straightforward compliance situation from emerging) (Winter and May 2001; Corner and Randall 2011; Chatterton and Wilson 2014; McLeod et al. 2015).

The behavioural expectations of policy tools

If target behaviour is not always utilitarian, though, then what is it, and how can it best be anticipated and linked in policy designs in order to promote the efficient and effective attainment of government goals, given that policy-makers themselves are behavioural agents (Viscusi and Gayer 2015) affected by the policy advice they receive and their own cognitive limitations?

Here it should be recalled that policy changes come about as governments and social actors wrestle with the basic problematic expectations of policy interventions and, in doing so, adopt policies composed of sets of tools which they expect to accomplish their goals, whatever these may be. *That is, the use of policy tools is expected to activate certain propensities on the part of policy actors, leading to more or less predictable changes in their behaviour and a different set of policy outputs than would have occurred with only a pre-existing mix.*

Tool deployment, thus, is a process which involves a complex causal chain centred on existing policy behaviours and policy-making contexts and how policy interventions trigger 'targets' to change their behaviour in some new direction compatible with government aims (Falleti and Lynch 2009; Hedström and Swedberg 1996, 1998; Hedström and Ylikoski 2010). This overall logic is set out in Figure 5.1.

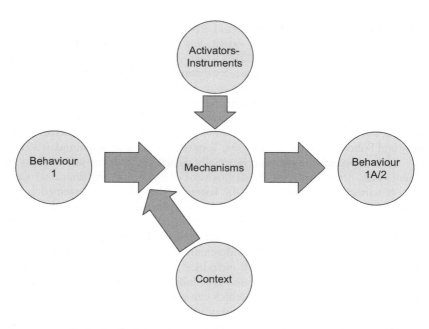

Figure 5.1 The behavioural expectations of policy design.
Source: Capano et al. (2019).

As Figure 5.1 illustrates, the idea is that policy-making can be viewed as largely about promoting or accomplishing behavioural changes in target populations, with policy instruments used as the means to influence a shift from behaviour (1) to a more desirable reformed or new behaviour (1A or 2). This occurs through the deployment of governing resources in the form of policy tools expected to affect behaviour in specified and more or less predictable ways (Balch 1980; Howlett 2018b).

The linkages between policy instrument invocation and behavioural or policy change are potentially very rich and involve a complex chain linking governing resources, such as funding, authority, and information, to particular behaviours. As Figure 5.2 shows, the process of behavioural change involves at least four linkages, all of which are affected by contextual aspects present at the moment at which instruments are invoked and mechanisms triggered. These are (1) the link between tools and the kinds of governing resources present at any moment in time, or governing capacity; (2) the link between resources and the mechanisms which tools activate, or target receptiveness to these resources; (3) the links between the mechanisms and the actual behavioural changes which occur post-activation, that is, the kinds and amounts of changes which actually occur when a tool is invoked; and (4) the link between changes in behaviour and changes in policy outputs, which may not exist in a linear kind of relationship but can also result in significant 'breaks' from past patterns and behaviours.

Significantly, all four of these linkages are susceptible to various barriers and impediments to resource availability, instrument choices, mechanism activation, reception, and impact, which make policy design and designing complex, uncertain, and error-prone activities (Falleti and Lynch 2009).

There are many such barriers and intermediating factors, which include such factors as the preferred policy style and governance mode, which can affect preferences for certain tools over others (Howlett 2017; Howlett and Rayner 2013); the various capacity strengths and weaknesses which can limit the capability of governments to use particular tools or eliminate them altogether (Wu et al. 2015b; Howlett and Ramesh 2016b);

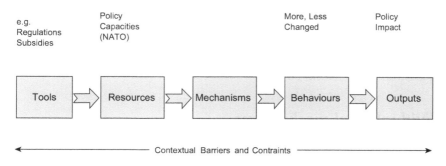

Figure 5.2 Links in the policy instrument–mechanism–output chain.

Source: Capano et al. (2019).

possible counter-vailing demands and constraints on behavioural change which can undermine the effect and impact of a mechanisms on subsequent behavioural change (Weaver 2014, 2015; Howlett 2018a); as well as various kinds of implementation and other issues which can lessen, or enhance, policy outputs (Lindqvist 2016; Hupe and Hill 2016) (see Figure 5.3).

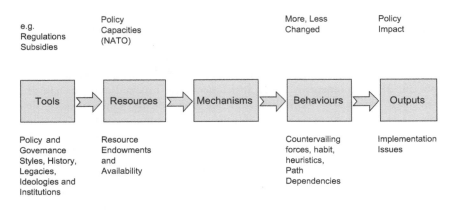

Figure 5.3 Context-related mechanism constraints.
Source: Capano et al. (2019).

Policy mechanisms activated in policy designs

This discussion of the general logic policy-making and policy design, of course, begs the question of what is in the 'black box' at the centre of the analysis. That is, what behavioural, group, and network mechanisms are affected by the use of governing resources in the form of policy tools? What are the mechanisms that lead more or less regularly to one type of output even if this regularity is limited in some circumstances and contexts by particular types of barriers and constraints?

Here, as noted above, a central distinction can be made between 'individual', 'group', and 'structural' mechanisms (Hedström and Swedberg 1998; Hedström and Ylikoski 2010).

Individual-level mechanisms

A great deal of the literature on social mechanisms in general and policy mechanisms in particular has focused on the individual level. As noted earlier, until recently, these studies focused almost exclusively on so-called 'system 2' mechanisms, that is, those which appealed to the more rational or utilitarian bases of human cognition, such as the ability to accurately assess the costs and benefits of specific proposed courses of action and decide upon a maximizing or optimal strategy (Elster 2009).

As we have seen, however, under the sway of behavioural economists and developments in other fields in recent years, many works dealing with 'system 2' or automatic and less reflective motivations and cognitive strategies have increasingly been added to this lexicon, such as tendencies toward risk aversion or the un- or semi-conscious adoption of attractive options, such as the purchase of comfort or junk food (Shafir et al. 1993; Shafir 2013; Sunstein et al. 2001; Ariely 2010). Although often pitched purely at the level of individuals, many of these same mechanisms also operate at the more collective or group level (Olson 1965; Buchanan et al. 1980; Riker 1986).

In this view, at the individual level, the mechanisms activated by policy instruments in order to trigger policy change are typically long-known characteristics of human behaviour, such as their moral posture, greed, pleasure-seeking, pride, fear, risk, or embarrassment aversion, bias confirmation, or the use of heuristics of different kinds which shortcut or otherwise affect the logics of calculation and appropriateness individuals might otherwise take and which affect their choices about whether or not to, for example, perform a crime or quit smoking, invest in a pension fund, or donate to a charity (March and Olsen 2004).

These kinds of mechanisms are the ones triggered or activated by 'substantive' policy instruments (Howlett 2000c), which are the typical kinds of policy tools found in most policy designs. Many of these mechanisms are hedonic, and mechanisms such as greed or self-interest, for example, as early utilitarian policy analysts observed, can be activated by economic incentives and disincentives, such as the provision of subsidies or the creation of penalty-based regulatory regimes or favourable or unfavourable tax treatment (Tupper and Doern 1981; Hood 1986c, 1995, 1991; Howlett 1991; Salamon 2002c). Other similar mechanisms, such as pride, can be activated and directed towards certain ends through the provision of prizes and praise, for example (Goodin 1980).

As we have seen in earlier chapters, policy tools rely on a set of governing resources for their effectiveness, including 'nodality' (or information), authority, treasure, or the organizational resources of government (Hood 1986c; Anderson 1975). And one of the main reasons a particular tool would be chosen over another is supply-oriented, that is, a government can only utilize specific kinds of tools when the resources it has to deploy it are in ample supply (Hood 1983). This is an important insight and driver of many tool and design decisions noted in previous studies.

But in addition to 'supply-side' capacity issues, 'demand-side' considerations are also very significant in policy design. That is, in general, each category of tool involves the use of a specific governing resource expected to trigger or lever a specific mechanism in targets, inducing a certain behavioural response. *Thus, the effectiveness of the deployment of such tools is linked not just to resource availability – a basic pre-condition of their use – but also to the existence of different characteristics on the part of policy targets which make them respond in a predictable way to the use of this resource.*

Table 5.3 presents some of the behavioural pre-requisites which governing tools rely upon for their effects.

Table 5.3 Behavioural needs for resource effectiveness

Tool type	Statecraft resource applied	Target behavioural pre-requisite
Nodality	Information	Credibility – willingness to believe and act on information provided by government
Authority	Coercive power/force	Legitimacy – willingness to be manipulated by government-invoked penalties and proscriptions
Treasure	Financial	Cupidity – willingness to be manipulated by gains/losses imposed by governments
Organization	Organization	Trust – willingness to receive goods and services from government and enter into partnership with it

Source: Howlett, (2011).

In the case of information use, for example, tool effectiveness relies both on the availability of knowledge and the means to distribute it ('resources') and also upon the target's belief in the accuracy of the messages being purveyed, or their *credibility* ('receptor'). Similarly, the effectiveness of the use of authoritative tools, as discussed earlier, depends not just on the availability of coercive mechanisms and their enforcement but also upon target perceptions of government *legitimacy*. Similarly, the effective use of treasure resources depends not just on the availability of government funding but also on target group financial need and especially their receptivity to government funding or their *cupidity*. Likewise, the effective use of organizational tools depends both on the existence of personnel and other organizational resource and also upon target group *trust* of government fairness and intent in the deployment and training of personnel to provide services and rules (Howlett 2017).

These are important considerations in policy design and especially in the calibration of policy tools. Thus, the use of authority-based tools such as laws and regulations, for example, involves considerations of legitimacy on the part of targets and must not over-reach or over-burden the extent of legitimacy which a government enjoys (Suchman 1995; Hanberger 2003). If a policy measure does so, it most assuredly will require much monitoring and enforcement activity in order for it to be even minimally effective. This can involve large administrative costs and burdens, which may well undermine its own efficiency and effectiveness, as has occurred in the past in many countries in areas such as marijuana, tobacco, or alcohol prohibition (Issalys 2005) where harsh penalities, taxes and bans led to high enforcement costs and the emergence of black markets.

Group-level mechanisms

This same logic can be applied to groups or collections of individuals who enter into coalitions in order to pursue collective aims and goals.

Such groups are sometimes viewed as mere aggregates of individual preferences with no interests or aims beyond those of their members (Olson 1965), although more careful study has shown that many complex motivations and proclivities exist at the collective or organizational level which are not reducible in such a fashion (Halpin and Binderkrantz 2011). These include propensities to search for new issues or retain existing issue orientations, decisions about whether to specialize or generalize in issue orientations, and the nature of membership appeals, for example, rather than simply an interest in membership or revenue growth (Halpin et al. 2018).

These groups have a different character than individuals, of course, but remain susceptible to the same kinds of motivations as do their members. That is, they have assets which can be replenished or jeopardized and react quickly to questions around organizational prestige and reputation (Coons and Weber 2014).

Structural- or subsystem-level mechanisms

A third set of mechanisms is composed of those whose focus affects the behaviour of policy subsystems. These have a different character than individual or group mechanisms, as they are more structure- than actor- or agent-oriented.

According to Sabatier (1998: 99), 'a subsystem consists of actors from a variety of public and private organizations who are actively concerned with a policy problem or issue, such as agriculture and who regularly seek to influence public policy in that domain'. Such subsystems, he argued, provide 'the most useful unit of analysis for understanding the overall policy process', superior to the use of other units such as government organizations or programmes.

A sizeable literature in the policy sciences has noted the importance to policy outputs and processes of two aspects of subsystem structure, namely, the number of type of actors arrayed in a subsystem or network and especially their ability to block off or close off entry of new actors, as well as the nature of the ideas which circulate within such subsystems (Howlett 2000c; Howlett and Ramesh 1998, 2002).

109

That is, changes in the ends of policies, be they conceptual or practical, require new ideas to be incorporated into policy-making processes (Sabatier 1999; Campbell 1998; Blyth 1997; Hall 1993), meaning, such ideas have to be able to penetrate into the policy communities and networks which control or dominate policy discourses (Howlett and Ramesh 1998). Similarly, another sizeable body of policy research links changes in the conceptual aspects of policy-making simply to the ability of actors in policy subsystems to achieve and retain 'monopoly' or hegemonic status within them and thus prevent serious discussion of new ideas and alternatives (Baumgartner and Jones 1993; Howlett and Rayner 1995; Hoberg 1996; Jacobsen 1995; Pontusson 1995).

This important third category of mechanisms is often ignored in the literature on policy mechanisms which overwhelmingly focuses on the micro or individual level, only occasionally venturing into a discussion of the meso or group level. These structural or network mechanisms, however, affect the propensity for subsystems to see the emergence of relatively consistent sets of policy actors and ideas interacting within more or less well-established relational parameters or whether more closed or chaotic relationships and interactions exist.

This third set of mechanisms can also be activated by policy tools, especially 'procedural' ones, which affect the manner in which individual and groups act and interact in attempting to affect policy outcomes (Howlett 2000c). That is, like any kind of networks, these subsystems are composed of nodes and links. And manipulating nodes and links – adding, subtracting, and changing them – constitutes a set of triggers which activate a variety of mechanisms at the network level, including the willingness of policy actors to enter into relationships with other proximate actors in the network (rather than more distant ones) or their ability to act as leaders, entrepreneurs, or brokers between other actors and governments.

Substantive tools deployment can affect network structure as when, for example, subsidies to an industry lead to the creation of more firms than otherwise would exist, altering the nature of production systems and industrial ecologies. However, procedural policy tools affect aspects of subsystem structure and behaviour more directly (de Bruijn and ten Heuvelhof 1997; Lang 2019, 2022) (see Table 5.4 below).

Examples of policy tools affecting networks with this procedural orientation include a government creating an advisory committee of select citizens or experts to aid it in its policy deliberations in contentious issue areas, such as local housing development or chemical regulation, or its creation of freedom-of-information or access-to-information legislation, making it easier for citizens to gain access to governments records, information, and documents. Re-organizing their own internal governmental structure can also have a similar effect on policy processes, for example, as occurs when a natural resource ministry is combined with an environmental one, forcing the two to adopt some form of new operating arrangements and changing the routes and routines through which industry and environmental lobbyists and interest groups previously interacted.

Table 5.4 Aspects of policy processes and structures affected by procedural policy tools

Process	Resource/Purpose	Network Structure Resource/Tools
Formulation	*Affect Actors and Preferences* Authority 　Restrict or Invite 　Participation	*Affect Deliberation Orientations* Authority 　Rules for decision-making 　(e.g. consensus vs 　majoritarian) 　Interaction Guidelines (e.g. 　joint declaration of intent)
	Information 　Issue Mission Statement	Information 　Providing and 　acknowledging interest 　positions
	Treasure 　Funding of participants	Treasure 　Establishing political 　opportunity structures (e.g. 　sponsoring of events/ 　funding secretariats
	Organization 　Trading influence for 　compromise and commitment	Organization 　Providing forums for 　deliberation
Implementation	*Affect commitment to* *deliver results* Authority 　Compliance mechanisms 　(binding vs non-binding) 　Accountability and control 　over implementing agencies	*Affect joint production* *orientation* Authority 　Establishing rules for 　joint production and 　collaboration
	Information 　Reporting 　Monitoring	Information 　Promotion/exhortation of 　participation 　Joint action plans
	Treasure 　Funding of participants	Treasure 　Incentives to collaborate and 　assume joint responsibility
	Organization 　Providing organizational 　home/support/resources	Organization 　Establishing coordinating 　and service delivery 　agencies

Source: Adapted from Lang (2019)

Improving policy designs through better linking tools, mechanisms, and targets

The fundamental design problem for governments, then, is not just determining resource endowments or calculating the range of prison sentences or the amount of fines and subsidies to levy in some situation based on a utilitarian compliance-deterrence. Rather it requires understanding on which basis expected and desired target behaviour is likely to occur (or not), by whom and how this is tied to the extent to which a government enjoys legitimacy, credibility, trust, and cupidity among target groups.

This is a design challenge which requires detailed empirical investigation and analysis in each case of tool deployment and continued monitoring over time to ensure these fundamental conditions have not changed or been undermined. Governments enjoying a high level of credibility, for example, may be able to undertake actions through moral suasion, while governments which do not enjoy that credibility will need to employ other tools. But whether or not this high level of credibility is being maintained is a key determinant of policy effectiveness, and continual monitoring and assessment are required to ensure this remains the case and that existing tools continue to function effectively over time.

The same non-utilitarian behavioural logic extends to the use of common traditional tools such as taxes and subsidies, although the behavioural characteristics of such treasure-based policy tools are not the same as for information-based ones. The former achieve their ends not through a legitimacy–coercion matrix of encouragement and deterrence but through the willingness of subjects to be manipulated, more or less voluntarily, by financial incentives and disincentives (Surrey 1970; Woodside 1979; Braithwaite 2003).

Calibrations or the settings of such tools are often claimed to be set on a purely utilitarian basis, but the extent of cupidity or greed on the part of policy targets varies dramatically by group and subject matter. Governments discover this whenever they attempt, for example, to discourage cigarette and tobacco by discouraging consumption through raising excise taxes on harmful products while reducing them on others (Gullberg and Skodvin 2011). Such actions may work in some cases and products or among some groups, like the elderly in the case of tobacco control, but fail in others, such as young women and younger people in general (Studlar 2002).

This behavioural pre-requisite also features in the use and effectiveness of the 'information' tools discussed earlier. As the poor experiences of the application of some of the insights of behavioural economics and psychology to policy-making in the form of 'nudges' or informational cues show, consideration by targets of the credibility of messages sent and received and the willingness of targets to trust their contents and promises are critical to what type and extent of behavioural response will ensue (Weiss and Tschirhart 1994).

This is true of many different public information campaigns, for example, in areas of obesity and the ingestion of dangerous products, which utilize this resource (Kersh 2015; Barreiro-Hurlé et al. 2010; Padberg 1992). Efforts at 'social marketing', such as these, feature the use of informational or 'nodality' tools (Hood 1986c) that appeal directly to sentiments of collective solidarity and moral duty of citizens and groups, invoking values well beyond those related to individual utility calculations (Corner and Randall 2011).

Finally, efforts at 'co-production' and co-design or co-management often aim at re-designing service delivery through various forms of partnerships in which some division of labour emerges between state and non-state actors (Pestoff et al. 2006; Voorberg et al. 2015; Alford 1998; Braithwaite and Levi 2003). These forms of service delivery are organizational tools which utilize state personnel and organizational resources to directly or indirectly deliver goods and services. But again, willingness of targets to partner in these activities, as in the case of more traditional, exclusively government-based ones, requires targets to assess and trust the competence of government agents to deliver or plan such services in a timely and appropriate way.

The key role of policy pilots and experiments in improving policy designs

In this complex design environment, policy experiments, including pilot projects, play an important role in producing design-relevant knowledge which can help clarify the behaviour(s) of target groups when they are unknown or poorly understood (Stromsdorfer 1985). The development sector, for example, has often conducted experiments to evaluate alternative strategies and accordingly allocate resources to those that emerge as most feasible in promoting development goals (Rondinelli 1983).

Although these might not be immediately feasible or popular on a large scale, designers can always advocate the development of pilot projects or policy experiments in which new designs and ideas are tried out and proven prior to their being 'scaled up' or 'scaled down' and put into widespread practice.

Such policy experimentation can be used to pre-test different programmes and policies for their likely impacts, process of implementation, and stakeholder acceptability and help assess their potential problems prior to launch. Policy experimentation provides meaning by helping in framing or projecting the future, deriving alternate response strategies, and monitoring any changes in the policy environment.

Policy pilots form a common and important form of policy experimentation and involve the introduction of major government policies or programmes at a 'controlled small-scale' (Weiss 1976) or in a phased manner, 'allowing them to be tested, evaluated and adjusted before being rolled out' (Cabinet Office 2003). Pilots can aid in policy appraisal (Turnpenny et al. 2009) and provide useful insights for dealing with complex policy issues and high uncertainty (Vreugdenhil et al. 2010). The small-scale and experimental nature of pilots can encourage policy innovations (Cabinet Office 2003), and policy-makers are thus often urged or consider pilot projects and other forms of policy experiments in order to test new policy and programme approaches (Martin and Sanderson 1999; Vreugdenhil et al. 2010).

Planning 'well-designed pilots' alongside a fully functioning policy can thus help test a policy's performance along with the identification of emerging issues and make necessary policy adjustments (Swanson and Bhadwal 2009). A pilot in this sense can form an important step of regular policy monitoring and evaluation over the long term.

Testing policy responses through such active experimentation is a key tool for policy-makers interested in developing more persuasive designs. Experiments and pilot projects help them deal with different kinds of uncertainty through improved knowledge of target group behaviour under different policy interventions to improve projections of the likelihood of future states of events. Transposing the idea of 'controlled experimentation' – a concept that is well-acknowledged in the social and natural sciences – into policy research has received much attention by policy scholars and practitioners alike attempting to deal with uncertainties in the policy environment (Anderson 1975).

Experiments have also served as a source of evidence for policy-making in many sectors, including education, healthcare, environment, and social welfare, among others (Bennion and Nickerson 2011). More recently, policy pilots have also gained attention in the transition management literature (Rotmans et al. 2001; Van den Bosch and Rotmans 2008), specifically those intended to generate long-term societal change (Bos et al. 2013; McFadgen 2019). Experimentation is an important instrument providing a 'space' for learning to occur and 'promoting variation' (Swanson and Bhadwal 2009) by crafting and field-testing multiple policy alternatives that can make the emergence of a successful solution more likely.

Enhanced experimentation and learning are thus instrumental in allowing design to keep pace 'with the dynamic drivers and expressions of risk' in a changing policy environment (O'Brien et al. 2012), but only if the experiments themselves are designed to address the level of uncertainty involved in a specific case. The underlying motivation in designing policy experiments is that these will provide results that are largely indicative of what outputs, outcomes, and challenges can be expected when programmes and policies based on results of these experiments are 'scaled up' or implemented fully, enhancing the persuasiveness of designs through better appreciation of the actual logics behind target behaviour in response to government initiatives (Vreugdenhil and Nair 2015).

However, there are several challenges posed to realizing the benefits of policy experimentation in practice which need to be overcome if success is to be achieved in this area. The study of the impact of pilots on policy development is often limited to 'learning from failure'. Furthermore, the factors leading to success of a pilot and links between pilot diffusion and transition to policies are not well-established, theoretically or empirically (Vreugdenhil et al. 2010).

Conclusion: policy designs as behavioural modifiers

A design approach to policy-making centered on this instrument-mechanism-behaviour logic has several advantages over other approaches, not least in how it clarifies the tool-to-output process of policy-making and the key factors and relationships existing in such processes.

It is a key technique for developing and implementing more persuasive designs and better achieving policy goals.

Readings

Australian Public Service Commission. (2009). *Smarter Policy: Choosing Policy Instruments and Working with Others to Influence Behaviour.* Canberra, ACT: Australian Public Service Commission.

Ayres, I. and J. Braithwaite. (1995). *Responsive Regulation: Transcending the Deregulation Debate.* Oxford: Oxford University Press.

Braithwaite, J., J. Walker and P. Grabosky. (1987). 'An Enforcement Taxonomy of Regulatory Agencies'. *Law and Policy 9*, no. 3: 323–351.

Bunge, M. (1997). 'Mechanism and Explanation'. *Philosophy of the Social Sciences 27*, no. 4 (1 December): 410–465.

Bunge, M. (2004). 'How Does It Work? The Search for Explanatory Mechanisms'. *Philosophy of the Social Sciences 34*, no. 2 (1 June): 182–210.

Capano, G. and M. Howlett. (2021). 'Causal Logics and Mechanisms in Policy Design: How and Why Adopting a Mechanistic Perspective Can Improve Policy Design'. *Public Policy and Administration 36*, no. 2 (1 April): 141–162.

Duesberg, S., Á. Ní Dhubháin and D. O'Connor. (2014). 'Assessing Policy Tools for Encouraging Farm Afforestation in Ireland'. *Land Use Policy 38* (May): 194–203.

Falleti, T. G. and J. F. Lynch. (2009). 'Context and Causal Mechanisms in Political Analysis'. *Comparative Political Studies 42*, no. 9 (1 September): 1143–1166.

Halpin, D. R., B. Fraussen and A. J. Nownes. (2018). 'The Balancing Act of Establishing a Policy Agenda: Conceptualizing and Measuring Drivers of Issue Prioritization within Interest Groups'. *Governance 31*, no. 2 (1 April): 215–237.

Harring, N. (2016). 'Reward or Punish? Understanding Preferences toward Economic or Regulatory Instruments in a Cross-National Perspective'. *Political Studies 64*, no. 3 (1 October): 573–592.

Hedström, P. and P. Ylikoski. (2010). 'Causal Mechanisms in the Social Sciences'. *Annual Review of Sociology 36*, no. 1: 49–67.

Heinmiller, B. T., M. A. Hennigar and S. Kopec. (2017). 'Degenerative Politics and Youth Criminal Justice Policy in Canada'. *Politics & Policy 45*, no. 3 (June): 405–431.

Howlett, M. (2018b). 'Matching Policy Tools and Their Targets: Beyond Nudges and Utility Maximization in Policy Design'. *Policy & Politics 46*, no. 1 (January): 101–124.

Leggett, Will. (2014). "The Politics of Behaviour Change: Nudge, Neoliberalism and the State." *Policy & Politics 42*, no. 1 (January 1, 2014): 3–19.

Lockton, D., D. Harrison and N. A. Stanton. (2016). 'Design for Sustainable Behaviour: Investigating Design Methods for Influencing User Behaviour'. *Annual Review of Policy Design 4*, no. 1 (28 October): 1–10.

Porumbescu, G. A., M. I. H. Lindeman, E. Ceka and M. Cucciniello. (2017). 'Can Transparency Foster More Understanding and Compliant Citizens?' *Public Administration Review 77*, no. 6: 840–850.

Redström, J. (2006). 'Persuasive Design: Fringes and Foundations'. In W. A. iJsselsteijn, Y. A. W. de Kort, C. Midden, B. Eggen and E. van den Hoven (eds.), *Persuasive Technology*. Lecture Notes in Computer Science 3962. Berlin, Heidelberg, Germany: Springer, 112–122.

Schneider, A. and H. Ingram. (1993). 'Social Construction of Target Populations: Implications for Politics and Policy'. *American Political Science Review 87*, no. 2: 334–347.

Schneider, A. and M. Sidney. (2009). 'What Is Next for Policy Design and Social Construction Theory?' *Policy Studies Journal 37*, no. 1: 103–119.

Vreugdenhil, H. and P. K. Rault. (2010). 'Pilot Projects for Evidence-Based Policy-Making: Three Pilot Projects in the Rhine Basin'. *German Policy Studies* (22 June).

Weaver, R. K. (2009a). *If You Build It, Will They Come? Overcoming Unforeseen Obstacles to Program Effectiveness*. The Tansley Lecture. Saskatoon, SK: University of Saskatchewan.

Weaver, R. K. (2009b). *Target Compliance: The Final Frontier of Policy Implementation*. Research Paper. Washington, DC: Brookings Institution.

Weaver, R. K. (2015). 'Getting People to Behave: Research Lessons for Policy Makers'. *Public Administration Review 75*, no. 6 (1 November): 806–816.

Part III

POLICY DESIGNING

Processes and practices

When does policy design occur and why? Policy designing as policy formulation in the face of uncertainty

The main focal points of design activities within the policy process, as the discussion in Chapters 1–5 has shown, are around policy formulation and implementation (Hood 1986c, 2007b; Linder and Peters 1991; Varone 1998; Varone and Aebischer 2001). It is at these two stages of the policy cycle that the possible techniques to be used in realizing policy are mooted and appraised and then later executed and put into practice (Goggin 1987). The key stage of policy design, however, is policy formulation, with successful implementation and overcoming the barriers to it being one concern of formulation and design activity (Villa Alvarez et al. 2022).

In general, within government, 'policy formulation' involves the pursuit of finding, devising, and defining solutions and takes place once a public problem has been recognized as warranting government attention. Formulation thus follows upon some initial 'agenda-setting' activity in policy-making and entails the various processes of generating options or alternative possible courses of action about what to do about an identified and prioritized problem.

As Charles Jones (1984: 7) observed, the distinguishing characteristic of policy formulation is thus, simply, that it is a process and stage of policy-making in which means are proposed in order to see if and how they could resolve a perceived societal problem or government goal. Goals may be given or emerge or be refined as formulation takes place. That is, once a social problem has been elevated to the formal agenda of the government, policy-makers are usually expected to act in devising alternatives or potential solutions to it. Although they may ultimately do nothing or react in a

DOI: 10.4324/9781003343431-9

purely symbolic way (Shroff et al. 2012), the essence of policy formulation is simply that various ways to deal with societal problems are proposed and deliberated upon by government officials and others knowledgeable about the problem.

During this period of policy-making, policy options that might help resolve issues and problems recognized at the agenda-setting stage are identified, refined, and formalized. However, it is also the case that many of these options may have been developed prior to the point in time at which they are suggested as solutions to particular problems in a process sometimes referred to as one of 'solutions chasing problems' (Beland and Howlett 2016; Halpin 2011).

Formulation activities are thus distinct from other aspects of policy-making, such as decision-making, which involves mainly authoritative government decision-makers choosing a particular course of action or its actual implementation on the ground (Schmidt 2008). Many modern governments have their own internal policy experts or 'policy professionals' (Svallfors 2017, 2020; Selling and Svalfors 2019) engaged in this formulation work and often have created smaller or larger kinds of 'policy shops' within government departments and agencies in which to house them (Migone and Howlett 2022; Lindquist and Desveaux 2007). These policy workers often lack the capability to undertake their own research and analysis, however, and instead act as policy brokers or champions of specific kinds of designs and tool uses put forward by others in the policy community (Knaggård 2015).

In most cases, external actors such as think tanks or academics are engaged alongside internal governmental ones in the process of devising possible policy mixes and tool applications. As a result of this interaction of state and non-state actors, the provision of potential solutions or alternative possible courses of action for governments often involves sometimes quite large sets or arrangements of internal and external experts and analysts and advisors which are often referred to collectively as composing a 'policy advisory system' (Craft and Howlett 2013), discussed in more detail in the next chapter.

It is also often the case that other governments are faced with similar problems whose actions can sometimes be replicated or emulated. This latter process is sometimes referred to as 'policy learning' or 'lesson-drawing' (Rose 1993; Bennett and Howlett 1992).

Learning, of course, is not automatic and may not occur due to time, information, ideologies, or other tensions. And poor learning may also lead governments down the wrong path in adopting inappropriate solutions for dealing with their problems or when they 'learn the wrong lessons' from this work (Dunlop and Radaelli 2018). In some cases, for example, little or not enough thought can go into learning, and emulation or 'policy transfer' can be an example of what Dimaggio and Powell (1983) referred to as 'institutional isomorphism' or 'isomorphic mimicry', in which similar organizations adopt similar routines and processes without fully understanding all their implications and without needed managerial or informational or other kinds of capacity required to make them work. Learning activity nevertheless can serve to reduce the differences found between the policies in different jurisdictions and can lead to large similarities or apparent convergences in policy design and content among even the most diverse societies (Bennett 1991a; Bennett and Howlett 1992).

Policy formulation as a distinct stage of the policy cycle

Public policies emanate from societies' efforts to affect changes in their own institutional or public behaviour in order to achieve some end goal that key policy actors consider to be important. They are determined by governments but involve other actors and institutions – private, commercial, family, and others – in often complex governance and governing arrangements and relationships (Howlett and Ramesh 2016a).

Devising what this course of action might entail is the subject of policy formulation. It is a stage of policy-making activity where options that might help resolve issues and problems recognized at the agenda-setting stage are identified, and often refined, appraised, and formalized in some fashion. Thus, in general, *policy formulation* refers to the process of both *generating and reducing* options about what to do about a social, political, or economic condition identified by a public authority as a public problem (Sidney 2007).

That is, during policy formulation, some range of available options is considered and then reduced to some set that relevant policy actors, especially in government, can agree may be usefully employed to address a policy issue. This generally occurs before the issue progresses onward to official decision-makers for some definitive determination, although those decision-makers may have, in their public pronouncements or electoral platforms and other statements, already signalled which kinds of efforts they might countenance and which they would not.

Proposals for action or inaction may come about during the initial agenda-setting discussions, during which a policy problem and a possible solution can become coupled on the government's agenda (Kingdon 1984); but they may also arise from past efforts, successful and otherwise, in the originating or other jurisdictions in dealing with an issue.

This depiction paints formulation as involving several disjointed activities within a larger policy-making process that will be carried out differently in each jurisdiction and situation given the different range of actors and institutions and histories found in each and their different levels of involvement in efforts to define and resolve policy issues. However, others have noted that it is still possible to identify general attributes of the formulation process which are similar across jurisdictions (Howlett et al. 2009).

Jones (1984: 78), for example, depicted the following general attributes of formulation in practice as follows:

• Formulation need not be limited to one set of actors. Thus, there may well be two or more formulation groups producing competing (or complementary) proposals.

- Formulation may proceed without a clear definition of the problem, or without formulators ever having much contact with affected groups.
- There is no necessary coincidence between formulation and particular institutions, though it is a frequent activity of bureaucratic agencies.
- Formulation and reformulation may occur over a long period of time without ever building sufficient support for any one proposal.
- There are often several appeal points for those who lose in the formulation process at any one level.
- The process itself never has neutral effects. Somebody wins and somebody loses even in the workings of science.

Actors and interests in the policy formulation process

Once a government has acknowledged the existence of a public problem and the need to do something about it, that is, once it has entered onto the agenda of government, policy-makers are often expected to decide on a course of action to follow in addressing it.

Although many such alternatives may have already emerged during or prior to agenda-setting and, in a sense, are 'sitting on the shelf', ready to be deployed or discussed (Kingdon 1984), even in this case policy formulation involves some initial assessment, no matter how cursory, of the feasibility and comparative costs and benefits of different policy options (May 1981; Wildavsky 1979; Salamon 1989, 2002c; Linder and Peters 1990b, 1990c, 1990d; Howlett 2000c; Howlett and Ramesh 2016a, 2016b; Howlett, Mukherjee and Woo 2015; Howlett, Ramesh and Woo 2015; Howlett, Rayner and Tollefson 2009; Jarvis 2011b; Montpetit 2003b, 2003c; Braathen 2007a, 2007b; Dunlop 2009a, 2009b).

Formulation activity encompasses consideration and discussion of several tasks which culminate in alternative possible programme designs and structures. These include problem conceptualization, theory evaluation and selection, specification of objectives, programme design, and programme structure, and may also involve activities such as pilot projects and 'prototyping' in which possible solutions are tried out on a limited or test basis (Wolman 1981; Nesta 2011; Villa-Alvarez et al. 2020; Leiter and Petersmann 2022).

Policy formulation, therefore, is a *process* of identifying and assessing possible solutions to policy problems or, to put it another way, a process of exploring the various options or alternatives available for addressing a problem through *policy analysis* and, often, trial and experiment (Linder and Peters 1990d). It is what Aaron Wildavsky (1979), one of the founders of the policy sciences, termed finding and establishing a relationship between 'manipulable means and obtainable objectives' (15–16).

In terms of *process*, Harold Thomas (2001) distinguished four aspects of policy formulation that are generally visible: appraisal, dialogue, formulation, and consolidation. During *appraisal*, information and evidence necessary to understand the issue at hand are sought and considered. This step in formulation is where data about policy problems and their solutions in the form of research reports, expertise, and input from stakeholders and the general public are often considered.

Following this, a *dialogue* phase between actors engaged in policy formulation typically ensues which is centred on the deliberation and exchange of different viewpoints about the policy goals and potential means to resolve them. Dialogues can be structured with the involvement of chosen experts and representatives from private sector, labour, or other interest groups, and they can take place as more open and unstructured processes or in a closed and secretive fashion. What structure is chosen can make a significant difference on the impacts of that participation in the formulation process (Hajer 2005). While established expert opinion is often sought, efforts to involve participants from less-established organizations and viewpoints can invigorate the discussion over policy alternatives and bring in new ideas and voices, which may sometimes prove advantageous.

Central to this process, at its core, lies the actual *formulation* phase, wherein typically administrators and public officials scrutinize the costs, benefits, challenges, and opportunities of various policy alternatives in the effort to consolidate a proposal or proposals about which alternatives or mix of alternatives will actually proceed through to consideration by authoritative decision-makers. This choice of some policy alternatives over others is likely to draw opposition from actors who have their preferred instruments sidelined, and these and other forms of feedback about shortlisted policy options are commonly considered during a final *consolidation* phase, in which proposed policy solutions are amended or refined before moving forward.

Formulation is a task undertaken ultimately by governments but is also affected by the ideas and interests held and promoted by a wide range of state and societal actors who are also often intimately involved in the formulation, promotion, and refinement of policy alternatives. It involves governments and other policy actors asking and answering questions about how societies can deal with various kinds of problems and conditions affecting citizens and organizations.

While some of the issues involved in formulation are technical and have a significant knowledge component, the issues that lead policy formulators to choose some policy options over others need not be based on facts (Merton 1948b). If powerful policy actors are of the belief that a policy option is unfeasible or unacceptable, this contention can be enough to exclude it from further discussion (Carlsson 2000), and the opposite may also be true in that support from such actors can carry a great deal of weight in determining what will successfully emerge from the formulation process (Ohberg et al 2015).

The exercise of framing problems and proposing alternatives which are expected to match policy goals and means is central to the tasks and activities of policy formulation, including policy design. Formulation activity entails not only calculations of the relative benefits and risks of the various policy means that can be considered to match stated policy goals but also their potential *feasibility* or likelihood of acceptance and thus involves both a technical as well as a political component (Huitt 1968). This is not a neutral or 'objective' or technical process. Although it may sometimes be written about or viewed in this way, as one of the earliest proponents of the policy sciences, Harold Lasswell, stated in 1936, it is a political activity thoroughly immersed and grounded in questions and conflicts about 'who gets what, when and how' in society (Lasswell 1936).

Design questions and concerns raised at the formulation stage of policy-making vary in range and scope, but addressing them typically involves deliberations among a wide range of actors about what kinds of activities governments can undertake and what kinds of policy instruments or levers they can employ in crafting solutions for the public and private dilemmas they identify or consider to be policy problems. Some problems may defy solution, such as poverty or homelessness in many countries and jurisdictions, and others may be resolvable more easily than others. But whatever solutions emerge from formulation activity are the basis of what, once adopted, becomes a public policy.

In this light, the formulation of policies and policy designs or the matching, and often mismatching, of goals and means, or policy aims and instruments, occurs through the interplay of knowledge-based analytics of problems and solutions with power-based political considerations. These include actor calculations of the costs and benefits of specific problem definitions and proposed solutions, but also the partisan and electoral concerns of governments and other actors and many other matters in the realm of ideological, religious, ethical, and other kinds of beliefs held by actors.

All this activity occurs within the context of the need for policy-makers to meet and placate the diverse interests of the public, social actors, and their own administrations. Not surprisingly, this process often ends with the adoption of complex assemblages or mixes of policy aims and policy tools both to address policy problems and the interests of actors that are somewhat unique to each jurisdiction and sector and which may or may not embody much in the way of 'technical' merit (Howlett and Cashore 2009).

Studying policy formulation: what does 'policy formulation' entail?

Many studies have engaged in the exploration of various kinds of policy tools and how they are implemented, but there is a less dedicated focus in the literature on how policy tools and outcomes can be better matched or 'designed'. While how policy instruments fare and how successful governments have been in their creation and deployment have always been subjects of interest among policy scholars, the literature on policy formulation has remained somewhat rudimentary and fragmented (Sidney 2007).

As discussed in earlier chapters, not all formulation activities match the criteria necessary to be called 'design'. The essence of what has come to be known as the policy design 'orientation' in the policy sciences (Howlett, Mukherjee and Woo 2015) requires a design process which is knowledge-based and intentional. While recognizing that often policy decisions and options may be made and developed in a more contingent and irrational or interest-driven fashion, policy design scholars highlight the desirability of identifying ideal 'technical' models of instrument use and the need to translate them sensitively in order to fit context-sensitive solution conditions.

Policy formulation in this sense involves identifying both the technical and political constraints on state action (May 1981; Sidney 2007) as well as simply articulating options. It involves recognizing limitations on state resources, such as a lack of credibility, fiscality, capacity, or legitimacy, which can limit what is considered to be feasible in specific circumstances (Majone 1989: 76). Politicians in most societies, for example, cannot do everything they consider would appeal to the public but also cannot ignore popular opinion and public sentiments and still maintain their legitimacy, credibility, trust, and electoral success.

Other constraints on policy design can arise from limits on a state's administrative and financial capacity. For example, governments that have an ownership stake in economic sectors such as energy, finance, and transportation may have more policy options open to them than states where the private sector exclusively delivers these goods and services, while states with well-developed and sophisticated administrative apparatuses generally also have a larger range of possible courses of action than those states lacking such resources (Ingraham 1987).

The study of policy tools and their design has been one major venue for building knowledge about policy options and choices and hence about policy formulation processes (Salamon 1989, 2002c). Policy instrument studies have, over the last several decades, been concerned with better understanding what Cochran and Malone (1999) deem to be the substantive 'what' questions of policy-making. That is:

What is the plan for dealing with the problem? What are the goals and priorities? What options are available to achieve those goals? What are the costs and benefits of each of the options? What externalities, positive, or negative, are associated with each alternative?

(Cochran and Malone 1999: 46)

However, in parallel with this effort, the study of policy design has also dealt with the 'how', or the procedural and process-orientated questions about how best to formulate policy solutions and how such solutions have evolved over time and spread over space (Howlett 2000c; Linder and Peters 1990c; Schneider and Ingram 1997; Considine 2012).

Much useful knowledge about formulation processes and designs has emerged from this area of study (Howlett et al. 2015). It has been shown, for example, that governments often find themselves in the position of being leaders or laggards in terms of recognizing and addressing problems and discussing or implementing possible solutions (Gunningham et al. 1998). While there are some advantages to being leaders, the risks of failure are higher when problem definitions and solutions are innovative, and laggards can benefit from both the positive and negative experiences of leaders and often can inherit an already well-discussed and elaborated set of policy solutions when they do eventually turn to address a particular problem already dealt with by other jurisdictions (Béland and Howlett 2016).

Throughout the formulation process and in subsequent activities involved in implementing initiatives and monitoring or evaluating the results of such actions, governments can and do learn from their own and others' experiences and can often improve their performance and more effectively attain their aims and goals.

Monitoring events in other jurisdictions and even other branches of the same government to see how various efforts and tools aimed at providing solutions to problems have fared is also often a major component of the policy formulation activity undertaken by governments and can be 'designed into' policy formulation through encouragement of comparative studies of policy successes and failures and by ensuring that evidence on 'best practices' in other jurisdictions enters into design deliberations and formulation practices.

Understanding the variety of inputs different actors bring to the policy formulation activity and the contexts within which they function can shed considerable light on topics related to why some policy options gain significant attention while others fall by the wayside. As mentioned earlier, formulation can take place even without a definite depiction of the policy problem at hand (Weber and Khademian 2008), and it often proceeds over time in successive 'rounds' of formulation and reformulation of policy goals and means (Thomas 2001; Teisman 2000). Within this iterative process, while some policy-makers may look for 'win-win' solutions that maximize complementarities between the views of different actors, the costs and benefits of different policy choices are often borne disproportionately by different participants, leading to contested processes of evaluation and deliberation (Wilson 1974).

Dealing with uncertainty in policy formulation through scenario analysis and prototyping

While this discussion says something about 'how' a policy is formulated, it is less clear 'what' is being formulated. Here it should be noted that the policy options that are considered during formulation are the embodiment of the techniques or tools of governance that, in some way, use resources of the state to define and attain government goals (Dahl and Lindblom 1953; Hood 2007b).

Policy goals result from the translation of multifaceted and interconnected societal problems into programmes of action, and since this translation has implications about what items are considered to be administratively achievable, technically feasible, and politically acceptable, the activities of goal selection and tool choice are often contentious (Majone 1975, 1989; Meltsner 1972; Dror 1969; Webber 1986). Indeed, even if policy-makers agree that a problem exists, they may not share an understanding of its causes or ramifications (Howlett et al. 2009: 113) or how it should be addressed.

Matching ends and means or policy goals and policy tools is thus a complex task and requires some knowledge of the problem area and potential solutions, as well as the context in which instruments will be deployed and their likely effects, including their level of support among powerful social and state actors.

But many uncertainties exist in these areas linked to the state of knowledge about 'how things are' as well as that concerning 'how things will be' in the future. A summary of these different kinds of uncertainty and their effects on formulation is set out in Table 6.1.

Table 6.1 Different kinds of uncertainty faced by policy-makers and types of policy-making responses

		Knowledge about Probabilities	
		Unproblematic	Problematic
	Unproblematic	**Character of uncertainty: risk** Ameliorative techniques • Risk assessment • Optimizing models • Expert consensus • Cost–benefit analysis • Aggregated beliefs	**Character of uncertainty: ambiguity** Ameliorative techniques • Interactive modelling • Participatory deliberation • Focus and dissensus groups • Multicriteria mapping • Q-method, repertory grid
	Problematic	**Character of uncertainty: uncertainty** Ameliorative techniques • Interval analysis • Scenario methods • Sensitivity testing • Decision rules • Evaluative judgment	**Character of uncertainty: ignorance** Ameliorative techniques • Monitoring and surveillance • Reversibility of effects • Flexibility of commitments • Adaptability, resilience • Robustness and diversity

Source: Based on Stirling (2010).

Overcoming or dealing with these problems is a key difficulty in policy formulation, and over the years, several common techniques have been developed to help deal with these uncertainty issues. Four of the most common – the use of measures and models, efforts at cost–benefit analysis, scenario planning, and prototyping – are set out next.

The use of measures and models as design aids

The need for the use of some level of expertise or expert advice in the formulation process in order to address uncertainties around problem (and solution) knowledge is well recognized. It has engendered the growth of a core of 'policy professionals' trained in specific techniques aimed at overcoming or at least managing or reducing the problems caused by present and future uncertainty.

One common source of formulated content and its evaluation or appraisal used in this process is often intricately tied up with the development, implementation, and interpretation of numerical *measures and indicators* capable of describing both the scope or origins of a problem as well as monitor its development and change over time (Lehtonen 2017, 2022). These can also sometimes be linked together in the form of a model of expected results and impacts of possible policy alternatives as is common, for example, in the public health and economic spheres, where such models affect the design and construction of hospitals and availability of surgical beds, or the setting of interest or mortgage or insurance rates.

It is no doubt true that many uncertainties stem from a lack of knowledge of cause-and-effect relationships between policy interventions and outcomes, and that the institution of some measurement system can be very helpful in developing such knowledge. However, only some kinds of problems and solutions are amenable to more precise specification or assessment through better data collection and analysis.

Very complex and dynamic relationships, for example, can be difficult to model or may involve a wide range of possible variation (Swanson and Bhadwal 2009) or involve activities like drug smuggling or money laundering which are intentionally made difficult to measure and trace. In such circumstances, measures and indicators may be biased or generate hard-to-interpret results (Lehtonen 2017).

Policy appraisal and cost–benefit analysis

For much of the history of the policy sciences, the key technique expected to be followed in the ranking and appraisal of policy alternatives was cost–benefit analysis. This technique involves an effort to quantify the purported benefits and costs of any alternative, and these estimates can sometimes be used by decision-makers to aid their choices. Typically, this involves a preference for the alternative which best maximizes benefits while minimizing costs (Boardman et al. 2001).

In many circumstances, sometimes by law, such *ex ante* evaluations or estimates of costs and benefits are mandated or expected to be completed as part of a formal policy development protocol. However, the quality and accuracy of such estimates are always suspect, and in many cases, the quantification or even monetization of costs and benefits may be difficult or impossible to accomplish (Vining and Boardman 2007), and such evaluations may be done poorly or purely symbolically (Hahn and Dudley 2007).

Scenario analysis

Many uncertainties figure or can figure even in these kinds of formal expert estimations and judgments, and policy-makers and implementers are often somewhat surprised when particular elements of policies or their expectations fail to occur as anticipated, but are not necessarily deeply shocked or disturbed when this happens.

This is because even when causal relationships and future scenarios are relatively well-known, there is always some uncertainty with respect to policy predictions due to statistical and uncertainties in data and estimates attached to expected relationships between policy interventions and target behaviour. Parameter and associated 'fuzzy' uncertainty, for example, is common in day-to-day policy-making, whereby it is often not known in real time, to give only one instance, what is the actual unemployment rate to be used to inform interest rates or other monetary policy tools expected to overcome it (Linder and Peters 1988; deLeon 1992).

One tool borrowed from futures studies and risk management to help conceptualize the future risks stemming from these kinds of uncertainties is *scenario analysis* (Volkery and Ribeiro 2009; Beh et al. 2015; Landuyt et al. 2016). In this technique, plausible and probable alternative future paths are identified and then described as existing as possible future paths within a broader 'cone' of all possible futures (Gall et al. 2022; Taylor 1988; Hancock and Bezold 1994; Voros 2017).

As Figure 6.1 shows, preferred, possible, plausible, and probable future scenarios can be thought of as alternative cones which grow in size as time moves forward but are nevertheless distinctly different in terms of their possible occurrence, and these distinctions can inform both policy choices and risk mitigation measures.

Other similar techniques have been developed to aid policy formulation in dealing with these kinds of uncertainty, such as Monte Carlo simulations and other kinds of statistical analyses which can provide likelihood estimates and probabilities which are good enough for action to be taken with the possibility of small errors and mistakes (Walker et al. 2010; Brugnach and Ingram 2012).

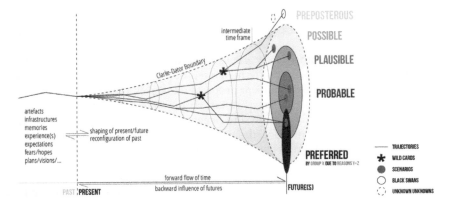

Figure 6.1 The cone of plausibility.
Source: Gall et al. (2022).

Policy actors, generally, are very aware of these issues around uncertainty and the difficulty of attributing weights to more plausible futures and planning accordingly (Jarvis 2011b; Morgan and Henrion 1990; Schrader et al. 1993). However, it is very easy to make mistakes, and rather than risk error, it is often preferable to design flexible or 'robust' packages of tools which are able to adapt and adjust as circumstances change, a subject which is discussed in depth in Chapter 14.

Prototyping as a design response to formulation uncertainty

One way in which some of the uncertainties involved in policy formulation can be reduced if and when institutional and ideological and other kinds of constraints on innovation can be removed is through 'prototyping'. As in the design of other kinds of products and processes, this means thinking through what a policy solution might look like and then developing a package of policy tools that could conceivably address these concerns (Gero 1990). This package can then be fleshed out in terms of possible calibrations and specifications into one or more 'prototypes' which can then be discussed in more detail (sometimes referred to as 'alpha' prototypes) or used as the basis for the pilot projects and experiments discussed in earlier chapters (so-called 'beta' prototypes) (Taeihagh et al. 2009).

Prototyping is sometimes linked closely to 'co-design' efforts, meaning, those with more extensive public or non-governmental input, although this is not a necessary condition and prototypes can be developed largely autonomously by government agencies (Sanders and Stappers 2014). As Villa-Alvarez et al. (2020) point out, they can also be used to test out many aspects of a policy design, including its evaluative components as well as those aspects related more closely to implementation (see Figure 6.2).

As Figure 6.2 shows, at the formulation stage, prototyping may be used to explore a policy problem, to help test or evaluate a possible solution, and to communicate ideas or current thinking of policy analysts, advisors, and governments to other members of the policy community.

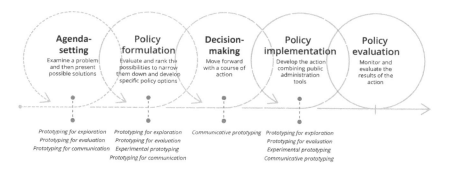

Figure 6.2 Possible subjects and uses of policy prototypes.
Source: After Villa-Alvarez et al. (2020).

The problems of policy formulation in space and time: policy horizons, zombie policies, and the pre-conditions of policy design

Ultimately, as Charles Anderson (1971) noted, policy design is virtually synonymous with 'statecraft', or the practice of government as 'the art of the possible'. It is always a matter of making choices from the possibilities offered by a given historical situation and cultural context. From this vantage point, the institutions and procedures of the state to shape the course of economy and society are the equipment provided by a society to its leaders to find the solution to public problems (121).

This applies very much to policy formulation, and skilful policy designers are those who can find appropriate possibilities in the institutional equipment of society to best obtain their goals.

In many cases, ranging from finance and immigration to pollution and healthcare, for example, a rapid pace of change in the technological, economic, and social environment may be coupled with a reduction in the ability of single jurisdictions to control internal and cross-border issue areas (Bakir 2017). And as has often been noted, tendencies of bureaucracies to develop standard operating procedures and to 'silo' policy work in specific agencies also can ossify policy-making and reduce the scope for changes needed to deal with problems as they develop and evolve (Yackee and Yackee 2010; Collins 2013).

Substantive constraints can also arise within the problem itself. The problem of global warming, for example, cannot be entirely eliminated because there is no known effective solution that can be employed without causing tremendous economic and social dislocations, which often leaves policymakers to tinker with options that barely scratch the surface of the problem (Howlett et al. 2009: 112). Such constraints can be considered 'objective', since reinterpreting them or recasting them in different terms does not eliminate them. Procedural constraints, on the other hand, are those that directly impinge upon the process of adopting policy options and are more subjective in nature and often react positively to reformulation and reinterpretation.

In general, it is often thought that 'designers' must avoid simply advocating 'stock' solutions unless this is called for by the limited nature of the space available for new designs (May 1981; Helms et al. 1993). Rather, they should consider the range of feasible options possible in a given circumstance and package these into sets of strategies capable of achieving policy goals (May 1981: 236, 238).

But different policy spaces exist which affect how prominent design is within formulation and condition what kinds of formulation processes are followed. Many such constraints on policy alternatives are embedded in the social and institutional contexts within which formulation unfolds and touch on issues related to, for example, constitutional specifications; difficult-to-change aspects of the organization of society, such as its ethnic or religious make-up; and the only slightly less difficult to alter, policy-making administration, electoral, and legislative systems.

Such established patterns of ideas, beliefs, and interactions can often lead decision-makers and formulators to favour some options or tools or problem definitions over others (Yee 1996; Montpetit 2003b; Falkner 2000; DeLeon 1992), constraining the consideration of alternatives.

The specific relationships existing between social groups and the state, for example, can create 'policy horizons' or limits to the acceptability of certain kinds of policy options for certain policy actors, such as treatment of disadvantaged populations for many social democratic groups and parties or various practices from abortion to same-sex marriages for various religious groups and parties (Warwick 2000; Bradford 1999). In worst-case scenarios, this can include continuously giving life to what Peters and Nagel (2020) call 'zombie' ideas – that is, thoroughly discredited notions, like moving world commerce back onto the gold standard – which do not 'go away' regardless of their demerits or poor experiences with them in the past.

The pre-conditions of policy design

As Weimer (1992b) has noted, 'instruments, alone or in combination, must be crafted to fit particular substantive, organizational and political contexts' (373). But formulation and design processes are wrought with both political and technical considerations and riddled with uncertainty about the future and the impact of any policy interventions. This reality, however, does not suggest that the systematic search for pairing policy means with goals is impractical and unworthwhile. Rather, it simply means that the implementation of some designs may be impossible in certain contexts and that those involved in crafting alternatives must be aware of the constraints under which they are working (Thomas 2001; Dryzek 1983).

In general, the extent to which this is possible in policy formulation depends on the governance structures, the state of knowledge on the subject, the 'tractability' of the problem, and the nature of the actors and interests involved in the evaluation. Policy-makers need to be, and generally are, cognizant about the internal mechanisms at work in their polity and in the policy sectors they are dealing with (Braathen and Croci 2005; Braathen 2007a; Grant 2010; Skodvin et al. 2010).

These factors determine the outside boundaries or the amount of 'elbow room' or *'degrees of freedom'* formulators have in a given formulation context, and this estimate heavily impacts how formulation activities proceed. Where earlier work on formulation and design often assumed a blank slate available to policy-makers, modern thinking about policy design better rooted in empirical studies and experiences has generally shown policy designers having to work within scenarios with already-established policy mixes with significant policy histories and legacies which constrain options and alternatives.

That is, legacies from earlier rounds of decision-making often affect the introduction of new elements which may conflict with pre-existing policy components (Thelen 2003, 2004). As Martin Carstensen has argued, as a result, policies often change through gradual processes and are often created much less through systematic reflection on (practice-derived) first principles than through processes of 'bricolage' or bespoke trial and error (Carstensen 2015).

As was discussed in Chapter 3, the contextual 'lock-in' of policy alternatives often impacts formulation processes by restricting a government's ability to evaluate alternatives and plan or design in a purely optimal fashion and often leads to *layering* rather than *replacement* (Howlett 2009a; Oliphant and Howlett 2010; Williams 2012). The former is a process of policy formulation and (re)design which alters only some aspects of a pre-existing arrangement and can thus be distinguished from processes proposing new policy packages or complete replacement.

While complete replacement or a brand-new 'package' of policies is rare, however, there are instances whereby entirely dedicated, or 'bespoke', policy packages are created to address an unprecedented policy problem. 'Customization' of policy is somewhat more common when lessons from other similar policy contexts are tailored into new policy options.

In any specific design circumstance, however, whether or not 'design' takes place at all can be seen to depend on the aim and intention of the government to undertake systemic thinking on a subject. But having such an intention is not enough in itself to promote replacement or design through packaging, since this also depends on the government's ability or capacity to alter the status quo. In many circumstances, even when a design intent is present, the difficulties associated with altering the status quo result in design through 'patching' rather than packaging.

Determining exactly what capacities are required in order to formulate and implement complex designs is thus a subject of much interest in the field today (Considine 2012) and is discussed in detail in later chapters.

Favourable design circumstances within policy formulation require not only the presence of high-quality information on the range and impacts of policy alternatives but also the presence of a high level of technical capacity and expertise on the part of policy analysts if that knowledge is to be mobilized effectively so that policy instruments are effectively and efficiently matched to policy goals and targets (Howlett 2009d, 2010; Dunlop 2009b; Radaelli and Dunlop 2013; Howlett and Rayner 2014). Design situations vary according to the nature of the resources available for design purposes and the constraints imposed by policy legacies. In the non-design world, where the intention to design is lacking, constraints on outcomes also exist, as do different processes which vary in their distance from the design ideal of public value and improving the public good (Holmberg and Rothstein 2012; Rotberg 2014).

When propitious conditions are present, purposive formulation activity resulting in good alternative generation and assessment is possible (Bhatta 2002; Locke 2009; Nutley et al. 2007). When conditions are not ripe, however, either poor designs will ensue from incomplete knowledge and information even with the best government intent or less technical and more overtly political forms of non-design policy-making are more likely (Davies 2004; Moseley and Tierney 2004; Howlett 2009b).

Policy formulators must be aware of these differences while developing policy options and making recommendations and providing advice to governments. Policies are the result of efforts made by governments to alter aspects of their own or public behaviour in order to carry out some end or purpose they consider important but take place within specific, context-bound, and temporally defined spaces (Angelides and Caiden 1994) affected by current realities, emerging trends, complexities, and future uncertainties.

Conclusion: policy formulation and policy design beyond the technical/political divide

Transforming policy ambitions into practice is a complex process. The efforts of policy-makers often have failed due to poor designs which have inadequately incorporated the complexity of policy formulation into their considerations (Cohn 2004; Howlett 2012). These experiences have led to a greater awareness of the various obstacles that can present themselves to policy design and have gradually fuelled a desire for better understanding the unique characteristics of policy formulation processes and the spaces in which design efforts are embedded as well as the merits and demerits of practical strategies and alternatives for resolving problems.

The design orientation calls for a broadening of thinking about formulation beyond policy tool choices, examining combinations of substantive and procedural instruments and their interactions in complex policy mixes. It also has focused on the need for a more detailed study of the actual formulation processes involved in tool and design choices as these occur and have evolved over time (Linder and Peters 1990c; Schneider and Ingram 1997; Considine 2012; Veselý and Petrúšek 2021).

The earlier discussion of different formulation modalities and processes does not preclude, but rather is built upon, the recognition and acceptance of the fact that some policy decisions and formulation processes are highly contingent ones in which 'design' considerations may be more or less absent and where the logical or empirical relations between policy components are ignored (Kingdon 1984; Cohen et al. 1979; Dryzek 1983; Eijlander 2005; Franchino and Hoyland 2009; Sager and Rielle 2013). This includes a variety of contexts in which formulators, for example, may engage in trade-offs or logrolling between different values or resource uses or, more extremely, engage in venal or corrupt behaviour in which personal gain from a decision may trump other criteria.

An optimal situation in public policy formulation from a design perspective is one wherein the interests and aims of both politicians and technical analysts and advisors are congruent and policy-makers seek to attain both policy and political objectives through the same tools. Understanding what kind of formulation process is likely to unfold or has unfolded is the key to understanding whether or not a design process is present and, if so, whether or not it is likely to generate a good or poor design effort. That is, the design of successful policies requires thinking about policy-making in such a way as to fully take into account the dual purposes – both technical/ problem and political – which policies can serve and the extent to which efforts to attain those ends are adequately resourced and capable, that is, to clearly understand the 'design space' (Hillier et al. 1972; Hillier and Leaman 1974; Gero 1990).

As we have seen, a very important aspect of such spaces concerns the general intention of the government in enacting policy. Much of the old design literature, as noted earlier, simply assumes a well-intentioned government and thus focused attention only upon 'technical' analysis, that is, upon efforts to better assess the functional potential of specific tools (Howlett 2014a). The new design literature keeps this focus but has added to it the need to also assess other factors, especially political ones, affecting the design space or context a subject discussed in depth in Chapter 15.

Readings

Béland, D. and M. Howlett. (2016). 'How Solutions Chase Problems: Instrument Constituencies in the Policy Process'. *Governance* 29, no. 3: 393–409.

Caplan, N. and C. H. Weiss. (1977). *A Minimal Set of Conditions Necessary for the Utilization of Social Science Knowledge in Policy Formulation at the National Level*. Lexington, MA: Lexington Books.

DeLeon, P. (1992). 'Policy Formulation: Where Ignorant Armies Clash by Night'. *Policy Studies, Review 11*, no. *3–4*: 389–405.

Dror, Y. (1969). 'The Prediction of Political Feasibility'. *Futures* (June): 282–288.

Dunlop, Claire A., and Claudio M. Radaelli, eds. (2018). Learning in Public Policy - Analysis, Modes and Outcomes | Claire A. Dunlop | Palgrave Macmillan. Palgrave Macmillan.

Freed, G. L. M. C. Andreae, A. E. Cowan and S. L. Katz. (2002). 'The Process of Public Policy Formulation: The Case of Thimerosal in Vaccines'. *Pediatrics 109*, no. *6*: 1153–1159.

Howlett, M. (2010). 'Stage Models of the Policy Process'. In Kurian, George Thomas, James E. Alt, Simone Chambers, Geoffrey Garrett, Margaret Levi, and Paula D. McClain, eds. *The Encyclopedia of Political Science*. First Edition. Washington, D.C: CQ Press.

Howlett, M. (2015). 'Policy Analytical Capacity: The Supply and Demand for Policy Analysis in Government'. *Policy and Society 34*, no. *3–4*: 173–182.

Howlett, M. and S. Nair. (2017). 'The Central Conundrums of Policy Formulation: Ill-Structured Problems and Uncertainty'. In I. Mukherjee (ed.), *Handbook of Policy Formulation*. New York: Routledge, 23–38.

Howlett, M., I. Mukherjee and J. Rayner. (2014). 'The Elements of Effective Program Design: A Two-Level Analysis'. *Politics and Governance 2*, no. *2* (9 June): 1–12.

Ingram, H., A. L. Schneider and P. DeLeon. (2007). 'Social Construction and Policy Design'. In P. A. Sabatier (ed.), *Theories of the Policy Process*. Boulder, CO: Westview Press, 93–126.

James, T. E. and P. D. Jorgensen. (2009). 'Policy Knowledge, Policy Formulation, and Change: Revisiting a Foundational Question'. *Policy Studies Journal 37*, no. *1*: 141–162.

Jordan, A. and J. Turnpenny (eds.). (2014). *The Tools of Policy Formulation: Actors, Capacities, Venues and Effects*. Cheltenham, UK: Edward Elgar.

Lasswell, H. D. (1936). *Politics Who Gets What, When and How*. New York: McGraw Hill.

Lehtonen, M. (2017). 'Operationalizing Information: Measures and Indicators in Policy Formulation'. In M. Howlett and I. Mukherjee (eds.), *Handbook of Policy Formulation*. Cheltenham: Edward Elgar, 161–181.

Linder, S. H. and B. G. Peters. (1987). 'A Design Perspective on Policy Implementation: The Fallacies of Misplaced Prescription'. *Review of Policy Research 6*, no. *3* (1 February): 459–475.

Linder, S. H. and B. G. Peters. (1990). 'Policy Formulation and the Challenge of Conscious Design'. *Evaluation and Program Planning 13*: 303–311.

Nilsson, M., A. Jordan, J. Turnpenny, J. Hertin, B. Nykvist and D. Russel. (2008). 'The Use and Non-Use of Policy Appraisal Tools in Public Policy Making: An Analysis of Three European Countries and the European Union'. *Policy Sciences 41*: 335–355.

Schwindt, R., A. Vining and S. Globerman. (2000). 'Net Loss: A Cost-Benefit Analysis of the Canadian Pacific Salmon Fishery'. *Journal of Policy Analysis and Management 19*, no. *1*: 23–45.

Sidney, M. S. (2007). 'Policy Formulation: Design and Tools'. In F. Fischer, G. J. Miller and M. S. Sidney (eds.), *Handbook of Public Policy Analysis: Theory, Politics and Methods*. New Brunswick, NJ: CRC, Taylor & Francis, 79–87.

Sørensen, C. H., K. Isaksson, J. Macmillen, J. Åkerman and F. Kressler. (2009). 'Strategies to Manage Barriers in Policy Formation and Implementation of Road Pricing Packages'. *Transportation Research Part A: Policy and Practice 60* (1 February): 40–52.

Thomas, H. G. (2001). 'Towards a New Higher Education Law in Lithuania: Reflections on the Process of Policy Formulation'. *Higher Education Policy 14*, no. 3: 213–223.

Turnpenny, J., C. M. Radaelli, A. Jordan and K. Jacob. (2009). 'The Policy and Politics of Policy Appraisal: Emerging Trends and New Directions'. *Journal of European Public Policy 16*, no. 4: 640–653.

Van der Steen, M. A. and M. J. W. van Twist. (2013). 'Foresight and Long-Term Policy-Making: An Analysis of Anticipatory Boundary Work in Policy Organizations in the Netherlands'. *Futures 54*, no. *Supplement C* (1 November): 33–42.

Walker, W. E., S. A. Rahman and J. Cave. (2001). 'Adaptive Policies, Policy Analysis, and Policy-Making'. *European Journal of Operational Research 128*, no. 2 (16 January): 282–289.

Chapter 7

Who are the policy designers and where do they work? Policy advice, policy advisors, and policy advisory systems

Public policies are ultimately made by decision-makers authorized to create them, but most often this is done on the basis of advice and information provided by other actors. While political and administrative leaders are the ones who eventually decide upon and thus 'make' public policy, in modern states, they do so by following the counsel of bureaucrats, civil servants, and other internal and outside advisors whom they trust to identify the sources of problems and evaluate and consolidate policy options into coherent designs to address them (Ohberg et al. 2021).

The nature and influence of the kinds of policy advice decision-makers receive are therefore key in understanding policy-making and policy design.

This advice typically arrives before decision-makers in the form of alternate proposals for action developed and put forward during policy formulation. As the account of the different substages and activities involved in policy formulation outlined in previous chapters suggests, different actors are involved in different aspects of these advisory processes.

Not all this advice about policy content and construction is internal, in the sense that it may well originate outside of government. Expert advice about the merits and risks of the proposals being considered typically arrives unasked from those interested in or affected by a policy ('stakeholders' and the public) and is often sought out by governments from a wide range of sources, including internal analysts, partisan advisors, lobbyists, and consultants, among others (MacRae and Whittington 1997; Heinrichs 2005).

DOI: 10.4324/9781003343431-10

It is useful to think about this wide array of policy advisors as being arranged in a 'policy advisory system' within which those most proximate to decision-makers occupy central positions. Studies of advisory systems in a variety of jurisdictions such as New Zealand, Israel, Canada, and Australia have furthered this idea of government decision-makers operating at the centre of a network of policy advisors who include both 'traditional' policy advisors, such as civil servants, as well as, increasingly, non-state actors from NGOs and think tanks, as well as less-formal forms of advice supplied by colleagues, members of the public and political party affiliates, and others (Maley 2000; Peled 2002; Dobuzinskis et al. 2007).

Having a large range of actors in a policy advisory system is generally considered beneficial, and Anderson (1996), for example, has argued that 'a healthy policy-research community outside the government can play a vital role in enriching public understanding and debate of policy issues' and can serve 'as a natural complement to policy capacity within' (Anderson 1996: 486).

Different kinds of advisory systems exist in different countries and within them in different sectors and the existence of these different types of policy advisory systems is linked with the nature of both the demand, supply and organization of knowledge and advice in particular policy areas and within specific governmental and sectoral contexts. These may prioritize of privilege certain types and purveyors of advice over others and thus understanding who provides advice and with what effect is a key question in studies of policy design (Halffman and Hoppe 2005).

In what follows, the general nature of the actors involved in such systems and the impact of the advice they provide for policy design is set out.

Policy analysis and the role of expertise in policy formulation

As Chapter 6 outlined, most policy formulation processes share certain characteristics. First and most obviously, formulation is not usually limited to one set of actors (Sabatier and Jenkins-Smith 1993a). Second, formulation may also proceed without a clear definition of the problem to be addressed (Weber and Khademian 2008) and may occur over a long period of time in 'rounds' of formulation and reformulation of policy problems and solutions (Teisman 2000). And third, the costs and benefits of different options fall disproportionately on different actors (Wilson 1974).

This implies, as Linder and Peters, among others, noted, that the capability of policy designs to be realized in practice remains subject to many political as well as technical variables, including who provides what kind of advice to whom about how to define a problem, what can be done about it and who should bear its costs (Dryzek 1983).

Of course, in the past, the nature and sources of policy advice received by decision-makers in the policy formulation process are subjects that have received their fair share of scholarly attention. Many journals and specialized publications exist on these subjects, and specialized graduate schools exist in most countries with the aim of training policy analysts to provide better advice to decision-makers (Geva-May and Maslove 2007; Jann 1991).

Studies have examined hundreds of case studies of policy-making and policy analysis in multiple countries (see for example the close to two dozen titles in the International Library of Policy Analysis series, such as Blum and Schubert 2013; Adachi and Hosono 2013; Head and Crowley 2015; Hird 2018; Vaitsman et al. 2013), and many texts exist which chronicle various analytical techniques expected to be used in the provision of policy advice (Weimer and Vining 2004). Yet surprisingly little systematic thinking exists about many aspects of this crucial component of policy-making activity (Howlett et al. 2009; Olejniczak et al. 2018).

Positivist and post-positivist understandings of policy advice

Early thinking about the content of policy advice often contrasted 'political', or partisan-ideological, value-based advice with more 'objective' or 'technical' advice and usually stressed the latter while ignoring or downplaying the former (Radin 2000). This 'positivist' or 'modern' approach to policy analysis dominated the field for decades (Radin 2000) and presupposed a sharp division between governmental advisors armed with technical knowledge and expertise and non-governmental actors possessing mainly non-technical skills and knowledge. And more to the point, although often implicit, a 'political' versus 'technical' advisory dichotomy often underlay such models of policy advice, with advice assumed to become more technical as it moved closer to proximate decision-makers so that external actors provided political advice and internal ones more technical ideas and evidence-informed policy alternatives.

Policy schools purporting to train professional policy advisors in government and the private and non-governmental sectors still mainly provide instruction in this positivist mode (Howlett and Jarvis 2021). They focus on only some of a possible range of qualitative and quantitative techniques that analysts are expected to use in providing technical advice to decision-makers, such as cost–benefit analysis, which are expected to generate optimal strategies and outcomes to pursue in the resolution of public problems.

This downplaying or ignoring of political or value-laden issues and concerns (MacRae and Wilde 1976; Patton and Sawicki 1993; Weimer and Vining 1989; Irwin 2003) provoked a reaction from those who argued these were intrinsic to the policy-making process and could not be ignored.

The extent to which policy advice and information is used and to what extent it can be considered 'objective' and 'expert' is also a continuing controversy in the policy sciences, and an emphasis on its intersubjective and political nature is a hallmark of the 'post-positivist' approach to the subject (Rein and White 1977a, 1977b; Lindblom and Cohen 1979; Shulock 1999; Adams 2004; Fischer and Forester 1993).

Policy advisory systems and their evolution

It is debatable, however, to what extent such a strict separation of political and technical advice was ever true in either theory or practice. And it is definitely the case that the supply of technical advice is no longer, if it ever was, a monopoly of governments. Various external sources of policy advice are now significant sources of substantive policy advisory content used by policy-makers both to support existing policy positions and as sources of new advice (Bertelli and Wenger 2009; McGann and Sabatini 2011).

Professional policy analysts, for example, are now employed not only by government departments and agencies but also by advisory system members external to government, ranging from private sector consultants to experts in think tanks, universities, political parties, and elsewhere (Svallfors 2020). They, like those in the employ of governments, are quite capable of providing specific suggestions about factors such as the costs and administrative modalities of specific policy alternatives (Boston 1994; Boston et al. 1996).

It is also the case that many advisors, both internal and external to governments, both today and in past years, provide political advice to decision-makers ranging from their personal opinion and experiences with public opinion and key stakeholder group attitudes and beliefs to explicit partisan electoral advice in the service of re-election (Rhodes et al. 2007).

This kind of advice has always been provided by prominent traditional inside actors, such as political advisors attached to elected officials and political parties, and has grown to include paid political staffers in many contemporary civil service systems (Connaughton 2010, 2015; Eichbaum and Shaw 2007, 2008). It is also the kind of advice which policy-makers have sought and received over many years from the public consultation and the stakeholder interventions which are increasingly prominent in contemporary governance (Edelenbos and Klijn 2005; Bingham et al. 2005; Pierre 1998).

While 'Westminster' or systems similar to and often modelled after the British parliamentary system continue to pride themselves on retaining at least part of a dichotomous political-administrative or 'civil service bargain' in the form of continuing conventions promoting civil service neutrality (Hood 2002a; Hondeghem 2011; Salomonsen and Knudsen 2011), even in this strong case, this convention has been eroded (Craft and Halligan 2020).

Maley (2000: 453) elaborated on the various policy roles now played there and in other kinds of governance systems by political advisors that exist in addition to their 'in-house' policy work: 'Dunn suggests an important brokering role within the executive; Ryan detects a significant role in setting policy agendas; Halligan and Power refer to advisers "managing networks of political interaction"'. Additional studies also point to the role 'political' advisors play in the brokerage, coordination, and integration of various endogenous and exogenous sources of policy advice in their reports and briefings to decision-makers (Dunn 1997: 93–97; Gains and Stoker 2011; Halligan and Power 1992; Maley 2011; OECD 2011; Ryan 1995).

In their study of New Zealand policy advice, for example, Eichbaum and Shaw (2008: 343) noted many instances of 'procedural politicization' that was 'intended to or has the effect of constraining the capacity of public servants to furnish ministers with (technical) advice in a free, frank and fearless manner'. This, they argued, was manifested whenever a 'political' advisor 'intervenes in the relationship between a minister and his or her officials'. This often occurred due to 'conduct by ministerial advisers which is intended to, or which has the effect of constraining the capacity of officials to tender frank and fearless advice by intervening in the internal workings of a department' (Eichbaum and Shaw 2008: 343). They also found many instances of 'substantive politicization' which dealt specifically with 'an action intended to, or having the effect of colouring the substance of officials' advice with partisan considerations' (Eichbaum and Shaw 2008: 343–344).

The increasingly plural and political nature of the policy advice available to decision-makers underscores that while under the older 'speaking-truth-to-power' customs policy advice might often have been largely a bipartite relationship involving public servants and executive politicians, with career officials offering only technical advice to cabinet ministers, this is no longer the case.

The sources of policy advice: actors in the problem, solution, and political streams

For many years, policy-making has been envisioned as a process in which subsets of policy actors engage in specific types of interactions involved in the definition of policy problems, the articulation of solutions, and their matching or enactment. This activity involves the definition of policy goals (both broad and specific), the creation or identification of the means and mechanisms that need to be implemented to realize these goals, and the set of bureaucratic, partisan, electoral, and other political struggles involved in their acceptance and transformation into action.

In much of the policy research published in recent decades, these actors are discussed in network terms as belonging to a 'subsystem' or policy 'community' (McCool 1998; Sabatier 1991). This is typically defined as a mostly undifferentiated group of actors originating in widely different areas of state and society who are united by a mutual concern for and knowledge of a specific policy area. They are not necessarily self-interested but share some ideas and knowledge about the policy area in question, which sets them apart from other policy actors (Howlett and Cashore 2009; Howlett et al. 2009; Kingdon 2001).

These sets of actors go by a variety of different names – policy networks, policy communities, issue networks, and the like – but all acknowledge the complex informal and formal exchanges that take place between both state and non-state policy actors in policy-making. This way of thinking improves on previous work that tended to emphasize the material, self-interested activity on the part of only a more limited range of actors, such as interest groups, lobbyists, bureaucrats, and politicians (McCool 1998).

Early studies on subsystems were seminal in the development of the discipline and included the articulation of a wide array of often-competing concepts and terminology to describe such collectivities, such as 'iron triangles', 'sub-governments', 'cozy triangles', 'power triads', 'policy networks', 'issue communities', 'issue networks', 'advocacy coalitions', 'policy communities', and others. All these terms refer to the propensity of policy actors to create alliances surrounding substantive issues that traverse institutional boundaries and to join together both governmental and non-governmental actors in groups sharing similar perspectives on policy issues, problems, and solutions (Arts et al. 2006; Freeman 1997; McCool 1998).

Subsystem theory helped distil the often-informal connections between actors, ideas, interests, and institutions that earlier policy studies had largely ignored when they focused on the more formal institutional linkages that exist between governmental and non-governmental agents active in policy-making (Howlett et al. 2009; McCool 1998; Freeman and Stevens 1987).

Such a unified or undifferentiated conception of a policy subsystem, however, is problematic on several scores when it comes to analyzing the sources of policy design–relevant information and advice. In particular, the grouping of all policy actors together in a single policy subsystem has confusingly juxtaposed similar but distinct sets of policy-related actors involved in problem definition, policy formulation, and policy-related political bargaining and conflict.

While past research on policy subsystems often assumed or implied that these tasks could be undertaken by any actor, more recent research argues that distinct sets of actors are involved in these tasks: *epistemic communities* that are engaged in discussions about policy dilemmas and problems (Haas 1992), *instrument constituencies* that define and promote policy instruments and alternatives (Voss and Simons 2014), and *advocacy coalitions* which compete to have their choice of policy alternative and problem frames adopted (Sabatier 1988).

Two of these three sets of actors are quite well-known and, indeed, have their own literature about what it takes to be a member of an epistemic community or advocacy coalition, although interactions between the two are rarely discussed. The third subset, the instrument constituency, is less well studied but is concerned exclusively with the articulation and promotion of policy solutions and is especially relevant to concerns about policy advice and policy design (Béland and Howlett 2016; Voss and Simons 2014; Mann and Simons 2014).

Distinguishing clearly between these sets of actors and activities allows researchers and practitioners to better capture how policy problems are designated and defined and how they move forward through the political processes and who does this. It allows each different subgroup to be analyzed as a discrete entity while, at the same time, recognizing their many interactions in the policy formulation process.

Actors in the problem stream: epistemic communities

While it would be possible, in answering the question about who is active in policy formulation and what they do, to develop new terminology to describe each subgroup, adequate terms already exist in the policy literature that can be used for this purpose. In this light, the concept of *epistemic communities*, which emerged out of the international relations literature to identify groups of scientists involved in defining and delimiting problem spaces in areas such as oceans policy and climate change (Gough and Shackley 2001; Haas 1992; Zito 2001), can be used to define a more general set of actors involved mainly in defining policy problems and providing and packaging policy advice related to those definitions.

Academic explorations of epistemic communities have thus far mainly used examples from environmental policy, a field that is constantly engaged in connecting scientific findings to policy-making. Haas (1992), for example, first described epistemic communities involved in deliberations in the environmental sector as 'a diverse group of policy actors including scientists, academics experts, public sector officials and other government agents who are united by a common interest in or a shared interpretation of the science behind an environmental dilemma' (Gough and Shackley 2001; Haas 1992). These communities, he found, influenced 'policy innovation not only through their ability to frame issues and define state interests but also through their influence on the setting of standards and the development of regulations' based upon them (Adler and Haas 1992: 378).

Information regarding a policy problem is the glue that bonds actors within an epistemic community together, differentiating them from those actors involved in political negotiations and practices around policy goals and solutions as well as from those, discussed later, who specialize in the development, design, and articulation of policy tools or solutions (Biddle and Koontz 2014; Lackey 2007; Meyer et al. 2010; Nelson and Vucetich 2009).

In his studies of global oceans research and policy, Rudd (2014, 2015), for example, provides important empirical findings related to scientists' framing of environmental dilemmas at the science–policy interface. In a large-N study spanning 94 countries and meant to comprehensively cover the role of scientists in oceans policy-making, Rudd conclusively shows the uniformity regarding research priorities in this group across the globe and how they are focused almost exclusively on problem definition while disregarding problem solutions.

Actors in the policy solution stream: instrument constituencies

Epistemic communities are thus conceptually distinct from a second group of actors, instrument constituencies, whose focus is much less upon problems than upon providing advice to governments about potential policy solutions. 'Instrument constituencies' is a term recently developed in the comparative public policy field to describe sets of these actors involved in solution articulation, often independent of the nature of the problem to be addressed (Voss and Simons 2014).

Such constituencies advocate for particular tools or combinations of tools to address a range of problem areas. They are united by their adherence to the design and promotion of specific policy instruments as the solutions to general sets of policy problems, usually in the abstract, which are then applied to real-world conditions.

That is, unlike epistemic communities that pursue the translation of broad issues and findings into distinct problems that policy-makers can act upon, instrument constituencies are more concerned with identifying and refining different kinds of policy tools and supplying policy-makers with information and advice about the design and mechanics of these tools. Think tanks and policy labs, for example, often fall into this category, as they provide policy-makers with 'basic information about the world and societies they govern, how current policies are working, possible alternatives and their likely costs and consequences' (McGann et al. 2014: 31).

In a series of studies on how various emission trading schemes emerged in Europe (Mann and Simons 2014; Voss and Simons 2014), Voss and Simons showed how, just as epistemic communities perpetuate and share collective ideas about the nature and sources of policy problems, members of instrument constituencies cohere around their identification and support for the use of particular policy tools or a specific combination of policy tools. These constituencies are thus 'networks of heterogeneous actors from academia, policy consulting, public policy and administration, business and civil society, who become entangled as they engage with the articulation, development, implementation and dissemination of a particular technical model of governance' (Voss and Simon 2014: 738).

The practices of such actors 'constitute and are constituted by the instrument' and develop a discourse concerning how an instrument may best be retained, developed, promoted, and expanded (Voss and Simons 2014).

What brings them together is the role they play in articulating 'the set of stories, knowledge, practice and tools needed to keep an instrument alive both as model and implemented practice' (Voss and Simons 2014).

Actors in the politics stream: advocacy coalitions

A third distinct set of actors – 'advocacy coalitions' – is most active in the political sphere and plays an important role bridging the gap between epistemic communities and instrument constituencies. Although the term 'advocacy coalition' is used by students of American policy-making in the context of earlier, less well-differentiated subsystem theories to refer to all the actors at work in a network (see Sabatier 1987, 1988, 1998; Sabatier and Jenkins-Smith 1993b; Sabatier and Weible 2007; Weible et al. 2009, 2011), it can also be used to describe the activities of only those involved in the political struggle surrounding the matching of problem definitions and policy tools

(Sabatier and Weible 2007; Schlager and Blomquist 1996; Weible 2018). It is also useful in this context for the analysis of this specific set of activities within policy-making and policy design.

These actors and advisors are often situated in key decision-making institutions of government and compete to get their choice of problem definitions as well as solutions adopted during the policy process, working within and against epistemic communities and instrument constituencies in order to do so.

Such politically active policy actors are usually more publicly visible than the substantive experts who collaborate in the formulation of policy alternatives or problem definition. More visible actors in the politics stream can include, as in the case of the US Congress John Kingdon examined, 'the president and his high-level appointees, prominent members of the congress, the media and such elections-related actors as political parties and campaigns' (Kingdon 1984: 64), while less-visible members include lobbyists, political party brokers and fixers, and other behind-the-scenes advisors and participants.

The organization of policy advice: the location of actors in policy advisory systems and in government

Generally speaking, the ideas held by central policy actors in government almost always play a key role in guiding efforts to construct policy options and assess design alternatives and have a direct influence on policy content. Those held by outside actors, on the other hand, have a less-direct impact as they are often mediated and massaged in internal policy development processes (Ingraham 1987; George 1969; Mayntz 1983; Jacobsen 1995; Chadwick 2000; Gormley 2007). But how these different actors are organized in specific issue areas is important to both what they do and how they do it.

As mentioned earlier, recent studies of advice systems have developed the idea that government decision-makers sit at the centre of a complex web of policy advisors which include both 'traditional' political advisors in government as well as non-governmental ones. These latter include, for example, those situated or employed by NGOs, think tanks, and other similar organizations, consultants, and less-formal or professional forms of advice from colleagues, friends, and relatives and members of the public and political parties, among others (Maley 2000; Peled 2002; Dobuzinskis et al. 2007; Eichbaum and Shaw 2007).

Given the range of players and substages that are involved in it, policy formulation and design can be a highly diffuse and often disjointed process. And procedural provisions such as conventions about cabinet secrecy or concerns about national security often mean that the workings of internal policy processes are difficult to discern. Nevertheless, examining the manner in which a *policy advice system* is structured in a particular sector can help us identify the more or less influential actors involved in policy assessments and design recommendations in specific issue areas (James and Jorgensen 2009).

The activities of policy advisory systems are central to the study of both policy formulation and policy design and to the understanding of the selection and reception given to different policy alternatives and arrangements (Brint 1990). Conceived of as knowledge utilization venues or 'marketplaces' of ideas and information, advice systems are comprised of separate components related to their role in the supply of policy advice, to its demand by government decision-makers, and to the set of brokers who work as intermediaries who match knowledge supply with demand (Brint 1990; Lindquist 1998). That is, members of policy advisory systems undertake one or more of these general types of activities linked to the types of positions participants hold in the creation and exchange of knowledge in the policy formulation process.

The exact configuration of each system varies by sector and by country and is heavily influenced by the nature of the civil service and political institutions present in each case (Hustedt and Veit 2017). The nature of policy formulation and design activities is thus different in different analytical contexts, and a central task in understanding advisory dynamics and influence involves discerning how the policy advice system is structured and operated in the specific sector of policy activity under examination (Brint 1990; Page 2010).

Nevertheless, policy advisory systems do share some common characteristics. First, they bring together members of epistemic communities and instruments constituencies with members of advocacy coalitions into a system in which problems, solutions, and politics are matched and discussed.

Secondly, they organize those different kinds of actors in different locations within a policy-making system and set of decision-making institutions. The first set of actors at the top of the system, for example, is typically composed of the 'proximate decision-makers' who act as consumers of policy analysis and advice – that is, those with actual authority to make policy decisions, including cabinets and executives, as well as parliaments, legislatures, and congresses and senior administrators and officials delegated decision-making powers by those other bodies. They form the demand for advice and are the targets of advisors' studies and entreaties.

The second set of actors is organized around the supply of advice and is composed of those 'knowledge producers' located in academia, statistical agencies, and research institutes who provide the basic scientific, economic, and social scientific data and studies concerning the severity and sources of problems and possible solutions upon which analyses are often based and decisions made.

The third set sits in between the first two and is composed of those 'knowledge brokers' who serve as intermediaries between the knowledge generators and proximate decision-makers, repackaging data and information into usable form (Lindvall 2009; Page 2010). These include, among others, permanent specialized research staff inside government as well as their temporary equivalents in commissions and task forces and a large group of non-governmental specialists associated with think tanks and interest groups. Although often thought of as 'knowledge suppliers', key policy advisors, almost by definition, exist in the brokerage subsystem, and this is where most professional policy analysts in governments and NGOs involved in policy formulation can be found (Lindvall 2009; Verschuere 2009; Howlett and Newman 2010; Page 2010).

In general, members of policy advisory systems can be found in one of four 'communities' of advisors, depending on the advisory role they perform and their proximity to central policy actors and upon their location either inside or outside of government (Table 7.1).

Table 7.1 The four communities of policy advisors

	Proximate actors	Peripheral actors
Public/governmental sector	Core actors: central agencies, executive staff, professional governmental policy analysts	Public sector insiders: commissions, committees, and task forces; research councils/scientists; international organizations
Non-governmental sector	Private sector insiders: consultants, political party staff, pollsters, donors	Outsiders: public interest groups, business associations, trade unions, academics, think tanks, media, international non-governmental organizations

Source: Howlett, M. (2014b).

The *core actors* are those members of the public sector who are closest to the official policy-making units of government and include central government agencies, executive staff, and professional government policy analysts. Governmental actors or *insiders* who work further away, at the periphery of policy advisory systems, are those who belong to commissions, special committees, and task forces; research councils; and scientists from international organizations. From the non-governmental sector, actors who are close to the decision-makers during formulation and are considered *private sector insiders* may include private sector consultants, political party staff, pollsters, as well as donor representatives. Actors who are considered to be farthest from the central core of policy formulators, or *outsiders*, often include those belonging to public interest groups, business associations, trade unions, independent academics, think tanks, members of the media, or international non-government organizations.

The content of policy advice: where policy ideas come from and how they influence policy-making and policy design thinking

It is important to note that even in Anglo-American 'Westminster'-style politi-cal systems, a shift from the largely internal, technical, 'speaking-truth' type of policy advising has occured toward the more diffuse and fragmented 'shar-ing of influence' between insiders and outsiders. This approach helps paints a picture of contemporary policy advising that features not only the pro-nounced influence of external or exogenous sources of technical and political advice but also the loss of whatever policy advisory monopoly or hegemony was once held or exercised by professional public service and advisors within government.

There is somewhat-reduced utility when such distinctions are applied to other systems (e.g. Napoleonic, Scandinavian) with alternative adminis-trative traditions where politico-administrative divisions have never been as pronounced, overlap, are configured differently than in Westminister ones (Peters and Pierre 2003; Painter and Peters 2010; van den Berg 2017; Craft and Halligan 2020). Nevertheless, moving beyond simple political-technical distinctions to a more robust model of policy advice is essential in order to improve thinking on the subject.

This includes more careful thinking about the content of the 'advice' pro-vided. A key component of this relates to the type of beliefs and ideas policy advisors and policy-makers have about the feasibility, desirability, and opti-mality of the deployment of various arrangements of policy tools to address social concerns and policy problems.

Understandably, the beliefs held by decision-makers, analysts, and advi-sors about the cost and effectiveness of different policy means and their views of the appropriateness or feasibility of policy goals play a key part in their efforts to construct policy alternatives and assess policy options, and advisors exist in both these areas to provide opinions and insights into these mat-ters (Ingraham 1987; George 1969; Mayntz 1983; Jacobsen 1995; Chadwick 2000; Gormley 2007).

In the policy realm, the notion of different kinds of ideas creating claims or demands on governments was taken up by Frank Fischer and John For-ester (1993) and Paul Sabatier (1987, 1988), among others, writing in the 1980s and 1990s (see George 1969). The concept of causal stories, for exam-ple, was applied to agenda-setting by Deborah Stone (1988, 1989). In Stone's view, agenda-setting usually involved constructing a 'story' of what caused the policy problem in question. As she has argued:

> Causal theories, if they are successful, do more than convincingly demonstrate the possibility of human control over bad conditions. First, they can either challenge or protect an existing social order. Second, by identifying causal agents, they can assign responsibility to particular political actors so that someone will have to stop an activity,

do it differently, compensate its victims, or possibly face punishment. Third, they can legitimate and empower particular actors as 'fixers' of the problem. And fourth, they can create new political alliances among people who are shown to stand in the same victim relationship to the causal agent.

(Stone 1989: 295)

But different types of ideas have different effects on different elements of policy-making and, hence, upon instrument choices and policy designs. Policy goals, for example, consist of a range of ideas from general philosophical and ethical principles to specific causal logics and sociological constructs (Petek et al. 2021). Different types of ideas impact goal formulation in different ways. For example, abstract policy-level goals, such as belief in the merits of economic development or ecological conservation, often combine ethical or political logics in efforts to alleviate poverty or protect the environment, while more specific cognitive causal constructs about how increasing household incomes can lead to greater economic gains or how limiting agriculture near ecologically sensitive areas can result in environmental gains, to name only two examples, are more relevant at the operational level.

And the same is true of policy means, which, as we've seen, can embody some knowledge of past practices and concepts of successful and unsuccessful policy implementation but also extend beyond this to ideological and other ideational structures which help define what choices are 'practical' or acceptable for goal attainment (Lindvall 2009). Ideas about what has 'worked' and why in the past are especially influential.

Differentiating between these different types of ideas in terms of their degree of abstraction and their normative appeal is an important step in understanding how policy advice impacts the creation of policy content (Campbell 1998). In their work on the influence of ideas in foreign policy-making situations, for example, Goldstein and Keohane (1993) and their colleagues noted at least three types of ideas that combined normative and cognitive elements but at different levels of generality: world views, principled beliefs, and causal ideas (see also Campbell 1998; Braun 1999), all of which can, and are, the subject of policy advice.

World views or ideologies, for example, have long been recognized as helping decision-makers make sense of complex realities by identifying general policy problems and the motivations of actors involved in politics and policy. These sets of ideas help motivate and separate political parties one from the other, and party organizations and officials serve as key advisors helping to define what state actions might be considered appropriate and which not.

Principled beliefs and causal stories, on the other hand, as Stone (1988) argued, can exercise a much more direct influence on the recognition of policy problems, on the designation of the worthiness of target populations, and on policy content itself. These kinds of ideas often influence policy-making

151

Table 7.2 Ideational components of policy contents

		Level of policy debate affected	
		Background	Foreground
Level of ideas affected	Normative (value)	Public sentiments	Symbolic frames
	Cognitive (causal)	Policy paradigms	Programme ideas

Source: Adapted from Campbell (1998)

by serving as 'road maps' for action, defining problems, affecting the strategic interactions between policy actors, and constraining the range of policy options that are proposed (Carstensen 2010; Stone 1988, 1989). At the micro level, as Schneider and Ingram argued, causal stories and beliefs about the behaviour patterns of target groups heavily influence choices of policy settings or calibrations (Stone 1989; Schneider and Ingram 1993, 1994).

As laid out in Table 7.2, ideas stemming from public sentiments associated with world views and ideologies often affect the perception of the appropriateness or 'legitimacy' of a certain policy choices and often lurk in the background of policy debated (Stimson 1991; Suzuki 1992; Durr 1993; Stimson et al. 1995; Goffman 1974; Surel 2000). The policy ideas found in *public sentiments*, for example, are generally too broad and normative in nature to have much of a direct impact on programme design. However, importantly, they serve to set the context within which that design activity occurs.

Conversely, *policy paradigms* have a much greater cognitive component, allowing them to significantly influence the details of policies and tool calibrations and choices. These paradigms are composed of 'a set of cognitive background assumptions that constrain action by limiting the range of alternatives that policy-making elites are likely to perceive as useful and work considering' (Campbell 2002; Surel 2000; Kuhn 1962, 1974; Hall 1990, 1992, 1993). Paradigm-inspired notions – such as the notion of 'public health' or 'sustained yield forestry' – are significant determinants of policy choices and constraints on alternative designs, although they, too, often sit behind the curtain in the back stage of the policy theatre (Hall 1990: 59; Huitt 1968; Majone 1975; Schneider 1985; Webber 1986; Edelman 1988; Hilgartner and Bosk 1988).

Symbolic frames, as Schneider and Ingram (1990) pointed out, are much more front and centre in policy deliberations and advice. They impact subjects, such as who is defined as a policy target and why. Policy advice from the media, for example, often trades in such frames and images, as do various public fora.

Programme ideas also affect policy content more directly. They represent a selection of possible solutions to problems thought to be appropriate and feasible within a prevailing policy paradigm (Stone 1989; Hall 1993). As

Table 7.3 Advisory system actors by policy level

	Content and source of advice		
Policy goals (normative)	General abstract policy aims	Operationalizable policy objectives	Specific policy targets
	Public, outsiders and insiders	*Insiders and core actors*	*Core actors*
Policy means (cognitive)	General policy implementation preferences	Operationalizable policy tools	Specific policy tool calibrations
	Public, outsiders and insiders	*Insiders and core actors*	*Core actors*

Source: Howlett, M. (2014b).

mentioned above, they are the bread and butter of advisory work done by experts in government policy shops, think tanks, and policy labs and other 'knowledge-based policy influence organizations' (KBPIOs) (Wellstead and Howlett 2022; Olejniczak et al. 2020).

Distinguishing between these types of ideas in terms of their level of abstraction and whether they directly affect the foreground of policy debate or its background helps clarify the content of policy advice and discern its impact on policy-makers and policy designs (Campbell 1998).

In terms of the specific contribution that policy advisors and their advice can make to different policy components, these sets of actors can be thought to exist on a spectrum of influence linked to whether their advice deals with larger issues about problem definition and the articulation of policy goals or to the technical details of policy tools and their calibrations (Table 7.3). Members of the general public, non-governmental outsiders and insiders, for example, often impact policy discourses at the broad level of abstract policy goals and general policy preferences, while insiders and core actors become more influential as formulation and design moves to programme-level operations and then on to specifying on-the-ground measures and instruments (Page 2010).

The forgotten fundamental in policy advisory systems: policy professionals and the organization of policy shops in government

While there is no doubt that more and different actors are now involved in providing policy advice than in past years, in focusing on these new additions, policy advisory system studies have often tended to neglect developments within the core internal policy actors and how their activities and organization have changed.

This is an important gap since, somewhat counterintuitively, trends such as the proliferation of external sources of policy advice have led, on the one hand, to the reduction of the quasi-monopoly that core civil servants had in the past when they advised politicians (Cairney et al. 2016; Cairney 2021) and, on the other, to an increase in the numbers of advisors internal to the public sector (Craft and Halligan 2020).

For the most part, research in the 1960s and 1970s identified 'policy shops' as the home of professional advisors and analysis in government. These workers were found to be clustered together into relatively small units (Lindquist 2006). Research in many countries since then have affirmed the continued existence of such units (Howlett and Wellstead 2009, 2011; Pattyn et al. 2020; Veselý et al. 2014; Veselý 2014).

However, recent work on some countries, like Canada, have suggested that a different pattern of deployment of policy professionals now exists, that not all professionals work in such shops, and that many shops are not all that small. Migone and Howlett (2022), in their study of policy professionals in the Ontario government, for example, found that these actors now work in at least four different kinds of organizational settings. These are:

- *Integrated policy shops*. The 'classic' model which they found to now mostly exist in single-function ministries, where policy professionals are concentrated to the exclusion of their appearance in other areas of the organization.
- *Gatekeeper shops*. Another version of the 'classic model', but larger and found mainly in central agencies, where policy professionals are located in higher-level positions in the department.
- A *distributed model*. In which many policy professionals are concentrated within a central policy shop but are also broadly distributed in small shops across a ministry.
- A *hired gun model*. That is, a model where policy professionals are concentrated within a policy shop, but at the same time, very small groups of policy advisors (often only individual senior advisors) are found in specific areas or units in the organization dealing with high-profile or priority policy areas (Migone and Howlett 2022).

The activities of policy professionals in each of these organizational situations vary, as does their need for specific kinds of resources and skills in order to perform their work.

Until recently, data limitations have prevented detailed structural analysis of the organization of internal policy advice. However, digitization of governments now allows more detailed pictures to be drawn concerning the nature and organization of policy advisors in government. Detailed comparative treatment suggests that one model – the distributed one – may in fact be the most common and dominant one in contemporary government, being found both in environmental agencies, where it might be expected, but also in ministries like justice, where it might not (Migone and Howlett 2023).

While more cases and more broadly transnational comparisons are needed to definitively establish this trend, the transition from an integrated to a distributed model of internal policy advice in government has several implications for government policy-making, policy advice, and policy design. These include not only a propensity for more but also potentially more conflicting advice, which can undermine other efforts, like moves toward evidence-based policy-making, for example, as it is unlikely that any such trends could deliver consistent and uniform advice, as would have occurred under the integrated policy shop model.

Taken together with the already-identified trends toward externalization and politicization cited above, this would mean that at a time when the organization of internal advice might offset some of the fragmentation expected from a greater number of more expert external advisors and more political-oriented internal ones, it would not do so. That is, rather than combatting this fragmentation and bringing some order to the policy process, the distributed model may, in fact, contribute additional uncertainty to the process and, in reducing the homogeneity of professional internal advice, may ultimately augment the influence of external and more political actors not only in setting overall goals and governance preferences but also in choosing tools and setting the calibrations and target included in policy designs.

Conclusion: policy design as constrained expert discourse in policy advice systems

Policy design is most productive when the government enjoys legitimacy and broad political support and members of epistemic communities, instruments constituencies, and advocacy coalitions are able to express their concerns and expertise clearly in policy deliberations. Designs will be strong or weak, depending on the organizational and analytical competences governments possess to formulate and implement their policy preferences, and this, in turn, is linked to the nature of policy advisors and their interactions with decision-makers.

Thus, it is common to find statements such as Halligan's (1995) assertion that a good advice system should consist of

> at least three basic elements within government: a stable and reliable in-house advisory service provided by professional public servants; political advice for the minister from a specialized political unit (generally the minister's office); and the availability of at least one third-opinion option from a specialized or central policy unit, which might be one of the main central agencies.
>
> (162)

Balancing political and technical objectives is only part of the policy design challenge and is only one kind of policy advice, however. The receptiveness of decision-makers to advice and their need for it will vary from case to case (Manwaring 2019). In many design situations, for example, general abstract policy definitions, aims, and implementation preferences can often be taken as given, establishing the context in which design decisions relating to programme-level and on-the-ground specifications are made by policy insiders and core actors, reducing the role played by epistemic communities in the provision of policy advice, while enhancing that of instrument constituencies.

How the temporal and spatial elements of a policy process fit together, then, is a critical determinant of how key actors view and articulate the range of policy alternatives available to them and their need and desire for specific kinds of advice. In all cases, however, a critical component of policy formulation and policy design is related to the ideas and knowledge policy-makers and advisors hold about the nature of policy instruments and their configurations and how they can best be arranged in policy packages aimed at achieving government aims, goals, and objectives.

This subject is set out in the six chapters which comprise the next part of the book.

Readings

Campbell, J. L. (1998). 'Institutional Analysis and the Role of Ideas in Political Economy'. *Theory and Society* 27, no. 5: 377–409.

Caplan, N. and C. H. Weiss. (1977). *A Minimal Set of Conditions Necessary for the Utilization of Social Science Knowledge in Policy Formulation at the National Level*. Lexington, MA: Lexington Books.

Craft, J. and M. Howlett. (2012). 'Policy Formulation, Governance Shifts and Policy Influence: Location and Content in Policy Advisory Systems'. *Journal of Public Policy* 32, no. 2: 79–98.

Craft, J. and M. Howlett. (2013). 'The Dual Dynamics of Policy Advisory Systems: The Impact of Externalization and Politicization on Policy Advice'. *Policy and Society* 32, no. 3: 187–197.

Craft, J. and M. Wilder. (2017). 'Catching a Second Wave: Context and Compatibility in Advisory System Dynamics'. *Policy Studies Journal* 45, no. 1: 215–239.

Eichbaum, C. and R. Shaw. (2008). 'Revisiting Politicization: Political Advisers and Public Servants in Westminster Systems'. *Governance* 21, no. 3: 337–363.

Fleischer, J. (2009). 'Power Resources of Parliamentary Executives: Policy Advice in the UK and Germany'. *West European Politics* 32, no. 1: 196–214.

Fraussen, B. and D. Halpin. (2017). 'Think Tanks and Strategic Policy-Making: The Contribution of Think Tanks to Policy Advisory Systems'. *Policy Sciences* 50, no. 1 (1 March): 105–124.

Goldstein, J. and R. O. Keohane. (1993). 'Ideas and Foreign Policy: An Analytical Framework'. In J. Goldstein and R. O. Keohane (eds.), *Ideas and Foreign Policy: Beliefs, Institutions and Political Change*. Ithaca, NY: Cornell University Press, 3–30.

Heinrichs, H. (2005). 'Advisory Systems in Pluralistic Knowledge Societies: A Criteria-Based Typology to Assess and Optimize Environmental Policy Advice'. In S.

Maasen and P. Weingart (eds.), *Democratization of Expertise?* Vol. *24.* Berlin, Heidelberg: Springer-Verlag, 41–61.

Howlett, M. (2019). 'Comparing Policy Advisory Systems Beyond the OECD: Models, Dynamics and the Second-Generation Research Agenda'. *Policy Studies 40,* no. *3–4* (4 July): 241–259.

Hustedt, T. and S. Veit. (2017). 'Policy Advisory Systems: Change Dynamics and Sources of Variation'. *Policy Sciences 50,* no. *1* (1 March): 41–46.

Jacobs, A. M. (2008). 'How Do Ideas Matter? Mental Models and Attention in German Pension Politics'. *Comparative Political Studies 42,* no. *2:* 252–279.

James, T. E. and P. D. Jorgensen. (2009). 'Policy Knowledge, Policy Formulation, and Change: Revisiting a Foundational Question'. *Policy Studies Journal 37,* no. *1:* 141–162.

Lindvall, J. (2009). 'The Real but Limited Influence of Expert Ideas'. *World Politics 61,* no. *4:* 703–730.

Maley, M. (2000). 'Conceptualising Advisers' Policy Work: The Distinctive Policy Roles of Ministerial Advisers in the Keating Government, 1991–96'. *Australian Journal of Political Science 35,* no. *3:* 449–470.

Manwaring, R. (2017). 'Understanding Impact in Policy Advisory Systems: The Australian Case of the "Thinker in Residence"'. *International Journal of Public Administration 41,* no. *11* (24 March): 1–12.

Radaelli, C. M. (2005). 'Diffusion Without Convergence: How Political Context Shapes the Adoption of Regulatory Impact Assessment'. *Journal of European Public Policy 12,* no. *5:* 924–943.

Rhodes, R. A. W., Paul 't Hart, and Mirko Noordegraaf, eds. (2007). Observing Government Elites: Up Close and Personal. Palgrave Macmillan.

Schmidt, V. A. (2010). 'Taking Ideas and Discourse Seriously: Explaining Change Through Discursive Institutionalism as the Fourth New Institutionalism?' *European Political Science Review 2,* no. *1:* 1–25.

Sidney, M. S. (2007). 'Policy Formulation: Design and Tools'. In F. Fischer, G. J. Miller and M. S. Sidney (eds.), *Handbook of Public Policy Analysis: Theory, Politics and Methods.* New Brunswick, NJ: CRC, Taylor & Francis, 79–87.

Simons, A. and J.-P. Voss. (2017a). 'The Concept of Instrument Constituencies: Accounting for Dynamics and Practices of Knowing Governance'. *Policy and Society 37,* no. *1* (2 January): 14–35.

Weible, C. M. (2008). 'Expert-Based Information and Policy Subsystems: A Review and Synthesis'. *Policy Studies Journal 36,* no. *4:* 615–635.

Zito, A. R. (2001). 'Epistemic Communities, European Union Governance and the Public Voice'. *Science and Public Policy 28,* no. *6:* 465–476.

Part IV

THE ELEMENTS OF POLICY DESIGN

Policy instruments and instruments mixes

Chapter 8

Policy designs and policy portfolios

The origins of policy instrument study as a field of academic inquiry

A significant part of policy design activity, as we have seen in previous chapters, involves matching policy goals with the ideas formulators and decision-makers hold about policy goals and about the feasible and desirable mixes of policy means or tools expected to achieve them. Understanding policy instrument choices and the range of possibilities present in any design situation is thus a key factor for both policy advisors and decision-makers.

This requires an understanding of what kinds of instrument options exist, which subset of those is generally considered possible in a given context, and which among that smaller subset of all possible tools is deemed by policy experts and the public to be the most appropriate to use at a given time to achieve some specific end. These questions have a 'technical' component but are also inherently political in the sense that they involve partisan, normative, and ideological judgments as well as considerations about their legality and technical ability to change behaviours in desired directions. And they are institutional in the sense that they build upon the foundations of the polity and policy regime in which they are located.

In the effort to help deal with these questions, students of policy formation and policy tools from a variety of academic disciplinary backgrounds have, over the years, developed several models or conceptual schemes which help explain how policy instruments differ from each other and how different ones are or can be used in specific circumstances to achieve specific purposes.

This study of the 'tools of government' has a long history and a rich tradition of research in the policy sciences, much of it borrowed from public administration, law and regulatory studies, business and public management, and from many sectoral fields, ranging from telecommunications and transportation studies to health and environmental regulation, social policy, criminology, and educational studies, to name only a few. The main findings and currents of thinking in this area are set out in what follows, providing a template for the study of the details and uses of specific kinds of tools listed in Chapters 9–12.

The tools approach in policy studies

Fields interested in studying public policy, such as political science and political sociology, have traditionally been concerned with studying policy 'inputs' or the dynamics of public policy formation. For example, in political science, a key focus has been upon the role played by public opinion, political party activities, elections, and similar phenomena in affecting policy-making processes and defining policy content, while, in the case of political sociology, a central focus has been on understanding the roles played by social structure in defining actor 'interests' and positions in policy-making processes (Mayntz 1983).

Studies in these disciplines revealed a great deal about policy formation processes but tended to neglect the implementation component of policy-making. Studies in other fields such as public administration and management and organization studies, on the other hand, traditionally focused their efforts on the study of the inner workings of government, especially upon the study of the behavioural and management issues involved in tasks such as financial administration and budgeting, ministerial responsibility and accountability, the operation of the merit principle, and human resources and personnel administration. While these studies often purposely avoided considering the more political aspects of policy processes, they provided a great deal of information on implementation issues and processes which helped inform policy instrument and policy design studies.

In his pathbreaking early works on public policy-making, Harold Lasswell drew on both these literatures not only to define public policy, as we have seen, but also to clarify important aspects of policy-making, such as the number and type of stages involved in policy deliberations, and emphasize the importance of context to its workings (Torgerson 1985, 1990).

Importantly, Lasswell (1954) also noted the extent to which governments could affect policy-making through manipulations involving, among other things, 'symbols, signs and icons' and argued that a principal task of the policy sciences must be to understand the nuances of these actions and their effects (Lasswell 1954, 1971).

Like others of Lasswell's insights, this orientation was retained by many later students of policy-making who developed flexible notions of the multiple means by which governments could affect, or give effect to, policy. In these early works, 'policy instruments' were defined very broadly so as to include a wide range of tools or techniques of governance used at different stages of the policy process. In the 1970s, as the effort to improve policy-making through improved policy designs took shape, work turned to focus mainly on the evaluation of the impact on policy outcomes of specific kinds of substantive implementation-related tools, primarily economic ones, like subsidies and taxes (Mayntz 1983; Woodside 1986; Sterner 2003).

Many authors and scholars, following this lead, argued for a fundamental recasting of policy studies with much more emphasis upon implementation research. In the United States, for example, Bardach (1980) and Salamon (1981) both argued in the early 1980s that policy studies had 'gone wrong' right at the start by defining *policy* in terms of 'issues', 'areas', or 'fields' rather than in terms of 'instruments', and that correcting this oversight would generate much more powerful and useful insights. As Salamon put it:

> The major shortcoming of current implementation research is that it focuses on the wrong unit of analysis and the most important theoretical breakthrough would be to identify a more fruitful unit on which to focus analysis and research. In particular, rather than focusing on individual programmes, as is now done, or even collections of programmes grouped according to major 'purpose', as is frequently proposed, the suggestion here is that we should concentrate instead on the generic tools of government action, on the 'techniques' of social intervention.
>
> Salamon (1981: 256)

Following these kinds of injunctions, other scholars began to investigate the links between implementation failures and policy success in more detail and turned their gaze directly onto the subject of how implementation alternatives were crafted and formulated (Mayntz 1979; Goggin et al. 1990; O'Toole 2000).

Many lessons about policy instruments and policy design were drawn from legal studies, for example, which revealed a great deal about how tools such as laws, regulations, and others involved in the delivery of various kinds of goods and services operate and upon procedural aspects of formulation and implementation activities, such as the passage of legislation and forms of administrative rule-making. Studies in economics and law which focused on the *ex post* evaluation of the impact of policy outputs (Bobrow 1977; Stokey and Zeckhauser 1978), for example, began the more systematic appraisal of implementation alternatives. And organization, management, and administrative studies provided insights into the links between administrative systems and governance modes and how these affected the macro-components of policies and policy-making (Peters and Nispen 1998; Pierre and Peters 2005).

Ultimately, insights gleaned from a wide body of interdisciplinary literature concerning both policy inputs and governmental processes were combined in the 1980s and 1990s in the dedicated study of policy instruments and their role in policy design.

One hallmark of studies from the early 1980s was their focus on the need to more precisely categorize types of policy instruments prior to analyzing the reasons for their use (Salamon 1981; Tupper and Doern 1981; Trebilcock and Hartle 1982; Bressers and Honigh 1986; Bressers and Klok 1988). Careful examination and systematic classification of implementation instruments and instrument choices, it was argued, would not only lead to insights into the factors driving the policy process and the characterization of long-term patterns of public policy-making, as Lasswell had hoped, but also allow practitioners to more readily draw lessons from the experiences of others with the use of particular techniques in specific circumstances and, hence, improve policy designs and outcomes (Mayntz 1983; Linder and Peters 1984; Woodside 1986).

During this period, studies in Europe and North America shed a great deal of light on the construction and establishment of regulatory and other political and administrative agencies and enterprises as well as upon the use of traditional financial inducements and the many 'command-and-control' regulatory measures favoured by administrative agencies during this period (Tupper and Doern 1981; Hood 1986a; Howlett 1991; Vedung 1997b; Landry et al. 1998).

This new emphasis upon the systematic study of policy instruments quickly generated a sizable academic literature and resulted in immediate application of its findings and concepts in the design of many new policy initiatives in emerging areas at that time, such as consumer protection regulation, pollution prevention, and professional regulation (Trebilcock 1983; Hippes 1988). Significant subjects such as the reasons behind shifts in patterns of instrument choices associated with the waves of privatization and deregulation which characterized the period also received detailed attention (Howlett and Ramesh 1993).

Most of these studies focused exclusively upon what were referred to in previous chapters as 'substantive instruments', that is, those which directly affect the production and delivery of goods and services in society. These early studies failed to adequately address procedural tools and, consequently, until around the year 2000, developed only a partial description of policy tools and an understanding of how instrument choices related to policy design (Howlett 2000).

Nevertheless, by the late 1980s, the field of instrument studies had advanced far enough that Salamon (1989) could argue that the 'tools approach' had indeed, by then, become a major approach to policy studies in its own right, bringing a unique perspective to the policy sciences with its focus on policy outputs. Salamon argued that this perspective had revealed that not only did, as traditional studies had maintained, 'politics determine policy' but also the reverse (Landry et al. 1998). That is, via the feedback mechanisms in the policy cycle (Pierson 1992, 1993), tool choices led to the establishment of a 'political economy' of a policy regime. Thus, for example, a tool choice such as a decision to use tax incentives to accomplish some end created a constituency for continuation of that incentive (and sometimes one opposed to it), affecting future policy deliberations and decisions, including those related to future instrument choices (Linder and Peters 1984; Bobrow and Dryzek 1987; Dryzek and Ripley 1988).

At this point, Salomon framed two important research questions to be addressed in future analyses of the tools of government action: 'What consequences does the choice of tool of government action have for the effectiveness and operation of a government programme?' and 'What factors influence the choice of programme tools?' (265). These questions were taken up by the 'tools approach' and the policy design literature in the 1990s.

The development of models of policy tool choices

Assessing and answering Salomon's questions required scholars interested in policy design to engage in a lengthy process of social scientific analysis and model-building related to the study of implementation tools. These efforts expanded the number of preliminary questions which needed to be answered before Salomon's queries could be addressed (Salomon 1981; Timmermans et al. 1998; Hood 2007b), to include:

1. What potential tools does any government have?
2. How can these be classified?
3. How have these been chosen in the past?
4. Is there a pattern for this use?
5. If so, how can we explain this (or these) pattern(s)?
6. Can we improve on past patterns of use?

In order to answer these questions, policy scientists pursuing the tools approach followed, although not always necessarily as systematically as might be hoped, a five-stage research and analytical model-building strategy, one quite typical of the social sciences (see Figure 8.1) (McKelvey 1978, 1982; Stevens 1994).

Each of the stages in this process is set out and described next.

The construction of empirical inventories

As Figure 8.1 shows, the first step in the systematic study of policy instruments, as in any other similar endeavour in the social sciences, is the establishment of an inventory of the dependent variable. While there were many scholars who had looked at specific tools in the past (such as Cushman's 1941 study of regulatory agencies which was often cited by early students of the field), the first effort to systematically define the range of possible instruments which could be used in a policy design originated in the post–World War II planning exercises undertaken by the United Nations and the Organization for Economic Co-operation and Development (OECD) in Europe.

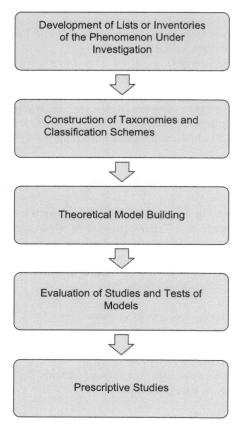

Figure 8.1 Analytical steps in social science model-building.

Key figures in this research included development economists such as E. S. (Etienne) Kirschen and nobel prize winner Jan Tinbergen, who published groundbreaking studies, including *Economic Policy in Our Times* (Kirschen et al. 1964), dealing with the instruments for economic policy they viewed in operation in the process of post-war European reconstruction. One of the first inventories of instruments was Kirschen et al.'s (1964) identification of well over 40 different types of implementation instruments then prevalent in European economic policy-making activities, ranging from public enterprises to various forms of government procurement and tax incentive and subsidy schemes.

Such studies were followed by many others examining the instruments prevalent in other areas, such as banking and foreign policy (Hermann 1982), adding to the list tools such as interest rate determination and other monetary and fiscal tools. These were pathbreaking studies which, although they did not make any distinctions between general implementation preferences, policy mechanisms, or calibrations and very often confused implementation tools and instruments used at other stages of the policy process, laid the groundwork for such future refinements by providing the raw data required for later classification efforts.

The development of taxonomies

Once a fairly exhaustive inventory has been created, the next major step in theory construction is to move toward taxonomy. That is, examining the list of the phenomena under consideration and attempting to classify or categorize the subject matter into a smaller number of mutually exclusive and exhaustive categories which, together, can simplify the often-idiosyncratic character of the original lists.

Many such schemes were developed in the policy instruments literature of the 1960s–1980s. Kirschen et al. (1964), for example, utilized a resource-based taxonomy of governing instruments to group instruments into five general 'families' according to the 'governing resource' they used: defined as public finance, money and credit, exchange rates, direct control, and changes in the institutional framework (16–17). However, this scheme was very sectorally specific and focused on the specific problem of achieving economic development goals. More generic schemes were developed, such as that put forward by Theodore Lowi (1966, 1972), which heavily influenced later thinking on the subject.

Lowi developed the insight first put forward by students of public administration in the USA, like Cushman (see Figure 8.2), that governments had only a small number of alternative choices in any given regulatory situation, depending on the amount of coercion they wished to employ in that situation – in Cushman's case, choosing either to regulate or not and, if so, to regulate either by the use of public enterprises or regulatory commissions. This analysis, among other things, introduced the idea that instrument choices were multi-level and nested, an insight which would be further developed in the years to come.

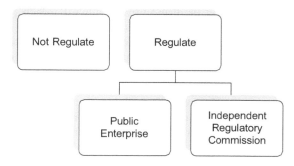

Figure 8.2 Cushman's three types of policy tools.

167

In his own work Lowi argued that a four-cell matrix based on the speci-ficity of the target of coercion and the likelihood of its actual application would suffice to distinguish all the major types of government implementa-tion activity. The original three policy types he developed included the weakly sanctioned and individually targeted 'distributive' policies, the individually targeted and strongly sanctioned 'regulatory' policy, and the strongly sanc-tioned and generally targeted 'redistributive' policy. To these three Lowi later added the weakly sanctioned and generally targeted category of 'constituent' policy (see Table 8.1).

Table 8.1 Lowi's matrix of policy implementation activities

		Specificity of target	
		Specific	General
Likelihood of sanctions	High	Regulatory	Redistributive
	Low	Distributive	Constituent

This was a significant advance, since it reduced the complexity of instru-ment choice to a single two-dimensional framework based on a simple set of dimensions. However, Lowi's categories of tools – distributive, redistributive, constituent, and regulatory – did not fit well with existing tool inventories and hence were difficult to operationalize and test (Roberts and Dean 1994), and his main purpose had been to discuss long-term patterns in tool prefer-ences by governments rather than develop a model or framework of choice. As a result, many other classification schemes emerged in the literature in the mid- to late 1980s.

Many of these later efforts, but not all, followed Lowi and Cushman's lead in focusing on some aspect of coercion as the key element differentiating policy instrument types. In a key development, however, some also introduced a greater number of differentiating criteria. Balch (1980), for example, talked about the need to differentiate between both 'carrots' (inducements or incen-tives) and 'sticks' (coercion or disincentives), while Bardach (1980) argued that governments had three 'technologies' which they could utilize in any given choice situation – enforcement, inducement, and benefaction – and that these strategies required different combinations of four critical governmental resources: money, political support, administrative competency, and creative leadership. Elmore (1987) identified four major classes of instruments: man-dates, inducements, capacity-building, and system-changing.

Further studies moving in the design direction refined this idea of only a limited number of 'governing resources' lying behind each tool. As we have already seen in earlier chapters, Christopher Hood (1983, 1986a) generated a major work on the subject in 1986 which was heavily influenced by detailed studies of the British and German policy implementation processes undertaken previously by Dunsire (1978) and Mayntz (1975). It involved the elaboration of a fourfold resource-based categorization scheme for policy instruments which served as an admirable synthesis of the other, earlier models.

Hood argued that governments have essentially four resources at their disposal which they can use to either effect changes in their environment or detect them: *nodality*, meaning, the resource that existed simply by nature of the fact that governments existed at the 'centre' of social and political networks but which can also be thought of as 'information' or 'knowledge'; *authority*; *treasure*; and *organization* (or 'NATO' in Hood's terminology). In Hood's scheme, implementation instruments are grouped together according to which of the NATO resources they *most* or *primarily* relied upon for their effectiveness, fully recognizing that most used some combination of these resources in practice (Anderson 1977; Hood 1986a).

That is, a government regulation requiring a license in order to use a particular pesticide, for example, is a policy tool expected to give effect to a set of policy objectives (in this case, a problem with externalities from pollution and information asymmetries between producers and consumers of sophisticated chemical products) within a set of aims (such as environmental protection and species preservation) and preferred implementation preferences (such as market-based service delivery within a market mode of governance). Such a tool requires an organization to implement it, some funding to pay the personnel involved in that activity, information notices to regulatees that a license is required and that the requirement will be enforced, and some legal authority to create a license scheme and enforce it. Such an instrument thus involves the use of many types of governing resources, but the primary resource it relies upon is the legal authority to enforce compliance, without which all the other resources would be ineffective and unnecessary (Bali et al. 2022).

That is, some tools (and resources) are 'primary' in the sense that they are central to achieving a stated objective and are expected to be the primary instrument(s) for changing a targeted behaviour. Others are 'secondary' in the sense that in themselves they are not expected to achieve primary policy goals but rather play a vital role in supporting primary tools. The primary and secondary or 'supplementary' tools used to target problems together form a policy 'portfolio' (see Table 8.2).

Table 8.2 Two orders of policy tools

Order	Definition
First order (primary)	The primary substantive and procedural tools used to meet policy objectives
Second order (Supplementary)	Other tools that are layered to increase effectiveness or sharpen the effect of first-order tools

The distinction between primary and secondary tools becomes clearer in the context of a particular policy goal or a policy function. That is, for example, in a portfolio of policy tools centred on the delivery of health services, public hospitals are expected to play the primary role. However, public hospitals are more effective in delivering quality services at affordable costs when used in conjunction with subsidies or regulatory tools that mandate certain standards (Ramesh 2008; Bali and Ramesh 2019). In this case, the performance of a primary tool (i.e. public hospitals) is sharpened by supplementary tools (i.e. subsidies and regulations). Similarly, fines or speeding tickets are the primary tools that governments use to ensure that motorists comply with safety regulations, while advertisements that nudge drivers to be cautious are supplementary tools. The larger point here is that individual policy tools do not operate in isolation, and that their impact is conditioned by supporting tools.

This taxonomy proved useful in providing a limited number of eight clearly differentiated categories of instruments (see Table 8.3) which could be taken to narrow the range of possible tools in the governing toolbox sufficiently to allow further considerations of topics such as the reasons that specific ones were selected in specific circumstances.

Table 8.3 Hood's 1986 taxonomy of substantive policy instruments

		Governing resource			
		Nodality	*Authority*	*Treasure*	*Organization*
Principle use	Detectors	Surveys	Licencing	Policing	Record-keeping
	Effectors	Public information campaign	Regulation	Subsidies	Government agencies

Source: Adapted from Christopher Hood (1986c).

Modelling policy tool choices

As Linder and Peters (1990b: 307) noted, once the tools of government have been inventoried and classified, 'the need to do something more becomes irresistible'. The next logical step was 'to explore functional connections' involving how to best match 'instruments to goals, policy problems, social impact and organizations'. Taking this next step toward the idea of policy design, as we have seen, requires clarifying the nature of the criteria by which experts assess policy tools and the nature of the contexts in which they can reasonably be anticipated to perform as expected.

Kirschen et al., in their early 1964 work, had already gone some distance toward that goal by arguing that the key determinants of policy choice in the case of the economic instruments they had identified were the economic objective or goal pursued and the structural and conjunctural context of the choice. The economic objectives, they argued, were determined by the interaction of political parties and their representatives in government, administrators, and interest groups while the structural and conjunctural context, in turn, was affected by the influence of long-term economic processes and structures and current economic conditions. They argued that the actual choice of instrument from within the set that fit these epistemic and contextual constraints should be made on essentially technical grounds, according to efficiency and cost criteria, although the political preferences of interest groups and governments – including sociological and ideological constraints – and the institutional limitations of the political system itself had to be taken into account as factors influencing key decision-makers.

This was a prescient analysis of the overall set of factors affecting instrument choices (Majone 1976, 1989), combining as it did both technical and political concerns. However, it was also one which was not adequately grounded in a classification of instruments so as to be able to produce specific recommendations or hypotheses concerning appropriate instrument selections and policy designs in different circumstances or times.

The first models of instrument choices which did so attempted to identify a limited number of criteria upon which policy tools varied, creating single or multiple 'spectrums' or 'continuums' of instrument characteristics which, it was hoped, could then be associated with specific government preferences among these criteria. Dahl and Lindblom, for example, as early as 1953, argued that although the number of alternative politico-economic instruments is virtually infinite, they varied along five dimensions which could be examined together to arrive at a measure of tool preferability in specific contextual situations (Dahl and Lindblom 1953).

Their first continuum ranged instruments according to whether they involved public or private enterprises or agencies, the second according to whether they were persuasive or compulsory, the third according to whether they involved direct or indirect controls over expenditures, the fourth according to whether they involved organizations with voluntary or compulsory membership, and the fifth according to whether government agencies were autonomous or directly responsible to legislators or executive members.

Although Dahl and Lindblom did not pursue any further the question of whether and to what extent governments actually used these criteria in order to choose a particular instrument, their idea of arranging instruments on a continuum in order to better clarify the reasons behind their choice was adopted by many authors. Salamon and Lund (1989), for example, suggested that different instruments involve varying degrees of effectiveness, efficiency, equity, legitimacy, and partisan support that affect their appropriateness in a particular situation.

A simplified version of this model was put forward by a group of Canadian scholars, including Bruce Doern, Richard Phidd, Seymour Wilson, and others, who published a series of articles and monographs in the late 1970s

171

and early 1980s that turned Lowi's two-dimensional matrix of policy choices into a single continuum of policy instruments based on the 'degree of government coercion' each instrument choice entailed. They first placed only self-regulation, exhortation, subsidies, and regulation on this scale (Doern 1981) but later added in categories for 'taxation' and public enterprise (Tupper and Doern 1981) and, finally, argued for an entire series of finer 'gradiations' within each general category (Phidd and Doern 1983) (see Figure 8.3).

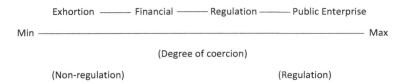

Figure 8.3 The Doern continuum.

For Doern and his colleagues, the development of this coercion spectrum model led to the hypothesis of a twofold rationale of instrument choice: one that fitted very well with the notion of Dahl and Lindblom's idea of a 'continuum' of choices and which offered a great deal of explanatory power in the context of the kinds of choices and preferences made by liberal-democratic states. This rationale was based on the assumption of an ideological preference of liberal-democratic governments for limited state activity and on the difficulties posed to this principle by the relative political 'strength' of the societal actors in resisting government efforts to shape their behaviour.

As Doern and Wilson put it:

> Politicians have a strong tendency to respond to policy issues, (any issue) by moving successively from the least coercive governing instrument to the most coercive. Thus they tend to respond first in the least coercive fashion by creating a study, or by creating a new or reorganized unit of government, or merely by uttering a broad statement of intent. The next least coercive governing instrument would be to use a distributive spending approach in which the resources could be handed out to constituencies in such a way that the least attention is given as to which taxpayers' pockets the resources are being drawn from. At the more coercive end of the continuum of governing instruments would be a larger redistributive programme in which resources would be more visibly extracted from the more advantaged classes and redistributed to the less advantaged classes. Also at the more coercive end of the governing continuum would be direct regulation in which the sanctions or threat of sanctions would have to be directly applied.
>
> (Doern and Wilson 1974: 339)

This model was lauded for its simplicity and elegance but, as critics pointed out, was still problematical in its application to policy design decisions since 'coercion' is difficult to operationalize with the degree of precision required by the model (Trebilcock et al. 1982).

Notwithstanding this concern, however, this kind of model has many advantages for policy analysis and policy design. It is not unidimensional, although it might appear so on first reading, because it, like Kirschen, does take into account several political and contextual variables, and it, like Cushman, assumes instrument choices are in fact multi-level, with finer calibrations of instruments emerging after initial broad selections have been made.

That is, the model also has a strong temporal dimension, lacking in many other models of instrument choice, since it assumes that both states and societal interests in liberal-democratic regimes prefer a minimal state and choose instruments accordingly after that initial decision has been made. Thus, preferring 'self-regulation', governments would first attempt to influence overall target group performance through exhortation and then add instruments only as required in order to compel recalcitrant societal actors to abide by its wishes, eventually culminating, if necessary, in the take-over of individual firms.

This is not an unreasonable conclusion, based as it is on much observation of the practices of such governments and hints at the 'nested' temporal nature of instrument choices, a subject not previously as well developed in instrument studies. However, empirically it was somewhat weakly supported since, as Woodside (1986) argued,

> experience suggest that governments do not always seek to avoid coercive solutions, but indeed, may at times seem to revel in taking a hard line from the start. While there are undoubtedly many reasons for these heavy-handed responses, surely some of the most important ones include the constituency or group at which the policy is aimed, the circumstances in which the problem has appeared and the nature of the problem involved.
> Woodside (1986: 786)

Trebilcock et al. also questioned the likelihood of state actors adhering to a minimalist notion of their own proper role in society, preferring more public choice-inspired notions about the desire for bureaucratic expansion and political credit-mongering motivating administrative and political policy-makers to grander initial plans, especially notions of a political cost–benefit calculus aimed at vote maximization (Trebilcock et al. 1982). These authors also questioned the notion of instrument substitutability found in Doern's work, arguing that constitutional restraints, financial limitations, and other technical criteria prevented certain instruments from being utilized in specific circumstances (Trebilcock and Prichard 1983).

Thompson and Stanbury did much the same, focusing on visibility and its linkages to political advantage and disadvantage as a criterion of instrument choice. Democratic politicians, they argued, are not simply ideologically predisposed toward a small state or minimal instruments but would adopt whatever instrument generates the most political benefits for them while minimizing the political costs (Howard and Stanbury 1984; Stanbury 1986). Baxter-Moore, from a neo-Marxist perspective, similarly challenged Doern's notion that the state is committed to a minimal role in society, arguing that 'the state will generally use less intrusive instruments when seeking the compliance of the dominant capitalist class and deploy more intrusive measures to direct or control the behaviour of subordinate classes' (Baxter-Moore 1987: 346).

Despite these criticisms, the Doern model remains an important one in studies of public policy tools, its virtues of simplicity and parsimony outweighing its empirical and conceptual difficulties.

Contemporary tool studies: improving on the modelling of policy instruments by adding in procedural tools and policy mixes

Since these early works, further studies developed tools thinking by extending and expanding their insights into the nature of policy tools and the reasons for their use. Some notable additions are set out below especially the expansion of the notion of policy tools beyond substantive implementation instruments and considering the relationships that exist between different kinds of tools, recognizing that most tools are deployed in 'mixes' or bundles, rather than singly, including mixes of substantive and procedural tools. These efforts and additions are discussed in turn in what follows.

Dealing with the relationships between different kinds of tools in a policy mix

While Hood's work focused mainly on 'substantive' policy tools, as we have seen, fortunately, earlier generations of implementation scholars had not completely neglected the manner in which governments deployed their resources to affect policy processed.

In the case of these 'procedural' instruments, several works dealing with this aspect of the subject provided a broad sense of which direction to pursue in attempting to elevate this area of instrument studies to the level that substantive implementation instrument research had attained through taxonomy construction and model-building (Walker 1983, 1991; Qualter 1985).

In their 1988 work, for example, Bressers and Klok (1988) had noted the ways in which 'subjective rational actors' can be influenced by manipulation of the alternatives placed before them and that different instruments can affect the number of policy options developed in the policy process or the calculations of costs and benefits of alternative courses of action made by policy actors. While some of the instruments they examined were 'substantive' (e.g. the use of licenses to affect the cost of certain activities), most of the instruments captured by their scheme were procedural, especially those dealing with the selective creation, provision, and diffusion of information to policy actors.

On the basis of this analysis, Schneider and Ingram, following Elmore and his colleagues, identified five general types of instruments corresponding to these 'behavioural assumptions'. These they called 'authority', 'incentives', 'capacity-building', 'symbolic and hortatory', and 'learning' instruments.

As was the case with Bressers and Klok, this scheme included both 'procedural' and 'substantive' tools. While their discussion, like many in the USA at that time, virtually ignored pure public provision of goods and services by government agencies and corporations (Leman 1989), the 'authority' and 'incentive' examples cited are typical substantive instruments involving mixed provision of goods and services by a combination of private and public actors. 'Capacity', 'symbolic', and 'learning' tools, however, are much more procedurally oriented, affecting the policy institutions and processes within which policy decisions take place.

Taken together, the works of Bressers and Klok, along with that of Schneider and Ingram and others in the USA and Europe, identified a large number of procedural instruments, their inventory, like that in the case of substantive tools, being accompanied by several ideas about how to classify them (Chapman 1973; Weiss and Tschirhart 1994). These authors identified, among others, tools involved in education, training, institution creation, the selective provision of information, formal evaluations, hearings, and institutional reform (Wraith and Lamb 1971; Chapman 1973; Kernaghan 1985; Peters 1992b; Weiss and Tschirhart 1994; Bellehumeur 1997).

Research into the tools and mechanisms used in intergovernmental regulatory design at the time also identified several other such instruments, including intergovernmental 'treaties' and a variety of 'political agreements' that can affect target-group recognition of government intentions, and vice versa (Bulmer 1993; Doern and Wilks 1998; Harrison 1999). Other research into interest-group behaviour and activities highlighted the existence of tools related to group creation and manipulation, including the role played by private or public-sector patrons in aiding the formation and activities of such groups (Burt 1990; Phillips 1991; Pal 1993; Finkle et al. 1994; Nownes and Neeley 1996; Lowry 1999). Still, other specialized research into aspects of contemporary policy-making highlighted the use of procedural techniques, such as the provision of research funding for and access to investigative hearings and tribunals (Salter and Slaco 1981; Gormley 1989; Cairns 1990; Jenson 1994).

While most researchers focused on the manner in which these instruments were used to enhance 'desirable' traits in public policy-making, such as enhanced participation and the wider dissemination of policy-relevant knowledge, some scholars like Saward (1992) also emphasized that procedural tools were also used to 'negatively' affect some interest groups and other actors' behaviour, that is, to restrict their freedom to associate and engage in policy-influencing activities.

This latter research highlighted the role such tools have played in the 'dark side' of politics and policy-making, for example, suppressing government enemies and rewarding friends via punishment, exclusions, and denial of information (Goodin 1980; Saward 1990, 1992), a subject which is discussed in depth in Chapter 16.

Examples of 'negative' procedural policy tools identified at this time included co-opting opponents through provision of funds and other privileges, denying information, keeping opponents' views from the public, penalizing opponents by denying funding or recognition and fragmenting opposition – divide and conquer – by selective rewarding, rewarding 'neutrals', adding administrative hurdles and costs to opponents, and many more. These latter studies, however, all existed outside the mainstream of policy instrument research, which continued to focus almost exclusively on substantive implementation tools but were ready to be used when policy design and implementation studies moved in a procedural direction in the late 1990s.

Hood's taxonomy of substantive instruments, set out earlier in the book, can be modified to help make sense out of this disparate list of procedural tools, and this task was undertaken in the late 1990s in several quarters. Classifying procedural instruments just as Hood had done for their substantive counterparts, that is, in accordance with the type of 'governing resource' on which they primarily rely for their effectiveness, generates a useful preliminary taxonomy of procedural tools.

Drawing a distinction between 'positive' and 'negative' uses of governing resources in terms of whether they encourage or discourage actor participation in policy processes further parallels the 'effector–detector' distinction made in Hood's original discussion of substantive tools (Howlett 2000c) (see Table 8.4).

As was the case with Hood's discussion of substantive instruments, this taxonomy is useful insofar as it highlights a small number of different basic resources used by different types of procedural tools and therefore allows a virtually unlimited number of such instruments to be placed in a limited number of general categories, preparing the ground for the development of

Table 8.4 A resource-based taxonomy of procedural policy instruments

| | | Governing resource | | | |
		Nodality	Authority	Treasure	Organization
Principle use	**'Positive'**	Freedom of information	Mandated participatory processes	Interest group funding	Conferences and commissions
	'Negative'	Propaganda	Preferential access to policy-makers	Targeted campaign funding	Red tape

Source: Adapted from Howlett (2000).

improved understandings of the basic contours and possibilities of tool selection and of policy designs.

This insight allows a simplified NATO model to be set out in Table 8.5, which includes both procedural and substantive tools as well as a clearer idea of what constitutes a basic governing resource. It is this model which is used in Chapters 9–12 to set out and describe the basic subtypes and most common individual kinds of implementation instruments used in contemporary policy designs.

Table 8.5 A simplified taxonomy of substantive and procedural implementation tools

		Governing resource			
		Information	Authority	Treasure	Organization
Purpose of tool	**Substantive**	Public information campaigns	Independent regulatory agencies	Subsidies and grants	Public enterprises
	Procedural	Official secrets acts	Administrative advisory committees	Interest group funding	Government reorganizations

As has already been noted, *substantive tools* – such as subsidies, taxes, public enterprises, etc. – seek to directly target the problematic conditions or subjects' behaviour, while *procedural policy tools* are used to alter the choice or use of decision processes (Howlett 2000). Procedural tools do not affect outcomes as directly as substantive tools do, but they are often essential for the latter to work effectively. Each substantive policy tool relies on a range of secondary complex administrative processes and procedures which are used to select, sequence, calibrate, and deploy the tool including the administrative processes and activities involved in selecting, deploying, and calibrating such tools.

Table 8.6 provides examples of such procedural tools in the healthcare sector.

Similar to substantive tools, these procedural tools appear in primary and secondary forms. That is, some procedural tools are often more 'primary', such as those related to designing governance arrangements (partnerships, degree and type of competition, accountability mechanisms, etc.) for delivering services or those which establish or change actors' positions or add actors to networks or change access rules for actors. But other procedural tools are more supportive or 'secondary', such as changing evaluation criteria or codes of conduct or for actors or establishing tribunals or commissions to adjudicate disputes, or those which otherwise change interaction procedures (Agranoff and McGuire 1999).

Table 8.6 Procedural tools in healthcare, examples

Policy formulation tools
- National health plan
- National targets, goals, and performance measures
- Multi-year strategic plan, medium-term expenditure frameworks, and national health accounts

Partnership tools
- Inter-ministerial and inter departmental committees
- Public–private task force
- Integrated budgets and accounting, co-funding arrangements, or earmarked grants

Information-gathering tools
- Inter-ministerial fact-finding commissions or task force; parliamentary investigations
- Periodic audits, public expenditure, and performance reviews
- Health technology assessments

Accountability tools
- Performance-based contracts
- Instruments of judicial redress, procedures to combat corruption
- Superintendent board/board of governors

Participation tools
- Open meetings, public workshops, national forums, citizen advisory committees, citizen juries
- Patient experience surveys
- Formal consultations in drafting legislation

Transparency tools
- Watchdog committees (facility boards, health authority, ombudsman, parliamentary committees)
- Freedom of information; right to information
- Inspectorates, fact-finding commissions

Source: Adapted from Barbazza and Tello (2014).

Dealing with measurement and typology issues in policy mixes

Earlier studies of policy tools focused almost exclusively on describing the types of tools governments used to advance their goals and the criteria which affected the choice of individual tools, be it regulation or public subsidies or some other policy mechanism (Lowi 1972; Hood 1983; Linder and Peters 1989; Schneider and Ingram 1990a; Peters and van Nispen 1998; Howlett 2000c; Salamon 2002). More recent studies brought about a renewed interest not only in issues such as how such specific tool choices evolve over time but also, importantly, how individual tools operate when combined with others, sometimes in very complex multi-level, multi-policy, and multi-tool 'policy mixes' or 'portfolios' (Howlett and Lejano 2013).

As we have seen in earlier chapters, choosing policy tools becomes more complex when multiple goals and multiple policies are involved within the same sector and government, as is very common in many policy-making situations (Doremus 2003; Jordan et al. 2012; Howlett et al. 2009). It has increasingly been recognized that most contemporary policy problems are too complex to be addressed by a single tool but rather require the use of multiple tools based on different 'governing resources' (Hood 2007).

Studies like those of Gunningham and his colleagues (Gunningham et al. 1998) on 'smart' environmental policy-making in Australia had begun to deal with the problem of the design of policy mixes in the mid-1990s. And as Peters (2018) recently reminds us, there are now very few policies composed of discrete and standalone policy tools. Mixes or 'combinations of different kinds of policy tools (market-based, hierarchical, network and others) whose exact configuration changes from location to location' (Rayner et al. 2017: 473) are far more common.

These latter kinds of multi-policy, multi-goal, and multi-instrument mixes – what Milkman et al. (2012) calls 'policy bundles', Chapman (2003) and Hennicke (2004) a 'policy mix', and Givoni et al. (2012) 'policy packages' – are all examples of complex portfolios of tools.

These mixes typically involve much more than functional logics linking tools to a goal but also deal with ideological or even 'aesthetic' preferences in tool choices and goal articulation which involve trade-offs and bargaining between actors in choosing one set of tools, goals, and policies over another (Béland and Waddan 2012; Williams and Balaz 1999). This makes their formulation or design especially problematic (Peters 2005b; Givoni 2014; Givoni et al. 2012). Most often, the focus should move from the design of specific instruments to the appropriate design of instrument mixes. This is more difficult to do when instruments belong to different territorial/administrative levels, however, or when they have gradually accreted through successive rounds of layering.

Developing a typology of policy mixes based on the level of complexity of their design has been a useful step in advancing design studies in this area. Mixes can be assessed at a general level by identifying spaces of conflicts, complementarities, and synergies between policy fields, but those interactions also depend on the type of tools being adopted and the specific design elements of the instruments adopted within those policy fields. The choice of specific instruments and design elements within interacting policy fields may contribute to mitigate conflicts and promote complementarities and synergies or not. Coordination is easier when certain instruments and design elements are deployed than it is with under others.

Constructing a basic taxonomy of policy portfolios needs to distinguish between mixes according to the number of instruments, goals, and policies found within them at a 'horizontal' or single-governmental level. Additional scenarios then exist for 'vertical' mixes in situations in which multiple instruments and goals exist across levels of governments. Like at the horizontal level, at these levels tools and goals may complement each other, while in others, or in some respects, they might not (Hull 2008; Flanagan et al. 2011) (See Table 8.7).

Table 8.7 Basic typology of policy portfolio design types and dimension

Dimension	Types							
	I	*II*	*III*	*IV*	*V*	*VI*	*VII*	*VIII*
Multi-level	No	No	No	No	Yes	Yes	Yes	Yes
Multi-policy	No	No	Yes	Yes	No	No	Yes	Yes
Multi-goal	No	Yes	No	Yes	No	Yes	No	Yes

What kind of mix exists is an important implication for its operation and design. A relatively simple mix design process, for example, may be dominated by expert actors (Dunlop 2009a) and decided upon largely according to technical or functional criteria (Braathen 2007a). But moving toward multiple policies and goals brings in additional actors (Marier 2008) and involves more sophisticated evidence and ideas than is found in more simple contexts (Sanderson 2002a). In multi-level government and governance contexts (Hooghe and Marks 2003), different levels of government are likely to have some common, but also different, goals and instrument preferences (Enderlein et al. 2011), and reconciling them typically involves the use of the most overt political calculus of intra- or intergovernmental bargaining and decision-making (Bolleyer and Borzel 2010; Kaiser et al. 2012).

Increasing complexity from horizontality to verticality can bring in cross-national actors (Haas 1992), including political ones, and often involves the assessment and use of politically contested evidence and criteria (Gilabert and Lawford-Smith 2012). The most sophisticated design spaces, like those around climate change, involve the most complex design processes and the full range of subsystem actors operating across multiple governance levels (McCool 1998; Hooghe and Marks 2003). Here, in a context of vested interests, lobbying pressures, and intergovernmental jurisdictional disputes, fully blown political criteria, such as blame avoidance, credit claiming, bargaining, and logrolling relevant information (Hood 2010), are likely to be features of policy formulation.

Within a mix, a variety of tools may be present, and mixes differ along several dimensions. For instance, many early studies of mixes stressed the importance of *policy density* (Knill et al. 2012), a measure which focuses on the number of tools in a policy mix, and *policy intensity*, which attempts to measure the coercive strength of individual tools. Others, like Attwell and Navin (2019), have offered more sophisticated models which attempt to capture the inter-relationships existing between tools and how the number and type of tools can determine the nature of a mix. They examine differences in mixes linked to their *scope* (which behaviours or outcomes are targeted),

Table 8.8 Five dimensions of policy mixes and their measurement

Mix aspect or dimension	Measure
Saturation	Number of policy tools
Scope	Number of policy goals
Sanctions	Extent of reliance on coercion
Severity	Extent of use of NATO resources
Selectivity	Number and type of policy targets
Salience	Effectiveness of the policy response

Source: Modified from Attwell and Navin (2019).

sanctions (what kind of tool is used), *severity* (how intensively the tool is used), and *selectivity* (which individuals and institutions are targeted or exempted), which, taken together, they argue, can provide a measure of the *salience* of a policy or its tendency to generate the behaviours or outcomes it aims at.

However, Attwell and Navin did not look at 'density', which remains a significant variable in mix construction. In keeping with their nomenclature, this can be thought of as 'saturation', that is, the degree to which a range of tools is used in a mix.

This generates the template found in Table 8.8, which emphasizes these six components of a mix and the need to examine each if the character of the mix is to be understood and one mix is to be compared with another.

Conclusion: from tools to toolboxes in contemporary policy design studies

In the late 1990s, work on instrument selection began to assess the question of the potential to develop optimal policy mixes and to move away from a focus on single-instrument choices (Grabosky 1994; Gunningham and Young 1997). Studies such as Gunningham, Grabosky, and Young's work on 'smart regulation' led to the development of efforts to identify complementarities and conflicts within instrument mixes or tool 'portfolios' involved in more complex and sophisticated policy designs (Barnett and Shore 2009; Buckman and Diesendorf 2010).

For these authors, the key question was no longer 'Why do policy-makers utilize a certain instrument?' as it was for earlier generations of students of policy instrument choice, but rather, 'Why is a particular combination of procedural and substantive instruments utilized in a specific sector?' (Dunsire 1993b; Howlett 2000c; Salamon 2002c; Cubbage et al. 2007; Gleirscher 2008; Gipperth 2008; Taylor 2008; Clark and Russell 2009; McGoldrick and Boonn 2010). This has important implications, of course, for policy design.

As this discussion has shown, over the course of the past 30 years, the study of policy implementation instruments has advanced through the various stages of social scientific theory construction and now contributes a great deal of knowledge to policy formulation and policy design (Hood 2007; Lascoumes and Le Galès 2007).

In general, however, current studies have focused on better identifying and measuring only the overall composition of policy portfolios or mixes (e.g. Kern and Howlett 2009; Schaffrin et al. 2014, 2015) in specific policy sectors and have not addressed in detail the key features of the inter- and intra-tool relationships they contain (McDermott et al. 2009, 2010; Auld et al. 2010; Schmidt and Sewerin 2019; for an exception, see Hou and Brewer 2010). The key question for most existing studies has been simply to describe what kind of policies or policy mixes exist and to grapple with the question of how overall policy configurations and specific policy components have developed and changed over time (e.g. Howlett and Lejano 2013) rather than to investigate their interactions in a manner which aids their design.

Many existing frameworks for modelling policy mixes still do not adequately recognize the hybrid and multilayered features of tool portfolios, how procedural and substantial tools operate and interact together in priority and supportive roles (Rogge and Reichardt 2016), and how important the micro-level of tools and settings are to policy effectiveness and outcomes. In particular, many existing policy tools frameworks do not adequately recognize the complexity of contemporary policy tools in policy mixes, especially their hybrid and multi-layered features, and how both procedural and substantial tools operate and interact together in priority and supportive roles (Bali et al. 2022).

Understanding such mixes and how their parts work (or not) together remains a significant area of interest and study in the field of policy design. The distinction in the type and mix of tools deployed in the effort to achieve policy goals, for example, is important and has significant implications for both implementation and programme success as governments and public sector agencies have differing capabilities and experience in designing, deploying, and managing specific types of tools and specific kinds of tool mixes (Levi-Faur 2014; Haber 2011).

In the next four chapters, the major types of tools which go into the creation of a policy mix are examined. Each chapter is not exhaustive, but illustrative, of the kinds of tools commonly found in policy portfolios, focusing mainly on the substantive and procedural tools deployed for implementation purposes, but also those involved in policy formulation, decision-making, evaluation, and often, agenda-setting (Howlett 2022).

Readings

Attwell, K. and M. C. Navin. (2019). 'Childhood Vaccination Mandates: Scope, Sanctions, Severity, Selectivity, and Salience'. *The Milbank Quarterly* 97, no. 4 (December): 978–1014.

Bali, A. S., M. Howlett and M. Ramesh. (2022). 'Unpacking Policy Portfolios: Primary and Secondary Aspects of Tool Use in Policy Mixes'. *Journal of Asian Public Policy 15*, no. 3 (2 September): 321–337.

Bemelmans-Videc, M.-L. and E. Vedung. (1997). 'Conclusion: Policy Instrument Types, Packages, Choices and Evaluation'. In M.-L. Bemelmans-Videc, R. C. Rist and E. Vedung (eds.), *Carrots, Sticks and Sermons: Policy Instruments and Their Evaluation*. New Brunswick, NJ: Transaction, 249–273.

Capano, G. and M. Howlett. (2020). 'The Knowns and Unknowns of Policy Instrument Analysis: Policy Tools and the Current Research Agenda on Policy Mixes'. *Sage Open* (24 January).

De Bruijn, J. A. and E. F. ten Heuvelhof. (1997). 'Instruments for Network Management'. In W. J. M. Kickert, E.-H. Klijn and J. F. M. Koppenjan (eds.), *Managing Complex Networks: Strategies for the Public Sector*. London: Sage, 119–136.

Doern, G. B. and V. S. Wilson. (1974). 'Conclusions and Observations'. In G. B. Doern and V. S. Wilson (eds.), *Issues in Canadian Public Policy*. Toronto, ON: Macmillan, 337–345.

Goodin, R. E. (1980). *Manipulatory Politics*. New Haven, CT: Yale University Press, 1–36.

Gunningham, N., P. Grabosky and D. Sinclair. (1998). *Smart Regulation: Designing Environmental Policy*. Oxford: Clarendon Press.

Gunningham, N. and M. D. Young. (1997). 'Toward Optimal Environmental Policy: The Case of Biodiversity Conservation'. *Ecology Law Quarterly* 24: 243–298.

Hood, C. (1983). 'Using Bureaucracy Sparingly'. *Public Administration 61*, no. 2: 197–208.

Hood, C. (1986). *The Tools of Government*. Chatham: Chatham House Publishers.

Hood, C. (2007). 'Intellectual Obsolescence and Intellectual Makeovers: Reflections on the Tools of Government After Two Decades'. *Governance 20*, no. 1: 127–144.

Howlett, M. (2000). 'Managing the "Hollow State": Procedural Policy Instruments and Modern Governance'. *Canadian Public Administration 43*, no. 4: 412–431.

Howlett, M. (2004). 'Beyond Good and Evil in Policy Implementation: Instrument Mixes, Implementation Styles and Second-Generation Theories of Policy Instrument Choice'. *Policy and Society 23*, no. 2: 1–17.

Howlett, M. and P. del Rio. (2015). 'The Parameters of Policy Portfolios: Verticality and Horizontality in Design Spaces and Their Consequences for Policy Mix Formulation'. *Environment and Planning C 33*, no. 5: 1233–1245.

Kickert, W. J. M. and J. F. M. Koppenjan. (1997). 'Public Management and Network Management: An Overview'. In W. J. M. Kickert, E.-H. Klijn and J. F. M. Koppenjan (eds.), *Managing Complex Networks: Strategies for the Public Sector*. London: Sage, 35–61.

Kirschen, E. S., J. Benard, H. Besters, F. Blackaby, O. Eckstein, J. Faaland, F. Hartog, L. Morissens and E. Tosco. (1964). *Economic Policy in Our Time*. Chicago, IL: Rand McNally.

Lascoumes, Pierre, and Patrick Le Gales. (2007). "Introduction: Understanding Public Policy through Its Instruments - From the Nature of Instruments to the Sociology of Public Policy Instrumentation." *Governance* 20, no. 1: 1–21.

Lowi, T. J. (1972). 'Four Systems of Policy, Politics and Choice'. *Public Administration Review 32*, no. 4: 298–310.

Salamon, L. M. (1981). 'Rethinking Public Management: Third-Party Government and the Changing Forms of Government Action'. *Public Policy 29*, no. 3: 255–275.

Saward, M. (1990). 'Cooption and Power: Who Gets What from Formal Incorporation'. *Political Studies 38*: 588–602.

Woodside, K. (1986). 'Policy Instruments and the Study of Public Policy'. *Canadian Journal of Political Science 19*, no. 4: 775–793.

Chapter 9

Organizational tools

Organizational-based policy instruments include a broad range of governing tools which rely upon the use of government and non-governmental institutions and personnel to affect policy output delivery and policy process change. There is a wide variety of *substantive organizational tools* available to affect both the production and consumption/distribution of goods and services in society. However, these generally fall into two main types, depending on the proximity of their relationship to government and, hence, the ability of the government to control the effects of their utilization: direct government and quasi-governmental or societally based organizational tools. *Procedural organizational tools* generally involve techniques such as the organization and reorganization of government agencies and policy processes in order to affect key parameters of governmental activity and that of the policy communities' governments face in making public policies.

The use of each type of organization-based tool is closely associated with a different mode of governance. Direct government tools, for example, are a principal component of legal modes of governance, while quasi-governmental tools are a feature of corporatist modes. Procedural organizational tools are commonly used to construct market and network governance arrangements and architectures, which, in turn, often utilize non-state-based tools to attain government ends.

Substantive organizational instruments

There are many types of substantive policy instruments which rely for their effectiveness upon the organizational resources of governments and non-governmental agencies and actors. Most involve (and rely primarily) on the use of government personnel to directly achieve government goals, usually operating in structures created and controlled by governments. These are commonly 'direct' government organizations, that is, owned and operated by the state, but can also include 'indirect' or quasi- or parastatal ones, the best-known example of which is the state-owned or 'public enterprise' – which itself comes in many shapes, sizes, colours, and flavours (Bernier 2011).

DOI: 10.4324/9781003343431-13

Direct government

The direct use of government agencies for substantive policy purposes involves the 'delivery of a good or service by government employees, funded by appropriations from government treasury' (Leman 1989, 2002). This is what has sometimes been referred to as 'the forgotten fundamental' (Leman 1989) within policy instrument studies, as its ubiquitous nature is often ignored in studies focusing on more esoteric kinds of tools.

Within this general type of direct government organizational tool, there are several common forms or subtypes.

Line departments

In most countries, government agencies undertake a wide variety of tasks on a direct basis. These include, but are certainly not limited to, those listed in Table 9.1.

These services are provided at all levels of government (central or federal, provincial, state, or regional, as well as urban or local) in slightly different configurations in different countries. Unemployment, welfare, or social security payments, for example, can be the task of central governments in some countries and eras and of state, provincial, or local governments in others.

Typically, modern government agencies follow what is known in the public administration literature as a Weberian 'monocratic bureaucracy' form of organization (Brubaker 1984; Beetham 1987). This is a type of organizational structure first systematically described and analyzed by the German political sociologist Max Weber in his early twentieth-century work *Economy and Society*. Weber argued that although bureaucratic forms of organization had a long history, a significant change had occurred in the modern era as such organizations came to be viewed as providing services to the public rather than being the property of a monarch or emperor to do with as they pleased. The main characteristics of a modern government agency, in Weber's view, were:

- Personnel are appointed on the basis of a merit system of appointment, retention and recruitment.
- Office holders do not own the office in which they work but hold it subject to the provisions of the merit system.
- Those offices tend to be organized in a hierarchical fashion with a relatively small span of control and multiple levels.

Activities in the agency operate according to the rule of law – office holders are not above the law and must operate within its limits (including provisions for their accountability – via some form of a 'chain of accountability' to representative assemblies in modern liberal democracies who actually establish and promulgate laws.

(Albrow 1970; Weber 1978)

Table 9.1 Tasks typically undertaken by government agencies

Task	Examples
Facilitating commerce	Mint, standards of weights and measures bureaus
Managing public lands	Commissioners of public lands, ministries of lands and parks, or environment or natural resources
Constructing public works	Departments of public works – airports, highways
Research, testing, and statistics	National statistical agencies
Law and justice	Courts, solicitor general or attorney general offices, corrections and prisons and policing
Technical assistance, record-keeping	Farm extension, ministries of agriculture, and libraries, national archives, national libraries
Healthcare	Ministries of health – hospitals, Clinics, dentists, nursing, home care
Social services	Ministries of welfare and social, family, or community services
Education and training	Ministries of education, post-secondary education, colleges, and universities, technical and training institutes
Labour relations	Ministries of labour and labour relations
Marketing	Tourism, ministries of small business, and ministries of trade and commerce
Defence	Ministries of defence, army, navy, air force, and coastguard
Supplying internal government needs	Ministries of supply and services, Queen's printers
Finance	Ministries of finance and treasury boards
International affairs	Ministries of external or foreign affairs

Source: Adapted from Hodgetts, 1973.

What are commonly referred to as 'line' departments (in order to distinguish them from central, headquarters, or 'staff' units) typically have this 'classic' hierarchical Weberian monocratic bureaucratic form. That is, such units are typically organized in a pyramidal shape linking offices of civil servants in various branches and sections to a single department head, such as a Department of Health or a Department of Highways. A subvariation of this is the 'ministry', a form in which typically multiple pyramids of departments culminate in a single head (for example, a Ministry of Lands, Parks and Housing) or an 'agency', which operates with some autonomy of managerial control (Verhoest et al. 2010).

Modern states have grown dramatically through the creation and expansion of ministries, departments, and agencies in areas such as defence, in transportation, and later, in areas such as social welfare, education, and health provision. This has resulted in the conversion of many sectors from legal modes of governance based on little government goods and service delivery to ones featuring larger and more active state organizations, often with a monopoly over the goods and services they provide.

These forms of government organization are the 'workhorses' of publicly provided goods and service delivery in most modern states. They can be very large (the US Department of Defense, for example, has close to two million employees, including approximately 750,000 civilians) and can be subdivided into hundreds of separate branches, bureaus, sections, and agencies. They employ the most personnel and deliver by far the largest percentage of state-provided goods and services in virtually all forms of modern government.

The 'government employees' employed in line departments are typically civil or public servants, whose salaries are paid out of general tax revenue. In most liberal-democratic countries, these are unionized and well-paid positions, and the use of public servants to directly deliver public services is often an expensive proposition, which in itself discourages its use. This is not the case in many other countries, where poorly paid officials may supplement their wages illegally through various forms of corruption ('kickbacks', bribes, 'service' payments, expediting 'fees', and the like), undermining the efficiency and effectiveness of this tool.

How well these officials are educated and trained and what kinds of facilities and information they have to work with also affect their capacity and competence, and these factors, along with cost, can play a significant role in their use within a policy design (Brunsson 2006). Countries or sectors with well-resourced administrative systems regarded as competent by their citizenry are more likely to feature smaller and more efficient direct government service provision in their policy designs than countries with corrupt or inefficient civil services, which tend to be large and bloated, with redundant and wasteful positions and expenditures.

Central support agencies

A second kind of organizational policy tool involves agencies which are very similar in appearance to line departments but often act more like private companies, delivering services within governments rather than to external constituencies. Some of these are very old (like government stationers and printers), while others (like government systems and information technology units) are much more recent. Many of these agencies are quite large, and since they often serve functions similar to private companies, they are, and have often been, primary targets for government efforts to save money by contracting out or privatizing government services – that is, they are simply turned into 'firms' supplying government services by severing their funding through general appropriations revenue and establishing autonomous boards of directors. Cost issues are typically a major factor affecting their creation and inclusion in policy designs.

Social and health insurance and pension plans

Other kinds of organizational forms also exist. Social and health insurance and pension schemes and unemployment insurance, for example, are used in many countries to provide services, such as elderly income support and healthcare, and are also often government organization–based schemes, ones in which all individuals in certain categories are mandated to make payments to a government agency or commission which acts, usually, as a monopoly insurance provider for that group (Katzman 1988; Moss 2002).

Some of these schemes, of course, are among the largest areas of government expenditure and are virtually identical in organizational form to direct government organizational tools, given their universal and mandated nature – with the main difference being that programme funds come from dedicated insurance payments rather than general tax revenue. These schemes are generally very high profile and targeted to specific kinds of outputs, such as pension or social security payments. They are often intended to be revenue-neutral, although any short-term shortfalls in these outlays typically have to be made up by governments.

They also can provide large pools of capital which governments can use to finance infrastructure and other kinds of investments. As such, they are very popular and found throughout the world, although their configuration and the extent of private sector involvement vary greatly from country to country. Countries which do not have such schemes typically cite reasons related to costs or intrusiveness upon already-existing private sector programmes as a reason not to use them.

Quasi-governmental organizational forms

Quasi-government agencies have an essentially bureaucratic organizational structure and exist largely as Weberian forms of administration – although some are structured in a more 'business-like' fashion, with fewer rules and regulations guiding their behaviour than government departments and agencies. These include the following main types.

Public enterprises and other corporate forms

Public enterprises, or 'state-owned enterprises' (SOEs), are the most common and well-known type of quasi-governmental substantive organizational tool. There are many different definitions of public enterprises, with different levels of public ownership ascribed to these organizations. Hence, for example, in Canada, the Ontario Auditor's Act defines a 'public enterprise' as

> a corporation which is not an agency of the Crown and having 50 percent or more of its issued and outstanding shares vested in the government or having the appointment of a majority of its Board of directors made or approved by the Lt. Gov in Council thus including a specified level of ownership and a means of control within the definition itself.
>
> (Prichard 1983)

SOEs undertake or have undertaken a wide variety of tasks in many jurisdictions (see Table 9.2).

Perry and Rainey (1988) developed an exhaustive typology of these kinds of government organizations by examining the different types of ownership, sources of funding, and mode of social control exercised over them. The key feature of these organizations, however, is that they have a corporate form and are not administrative agencies. That is, they typically operate under separate legislation or under general corporate legal principles, and government control is exercised less directly as a function of government share ownership, typically through voting control over appointments to the company board of directors – who usually can be removed 'at pleasure' by the government – thanks to their ownership of company stock. The board of directors then hires and fires senior management so that government control is indirect and 'arm's-length', unlike the management and control of direct government administrative agencies.

Some public enterprises can raise and borrow money on their own authority, while others are limited in their sphere of independence and must seek funding or permission to borrow from governments. Similarly, some are free to set whatever prices they would like for their products, while others must seek government permission to alter prices and may be subsidized to provide a good or service at below market value. While government share ownership can drop below 50 percent and still exercise control if the remainder of the shares is widely held, it is more common for a government to own 50 percent or more of voting shares (in fact, it is very common for them to own 100 percent, often in a so-called 'golden share' scheme, where there is only one share of the company and the government owns this). There is also a growing number of 'mixed' enterprises with joint public–private or multiple government ownership

These companies can be exceedingly large, although they can also be much smaller, in some cases limited to one or two factories or offices.

Table 9.2 Examples of tasks undertaken by public enterprises (Canada – twentieth century)

Task	Example (Canada, twentieth century)
Housing	Canadian Mortgage and Housing Corporation
Finance	Bank of Canada, Small Business Development Bank, Caisse de Depot et Placement de Quebec
Wartime production	Canadian Arsenals
Transportation	Canadian National Railways, Via Rail, Air Canada/ Trans-Canada Airlines, St Lawrence Seaway Co., BC Ferries, Northern Transportation Company Ltd
Strategic industries	Atomic Energy of Canada Ltd, Petro-Canada
Communications	Canadian Broadcasting Corporation, Radio-Canada
Cultural industries	Canadian Film Development Corporation, National Film Board, National Museum Corps
Utilities	SaskTel, Hydro Quebec, Ontario Hydro, and BC Hydro
Infant industries	Petrosar, Athabaska Tar Sands, Canadian Development Corporation
Sick industries	Skeena Cellulose, BC Resources Investment Corporation
Property management	British Columbia Building Corporation
Regional development	Prince Rupert Coal Corporation, DEVCO, Cape Breton Development Corp
Lotteries and vice	BC Liquor Stores, Société des Alcools de Quebec, Casino Nova Scotia, Lotto-Canada
Local utilities	Translink, Edmonton Telephones
Marketing boards	Canada Wheat Board, British Columbia Egg and Milk Marketing Board and Freshwater Fish Marketing Board

Source: Adapted from Vining and Botterell. 1983.

Sovereign wealth funds, holding the proceeds of oil and gas, or pension revenues in countries such as Singapore and Dubai, for example, are among the largest firms in the world in terms of assets and can control hundreds of billions of dollars in investments (Elson 2008), while large public hydroelectrical or petrochemical utilities in countries such as Canada, Norway, Mexico, Iran, and Venezuela also rank first among companies in those countries based on size of assets controlled (Laux and Molot 1988).

The use of state-owned enterprises is common in many situations where governments wish to undertake specific kinds of goods and service delivery, but in a less-bureaucratic and more corporate fashion. Governments prize the high levels of automaticity, intrusiveness, and visibility, as well as the generally low cost and ability of public enterprises to be precisely targeted to different sectors and policy areas. However, there have been many efforts to privatize these companies or move their ownership from the government to the private sector, as some governments have attempted to shift from corporatist to more market modes of governance or cut costs or reduce their balance sheets or levels of debt by transferring these to the private sector (Savas 1989).

Many of these efforts have been successful in sectors where competition exists, such as efforts to privatize marketing boards, product-producing companies, and property management (Savas 1987; Laux 1993), but have often foundered in other areas where the privatized corporation has simply become a privately owned monopoly service provider. This has often been the case with efforts to privatize large-scale utilities such as water, electricity, or public transportation providers, where natural monopoly conditions often exist (Chapman 1990; Gayle and Goodrich 1990; Bos 1991). In these cases, these companies have often been re-nationalized and returned to the public sector or re-regulated through the creation of regulatory oversight agencies and mechanisms to rein in their monopoly behaviour (see Chapter 9) (Mees 2005; Leland and Smirnova 2009). Policy designers now very much take these contextual circumstances into account in proposing or recommending either the creation or privatization of SOEs.

Organizational hybrids (quangos and SOAs)

In recent years, numerous other hybrid forms of indirect government organizations have also been developed and implemented in many jurisdictions. These have often been proposed in situations where governments would like to privatize or contract out government services but where there is not a competitive market, thereby limiting the utility of outright sale or divestment by a government (Mathur and Skelcher 2007).

Examples of these types of tools include so-called 'special operating agencies' (SOAs) (Koppell 2003; Birrell 2008) which were established in many countries in the 1980s and 1990s in the effort to grant more autonomy to central service agencies and remove them from day-to-day government control. This was typically done by 'outsourcing' whatever services could be secured from a competitive external marketplace while allowing agencies providing those goods and services which could not be so relocated, such as confidential or high-security printing and data storage activities, to charge real prices to purchasers and to retain their earnings and make their own reinvestment decisions (Aucoin 2006; Flumian et al. 2007).

A second type of hybrid is the so-called 'quasi-autonomous non-governmental organization', or *quango*, an organizational form in which a non-governmental agency is established and given a grant of authority by a government to provide a particular good or service (Hood 1986b). These can be precisely targeted, and many airports, ports, and harbours, for example, are run by such 'independent authorities', which rely on governments for their monopoly position but which are answerable to their own boards for their activities rather than to the government itself (Kickert 2001). These agencies are usually then able to charge their own prices for the good or service they provide, retain their earnings, and raise funds on capital markets for investments, removing these items from government books and balance sheets (Flinders and McConnel 1999; Lovink 1999; Advani and Borins 2001).

There can be serious principal–agent problems with these kinds of agencies, however, which can affect their use in many fields (Koppell 2003). Maintaining the arm's-length nature of the relationship of public enterprises and quangos to government is difficult, for example, when their decisions and actions, such as expanding an airport or closing one, may impact a large section of the populace. And such agencies may not have enough autonomy for governments to avoid the consequences of any scandals or other problems associated with them which many in the media and elsewhere will still attribute to lax government oversight, no matter the legal niceties about who owns what and, thus, who is responsible for what.

That is, these relationships can be either too close (day-to-day interference) or too distant (agencies become distant and aloof powers unto themselves). Utilizing this form of substantive organizational tool can also be very expensive and linked to unpopular actions with political and economic consequences for governments – such as price increases, political scandals, and high-profile financing and operational issues. Many public agencies also do not have to face the discipline of the market in terms of meeting shareholder or investor expectations for profitability and hence lack at least this incentive to operate in a cost-efficient manner, raising difficulties for the governance of specific sectors of government activity (Kernaghan 1993; Ford and Zussman 1997; Flumian et al. 2007). These kinds of visibility and cost issues discourage the inclusion of these agencies in many policy designs.

Public–private partnerships, commissioning, and contracting out

More recent efforts on the part of some governments to offload legal and financial responsibility for specific kinds of goods and service delivery by having them delivered through the private or quasi-governmental sector have evolved into several distinct forms of organization which are more private than public, with the public sector acting mainly as a purchaser of goods and services provided by private companies (Grimshaw et al. 2001; Grimsey and Lewis 2004; Greener 2006).

One typical form of such activity is 'contracting out', or outsourcing, mentioned earlier, in which internal provision of some good or service is simply replaced with a source external to government (Zarco-Jasso 2005). Contracting is probably the most well-known such activity and involves governments in reducing the level of direct state involvement in the provision of public services, including internal state services, through the replacement of civil servants and internal procurement processes with contractual arrangements with, usually, non-governmental organizations, primarily businesses (Ascher 1987; Vincent-Jones 2006).

Various forms of contracting out exist, such as the PPPs, or public–private partnerships, discussed in more detail later, which have grown in popularity in areas involving large-scale infrastructure investments, whereby private firms absorb many investment costs and construct or rehabilitate infrastructure projects in water, highways, dams, and other such areas in exchange for long-term contracts to operate and profit from them (English and Skellern 2005; Vining et al. 2005). Other, less-rigorous forms of contracting out exist in areas such as healthcare, education, and prisons, in which contracts may not involve large investments and profit sharing but rather simply remove major expenditure areas, such as penitentiaries, from government books and budgets (Thadani 2014; Roehrich et al. 2014).

In the case of contracting, many supporters of the concept have noted significant limitations which can prevent contracting from functioning effectively. The 2016 Nobel Prize in Economics, for example, was awarded to two economists who specialize in detailing the significant flaws and limits of contracting in areas such as prisons and healthcare (Hart 2017; Holmström and Milgrom 1991). Their concern was with the difficulty encountered by governments in enforcing quality control in such contracts when the nature of the service provided (i.e. its quality) is dependent on difficult-to-monitor interactions between, for example, patients and doctors or prisoners and prison guards. However, many other criticisms of such partnerships exist (Newman 2014) which highlight the need to carefully negotiate realistic contracts and deal with the information asymmetries and knowledge gaps linked to them, as well as other issues, such as difficulties encountered cancelling contracts or preventing contractees from simply reneging on their contracted obligations (Jensen 2017).

Contracting out can be more complicated if a non-governmental provider does not exist for a particular product or service, so that a government must first, or simultaneously, create a non-governmental provider (Brown et al. 2008). Outsourcing of highway and railway maintenance in many countries in the 1980s and 1990s, for example, involved government managers creating their own firms, which then bid on and received government contracts to provide already-existing maintenance services previously provided by the government agencies they managed. Often, those companies then immediately hired former government workers and, in some cases, used former government equipment to provide the same service, often with very little savings to government, save that those costs became contract costs and governments could show a reduction in their levels of employment (McDavid and Clemens 1995).

More recently, this form of activity moved to the capital goods sector with the development of so-called 'P3s', or 'public–private partnerships', in which governments encourage private sector firms to build and operate public infrastructure, such as schools, office buildings, hospitals, and sports facilities, and even prisons and transportation infrastructure, such as bridges and roads, in return for a government guarantee of a long-term lease or use agreement with the provider (English and Skellern 2005). These so-called 'supply, build, operate' agreements again often involve few savings for government, save the carrying (capital) costs of buildings which instead appear as rent, allowing a government to claim it has not grown in terms of overall levels of asset ownership. The net effect of this activity is essentially to remove capital costs from government budgets while retaining the service (Rosenau 1999; Boase 2000).

Many different kinds of such partnerships exist, such as collaborative partnerships with NGOs to control hospital admissions for the disabled, operational partnerships with companies and other governments to share costs for many of the items discussed earlier, and contributory partnerships, where governments may provide funding without necessarily controlling the use of such funds, as occurs when matching funds are provided for local or community-based environmental improvement projects (Kernaghan 1993; Daniels and Trebilcock 1996; Hodge and Greve 2007). Some of these arrangements with social groups rather than the private sector are sometimes referred to as 'commissioning' rather than 'contracting out', although the net effect and outcome are the same.

Commissioning

Commissioning is a recently recognized collaborative technique which, as Taylor and Migone (2017) put it

> generally refers to a more strategic and dynamic approach to public service design and delivery with a clear focus on aligning resources to desired outcomes by injecting greater diversity and competition into the public service economy. By creating public service markets, the expertise and resources of the private and not-for-profit sectors can be harnessed and leveraged through new business and delivery models.

Commissioning sometimes goes well beyond traditional procurement and outsourcing agendas (Tanner 2007; Macmillan 2010; Martikke and Moxham 2010), with the aim of increasing service levels from both private and community partners by involving 'third sector' actors, such as NGOs, in both service target formulation and design ('co-design'), as well as service delivery ('co-management'). The provision of stable funding and ongoing interactions with government funding agencies, it is argued, allows the capacity of third sector actors to be enhanced at the same time that co-design and co-management ensure that outcomes match the expectations of clients rather than agencies (Bovaird et al. 2014).

Commissioning suffers from many capacity issues, however. Although popular in some countries and sectors in recent years as examples of 'collaborative' or 'joined-up' government, such schemes often stretch the resources of non-profit or volunteer organizations and can result in inefficient or incompetent goods and services delivery (Evans et al. 2005; Riccucci and Meyers 2008; Smismans 2008; Tsasis 2008). These kinds of cost and reliability issues increasingly have affected considerations of such tools and their inclusion in policy designs.

Again, as Taylor and Migone (2017) also note:

> This means that the various organizations involved redefine their relations with the public administration on one level, with the clients/ users of the services on another and finally with each other. A critical element in this relationship is the creation of high-level trust relations among the stakeholders. This trust will affect the flow of information and help in the creation of a contestable environment where multiple parties can move away from hindrances to outcome-based approaches such as overly legalistic contracts, enable the devolution of meaningful autonomy to those who are ultimately accountable and responsible for the delivery of services.

These new relationships can also modify established sets of government–NGO relationships in unintended ways, such as when increased competitiveness of non-profit organizations results in decreased cooperation among the providers (Buckingham 2009; Mills et al. 2011).

Co-production

Many of these collaborative-type relationships involve a form of 'co-production'. *Co-production* is a shorthand term for a variety of governance arrangements which involve citizens in the production and delivery of public services.

In the United States, these ideas generated interest among public administration scholars in the 1970s and the 1980s (Parks et al. 1981; Brandsen and Pestoff 2006) and experienced a revival in the decades after the turn-of-the-century (Pestoff et al. 2012). The idea has since been picked up and studied by scholars around the world (e.g. Whitaker 1980; Parks et al. 1981; Ostrom 1996; Alford 2002; Brandsen and Pestoff 2006; Prentice 2006; Bovaird 2007; Pestoff and Brandsen 2009; Pestoff et al. 2012).

First described in detail by Elinor Ostrom (Parks et al. 1981) in her work on community policing in the 1960s, the term has been expanded and popularized by Victor Pestoff and Taco Brandsen in their many books and writings in the years since then (Brandsen and Pestoff 2006; Pestoff et al. 2012).

Originally, *co-production* was narrowly defined as the 'involvement of citizens, clients, consumers, volunteers and/or community organizations in producing public services as well as consuming or otherwise benefiting from them' (Alford 1998: 128). Drawing on the experience of countries in Scandinavia in areas such as parent–teacher associations, Brandsen and Pestoff highlighted the extent to which many governance arrangements, even those thought to be purely hierarchical, such as public schooling, in fact combine aspects of hierarchical or state-based governance with elements of civil society mobilization (Pestoff 2006).

In early studies of activities such as parent–teacher interactions, this involvement in co-production activity was typically voluntary, meaning, it existed as a positive externality reducing production and delivery costs of public services. This made it very attractive as a tool to governments seeking cost reductions in public service delivery, especially ones favourable to notions of 'social enterprise' and enhanced community participation seen as an end- or good-in-itself (Parks et al. 1981; Salamon 1981, 1987).

Although co-production emerged as a concept that emphasized citizens' engagement in policy designs and service delivery, its meaning has evolved in recent years to include both individuals (i.e. citizens and quasi-professionals) and organizations (citizen groups, associations, and non-profit organizations) collaborating with government agencies (Alford 1998; Poocharoen and Ting 2015). In this sense, as public management studies have showed, non-governmental organizations can act as effective facilitators of the participation by individual citizens, while managerial reliance on trust and shared responsibility can discourage competitiveness and foster knowledge sharing among participating organizations (Pestoff and Brandsen 2010; Poocharoen and Ting 2015).

Two aspects of the use of co-production as a policy tool are critical. First, at the macro-level, governance arrangements, actors, and their interaction matter to co-production success, just as is the case with any policy tool, highlighting the need to combine policy and public management thinking in order to achieve service delivery success. Second, at the meso and micro level, some balancing of state and societal roles is required if co-production is to be sustained (Howlett 2000c, 2004a).

Like all others, co-production also has a downside as a policy tool. In the case of co-production, it has long been recognized that expectations of free labour from co-producers may not materialize (Sorrentino 2015; Brudney and England 1983), and schemes to incentivize co-producers through payments are susceptible to all the usual harms of public expenditures, including corruption, clientelism, and goal displacement, among others (Howlett et al. 2017).

Procedural organizational instruments

Substantive tools, of course, are only one half of the uses toward which government and non-governmental organizational resources can be put. The second use is procedural. This involves the use of the organizational resources such as personnel, staffing, institutionalization, and internal procedures to alter or affect policy processes in order to better achieve general government aims or specific programme activities.

It bears repeating that these tools are neither direct nor indirect goods and service delivery mechanisms, as are their substantive counterparts, but rather affect procedural activities, generally efforts aimed at creating or restructuring policy community structure and/or behaviour through government leadership or 'network management' efforts.

As Agranoff and McGuire (1999: 21) note, this latter activity involves 'network managers' in 'selecting appropriate actors and resources, shaping the operating context of the network and developing ways to cope with strategic and operational complexity'. The key dimensions or tasks involved in these kinds of network management activities include the identification of potentially compatible network actors, given the issue at hand; limiting potential conflicts that would hinder flexibility; recognizing legal requirements; balancing political objectives/conflicts with policy objectives; and assigning costs in implementation.

That is, in any policy process, policy managers need to work with the structure and operation of any network which already exists in the area; recognize potential new actors and limit the role of ineffective actors; balance their time and resource commitments (money, technology, expertise, etc.); maintain the focus of the network in achieving goals; and build trust between actors/reduce possible conflicts (Mandell 1994, 2000; Agranoff 1998; Agranoff and McGuire 1999; Koppenjan and Klijn 2004; Wu et al. 2010). In order to achieve these ends, various kinds of organization-based network management tools can be used. Several of the most common of these are set out next.

Network management tools

There are many different types of procedural tools linked with the use of specific government organizational resources which can affect various aspects of policy subsystem behaviour in policy processes.

Staff or central (executive) agencies

This is an old form of government organization, one in which a small coordinating government agency, rather than one which directly delivers services to the public, is created to centralize and coordinate government initiatives in different areas. Such 'staff' or 'central' agencies are generally created as a means to control other administrative agencies and are often linked very closely to the political executive (Bernier et al. 2005). In Westminster-style parliamentary systems, for example, older examples include Privy Council offices and treasury board secretariats, while newer ones include presidential, premier, and prime minister's offices, ministries of state, communication units, intergovernmental secretariats, and various kinds of implementation units (Chenier 1985; Savoie 1999; Lindquist 2006).

Although small (even most prime minister's offices, until recently, had less than 100 personnel, most of whom handled correspondence), these are central coordinating units which exercise a great deal of control over other bureaucratic agencies through their links to the executive and to the budgetary and policy processes in government. They have seen much growth in recent years as political executives have sought to re-establish control over far-flung administrative apparatuses (Campbell and Szablowski 1979; Rhodes and Weller 2001; Bevir et al. 2003; Bernier et al. 2005).

Unlike line departments, these staff or central agencies are less- or non-hierarchical, flatter organizations typically staffed by political appointees, although others also employ permanent officials as well. Key officials are chiefs of staff, principal secretaries, and specialized positions, such as a clerk of the Privy Council or a cabinet secretary. These agencies play a major and increasing role in designing and coordinating policies and policy-making, ensuring accountability to legislatures, and controlling the budgets, activities, and plans of line departments and ministries. They often have a strong research orientation and deploy various kinds of personnel and resources in a variety of organizational settings in order to vet and develop policy options and tool uses (Migone and Howlett 2022).

Tribunals and other quasi-judicial bodies

Other kinds of procedural tools exist which are designed to help manage or process policy issues, especially those related to dispute adjudication and the processing of various kinds of claims against government ministries or officials. These are typically created by statute and perform many administrative functions, such as hearing appeals concerning licencing (e.g. of pesticides), certification (of personnel or programmes), and permits (e.g. for disposal of effluents). Appointed by government, they usually represent, or purport to represent, some diversity of interests and expertise needed to deal with complex policy issues and concerns.

Administrative hearings conducted by these tribunals typically unfold in a quasi-judicial fashion. These hearings are bound by rules of natural justice and legal procedures dictated by statutory provisions concerning administrative behaviour and processes. The decisions of tribunals are often designed to be binding on the ministry in question but may be subject to various political, administrative, and judicial levels of appeal. Public hearings may also be statutorily defined as a component of these administrative processes. However, in most cases, proceedings are held at the discretion of a decision-making authority, and public hearings are often 'after the fact' public information sessions rather than being true consultative devices (Grima 1985; Stewart and Sinclair 2007).

In the framework of public administration and public policy-making, tribunals are directed toward securing compliance with administrative edicts and the achievement of identified standards of behaviour by both governmental and non-governmental actors. They can be precisely targeted and are an important component of legal modes of governance. They are generally low cost and often nearly invisible, despite often having an important influence on many aspects of policy-making and policy implementation.

Creating or reorganizing government agencies

Another fairly commonly used procedural organizational tool is to establish new government agencies or reform existing institutions in order to focus or re-focus state and societal activities on specific problems or issue areas (Goetz 2007; Durant 2008). Setting up a new government ministry for technology or a new research council to promote advanced technologies such as biotechnology, e-technologies, or other high-technology sectors, for example, is a common action on the part of governments wanting to target a new area of activity for further development (Hood 2004; Lindquist 2006; van Thiel 2008). However, such actions are highly visible and, if repeated too often, quite costly. They are also quite intrusive and, as a result, are proposed and used only infrequently (Fleischer et al. 2023).

Establishing analytical units

New analytical units such as those policy shops created in many jurisdictions in the 1970s and 1980s in order to promote formal policy analysis and what is now referred to as 'knowledge-based' or 'evidence-based' policy-making, are good examples of procedural organizational tools (Prince 1979; Prince and Chenier 1980; Chenier 1985; Hollander and Prince 1993; Lindquist 2006).

In addition to the policy shops previously mentioned, some governments have also set up internal think tanks or research institutes or, more recently, 'policy labs' in order to provide policy advice to governments (Dobuzinskis et al. 2007; Marchildon 2007; Wellstead 2020; Wellstead et al. 2021). Many government departments and agencies now have these kinds of specialized policy units designed to generate studies and reports which can influence or help persuade both government officials and non-governmental actors of the merits of government plans. These agencies also often employ outside consultants to bring additional expertise and knowledge to policy formation, implementation, and evaluation (Schwartz 1997; Perl and White 2002; Speers 2007). The knowledge they generate is used to inform internal policy-making processes and also to garner support for government positions from outside groups (Whiteman 1985, 1995).

These agencies can be precisely targeted and are generally low cost and have low visibility. However, their impact on policy-making can raise the ire of stakeholders and others in market, corporatist, and network forms of governance, while other agencies in more legal modes also find them to be rivals. Such considerations have dampened enthusiasm for such units in many jurisdictions and sectors and reduced their appeal in policy designs in recent years.

Establishing clientele units

New administrative units in areas like urban affairs, science, technology, and other areas flourished in many governments in the 1970s, as did new environmental units in many countries in the 1980s and 1990s; they were joined by units dealing with areas such as youth and small business in the 1990s, while in the post-1990 period, other new units were developed in countries such as Canada and Australia to deal with pressing issues, such as aboriginal affairs, and in many countries to support and promote areas such as multiculturalism, women, and immigration. Human rights units dealing with minorities and the disabled are good examples of network mobilization and activation occasioned by this kind of government organizational (re)engineering (Malloy 1999, 2003; Teghtsoonian and Grace 2001; Teghtsoonian and Chappell 2008; Osborne et al. 2008).

In general, these agencies undertake the kinds of management and policy development functions set out in Table 9.3. They are very popular in network governance modes, given their generally low cost but higher visibility than

Table 9.3 Analytical agency network managerial tasks

1	Vertical and horizontal coordination
2	Overcome institutional blockages, such as federalism and divisions of power
3	'Mainstreaming'
4	Building commitments
5	Building legitimacy/developing visions and agreement on alternatives
6	Building coalitions
7	Structuring NGO activity, for example, lobbying activities

Source: Adapted from Mandell, (2000)

policy labs and other such entities, which underscores and highlights the significance attributed to government efforts in the areas concerned.

Establishing government reviews, ad hoc task forces, commissions, inquiries, and public hearings

A sixth common procedural organization-based tool used by governments is the establishment of an *ad hoc* government review. These range from formal, mandated, periodic reviews of legislation and government activity by congressional or parliamentary committees and internal administrative bodies to more *ad hoc* processes, such as task forces or inquiries designed to activate or mobilize network actors to support government initiatives (Gilmore and Krantz 1991; Bellehumeur 1997; Marchildon 2007; Sulitzeanu-Kenan 2007, 2010; Rowe and McAllister 2006).

These are typically temporary bodies, much shorter-term and often more issue-related than institutionalized advisory committees, and are often created as instruments to consult a variety of interests with regard to economic and other areas of planning activity. These range from the presidential or royal commissions to those created at the departmental level. Presidential and royal commissions are the most formal and arm's-length and, therefore, are the most difficult for governments to control and predict and therefore are used less often (Maxwell 1965; Doern 1967; Clokie and Robinson 1969; Wilson 1971; Chapman 1973; Flitner 1986; Salter 1990; Jenson 1994).

Task forces have similarly been created in many jurisdictions for planning, consultation, or conflict resolution concerning many specific issues. The task force may be invoked by a government when there is an area of conflict in which different groups have different interests and perspectives or where they require more information in order to arrive at a decision or judgment (Marier 2009; Rowe and McAllister 2006). They are generally easier to set up and report faster than more formalized inquiries.

The subject matter of an *ad hoc* commission is typically urgent, of concern to more than one ministry and level of government, and is the subject of some controversy (Resodihardjo 2006; Sulitzeanu-Kenan 2010). They are invoked at the discretion of government and are often subject to many political, economic, and social pressures. Indeed, the very initiation of the commission is likely to have been the product of concerted pressure by some public groups. But as Chapman (1973: 184) noted, 'commissions may also play a significant political role and are often used as a method for postponing to an indefinite future decision on questions which appear to be embarrassing but not urgent'. Employment of these instruments for this purpose can thus result in serious legitimation problems for governments utilizing these policy tools, given their high level of visibility (Heinrichs 2005; Hendriks and Carson 2008; Stutz 2008; Marier 2009).

Public participation through *hearings* is the most common type of public or network consultation in many sectors (Rowe and Frewer 2005). Hearings vary by degree of formalization and when they occur in a policy process.

The most effective and influential are often flexible processes that are geared toward policy formulation, such as project reviews or environmental assessments, but the most common are rigid processes that take place in or after the implementation stage of a process, such as a formal policy evaluation exercise (Dion 1973; Baetz and Tanguay 1998; Edelenbos and Klijn 2005). Public hearings are often mandated by legislation and most often occur after a decision has been taken – that is, purely as information and/or legitimation devices. Actual instances of open, truly empowered public hearing processes are very rare (Riedel 1972; Grima 1985; Torgerson 1986).

Although sometimes used for other purposes such as information collection or blame attribution, these tools are often also used to overcome institutional 'blockages' and veto points such as those which are commonly found in federal–state or intergovernmental relations or in interdepartmental jurisdictional struggles (Ben-Gera 2007). They can also help bolster the capacity of groups to become more involved in the policy process if funding is extended to their participants, thereby promoting network governance (Robins 2008). They can be precisely targeted and are generally low-cost. However, their high level of visibility can cause problems for governments and results in their less-frequent appearance in policy designs than would otherwise be the case (Rowe and Frewer 2005).

Legislative and executive oversight agencies

This category of organization-based procedural tools also includes specialized agencies with very different policy-making functions, such as arm's-length independent auditor-generals or access to information commissioners, which are units typically attached to legislatures, providing some oversight or control over executive branch activities (Campbell-Smith 2008). Administrative procedures mandating oversight agency reviews of government actions are very common in some jurisdictions (McCubbins and Lupia 1994; McCubbins et al. 1987), especially if these are linked to ongoing monitoring of funding and budgetary issues (Hall 2008).

These units are usually fairly small, inexpensive, and highly visible, and there has been a proliferation of them in recent years dealing in areas such as corruption, human rights, and the promotion of ethnic and gender equality (Malloy 2003; Graycar 2015; Graycar and Prenzler 2013).

Conclusion: organizational tools – the forgotten fundamental in policy design studies

Practical experience and ideological predilections have shaped the substance of much of the debate on governance and the tools of government, ranging from preferences for democracy, popular participation, and collaboration to concerns about budget deficits and public sector inefficiencies in hierarchy-based systems. These have often driven preferences for the use of specific forms of governance, from hierarchical ones to market- or network-based ones.

In recent years, however, for a variety of reasons, a strong preference for shifts toward non-hierarchical forms of governance, coupled with discontent with the results of market-based reforms in the 1970s–1990s, has led to increasing attention being paid to different kinds of more civil society or networked forms of governance, often referred to by the shorthand term 'collaborative governance' (Meuleman 2009). These tendencies are discussed in more detail in Chapter 13.

Direct organization-based implementation tools are generally costly and have high visibility. This is because they rely on government personnel funded by appropriations from general revenue raised through taxes or royalties, although some are also funded from market revenue stemming from the sale of goods or services. The use of tax-based funding makes the use of public servants expensive in the sense that governments tend to have a limited capacity to tax citizens to pay for services and incur opportunity costs no matter which activity they choose to adopt. It can also lead to governance failures, as the link between system outputs and inputs (expenditures and revenues) is usually not clear, providing the opportunity for funds to be misallocated and effort misspent, all in the fishbowl environment of public government (Le Grand 1991).

However, in some countries, additional sources of revenue – such as those accruing from natural resources rents or 'royalties', especially from oil and natural gas activities in many states in the contemporary era – can make the expenses involved in direct delivery appear less onerous for the public at large, and in such circumstances, such tools are much easier for governments to establish and maintain. It is also the case that some publicly delivered goods and services can be charged for – for example, through highway or bridge tolls, or publicly run electricity, fuel, or food services, among many others – and can be priced like any other private good or service, helping to explain why many resource-rich countries have large public sectors and why many countries of all types have large public sectors and state-owned enterprises.

Much attention has been focused in the past three decades on the privatization of public goods and service production and distribution facilities and organizations, and many efforts have been made to replace chargeable publicly provided goods ('toll' or 'club' goods, such as toll bridges or publicly run recreational facilities) (Potoski and Prakash 2009) with privately supplied ones. This has been done largely in the effort to improve productivity or reduce the burden on taxpayers and governments of the wages of public servants involved in direct government provision (Dunleavy 1986; Ascher 1987; Cook and Kirpatrick 1988; Donahue 1989; Finley 1989; Cowan 1990; Hanke and Walters 1990; Heald 1990; Connolly and Stark 1992).

Many new hybrid and non-state practices, from contracting to partnerships, were also a key component of 'new public management' (NPM) thinking in the 1980s and 1990s in many countries and are a key component of many contemporary efforts to promote 'public–private partnerships' and 'collaborative government' (Linder 1999). Many of these innovations in organizational forms, from special operating agencies to quangos, private–public partnerships, and various kinds of hybrid organizations, have emerged largely in the effort to reduce the size of existing state organizations and transform some sectoral activities from legal and corporatist to market or network modes of governance (Hardiman and Scott 2010). This is done in the name of improving the efficiency of service delivery or in order to try to reduce the resource burden large public service delivery agencies place on budgets and taxpayer loads (Verhoest et al. 2007; O'Toole and Meier 2010).

Efforts at policy reform have been omnipresent in many developed and developing countries over the past several decades and have often featured efforts to reduce the number of state-based tools and shift their activities toward either hybrid instruments or, in some cases, away from state-based organizations altogether. Many of these efforts have featured waves of management reforms and administrative re-structuring, including privatizations, de-regulation, and re-regulation and the like (Ramesh and Howlett 2006). 'Anything but the government', for example, was a popular sentiment in public policy reform for at least two decades (Christensen and Lægreid 2008). These efforts led to the articulation and promotion of several alternative modes of governing to more traditional 'hierarchical' or state-led ones.

Many of these techniques are 'market-based' and constitute efforts to replace government activity with private sector actions (Savas 1987). However, others are focused less on zero-sum notions of state–market relations but rather involve more complex ideas about involving 'civil society' actors more directly in 'collaborative' policy-making, administration, and implementation (Brudney 1987; Salamon 1989), and these developments have promoted the frequent appearance of small scale experiments in alternate instruments and policy designs, although much less often their realization in practice or at scale.

These efforts have generally been less successful than often thought or alleged. Most successes have come in either small-scale direct service privatizations or in single-industry company privatizations, which have generally not altered earlier governance modes (Verhoest et al. 2010). And significant areas of public expenditure and effort such as healthcare and education, for example, have generally proved immune to privatization efforts, given their overall cost structures, mandatory service delivery nature, and high levels of citizen support (Le Grand 2009).

Often lost in the effort to identify alternative tools to these traditional, direct government has been the understanding of the demerits of these kind of collaborative governance arrangements. All collaborative tools are vulnerable to specific kinds of failures due to their inherent vulnerabilities and capacity and accountability issues. Policy-makers and advisors need to understand not only the nature of the problem they are trying to address and the skills and resources they have at their disposal to address it but also the innate features of each potential governance tool and the capabilities and competences each requires in order to operate at a high level of performance (Choi et al. 2020).

How specific government capabilities and competences can be bolstered or augmented by collaborative arrangements when governance reforms are contemplated or implemented will vary from case to case, depending on the distribution of available capacities in 'partner' organizations and upon the capacity of the state in terms of carrying out appropriate network management activities.

Despite their real or perceived cost, and in spite of many efforts to create or replace them with other forms of service and goods delivery, direct delivery of goods and services by public agencies remains 'the forgotten fundamental' of implementation instruments and policy designs. However, it is sometimes over-looked that 'old-fashioned' government agencies are still the most common and pervasive policy instrument in most sectors (Leman 1989; Aucoin 1997; Olsen 2005). Even in the ostensibly most private sector–oriented market governance systems (like the USA or, more recently, New Zealand), direct government goods and service production usually reaches close to 50 percent of gross national product (GNP) – that is, half of the dollar value of all goods and services produced in a country in one year – while direct civil service employment typically hovers in the area of 15–20 percent of the labour force but can also be much higher (Christensen and Pallesen 2008; Derlien 2008; Busemeyer 2009). The difference between the two figures has to do with the fact that many expenditures are composed of transfers to individuals which can involve large sums but only a small administrative overhead – for example, unemployment insurance or old age security payments.

Procedural organizational instruments have also been growing in frequency of appearance in conjunction with these reform efforts. Government reorganizations are increasingly common, and these reorganizations and the new agencies often created alongside them often are intended to use government organizational resources to refocus government efforts and interactions with policy community/network members rather than directly improve the delivery of particular types of goods and services (Herranz 2007; Bache 2010).

As Peters (1992a) noted, re-organization of existing departments and agencies serves to refocus government efforts and reposition government administration within policy networks, bringing together policy community members to reconsider the effectiveness of network management activities (Banting 1995; de la Mothe 1996), improving management of complex areas by restructuring relationships (May 1993; Metcalfe 2000), and can insert government actors between competing private actors in networks by, for example, creating consumer departments to sit between producers and (un) organized consumers (Bache 2010). These moves are often accompanied by the increasing use of government reviews and inquiries, as well as consultative conferences and other similar organizational forms for stakeholder and public consultation (Crowley 2009)

Readings

Alford, J. (1998). 'A Public Management Road Less Travelled: Clients as Co-Producers of Public Services'. *Australian Journal of Public Administration 57*, no. 4 (1 December): 128–137.

Bellehumeur, R. (1997). 'Review: An Instrument of Change'. *Optimum 27*, no. 1: 37–42.

Bernier, Luc, Philippe Bance and Massimo Florio, eds. (2020). *The Routledge Handbook of State-Owned Enterprises*. Routledge International Handbooks. New York: Routledge.

Bovaird, T., I. Briggs and M. Willis. (2014). 'Strategic Commissioning in the UK: Service Improvement Cycle or Just Going Round in Circles?' *Local Government Studies 40*, no. 4 (4 July): 533–559.

Brandsen, T. and V. Pestoff. (2006). 'Co-Production, the Third Sector and the Delivery of Public Services'. *Public Management Review* 8 (December): 493–501.

Cairns, B., M. Harris and P. Young. (2005). 'Building the Capacity of the Voluntary Nonprofit Sector: Challenges of Theory and Practice'. *International Journal of Public Administration* 28: 869–885.

Cantor, R., S. Henry and S. Rayner. (1992). *Making Markets: An Interdisciplinary Perspective on Economic Exchange*. Westport, CT: Greenwood Press.

Fledderus, J., T. Brandsen and M. E. Honingh. (2015). 'User Co-Production of Public Service Delivery: An Uncertainty Approach'. *Public Policy and Administration 30*, no. 2 (1 April): 145–164.

Goldsmith, S. and W. D. Eggers. (2004). 'Designing the Network'. In *Governing by Network: The New Shape of the Public Sector*. Washington, DC: Brookings Institution, 55–92.

Hatanaka, M., C. Bain and L. Busch. (2005). 'Third-Party Certification in the Global Agrifood System'. *Food Policy 30*: 354–369.

Hood, C. (2004). 'Controlling Public Services and Government: Towards a Cross-National Perspective'. In C. Hood, O. James, B. G. Peters and C. Scott (eds.), *Controlling Modern Government; Variety, Commonality and Change*. Cheltenham, UK: Edward Elgar, 3–21.

Howlett, M., A. Kekez and O.-O. Poocharoen. (2017). 'Understanding Co-Production as a Policy Tool: Integrating New Public Governance and Comparative Policy Theory'. *Journal of Comparative Policy Analysis: Research and Practice 19*, no. 5 (20 October): 487–501.

Kelman, S. J. (2002). 'Contracting'. In L. M. Salamon (ed.), *The Tools of Government: A Guide to the New Governance*. New York: Oxford University Press, 282–318.

Kernaghan, K. (1993). 'Partnership and Public Administration: Conceptual and Practical Considerations'. *Canadian Public Administration 36*, no. 1: 57–76.

Leman, C. K. (2002). 'Direct Government'. In L. M. Salamon (ed.), *The Tools of Government: A Guide to the New Governance*. New York: Oxford University Press, 48–79.

Migone, A. and M. Howlett. (2012). 'From Paper Trails to DNA Barcodes: Enhancing Traceability in Forest and Fishery Certification'. *Natural Resources Journal 25* (Fall): 421–441.

Olsen, J. P. (2005). 'Maybe It Is Time to Rediscover Bureaucracy'. *Journal of Public Administration Research and Theory 16*, no. 1: 1–24.

Peters, B. G. (1992). 'Government Reorganization: A Theoretical Analysis'. *International Political Science Review 13*, no. 2: 199–218.

Poocharoen, O. and B. Ting. (2013). 'Collaboration, Co-Production, Networks: Convergence of Theories'. *Public Management Review 18* (December): 1–28.

Posner, P. L. (2002). 'Accountability Challenges of Third-Party Government'. In L. M. Salamon (ed.), *The Tools of Government: A Guide to the New Governance*. New York: Oxford University Press, 523–551.

Riccucci, N. M. and M. K. Meyers. (2008). 'Comparing Welfare Service Delivery among Public, Nonprofit and For-Profit Work Agencies'. *International Journal of Public Administration 31*: 1441–1454.

Savas, E. S. (1989/90). 'A Taxonomy of Privatization Strategies'. *Policy Studies Journal 18*, no. 2: 343–355.

Stanton, T. H. (2007). 'The Life Cycle of the Government-Sponsored Enterprise: Lessons for Design and Accountability'. *Public Administration Review 67*, no. 5: 837–845.

Stanton, T. H. and R. C. Moe. (2002). 'Government Corporations and Government-Sponsored Enterprises'. In L. M. Salamon (ed.), *The Tools of Government: A Guide to the New Governance*. New York: Oxford University Press, 80–116.

Vining, A. R., A. E. Boardman and F. Poschmann. (2005). 'Public – Private Partnerships in the US and Canada: 'There are No Free Lunches'''. *Journal of Comparative Policy Analysis 7*, no. 3: 199–220.

Chapter 10

Authority-based policy tools

There are many types of policy instruments that are based not on the organizational resources of government but on their authority. These are often central features of many policy designs in which governments wish to set various standards of conduct and then exercise 'legitimate coercion' in attaining them (Frieberg 2018). All these kinds of tools involve and rely primarily upon the ability of governments to direct or steer targets in the directions they would prefer them to go through the use of the real or perceived threat of state-enforced sanctions. While treasure resources, discussed in Chapter 11, are often used to encourage 'positive' behaviour – that is, behaviour which is aligned with government goals – and authoritative actions can be used for this purpose, the latter are more often used in a 'negative' sense, that is, to prevent or discourage types of behaviour which are incongruent with government expectations (Ajzen 1991).

The use of the coercive power of the state to achieve government goals through the control or alteration of societal (and governmental) behaviour is the essence of *regulation*, one of the most common types of governing instrument found in this category and the one most compatible with legal forms of governance.

With regulation, the government does not provide goods and services 'directly' as it would through the use of its organizational resources but rather allows this to occur in a controlled fashion through an intermediary – usually a private company or market enterprise, but also sometimes state-owned enterprises and various kinds of NGOs, such as churches, voluntary organizations and association, trade unions, and professional bodies (Mitnick 1978; Scott 2001; Abbott et al. 2017). Other procedural authoritative tools are also commonly deployed in the pursuit of effective network management and governance.

Substantive authoritative instruments

In general, all types of regulation involve the promulgation of more or less binding rules which circumscribe or alter the behaviour of particular target groups

DOI: 10.4324/9781003343431-14

(Hood 1986a; Kiviniemi 1986). As has been succinctly described by Barry Mitnick, this very often involves the 'public administrative policing of a private activity with respect to a rule prescribed in the public interest' (Mitnick 1978).

The rules that are created take various forms and include standards, permits, prohibition, and executive orders, among others.

Some regulations, like ones dealing with criminal behaviour, are *laws* and involve the police and judicial system in their enforcement. Most regulations, however, are *administrative edicts* created under the terms of enabling legislation and administered on a continuing basis by a government department or by specialized, quasi-judicial government agencies sometimes referred to as 'independent regulatory commissions', or IRCs (Rosenbloom 2007). In relatively rare cases, the authority to enact, enforce, or adjudicate regulations can also be delegated to private firms or NGOs in various forms of 'voluntary' or 'self-regulation'. All these types are set out, and their strengths and weaknesses in policy designs described, in what follows.

Laws

As mentioned earlier, laws are an important tool of modern government and the very basis of legal modes of governance (Ziller 2005). Several different types of laws exist, however. These include distinctions often drawn by legal scholars between private and public law, private civil or tort law and common law, public criminal and administrative law, and hybrids, such as class action suits, which combine features of public and private law. These different types of law vary substantially in terms of what kinds of situations they can be applied to, by whom, and to what effect (Keyes 1996; Scheb and Scheb 2005).

Laws can be thought of as 'regulations' since all involve the creation of rules governing individual behaviour (Williamson 1975, 1996a; Ostrom 1986). However, in the form usually discussed by policy scholars, 'regulation' is typically thought of as a specific form of public law – although it can also involve criminal and individual or civil actions – rather than being synonymous with the subject (Kerwin 1994, 1999; West 2005).

Keyes (1996) has usefully described six types of legal instruments used by governments when they wish to invoke their authority to try to direct societal behaviour (see also Brandsen et al. 2006). These are shown in Table 10.1.

Laws can prohibit or proscribe many kinds of behaviour (and encourage others either by implication or overtly) but, in order to move beyond the symbolic level, require a strong enforcement mechanism, which includes various forms of policing and the courts (Edelman 1964, 1988). A desire for high levels of compliance with laws on the part of governments requires a high level of scrutiny and thus some kind of ongoing, institutionalized, and regulatory presence within a government organization or agency: typically a line department such as a police department or some other similar administrative bureau with investigatory and policing powers.

But even here a considerable amount of variation and discretion is possible since inspections and policing can be more or less onerous and more or

Table 10.1 Six types of legal instruments

1	Statutes
2	Delegated legislation between levels of government
3	Decisions of regulatory bodies and courts
4	Contracts or treaties
5	Quasi-legislation, such as tax notices and interpretative bulletins
6	Reference documents, such as background papers, other legislation, standing orders, etc.

Source: Adapted from Keyes, 1996.

less frequent, can be oriented toward responding to complaints or actively looking for transgressions ('police patrols' vs 'fire alarms'), and can be focused on punishment of transgressions or prevention, in the latter case often with a strong educational component designed to persuade citizens and others to adopt modes of behaviour more congruent with government aims (McCubbins and Schwartz 1984; Hawkins and Thomas 1989; McCubbins and Lupia 1994; May and Winter 1999).

All laws are intrusive, and many are highly visible. A significant problem with the use of laws in policy designs, however, pertains to cost, lack of automaticity, and precision of targeting. With respect to the first two, while passage of a law is usually not all that costly, the need for enforcement is. Laws have a low degree of automaticity as they rely upon citizens' goodwill and perceptions of legitimacy for them to be obeyed. Inevitably, this will not ensure 100 percent compliance and will thus require the establishment of an enforcement agency, such as the police, customs agencies, immigration patrols, coastguards, and the courts. Precision of targeting is also an issue since most laws have general applicability and often cannot single out specific groups or targets for differential treatment. These problems have led to the use of alternate forms of regulation expected to reduce these costs and allow for improved targeting of specific actors, such as firms involved in specific kinds of economic activities, as well as superior monitoring and enforcement.

Direct government regulation

Regulation is a fundamental technique of legal governance. There are numerous definitions of *regulation*, but a good general one is offered by Michael Reagan (1987), who defines it as

a process or activity in which government requires or proscribes certain activities or behaviour on the part of individuals and institutions, mostly

211

private but sometimes public and does so through a continuing administrative process, generally through specially designated regulatory agencies.

Regulation is thus a prescription by the government which must be complied with by the intended targets; failure to do so usually involves a penalty, sometimes financial, but also often involving incarceration and imprisonment. Although citizens may not always be aware of their presence, among other things, regulations govern the price and standards of a wide variety of goods and services they consume, as well as the quality of water they drink and the air they breathe.

This type of instrument is sometimes referred to as 'command and control' regulation since it typically involves the government issuing a 'command' to some target group, followed by enforcement efforts to 'control' their behaviour. 'Control' thus refers to the need for governments to monitor and enforce target group activity in order for a 'command' to be effective.

This type of regulation is very common in many social and economic spheres and has often been put in place in order to encourage 'virtues' by discouraging or punishing 'vices', however those are defined at that time. Thus, the criminal law, for example, which prohibits or restricts different types of behaviour through the provision of penalties such as jail or fines is a kind of regulatory activity, as are common laws and civil codes, which do the same for different kinds of offenses. All countries have such systems which states develop and implement, usually relatively non-controversially (May 2002; Cismaru and Lavack 2007).

Although less significant in terms of the day-to-day lives of many citizens, much more attention has been paid in the policy tools literature to economic regulation which affects aspects of established markets for goods and service production by establishing standards, property rights, and licencing regimes governing commercial and industrial conduct. Such regulation is often resisted by target companies and industries if they feel it undermines their competitive position either domestically or internationally. It is sometimes difficult for governments to 'command and control' their targets if these targets resist regulatory efforts (Scholz 1991) or if governments do not have the capacity or legitimacy required to enforce their orders, and this conflict has inspired many studies and research into the sources, conditions, and preconditions of effective economic regulation (Baldwin and Cave 1999; Crew and Parker 2006).

Independent regulatory commissions

Direct administration of legislated rules and regulations is very common in government. However, in the economic realm, especially, it often raises concerns about issues such as corruption and patronage as well as concerns for the inefficiencies and distortions in market signals rule observation and evasion can incur for regulated actors. The abuse of administrative discretion to either ease enforcement in certain cases or administer it capriciously in others is generally controlled through associated procedural instrument deployment, such as audits, or the use of corruption agencies and commissioners. Other checks on administrative discretion usually exist through the court system, whereby those who feel they have been unfairly treated can often appeal administrative decisions and seek to overturn them (Jaffe 1965; Edley 1990). This can be a very time-consuming and expensive process, however, and several distinct forms of regulatory agencies with semi-independent, quasi-judicial status have been developed in order to avoid governance problems associated with direct departmental or agency-based regulation.

The most well-known of these is the *independent regulatory commission*, or IRC, which is used extensively in some countries, like the United States where it was created. Although some early exemplars of this instrument can be found in canal authorities in Great Britain and other European railway, highway, and transportation authorities of the eighteenth and nineteenth centuries, the IRC as it is currently known stems mainly from concerns raised in the post–Civil War USA about unfair practices in railway transportation pricing and access. These led to the creation of an innovative organizational regulatory form in the 1887 US Pendleton Act, which established the US Interstate Commerce Commission, a quasi-judicial body operating at arm's length from government, which was intended to act autonomously in the creation and enforcement of regulations and which remained in operation for over 100 years (until 1995) (Cushman 1941).

Independent regulatory commissions evolved from the transportation sector model to become common in many other sectors, not limited to those dealing with economic issues. They quickly moved into the production realm, and in the post–World War I era in many countries, IRCs were implemented in areas such as labour and industrial dispute regulation, as well as the commodity-based marketing boards mentioned earlier. In the post–World War II era, they were used to cover a range of emerging consumer and consumption issues, such as consumer rights, landlord–tenant interactions, human rights disputes, and others (Hodgetts 1973).

IRCs are 'semi-independent' administrative agencies in the sense that, as was the case with public enterprises, government control is indirect and exercised via the appointment of commissioners who are more or less difficult to remove from office (Stern 1997; Gilardi 2005b, 2005c; Jacobzone 2005; Majone 2005; Christensen and Lægreid 2007). These commissioners follow quasi-legal procedures and processes in arriving at more or less binding decisions.

Irene Wu has listed 11 aspects of the organization, staffing, and function of IRCs which make such agencies 'independent' (Wu 2008; Wonka and Rittberger 2010) (see Table 10.2).

IRCs are quasi-judicial in the sense that one of their main activities is adjudicating disputes over the interpretation and enforcement of rules – a task taken away from the courts in order to ensure that expertise in the specific activities regulated is brought to bear on a case and in the hope of more expert, timely, and predictable results in what are often very repetitive cases.

Table 10.2 Requisites for regulatory agency independence

1	An independent leader
2	Exclusive licensing authority
3	Independent funding
4	Private sector regulatees
5	Little movement of staff between industry and regulator
6	Consumer offices
7	Universal service offices
8	Notice-and-comment decision-making
9	Rules against gifts
10	Rules against conflicts of interest
11	Post-employment rules

Source: Adapted from Wu, (2008).

Decisions of independent regulatory commissions are still subject to judicial review, although often this is only in terms of issues relating to procedural fairness rather than the evidentiary basis of a decision (Edley 1990; Berg 2000; Lægreid et al. 2008; Lehmkuhl 2008).

With respect to targeting, including precision and selectivity among groups and policy actors, the information needed to establish regulation is less than with many other tools, because a government need not know in advance the subject's preferences, as is necessary in the case of some other instruments. It can just establish a standard, for example, a permitted pollution level, and expect compliance. This is unlike the situation with financial incentives, for example, which will not elicit a favourable response from regulatees unless their intended subjects have a preference for them (Mitnick 1980).

IRCs are relatively inexpensive, specialized bodies that can remove a great deal of the routine regulatory burden from both departments and the courts in many areas of social and economic life and are quite popular with governments wishing to simplify their agendas and reduce their need to supervise specific forms of social behaviour on a day-to-day basis.

As Berg (2000) and Stern and Holder (1999) noted, in addition to questions related to their level of independence or autonomy, additional design criteria include the clarity of their roles and objectives, their degree of accountability of governments or the public, their level and type of participation and transparency, and ultimately, their predictability in terms of being bound by precedents either of their own making or through judicial review (see also Berg et al. 2000).

Marketing boards

In the contemporary period, independent regulatory commissions are involved with many aspects of market behaviour, production, distribution, and consumption, as well as many areas of social life. Many specialized forms of such agencies exist, and one such use is the creation of 'marketing boards', or arm's-length regulatory bodies, often staffed by elected representatives of producers and granted specific rights to control prices and/or supply, thereby creating and enforcing pricing and supply regimes on producers. This has occurred primarily in areas affected by periodic bouts of over- or under-supply and can be found in areas such as bulk agricultural commodities, such as wheat or milk, which are very sensitive to price fluctuations, but also in areas such as liver and heart transplants subject to chronic supply shortages (Weimer 2007; Royer 2008). These boards typically act to ration and allocate supply quotas and set prices in order to smooth out supply fluctuations in the activity involved.

De-regulation

IRCs, and marketing boards, like more direct government regulation, have been the subject of efforts at *deregulation* in recent decades as some governments attempted to move some sectors away from legal and corporatist governance forms toward more market modes of operation. Some high-profile privatization and deregulation in transportation, telecommunication, and financial industries in many countries occurred as a result of these efforts (Levi-Faur 2003).

Understanding why deregulation occurs has proven to be a challenge to regulatory theorists, since many of the imperatives regarded as the source of regulation – such as industry collusion and the desire to retain market share through the erection of barriers to entry to new firms – continue to be vital in the deregulatory context (Crew and Rowley 1986). Some analysts have therefore searched for exogenous causes – such as foreign or technical pressures for regulatory harmonization (Derthick and Quirk 1985; Libecap 1986; Quirk 1988; Lazer and Mayer-Schonberger 2002; Garcia-Murillo 2005).

However, it must also be noted that at the same time that some deregulation has occurred, re-regulation of many sectors has also taken place. And as the discussion in this chapter has shown, an explosion of the use of procedural authoritative implementation tools has also occurred. While some of this activity can be traced to attempts to shift governance modes in various sectors, it is also the case that changes have occurred as policy design ideas and technologies have changed, resulted in different configurations of costs and other instrument attributes in some sectors, and sometimes undermining long-established policy styles and policy-making routines.

The reality is that there has been no across-the-board reduction in the use of more directive tools (Drezner 2001a; Vogel 2001; Wheeler 2001). Like privatization, deregulation is nowhere as widespread as claimed by both enthusiasts and critics (Iacobucci et al. 2006). Even in banking, the most globalized sector, there is little or no evidence of an overall decline of regulation, and the market and credit crises of 2008 have led to *increased* moves in a re-regulatory direction in many countries, from Iceland to the USA (Busch 2002; Harris 2004). Indeed, regulations have been expanded in many sectors to compensate for the loss of state control following privatization of public enterprises (Jordana and Levi-Faur 2004b; Braithwaite 2008), and IRCs are among the most favoured means of re-regulating previously deregulated or privatized industries and activities (Ramesh and Howlett 2006).

There are still some concerns about the use of this instrument in policy designs, however, linked to considerations of cost and visibility. The cost of enforcement by regulatory commissions can be quite high, depending on the availability of information, and the costs of investigation and prosecution in highly legalistic and adversarial circumstances can also be very large. Regulations also are often inflexible and do not permit the consideration of individual circumstances and can result in decisions and outcomes not intended by the regulators (Bardach 1989b; Dyerson and Mueller 1993). They quite often distort voluntary or private sector activities and can promote economic inefficiencies, for example. Price regulations and direct allocation, for example, restrict the operation of the forces of demand and supply and affect the price mechanism, thus causing sometimes-unpredictable economic distortions in the market place. Similarly, restrictions on entry to and exit from industrial sectors, for example, can reduce competition and thus have a negative impact on prices. Regulations can also inhibit innovation and technological progress because of the market security they afford existing firms and the limited opportunities for experimentation they might permit. For these and other reasons, they are often labelled as overly intrusive by many firms and actors.

Indirect government regulation

A third form of regulation is 'indirect regulation', in which third parties or 'regulatory intermediaries' (Abbott et al. 2017; Medzini and Levi-Faur 2023) conduct much of the regulatory activity rather than government or public agencies. There are several different types of such regulation, however, which vary in terms of their design attributes.

Delegated professional 'self'-regulation

One prominent form of such delegated regulation is professional self-regulation. This is a relatively rare form of regulatory activity which occurs when a government transfers its authority to license certain practices and discipline transgressors to non-governmental or quasi-governmental bodies whose boards of directors, unlike the situation with independent regulatory commissions, they typically do not appoint (Elgie 2006; Kuhlmann and Allsop 2008).

This form of delegated self-regulation typically involves legislatures passing special legislation empowering specific groups to define their own membership and regulate their own behaviour. Brockman (1998) defines it as

> the delegation of government regulatory functions to a quasi-public body that is officially expected to prevent or reduce both incompetence (lack of skill, knowledge or ability) and misconduct (criminal, quasi-criminal or unethical behaviour) by controlling the quality of service to the public through regulating or governing activities such as licencing or registration – often involving a disciplinary system (fines, licences, suspension or revocation) and codes of conduct/ethics, etc.

This occurs most commonly in the area of professional regulation, where many governments allow professions such as doctors, lawyers, accountants, engineers, teachers, urban planners, and others to control entrance to their profession and to enforce professional standards of conduct through the grant of a licencing monopoly to an organization such as a bar association, a college of physicians and surgeons, or a teachers' college (Tuohy and Wolfson 1978; Trebilcock et al. 1979; Tuohy 1992, 1999; Sinclair 1997). Typically, appeals of the decisions of delegated bodies may also be heard by the courts or specialized administrative tribunals (Trebilcock 2008).

The idea behind delegated regulation, as with independent regulatory commissions, is that direct regulation through government departments and the courts is too expensive and time-consuming to justify the effort involved and the results achieved. Rather than tie up administrators and judges with many thousands of cases resulting from, for example, professional licensing or judicial or medical malpractice, these activities can be delegated to bodies composed of representatives of the professional field involved who are the ones most knowledgeable about best practices and requirements in the field. Governments have neither the time nor expertise required to regulate multiple interactions between lawyers and their clients, teachers and students, or doctors and patients, for example, and a form of 'self-regulation' is more practical and cost-efficient.

Scandal in self-regulated areas such as business accounting in many countries in recent years, such as the Enron scandal in the US, however, can undermine confidence in a profession's ability or even willingness to police itself and can lead to a crisis in confidence in many aspects of delegated self-regulation (Vogel 2005; Bernstein and Cashore 2007; Tallontire 2007). Of course, any delegation of government regulatory authority can be revoked if misbehaviour ensues, and this has occurred in some areas from time to time.

Voluntary or incentive regulation

Another form of indirect or 'self-regulation' has a more recent history than delegated regulation and has been extended to many more areas of social and economic life. This is typically a form found in market governance systems in which, rather than establish an agency with the authority to unilaterally direct targets to follow some course of action with the ability to sanction those actors who fail to comply, a government instead tries to persuade targets to voluntarily adopt or conform to government aims and objectives.

Although these efforts often exist 'under the shadow of hierarchy' (Heritier and Lehmkuhl 2008) – that is, where a real threat of enhanced oversight exists should voluntary means prove insufficient to motivate actors to alter their behaviour in the desired fashion – they also exist in realms where hierarchies don't exist, such as the international realm, when a strong treaty regime, for example, cannot be agreed upon (Dimitrov 2002, 2005; Dimitrov et al. 2007).

A major advantage often cited for the use of voluntary standard-setting is cost savings, since governments do not have to pay for the creation, administration, enforcement, and renewal of such standards, as would be the case with traditional command-and-control regulation, whether implemented by departments or independent regulatory commissions. Such programmes can also be effective in international settings, where establishment of effective legally based governmental regimes can be especially difficult (Schlager 1999; Elliott and Schlaepfer 2001; Cashore et al. 2003; Borraz 2007). The Corporate Social Responsibility (CSR) movement around manufacturing and industry conditions in many countries is a good example of such initiatives (LeBaron et al. 2017).

Moffet and Bregha set out the main types of voluntary regulation (see Table 10.3) found in areas such as environmental protection.

Table 10.3 Types of voluntary regulation

1	Legislated compliance plans
2	Regulatory exemption programmes
3	Government–industry negotiated agreements
4	Certification
5	Challenge programmes
6	Design partnerships
7	Standards auditing and accounting

Source: Adapted from Moffet and Bregha. 1999

These tools attempt such activities as inducing companies to exceed pollution targets by excluding them from other regulations or enforcement actions, establishing covenants in which companies agreed to voluntarily abide by certain standards, establishing labelling provisions or fair trade programmes, providing favourable publicity and treatment for actors exceeding existing standards, promoting co-operation over new innovations, and attempting to improve standards attainment by targeted actors through better auditing and evaluation. These are all forms of what Sappington (1994) has termed 'incentive regulation'.

The role played by governments in voluntary regulation is much less explicit than in traditional direct or delegated regulation but is nevertheless present. Unlike the situation with command-and-control or delegated regulation, in these instances governments allow non-governmental actors to regulate themselves without creating specific oversight or monitoring bodies or agencies or empowering legislation. As Gibson (1999: 3) defined it:

> By definition voluntary initiatives are not driven by regulatory requirements. They are voluntary in the sense that governments do not have to order them to be undertaken . . . [but] governments play important roles as initiators, signatories, or behind-the-scenes promoters.

While many standards are invoked by government command-and-control regulation, others can be developed in the private sphere, such as occurs in situations where manufacturing companies develop standards for products or where independent certification firms or associations guarantee that certain standards have been met in various kinds of private practices (Gunningham and Rees 1997; Andrews 1998; Iannuzzi 2001; Cashore 2002; Eden 2009; Eden and Bear 2010).

These kinds of self-regulation, however, are often portrayed as being more 'voluntary' than is actually the case. That is, while non-governmental entities may, in effect, regulate themselves, they typically do so, as Gibson notes, with the implicit or explicit permission of governments, which consciously refrain from regulating activities in a more directly coercive fashion (Gibson 1999; Ronit 2001). As long as these private standards are not replaced by government-enforced ones, they represent the acquiescence of a government to the private rules, a form of delegated regulation sometimes refered to a regulation 'in the shadow of hierarchy' (Haufler 2000, 2001; Knill 2001b; Heritier and Eckert 2008; Heritier and Lehmkuhl 2008).

That is, as a 'public' policy instrument, 'self-regulation' still requires some level of state action – either in supporting or encouraging development of private self-regulation or retaining the 'iron fist' or the threat of 'real' regulation if private behaviour does not change (Cutler et al. 1999; Gibson 1999; Cashore 2002; Porter and Ronit 2006). This is done both in order to ensure that self-regulation meets public objectives and expectations (see, for example, Hoek and King's (2008) analysis of the ineffective self-regulation practiced by TV advertisers in New Zealand) and to control the kinds of 'club' status which self-regulation can give to firms and organizations which agree to adhere to 'voluntary' standards (Potoski and Prakash 2009).

As Delmas and Terlaak (2001) noted, joining or participating in voluntary schemes entails both costs and benefits to companies, which undertake detailed cost–benefit calculations about whether or not to join voluntary associations. This is one of the 'limits of virtue' which David Vogel (2005) noted in his studies of various corporate social responsibility (CSR) schemes in the late 1990s and first decade of the twenty-first century (see also Tallon-tire 2007; Steurer 2009; Natural Resources Canada 2003).

It is also the case that any possible savings in administrative costs over more direct forms of legal regulation must be balanced against additional costs to society which might result from ineffective or inefficient administration of voluntary standards, especially those related to non-compliance (Gibson 1999; Karamanos 2001; Henriques and Sadorsky 2008).

Certification

Certification is a term used to capture the activities of non-state actors involved in areas such as forestry, fisheries, organic foods, and other similar areas in which quality control and enforcement of standards is accomplished less directly than is the case with traditional command-and-control regulation through the use of private or non-governmental intermediaries (Cashore et al. 2004; Cutler et al. 1999; Gulbrandsen 2010; Abbott et al. 2017). In these cases, for a variety of reasons from cost to ideology, 'certification' of standards is undertaken by civil society organizations, such as the Forestry Stewardship Council or the Marine Stewardship Council, which lack the formal authority to compel business and industries to abide by regulatory standards but which utilize (often negative) publicity, boycotts, and other actions to encourage compliance (Cashore 2002; Pérez-Ramírez et al. 2012).

Certification is a form of 'self-regulation' which has grown substantially in recent years. Almost all products can be certified in this sense, although many do not need to be if consumers can themselves judge their quality and desirability. When information is lacking on, for example, the provenance or production techniques used in wine or food products such as olive oil, however, certification can enhance prices and encourage consumption, as occurs, for example, with the certification of 'pre-owned' (i.e. used) cars, electronic equipment, or artworks.

These tools are sometimes referred to as non-state market-based (NSMD) tools (Cashore 2002) since they do not rely upon state authority for their power and legitimacy to regulate private sector activity but rather do so through market activities such as product labelling and producer certifications, affecting consumer behaviour and preferences for, for example, organic produce or sustainably harvested timber, fish, or coffee, among others.

Although technically not 'public' policy tools in the sense that they are often fully provided by non-state organizations, states do allow these third-party standard-setting and reviewing organizations to operate and legitimate them by declining to take on these duties and tasks themselves. Thus, they exist in a netherworld in the private or civil society sector but operating with state blessing or acquiescence.

While it is debatable if they could work without the 'iron fist' of a threat of potential government regulation lurking in the background, it is clear that their impact and operation are through market mechanisms, affecting the supply and demand for products and services by affecting consumer views of their costs and benefits.

Such schemes rely heavily on the reputation of the certifier for honesty, accuracy, and precision. In the case of certification, legitimacy and trust are key aspects of the certifying organizations and predictors of the success of voluntary certification arrangements (Bernstein and Cashore 2007). Certification thus only functions effectively if trust exists between the public and certifiers and between the certifiers and certified companies and governments.

Concerns about second-class regulation or corrupt standards can easily undermine years of work building up a certified brand. Similarly, competing or duelling certifiers can also undermine existing schemes and lead to their ineffectiveness (Zelli et al. 2017). If their reputation is damaged, as has happened from time to time with products such as wine or olives in which additives were added or cheaper products substituted for expected ones, such schemes can collapse and require either substantial reform or government takeover, revealing their dependence on government, ultimately, to serve as the guarantor of quality.

Market creation and maintenance

Paradoxically, as it might seem from its title, another form of an indirect regulatory instrument used by the government is the use of other kinds of 'market-based' instruments by creating property rights where none previously existed, allowing private markets to undertake particular kinds of activities in particular ways preferred by governments (Hula 1988; Fligstein 1996).

These are activities, such as pollution prevention or climate change reduction efforts, in which governments establish property rights frameworks or regimes which establish various kinds of limits or prices for certain goods and services and then allow market actors to work within these 'markets' to allocate goods and services according to price signals (Averch 1990; Cantor et al. 1992).

Such schemes have often been proposed or exist in many areas related to environmental and resource policy, for example, from land and water use (Murphy et al. 2009) and bio-conservation (ecosystem services) (Wissel and Watzold 2010) to climate change–related greenhouse gas emissions control systems (Sovacool 2011). But they have also been used in areas such as fisheries and taxi services, in the form of individual transferable quotas (ITQs) or tradeable tokens (Pearse 1980; Townsend et al. 2006), which allow companies and individuals to purchase and trade certain rights to produce or harvest certain products while capping the total amount produced, thus effectively regulating these activities in an indirect way. These kinds of systems have been proposed for the control of greenhouse gas regulation, such as the 'cap and trade' systems created in the European Union and other countries associated with the Kyoto Protocol and other kinds of climate change mitigation efforts, although with mixed results (Heinmiller 2007; Voss 2007; Hahn 2008; Toke 2008; Pope and Owen 2009).

Few of these schemes have been implemented despite much publicity and their promotion by industry and government, due to the difficulties involved in setting prices and overall caps or limits on items such as pollutants, problems with leakage when companies evade caps, and poor enforcement in the system. While governments often want to use such techniques to transfer responsibility for activities to the private or non-governmental sector, the inability of governments to avoid the blame for problems with these systems, despite their ostensibly arm's-length character, makes them risky and sometimes unpalatable (Stavins 1998, 2001; Mendes and Santos 2008; Keohane and Victor 2011). Unlike traditional regulation, where the direct costs and risks of public administration are well-known, these market designs can be higher cost and much less automatic than often expected when they are suggested and promoted (Krysiak and Schweitzer 2010; Mickwitz et al. 2008).

Procedural authoritative instruments

Like with organization-based tools, there are also procedural authority-based instruments. These typically involve the exercise of government authority to recognize or provide preferential access or treatment in policy processes to certain actors over others – and hence often to fail to recognize others in those processes. This is accomplished by mandating certain procedural requirements in the policy-making process in order to ensure it takes certain views or perspectives into account when decisions are made, or reforms proposed.

These instruments perform a wide variety of network management functions (Agranoff and McGuire 1999), very often in order to gain support or marginalize policy opponents, but also to ensure representation of marginal groups and to ensure certain standards and standard practices are followed in policy choices (Goodin 1980; Saward 1992).

Policy network activation and mobilization authority-based tools

In terms of network management activities, many procedural authoritative tools are involved in the 'selective activation' of policy actors and/or their mobilization through the extension of special recognition in policy deliberations and other activities like judicial or administrative assessments and policy reviews. The key use of authority is in the extension of preferential access to decision-makers or regulators of certain views and actors and not others, or at least to a lesser extent (Doerr 1981).

Procedural authoritative tools attempt to ensure efficiency and effectiveness of government actions through activation of policy actor support. Networks may be structured, for example, through the creation of various advisory processes which rely on the exercise of government authority to recognize and organize specific sets of policy actors and give them preferential access to government officials and decision-makers (Pierre 1998; Hall and O'Toole 2004). These include advisory councils, *ad hoc* task forces and inquiries, consultations, and public hearings oriented toward extending special authoritative status to certain societal interests or 'stakeholders', that is, those actors with a financial or some other form of 'stake' in a particular state activity (Hall and O'Toole 2004).

Phillips and Orsini (2002) list the types of policy process activities which advisory committees undertake (see Table 10.4).

Table 10.4 Actions undertaken by procedural authoritative instruments

Problem identification
Mobilizing interest
Spanning and bridging activities
Claims-making
Knowledge acquisition
Convening and deliberating
Community capacity-building
Transparency, evaluation, and feedback

Source: Adapted from Phillips and Orsini. 2002.

Several distinct types of authoritative network management tools can be identified in this group. Prominent ones include the following list.

Advisory councils

Advisory councils are the best example of procedural authoritative instruments and are very common in market and corporatist governance arrangements. These are more or less permanent bodies established to provide advice to governments – either political-executive or administrative – and co-ordinate policy-making on an ongoing basis. They are often established on a sectoral (e.g. industry-specific, such as an automobile trade advisory committee) basis but also can be topical (e.g. biomedical ethics) (Gill 1940; Brown 1955; Smith 1977). These committees play a major role in many areas but are especially prominent in areas of new technologies, where they play a significant role in linking governments to various kinds of expert or 'epistemic' communities (Haas 1992; Jasanoff 1998; Heinrichs 2005; Dunlop 2009a).

The archetypal advisory council is a more or less permanent body used to institutionalize interest group members in government deliberations (Heinrichs 2005). They are at least partially, if not fully, co-optive in nature and intended to align the ideas and actions of the regulated group and the government ministry to which they are attached. However, they can also be more standalone and independent sources of expert advice to governments, such as science and technology councils, councils of economic advisors, and others (Phidd 1975; Doern 1971).

Smith (1977) and Brown-John (1979) identify eight main types of advisory committees commonly found in modern liberal-democratic governments. These are set out in Table 10.5.

Table 10.5 Types of advisory committees

1	General advisory committees – to discuss policy alternatives generated by government, comment on current policies, examine trends and needs, and suggest alternatives to status quo
2	Science and technology advisory committees – to provide expert advice in narrow specialist areas
3	Special clientele advisory committees – to assist governments to make and implement policies in special sectors of the economy or society
4	Research advisory committees – lengthy, research-oriented to tackle large questions
5	Public conferences – for example, citizens' assemblies, national forest congresses, etc.
6	Geographic-based advisory committees – to deal with geographic particularities, for example, in agriculture
7	Intergovernmental advisory committees – to coordinate between government levels
8	Interdepartmental committees – to achieve vertical and horizontal coordination in government

Sources: Adapted from Smith (1977); Brown-John (1979).

Brown (1955) lists several purposes of such bodies which stress their network nature (see Table 10.6).

These boards are generally very inexpensive and often almost invisible, although they can be quite powerful and influential. They can be precisely targeted and enhance the automaticity of government and are also viewed favourably by many stakeholders and policy participants. As a result, they

Table 10.6 Purposes of advisory boards

1   Source of advice

2   A source of support for regulators

3   A means of popularizing a regulatory regime

4   A 'listening post' for industry and government to listen to each other

5   A means of reaching an agreement and resolving conflicts between government and interests

6   An agency for special inquiries

7   A device for patronage

8   A set of ambassadors for an administrative agency

Source: Adapted from Brown (1955).

have proliferated in all governments in recent years. This proliferation has led in some countries to the passage of legislation to control and standardize the number of advisory committees and their behaviour. The US Advisory Committee Act (1972), for example, specifies membership and guidelines and standard operating procedures for these types of committees (Brown 1955; Cronin and Thomas 1970; Brown 1972; Smith 1977; Heinrichs 2005) (see Table 10.7), although many countries lack such fundamental mechanisms for ensuring transparency and accountability of such groups.

Table 10.7 US Advisory Committee Act (1972) criteria

1   Written charter explaining role of committee

2   Timely notice of committee meetings in federal register

3   Fair and balanced representation on committees

4   Sponsoring agencies prepare minutes of meetings

5   Open committee meetings to the public wherever possible

6   Provide public access to information used by the committee

7   Government given sole authority to convene and adjourn meetings

8   Committees terminated in two years unless renewed or otherwise provided by statute

Source: Adapted from Smith (1977).

Public consultation, stakeholder, and consensus conferences

In addition to more permanent bodies, governments can also organize shorter-term or longer-range mechanisms to provide input and legitimate government policy-making (Leroux et al. 1998). Increasingly, the role of the public in these processes has been expanded to include participation in the design of the consultation process as well as in making policy recommendations to the government (Abelson et al. 2003; Dryzek and Tucker 2008). Sometimes mandated by legislation, different levels of government also often elicit public involvement in policy deliberations through such forms as 'constituent assemblies" and 'mini-publics' (Pattberg 2023; Vrydagh et al. 2023) as well as administrative activities, such as regulatory monitoring and environmental impact assessment.

Abelson et al. (2003) have noted that these participation efforts can be classified by looking at the procedures, representation, and information involved and by looking at their outcomes. Key issues in the design of consultative processes are, first, who is involved and who is not (e.g. whether elites or the public are involved, or whether only stakeholders rather than the public, per se, are consulted) and who makes this determination, for example, government or representative groups (Howlett 1990).

Many of these efforts are structured as 'stakeholder' representative arrangements; although the term 'stakeholder' is very poorly defined and often unclear. Glicken (2000: 306), for example, defines it very broadly as: 'A stakeholder is an individual or group influenced by – and with an ability to significantly impact (either directly or indirectly) – the topical areas of interest', which covers a wide range of possible members.

It is also critical what resources are provided to members – such as access to funding, staff, politicians, information, or to witnesses in the case of inquiries (Salter and Slaco 1981) – and whether or not any recommendations they make are binding (Webler and Tuler 2000; Margerum 2008). Dion lists several of these design criteria in Table 10.8.

Table 10.8 Types of public consultation – design criteria

1	From the point of view of publicity: how private and secret these consultations are versus public, open, and transparent
2	From the point of view of official status: whether consultations are unofficial, semi-official, or official
3	From the point of view of origin: whether the consultations are 'organic' (traditional) or 'inorganic' (imposed)
4	From the point of view of imperiousness: whether participation is optional or compulsory

Source: Adapted from Dion (1973).

Consultations can cover an extraordinarily wide range of topics – from constitutional issues related to voting systems and the like (Kogan 2010) to much more mundane ones, such as city zoning changes. They are typically organized by government agencies, although in some jurisdictions, such as Australia, consultants specializing in the organization and delivery of consultation exercises have become much more prominent in recent years, leading to some concerns about their effects on the legitimacy and transparency of such arrangements (Hendriks and Carson 2008; Althaus et al. 2021; Levin 2023; Marciano 2023).

Conclusion: regulation – a very flexible instrument

The evolution of regulation as a key policy instrument in the toolbox of modern government is a well-known story. From the development of the principle of delegated legislation in the early years of the evolution of the modern state (Page 2001; Gilardi 2002; Thatcher and Stone-Sweet 2003) to the first creation of specialized quasi-judicial independent regulatory commissions in the USA after the Civil War (Huntington 1952; Eisner 1994a, 1994b), the gradual development of bureaucratic expertise and capacity in the social and economic realms is a defining characteristic of the legal and corporatist modes of governance found in many counties and a central feature in many policy designs (Berg 2000; Howlett 2002b, 2004b; Scherer 2008).

Debates about the merits of this development continue in many corners, however, especially in those economic sectors in which participants feel they could be organized along less-direct market lines. For example, a large literature exists on whether or not regulations serve the public or the private interest (Posner 1974; Stigler 1975a) and whether or not they contribute to economic efficiency by correcting market failures (Croley 2007) or instead create new government-driven ones (Wolf 1979, 1987; Le Grand 1991; Zerbe and McCurdy 1999). The discussion has generated a plethora of studies about the merits of particular types of regulation over others (Hawkins and Thomas 1989; Williams 2000; Ringquist et al. 2003), the problems of 'regulatory capture' – when the interests of regulated groups precede that of the public in regulatory decisions and activities (Laffont and Tirole 1991) – and the continued difficulties of legislative and judicial oversight of regulatory activities to avoid over-reach and duplication of effort (de Smith 1973; Angus 1974; McCubbins and Schwartz 1984; McCubbins and Lupia 1994; Gilardi 2005a).

This discussion has often linked regulatory instrument choices to larger issues such as levels of trust in government (Levy and Spiller 1994) and other aspects of administrative traditions and governance modes which favour or support certain kinds of regulation over others (see McAllister 2009; Kagan 2001; Klijn et al. 2010). A general tendency to shift regulatory activity from enforcement to persuasion, in recent years, for example, has been noted, but so have significant variations by nation and sector in these efforts (Pautz 2009; McAllister et al. 2010) as governments attempt to deal with targets' behaviour in complex coercion-avoidance-persuasion games (Scholz 1984, 1991).

The early 1980s were a turning point in the debate on regulation in many countries, as the idea that regulations were conceived and executed solely in the public interest came under heavy attack from a wide range of critics. Much of this criticism relied heavily on works by authors and economists of the Chicago (Stigler 1975b; Peltzman 1976; Becker 1983) and Virginia (Posner 1974; Landes and Posner 1975; Buchanan and Tollison 1984; Tollison 1991) schools of political economy who argued that many regulations were inefficient as well as inequitable. Governments led by right-wing politicians in many countries, such as Ronald Reagan in the USA and Margaret Thatcher in the UK, but also labour governments in New Zealand and elsewhere, further fanned popular sentiment against regulations by putting deregulation and the search for alternatives to traditional 'command-and-control' regulation at the centre of policy reform agendas designed to address declines in productivity and persistent inflation and high unemployment present at that time (Howlett and Ramesh 2006). Many governments began at this time to experiment with forms of 'voluntary regulation'.

Many so-called 'deregulation' measures, however, were common-sense reforms intended to iron out shortcomings, anomalies, and obsolescence in existing regulations rather than a response to any particular systemic pressure (Wilson 2003; Frischtak 1995).

The campaign for removal or at least weakening of many regulations is often led by businesses which find complying with them in new technological environments to be onerous. Their efforts often find ready support among voters, who have their own reasons for disaffection with outdated, inappropriate, and seemingly meaningless regulations which can impose costs on them for various services – such as telephones and television – which seem unwarranted. The regulators' own frustration with the costs of implementation further reinforces calls for reform.

Readings

Abbott, K. W. David Levi-Faur, and Duncan Snidal. (2017). "Introducing Regulatory Intermediaries". *The ANNALS of the American Academy of Political and Social Science 670*, no. *1* (1 March): 6–13.

Bryson, J. M. and B. C. Crosby. (1993). 'Policy Planning and the Design and Use of Forums, Arenas, and Courts'. In B. Bozeman (ed.), *Public Management: The State of the Art*. San Francisco, CA: Jossey-Bass, 323–344.

Cantor, R., S. Henry and S. Rayner. (1992). *Making Markets: An Interdisciplinary Perspective on Economic Exchange*. Westport, CT: Greenwood Press.

Cashore, B., G. Auld and D. Newsom. (2003). 'Forest Certification (Eco-Labelling) Programs and Their Policy-Making Authority: Explaining Divergence Among

North American and European Case Studies'. *Forest Policy and Economics 5*: 225–247.

Cook, D. (2002). 'Consultation, for a Change? Engaging Users and Communities in the Policy Process'. *Social Policy and Administration 36*, no. 5: 516–531.

Cordes, J. J. (2002). 'Corrective Taxes, Charges and Tradable Permits'. In L. M. Salamon (ed.), *The Tools of Government: A Guide to the New Governance*. New York: Oxford University Press, 255–281.

Crew, M. A. and C. K. Rowley. (1986). 'Deregulation as an Instrument in Industrial Policy'. *Journal of Institutional and Theoretical Economics 142*: 52–70.

Doern, G. B. (2004). 'Institutional and Public Administrative Aspects of Voluntary Codes'. In K. Webb (ed.), *Voluntary Codes: Private Governance, the Public Interest and Innovation*. Ottawa, ON: Carleton Research Unit on Innovation, Science and Environment, 57–76.

Eisner, M. A. (1994). 'Economic Regulatory Policies: Regulation and Deregulation in Historical Context'. In D. H. Rosenbloom and R. D. Schwartz (eds.), *Handbook of Regulation and Administrative Law*. New York: Marcel Dekker, 91–116.

Freiberg, A. (2018). 'Authority Tools: Pervasive, Persistent and Powerful'. In M. Howlett and I. Mukherjee (eds.), *Routledge Handbook of Policy Design*. New York: Routledge, 261–273.

Hall, T. E. and L. J. O'Toole. (2004). 'Shaping Formal Networks through the Regulatory Process'. *Administration and Society 36*, no. 2: 186–207.

Heinrichs, H. (2005). 'Advisory Systems in Pluralistic Knowledge Societies: A Criteria-Based Typology to Assess and Optimize Environmental Policy Advice'. In S. Maasen and P. Weingart (eds.), *Democratization of Expertise? Exploring Novel Forms of Scientific Advice in Political Decision-Making*. Dordrecht, Netherlands: Springer, 41–61.

Keyes, J. M. (1996). 'Power Tools: The Form and Function of Legal Instruments for Government Action'. *Canadian Journal of Administrative Law and Practice 10*: 133–174.

LeBaron, Genevieve, Jane Lister, and Peter Dauvergne. (2017). "Governing Global Supply Chain Sustainability through the Ethical Audit Regime." *Globalizations 14*, no. 6 (September 19, 2017): 958–975.

Lowndes, V. and C. Skelcher. (1998). 'The Dynamics of Multi-Organizational Partnerships: An Analysis of Changing Modes of Governance'. *Public Administration 76* (Summer): 313–333.

McCubbins, M. D., R. G. Noll and B. R. Weingast. (1987). 'Administrative Procedures as Instruments of Political Control'. *Journal of Law, Economics, and Organization 3*, no. 2: 243–277.

Medzini, R. and D. Levi-Faur. (2023). 'Self-Governance via Intermediaries: Credibility in Three Different Modes of Governance'. *Journal of Comparative Policy Analysis: Research and Practice* (20 January): 1–23.

Mitchell, R. K., B. R. Agle and D. J. Wood. (1997). 'Toward a Theory of Stakeholder Identification and Salience: Defining the Principle of Who and What Really Counts'. *Academy of Management Review 22*, no. 4: 853–886.

Pal, L. A. (1993). *Interests of State: The Politics of Language, Multiculturalism, and Feminism in Canada*. Kingston, ON: McGill-Queen's University Press.

Patberg, Markus. (2023). "Farewell to Constituent Power? The Conference on the Future of Europe, Citizens' Assemblies and the Democratic Minimum." *Global Constitutionalism*, October 11, 2023, 1–18.

Phillips, S. D. (1991). 'How Ottawa Blends: Shifting Government Relationships with Interest Groups'. In F. Abele (ed.), *How Ottawa Spends 1991–92: The Politics of Fragmentation*. Ottawa, ON: Carleton University Press, 183–228.

Pierre, J. (1998). 'Public Consultation and Citizen Participation: Dilemmas of Policy Advice'. In B. G. Peters and D. J. Savoie (eds.), *Taking Stock: Assessing Public Sector Reforms*. Montreal, QC: McGill-Queen's Press, 137–163.

Salamon, L. A. (2002). 'Economic Regulation'. In L. M. Salamon (ed.), *The Tools of Government: A Guide to the New Governance*. New York: Oxford University Press, 117–155.

Sovacool, B. K. (2011). 'The Policy Challenges of Tradable Credits: A Critical Review of Eight Markets'. *Energy Policy 39*, no. 2 (February): 575–585.

Townsend, R. E., J. McColl and M. D. Young. (2006). 'Design Principles for Individual Transferable Quotas'. *Marine Policy 30*: 131–141.

Vrydagh, Julien, Sophie Devillers, and Min Reuchamps. (2023). "The Integration of Deliberative Mini-Publics in Collaborative Governance Through the Perspectives of Citizens and Stakeholders: The Case of the Education Reform in French-Speaking Belgium." *Representation 59*, no. 1 (January 2, 2023): 95–116.

West, W. (2005). 'Administrative Rulemaking: An Old and Emerging Literature'. *Public Administration Review 65*, no. 6: 655–668.

Windholz, E. (2018). *Governing Through Regulation: Public Policy, Regulation and the Law*. London: Taylor & Francis.

Wu, I. (2008). 'Who Regulates Phones, Television, and the Internet? What Makes a Communications Regulator Independent and Why It Matters?' *Perspectives on Politics 6*, no. 4: 769–783.

Chapter 11

Financial or treasure-based tools

Financial substantive tools are not synonymous with all government spending, since much of this goes to fund direct service delivery and also support regulatory agencies (as well as to provide information, which will be discussed in Chapter 12). Rather, such tools are specific techniques of governance involved in transferring treasure resources to or from other actors in order to encourage them to undertake some activity desired by governments through the provision of financial incentives, or to discourage them through the imposition of financial costs.

Like organizational and authoritative tools, there are many different permutations of these instruments and mechanisms. In fact, they can be calibrated down to the decimal point, since they involve the transfer of money or goods and services with a calculable dollar value between governments and between governments and non-governmental actors and organizations. And as such, their exact configuration is virtually infinite in variety. Nevertheless, like organizational and authority-based tools, their basic types are few and categorizable according to what kind of treasure resource they rely upon to extract expected behaviour from targeted organizations, groups, and individuals. Transfers can be either in cash or tax-based but also can be made through a wide range of 'cash equivalents', for example, procurement, loan guarantees, insurance, or vouchers, among others. Both principal types and some of the many alternate means and variations of both substantive and procedural treasure-based tools are discussed next.

Substantive financial instruments

The use of treasure resources in policy designs in order to allow states to attain their substantive goals is, of course, very common. Modern liberal democratic states spend billions annually on many different programmes involving the use of these tools across a wide range of areas, from welfare

DOI: 10.4324/9781003343431-15

policy to health and economic policy, to name only a few. In some areas, such as industrial activity, some efforts have been made in recent years – through provisions of free trade treaties and the like – to restrict their use. Like the situation with privatizations and contracting out of government services and deregulation, these efforts have been only partially successful, often resulting in the transformation of cash-based incentives and disincentives to other forms of financial tools rather than their complete elimination or abandonment.

Cash-based financial tools

Grants, subsidies, and user fees

Haider defines *grants* as 'payments in cash or in kind . . . to lower units of government, non-profits or profit-seeking companies, NGOs (and individuals) to support public purposes' (Haider 1989: 94). All substantive grants are subsidies or 'unearned savings to offset production costs' and are one of the oldest forms of the financial tools through which governments pay companies, organizations, or individuals to do (or not to do – such as agricultural subsidies for not growing corn or wheat) some (un)desired form of activity (Lybecker and Freeman 2007). They are the 'carrot' in instrument and implementation models based on the idea of the use of 'carrots and sticks' (regulations or penalties by governments in their efforts to influence non-governmental actors).

Many, many such schemes exist, from the use of feed-in tariffs to promote the use of renewable energy alternatives, such as solar panels and wind power (DeShazo et al. 2017), to the payment of cash to parents to send their children to school in various kinds of 'conditional cash transfers', or CCTs, found in many countries from the Philippines, and Brazil to Ghana (Brooks 2015).

User fees are the most straightforward financial disincentive (one of the 'sticks' available to governments) as they, too, affect target behaviour through the use of treasure resources, but this time by increasing rather than decreasing the cost of doing some action.

While straightforward in principle, however, in practice the design of tools such as subsidies and user fees can be quite complex, depending on exactly what it is that a government wishes to accomplish through their imposition – for example, revenue generation, goods or service production or rationing, or some combination of the two – and upon how non-governmental actors actually react to such grants and charges (Deber et al. 2008).

These kinds of cash-based tools use the direct transfer of treasure resources from governments to some other actor or vice versa in the form of monetary payments. These vary along several dimensions. They can, to cite only a few examples, be large or small, a single instance or multi-year in nature, tax-deductible (which increases their size) or not, used alone or in combination with other instruments (for instance, in conjunction with the use of public enterprises in regional development programmes to promote local industry investment or hiring), matched or not by recipients and to what degree, or linked to some other item (e.g. a per capita grant) in a total subsidy package (Woodside 1979; Leeuw 1998; Haider 1989). They typically can be very precisely targeted down to the level of the individual and individual firm or plant and can be very precisely calibrated. They are also quite visible, as they appear in public accounts and are considered to be more intrusive than information-based tools (see Chapter 12), but less so than authority or organization-based ones. They can also be designed in such a way as to enhance their automaticity, although this is more the case with tax- and royalty-based payments, as discussed in what follows below.

Tax- or royalty-based financial instruments

The second main type of substantive treasure-based instrument involves those which are based not on direct cash transfers but rather on indirect transfers mediated through the tax system or, in some countries, through the royalty systems designed to capture natural resource rents. Using these systems, a government can spend or forego tax or royalty income they would otherwise have collected from an individual, organization, or firm, which serves as an incentive to targets to undertake the activity receiving favourable tax treatment, or, in the case of tools which increase taxes on certain kinds of activity, to not undertake that activity or to undertake less of it.

Tax- and royalty-based expenditures

Tax expenditures or 'tax incentives' come in many kinds. Maslove defined them as 'special provisions in the tax law providing for preferred treatment and consequently resulting in revenue losses (or gains)' (Maslove 1978; Surrey 1979). These can be 'paid in advance' and can be carried forward for numbers of years and, like cash-based schemes, can be 'matched' by other sources of funds, range in size and significance, and be used in conjunction with other instruments.

Different subtypes exist, depending on 'where' government tax revenue is forgone. *Tax incentives* generally involve deductions from corporate or personal income, meaning their actual effect on a target group is determined by the marginal rate of taxation individual persons or firms must pay. Their effect, therefore, varies from group to group. *Tax credits*, on the other hand, are direct deductions from taxes owed, and their size is typically the same regardless of the tax rate individual taxpayers or firms face. Tax credits are typically the only ones which can be 'negative', in the sense that they can be used to push a taxpayer's tax load beyond zero so that a refund (or real cash transfer) may ensue. However, most tax expenditures will only push a taxpayer's tax to zero, meaning, their effect also remains conditional on the amount of tax targets pay.

These same schemes can also be developed with transfers from non-tax-based revenue, such as resource royalty payments or other forms of economic rents, which can similarly be waived or reduced. Governments often, for example, promote oil and gas exploration by allowing energy companies to write off some portion of their exploration costs against royalties they would otherwise have to pay.

Excise taxes

Excise taxes are another treasure-based tool, one that acts as a disincentive for individuals, organizations. and groups to undertake specific actions and activities. Cnossen (2005: 2) defines these as 'all selective taxes and related levies and charges on goods and services'. They have several general purposes: (1) to raise revenue for general purposes, (2) to offset 'external costs', (3) to discourage consumption, and (4) to pay for public goods (Nowlan 1994).

Raising revenue through taxes is, of course, the oldest technique of government practiced, from taxes placed on road use by the Romans to the tea tax US colonists rebelled against at the Boston Tea Party. In this form, the funds raised by excise taxes typically support government actions of all kinds. Using taxes to offset costs of production – to pay for pollution clean-up or health consequences of tobacco use in order to correct production or consumption 'externalities', such as pollution or carbon emissions or ill-health, which otherwise would be passed onto the general public – is a much newer form and is more compatible with modern market modes of governance (Mandell 2008; Toke 2008; Pope and Owen 2009).

A similar effort involves so-called 'vice taxes' for activities such as gambling, alcohol consumption, lotteries, or more frequently, in recent years, various forms of 'virtuous' 'green' taxes, such as those designed to cover the cost of recycling car batteries or used oil or paint, or even returnable bottle deposits, all designed to offset the social costs of the activities concerned (Cnossen 2005; Eloi 2009). The use of motor fuel taxes to cover the cost of road construction or mass transit is an example of the fourth of Nowlan's purposes.

Such taxes generally aim to discourage the taxed activity by raising its price. This, of course, can be a mixed blessing for activities such as public transit and can often result in unintended consequences for items taxed in order to raise revenues, both in terms of taxpayer resistance and upset and in the often-unintended encouragement of the increased use of non-taxed items or substitute goods and services, such as an increase in motorcycle use if cars and fuel are heavily taxed.

Tax-based subsidies and disincentives are generally inexpensive to establish, although they require an extensive revenue collection and enforcement presence to avoid evasion and can be either highly visible, if added onto prices, or almost invisible, if included with posted prices. They can be targeted to specific kinds of goods and services and set up to be highly automated. They are generally considered to be quite intrusive by those paying them, however, which is the main reason they are often excluded from many policy designs.

Other kinds of financial tools

Both cash and tax or royalty-based transfers can provide financial incentives and disincentives to policy actors to undertake or refrain from undertaking specific activities encouraged or discouraged by governments. However, such encouragement and discouragement do not always require a direct or indirect cash transfer. Governments are also often able to provide financial incentives through the much less direct use of their spending powers to offset costs or provide additional benefits to policy targets. Several of the more prominent of these tools are discussed next.

Preferential or 'strategic' procurement

Preferential or 'strategic' procurement involves the use of government purchases to subsidize companies or investors which agree to abide by specific provisions of government contracts which reflect and seek to achieve government aims of various kinds. These can extend to preferential treatment for firms which, for example, employ the disabled or women, or ethnic or linguistic minorities, or produce 'green' or ecologically benign or beneficial products. But these also often extend to other areas, such as special favourable treatment for small businesses, in order to enhance their access to contracts; national defence contractors, in order to promote indigenous sources of military weapons and weapons platforms; and regional development schemes, in which, for example, investors receive government contracts if they agree to locate factories or distribution or other services in specially designated regions (Bajari and Tadelis 2001; Rolfstam 2009).

Such procurement schemes also often play a major part in efforts by governments to promote 'third sector' or volunteer and community group–based delivery of public services. In many cases, it may be illegal or unconstitutional for a government to directly deliver funding to such groups if they represent or are associated with activities such as drug use or prostitution or if they have a religious or 'faith base', which can violate constitutional limits separating church and state activities (Dollery and Wallis 2003; Black et al. 2004; Kissane 2007; Hula et al. 2007; Zehavi 2008). However, these groups may still be able to receive favourable treatment, such as in bidding for government contracts, making procurement an important part of their funding base, and of efforts to enhance their policy delivery capacity (Carmel and Harlock 2008; Chapman et al. 2008; Diamond 2008; Hasan and Onyx 2008; Walsh et al. 2008).

Like direct cash subsidies, many trade agreements attempt to ban procurement plans which favour domestic over international suppliers, but these provisions do not extend to favourable treatment for marginalized groups or individuals or to national security. Such procurement schemes, of course, by extending favourable treatment to some contractors, also act as a disincentive to non-favoured groups and firms, which are discouraged from bidding for contracts and other services to the extent of the subsidy provided (McCrudden 2004). The main advantage of such forms of subsidy over other forms of payments in these cases, however, is their low visibility, which encourages their use.

Favourable insurance and loan guarantees

Insurance or loan guarantees can also act as a subsidy to the extent that government backing helps secure loans by raising the reliability of borrowers, altering the types of borrowers who might otherwise fail to qualify for loans, or reducing interest payments and charges that individuals and companies would otherwise have to pay (Maslove 1983). The difference in cost constitutes a subsidy.

Such guarantees are very common in areas such as student loans, for example, in which governments agree to serve as the guarantor of loans to banks which otherwise would reject most students as too risky. They are also common in areas such as export development, whereby a government may provide insurance to a domestic firm to help it offset the risk of undertaking some action in a foreign country or provide a foreign company or government with assurance that a contract will be fulfilled by the supplying firm.

Some loans can also be made directly to individuals and firms on a 'conditionally repayable' basis, that is, whereby a loan turns into a grant if some conditions are successfully met, for example, in meeting employment targets for minority groups or the homeless. These tools are almost invisible, can be precisely targeted, and are often considered to be less-intrusive than grants and direct cash or tax transfers, making them a popular choice for many policy designs.

Vouchers for public services

Another such tool is the voucher. Vouchers are 'money replacements' provided by governments to certain groups in order to allow them to purchase specified goods and services in specific amounts. These are typically used when a government does not trust someone to use a cash transfer for its intended purpose, for example, with vouchers provided to low-income or welfare recipients for food (food stamps), childcare, or hotel/housing payments.

Some governments such as Denmark and Sweden, however, also use these to provide some freedom of choice for consumers to select particular kinds of public services (usually education) in order to promote competition within monopoly provision systems or to allow equitable funding arrangements between providers based on specific attributes – such as schools provided by different religious denominations (Le Grand 2007; Andersen 2008; Klitgaard 2008).

These can lead to grey markets (when food stamps, for example, are sold at a discount to 'undeserving' recipients) and may not improve service delivery if there is little choice provided in the supply of goods and services for which vouchers are issued (Valkama and Bailey 2001). As a result, although often mooted, vouchers appear only rarely in policy designs.

Sales of state assets at below market prices

Governments can also sell off or 'rent out' certain items – from the TV and radio spectrum to old or surplus equipment, buildings, and land. If prices are set below market rates, then this is a subsidy to investors and businesses (Sunnevag 2000). Many privatizations of formerly state-owned firms in collapsed socialist countries in the 1990s, for example, involved this kind of sale, including for lucrative mineral and oil and gas rights, which made billions of dollars for the many former officials who were often favoured in these arrangements (Newbery 2003). Given the costs involved and their generally high profile, however, this tool also does not feature very often in policy designs in countries which are stable and solvent.

Procedural financial instruments

Treasure resources, of course, just like organizational and authoritative ones, can also be used to alter the nature of policy processes. Procedural financial tools are generally used to attempt to alter or control aspects of the interest articulation and aggregation systems in contemporary states by creating or encouraging the formation of associations and groups where this activity might not otherwise occur, or, more prosaically, by rewarding government friends and punishing enemies through various kinds of payment schemes or penalties, strengthening or weakening their general positions in society.

Phillip Schmitter, in his comparative studies of European systems, argued that the interest articulation systems in different countries form a spectrum from 'free market', 'competitive' pluralism to 'state-sponsored oligarchic corporatism' (see Figure 11.1). In Schmitter's (1977, 1985) view, pluralism is a

Figure 11.1 Spectrum of interest articulation systems.

system of interest articulation in which interest groups are 'free-forming', have voluntary membership, and are multiple and non-monopolistic/competitive. That is, more than one group can represent individual members.

Corporatist regimes, on the other hand, are the opposite – they require state licensing, have compulsory membership, and are monopolistic. Corporatism was the official mode of social organization in many fascist governments after World War I, and in order to avoid this association and connotation, modern studies tend to use the term 'neocorporatism' to distinguish modern forms of (liberal-democratic) corporatism found in states such as Austria or Sweden from older ones – though examples also exist of this form in liberal-democratic states when they are in crisis, for example, during wartime or during the Great Depression–era Rooseveltian New Deal, which had strong roots in corporatist thinking.

Other variants also exist, such as, for example, consociationalism, where corporatist systems exist but divisions are along ethnic or religious grounds (e.g. the Netherlands) rather than between industry and workers, as was the case in Italy or Germany before and during World War II, or 'concertation' (France), where there is more pluralism in some areas than others (e.g. social vs economic planning), or 'parentela pluralism' (Atkinson and Coleman 1989a), where divisions are partisan (e.g. Italy) (Lijphart 1969; Lehmbruch 1979).

Until recently, interest group theorists in North America claimed it was largely pluralist (Bentley 1908; Truman 1964) and argued that interest group formation was a quasi-automatic, 'naturalistic process' in which state activity was minimal. The empirical basis for this assessment, however, was lacking (see Mancur Olson 1965; Salisbury 1969; Bachrach and Baratz 1970; and especially Jack Walker 1991 and, later, Anthony Nownes 2000). Neo-pluralism is a modern version of pluralism which takes into account some state activity in this area.

Olson's (1965) view of the 'collective action problems' interest groups face in these different governance contexts is an important insight helpful to understanding the rationales for the government use of procedural financial instruments in these different systems.

Olson argued that in any political system, some individuals have fewer incentives and more disincentives to form and join interest groups than others – for example, someone benefiting from some proposed government action might have a stronger motivation to lobby for it than would someone who stood neither to gain nor suffer from it. As a result, in a 'free association' system, there would be a tendency for specific affected interests – for example, businesses negatively affected by regulation – to form groups and pressure governments, while other, more general interests – for example, to retain tough environmental standards on industry – would be poorly represented. Due to this unequal distribution of the costs and benefits of political action, in many issue areas in pluralist systems, Olson argued, 'general interest' groups were unlikely to form or, if they did, would be quickly captured by 'special interests' who had more to gain from their existence and activities (Strolovitch 2006).

Olson had the idea that this could be overcome by providing 'selective incentives' for membership in mass groups – a practice followed, for example, by many environmental groups who offer a variety of services and free goods, such as calendars and book discounts, to attract and retain members. More recent works, however, point to the significance of a variety of factors in the process of group creation, such as the nature of a country's associational rights, the existence of 'focusing events' raising the public profile of an issue, and especially the presence of outside funds for seed money, as key factors in the creation and growth of interest groups.

Governments can still play a major, though little-studied, role in affecting this general pattern of interest group behaviour by either encouraging or discouraging interest group formation and activity. These activities are little studied but quite common in many countries. Governments can do this, for example, by creating (or not) systems of associational rights which allow groups to form, using their actions and resources to publicize events and issues and providing funds for the creation and maintenance of groups. Procedural financial tools are key ones used to affect these kinds of interest group system behaviour.

These tools generally fall into two types, those which are used to create or help support the formation of interest groups and those which help activate or mobilize them. The latter can be thought as 'network creation tools', while the latter can be considered as 'network mobilization tools'.

Financial policy network creation tools

Although their activities in this domain are often hidden from view, governments are very often quite actively involved in the creation and organization of policy networks and fund many key policy actors. An important activity in this regard is the use of government financial resources to create either the organizations themselves which go into the establishment of a policy network – research institutes, think tanks, government departments, and the like – or to facilitate the interaction of already-existing but separate units into a more coherent network structure (Hudson et al. 2007).

Funding is very often provided to think tanks and other policy research units and brokers by governments, either in the form of direct funding or as contracts (Rich 2004; Abelson 2007). More controversial, however, and at the same time not very well understood, is the role governments play in funding interest groups (Anheier et al. 1997).

Interest group creation

Provision of seed money is a key factor in interest group creation (Nownes 2004). King and Walker (1991), for example, found that the percentage of groups that received aid from outside groups in start-ups in the USA was 34 percent for profit sector groups; non-profit, 60 percent; and citizens'

Table 11.1 Average percentage of 'seed money' obtained by groups from each source by group type

Source	Type of group (%)				
	Patronage	Societal disturbance	Personal disturbance	Splinter	Generic entrepreneurial
Foundations	38	38	0	23	19
The government	0	0	0	0	0
Corporations	0	1	17	3	2
Other associations	32	11	3	0	2
Individuals	19	18	3	28	29
Personal funds	0	31	60	43	43
Other*	11	1	17	3	5
Total	100	100	100	100	100
n	10	12	6	16	16

* Includes loans, merchandise sales, fees for service, and special events.
Source: Adapted from Nownes and Neeley (1996).

groups, 89 percent. Nownes and Neeley (1996) similarly surveyed 121 national public interest groups in the USA in the mid-1990s and uncovered a pattern of extensive foundation support in terms of how their origin was financed (Table 11.1). While this survey revealed no direct government involvement, it did show that foundations provided a large percentage of the funding for pressure group creation, and since these operate under special tax treatment in the USA, this gives the US federal government a substantial indirect role in interest group creation in that country (Lowry 1999; Carmichael 2010).

In other countries, however, a much more direct role is played by governments, sometimes also with a substantial indirect role through foundations, but sometimes not. In Canada, for example, Pal (1993) noted that many of the prominent national interest groups in specific sectors, such as the Canadian Day Care Advocacy Association, the Canadian Congress for Learning Opportunities among Women, the Canadian Ethnocultural Council, and others, had emerged from conferences and workshops organized by federal government departments in the 1980s and 1990s (see also Finkle et al. 1994). Similar results can be found in many other jurisdictions. This activity is generally low profile and inexpensive but can be considered intrusive and is not all that easily targeted, making it a less-popular instrument in policy designs than network mobilization (see following text). However, where interest groups do not exist, governments may have little choice but to facilitate their creation if they wish to have their interests represented in policy deliberations and practices.

Financial network mobilization tools

A second key type of activity undertaken by governments through the use of procedural financial policy tools relates less to the creation of new groups and networks than to the reorientation of older, already-existing ones. Again, in the case of think tanks and other such actors, this can be accomplished through various forms of government contracting and procurement, notably for consulting (Speers 2007). A significant target for this kind of funding, however, are interest groups.

Interest group alteration/manipulation/co-optation

Cash funds or the tax system is used in many countries to alter interest group behaviour. The aim may be simply to neutralize or co-opt a vocal opponent of government (Kash 2008) but can also be a more broad-based effort to 'even out the playing field' for groups which lack the kinds of resources available to other groups (such as business) to mobilize and pressure governments to adopt policies of which they approve (Furlong and Kerwin 2004; Boehmke 2005).

Designing these programmes can, therefore, be quite complex (Phillips et al. 2010). Governments often use this tool to counterbalance, for example, lobbying on the part of business interests.

Most business groups, as well as many others, prefer 'insider action' and only revert to 'outside agitation' in order to attract new members in a competitive situation with other groups (Binderkrantz 2005). In some countries, however, like Sweden or Germany, companies and industrial groups and associations form foundations which take an active role in promoting their interests. Similarly, Lowry (1999) found that two main types of foundations exist in the USA – company-sponsored and independent – and both take active roles not only in interest group creation (discussed above) but also in funding interest group activities. In the USA in 1992, for example, he uncovered 463 grants made by 37 company foundations and 125 independent foundations just to environmental groups, $32.6 million from independent foundations versus only $1.5 million from company-sponsored foundations. Again, given the favourable tax treatment foundations enjoy in the USA, this gives the US government a substantial indirect role in funding interest group activity as well as in their creation.

In other countries, however, as with interest group creation, foundations are less important, and governments instead more directly provide 'sustaining' funding after groups are created. This has been ongoing for some time, with long-term impacts on policies and programme development. Stanbury, for example, examined the Canadian federal public accounts for 1986–1987 and found that 17 federal departments gave $185 million to over 500 groups (excluding non-policy groups, like those providing shelters for battered women). Over 50 organizations in Stanbury's sample were funded by a single federal agency – the Federal Secretary of State – mainly in the area of multiculturalism, which is now a key policy sector and issue area in the country.

Similarly, Pal found a total of $80 million going from the Federal Secretary of State to minority language groups over the period of 1970–1982, $50 million in 1978–1982 alone, while multicultural groups received over $125 million from 1976 to 1988 and $94 million in 1983–1988. Women's programmes received $63 million from 1973 to 1988, and $46 million over 1984–1988 (Stasiulis 1988; Pal 1993; Stanbury 1993). Phillips (1991) found the Federal Secretary of State to have spent $130 million over much the same period on over 3,000 groups with five major areas accounting for about one-third of all recipients: 337 groups for official languages; 457 women's groups; 195 disabled groups; 160 aboriginal groups; and 175 multicultural groups.

A total of 160 of these groups was defined only as 'public interest groups' (or classical pressure groups) and received $24 million from federal departments alone that year. Burt (1990) similarly surveyed the sources of funding received by 144 women's groups (24 percent of the estimated 686 such groups in Canada at that time) in the early 1980s and found the government was the single largest donor by far for most types of groups, far outstripping membership dues (see Table 11.2).

In Europe, Mahoney and Beckstrand (2009) similarly identified 1,164 civil society groups that received funding from the European Commission in

Table 11.2 Source of funding for women's groups (Canada)

Most important source of funds	Type of group (%)			
	Traditional	Status of women	Service	Shelter
Government	33	40	38	52
Dues	8	20	9	0
Fund-raising	17	7	2	11
Other, n/a	42	33	51	37
	100	100	100	100

Source: Adapted from Burt (1990).

2003–2007. They shared in 120 million euros of funding at the EU level and another 75 million in international-, national-, and subnational-level funding. These were primarily groups operating at the EU level in areas such as youth, sports, education, and cultural activities in support of the EC mandate to develop a supra-national EU civil society.

This funding is almost invisible, can be precisely targeted, and although often considered intrusive in legal and market governance modes, is quite compatible with network and corporatist governance activities. As a result, it is a growing area and a prominent feature of many contemporary policy designs, although this is often not clearly acknowledged or recognized.

Conclusion: treasure – an effective but depletable resource

The use of financial resources is one of the oldest forms of government activity and instrument use. The use of substantive treasure-based instruments is quite common in designs, and in terms of size and impact, it is as significant as direct government service delivery or regulation.

The use of this resource, as Hood (1983, 1986c) noted, is sometimes restricted by a lack of treasure resources, either because a country is poor and simply cannot generate revenue or, as has happened in jurisdictions such as California, for example, because of various measures which prevent or limit government access to substantial taxpayer wealth. However, notwithstanding these limitations, in general, all governments spend considerable sums encouraging certain activities and discouraging others through the use of various kinds of fiscal and monetary tools and techniques. An important trend in this area, as noted by Howard (1993, 1995, 1997), is toward the increased use of tax-based incentives rather than subsidies. This is due to a number of reasons and will be discussed in more detail in Chapter 13 but often reflects concerns with visibility and automaticity.

As for procedural financial tool uses, as mentioned earlier, the use of these techniques is also increasing at a substantial rate, although the exact mechanisms used vary from country to country, such as the use of indirect foundations in the USA, compared to more direct government allocations in many other jurisdictions.

Readings

Bangalore, M., G. Hochman and D. Zilberman. (2016). 'Policy Incentives and Adoption of Agricultural Anaerobic Digestion: A Survey of Europe and the United States'. *Renewable Energy* 97 (November): 559–571.

Beam, D. A. and T. J. Conlan. (2002). 'Grants'. In L. M. Salamon (ed.), *The Tools of Government: A Guide to the New Governance*. New York: Oxford University Press, 340–380.

Brooks, S. M. (2015). 'Social Protection for the Poorest: The Adoption of Antipoverty Cash Transfer Programs in the Global South'. *Politics & Society 43*, no. 4 (1 December): 551–582.

Cnossen, S. (2005). 'Economics and Politics of Excise Taxation'. In S. Cnossen (ed.), *Theory and Practice of Excise Taxation: Smoking, Drinking, Gambling, Polluting and Driving*. Oxford: Oxford University Press, 1–19.

Cordes, J. J. (2002). 'Corrective Taxes, Charges and Tradable Permits'. In L. M. Salamon (ed.), *The Tools of Government: A Guide to the New Governance*. New York: Oxford University Press, 255–281.

Deber, R., M. J. Hollander and P. Jacobs. (2008). 'Models of Funding and Reimbursement in Health Care: A Conceptual Framework'. *Canadian Public Administration 51*, no. 3: 381–405.

DeShazo, J. R., T. L. Sheldon and R. T. Carson. (2017). 'Designing Policy Incentives for Cleaner Technologies: Lessons from California's Plug-In Electric Vehicle Rebate Program'. *Journal of Environmental Economics and Management 84* (July): 18–43.

Howard, C. (2002). 'Tax Expenditures'. In L. M. Salamon (ed.), *The Tools of Government: A Guide to the New Governance*. New York: Oxford University Press, 410–444.

Juillet, L., C. Andrew, T. Aubry and J. Mrenica. (2001). 'The Impact of Changes in the Funding Environment on Nonprofit Organizations'. In K. L. Brock and K. G. Banting (eds.), *The Nonprofit Sector and Government in a New Century*. Montreal, QC: McGill-Queen's University Press, 21–62.

Klitgaard, M. B. (2008). 'School Vouchers and the New Politics of the Welfare State'. *Governance 21*, no. 4: 479–498.

Leeuw, F. L. (1998). 'The Carrot: Subsidies as a Tool of Government'. In M.-L. Bemelmans-Videc, R. C. Rist and E. Vedung (eds.), *Carrots, Sticks and Sermons: Policy Instruments and Their Evaluation*. New Brunswick, NJ: Transaction, 77–102.

Louhaichi, M., Y. A. Yigezu, J. Werner, L. Dashtseren, T. El-Shater and M. Ahmed. (2016). 'Financial Incentives: Possible Options for Sustainable Rangeland Management?' *Journal of Environmental Management 180* (15 September): 493–503.

Maddison, S. (2005). 'Democratic Constraint and Embrace: Implications for Progressive Non-Government Advocacy Organisations in Australia'. *Australian Journal of Political Science 40*, no. 3: 373–389.

McIlroy-Young, B., D. Henstra and J. Thistlethwaite. (2022). 'Treasure Tools: Using Public Funds to Achieve Policy Objectives'. In M. Howlett (ed.), *The Routledge Handbook of Policy Tools*. New York: Routledge, 332–344.

Nownes, A. and G. Neeley. (1996). 'Toward an Explanation for Public Interest Group Formation and Proliferation: 'Seed Money'', Disturbances, Entrepreneurship, and Patronage'. *Policy Studies Journal 24*, no. 1: 74–92.

Pal, L. A. (1993). *Interests of State: The Politics of Language, Multiculturalism, and Feminism in Canada*. Kingston, ON: McGill-Queen's University Press.

Phillips, S. D. (1991). 'How Ottawa Blends: Shifting Government Relationships with Interest Groups'. In F. Abele (ed.), *How Ottawa Spends 1991–92: The Politics of Fragmentation*. Ottawa, ON: Carleton University Press, 183–228.

Sharpe, D. (2001). 'The Canadian Charitable Sector: An Overview'. In J. Phillips, B. Chapman and D. Stevens (eds.), *Between State and Market: Essays on Charities Law and Policy in Canada*. Toronto, ON: University of Toronto Press.

Stanton, T. H. (2002). 'Loans and Loan Guarantees'. In L. M. Salamon (ed.), *The Tools of Government: A Guide to the New Governance*. New York: Oxford University Press, 381–409.

Steenblik, R. (2018). 'Treasure Tools: A Primer on Subsidies'. In M. Howlett and I. Mukherjee (eds.), *Routledge Handbook of Policy Design*. New York: Routledge, 261–273.

Surrey, S. S. (1970). 'Tax Incentives as a Device for Implementing Government Policy: A Comparison with Direct Government Expenditures'. *Harvard Law Review 83*, no. 4 (1 February): 705–738.

Woodside, K. (1979). 'Tax Incentives vs. Subsidies: Political Considerations in Governmental Choice'. *Canadian Public Policy 5*, no. 2: 248–256.

Wu, J. and A. Tal. (2017). 'From Pollution Charge to Environmental Protection Tax: A Comparative Analysis of the Potential and Limitations of China's New Environmental Policy Initiative'. *Journal of Comparative Policy Analysis: Research and Practice* (25 September): 1–14.

245

Chapter 12

Information-based policy tools

Information-based tools are those based on the last of the four categories of resources set out by Hood (1986c): 'nodality' or 'centrality' or, as we have defined it, being in a position to monitor and communicate 'knowledge' or 'information' to target groups in the expectation this will alter their behaviour. These are the 'sermon' in the 'carrots, sticks, and sermons' formulation of policy instruments (Bemelmans-Videc et al. 1998).

Exactly what is meant by the term 'information' or 'communication' varies from author to author, ranging from its association with all forms of political activity (Deutsch 1963; Bang 2003) to a very specific focus on one type of action, like public service or political advertising (Firestone 1970; Young 2007). These different foci make classifying and analyzing the wide range of activities and tasks which involve policy-relevant government information provision and collection more difficult than it should be (Ledingham 2003).

As Evert Vedung defines them, information-based policy tools are 'efforts to use the knowledge and data available to governments to influence consumer and producer behaviour in a direction consistent with government aims and wishes and/or gather information in order to further their aims and ambitions' (Vedung and van der Doelen 1998).

This definition, while useful, is limited in that it conceals or elides the two different general purposes to which these tools can be put to use (Howlett et al. 2010). These are the familiar procedural versus substantive distinction used throughout this book – whether these activities are intended to serve as devices primarily oriented toward the manipulation of the behaviour of policy actors in policy processes (Edelman 1988; Saward 1992; Mikenberg 2001; Sulitzeanu-Kenan 2007) or as social and economic ones involved in and affecting the production, distribution, and consumption of different types of goods and services (Hornik 1989; Salmon 1989a, 1989b; Jahn et al. 2005; Howlett 2009b). Disentangling the two is necessary in order to provide a clear analysis of the role each plays in policy designs.

It is also important to note that many new communication practices have emerged in recent years, at least in part due to the development of new

DOI: 10.4324/9781003343431-16

information technologies, notably computerization and the internet (Feldman and Khademian 2007), which have broadened the range and menu of government nodality tools to include social media. These tools include the development and use of instruments which promote citizen empowerment, such as freedom of information (FOI) legislation, the use of public performance measures, various forms of e- or 'digital' government, and the increased use of government surveys and advertising, among others (Hood and Margetts 2007). The growth in such activities has led at least one commentator to suggest that 'all tools are informational' now (John 2013).

Substantive informational instruments

Following Vedung's lead, we can define substantive government communication instruments as those policy techniques or mechanisms which rely on the use of information to directly or indirectly affect the behaviour of those involved in the production, consumption, and distribution of different kinds of goods and services in society.

The highest profile and thus most commonly observed and chronicled type of substantive tool is the instrument focused on the targeted effort to alter specific kinds of public or consumer behaviour: the *government information campaign*. This includes various campaigns waged by governments to encourage citizens to, for example, eat well, engage in fewer vices, and otherwise behave responsibly, which are common in all forms of governance.

However, communication activities aimed at altering producer behaviour through provision of product and process information to customers (*labelling and product information*) are also very prominent. As Hood (1986c) noted, these kinds of tools can be targeted at different levels of society – individuals, groups, and populations as a whole and according to whether they are intended to collect or disseminate information.

Information dissemination tools

Information dissemination tools like public service advertising are classic 'persuasion instruments' and are the most studied substantive information implementation tools. Adler and Pittle define these instruments as those 'persuasion schemes [which] convey messages which may or may not contain factual information which overtly seek to motivate target audiences to modify their behaviour' (Adler and Pittle 1984: 160). These tools are used often, as they are fairly inexpensive. However, they remain controversial as the line between communications and intrusive propaganda is one which is easily blurred, and their effectiveness is difficult to gauge (Gelders and Ihlen 2009, 2010).

Exhortation and moral suasion

The most prominent type of substantive information tool designed to persuade is the appeal from political leaders to various social actors, urging them to follow a government's lead in some area of social or economic life. Stanbury and Fulton (1984) provide a list of 'exhortation' and 'moral suasion' activities which include 'pure political leadership such as appeals for calm, better behaviour, high principles and whereby voluntary action is urged under threat of coercion if refused' (304).

Such forms of 'moral suasion' are often specifically aimed or targeted at individual producers or sectors and are typically used within the context of an already-existing regulatory regime. These can help governments regulate a variety of activities without necessarily creating new legal instruments in order to do so. Many countries, for example, administer important aspects of their financial systems in this fashion, asking banks, taxpayers, and other financial institutions to act in a certain way (e.g. keep interest rates low or allow certain groups to borrow funds), with the implicit or explicit threat of direct government regulation if such requests are ignored or go unfulfilled (Bardach 1989a). Government requests are often very focused and can be quite secretive (e.g. in the immediate aftermath of the 9/11 airline hijackings, when the US government urged credit card companies to provide them with records of suspicious activities by suspected hijackers).

Information campaigns

Mass media and targeted social media information campaigns, on the other hand, are much more visible, by definition, and tend to be aimed less at producers than at consumers. Adler and Pittle (1984) describe these tools as 'notification instruments' which

> convey factual information to the intelligent target. Implicit in the notification approach is the belief that the target, once apprised of the facts, will make the appropriate decision.

Some notification tools do attempt to be purely factual, ongoing, and passive in nature, such as nutritional labelling on foodstuffs or health warnings on cigarettes (Padberg 1992; Baksi and Bose 2007). They are usually enacted in regulations (i.e. disclosure is mandatory) and are aimed at providing information to consumers allowing them to make better decisions or overcome information asymmetries between producers and consumers. The expectation is that after receiving a 'message' consumers will change their behaviour in some way consistent with government goals – for example, reducing smoking when informed of its dangers, exercising more when informed of its health benefits, or eating nutritional foods rather than snacks when the dangers of the latter are made clear (Jahn et al. 2005). Although the evidence of the effectiveness of such campaigns is mixed (Mann and Wuste-mann 2010; Barreiro-Hurlé et al. 2010), this has not dampened their growth.

Other information campaigns are more active and less factual but have the same intent, that is, providing social actors with more information about some aspect of their behaviour and its advantageous or deleterious quality, urging enhancement of the former and a diminishment of the latter. The infor-mation often transmitted through such information instruments is not always so factual, however, but can be used to 'sell' a government's policies in the same way that other products are marketed. Such campaigns are often con-ducted at the mass level and use a variety of mass media delivery mechanisms (commercials, broadcasts, newspaper advertisements, social media influenc-ers and the like). High-profile campaigns in many countries to prevent drink-ing and driving or encourage the purchase of war bonds during wartime are good examples of the use of this kind of instrument, which often features information which is emotional, rather than factual, in nature.

This kind of mass campaign began with the emergence of mass media and is now common in most countries. Many national governments are now the largest purchasers of advertising in their countries and far outstrip national brands well-known for their advertising overkill, such as alcoholic beverage and soft drink companies, as well as fast-food chains. The federal government of Canada, for example, has been the largest advertiser in the country since 1976 (Stanbury et al. 1983), with the larger provincial governments in the top 10 as well. Ryan (1995) noted that federal advertising expanded from $3.4 million in 1968 to $106.5 million in 1992, a 3,000 percent increase. Even inflation-adjusted, this amounted to a 665 percent increase in 25 years.

Specific national issue campaigns, however, can be very costly. Alasdair Roberts and Jonathan Rose (1995), for example, conducted an in-depth study of a mass media campaign conducted by the federal government of Canada to introduce a new goods and services tax (GST) in 1989–1990. They found the federal Department of Finance to have spent $11.6 million on public educa-tion in a combined print/radio/TV campaign, $5 million on direct mail mate-rials, $5 million on a call centre; Revenue Canada (Customs) to have spent $10.6 million on advertising, $9.2 million on instructional material; Revenue Canada (Taxation) to have spent a further $28 million advertising a GST credit; while a specially created GST Consumer Information Office spent $7.4 million on advertising and $6.9 million on production. The total for this one campaign was $85 million. This was more than the largest private sector advertisers spent in all of 1989. For example, Procter & Gamble, with its hundreds of consumer products, had a total advertising budget of $56.7 million. This has led to some calls in some countries for greater regulation or control on govern-ment advertising, but these proposals have shown few results (Young 2007).

Although they can be costly, such campaigns are generally less expensive than many other alternatives, although the costs of non-compliance must also be taken into account (Pellikaan and van der Veen 2002). Generally, governments will tend to include information tools and government communications in policy designs only when:

- 100 percent compliance is not required for a policy to be effective
- Government and public interests coincide (e.g. on health awareness) so that government appeals are likely to be favourably received.
- Only in relatively short-term crisis situations, when other tools may require too much lead time to be effective.
- It is otherwise difficult to impose sanctions.
- The issue in question is not very complex (technological or legal) in nature but can be reduced to the level of advertising slogans.
  (see Rose 1993; Romans 1966; Vedung and van der Doelen 1998)

Nudges and information-based choice architectures

In recent years, as we have seen in earlier chapters, much attention has been paid to information provision as a governing tool as a result of work based in behavioural economics which promotes the use of 'nudges' or informational cues to encourage or discourage certain kinds of behaviour at a less-'conscious' level (Thaler and Sunstein 2009). These cues are more subtle than traditional information- and media-based campaigns and are often targeted at the unconscious or semi-conscious level of individual behaviour. They can include such micro-level interventions as changing the default opt-in on organ donation forms to a default opt-out, for example, or painting walking path lines in subway stations that lead to stairs rather than escalators in order to encourage exercise.

Sunstein (2014) identified ten important types of nudges, many of which have been discussed in earlier chapters. They are all efforts to alter citizen behaviour by altering the informational environment in which they operate, especially through activation of so-called 'system 1' or quasi-automatic cognitive responses (Kahneman 2013b; Strassheim 2021). These include:

1. Changing default rules, such as making people opt out rather than into some scheme.
2. Simplification of the options presented to individuals, such as a shortened contract.
3. Use of social norms to encourage people to conform with certain practices, such as not littering or jaywalking.
4. Increases in ease and convenience, such as making bike paths and exercise areas common and easily accessible.
5. Disclosure, that is, mandating the provision of certain kinds of information, like the real interest rate charged to credit card debt.
6. Warnings, graphic or otherwise, to discourage behaviour, such as mandatory pictures of cancer victims on cigarette packages.

7. Pre-commitment strategies, such as the provision of peer-supported anti-obesity or alcoholism support groups, such as Weight Watchers or Alcoholics Anonymous.
8. Reminders of important activities, such as children's dental appointment or vaccination schedules.
9. Eliciting implementation intentions through various campaigns, such as voter registration drives or pension planning.
10. Informing people of the nature and consequences of their own past choices, such as informing them of the amount they have spent on electricity in past months or years on their current bill.

Many of these items are included in bills or forms or mailings of various kinds and are intended to provide information about their behaviour to consumers which might otherwise be difficult or impossible for them to collect, such as the fluctuations in their monthly electricity or water consumption, with the idea that having this information will alter their use of these resources. This kind of 'choice architecture' involves careful consideration and design of the kinds of choices 'behavioural architects' place before policy targets and the public in order to encourage them to undertake some kinds of actions rather than others (Olejniczak et al. 2019).

Although the idea of 'nudging' received a surge of attention after the publication of Thaler and Sunstein's book in 2010, the effectiveness of such measures remains unclear. Evidence suggests, for example, that they may have a role to play in solving large-scale policy issues, but only when they are exercised in tandem with other policy tools, such as financial incentives or penalties such as a sliding scale of water or electricity prices, in the preceding example, designed to discourage higher levels of consumption (Weimer 2020).

Moreover, there may be unintended and undesirable 'behavioural spillovers' from nudges (Dolan and Galizzi 2015). That is, there is a risk of infantilizing and diminishing people's autonomous decision-making capacities by constantly manipulating them (Hausman and Welch 2010; Bovens 2009), and also a concern regarding the potential for abuse in the use of nudging to shape people's choices in pro-government ways (Hausman and Welch 2010). Governments may also be unable to counter 'nudge'-style tactics employed by private market institutions which, for example, encourage people to spend rather than save, or smoke or gamble rather than abstain, to name only a few (Bovens 2009; Loewenstein et al. 2015).

Hagman et al. (2015) also found significant differences in the receptiveness of different populations to nudging activity. They find a high degree of acceptance toward 'nudge' policies among a sample population drawn from Sweden and the USA, for example, but also a majority of the respondents perceiving such policies to be intrusive to their freedom of choice. Policies that the researchers classified as pro-social (i.e. focusing on social welfare) also had a significantly lower acceptance rate compared to pro-self-nudge policies (i.e. those focusing on private welfare). In addition, 'overt' nudges, that is, those that target conscious, higher-order cognitive processes of decision-making, were preferred by people over 'covert' nudges (i.e. those that target subconscious, lower-order processes of decision-making). However, while this was true in most contexts, such as eating, purchasing, exercising, and making investment decisions, it wasn't true in other contexts, that of work-place productivity decisions (Felsen et al. 2013).

Regardless of the behavioural tool being employed, whether a nudge, shove, or budge, in cases where incentives for non-compliance are high, such information-based tools may be unlikely to secure compliance by themselves. In such cases, policy-makers need to think about both the barriers that may be preventing compliance and how to match a variety of policy tools to the most important barriers, taking into account the heterogeneity within the given population in terms of their receptiveness to different tool use (Weaver 2015).

Information and knowledge collection tools

Information collection is the key to many and better policies (Nutley et al. 2007), and as Hood (1986c) pointed out, many implementation instruments exist to collect information for governments and can contribute to enhanced 'evidence-based' policy-making in this way. This extends to the use of licensing provisions in which information may be collected before or after a driver, business, building, or some other form of license is granted but can also involve the use of research and generation of new policy-relevant knowledge through special forums, such as inquiries and commissions.

Inquiries and commissions

One fairly common and high-profile means by which governments collect information is the use of official inquiries, such as a judicial inquiry or executive commission, discussed in part earlier in Chapter 9. These exist on a spectrum, depending on their relationship to government agencies and according to their functions. Some inquiries and task forces are largely internal to government and intended to mobilize network actors. These have been discussed in Chapter 9 in the context of their role as procedural organizational tools.

Other kinds of commissions, however, are designed primarily to collect information (Sulitzeanu-Kenan 2010; Rowe and McAllister 2006). Many judicial inquiries fall into this category and have a great deal of autonomy from governments. They are a common feature of most modes of governance and enjoy a variety of different relationships with their commissioners (Inwood and Johns 2016). Presidential and royal commissions, for example, are independent and autonomous, although they still depend on government for budgets and resources. Others are less 'arm's-length' and expected to report back to specific agencies on specific subjects with no guarantee that their reports will ever be released to the public.

All these devices can be used to summarize existing knowledge or generate new data on a subject (Chapman 1973; Bulmer 1981; Sheriff 1983; Clark and Majone 1985; d'Ombrain 1997; Elliott and McGuinness 2001; Montpetit 2003c, 2008; Salter 2003; Prasser 2006).

Statistical agencies and units

Another information collecting and disseminating tool is the use of agencies which are specifically tasked with collecting statistical data on a wide variety of social activities of individuals, groups, and firms. Some, like national statistics bureaus, typically operate using internationally recognized standards for classifying these activities and may rely more or less heavily on voluntary disclosure of information. These agencies may also conduct surveys on specialized topics and/or periodic censuses of national or subnational populations (Anderson and Whitford 2018).

This information is often used to determine such factors as the level of per capita grants transferred between governments or the number and types of hospitals and medical facilities which should be built and where these and other public institutions like schools and offices should be located.

National- and other-level statistical agencies are expensive to establish and maintain but, once in operation, can be used to collect information on many subjects at relatively low cost and often provide otherwise very hard-to-collect information to the public as well as governments through, for example, time series databases on a wide range of issues from housing starts to consumer savings rates.

Surveys and polling

In many countries, governments are now the largest purchasers of surveys (Hastak et al. 2001), and many government agencies now undertake polling on a regular basis, both as environmental scans in order to try to anticipate issues but also in order to determine public opinion on agency performance and plans (Rothmayr and Hardmeier 2002; Page 2006).

Procedural informational instruments

In order to pursue their preferred policy initiatives, governments can also use procedural tools based on government information resources in order to attempt to alter the behaviour of policy network members involved in policy-making processes (Burris et al. 2005), just as they attempt to alter consumer and producer behaviour through the employment of substantive information-based tools.

Information-based procedural policy tools are those designed to affect policy processes in a way consistent with government aims and ambitions through the control and selective provision of information. As Hood suggested, these are 'nodality' instruments because the information exchanged is valuable largely as a function of the government's position as a key nodal link in a policy network (Margetts and John 2023). Some of these efforts are aimed at promoting information release, while others are aimed at preventing it.

Both European and American studies have found that governments have increasingly employed a variety of procedural information-based instruments to indirectly affect the outcomes of the policy process in ways that are consistent with their aims and objectives (Kohler-Koch 1996; Johansson and Borell 1999; Hall and O'Toole 2000).

The most commonly observed and chronicled category of procedural tool is the type which focuses on the use of general information prevention or disclosure laws and other such tools – such as access to information laws – in order to provide policy network actors with the knowledge required to effectively filter and focus their demands on government for new policy measures or reforms to older ones. However, governments are also very much involved in the use of communications on government websites, on social media, and through other means (Gandy 1982; Hood and Margetts 2007) to provide additional information to policy network members in specific sectoral or issue areas in order to both enhance their credibility and effectiveness and also to promote evidence-based rather than pure advocacy activity (Clarke 2019).

These tools fall into two types, depending on whether they facilitate or withhold information.

Information release tools

Stanbury and Fulton (1984) describe two common types of procedural information release or disclosure tools: *information disclosure* (e.g. through formal FOI and privacy laws) and *consultation/co-optation tools*, such as public hearings, the discreet use of confidential information such as planned leaks to the press or planned public disclosure of government intentions.

Freedom of information and e- or digital government legislation and other initiatives

FOI provisions allow access to an individual's own records – with numerous mainly benign exemptions (to protect other individuals from unnecessary disclosure) – and allow access to documents and records of others – with numerous exemptions, again mainly benign and intended to protect individuals from unnecessary disclosure.

These legislative arrangements were a feature of the centuries-old Scandinavian ombudsman system of administrative control and were introduced in many other countries in the 1970s and 1980s. The idea generally being that citizen's cannot hold a government accountable for its actions if they don't fully understand what those actions are and how they came about (Relyea 1977; Bennett 1988, 1990, 1991a, 1992; Bennett and Raab 2003; Bennett and Bayley 1999; Howe and Johnson 2000).

These are sometimes accompanied by other tools, for example, in the Scandinavian case by 'ombudsmen' or public officials able to raise complaints with governments and publicize the outcomes of their investigations (Cheng 1968). Others, such as 'whistle-blower' acts – that is, bills intended to protect people who speak out about problems in the government's bureaucracy – have also grown in number and coverage (Kang 2022). Through such legislation, bureaucrats are often offered legal protection against reprisals for reporting government wrongdoing. Both represent popular forms of procedural information tool designs.

Various kinds of open data and e-government projects, often referred to collectively as 'digital government', which move previously in-person service delivery online, also often have an information release component to them, collecting data on users or providing additional venues for users to obtain information on government programmes and other options (Clarke and Craft 2017; Clarke et al. 2017). In the form of various 'open government' initiatives, these programmes and rules can greatly augment both the ability of the citizenry to hold a government accountable and also to benefit from the massive amount of data governments collect and create each year in the course of their activities (Ruijer et al. 2020). Such efforts, while plentiful, however, require a great deal of planning in order to deal with problems linked to the release of sensitive information, including national security and personal health data, for example, which have proved very challenging to their implementation (Moon and Lee 2022).

Information release prevention tools

There is also a wide range of such tools designed to protect certain kinds of information on government activities or in government files and prevent its distribution to the public. These include protecting not only information collected by governments but also that which comes into their possession (for example from a foreign government or via documents filed in court cases and the like).

These range from wartime (and peacetime, for example, a film review board) censorship and bans on political parties and speech such as hate crimes legislation, to official secrets acts with various levels of confidentiality and penalties imposed for publicizing or releasing government secrets, especially, but not exclusively, around areas such as national security.

Censorship

This has occurred in many countries during wartime but also in peacetime, for example, as media, film, or theatre censorship. This latter use has been slowly whittled away in most advanced countries as individual rights in democratic states have been ruled to trump government or collective ones, but wartime prohibitions remain very common (Qualter 1985).

Official secrets acts

Official secrets acts are a replacement for censorship in many areas. They are often the most important statute relating to national security in many countries and are designed to prohibit and control access to and the disclosure of sensitive government information (Pasquier and Villeneuve 2007). Offences tend to cover espionage and leakage of government information. The term 'official secret' varies dramatically in meaning from country to country but, broadly, allows governments to classify documents and prohibit release of different categories for sometimes very long periods of time (e.g. 50–75 years).

All countries have some form of official secrecy, although the legislative and executive basis for such laws varies quite dramatically between countries.

Privacy and data protection acts

These acts exist in many jurisdictions as a counterpoint to access-to-information laws in which various types of personally specific information is excluded from such acts. Some jurisdictions have specific legislation devoted to this subject, usually with a focus on protecting personal information in areas such as health, financial, or tax matters and with respect to criminal proceedings.

These instruments are also quite varied, but in general, it is fair to say that restricting information is low cost to initiate but high cost to monitor and maintain, while the reverse is true of information disclosure. In terms of targeting, it is true of both sets of instruments that it is very difficult to target either secrecy or disclosure on specific groups. As a result, these actions are typically more difficult to set up and take more time and effort than is often thought to be the case, making them an infrequent component of many policy designs, although increasingly demanded in an era of computer hacking and data breaches.

Conclusion: information – cost-efficient but often ineffective

As has been set out earlier, there are many different kinds of government communication and information activities, and in the past the lack of an effective taxonomy or framework for their analysis has made generalizing about their impact and patterns of use quite difficult.

Describing information-based policy tools in the terms set out in this chapter helps highlight the similarities and differences between different instruments and helps develop a relatively parsimonious taxonomy of their major types which can facilitate national and cross-national studies of their use and impact.

Information dissemination activities remain relatively low cost in terms of financial and personnel outlays, but compliance is a major issue, and as in all advertising activities, evaluating the impact of these campaigns in changing behaviour in desired ways is very uncertain (Salmon 1989a, 1989b). Adler and Pittle (1984: 161), for example, found 'many of these programmes require more careful planning, larger expenditures and longer implementation periods than they usually receive' if they are to have any effect.

The assumption that greater knowledge always equals greater compliance with government aims, for example, is not always the case. Alcoholism and drug abuse, to give only two prominent examples, are complex problems that are not 'rational' in the sense that individuals continue to consume or engage in them while knowing their destructive attributes (so-called 'demerit goods') (see Walsh 1988; Weiss and Tschirhart 1994). Greater knowledge may not affect or alter behaviour in such cases.

Thus, while it may be the dream of many governments that simply monitoring and communicating with people will accomplish all their ends, this is not usually the case. The benefits to government in using such tools may thus be much lower than anticipated if such a high-visibility instrument is perceived to have failed and the blame for a continuing policy problem is focused squarely on governments (Hood 2007b). Such considerations are a prominent feature in the design of policy alternatives envisioning the use of such tools, often resulting in their use in combination with other tools rather than as the sole tool deployed in a policy area of interest.

Readings

Anderson, D. M. and A. Whitford. (2018). 'Designing Systems for the Co-Production of Public Knowledge: Considerations for National Statistical Systems'. *Policy Design and Practice 1*, no. 1 (2 January): 79–89.

Bardach, E. and R. A. Kagan. (1982). 'Mandatory Disclosure'. In E. Bardach and R. A. Kagan (eds.), *Going by the Book: The Problem of Regulatory Unreasonableness.* Philadelphia, PA: Temple University Press, 242–270.

Bennett, C. and R. Bayley. (1999). 'The New Public Administration: Canadian Approaches to Access and Privacy'. In M. W. Westmacott and H. P. Mellon (eds.), *Public Administration and Policy: Governing in Challenging Times.* Scarborough, ON: Prentice Hall/Allyn & Bacon, 189–201.

Bougherara, D., G. Grolleau and N. Mzoughi. (2007). 'Is More Information Always Better? An Analysis Applied to Information-Based Policies for Environmental Protection'. *International Journal of Sustainable Development 10*, no. 3: 197–213.

Bulmer, M. (1981). 'Applied Social Research? The Use and Non-Use of Empirical Social Inquiry by British and American Governmental Commissions'. *Journal of Public Policy 1*: 353–380.

Cairns, A. C. (1990). 'Reflections on Commission Research'. In A. P. Pross, I. Christie and J. A. Yogis (eds.), *Commissions of Inquiry*. Toronto, ON: Carswell, 87–110.

Chapman, R. A. (1973). 'Commissions in Policy-Making'. In R. A. Chapman (ed.), *The Role of Commissions in Policy-Making*. London: George Allen & Unwin, 174–188.

Cheng, H. Y. (1968). 'The Emergence and Spread of the Ombudsman Institution'. *The Annals of the American Academy of Political and Social Science* 377: 20–30.

Clarke, A. and J. Craft. (2017). 'The Vestiges and Vanguards of Policy Design in a Digital Context'. *Canadian Public Administration* 60, no. 4 (1 December): 476–497.

Howells, G. (2005). 'The Potential and Limits of Consumer Empowerment by Information'. *Journal of Law and Society* 32, no. 3: 349–370.

Howlett, M. (2009). 'Government Communication as a Policy Tool: A Framework for Analysis'. *Canadian Political Science Review* 3, no. 2: 23–37.

Jahn, G., M. Schramm and A. Spiller. (2005). 'The Reliability of Certification: Quality Labels as a Consumer Policy Tool'. *Journal of Consumer Policy* 28: 53–73.

John, P. (2013). 'All Tools Are Informational Now: How Information and Persuasion Define the Tools of Government'. *Policy & Politics* 41, no. 4 (1 October): 605–620.

Kang, M. M. (2023). 'Whistleblowing in the Public Sector: A Systematic Literature Review'. *Review of Public Personnel Administration 43*, no. 2 (1 June): 381–406.

Moon, M. J. and S. Lee. (2022). 'The Future of Informational Tools with Big Data Informatics: Opportunities and Challenges for Evidence-Based Policymaking'. In M. Howlett (ed.), *The Routledge Handbook of Policy Tools*. London: Routledge, 559–569.

Ruijer, E., F. Détienne, M. Baker, J. Groff and A. J. Meijer. (2020). 'The Politics of Open Government Data: Understanding Organizational Responses to Pressure for More Transparency'. *The American Review of Public Administration 50*, no. 3 (1 April): 260–274.

Salmon, C. (1989). 'Campaigns for Social Improvement: An Overview of Values, Rationales, and Impacts'. In C. Salmon (ed.), *Information Campaigns: Managing the Process of Social Change*. Newbury Park, CA: Sage, 1–32.

Sheriff, P. E. (1983). 'State Theory, Social Science, and Governmental Commissions'. *American Behavioural Scientist 26*, no. 5: 669–680.

Vedung, E. and F. C. J. van der Doelen. (1998). 'The Sermon: Information Programs in the Public Policy Process – Choice, Effects and Evaluation'. In M.-L. Bemelmans-Videc, R. C. Rist and E. Vedung (eds.), *Carrots, Sticks and Sermons: Policy Instruments and Their Evaluation*. New Brunswick, NJ: Transaction, 103–128.

Weiss, J. A. (2002). 'Public Information'. In L. M. Salamon (ed.), *The Tools of Government: A Guide to the New Governance*. New York: Oxford University Press, 217–254.

Chapter 13

Traditional policy styles and contemporary design trends

As the discussion in Chapters 9–12 has shown, there are many different kinds of instruments which can be used in a policy design and many ways in which instruments of different types can be combined into a policy mix.

Given this variation, the extent of the permutations and combinations possible within it, and the complex nature of the policy advice systems in which design decisions are taken, one might expect each policy design to be idiosyncratic and for there to be an incredibly wide range of designs, much as there is in the area of naval design, for example, whereby boats can take on almost any shape and structure imaginable.

However, this is not the case in the policy sphere. Rather, like with automobiles, the standard range of designs is fairly limited, and the same general design, for example, one utilizing a combination of regulation and stakeholder advisory councils, is very common and operates in a very similar manner across a wide range of domains and problem areas.

This is fortunate because if there was an extremely wide range of designs and design permutations, it would be very difficult, if not impossible, to identify and talk about any specific trends in design activity or to formulate many conclusions about the superiority of any one design over any other. However, with a much smaller number of designs, it is possible to identify general trends and directions in policy designs.

As we saw in Chapter 2, for example, many scholars have argued that in coming to terms with the challenges of globalization and the increasing networkization of society, governments developed a renewed interest in a particular set of policy tools appropriate to market or network modes of governance. Alongside this purported shift in governance contexts – the presence of more flexible social, economic, and political circumstances than have existed in the past (Lenihan and Alcock 2000) – contemporary policy designs in many advanced countries, it has been argued, have changed. Specifically, unlike in past epochs, they are argued to have become more indirect and subtle, more

DOI: 10.4324/9781003343431-17

often much less visible than was previously the case, and also more similar in that they rely on many of the same types of tools (Rhodes 1997).

That is, it has been argued in many circles that in response to the increased complexity of society and the significance of changes in the international environment, governments in many countries have turned away from the use of traditional, more or less direct and command-and-control-oriented, 'substantive' policy tools, such as public enterprises, regulatory agencies, subsidies, and exhortation, and begun to increasingly use their resources to support a different set of less-coercive and more-collaborative tools. This includes using many more 'procedural' tools in policy mixes, such as government reorganizations, reviews and inquiries, government–NGO partnerships, and stakeholder consultations of various kinds, than in the past (Klijn and Teisman 1991; Peters 1998; Bingham et al. 2005).

As Hood et al. and Majone have argued in the European case, for example, 'modern states are placing more emphasis on the use of authority, rules and standard-setting, partially displacing an earlier emphasis on public ownership, public subsidies and directly provided services' (Hood et al. 1999; see also Majone 1997).

Even contemplating statements of this kind would be impossible if designs were plentiful and hundreds or even thousands of discrete types existed. However, even here, most sectors in Europe remain firmly entrenched in traditional and long-lasting corporatist governance modes, and public enterprises are by no means rare and continue to dominate many critical sectors, from mass transportation to power generation and distribution, healthcare, and education, to name only a few.

Why constant and frequent change in governance modes and tool use is not the case and what it is that holds variation in policy designs down to a minimum are discussed in this chapter, which also identifies more accurately what are the main trends in designs over the past two to three decades, utilizing the information set out in Chapters 9–12.

As this discussion shows, the basic context of institutions and structures in which design activities occur serves to create a jurisdiction's 'policy style' (Richardson et al. 1982; Howlett and Tosun 2019) or long-term preference for a certain mode of policy-making and a certain choice of instruments. This style is more difficult to change than often assumed and structures instrument choices and design decisions in predictable ways.

Understanding contemporary policy designs: continuity and change in patterns of instrument choices

Table 13.1 shows how each of the modes of governance discussed earlier in the book includes a specific set of tool preferences, the use of those tools and their interactions being more or less coherent and compatible with that mode.

Table 13.1 Propensity for tool use by governance mode and resource category

		Governance mode			
		Legal	Corporatist	Market	Network
NATO resource category	Organization	Direct government Administrative tribunals	State-owned enterprises	Privatization Contracting out Special operating agencies Private–public partnerships	Clientele agencies Task forces Public hearings
	Authority	Laws Direct regulation Administrative procedures	Independent regulatory commissions Delegated regulation Advisory councils	Deregulation Voluntary and self-regulation	Stakeholder conferences
	Treasure	Excise taxes Insurance	Subsidies, grants, and interest group mobilization	Tax incentives Procurement and vouchers Exhortation and suasion	Interest group creation
	Informational	Product information campaigns Censorship official secrets	Government information campaigns Surveys	Statistics and data collection	Freedom of information

Legal governance modes, for example, are correlated closely with preferences for the use of direct government, laws and direct regulation, excise taxes and insurance, and often, censorship and privacy laws, while alternate modes, such as corporatist governance, are correlated with a preference for the use of state-owned enterprises, independent and other forms of delegated regulation, subsidies and grants, interest group mobilization, and information campaigns. The same is true of market governance modes, to provide another example, which are correlated with a preference for tools such as contracting out, voluntary regulation and deregulation, tax incentives, and data collection. And network governance modes involve the use of tools such as clientele agencies, co-production, consultation mechanisms, interest group creation, and access to information.

Experts in government are familiar with these modes and see the links between them and policy components in terms of the compatibility of the latter with each mode as well as their inner coherence within a policy mix. From their positions in policy advisory networks, they commonly develop policy alternatives which combine these elements in more or less consistent ways, leading to the association of each mode of governance with a particular kind of policy style or manner in which government initiatives are commonly undertaken.

Modes and styles do change as the context of policy-making changes and shifts in governance modes and policy regime logics occur; however, neither changes quickly, and changes are also infrequent (Howlett and Tosun 2019; Howlett and Tosun 2019, 2021). This means there is typically a great deal of continuity and less variation in policy designs across most sectors and issue areas than might be expected. As the discussion in Chapter 2 highlighted, even such 'mega-trends' as globalization and the networkization of society have had only a limited impact on changing the kinds of tools and instruments used in most countries to address their problems.

Rather than see a single change in direction in instrument use in recent decades, in fact, the discussion of individual kinds of policy tools in Chapters 9–12 has indicated that several distinct meso-level trends can be observed in the use of particular types of governing tools in contemporary public policy designs.

These trends in the use of each kind of tool are set out in more detail in what follows.

Patterns of organizational tool use: direct and indirect instrument designs

Despite some moves toward the increased use of procedural tools more compatible with network modes of governance – such as public hearings, task forces, and the establishment of clientele agencies – most policy sectors in most governments remain firmly based in legal or corporatist modes of governance established decades ago. And these continue to feature a prominent role for direct government goods and service delivery – what Chapter 9 described as the 'forgotten fundamental' of policy instruments and policy designs (Leman 1989; Majone 1997).

In recent years, these direct forms of government goods and service delivery have continued to grow in most sectors, although the attention paid to this continued growth has often been overshadowed in the academic literature by that paid to much smaller-scale experimentation with alternate forms of indirect government organization (Aucoin 1997). Patterns of change in the use of this dominant policy tool have been very uneven as governments have expanded in spurts and starts punctuated by major crises, especially in times of war or financial crises or health crises, such as COVID-19, and their aftermath (Bird 1970; Hodgetts 1973).

Public enterprises, for example, grew dramatically in many countries over the course of the twentieth and twenty-first centuries, both in the developed world in association with war efforts and in developing countries as a function of decolonization and drives toward economic development. The spread of privatization in almost every country over the last three decades reflected a rapid and fundamental change in expert attitudes toward the use of this instrument, as governments tried to move many sectors away from corporatist modes of governance under the pressure of cost and other constraints (Le Grand 1984; Walker 1984; Savas 1987; Veljanovski 1988; Kamerman and Kahn 1989; MacAvoy et al. 1989; Salamon 1989; Starr 1989, 1990a; Ikenberry 1990; Richardson 1990; Suleiman and Waterbury 1990; Kemp 1991; Marsh 1991).

The term 'privatization', however, carries at least two different, albeit related, meanings (Starr 1989, 1990a, 1990b). In one common usage, the term is sometimes inaccurately used as a shorthand reference for general efforts made to reduce the scale or scope of government. In this sense, the term is used to denote a basic shift in governance modes toward a more market mode of coordination. In the second sense, however, privatization refers only to those specific efforts made by the state to replace specific organizational instruments based on government ownership with those based on more indirect controls – such as independent regulatory commissions – which does not necessarily entail a corresponding shift toward an overall market governance mode.

In this more restricted sense, a government's commitment to an existing mode of governance can remain unchanged; what changes instead is the general manner in which it meets its commitments: shifting from the use of organizational resources to more authoritative ones. Similarly, instead of regulating a company's polluting activities, to provide another example, the government may offer it a financial incentive to modernize its equipment and curb pollution.

It is this latter development which characterizes the use of organizational tools, and again, this does not represent a fundamental shift in governance mode but rather a limited change of instruments in some sectors within an existing one.

Patterns of authoritative tool use: indirect regulation and increased public participation

Looking at the use and promotion of authority-based substantive policy tools, the discussion in Chapter 10 showed that regulations are compatible with most modes of governance, depending on how state-directed they are. Many policy designs have indeed changed over the past two decades in this tool area as, for example, many regulatory activities have shifted from 'enforcement' to 'compliance' regimes (Hawkins and Thomas 1989; Doern and Wilks 1998). But these activities remain compatible with pre-existing modes of governance and do not necessarily infer a shift toward market or network forms of governance, as many proponents of phenomena such as deregulation have alleged.

Nevertheless, it is true that many governments in recent years indeed have made varying levels of efforts, albeit often more in formulation than implementation, to deregulate important sectors of their economies, that is, to shift from earlier legal or corporatist governance modes to a more market or network mode (Swann 1988; Rubsamen 1989; Gayle and Goodrich 1990; Richardson 1990; Beesley 1992; Collier 1998; Crew and Rowley 1986; Derthick and Quirk 1985; Hammond and Knott 1988; Daugbjerg 1997; Lazer and Mayer-Schonberger 2002). Many such efforts, however, failed to produce qualitatively superior results to the regimes they replaced, leading to a movement back toward 're-regulation' in the policy designs adopted or proposed in many jurisdictions (Jordana and Levi-Faur 2004a; Ramesh and Howlett 2006).

In fact, many of these changes are compatible with other explanations besides a shift in governance mode. Bernstein (1955), for example, postulated close to 75 years ago that a regulatory 'life cycle' existed with regulatory agencies moving from birth to senescence and regulatory decline and termination (or deregulation). In Bernstein's work, the idea was that a regulatory agency or regime would gradually suffer a decline in autonomy due to the accumulation of decisions which would generate a cadre of skilled regulators who moved back and forth between regulators and regulatees, undermining the independence of the regulating body and its legitimacy as an impartial protector of the public interest. Eventually, the regulator would be 'captured' by the regulatee, and the regime would decline into oblivion (Bernstein 1955).

Historical studies generally show that regulatory regimes everywhere evolved gradually, emerging in response to the turbulence caused by industrialization and the growth of unfettered market capitalism (Eisner 1993, 1994a, 1994b). The development of independent regulatory commissions, in fact, is co-terminate with that of the enhancement of the bureaucratic capacity of the modern state (Hodgetts 1964; Skowronek 1982). As an inexpensive and plentiful source of government control, regulation was often invoked by governments eager to reduce their direct government agency–level involvement in the provision of goods and services in society but unwilling to fully trust politically important functions entirely to market actors.

Although regulation was often initially opposed by industry and many professional economists as promoting inefficiency, it was generally accepted in mainstream policy circles as essential for addressing market imperfections and dealing with the uncertainties of modern economic and social life. It is only recently that a broad body of opinion emerged which regards all regulations as inefficient and burdensome for the state itself, and this opinion is not shared widely among government officials and their advisors (Cheung 2005).

The expansion of reservations toward regulations involves two quite distinct movements: on the one hand, toward 'regulatory reform' and, on the other, 'deregulation'. Regulatory reform, for example, involves activities such as the mandating of cost–benefit analyses before the enactment of any new rules, while deregulation involves the wholesale rollback and even abolition of existing rules (McGarity 1991). These two movements represent two separate approaches to resolving 'the regulatory dilemma' highlighted in Bernstein's work (Birch 1984). However, as Eisner has pointed out, these two activities are often incorrectly juxtaposed (Eisner 1994a).

With respect to procedural authoritative instruments, Chapter 10 also underscored the increased use of these tools in response to demands for enhanced participation and consultation in government policy-making driven by domestic groups (Kernaghan et al. 2000).

But this is also not a new phenomenon, and there has been substantial growth in the use of consultative forums and mechanisms in many sectors and countries over the past century. Institutionalized forms of citizen involvement in policy-making attempt to replace agenda-setting and policy influence by only those actors intimately involved in project or policy proposals with a process in which 'outsiders' as well as 'insiders' can promote new and alternative perspectives on these issues (Marchildon 2007). But advisory committees, commissions, task forces, and round tables already existed in many sectors.

Authoritative procedural tool use extending from the increased use of public hearings to the increased creation (and regulation) of advisory committees, for example, has been an ongoing process close to a century. As David Brown noted as early as 1955 in the USA, for example, while in 1938 there were perhaps 100 advisory boards in the US federal government, by 1955 there were 50 in the US Department of Agriculture alone (vs 4 in 1938). But Smith (1977) also noted that this phenomenon varied by jurisdiction and that while by 1962–1963 the US federal government had over 900 advisory committees and the UK in 1960 about 500, Australia only had about 200 by 1975 (see also Brown-John 1979).

As Dion argued as early as 1973, at least part of the growth noted by Brown, Smith, and others was due to the decline of political parties as a vehicle to aggregate public interests and of legislative and representative institutions to articulate them, rather than due to enhanced communications and network activity in society (Dion 1973).

Over the past half-century, these avenues for public participation have provided more institutionalized means for citizen involvement. In many countries and sectors, the 1990s in particular ushered in an era in which a number of new procedural authoritative instruments were established through which enhanced public participation was actively sought by the state both to legitimate state action and to defuse possible conflicts and co-opt dissent (Saward 1992). Environmental task forces, round tables, land-use planning commissions, and other advisory tools, for example, were used by governments in various countries and sectors in the environmental sector as concerns grew around topics such as pollution, deforestation, biodiversity loss, and others, while new legislation embodying processes such as mandatory environmental assessment reviews also created additional instruments mandating public participation. These actions were sector-specific.

It is also the case that problems with limited community group resources and too many consultative exercises can lead to diminishing returns and ineffectiveness if they are utilized too often (Cook 2002; Ross et al. 2002), and some reluctance to engage in continual participatory exercises can be seen in many countries and issue areas. Regulations preventing participatory abuses, such as legislation controlling lobbyists through mandatory registration, have also been deployed, which limit some of these activities (Chari et al. 2007).

Patterns of financial tool use: from visible to invisible instruments

There have been some interesting developments in the patterns of use found in this very old set of instruments and some interesting tool dynamics well worth additional study. While most economic theories push for visible taxes and incentives in order to promote virtues and discourage vice, the reality in most countries is a trend toward the use of more and more hidden financial tools – especially tax-based ones, which are more difficult to trace and quantify than cash-based ones.

Since the tax system is already in place, along with a collections and enforcement apparatus, changes to create new incentives or disincentives through taxes are largely matters of administration. There is some risk involved in their use, though, as it is often difficult to control whether or not a recipient will actually do what a government wants them to with the transferred funds. Agents can often simply take the money offered with few results in terms of achievement of a principal's intentions. Avoiding such principal–agent problems can involve costly and visible enforcement agencies, which negates some of the advantages of the use of these instruments in contemporary policy designs but does not negate their ability to hide large-scale government expenditures while claiming to have cut them.

But again, these trends are not recent. Howard (1993, 1995, 1997, 2002), for example, estimated that the US welfare system by the mid-1990s included $896 million in direct expenditures, but also $437.9 million in more or less hidden tax expenditures (1995: 26). He estimated that while tax expenditures in the USA grew by an average 4.8 percent over the period of 1967–1995 versus 5.9 percent for direct expenditure on income security, health, and housing, over the period of 1980–1990, they grew at a faster rate than direct expenditures (3.9 vs 3.1 percent annual growth), with a similar pattern over the period 1975–1995 (the 'Republican era' in US politics), in what was ostensibly a deficit cutting/free trade era of market-based governance.

This expansion thus represents an effort to mask continuity in governance arrangements based on subsidies and government spending rather than the development of an entirely new mode of governance or policy style.

With respect to procedural financial tools, a pattern in many countries and sectors has been for their increased use over the past 30 years in the effort to enhance and control the operation of interest articulation and aggregation systems in many sectors.

Again, however, this is compatible in many jurisdictions with pre-existing modes of governance and, again, does not necessarily imply a major shift in government behaviour. As we have seen, many groups receive direct or indirect funding from governments, while others are funded indirectly through tax systems which allow for transfers of funds to non-profit and charitable groups either directly or through foundations (Pross and Stewart 1993; Phillips 2001; Sharpe 2001; Carmichael 2010; Wood and Hagerman 2010).

Rather than enhance the activities of social actors, this pattern of government funding typically has some negative consequences for recipient groups (De Vita and Twombly 2005; Pittel and Rubbelke 2006; Guo 2007; Knott and McCarthy 2007) and has not been universally applauded by them. As Laforest and Orsini argued:

> Rather than seeing a multiplicity of innovative practices, voluntary organizations are actually using fewer tools and fewer strategies to influence the policy process, investing most of their energy in research and evidence-based advocacy . . . becoming depoliticized and professionalized as they engage more in research and develop finely honed analytical skills. . . . While voluntary organizations are increasingly being consulted and engaged in policy-making, the basis of these interventions too often lies in their capacity to generate empirical evidence and data, not in their ability to articulate the interests of their constituents.
>
> (Laforest and Orsini 2005: 482; *see also* Cairns et al. 2005)

The use of such procedural financial tools is generally very inexpensive and can be precisely targeted, making them a preferred tool for government managers eager to control their policy environments. But there are some risks involved in such activities, since outside funding promotes oligarchy/formalization in voluntary associations and can lead to discontent both among 'co-opted' group memberships as well as from groups which do not receive funding (Saward 1990, 1992; Lowndes and Skelcher 1998; Smith 2005a, 2005b). Ideological predispositions toward 'free association' in deliberative democratic practices, too, are jeopardized by government manipulation of interest articulation systems, which can lead to further difficulties for governments who engage in this practice in a substantial way, although the lack of visibility and accountability of such practices reduces this concern (Beetham 1991; Phillips 1991; Stanbury 1993; Webb 2000; Maddison 2005; Carmichael 2010).

Patterns of informational tool use: the growth of exhortation, nudges, and public information campaigns

It is now very much a matter of course for information campaigns to accompany many government initiatives, and Chapter 12 showed how expenditures, laws, and programmes in this area have grown as they have been included in more and more policy designs. This is explicable, given the non-coercive and fairly low-cost nature of this tool, which accords well with the ideology and imperatives of liberal-democratic governments and their preferred modes of governance (Margetts and John 2023).

Information dissemination is indeed relatively low cost in terms of financial and personnel outlays as well, but the level of compliance with government urgings which results from its deployment is a major issue. And as in all product advertising, evaluating the impact of these campaigns is very uncertain (Salmon 1989a, 1989b).

Consumers may not pay attention to information provided by, for example, nutritional or eco-labels or may become inured to messages repeated too often (Howells 2005). Effective campaigns can also take some time to get started and evoke any behavioural response, and behaviour can revert back to old habits and patterns once a campaign stops. Or where too much information is provided ('information overload'), intended targets may stop listening, also leading to diminishing returns over time (Bougherara et al. 2007).

The political risks to government in using such tools also may be high if such high-visibility instruments are perceived to have failed to alter behaviour in the desired direction, for example, in reducing greenhouse gas use, this can lead to demands for greater government efforts, such as mandated caps on energy use or carbon taxes.

Moreover, as the discussion of privacy and official secrets legislation in Chapter 12 showed, any moves in a more network governance direction which might be associated with this tool use have been offset by equal moves in the opposite direction toward knowledge suppression, either for state or individual privacy purposes. Freedom of information versus privacy balancing, for example, is very important ideologically in many liberal-democratic countries as it pits individual rights to know what a government is doing against individual rights to privacy (De Saulles 2007). And concerns with state and collective security in times of war or terrorism can lead to a renewed emphasis on restricting information disclosure, as we have seen recently in many countries. Any general diminishment of state power in this area can be easily reversed in times of war or crisis, as was the case in many countries in the post-9/11 environment of the US-led 'war on terror'.

While in recent years more attention has been paid to information-based tools as a result of the 'nudge' movement described in Chapter 12 and in earlier chapters, to date the actual implementation of such measures has been very minor, extending largely to re-writing forms and contracts to alter defaults, as in the case of organ donation provisions on driver's licences and some minor adjustment to traffic laws, and efforts to have citizens engage in more healthy life choices, such as walking upstairs rather than always riding escalators (Lourenco et al. 2016; Moseley and Stoker 2015).

Overall patterns and trends in contemporary policy designs

As this discussion has shown, the patterns of tool use in contemporary policy designs are much more varied than simply involving a cross-sectoral, government-wide shift toward policy mixes associated with a shift toward enhanced market or network governance, as is sometimes alleged, but the actual developments are also not wildly disparate in terms of their content and evolution.

In the case of organizational tools, there has been a noticeable movement in many sectors away from the use of direct government instruments and public enterprises and toward the use of more indirect means of goods and service delivery, such as partnerships, special operating agencies, and quangos. However, this movement should not lead us to underestimate the resilience and continued presence of traditional direct government tools, especially line departments, which remain the backbone of most policy sectors.

In the case of organization-based procedural tools, there has been a simultaneous movement toward the use of government organizational resources to involve larger components of the public or affected 'stakeholders' in policy deliberations. These moves, again, while certainly not new, do reflect a shift in some policy sectors from state-led toward more societally driven modes of organization, as efforts have been made in many countries to implement some aspects of network governance, but again, the breadth and depth of such movements should not be exaggerated.

With respect to authoritative substantive instruments, this same pattern appears once again as the traditional direct and indirect regulatory mechanisms which are a long-term feature of implementation in legal and corporatist modes of governance remain predominant, although they have been augmented by some efforts to promote more voluntary regulatory regimes in some areas such as food safety, forestry, and the fishery.

Again, however, these developments should not be exaggerated. Deregulatory movements in some areas have been offset in many jurisdictions and sectors by the return to direct or indirect regulation through re-regulation of areas such as telecommunications, water, and energy in many countries (Majone 1997). And the relative stasis in this category of tool choice is also visible in its procedural components, as traditional mechanisms such as advisory committee creation continue to be extensive, but has also been that way for decades.

In the area of financial tools, changes in policy designs have been more unidirectional, with most countries seeing a cross-sectoral, government-wide shift in recent years from an emphasis on the use of more visible subsidies to a preference in many sectors for less-visible forms of tax- and royalty-based expenditures. This movement, however, mainly concerns a shift in the visibility of government expenditures in the face of criticisms around debts and deficits and continued government growth. The actual amounts expended, in total, are much the same and typically have increased rather than declined.

On the procedural front, although there is not a great deal of information available from which to judge, it appears that, in many countries, more or less covert efforts to correct collective action problems through the use of tools such as interest group creation have been attempted in many sectors (Bali and Halpin 2021). But this, again, is a policy tool use which is compatible with already-existing modes of governance.

Finally, in the area of information-based tools, the propensity for governments to undertake large-scale public information campaigns has accelerated, as has their use of devices such as surveys and other techniques for monitoring their populations and, more recently, their creation of an extensive social media presence (Margetts and John 2023). On the procedural side, however, an earlier generation's efforts at enhancing information access for the public has been somewhat curtailed in the post-9/11 environment of enhanced security and state secrecy.

The general picture this provides, in terms of measures of government involvement in specific tool choices and policy designs, is of a number of shifts, but much less *between* governance modes than *within* them.

This is not to say that major shifts in governance arrangements never happen but, again, to emphasize that they are rarer than many have argued. The actual trends in instrument set out earlier are much less dramatic than often suggested and suggest a much greater resilience in governance practices and policy styles than is often alleged (Aucoin 1997; Lynn 2001; Hill and Lynn 2004; Hamelin 2010).

It suggests, among other things, that governance modes are more difficult to change than is often argued and provides additional evidence for the contention that policy designs most often must be compatible with previously existing governance modes and preferences if they are to survive the formulation process and be implemented successfully. Empirical evidence of the existence of these kinds of long-term overall governance arrangements exists in the work of Theodore Lowi cited earlier, for example, who noted that while the historical record in general throughout the world has been one featuring the constant expansion of the range and scope of instruments used in governance, in the case of the USA, at least, over a 200-year-plus period, these arrangements proceeded through only four distinct periods.

As he argued in 'Four Systems of Policy, Politics and Choice' (Lowi 1972: 300), 'it is not hard to document historically that the overwhelming proportion of policies produced by the U.S. federal government during the 19th century were distributive', while regulatory policies were introduced in the late nineteenth century and redistributive ones in the twentieth (see also Orren and Skowronek 1998; Skowronek 1982).

Explaining long-term policy design patterns: the persistence of governance modes and policy styles

As this discussion has shown, the insights gained from studies of policy instruments and policy designs are that, because macro-level arrangements such as governance modes typically change only very slowly over time, patterns of government instrument choices tend to exhibit a surprising amount of similarity within policy sectors over time (de Vries 1999, 2002, 2005).

A focus on relatively long-standing structural or institutional factors in the policy formulation process which affect state capacity and network complexity helps explain why long-lasting patterns of instrument choice, such as those discussed earlier, exist at both the sectoral and national levels in most countries.

Studies of this type have identified the key agents responsible for this lack of movement, underlining the key role played by policy experts at the policy formulation stage of the policy-making process in promoting and enhancing continuity. These policy experts, as guardians of knowledge and ideas about the appropriate relationships existing between policy tools and governance modes, occupy key positions in policy advice systems and ensure policy alternatives are developed, which accord with their conceptions of feasibility, meaning, focusing a great deal of attention on their congruence with existing governance norms and contextual dynamics. They play a key role in influencing policy formulation in such a way as, normally, ensures continuity in favoured policy designs or the adoption and maintenance of a distinct policy style (Ohberg et al. 2021).

Conclusion: toward the understanding of best practices in policy design

Students of public policy-making in many countries have begun to move beyond simple macro-level models and theories of policy design and change and have developed a renewed interest in the meso- and micro-aspects of policy formulation and the investigation of the ways in which governments actually propose and utilize the multiple different types of policy instruments available to them (Goggin et al. 1990; Dunsire 1993a). And this is just as true for practitioners as it is for theorists and academics.

As Evert Lindquist (1992) argued close to two decades ago, in the modern era, policy-makers need

> new analytical tools that will help them to diagnose and map the external
> environments of public agencies, to recognize the inherent tensions and
> dynamics in these environments as they pertain to policy development
> and consensus-building and to develop new strategies for 'working' these
> environments in the interests both of their political masters and those of

the broader communities they serve. . . . If public servants are to learn from the experience of colleagues working in other sectors and levels of government, they will need a vocabulary to facilitate the dialogue.

(128–9)

Concepts such as governance modes and policy styles are critical in this regard and form the necessary backdrop to any efforts to outline or detail 'best practices' in policy design and designing.

It is to the articulation of these best principles and practices that we now turn in Part 5.

Readings

Adam, C., S. Hurka and C. Knill. (2015). 'Four Styles of Regulation and Their Implications for Comparative Policy Analysis'. *Journal of Comparative Policy Analysis: Research and Practice* (21 September): 1–18.

Agranoff, R. and M. McGuire. (2001). 'Big Questions in Public Network Management Research'. *Journal of Public Administration Research and Theory 11*, no. 3: 295–326.

Bingham, L. B., T. Nabatchi and R. O'Leary. (2005). 'The New Governance: Practices and Processes for Stakeholder and Citizen Participation in the Work of Government'. *Public Administration Review 65*, no. 5: 547–558.

Derthick, M. and P. J. Quirk. (1985). *The Politics of Deregulation*. Washington, DC: Brookings Institution.

Dion, L. (1973). 'The Politics of Consultation'. *Government and Opposition 8*, no. 3: 332–353.

Eisner, M. A. (1994). 'Discovering Patterns in Regulatory History: Continuity, Change and Regulatory Regimes'. *Journal of Policy History 6*, no. 2: 157–187.

Enkler, J., S. Schmidt, S. Eckhard, C. Knill and S. Grohs. (2016). 'Administrative Styles in the OECD: Bureaucratic Policy-Making beyond Formal Rules'. *International Journal of Public Administration 40*, no. 8 (13 July): 1–12.

Freeman, G. P. (1985). 'National Styles and Policy Sectors: Explaining Structured Variation'. *Journal of Public Policy 5*, no. 4: 467–496.

Hammond, T. H. and J. H. Knott. (1988). 'The Deregulatory Snowball: Explaining Deregulation in the Financial Industry'. *Journal of Politics 50*, no. 1: 3–30.

Howard, C. (1993). 'The Hidden Side of the American Welfare States'. *Political Science Quarterly 108*, no. 3: 403–436.

Howlett, M. and M. Ramesh. (1993). 'Patterns of Policy Instrument Choice: Policy Styles, Policy Learning and the Privatization Experience'. *Policy Studies Review 12*, no. 1: 3–24.

Howlett, M. and J. Tosun. (2021). 'National Policy Styles in Theory and Practice'. In M. Howlett and J. Tosun (eds.), *The Routledge Handbook of Policy Styles*. New York: Routledge, 15–24.

Jordana, J. and D. Levi-Faur. (2004). 'The Politics of Regulation in the Age of Governance'. In J. Jordana and D. Levi-Faur (eds.), *The Politics of Regulation: Institutions and Regulatory Reforms for the Age of Governance*. Cheltenham, UK: Edward Elgar, 1–28.

Kammerman, S. B. and A. J. Kahn. (1989). *Privatization and the Welfare State*. Princeton, NJ: Princeton University Press.

Libecap, G. D. (1986). 'Deregulation as an Instrument in Industrial Policy: Comment'. *Journal of Institutional and Theoretical Economics 142*: 70–74.

Majone, G. (1997). 'From the Positive to the Regulatory State: Causes and Consequences of Changes in the Mode of Governance'. *Journal of Public Policy 17*, no. 2: 139–167.

Moran, M. (2002). 'Review Article: Understanding the Regulatory State'. *British Journal of Political Science 32*, no. 2: 391–413.

Rhodes, R. A. W. (1994). 'The Hollowing Out of the State: The Changing Nature of the Public Service in Britain'. *The Political Quarterly 65*, no. 2: 138–151.

Vogel, D. (2005). *The Market for Virtue: The Potential and Limits of Corporate Social Responsibility*. Washington, DC: Brookings Institution.

Part V

LESSONS FOR POLICY DESIGNS AND DESIGNERS

Chapter 14

How best to assemble and evaluate a policy design

Character and context in contemporary policy designs

As Stephen Linder, B. Guy Peters, Davis Bobrow, Peter May, Patricia Ingraham, Christopher Hood, Renate Mayntz, and the other pioneers of policy design research in the 1980s and 1990s argued, like other kinds of design activities in manufacturing and construction, policy design involves three fundamental aspects: (1) knowledge of the basic building blocks or materials with which actors must work in constructing a (policy) object; (2) the elaboration of a set of principles regarding how these materials should be combined in that construction; and (3) understanding the process by which a design becomes translated into reality.

The previous chapters in the book discussed two of these topics. Chapters 1–8 outlined the processes by which designs occur, while Chapters 9–12 augmented this analysis with a detailed discussion of the basic building blocks of policy designs. What remains to be done, then, is to look at the second topic and outline the principles or best practices for policy design which have been described in the literature on the topic. It is to this subject that this part of the book is addressed.

The role of design in policy success and failure

Design is a crucial activity in policy-making and in considerations of potential and actual policy success or failure (Marsh and McConnell 2010; McConnell

DOI: 10.4324/9781003343431-19

2010). This is because it can embody the lessons learned (or not) from other policy activities at the moment in time when a new policy is being developed or an old one reformed, with the usual expectation being that the possibility of success of the new or revised policy would be enhanced as a result of good design.

Of course, what exactly constitutes policy success and failure has been a subject which has pre-occupied both policy scholars and practitioners for decades (Kerr 1976; McConnell 2020). Many of these studies have suffered from a wealth of incompatible terms and concepts used to ascertain success or failure, from attainment of original government objectives to normative arguments to a focus on results or an emphasis on continued support by key policy actors and stakeholders, and these different approaches and criteria have, until recently, greatly diminished their cumulative impact.

McConnell (2010), for example, usefully listed nine criteria which are commonly used to define and assess success and failure in the policy literature (see Table 14.1).

Failures, like successes, differ significantly in cause and also in extent and magnitude. They can be large or small, long-term or short-term, for example, and some may be highly visible while others discernible only to experts. These central characteristics of policy success and failure are set out in Table 14.2 (Howlett 2012).

As the table shows, failures vary along several key dimensions, from extent to visibility, duration, and intensity, but also in terms of intentionality or avoidability.

Table 14.1 Criteria for policy success and failure (after McConnell)

Basis of claim	Claim of success	Claim of failure
Original objectives	Achieved	Not achieved
Target group impact	Positive impact	Negative impact
Results	Problem improvement	Problem worsening
Significance	Important to act	Failing to act
Source of support/ opposition	Key groups support	Key groups oppose
Jurisdictional comparisons	Best practice or superior performance	Someone is doing this better elsewhere
Balance sheet	High benefits	High costs
Level of innovation	New changes	Old response
Normative stance	Right thing to do	Wrong thing to do

Source: Adapted from McConnell (2010).

Table 14.2 Six dimensions of policy success and failure

Attribute	Range
Extent (size)	From large (regime) to small (event)
Avoidability	From low to high
Visibility	From low to high
Intentionality	From low to high
Duration	From long to short
Intensity	From low to high

Source: Howlett (2012).

Combining several of these elements together and focusing on their magnitude and salience, it is possible to arrive at a more concise taxonomy of failure types (see Table 14.3). This allows distinctions to be made between major and minor failures, and focused and diffuse ones, clarifying the dependent variable in studies of failures and better informing considerations of the kinds of efforts that might contribute to them.

Table 14.3 Principal types of policy success and failure by magnitude and salience

		Magnitude (extent and duration)	
		High	Low
Salience (intensity and visibility)	High	**Type 1 – major failure** For example, climate change (international treaty) policy failure	**Type 2 – focused failure** For example, sports crowd control (riots) policy failure
	Low	**Type 3 – diffuse failure** For example, anti-poverty policy failure	**Type 4 – minor failure** For example, charities (fraud) policy

Source: Howlett (2012).

Another important dimension of the subject, however, is when failures occur in policy making. Some failures originate immediately in the agenda-setting process, while others emerge later due to problems encountered in formulation or decision-making, while others are linked to implementation or evaluation (Howlett et al. 2020) (see Table 14.4).

Table 14.4 Policy failures by stage of the policy cycle

Policy stage	Example of source of policy failure
Agenda-setting	Over-reaching governments establishing or agreeing to establish over-burdened or unattainable policy agendas
Policy formulation	Attempting to deal with problems without investigating or researching problem causes and identifying the probable effects of policy alternatives
Decision-making	Failing to decide on a policy within a reasonable period of time or distorting its intent through bargaining and logrolling
Policy implementation	Failing to deal with implementation problems, including lack of resources, principal–agent problems, oversight failures, and others
Policy evaluation	Lack of learning due to lack of, ineffective, or inappropriate policy monitoring and/or feedback processes and structures

As Table 14.4 shows, this means some policies can fail 'early on' in the policy process – including in the process of policy design – if and when governments 'bite off more than they can chew' or take on too many issues beyond their capacity to deal with (Howlett et al. 2017). Others emerge later, including the failure to draw any or appropriate lessons from policy evaluations.

Some of the better-known policy tools that can help offset or manage risk and volatility discussed in this literature are set out in Table 14.5. Better management of policy processes along these lines to avoid or restrain malevolent behaviours and results is often the key if these problems are to be avoided (Banks 1995).

Table 14.5 Sources of policy malignancy and design alternatives

Tool type	Flaw	Examples	Procedural tool solutions
Organization	**Agency failure or co-optation**	Corruption Contracting and procurement issues Perverse co-production/ clientelism	Accountability/ transparency rules Anti-corruption bureaus Blockchain bidding and procurement/ contracting records Fraud squads

Tool type	Flaw	Examples	Procedural tool solutions
Authority	**Corruption, favouritism, and gaming**	Capture and venue-shopping Bribes and kickbacks Extortion	Whistle-blower laws Sunset laws Merit appointments Conflict of interest laws
Treasure	**Fraud and gaming**	Misrepresentation False claims Swindles Cheating	Complete contracts Careful subsidy/tax design Monitoring Verification/ enforcement/ inspections
Nodality	**Biased information**	Propaganda Slander Improper secrecy	More carefully targeted messages Truth in advertising laws Libel and slander laws Access to information laws

These distinctions and their correctives are important in studying policy designs and understanding their possibility of success and failure. Design studies, therefore, need to recognize the principal sources and nature of policy success and failure, their role within them and design policies accordingly.

Principles of effective policy designs based on the character of tools

Like architecture or engineering, it is critical to policy-making that the lessons of past efforts – both successes and failures – are encapsulated into principles of sound design which can offer the best chance of the attainment of government goals and objectives in prevailing circumstances (May 1981; Schneider and Ingram 1988; Weimer 1992a; Rose 1993, 2005; Grabosky 1995; Gunningham and Sinclair 1999a).

Policy designs are expected to, as much as possible, avoid failure and to result, instead, in successful policies, namely, ones which are reasonably effective and efficient in achieving government goals. Developing basic principles expected to result in superior or more effective designs and continually testing and refining these designs and principle in practice is one way in which the prospects of success can be enhanced.

The literature on policy design reviewed in earlier sections of the book has, over the years, highlighted several such key principles for effective policy designs based on the 'character' or innate characteristics of the tools set out in Chapters 9–12 and upon the design 'context' discussed in earlier chapters.

These principles are expected to inform policy design considerations in this area. The lessons that can be taken from past design experiences often take the form of heuristics or guides to action articulated as policy principles. Three of these principles linked to tool character are listed in what follows. More contextual concerns then follow this discussion.

Parsimonious tool use and the Tinbergen rule

One design question involves determining how many tools are required for the efficient attainment of a goal or goals. The older literature on policy design suggested several maxims or heuristics which can be used to head off some common errors in policy-making. The first and oldest of these is to observe parsimony in tool selection.

This concern has animated policy design studies from their outset, and an example of an oft-cited rule in this area originating in the very early years of policy design studies is that the optimal ratio of the number of tools to targets or goals in any portfolio is 1:1 (Knudson 2009). This is a rule-of-thumb design principle toward which the Nobel Prize winner Jan Tinbergen (1952) provided some logical justification in his discussion of the information and administrative costs associated with the use of redundant tools in the area of economic policy.

The issue of potentially under- or over-designing a mix arises in all policy-making circumstances and is made more complex because in some instances, for example, arrangements may be unnecessarily duplicative while in others some redundancy may be advantageous in ensuring that goals will be met (Braathen and Croci 2005; Braathen 2007a). Tinbergen analyzed what he termed the 'normal' case, in which it was possible to match one goal with one target so that one instrument could fully address its task and accomplish the goal set out for it.

Prima facie, however, as we have seen, simple Tinbergen-type single-instrument, single-goal, single-policy, single-government instrument mixes represent only one of many possible types of such mixes and a relatively rare one. Most observers, instead have found that combinations of tools are more typical in efforts to address multiple policy goals (Jordan et al. 2012).

This means that the standard Tinbergen design maxim of 'one goal, one tool' proposed as a suitable design maxim to address the issue of instrument optimality is unlikely to be put into practice very often, and other principles need to be developed to take its place within more complex designs. In fact, even Tinbergen (1952: 37) himself argued, '*a priori* there is no guarantee that the number of targets always equals the number of instruments', and (71) 'it goes without saying that complicated systems of economic policy (for example) will almost invariably be a mixture of instruments'.

A more modern interpretation of the Tinbergen rule is that it reflects a concern for parsimony, meaning utilizing only the number of tools required to reasonably attain policy goals and achieve compliance with government wishes and no more than that. While it may not be clear at the start what is that number, beginning with a smaller number and adding tools as needed to ensure compliance and monitoring the impact and effect of each additional tool can help identify it (see the discussion of 'sequencing' in what follows and the ideas on this point raised by Doern and his colleagues outlined in earlier chapters).

Avoiding over- and under-designing when not necessary: (dis)proportionality in policy designs

As has also been discussed in earlier chapters, in an ideal world, designing policies involves governments always acting as efficient policy-makers. As a consequence, any errors in decision-making – over- or under-reacting to the nature of a problem – can be attributed to idiosyncratic errors, such as poor information control and management, personality conflicts, or miscalculation of costs and benefits of public action. In this sense, the task of policy advisors and of a policy advisory system as a whole is to provide templates for government action appropriate or 'proportionate' to the objective characteristics and severity of a policy problem.

However, it is well-known that this simple situation of 'proportionality' is less common than might be assumed (deLeon 1999a; Hargrove 1975). In fact, studies of policy success and failure suggest more complex patterns in which many policy efforts intentionally under- or over-react to problems or oscillate between these two states (Maor 2012a, 2014a; de Vries 2010).

That is, some poorly calibrated efforts may only be temporary in nature, reflecting a sort of poor marksmanship in the early stages of a trial-and-learning approach to resolve a problem which will be corrected in future. But many instances involve sustained periods of over- and under-reaction in which either government resources are wasted or problems continue to be unresolved (de Vries 2010). These systematic over- and under-reactions and specifically sustained under-reactions are the subject of much current research interest (Maor 2014a, Jones et al. 2014).

At least some of the blame for over- and under-reactions and over- and under-designs often falls on policy advisors and poor policy designs. The social and political construction of underlying policy problems (Zuckerman 2012) always gives room for political controversy and disagreement in assessing exactly what is the nature of the problem at hand and, therefore, what is a reasonable or proportionate response to it. In this sense, as many have argued, feedback loops between policy-makers, expert advisors, and the public also play a major role in creating both inflationary and deflationary pressures upon problem definitions and policy solutions (Jacobs and Weaver 2014; also Patashnik 2003).

Jones et al. (2014), for example, argue the origins of a many over-reactions are biases in information processing which occur at least in part due to the insulation of policy-making elites from public sentiments. Maor (2014a) also explains policy over-reaction by looking at valence politics or differences between the emotional and unemotional content of specific policy issues, especially considering the role extreme forms of public sentiment, such as moral outrage or panics, can play in promoting policy over-reactions.

In the case of such over-reactions, Maor argues that this reaction is sustained by cognitive, ideational, and institutional processes, such as interest group support or the persuasiveness of causal narratives favouring action over inaction (Stone 1988). Institutional fragmentation into several policy subsystems more susceptible to groupthink and less autonomous from interest groups and the public than larger, more unified ones has also been noted to lead to this type of disproportionate response (May et al. 2009).

However, even in larger subsystems, over-reactions can follow a 'naïve' contagion process in which policy (mis)learning contributes to over-reaction. Herd behaviour of advisors in support of particular actions can lead governments – similar to the financial investors acting in concert in the case of asset bubbles – to copy policy practices from other jurisdictions without considering their limitations or contextual constraints (Jarvis 2014; Daugbjerg and McConnell 2021).

Compared to that on over-reactions, the literature on under-reactions is much less well developed (but see Maor 2014b). Empirically, of course, one can find many illustrations of this phenomenon. Harmful international tax competition (e.g. Kemmerling 2009; Holzinger 2005) in which countries are slow to respond to changes in other jurisdictions. The slow reaction of agencies to epidemics such as the 'mad cow disease' (BSE) is one example and other health issues (Leiss and Powell 2004; Smith 2004; Oosterveer 2002) are prime examples of policy underinvestment which, again, are closely linked to the nature of the advice policy-makers receive from epistemic communities, instrument constituencies, and advocacy coalitions often acting in their self-interest to promote policy inaction (McConnell and t'Hart 2019).

Policy analysts and formulators need to be aware of these possibilities and formulate policy options and alternatives accordingly.

Sequencing: moving up the scale of coercion in instrument choices

A third principle of good policy design found in the literature is not only to be parsimonious and proportionate in the number of instruments chosen at a specific point in order to attain a goal but also to be so dynamically or sequentially.

As we saw in Chapter 8, in the mid-1970s and early 1980s, for example, Bruce Doern, Richard Phidd, and Seymour Wilson argued that different policy instruments varied primarily in terms of the 'degree of government coercion' each instrument choice entailed (Doern 1981; Doern and Phidd 1983; Doern and Wilson 1974; Tupper and Doern 1981) and that tool choices should only 'move up the spectrum' of coercion or be sequenced from minimum toward maximum if and when necessary this rationale for the sequencing of policies in terms of increased stringency of the tools deployed.

This rationale is based on a cost–effort calculation and can occur in an effort to proportionally calibrate a policy but can also be linked to preferred governance modes. Doern and his colleagues, for example, linked it to an appreciation of the ideological preferences of liberal-democratic governments for limited state activity combined with the difficulties posed to the exercise of state power and policy compliance by the relative political 'strength' or ability of societal actors to resist government efforts to shape their behaviour.

Doern and his colleagues argued that in a liberal democratic society, governments, for both cost and ideological reasons, would prefer to use the least-coercive instruments available and would only 'move up the scale' of coercion as far as was necessary in order to overcome societal resistance to attaining their policy goals (Howlett 1991). Preferring 'self-regulation' as a basic default, for example, they argued that governments should first attempt to influence overall target group performance through exhortation and then only add instruments as required in order to compel recalcitrant societal actors to abide by their wishes, eventually culminating, if necessary, in the fully public provision of goods and services.

Principles of good policy design based on the character of tool mixes

The studies cited in earlier chapters also provide admonitions to policy designers and articulate principles of good policy formulation and design linked to the characteristics of policy *portfolios* as well as that of individual tools. Three of these are set out here.

Integrating policy elements: utilizing coherence, consistency, and congruence as measures of the superiority of a policy mix

As we have seen, much work on policy design and policy mixes has focused on the need for the various parts of a mix or portfolio to be *integrated* for maximum effectiveness (Briassoulis 2005a, 2005b; Howlett and Rayner 2007; Lanzalaco 2011; Mandell 2008; Howlett and Rayner 2007; Kern and Howlett 2009).

Policies are composed of several elements, and some correspondence across these elements is required if policy goals are to be integrated successfully with policy means (Cashore and Howlett 2007; Trein et al. 2020, 2023).

The criteria which allow the assessment of integration include '*consistency*', or the ability of multiple policy tools to reinforce rather than undermine each other in the pursuit of policy goals; '*coherence*', or the ability of multiple policy goals to co-exist with each other and with instrument norms in a logical fashion; and '*congruence*', or the ability of goals and instruments to work together in a uni-directional or mutually supportive fashion (Lanzalaco 2011; Howlett and Rayner 2007; Kern and Howlett 2009).

While clear enough in theory, empirical work on the evolution of policy mixes has highlighted how these three criteria are often weakly represented in existing mixes, especially those which have evolved through successive patching and layering processes over a long period of time (Howlett and Rayner 2006b; Rayner and Howlett 2009; Miller 1990).

Many existing studies assume, whether explicitly or implicitly, that *any* combination of tools is possible in any circumstance. That is, that decision-makers have unlimited *degrees of freedom* in their design choices. But as we have seen and has been noted in earlier chapters, empirical studies have noted this kind of freedom in combining design elements is only to be found in very specific circumstances – what Thelen (2003) terms 'replacement' or 'exhaustion' – when older tool elements have been swept aside or abandoned and a new mix can be designed or adopted *de novo*. These circumstances are quite rare, and most existing mixes or portfolios rather have emerged from a gradual historical process in which the elements of a policy mix have slowly built up over time through processes of incremental change or successive reformulation – processes that historical institutionalists such as Thelen (2003) or Hacker (2004b, 2005) term 'layering', 'drift', or 'conversion' (Bode 2006).

Intelligent design of policy mixes needs to ensure a good fit of policy elements not only between packages of tools and government goals and their institutional and behavioural contexts at a specific moment in time (Considine 2012; Lejano and Shankar 2013) but also across time periods as new instruments appear and old ones evolve or are eliminated (Larsen et al. 2006; Kay 2007; Feindt and Flynn 2009).

Recognizing the drawbacks of layering, conversion, and drift as often promoting poorly integrated mixes, many critics have increasingly argued for the promotion of complex policy mixes through processes of 'smart patching', in which goal and instrument coherence can be achieved by, over time, removing or altering inconsistent and incongruent elements to consciously create a more integrated and interlocking packages of measures (Feindt and Flynn 2009; Kay 2007; Howlett and Rayner 2014).

Smart designing: maximizing complementary effects and minimizing counterproductive ones

Recent design thinking and earlier work on 'smart regulation' both underlined the importance of considering the full range of policy instruments when designing a mix rather than assuming that a choice must be made between only a few alternatives, such as regulation versus market tools (Gunningham et al. 1998).

However, a major issue for such studies is the fact that not all the tools involved and invoked in a mix are inherently complementary (Tinbergen 1952; Grabosky 1995; Gunningham et al. 1998; Gunningham and Sinclair 1999a; del Rio et al. 2011; Boonekamp 2006) in the sense that they evoke contradictory responses from policy targets (Schneider and Ingram 1990a, 1990b, 1993, 1994, 1997, 2005). Some combinations, of course, may also be more virtuous in providing a reinforcing or supplementing arrangement (Hou and Brewer 2010). And some other arrangements may also be unnecessarily duplicative, while in others some redundancy may be advantageous (Braathen and Croci 2005; Braathen 2007a).

That is, as Grabosky (1995) and others suggested, some tools counteract each other – for example, using command-and-control regulation while also attempting voluntary compliance – while, as Hou and Brewer (2010) argued, other tools complement or supplement each other – for example, using command-and-control regulation to prevent certain behaviour deemed undesirable and financial incentives to promote more desired activities.

A key principle of current policy design thinking, therefore, is to try to maximize supplementary effects while minimizing counterproductive ones. 'Smart' design implies creating packages which take these precepts into account in their formulation or packaging (Gunningham et al. 1998; Gunningham and Sinclair 1999b; Eliadis et al. 2005).

That is, when multiple tools are involved in a mix, the tools involved and invoked in a mix may be inherently contradictory, and this kind of relationship should be avoided in a 'smart' design.

Although a consensus does not exist on the terms and definitions of actual and potential conflicts and complementarities (Oikonomou and Jepma 2007; Oikonomou et al. 2010, 2011a), the types of interaction found between tools logically include the possibilities of:

1. A strong conflict, where the addition of an instrument (X) leads to a reduction of the effect of a second instrument (Y) in the combination: $0 < X + Y < 1$.
2. A weak conflict (partial complementarity), where the addition of an instrument to another leads to a positive effect on the combination, but lower than the one that would take place if both were used separately: $1 < X + Y < 2$.
3. A situation of full complementarity, where X adds fully to the effect of Y in the combination: $X + Y = 2$.
4. A situation of synergy, where adding X to Y magnifies the impact of the combination: $X + Y > 2$.

(del Río 2014)

Such interactions thus can range from 'no effect' to 'direct interaction', with effects ranging from 'duplication' (positive or negative redundancy) to 'extended coverage' (positive redundancy) (del Rio 2007; da Costa 2013).

Effective design should, wherever possible, involve avoiding strong conflicts, minimizing weak ones, and promoting complementarity and synergies. While this becomes more difficult to do as the level of complexity of the design space increases, it remains a central goal of portfolio design. Although it may not be possible to eliminate all conflicts, they can be made explicit, allowing policy-makers to decide on what trade-off might be involved according to their preferences rather than discovering them later (Pluchinotta et al. 2020; Leong and Howlett 2022b).

But both horizontal and vertical integration are very difficult to achieve in complex mixes of this type. The existence of different goals at different administrative levels complicates vertical coordination (Petek et al. 2021, 2022). Different benefits and costs for different constituencies may lead to low levels of social acceptability and jeopardize political feasibility. Different goals may create winners and losers at lower administrative levels and thus lead to unacceptable distributional effects at others or involve trade-offs between goals and actors. And, as mentioned earlier, attention also needs to be focused on the need to properly sequence instrument choices within mixes (Taeihagh et al. 2009, 2013; Daugbjerg 2009).

Better matching tools and target behaviours in compliance regimes

As we have also seen in earlier chapters, there also is a significant behavioural component to the design of policy mixes which is critical to policy success and failure (Weaver 2009b; Lynn 1986; Schneider and Ingram 1990a; Shafir 2013). That is, as discussed in Chapter 5 in some detail, it is critically important for policy-making that the behaviour resulting from policy activity and the expenditure of governing resources match that anticipated prior to deployment (May 2004; Kaine et al. 2010; Duesberg et al. 2014).

Policy tool use and behavioural expectations are linked in the sense that the use of policy tools involves implicit or explicit assumptions and expectations about the effect tool deployment will have upon those impacted by it. In most cases, with the exception of those symbolic instances where 'over-design' is welcomed, such as in areas such as national security or crime prevention (Maor 2013, 2014a, 2017), efficient policy designs are those that affect only those targets whose behaviour it is necessary to change and with only the minimum necessary levels of coercion and display.

Policy designs themselves, however, have often been developed with only the most rudimentary and cursory knowledge of how those expected to be affected by an instrument are in fact likely to react to it (Lewis 2007; Corner and Randall 2011; Taylor et al. 2013; Duesberg et al. 2014). Regardless of whether those targets are purely social constructions with few empirical referents (Schneider and Ingram 1993, 2005) or if they reflect more objective assessment of the actual behaviour of relevant groups of policy actors, however, it is critical for effective policy-making that actual target behaviour matches expectations, and this is thus a key aspect of effective policy design (Grabosky 1995; Weaver 2009a, 2009b, 2014, 2015; Winter and May 2001; Nielsen and Parker 2012).

When designing for high levels of compliance, for example, Weaver (2009a, 2014, 2015) argues that the appropriate responses of governments to these challenges and barriers is to create a 'compliance regime' involving a mix of tools and elements.

A basic regime of this kind includes such traditional arrangements as:

- Providing positive incentives for compliance
- Having negative incentives for non-compliance
- Providing prohibitions and requirements with punishments attached

But it also includes less-traditional elements, such as:

- Providing information about what behaviour is compliant, how to comply, and the advantages of compliance
- Providing admonitions to comply on moral, self-interested, or other grounds, as well as utilitarian ones
- Providing resources to comply which may be targeted to those who would otherwise lack those resources
- Manipulating options and defaults (choice architecture) without substantially affecting the pay-off to individuals of so doing (Weaver 2015: 6)

Weaver (2009b: 5) also enumerated the various 'compliance problems' or 'barriers' to compliance which targets and governments face and which should be the subject of investigation and design action. These include:

- **Incentive and sanction problems,** where positive and/or negative incentives are insufficient to ensure compliance
- **Monitoring problems,** where target compliance may be difficult or costly to monitor
- **Resource problems,** where targets lack the resources to comply even if they want to
- **Autonomy problems,** where targets do not have the power to make decisions that comply with policy even if they want to
- **Information problems,** where targets lack information that would make compliance more likely
- **Attitude and objectives problems,** where targets are hostile/mistrustful toward providers or programmes

What is needed for effective designs, he argues, is that policy-makers and designers take these problems and barriers into account and ensure their choices and designs are underscored by a systematic analysis and understanding of the motivations of policy targets. This allows better matching of tools and targets right at the outset of policy-making than would occur by relying only upon utilitarian pre-conceptions of such behaviour (Weaver 2009a, 2009b; Schneider and Sidney 2009; Chatterton and Wilson 2014). This may also involve, as Braithwaite (2003) noted, the intentional scaling up or down of the resource-intensiveness of various tools and policy packages as behaviour changes or, as the case may be, does not.

Principles of good policy design based on the design context

While knowledge of the character of individual tools and of how tools and goals interact in policy mixes is critical in developing principles for good policy designs, the policy design *context* is equally so (deLeon 1988).

While the choice of a specific instrument could be made on essentially technical grounds, according to criteria such as efficiency, cost, or effectiveness, it is also affected by the political preferences of interest groups and governments, and a variety of sociological and ideological constraints inform tool choices and preferences.

A host of contextual factors comes into play in instrument choices and affects design decisions. Decisions about tools and designs are not random, and context, like character, can be systematically modelled and analyzed in its effects on the process of policy designing. As the discussion in Chapter 13 noted, aspects of the policy environment, including the nature of preferred and existing governance modes and policy styles, influence assessments of the desirability, feasibility, and appropriateness of specific kinds of tools and help explain common patterns and motifs in the construction of policy designs in different jurisdictions (Richardson et al. 1982; Howlett 2004a; Howlett 2009d).

In other words, the design of a good policy mix requires ensuring a good fit not only between types of tools and government goals but also with their institutional and behavioural contexts (Considine 2012; Lejano and Shankar 2013).

The need for high levels of policy capacity

As noted in earlier chapters, existing work on the subject of policy portfolio design has helped address this issue by differentiating between design spaces which are simple and more complex (Howlett 2004b, 2011; Howlett et al. 2006), and this work has broached the question of the ability or capacity and intent of governments to undertake specific kinds of design activity.

Having the necessary skills or *competences* to make policy is crucial to policy and governance success. However, they also rely on their availability and the availability of adequate resources to allow them to be mobilized. These resources or *capabilities* must exist at the individual, organizational, and system levels in order to allow individual policy workers and managers to participate in and contribute to designing, deploying, and evaluating policies. It includes their ability not only to analyze but also to learn and adapt to changes as necessary (Wu et al. 2015a).

Analytical competences allow policy alternatives to be effectively generated and investigated, managerial capacities allow state resources to be effectively brought to bear on policy issues, and political capacities allow policy-makers and managers the support required to develop and implement their ideas, programmes, and plans. The skills and competences of key policy professionals, such as policy-makers, public managers, and policy analysts, play a key role in determining how well various tasks and functions in policy process work but require various kinds of resources if they are to be exercised fully or to the extent they are needed. But resources must also be available at the level of the organization if their members' ability to perform policy functions as needed is to exist.

System-level capabilities include the level of support and trust a public agency enjoys from its political masters and from the society at large, as well as the nature of the economic and security systems within which policy-makers operate. Such factors are a critical determinant of organizational capabilities and thus of public managers' and analysts' capability to perform their policy work. Political support for both from both above and below is also vital because agencies and managers must be considered legitimate in order to access resources from their authorizing institutions and constituencies on a continuing basis, and such resources must also be available for award in the first place (Woo et al. 2015).

Goodness of fit and degrees of freedom: the need for designs to match governance mode and policy regime capacities

Just as was the case with single-instrument and mix characteristics, it is possible to highlight several design principles which flow from the analysis of the design contexts set out above. These include the question of *goodness of fit* of proposed designs with pre-existing governance preferences and the need for an accurate analysis of the *degrees of freedom* designers have to innovate at any specific moment in time.

'Goodness of fit' between tool choices and choice contexts is a key concern in contemporary policy design considerations and can be seen to occur at several different levels (Brandl 1988). As the discussion in Chapter 13 highlighted, pre-existing policy styles and governance modes affect tool and design choices and significantly impact the ultimate success of mooted policy options and alternatives.

Different orientations toward state activity require different capabilities on the part of state and societal actors, and since different governance modes or styles rely on these to greater or lesser degrees, policy designs must take into account both the existing governance context and the resources available to a governmental or non-governmental actor in carrying out its expected role.

Thus, for example, planning and 'steering' involve direct coordination of key actors by governments, requiring a high level of government policy analytical and political capacity to identify and utilize a wide range of policy tools in a successful policy 'mix' or 'arrangement' (Arts et al. 2000, 2006).

Also, as noted earlier, empirical studies in many policy areas have shown that many existing policy mixes were not 'designed' in the classical sense of conscious, intentional, and deliberate planning according to well-established or oft-used governance principles but rather evolved through layering and other similar processes. As Christensen et al. (2002) have argued, the issue here is the leeway or *degrees of freedom* policy designers have in developing new designs, given existing historical arrangements, path dependencies, policy legacies, and lock-in effects.

That is, in addition to the requirements of 'goodness of fit' with prevailing governance modes, constraints are imposed on designs by existing sectoral trajectories of policy development and policy capacities. As Christensen et al. note, 'these factors place constraints on and create opportunities for purposeful choice, deliberate instrumental actions and intentional efforts taken by political and administrative leaders to launch administrative reforms through administrative design' (2002: 158).

Determining how much room to manoeuvre or the degrees of freedom designers have to be creative (Considine 2012) or, to put it another way, to what degree they are 'context bound' in time and space (Howlett 2011) is a key requisite of contemporary design studies.

Designing to deal with temporal uncertainty: agility and robustness as hallmarks of good policy design

As we saw in earlier chapters, how to deal with uncertainty and surprise is an issue which has troubled policy studies for some time and one which has many implications for policy design. That is, it is often not enough to design for policy success in the short term but rather requires a longer-term horizon and special measures so that policy success may persist in future years, often well beyond the electoral lifespan of an enacting government.

This is inevitably the case with many policy issues, from re-forestation and timber management to pension or highways planning, which entail long policy horizons for regeneration and operation and construction, but also extends to many other issues as well, such as unemployment insurance or social welfare policy, which have shorter-term goals but also a long lifespan (Jacobs 2011).

How can this best be done?

Designing for the long term: robustness and resilience in policy designs

The modern policy sciences are founded on the idea that accumulating and utilizing knowledge of the effects and impacts of a relatively well-known set of policy means developed over many years of state-building experience allows policy-makers to effectively marshal and utilize those lessons (Lerner and Lasswell 1951; Howlett and Mukherjee 2014).

However, there has also been a recognition that even in cases of well-thought-out and well-intentioned or otherwise well-designed policies, failures commonly occur as time elapses and circumstances change (Nair and Howlett 2017; Howlett et al. 2015). That is, even when policies are designed with a clear evidentiary basis in a model process, they may still fail if they do not adapt to changing circumstances and concerns as policy implementation proceeds and the policy is put into action (Nair and Howlett 2017).

Studies of policy uncertainty and policy failure have emphasized the need to enact policies able to cope with the many anticipated and unexpected events which might occur over the lifespan of a programme or policy. As noted in earlier chapters, the future is always very uncertain, meaning, there is a need to design and adopt many policies in a manner which encourages agility, improvisation, and flexibility. Over the course of a policy, governments may well have to grapple not only with complex problems involving situations in which they must deal with multiple actors, ideas, and interests but to also do so in the context of complex problem environments in which these elements typically evolve and change over time (Arts and van Tatenhove 2004; Lasswell 1958; Stone 1988).

The kinds of designs needed to deal with such issues often require redundant resources and capabilities in order to remain 'robust' or 'resilient' in the face of change, and this need is in strong opposition to ideas about design which equate better designs purely with short-term efficiency and the allocation of the absolute minimum amount of resources required at the present time. And it also stands in contrast to views of effective designs which emphasize routinization and the rote replication of standard operating procedures and programme elements.

While these latter kinds of designs may be appropriate in some circumstances where risks are well-known and environments are stable, so that surprise is unlikely, this is not true of many public sector activities, where government is the sole provider of specific goods and services and future scenarios are unknown, contested, or unpredictable. As studies of crisis management and other similar situations have emphasized, in these instances, policy robustness is needed and needs to be planned for.

Efforts to preserve a policy's original intent by continuing to adhere to the original policy goals and alter some aspects of policy tools, objectives, specifications, and/or calibrations in the face of changes in the policy environment constitute a form of adaptive robustness (Jordan and Matt 2014). When an object is able to respond to changes in its environment, it is 'adaptive'. It can be said to be 'resilient' when it is able to retain its original purpose in the face of the changes (Holling 1973). Both such relationships may be described as 'robust' in the sense that the object does not disappear or collapse in the face of such changes.

One kind of common design promotes 'pure' resilience, that is, allowing a policy to bounce back to its original state after some initial shock (Walker et al. 2004; Folke 2006). They represent efforts to create policies which are 'sticky' and durable, thereby avoiding unnecessary or unhelpful policy variation or 'churn' (Jordan and Matt 2014; Monios 2016) due to short-term fluctuations in the policy environment. But such design efforts are less helpful if and when the policy environment changes, or is expected to change, substantially.

It has been shown, for example, that the classic practice of developing standard operating procedures and to 'silo' policy work in specific agencies with the purpose of promoting resilience can undermine rather than promote robustness by reducing agility in volatile times (Yackee and Yackee 2010; Moynihan 2009b; Pina e Cunha et al. 1999; Cunha et al. 2002). Machine-like resilience is problematic when circumstances change, such as, for example, when a government's fiscal situation is altered dramatically by a financial crisis and it becomes imperative to 'do more with less' (Le Grand 1984), or when a pandemic wreaks such havoc on the society that changes in tools calibrations alone are insufficient in retaining policy effectiveness in many different areas of social life (Capano et al. 2020, 2022; Xu and Basu 2020). Policy designs need to accurately reflect these dynamic scenarios and introduce tools - mainly procedural ones - which promote agility.

Overcoming policy myopia and the challenges of robust designs

While some policies are intended only to be short-term fixes, studies of policy uncertainty and policy failure have emphasized the need in many cases for policies to be able to adapt to deal with uncertain futures over the medium to the long term (Walker et al. 2010, 2013; Kwakkel et al. 2010; Capano and Woo 2017). This means to design adaptable policies capable of maintaining the same or equivalent performance in the face of any type of internal/external perturbation (Capano and Woo 2017; Howlett et al. 2015).

Studies of policy uncertainty, crisis management, policy learning, and policy capacity (Moynihan 2009a) have all emphasized this need. Swanson and Bhadwal (2009), for example, emphasize the importance of formal policy review and continuous learning through regular review process even when the policy is functioning well as one of several procedural policy tools that can help policies deal effectively with both anticipated and unanticipated conditions.

The European Environment Agency (2001) report on long-term policies, for example, has repeatedly emphasized the importance of building into policies various processes to recognize early warnings of changes in policy environments, especially as new knowledge emerges. The report noted the rising degrees of uncertainty about the suitability of existing policy solutions to address specific policy problems in the future, but that many of the serious problems posed by deep uncertainties at present could be reduced if policy-making remained flexible and adaptive, or robust and resilient.

To continue to operate effectively in the face of change and respond to policy feedback from policy actors and outputs, policy mixes must be robust. But robustness is of two types: *static robustness*, in which policy means are designed to adapt while policy goals remain unchanged, and *dynamic robustness*, in which both goals and tools are designed to change. As discussed above, the first equates robustness with resilience – that is, the ability to bounce back to a previous state and attain original goals in altered contexts caused by some change in internal or external conditions (Howlett and Ramesh 2023). The second, however, is more complex, as it can involve changes in aspects of policy goals as well as means in order to allow policies to adapt more broadly by altering their form in response to changing circumstances. This second type of 'dynamic robustness' focuses attention on the need for agility and upon the requisites for the creation of policy designs which allow for substantive changes in form as well as state.

Designing policies which are robust and resilient over such a wide range of unknowns and uncertainties is a major challenge. On a substantive level, 'robust' policies are those which incorporate some slack, allowing room for adjustments as conditions change. Robust policies, as in the case of a bridge or building, often need to be 'overdesigned' or 'over-engineered' in order to allow for a greater range of effective responses across contexts and time. This can be effective and even efficient over the long term, for example, in the case of 'automatic stabilizers,' such as welfare payments or unemployment insurance payments in the event of an economic downturn, maintaining some level of spending and saving despite a general economic contraction and removing some funds from investment availability during boom times (Salamon 2002b; Sterner 2003) in order to fund responses to future crises. Organizations can become too lean (Radnor and Boaden 2004) and may eliminate elements that could be useful when circumstances change, thus restricting the ability of an organization to respond to surprises (Lai 2012).

Such minimum levels of robustness, however, may not be enough in dealing with deeper levels of uncertainty. These circumstances require not just robust policies but also policy processes that promote robustness. That is, policy robustness in such circumstances requires responses to surprises to be improvised and implemented in an effective way *as they occur* (Room 2013a, 2013b).

However, the ability to alter and adapt policies on the fly – to improvise effectively – requires not only greater levels of redundancy in programme resources and parameters but also significant administrative and other redundancies and expenses, such as built-in policy reviews and mechanisms for outside evaluation and control, including provisions for future public hearings and information access, disclosure, and dissemination, which can allow more significant adjustments to changing circumstances to occur (Lang 2019). This can include actions promoting informal relationships, personal connections, and past experiences, which are the prerequisites for collaboration in extreme events or what Lai (2012) calls 'auto-adaptation to initial conditions', the frequent re-examination and adaptation to changes of initial conditions and assumptions. This often makes such designs more expensive in the short term than leaner efforts, however, which may make them difficult to enact or implement.

This second form of robustness is highly dynamic in the sense that it allows for continuous adaptation of almost all policy elements in the face of environmental instability. This makes it highly desirable in dealing with long-term challenges which are expected to fluctuate over the short, medium, and long term and transcend existing policy arrangements. This is the case in important areas of activity, such as banking system stability or sustainability efforts, for example (Selmier 2016; Bakir 2017). These are areas in which responses to long-term challenges must be anticipated and designed at the outset and not just adjusted incrementally as circumstances change. And this must be done despite many uncertainties in both short and long terms regarding the timing and content of required changes.

Many studies of policy uncertainty, crisis management, policy learning, and policy capacity (Moynihan 2009a) have emphasized the need to go beyond limited conceptions of static robustness like resilience in order to deal with changes and surprises that may undermine a policy (Mergel et al. 2018; Hamalainen et al. 2012; OECD 2011; Weick and Sutcliffe 2001; Jordan and Matt 2014). Moving beyond considerations of redundancy to fully dynamic designs requires procedural tools to be deployed to monitor changes in the external environment in order to trigger the kinds of changes needed to continue to achieve the original intent of a policy (Bali et al. 2021). This can involve, for example, agencies and actors placed in positions to monitor the environment and implement alterations in policy outputs based on changes in key indicators and metrics (MacRae 1985; Innes 1990) in a 'manual' way (Salamon 1989), allowing them to adjust not only tool calibrations, for example, but also programme objectives and goals.

Conclusion: the need to design intelligently but also dynamically

As we have seen in earlier chapters, design tasks are typically undertaken during policy formulation by experts and others operating in policy advice systems, utilizing the different sets of ideas they and other policy actors have about the normative and cognitive contents of policies. It is in this sense that one can talk about policies being designed or consciously crafted and constructed.

As we have also noted, this does not mean that design is always done or is always done well – no more than this is the case in architecture or industrial design – and it does not mean that design is the only activity important to studying or making public policy. Other activities equally important to policy studies include 'understanding' policy-making, or researching its nature and processes (Howlett et al. 2009); 'managing' public policy, or ensuring that planned objectives are actually met in practice (Wu et al. 2010); and 'analyzing' public policy, for example, that is, developing and implementing the techniques needed to evaluate the experiences of past or existing policies in order to better inform future policies, and developing better methodologies for policy alternative appraisal and evaluation (Weimer and Vining 2004; Dunn 2008). But design is a central component.

Like all these other tasks, design can be done well or poorly, depending on the skills and knowledge of the designers and the amount of time, information, and other resources at their disposal in the design task. While policy-makers should not always be simply reacting to circumstances or engaging in unthinking processes of incremental policy-making, if design is to occur in any meaningful sense of the term, some autonomy and capability to systematically evaluate circumstances and the range of possible instrument choices are required if better policy designs are to emerge.

The existing evidence, for example, shows that sub-optimal situations are very common in many existing mixes which have developed through processes of policy layering (Thelen 2004; van der Heijden 2011). These kinds of 'unintentional' mixes can be contrasted with 'smarter' designs, which involve creating new sets of tools specifically intended to overcome or avoid the problems associated with layering but which may be harder to put into practice (Gunningham et al. 1998; Kiss et al. 2012). In both cases of 'packaging' and 'patching', however, following the basic principles of good policy design can help ensure expected outcomes are achieved in an effective fashion.

There is a temporal dimension to the policy design efforts, however, which is often unspoken or unacknowledged but must be addressed. That is, most policies are expected not only to be effective in the immediate situation after their enactment but also to retain that effectiveness into the future (Howlett 2019). The answer to the question concerning what kinds of policy tools should be chosen and deployed if the expectation is that they will continue to work effectively over extended periods of time, however, is by no means straightforward. And while long-term performance may be a straightforward ambition, it may also be a tall expectation to meet, given that the nature of policy problems and their contexts themselves change constantly.

That is, as even the most rudimentary analysis displays, even when the causes of a problem are clear and solutions well-known, or so-called 'tame' problems (Newman and Head 2017; Head 2019), governments commonly face turbulent environments which pose significant adjustment challenges to existing policy goals and tools (Bennett and Lemoine 2014a, 2014b). In many cases, ranging from finance to pollution and healthcare, rapid changes in the technological, economic, and social environment may be coupled with a reduction in the ability of single jurisdictions to control internal and cross-border issue areas, undermining policy effectiveness and making an already-complex situation yet more difficult to address (Howlett et al. 2017).

While many principles of good design exist which can help strengthen a policy mix and reduce its conflicts and internal contradictions, in order for even relatively simple policies to continue to operate effectively over time in the face of change, they must feature a minimum level of robustness sufficient to withstand the turbulence while retaining their essential character (Comfort et al. 2010). This is the essence of policy 'resilience' or 'static robustness' and is associated with somewhat over-designing policy mixes by including what may appear in the short term as redundant measures.

However, in many cases, changes in the policy environment may be more significant and require higher levels of robustness. Achieving dynamic robustness requires a different approach than does attaining a more static form of resilience. As noted earlier, it involves avoiding short-term orientations toward limited forms of robustness and ensuring that policies contain procedures and practices which allow re-orientation of goals and governance arrangements as events unfold (Edelenbos et al. 2011).

Effective policy designs embracing dynamic robustness require the inclusion of elements that ensure sensitivity to 'trends, the risks of discontinuities, and the real-time sense-making of strategic situations as they develop and evolve' (Doz and Kosonen 2014). This, in turn, requires not just 'positive' steps to create bodies and policy elements capable of such adjustments but also avoiding the widespread tendency to promote the ossification of routinization and narrowly defined considerations of efficiency in public administration (Howlett and Mukherjee 2014; Junginger 2013; Bason 2014; Mulgan 2008; Chiarini 2012).

Readings

Béland, D., M. Howlett, P. Rocco and A. Waddan. (2020). 'Designing Policy Resilience: Lessons from the Affordable Care Act'. *Policy Sciences 53*, no. 2 (June): 269–289.

Bennett, N. and G. James Lemoine. (2014). 'What a Difference a Word Makes: Understanding Threats to Performance in a VUCA World'. *Business Horizons 57*, no. 3 (1 May): 311–317.

Berg, S. V., A. N. Memon and R. Skelton. (2000). 'Designing an Independent Regulatory Commission'. *IRC Research Paper*.

Boin, Arjen, Louise K. Comfort and Chris C. Demchak. (2010). 'The Rise of Resilience'. In L. K. Comfort, A. Boin and C. C. Demchak (eds.), *Designing Resilience: Preparing for Extreme Events*. Pittsburgh, PA: University of Pittsburgh Press, 1–12.

Bryson, J. M., K. S. Quick, C. S. Slotterback and B. C. Crosby (2013). 'Designing Public Participation Processes'. *Public Administration Review 73*, no. 1 (1 January): 23–34.

Capano, G., M. Howlett and M. Ramesh. (2018). 'Designing for Robustness: Surprise, Agility and Improvisation in Policy Design'. *Policy & Society 37*, no. *4*: 1–22.

Capano, G. and J. J. Woo. (2017). 'Resilience and Robustness in Policy Design: A Critical Appraisal'. *Policy Sciences 37*, no. *4* (5 January): 1–28.

del Río, Pablo. (2014). "On Evaluating Success in Complex Policy Mixes: The Case of Renewable Energy Support Schemes." *Policy Sciences*, 1–21.

Fung, A. (2003). 'Survey Article: Recipes for Public Spheres: Eight Institutional Design Choices and Their Consequences'. *Journal of Political Philosophy 11*, no. *3* (1 September): 338–367.

Gilardi, F. (2005). 'The Formal Independence of Regulators: A Comparison of 17 Countries and 7 Sectors'. *Swiss Political Science Review 11*, no. *4*: 139–167.

Grabosky, P. (1995). 'Counterproductive Regulation'. *International Journal of the Sociology of Law 23*: 347–369.

Hamalainen, Timo, Mikko Kosonen and Yves L. Doz. (2012). *Strategic Agility in Public Management*. SSRN Scholarly Paper. Rochester, NY: Social Science Research Network, 12 March.

Holland, S. P. and M. R. Moore. (2013). 'Market Design in Cap and Trade Programs: Permit Validity and Compliance Timing'. *Journal of Environmental Economics and Management 66*, no. *3* (November): 671–687.

Hou, Y. and G. Brewer. (2010). 'Substitution and Supplementation between Co-Functional Policy Instruments: Evidence from State Budget Stabilization Practices'. *Public Administration Review 70*, no. *6*: 914–924.

Howlett, M. (2019). 'The Temporal Dimension(s) of Policy Designs: Resilience, Robustness and the Sequencing of Tools in Policy Mixes'. *International Review of Public Policy 1*, no. *1*: 27–45.

Howlett, M., I. Mukherjee and J. Rayner. (2014). 'The Elements of Effective Program Design: A Two-Level Analysis'. *Politics and Governance 2*, no. *2* (9 June): 1–12.

Howlett, M. and M. Ramesh. (2016). 'The "Achilles" Heels of Governance: Critical Capacity Deficits and Their Role in Governance Failures'. *Regulation & Governance 10*, no. *4* (1 December): 301–313.

Howlett, M. and M. Ramesh. (2023). 'Designing for Adaptation: Static and Dynamic Robustness in Policy-Making'. *Public Administration 101*, no. *1*: 23–35.

Howlett, M., J. Vince and P. del Río. (2017). 'Policy Integration and Multi-Level Governance: Dealing with the Vertical Dimension of Policy Mix Designs'. *Politics and Governance 5*, no. *2* (5 May): 69–78.

Jordan, Andrew and Elah Matt. (2014). 'Designing Policies That Intentionally Stick: Policy Feedback in a Changing Climate'. *Policy Sciences* (11 June): 1–21.

Justen, A., N. Fearnley, M. Givoni and J. Macmillen. (2014). 'A Process for Designing Policy Packaging: Ideals and Realities'. *Transportation Research Part A: Policy and Practice, Policy Packaging 60* (February): 9–18.

Kay, Adrian. (2007). "Tense Layering and Synthetic Policy Paradigms: The Politics of Health Insurance in Australia." *Australian Journal of Political Science 42*, no. *4*: 579–591.

Kemmerling, Achim. (2009). *Taxing the Working Poor: The Political Origins and Economic Consequences of Taxing Low Wages*. Cheltenham; Northampton, MA: Edward Elgar.

Maor, Moshe, Jale Tosun and Andrew Jordan. (2017). 'Proportionate and Disproportionate Policy Responses to Climate Change: Core Concepts and Empirical Applications'. *Journal of Environmental Policy & Planning* (24 January): 1–13.

May, P. J. (1981). 'Hints for Crafting Alternative Policies'. *Policy Analysis 7*, no. *2*: 227–244.

Mayntz, R. (1983). 'The Conditions of Effective Public Policy: A New Challenge for Policy Analysis'. *Policy & Politics 11* (April): 123–143.

McInerney, David, Robert Lempert and Klaus Keller. (2012). 'What Are Robust Strategies in the Face of Uncertain Climate Threshold Responses?' *Climatic Change 112*, no. *3–4* (3 January): 547–568.

Mees, H. L. P., J. Dijk, D. van Soest, P. P. J. Driessen, M. H. F. M. W. van Rijswick and H. Runhaar. (2014). 'A Method for the Deliberate and Deliberative Selection of Policy Instrument Mixes for Climate Change Adaptation'. *Ecology and Society 19*, no. *2*: 58.

Mergel, Ines, Yiwei Gong and John Bertot. (2018). 'Agile Government: Systematic Literature Review and Future Research'. *Government Information Quarterly 35*, no. *2* (April): 291–298.

Optic, Optimal Policies for Transportation in Combination. (2014). 'Best Practices and Recommendations on Policy Packaging'. *Annual Review of Policy Design 2*, no. *1* (8 November): 1–10.

Swanson, Darren and Suruchi Bhadwal (eds.). (2009). *Creating Adaptive Policies: A Guide for Policy-Making in an Uncertain World | IISD*. Winnipeg: IISD.

Taeihagh, A., M. Givoni and R. Bañares-Alcántara. (2013). 'Which Policy First? A Network-Centric Approach for the Analysis and Ranking of Policy Measures'. *Environment and Planning B: Planning and Design 40*, no. *4*: 595–616.

Vining, A. R. and A. E. Boardman. (2008). 'Public – Private Partnerships: Eight Rules for Governments'. *Public Works Management & Policy 13*, no. *2* (1 October): 149–161.

Weaver, R. K. (2014). 'Compliance Regimes and Barriers to Behavioural Change'. *Governance 27*, no. *2* (1 April): 243–265.

Whitten, S. M. (2017). 'Designing and Implementing Conservation Tender Metrics: Twelve Core Considerations'. *Land Use Policy 63* (April): 561–571.

Chapter 15

Dealing with the dark side of policy design

Policy design studies to date have focused almost exclusively on the "good" or bright side of policy formulation, that is, dealing with concerns around ensuring that knowledge is marshalled toward developing the best feasible policy under the assumption of well-intentioned governments and accommodating policy targets. This work has not examined carefully enough, or allowed for the possibility, that government intentions may not be solely oriented toward the creation of public value or that policy targets may indulge in various forms of 'misconduct' – from fraud to gamesmanship – which undermine government intentions.

Although self-interested, corrupt, and other similar kinds of policy-making have been the subject of many studies in administrative and regulatory law this work has generally been ignored or paid only lip service by policy studies. This is changing, however, as the question of the behaviour of policy targets in particular has increasingly become a source of interest among policy scholars and begun to inform policy design studies.

This chapter reviews these developments and behaviours in order to aid the process of improving policy designs to deal with this 'dark side' of policy-making.

The assumption of well-meaning behaviour in the policy sciences

Current work on policy-making and policy design often adopts an almost-Panglossian vision of the subject, viewing policy-making activity as always embodying a well-intentioned effort on the part of governments to address and resolve public problems in a manner that best serves the public interest and delivers public value (Arestis and Kitromilides 2010; Moore 1994, 1995).

This is despite the fact that the general problem of less-benign or self-interested behaviour on the part of politicians and administrators interfering

DOI: 10.4324/9781003343431-20

or undermining efforts to promote the public good, of course, is one of the oldest in political study (Saxonhouse 2015). These range from the abuse of public authority to promote the interests of ethnic, religious, and other favoured groups or specific sets of 'clients' (Gans-Morse et al. 2014; Goetz 2007) or to penalize or punish others (Howlett et al. 2017); its (mis)use to enrich or otherwise benefit policy-makers and administrators (Uribe 2014); and its use to manipulate a variety of activities of target groups through, for example, vote-buying or other forms of electoral pandering (Brancati 2014; Manor 2013).

These kinds of policy-maker behaviour are generally ignored in the policy literature, although they are highly policy-relevant. Even those studies which do include consideration of the political and power-based nature of policy narratives and target constructions often still hold out hope that such 'distortions' can be corrected through the workings of competitive political markets (Schultze 1977; Blanc 2018) or that clearer visions of evidence-based policy solutions can emerge from policy processes and be implemented effectively, self-interested behaviour notwithstanding (Schneider and Ingram 2005; Feldman 2018; Oliver and Pearse 2017).

Most of the concerns raised in the preceding text, when they have been examined at all in design studies, have been analyzed in the case of policy-maker behaviour. But there is also a large second area of concern which exists: that related to adverse or malicious behaviour of policy 'takers' evading or otherwise undermining government initiatives. This behaviour on the part of policy-takers to deceive, 'game', or otherwise evade the intentions and expectations of the government when 'complying' with regulations, subsidies, and other forms of government action is a subject often entirely glossed over in studies of policy compliance.

As we have seen in earlier chapters, any consideration of 'target behaviour' is often couched in utilitarian language and assumptions (Howlett 2018), and the idea commonly found in the policy literature is that the only real issue in policy compliance is 'getting incentives (and disincentives) right', with expected target behaviour sure to follow when this occurs (Howlett 2018). This not only ignores both aspects of the social and political construction of targets highlighted in the policy design literature (Schneider and Ingram 1990a, 1990b) but also minimizes the complex behaviours which go into compliance, most notably considerations of legitimacy, but also those related to a wide variety of descriptive and injunctive social norms which affect policy target or 'taker' behaviour (Howlett 2019; Bamberg and Moser 2007; Thomas et al. 2016; Weaver 2014, 2015).

Ignoring these behaviours does a disservice to policy studies by failing to address head-on the facts that (a) policy-makers are often driven by malicious or venal motivations rather than socially beneficial or disinterested ones, and (b) policy-takers or target populations also have proclivities and tendencies toward activities such as free-ridership and rent-seeking which serve to undermine even the best of government intentions (Hoppe 2017; Feldman 2018).

Designing for the dark side

The fact that false, biased, or misleading information enters into political discussions and policy deliberations, of course, is not new, and the policy sciences have always recognized and incorporated into their models the idea of the limits or bounds of 'perfect' policy-making (Simon 1967, 1978; Jones 2002). Similarly, the idea that policy problems are, at least in part, socially constructed and that the nature of policy problems, solutions, and targets is biased in various ways is also an old insight which has also, although to a more limited degree, penetrated into the policy sciences and thinking around policy design (Schneider and Ingram 1993, 1997; Foucault 1979; Lemke 2002).

Although both of these latter subjects have been a steady subject of debate and interest in the field for decades (Fischer 1987; Fischer and Forrester 1993), epistemologically speaking, the underlying theory of knowledge behind the mainstream policy sciences, existing as a presupposition for much analysis and deliberation, has always been a 'realist' one, that is, a stance toward the world in which it is assumed that 'evidence' objectively exists and can be marshalled by careful study and analysis to address specific kinds of policy problems. Thus, policy scientists and the policy analysis profession in general have typically viewed themselves as following a mode of 'speaking truth to power' (Wildavsky 1979), that is, assembling and presenting verifiable facts and evidence about what works and what does not to policy-makers, taking steps to offset biases and overcome limitations on knowledge and behaviour in so doing.

Following these precepts, generations of policy scholars have advanced, applied, and refined rational or instrumental models and approaches to policy-making that portray the policy-making process as one in which policy participants are able to distinguish fact from fiction and operate with good intentions, even if conflicts over meaning, strategy, and resources may be endemic to the politics of policy-making (Tribe 1972; Goodin 1980; Saward 1992; Hawkesworth 1992).

The policy sciences, for example, are well-prepared to deal with the issue of correcting a deficiency in *existing* knowledge. This, it is commonly argued, can be ameliorated by careful knowledge transmission and persistent education activities directed either toward policy-makers, who may be ignorant, for example, of the latest science on an issue such as climate change, or of policy targets, who likewise may not know about a programme or subsidy for which they are eligible. In fact, some scholars have characterized the work of policy analysis as a whole in precisely these terms, that is, as involving principally the effort to generate and disseminate as much policy-relevant knowledge ('evidence') as possible, ensuring decisions are taken which are fully cognizant of all 'known-knowns' (Hawkesworth 1992; Chow and Sarin 2002; Logan 2009).

The policy literature is also replete with precepts and proposals for how to deal with fundamental limits or the 'boundedness' of knowledge, discussed in earlier chapters, arguing that policy-makers need to be cognizant of such limits and avoid hubris and excessive confidence when assessing policy options and determining specific courses of action (Manski 2011, 2013; Morgan and Henrion 1990; March 1978; Forester 1984; Jones 2001, 2002).

These kinds of precautionary and prudent marshalling of best available evidence, however, are built on the assumption that the end of policy-making is to serve the public interest and enhance public value (Mintrom and Luetjens 2018; Moore 1995) and that what can be thought of as errors of omission and commission in policy-making are largely unintentional, with all participants amenable to enhanced learning and more carefully considered action. This approach has only rarely dealt with the perpetual desire of self-interested parties, from decision-makers to policy targets, to hijack, distort, or otherwise re-orient public processes toward their ends and goals (Jones 2002; Habermas 1974).

Lessons for design processes: learning from past experience to mitigate dark-side policy risks

There are several 'dark-side' policy risks that design, and designers, must deal with. Many are external, but some are 'vices' which are 'inherent' or built into policies, programmes, and processes which governments must, but often do not, adequately address in policy designs and deliberations. They include 'unpreparedness', for example, a policy vice or common problem which events such as the 2020–2022 coronavirus underscored (Capano et al. 2020). As t'Hart et al. (2001) have noted, the timing and nature of government interventions in crises vary according to the nature of the crisis, as rapid and severe crises demand more from leaders and systems than their 'slow-onset' counterparts and require some level of preparedness (Kehinde 2014; Staupe-Delgado 2019).

Preparedness, of course, is often linked to previous experience with a problem, but unpreparedness can also occur even when this previous experience exists. In the case of the responses to the COVID-19 crisis, for example, a key determinant of governments' initial responses to the pandemic typically related to their existing capabilities, which, in turn, were related to their preparation and planning for such pandemics and the managerial and organizational resources they had at their disposal when first encountering the virus (Capano et al. 2020; see also McConnell and Drennan 2006).

Governments which were prepared for pandemics and had recent similar past experience, such as those in Asia which had dealt with SARS-CoV-1, H1N1, and MERS, for example, were most likely to have been prudent and have a realistic level of confidence in the capability of their existing public health and financial systems to handle new communicable diseases. They were well-informed about their actual capabilities and also of the potentially very dangerous nature of the disease. This led them to be wary of the disease and, *ceteris paribus*, pushed them toward relatively early, slow but steady, and strong responses in terms of rolling out elements of the standard portfo-lio of policy tools, from quarantines to vaccines, used to deal with epidemics. Countries which were both unprepared and had no recent relevant past expe-rience were often complacent initially and then shocked as the true nature of the pandemic and their lack of preparedness were revealed (Howlett 2021b).

Learning from past experiences can thus help play a key role in overcom-ing this source of failure, but only if the lessons are translated into designs and activities which promote effective preparation.

A second inherent problem, which manifests itself most clearly at the formulation stage of policy-making is, as we have seen, 'uncertainty'. Policy-makers face many different kinds of uncertainties (Howlett and Nair 2017) which surround the choice of policy options, their consequences, confidence in available information, and the values of multiple stakeholders. When these are not well understood, this leads to a great deal of ambiguity concerning what might be the correct action to follow (Knight 1921; Hansson 1996; van der Sluijs 2005). As described in earlier chapters, the types of uncertainty common in policy-making include:

1. Substantive uncertainty that relates to lack of relevant information related to the nature of the complex problem, and the different interpretations of information arising from different 'frames of reference' of the social actors.
2. Strategic uncertainty that arises due to unpredictability of strategies deployed by different actors based on their perception of the problem and strategies likely to be deployed by other actors.
3. Institutional uncertainty that arises owing to the complexity of interaction of different actors guided by institutional frameworks, that is, rules and procedures of the organizations they represent.

(Koppenjan and Klijn 2004)

These forms of uncertainty have been widely studied in diverse disciplines, from psychology to organization theory, and studies in these fields have had some impact on policy analysis and policy-making (Morgan and Henrion 1990; Manski 2011). As earlier discussions in this book have noted, in the policy world, much of this discussion has centred on clarifying the nature, causes and consequences nature of what Simon (1973) termed 'ill-structured problems', or ones in which the nature of policy problems and solutions is unknown. The concepts of 'wicked' and 'tame' problems, which for decades have dominated thinking around uncertainty in the policy sciences, are examples of this distinc-tion (Churchman 1967; Rittel and Webber 1973; Alford and Head 2017; Levin et al. 2012), and we have seen how better knowledge acquisition and manage-ment practices can help address these kinds of issues.

But other problems also exist. 'Non-compliance', for example, is another form of uncertainty which affects implementation negatively. Implementation is by no means straightforward and involves a plethora of problems related to administrative behaviour and issues linked to problems such as the complex principal–agent chains policies often involved in translating policy intentions into action (Ellig and Lavoie 1995). And as we have seen in earlier discussions, compliance problems are endemic in implementation and need to be incorporated into design studies. This is a problem because policy 'takers' often fail to comply with government wishes, even when these are expressed or enacted with the best of intentions. While such behaviour is an essential component of studies in cognate fields such as law and accounting (Howlett 2018; Doig and Johnson 2001; Kuhn and Siciliani (2013), it is glossed over almost completely in studies of public policy. Yet this is a key question in policy design, related to better understanding the conditions of policy success and failure and the kinds of designs and activities more likely to attain success with minimal effort and expenditure (Feeley 1970; Mulford and Etzioni 1978; Schneider and Ingram 1990a, 1990b).

A fourth vice is 'non-learning', which is another major problem set out in earlier chapters. It is an outcome of policy analysis and evaluations which either do not accurately derive appropriate lessons or which 'learn the wrong lessons' (Dunlop 2017a, 2017b; Dunlop and Radaelli 2018a, 2018b) and is also a significant issue facing policy formulation and alternative design.

And, as has also been discussed in depth in earlier chapters, a fifth vice is 'maliciousness', which affects decision-making when the criteria undergirding policy choice are not benevolent and public-spirited and do not enhance public value (LeGrand 2022).

Such vices – 'unpreparedness', 'uncertainty', 'non-compliance', 'non-learning', and 'maliciousness' – can usefully be organized according to the stage of policy-making they most affect (Howlett 2000a; Lang 2019) (see Table 15.1). Each is a potentially important source of policy failure which injects volatility into policy-making. Each can be addressed through the use

Table 15.1 The inherent vices of public policy

	Policy stage/task	Central policy risk	Cause/source
Sources of policy volatility	Agenda-setting	Unpreparedness surprise)	Lack of attention
	Policy formulation	Uncertainty (wickedness)	Lack of knowledge
	Decision-making	Maliciousness (poor decisions)	Self-interestedness
	Policy implementation	Non-compliance (misaligned target behaviour)	Unknown behavioural mechanisms
	Policy evaluation	Non-learning (poor learning)	Unknown intervention effects

of specific kinds of policy tools and thus each should properly be within the purview of studies of policy design (Howlett and Mukherjee 2017a, 2019).

Other fields have also encounterd these problems and have developed ideas and mechanisms which can help deal with them, and policy design efforts should be aware of and utilize these techniques.

This work has shown that each of these risks can be mitigated or managed through a variety of means – from institutionalizing foresight agencies to deal with the risk of surprises affecting government agendas to evaluation and measurement activities to reduce the risk of poor or non-learning in policy evaluation – if not always completely eliminated (see Table 15.2)

Table 15.2 Potential policy risk management strategies

	Policy stage/ task	Central policy risk	Cause/ source	Management strategy (procedural tools)	Result
	Agenda-setting	Unpreparedness (surprise)	Lack of attention	Institutionalized foresight/issue management	Reduced surprise
	Policy formulation	Uncertainty (wickedness)	Lack of knowledge	Institutionalized policy analysis/risk management/ modelling	Reduced ignorance
Sources of policy volatility	Decision-making	Maliciousness (poor decisions)	Self-interestedness	Institutionalized Evidence-based policy-making	Reduced opportunity for political or personal gain from poor decisions
	Policy implementation	Non-compliance (misaligned target behaviour)	Unknown behavioural mechanisms	Institutionalized policy design/policy labs	Reduced non-compliance
	Policy evaluation	Non-learning (poor learning)	Unknown intervention effects	Institutionalized evaluation and measurement	Separates signal from noise

Dealing with the adverse behaviour of policy-takers and policy-makers through procedural tool deployment

As we have seen in the book, contemporary studies of policy design have increasingly focused on better understanding 'policy mixes', that is, bundles of tools and instruments commonly assembled into policy programmes to attain a government aim (Howlett 2011; Rogge and Reichardt 2016). Recent research has examined the manner in which such mixes have been constructed, how they have evolved over time, and how they can be designed to be more robust and resilient in the face of various kinds of challenges post-enactment (Beland et al. 2019; Jordan and Matt 2014).

Although they have not dealt explicitly with issues around poor or adverse policy-maker and policy-taker behaviour, studies of how policy mixes can be designed to remain effective over a range of alterations in their contexts and targets (Capano and Woo 2017; Capano et al. 2018) and withstand challenges when deliberate efforts are made to alter, adapt, or repeal all or part of it (Comfort 2010; Duit 2016; Folke 2006; Holling 1973; Wilts and O'Brien 2018; Howlett 2019) provide some hints about how averse policy behaviour can be controlled or constrained though the use of specific kinds of policy tools. Each of these is examined in turn next.

Constraining policy-maker behaviour through the use of procedural tools

It is well recognized that even when policies are designed with a clear evidentiary basis in a model formulation process, they may still fail over time if they do not adapt to changing circumstances and concerns as policy implementation proceeds and the policy is put into action (Nair and Howlett 2017; Bennett and Lemoine 2014a, 2014b).

This suggests a need to be able to design and adopt policies featuring some level of agility and flexibility in their components and processes if they are to respond to challenges, including behavioural ones (Room 2013a, 2013b). In turbulent circumstances, for example, where policy ideas and actors change frequently (Howlett and Ramesh 1998), policies must be flexible. In practice, this mean policies and policy-making require additional and redundant resources and capabilities which allow them to change course as conditions change, including such procedural devices as feedback mechanisms and procedures for automatic or semi-automatic adjustment (Pierson 1992, 1993; Baumgartner and Jones 2002a). Other such devices include procedural tools, such as built-in policy reviews, and mechanisms for outside evaluation and control, such as provisions for future public hearings and information access, disclosure, and dissemination, which allow significant adjustments to changing circumstances to occur in more or less realtime (Lang 2019).

In the case of policy 'vices', exactly which kind of procedural tool is required depends on the nature of the behaviour to be curbed. Hence, the targets of corrupt behaviour are often organizational in nature and can be addressed through a combination of organizational and regulatory activity, such as the creation of anti-corruption agencies and the development of more effective financial and recruitment controls, including ones such as limits on party funding and government contracting and procurement activity (Graycar 2015; Graycar and Prenzler 2013; Phillips and Levasseur 2004).

Other adverse behaviours have a more quasi-governmental aspect and affect other policy tools, such as authority-based (regulatory) ones or financial instruments. These range from forms of regulatory capture (Levine and Forrence 1990) to the gaming of regulations and sophisticated swindles and abuses of government treasury and tax largesse (Doig and Johnson 2001; Raghunandan 2018).

These require the use of careful monitoring of policies and regulatory behaviour and typically the use of disclosure acts – such as the Federal Advisory Commission Act in the United States or various lobbyist registries controlling regulator–regulatee interactions through enhanced mandatory transparency (Chari et al. 2007; Carpenter and Moss 2013; Karty 2002). Other procedural devices, such as sunset clauses and term limits, conflict of interest rules, ethics commissioners, and similar kinds of administrative procedures, are also useful in this area (McCubbins et al. 1987). Other problems around incomplete contracts and poor procurement practices, for example, can require better legal construction and contract design (Scott and Triantis 2005).

This discussion is summarized in Table 15.3.

When policy tools are utilized which are subject to gaming, fraud, or misrepresentation on the part of policy-takers, additional resources are required to build in the accountability, monitoring, and auditing functions required for such mixes to operate effectively (Blanc 2018). Designs based on nodality and nudges and/or treasure resources, such as those most closely associated with 'modern' collaborative governance, for example, are always highly volatile, as the opportunities are ripe for cheating and gaming, and protections against such behaviour are often low and rely on trust. Therefore, there is a need to 'design in' correctives, such as stricter accountability mechanisms, verification, and monitoring plans right at the outset in order to ensure these are locked in and left in place as the programme or policy matures (Plaček and Ochrana 2018; Vine and Sathaye 1999). That is, there is a need to better assess and address the risks of failure when a policy alternative is first considered (Falco 2017; Taylor et al. 2019).

It is also necessary to have better and continuous monitoring and assessment or evaluation of policy impacts and outcomes and the ability to respond to any compliance deficits with new tools or altered calibrations (e.g. higher fines or greater subsides, as the case may be) in order to ensure desired levels of compliance are realized. This fits nicely with Weaver's (2014, 2015) admonition that designers need to think not in terms of compliance per se but rather in terms of 'compliance regimes' in which different policy targets can be treated in different ways, depending on the actual behaviour envisioned and encountered. This is a subject which requires a high level of policy

Table 15.3 Tool volatility and procedural tool alternatives

Tool type	Flaw	Results	Solutions
			Procedural tools
Organization	Public failure Corruption SOEs contracting Co-production – clientelism	Diversion of public resources to private aims/ end	Accountability/ transparency/etc. Anti-corruption bureaus Blockchain bidding and procurement/contracting records Fraud squads
Authority	Regulatory gaming Capture Bribes and kickbacks	Diversion of public ends to private	Careful design, monitoring, and learning Whistle-blower laws Sunset laws Merit appointments Conflict of interest laws
Treasure	Gaming/fraud	Diversion of public resources to private	Complete contracts, careful subsidy/tax design Monitoring and verification/ enforcement/inspections
Nodality	Diversion of individual/group message for private ends, for example, propaganda or blackmail	Private gain	More carefully targeted messages Truth in advertising laws

acumen and analytical/evaluation capacity on the part of government, however, and capacity building in this area may be required as a pre-requisite for the design and employment of procedural tools against adverse policy-taker behaviour (Wu et al. 2015; Howlett 2015).

Conclusion: controlling volatility in policy design through better risk identification and mitigation

Political scientists, sociologists, anthropologists, and others often invoke a sizable literature on policy advice in the tradition of Machiavelli's advice to princes (Machiavelli et al. 1988; Goldhamer 1978; Shore et al. 2011;

Colebatch 2018). This literature has a long history of warning against the use of state power in the pursuit of personal and political gain, but this long record of activity has been largely ignored by policy textbooks and studies. Whether it is policy design in the sense of policy studies – that is, dealing with the design of policy instruments and instrument mixes (Howlett 2019) – or with the application of 'design thinking' to policy formulation, in the form of more publicly driven participatory efforts to define problems and identify solutions in a 'thinking-outside-the-box' style (Blomkamp 2018; Clarke and Craft 2017), both orientations can be criticized for having neglected the *real-politik* of policy-making and policy-taking (Colebatch 2018; Turnbull 2018).

Although omnipresent in popular accounts and traditional and social media visions of policy-making, the possibility of adverse behaviour on the part of policy-makers and policy-takers is generally absent from standard textbooks and other works on policy-making and policy design (Howlett et al. 2009; Anderson 1975; Weimer and Vining 1989). Rather, these often adopt as self-evident the idea that policy-making and policies should be developed in accordance with the best evidence and practice in order to generate public value and that attaining the co-operation of policy targets in this endeavour is unproblematic (Mintrom and Luetjens 2018; Moore 1994, 1995). While this is a noble thought, however, the evidence of corruption, collusion, clientelism, and other such self-interested and destructive policy-making behaviour is all around us (Dahlström et al. 2012) and is a pervasive trope in the popular media, just as are stories of welfare fraud and other kinds of policy-taker malfeasance (Cappella and Jamieson 1996).

This part of the 'dark side' of policy-making is almost never referred to, let alone studied and analyzed in the policy sciences. Yet the existence and nature of 'manipulatory politics' (Goodin 1980) are well-known and often observed. Instead of dealing head-on with the diverse motivations which drive policy-makers, including such topics as corruption, venality, unpreparedness and the desire to punish enemies and reward supporters, these works typically begin from the premise that policy-makers and actors, especially those in authoritative positions in governments and bureaucracies, are motivated by the best of intentions to improve the public weal or may be plagued only by relatively minor concerns around bureaucratic budget maximization or other behaviours interfering with generally good intentions. In such work, errors are often attributed to poor information or poor timing, for example, rather than to maliciousness, and problems in implementation and formulation, especially, are ascribed to barriers to effectiveness, such as poor analytical, managerial, or political capabilities and competences (Wu et al. 2015), rather than to adverse policy behaviour. Rather than be ignored, however, such behaviour is a subject worthy of systematic study in a more full-formed policy science.

The same is true of the (mis)behaviour of 'policy-takers', that is, the targets of public policies. Again, while early policy studies had a more well-rounded notion of the kinds of activities undertaken by policy targets (Edelman 1988), these aspects of policy-making and compliance were largely lost in the 1970s and 1980s (Radin 2000). Most policy studies continue to focus exclusively on the behaviour of 'rational' individuals faced with government incentives and disincentives and approach these subjects from a hedonic, utilitarian perspective. Not only does this ignore non-utilitarian aspects of target behaviour such as addiction or self-harm, but also, generally, moral sentiments and orientations linked to religious, ethical, and other sets of widely or individually held beliefs (Howlett 2018), as well as malicious and poorly intended behaviour toward government efforts.

Both these kinds of behaviour should not be ignored but rather should serve as a cautionary note for erstwhile policy-designers, who should consider additional sets of criteria for developing and evaluating effective policy designs which deal head-on with these problems and their impact on the risks of policy failure (Peters et al. 2018; Taylor et al. 2013, 2019). This is especially the case with designs which implicitly or explicitly rely on engaged, compliant, target group behaviour for their effectiveness, such as co-production, collaboration, and other forms of voluntary regulation (Ansell et al. 2017). But this also extends to all other forms of policy activity and instrument use, from the provision of loans and subsidies to the creation of administrative rules and the provision of information, which also need to be designed and operated with a clear vision of the nature of policy-taker compliance and policy-maker self-interest (Howlett 2019).

A more fully fledged policy design science needs to be more open-minded about how the minds of targets and policy-makers work and to be fully informed by empirical and experimental work into these subjects, including those behaviours which form the 'dark side' of policy-making. The policy realm is not the place for naivete about altruism and the good intentions of either policy-makers or policy-takers.

As this discussion has noted, learning to properly diagnose policy risks and the volatility they bring to policy-making and policy outcomes is crucial to drawing meaningful lessons about effective policy and programme design and operation. That is, all the policy-making vices listed earlier can be thought of as 'policy risks' affecting the programme, political, and problem dimensions of policy-making, ranging from unpreparedness in agenda-setting to non-learning in policy evaluation, and include poor decision-making, policy implementation, as well as problems in policy formulation (Howlett 2012), and all are properly subjects of studies of policy learning. Better understanding and managing these risks, which are the *sources* of failure and barriers to policy success, is important to learning useful lessons from policy studies and evaluations. Incorporating measures to correct, offset, or at least mitigate such risks into policy designs is crucial.

Readings

Blanc, Florentin. (2018). *From Chasing Violations to Managing Risks: Origins, Challenges and Evolutions in Regulatory Inspections.* Cheltenham: Edward Elgar Publishing.

Braithwaite, V. A. (ed.). (2013). *Taxing Democracy: Understanding Tax Avoidance and Evasion*. Aldershot, Hants, England and Burlington, VT: Ashgate Pub Ltd.

Brancati, Dawn. (2014). 'Democratic Authoritarianism: Origins and Effects'. *Annual Review of Political Science 17*, no. 1: 313–326.

Cappella, Joseph N. and Kathleen Hall Jamieson. (1996). 'News Frames, Political Cynicism, and Media Cynicism'. *The Annals of the American Academy of Political and Social Science 546*: 71–84.

Carpenter, Daniel and David A. Moss (eds.). (2013). *Preventing Regulatory Capture: Special Interest Influence and How to Limit It*. New York: Cambridge University Press.

Chari, Raj, Gary Murphy and John Hogan. (2007). 'Regulating Lobbyists: A Comparative Analysis of the United States, Canada, Germany and the European Union'. *The Political Quarterly 78*, no. 3: 422–438.

Dahlström, Carl, Johannes Lindvall and Bo Rothstein. (2013). 'Corruption, Bureaucratic Failure and Social Policy Priorities'. *Political Studies 61*, no. 3: 523–542.

Delbosc, Alexa and Graham Currie. (2016). 'Four Types of Fare Evasion: A Qualitative Study from Melbourne, Australia'. *Transportation Research Part F: Traffic Psychology and Behaviour 43*, no. 4 (1 November): 254–264.

Doig, A. and S. Johnson. (2001). 'New Public Management, Old Populism and the Policing of Fraud'. *Public Policy and Administration 16*, no. 1: 91–111.

Feldman, Yuval. (2018). *The Law of Good People: Challenging States' Ability to Regulate Human Behavior*. Cambridge, UK and New York, NY: Cambridge University Press.

Foucault, Michel. (1979). 'On Governmentality'. *Ideology and Consciousness 6*: 5–21.

Goetz, Anne Marie. (2007). 'Manouevring Past Clientelism: Institutions and Incentives to Generate Constituencies in Support of Governance Reforms'. *Commonwealth and Comparative Politics 45*, no. 4: 403–424.

Goldhamer, Herbert. (1978). *The Adviser*. New York: Elsevier.

Goodin, R. E. (1980). *Manipulatory Politics*. New Haven: Yale University Press.

Graycar, Adam. (2015). 'Corruption: Classification and Analysis'. *Policy and Society 34*, no. 2 (1 June): 87–96.

Karty, Kevin D. (2002). 'Closure and Capture in Federal Advisory Committees'. *Business and Politics 4*, no. 2: 213–238.

Kuhn, Michael and Luigi Siciliani. (2013). 'Manipulation and Auditing of Public Sector Contracts'. *European Journal of Political Economy 32* (9 September): 251–267.

Lang, Achim. (2019). 'Collaborative Governance in Health and Technology Policy: The Use and Effects of Procedural Policy Instruments'. *Administration & Society 51*, no. 2 (1 February): 272–298.

Marion, Justin and Erich Muehlegger. (2007). *Measuring Illegal Activity and the Effects of Regulatory Innovation: A Study of Diesel Fuel Tax Evasion*. Cambridge: John F. Kennedy School of Government Faculty Research Working Paper Series RWP07–026.

McCubbins, M. D., R. G. Noll and B. R. Weingast. (1987). 'Administrative Procedures as Instruments of Political Control'. *Journal of Law, Economics, and Organization 3*, no. 2: 243–277.

Oliver, J. Eric and Thomas J. Wood. (2014). 'Conspiracy Theories and the Paranoid Style(s) of Mass Opinion'. *American Journal of Political Science 58*, no. 4: 952–966.

Oreskes, Naomi and Erik M. Conway. (2011). *Merchants of Doubt: How a Handful of Scientists Obscured the Truth on Issues from Tobacco Smoke to Global Warming*. Export edn. New York, NY: Bloomsbury Press.

315

Pasek, Josh, Tobias H. Stark, Jon A. Krosnick and Trevor Tompson. (2015). 'What Motivates a Conspiracy Theory? Birther Beliefs, Partisanship, Liberal-Conservative Ideology, and Anti-Black Attitudes'. *Electoral Studies 40*: 482–489.

Perl, Anthony, Michael Howlett and M. Ramesh. (2018). 'Policy-Making and Truthiness: Can Existing Policy Models Cope with Politicized Evidence and Willful Ignorance in a "Post-Fact" World?' *Policy Sciences 51*, no. 4 (December): 581–600.

Proctor, Robert and Londa Schiebinger (eds.). (2008). *Agnotology: The Making and Unmaking of Ignorance*. Stanford, CA: Stanford University Press.

Riker, W. H. (1986). *The Art of Political Manipulation*. New Haven: Yale University Press.

Saward, M. (1992). *Co-Optive Politics and State Legitimacy*. Aldershot: Dartmouth.

Schultz, David. (2017). 'Alternative Facts and Public Affairs'. *Journal of Public Affairs Education 23*, no. 3: 775–778.

Part VI

CONCLUSION

Chapter 16

The capacity challenges of policy design over space and time

The modern policy studies movement began with the recognition that large gaps exist between policy intentions and implementation realities (Pressman and Wildavsky 1973), a phenomenon which led to many ensuing efforts to describe and plug these gaps, including a new emphasis on the difficulties and challenges of policy design (Arts and van Tatenhove 2004; Lasswell 1958; Stone 1988).

However, transforming policy intentions into practice is a complex process, and crafting the best possible policy is by no means simple or automatic. Not only may policy-makers fail to correctly identify the source of the problems they seek to address, and thus choose misdirected policies, but in other instances, criteria such as scoring political points or obtaining a legislative majority vote may also matter more to policy-makers than selecting the most effective policy (Howlett 2021). Worse, in some cases, policy-makers' efforts may be guided by malice and caprice rather than a spirit of public service, reducing the prospects for achieving any kind of public value (Legrand and Jarvis 2014; Osborne et al. 2021).

Notwithstanding these latter concerns (Leong and Howlett 2022c), the modern policy sciences were founded on the idea that accumulating and utilizing knowledge of the effects of current and past policies is vital for better understanding policy problems and fashioning appropriate solutions to them (Lerner and Lasswell 1951). The operating principle for both research and practice in this view is that this knowledge should be brought to bear on the design and creation of policies, which can then be expected to be more likely to accomplish government goals than those formulated in other, less evidence-driven ways (Mukherjee et al. 2021).

In what follows, two central points in the book concerning the nature of policy design and the pre-conditions for its success are set out. These are (1) the need for designers to thoroughly analyze and understand the 'policy space' in which they are working, and (2) the need for them to be aware of, and deal with, the temporal and contextual dimensions of this space.

DOI: 10.4324/9781003343431-22

Understanding the design space

The chapters in this book have highlighted many significant aspects of the policy formulation and design processes, describing both how these processes work, who is involved with them, their impact on policy outcomes, and the lessons from the existing design literature on best practices for practitioners and erstwhile designers as they go about their work.

This is ongoing work, and the ongoing research agenda of the new design orientation is focused on many questions which an earlier literature on the subject largely neglected, such as the trade-offs existing between different tools in complex policy mixes and how to deal with the synergies and conflicts which result from tool interactions, as well as the different means and patterns – such as layering – through which policy mixes evolve over time (Thelen 2004).

Understanding the design space available in any design situation is critical in this work. Many formulation situations, for example, involve information and knowledge limits or involve multiple actors whose relationships may be more adversarial or competitive than is typically associated with the idea of a designed process and outcome (Schon 1988; Gero 1990). That is, not all policy-making is logic- or knowledge-driven, and how closely policy-makers approximate the instrumental logic and reasoning which is generally thought to characterize an intellectually driven design, in this field or any other, is in large part a function of the 'space' in which formulation considerations take place (Howlett et al. 2009). As we have seen, some of these spaces are conducive to knowledge-driven policy design, while others – 'non-design' spaces – are not.

But even within a favourable design space, some situations are more propitious for large-scale or fundamental reforms or policy 'packaging' than others which tend toward policy 'patching' or 'stretching'. As we have seen, policy formulation typically occurs within the confines of an existing governance mode and policy logic which both simplifies and constrains the task of policy design. It does this by restricting the number of alternatives which are considered feasible in any given situation. This can reduce to manageable proportions the otherwise almost-infinite range of possible specific micro-level instrument choices (Meuleman 2010b) and promote 'smart' layering, but only if these contextual constraints are diagnosed accurately.

Establishing the nature of the policy design 'space' is, therefore, a crucial activity for policy designers. That is, the process of design and instrument selection is made simpler once it is recognized that in some circumstances some of the elements of public policies are more amenable to careful thought and deliberate government manipulation than others.

Designing successful policies also requires thinking about policy-making in such a way as to fully take into account the dual purposes – substantive and procedural – which policies and policy tools can serve and the nature of the multiple levels of policy elements or components which make up a typical policy. But understanding exactly how instrument choices and calibrations are constrained by higher-order sets of variables is crucial to making good policy design decisions in specific policy-making contexts.

As set out in this book, adopting a multi-level, nested model of policy-making helps clarify what 'room' exists at what level of policy for new or alternative policy design elements (Hamdouch and Depret 2010). As the discussion here has shown, high-level abstract 'macro'-level policy goals like the nature of the governance mode found in a particular sector at a specific point in time change only very slowly, as do the sets of political actors, ideas, and institutional rules which create and work within it (Moore 1988; Braun 1999; Howlett and Ramesh 2003). The existence of these fairly long-term and stable governance arrangements helps maintain relatively constant formulation and implementation preferences or 'styles', since these derive from and are constrained by the same set of factors which influence and inform the development and articulation of abstract policy goals and means (Howlett 1991; May 1991; Dunsire 1993a; Kooiman 2000, 2008).

As the discussion in Chapters 9–12 has shown, the existence of a dominant governance mode in a particular sector or issue area generates certain propensities for the use of specific kinds of tools and their calibration. That is, these different governance modes involve different overall preferences for general kinds of substantive and procedural policy instruments expected to attain the general aims of government. Different countries and sectors share these preferences or styles, and they are an important overall determinant of the policy design preferences and choices made in specific policy and issue areas (Meuleman 2010a; Hardiman and Scott 2010; Howlett and Tosun 2019).

As we have seen in many countries, for example, the preferred instruments for policy implementation in many sectors have been configured historically as largely legal and corporatist rather than market- or network-based. Although the context, style, and substance of both the marketplace and the network have infiltrated the policy formulation process in most countries in recent years (Majone 1989), as the discussion in the book has shown, the policy design space in many countries remains firmly fixed within legal modes or, especially in many countries in Europe, Asia, and Latin America, within corporatist ones (Heritier et al. 1996; Knill 2001b; Pollitt 2001a). Hence, although compliance with government intentions has been approached in some sectors in these countries in terms of market-based factors – profit margins and the economic viability of industry, employment patterns, and international competitiveness – any new emphasis on the deployment of market-based policy tools often has little effect on already long-standing policy designs (Rhodes 1996; Salamon 2001; O'Toole and Meier 2010).

This underlines the linkages which exist between patterns of policy instrument choices and general governance preferences and the need for policy designers to be thoroughly aware of this aspect of the nature of the design space within which they are working. The basic nature of possible governance regimes is well-known, and the general implementation preferences they entail are also quite clear. That leaves the essential design challenge in many sectors as one of the identification and articulation of specific policy measures, more or less carefully calibrated, from within each category of tools, to secure compliance with government wishes in an already-existing governance mode.

But there is more to the impact of design spaces on policy designs and designing than this. Promoting 'integrated' policy mix designs congruent with existing design spaces, for example, multiplies the problems designers face in making choices and selecting instruments (Meijers and Stead 2004; Stead et al. 2004; Briassoulis 2005b, 2005c). Doing so requires a great deal of administrative and analytical capacity on the part of state actors that may or may not exist in different sectors and countries (Howlett 2009d; Howlett and Newman 2010).

That is, in order for 'design' to meaningfully occur at all, policy designers need a great deal of knowledge and insight into the workings of their polity and specific policy sectors, raising to the forefront questions about the capacity of policy experts and advisors involved in the policy formulation process to provide this information (Bye and Bruvoll 2008; Schön 1992). In order to be able to make an appropriate decision about when to introduce new instruments and when to renew old ones, for example, they must be familiar not only with the technical aspects of the menu of instruments before them but also with the nature of the governance and compliance contexts in which they are working and thus require training and experience in both these aspects of the policy design process if successful designs are to emerge (Braathen 2005, 2007b; Grant 2010; Skodvin et al. 2010).

Thus whether or not such expertise exists within a design space is a key criteria of design success of which both students and practitioners of policy design must be fully aware. And where it does not exist it must be created and encouraged.

Understanding the temporality of design choices

As the discussion in the book has also repeatedly noted, specific instrument choices are embedded decisions, not only existing within a nested, multi-level environment of governance modes, policy regime logics, and tool calibrations, but also being heavily context-laden.

The common existence of fairly 'routine' design situations and choices should not be taken to suggest complete stability in all areas, and it is certainly the case that designs can change as governments move away from earlier governance arrangements toward others. Any large-scale movements, as adherents of the globalization and government-to-government hypotheses have articulated, can have a large impact on the types of policy design choices taken by government, such as a shift away from 'direct' government activities toward an increased reliance on the indirect manipulation of market and policy network actors as has been observable in some sectors, such as energy and education policy in recent years.

There is thus a temporal aspect to policy designs contexts which policy designers must also take into account. As Christensen et al. (2002) have argued, the leeway or degree of manoeuvrability policy designers have in developing new designs is influenced not only by existing arrangements and polity features but also by historical-institutional processes and temporal dynamics.

That is, except in the case of completely new policy areas, which are relatively rare, designers are typically faced with situations in which an existing set of policy goals and a mix of policy instruments are already in place (Thelen 2003, 2004). These arrangements commonly have emerged or evolved over relatively long periods of time through previous design decisions, and as the discussion in this book has shown, even if they had a clear logic and plan at the outset, they may no longer do so (Bode 2006). Having evolved through such temporal processes as layering, in which instruments and goals are simply added to existing ones without abandoning the previous ones, can lead to both incoherence among the policy ends and inconsistency with respect to policy means (Howlett and Rayner 1995; Orren and Skowronek 1998; Rayner et al. 2001).

In these contexts, designers are faced with the challenge of re-design or the replacement of only some of the existing regime elements while working in a design space that is characterized by the continued existence of the remnants of earlier policy efforts. In such situations, designers often attempt to patch or re-structure existing policy elements rather than propose alternatives *de novo* (Gunningham and Sinclair 1999a; Thelen 2003, 2004; Eliadis et al. 2005). In such re-designs, Howlett and Rayner (2007) and Kern and Howlett (2009) have focused attention on the importance of designers aiming to achieve principles of good design, such as maintaining the 'coherence, consistency and congruence' of the elements in any new, or old, design. That is, designers typically strive to ensure that any new design elements are coherent in the sense that they are logically related to overall policy aims and objectives, that they be consistent in that they work together to support a policy goal, and that both policy goals and means should be congruent, rather than working at cross-purposes.

And as other chapters in the book have highlighted, this temporality is important in many ways. It affects not only how policy elements are sequenced but also the nature of overall policy goals when longer-term time horizons require policies to be robust or resilient, agile or adaptable.

The achievement of such characteristics in policy designs, however, requires a great deal of analytical and implementation capacity on the part of policy-makers and policy designers. Capacity, therefore, emerges as a second key pre-requisite for designing effective policies over both space and time and, again, is something those interested in successful policy design should understand.

Overcoming capacity and competence challenges to effective design

As the preceding discussion suggests, in dealing with the difficulties of design, governments face a variety of empirical, capacity, and knowledge-related circumstances which pose significant challenges to the design of effective policies. Transforming policy ambitions into practice is a complex process, and intentionally creating the best possible arrangement of policy elements is not always the first item on a government's mind or necessarily within its reach.

Nevertheless, many noble efforts of policy-makers have failed due to poor design capacity or the inability or lack of desire to alter elements of existing policies in a more logical, instrumental fashion (Howlett 2012; Cohn 2004). These experiences have led to a greater awareness in recent years of the various obstacles that can present themselves to policy design efforts and have gradually fuelled a desire for better understanding both the unique characteristics of each policy instrument and the different contexts in which policy design work proceeds, as well as to articulate principles of policy design which are themselves robust across jurisdictions, sectors, and time periods and can provide instructions to those attempts to improve policy-making and policy outcomes.

The desire to create effective policies in areas such as climate change, for example, where problems are expected to mount in number and persist over the long term, needs to not only be based on evidence and logic but also embody flexibility in order to be able to deliver on expectations about programme and policy goals and objectives over the long-term (Jordan and Matt 2014; Leone 2010).

Attaining robust, resilient, and effective policies in such areas requires a conscious effort to diagnose existing arrangements and existing levels of uncertainty and the existence of policy-making processes capable of adapting to a wide range of potential future circumstances (Day and Klein 1989; Capano and Woo 2017). Formulating and implementing policy processes and programmes which promote agility is not automatic but requires care and forethought. Failing to correctly identify the bounds and range of uncertainties, for example, is a major cause of policy over- and under-reaction (Maor 2012a, 2012b) and unwanted over- and under-policy design.

A critical enabling condition identified in many studies as a requirement for effective policy designs to emerge from policy formulation activity is enough *policy analytical capacity* to allow a government to acquire and process the information and knowledge required to conduct a sophisticated analysis of problems and alternatives (Wu et al. 2015a; Howlett and Ramesh 2016b).

This capacity relates to the sets of skills, competences, resources, and institutional arrangements and capabilities with which key tasks and functions in policy-making are structured, staffed, and supported, including the provision of policy advice from a policy advisory system. The extent to which the principal actors involved in the policy process are able to gather this advice, evaluate its merits, and carry out their functions depends on their organization's data collection and analysis capabilities. This includes their ability or capability to store and disseminate operationally relevant information. And each organization's analytical competences allow its members to identify and understand policy problems, canvass for solutions, assess

Table 16.1 Capacity issues in policy design outcomes

		Level of governance (political and operational) capacity	
		High	Low
Level of analytical capacity	High	**Capable design** Effective policies are possible	**Poor political design** Good technical designs may be weakly supported
	Low	**Capable political design** Good political designs are possible which may be technically poor	**Poor design** Only ineffective and poorly supported policies are possible

alternatives based on comparative assessment, and evaluate the impacts of chosen policies (Howlett 2009d, 2015) to a greater or lesser extent.

Effective policies can emerge only if governments possess high levels of governance capacity as well as a high level of analytical capability. Conversely, the absence of both types of capabilities allows for only weak design efforts and increases the probability of ineffective policies emerging from design processes (see Table 16.1).

Capacity constraints may be so strong that the ultimate design of policies is only distantly related to solving the originally highlighted problem. When policy tools are used in combination, as is often the case in social policy, for example, or when they are layered on top of earlier tools, there are additional complexities that promote synergies and complementarities but also allow for contradictions and conflicts in expected and unexpected ways. Only a high level of policy capacity can help advisors and analysts predict these relationships and avoid them in their policy recommendations (Howlett and Rayner 2007).

Other problems in policy design: decision-maker heuristics, disproportionality, and the social construction of policy targets

As previous chapters have set out, decision-makers are cognitively constrained in terms of their information processing capacities. Uncertainties and ambiguities abound and neither decision-makers nor formulators have complete knowledge of all the consequences of their actions or of all possible alternative actions, and face difficulties associated with anticipating them.

In order to deal with these gaps, decision-makers seek out advice but also frequently employ heuristic principles in order to reduce complex tasks that involve assessing probabilities and predicting values, to simpler judgmental operations (Tversky and Kahneman 1974: 1124). These heuristics are mental shortcuts that reduce the cognitive burden associated with decision-making (Shah and Oppenheimer 2008). Some are very useful in surmounting challenges of complexity, uncertainty, compliance, and malice, but others are not and the two must be carefully distinguished.

Decision-maker heuristics and the social construction of policy targets

One such important heuristic particularly relevant in policy analysis which affects policy designs is the use of mental models of policy problems, circumstances, and target populations (Hendrick 1994; World Bank 2015). These models are internal representations created by individual cognitive systems, with some types of mental models shared inter-subjectively (Denzau and North 1994).

Socially reinforced choices and shared mental models can affect policy design by blocking choices, preventing even conceiving of certain courses of action while promoting others. To the extent that policy-makers themselves are behavioural agents, their judgments all suffer from such psychological biases (Viscusi and Gayer 2015). The social constructions of target populations discussed earlier in the book are an example of how such heuristics may exert a powerful and often unintended influence on policy design (Schneider and Ingram 1993).

These biases can present themselves in the selection of policy advice and its utilization, for example. For instance, one bias frequently identified with policy-makers is 'confirmation bias', that is, the selective gathering of, or giving undue weight to, certain information in order to support a previously held belief (Nickerson 1998). Another bias that policy-makers often exhibit is their tendency to continue on a project once an initial investment of resources has been made: the 'sunk cost bias' (Arkes and Blumer 1985).

Both these and the impact of other kinds of biases need to be guarded against in both proposing and choosing policy alternatives.

The need for leadership, brokerage, and entrepreneurship in policy design implementation

Even where suitable capacity exists to design an effective policy and avoid the most obvious kinds of biases, this does not guarantee that a design will effectively be implemented. Policy-makers must operate as 'continuous policy-fixers' (Ingraham 1987), and their role oscillates between that of a policy 'architect', 'facilitator', and 'learner' in the policy process in order to appropriately 'adjust' a design in response to changing conditions over time (Howlett and Mukherjee 2014; Junginger 2013; Bason 2014; Mulgan 2008; Chiarini 2012).

Brokerage, for example, is an important task that needs to be undertaken in ensuring not only that knowledge and power are brought together in the right combination to result in problem-centred and evidence-informed policy-making (Christopoulos and Ingold 2011; Peters 2018) but also that implementation proceeds effectively. The prevailing function of brokerage in a policy design perspective is bridging and connecting different groups in a network of different actors involved in a common project of design, or in channelling improvisation according to the planned design in order to maintain or facilitate agility. Attention needs to be paid to this aspect of policy-making when implementation issues are considered.

Entrepreneurship (Schneider and Teste 1995; Kingdon 1984; Mintrom 1997; Mintrom and Norman 2009; Wijen and Ansari 2007; Levy and Scully 2007) is also important, as entrepreneurs can be the bearers of innovation or act to enlighten policy-makers with respect to the real meaning of new evidence-based knowledge (Argote et al. 1990; Darr et al. 1995). Again, governments can encourage or discourage this kind of policy and design-relevant activity with signicant consequences for the kinds of alternatives that emerge from design processes.

And, of course, leadership is also significant (Weber 1978; Blondel 1987), as transformational and transactional leadership (cf. Burns 2012; Selznick 1984; Gronn 2009; Pfeffer 1977; Svara 1994; Stiller 2010) each activates different types of followership. The former in particular can be critical in steering the policy design process by encouraging policy-makers to maintain their commitment toward design-orientated formulation and implementation (OECD 2011; Tosun et al. 2022).

Conclusion: dealing better with uncertainty and delivering public value – the task of policy design in contemporary government

As stated in the introduction to this volume, policy design is a specific form of policy formulation based on the gathering of knowledge about the effects of policy tool use on policy targets and the application of that knowledge to the development and implementation of policies aimed at the attainment of specifically desired public policy outcomes and ambitions (Bobrow 2006; Bobrow and Dryzek 1987; Montpetit 2003b; Weaver 2009b, 2010b). It involves the deliberate and conscious attempt to define policy goals and connect them in an instrumental fashion to tools expected to realize those objectives (Gilabert and Lawford-Smith 2012; Majone 1975; May 2003).

Within the policy sciences, the 'design' orientation addresses key questions about policy instrument characteristics and choice and about the factors behind successful design formulation and implementation (May 2003; Linder and Peters 1990a). These include such important questions as the trade-offs existing between different tools in complex policy mixes and how to deal with the synergies and conflicts which result from tool interactions, as well as the different means and patterns – such as layering – through which policies evolve over time (van der Heijden 2011; Howlett and Lejano 2013; Howlett et al. 2014; Doremus 2003; Howlett 2014b; Jordan et al. 2011, 2012; del Río and Howlett 2013). These activities all aim, as Moore (1994) suggested, one way or another, to enhance public value or the benefits citizens receive from the activities of their governments.

But studies in fields such as political science, economics, law, and public administration have all underlined that translating policy aims and objectives into practice is not as simple a task as might at first appear and public value may not always be at the forefront of policy-makers minds and intentions. And policies are made by a variety of different actors interacting with each other over a relatively long period of time within the confines of a set of political and economic institutions and governing norms, each with different interests and resources and all operating within a climate of uncertainty caused both by context and time-specific knowledge and information limitations, making the continual achievement of public value a challenging task (Bressers and O'Toole 1998, 2005).

Understanding who these actors are and why and how they act the way they do is a critical aspect of all public policy-making activity, including policy instrument selection and policy design (Skodvin et al. 2010), and is a central concern motivating research in the discipline.

The analysis presented in this book suggests that many traditional ways of thinking about these activities and their impact on policy instrument choices and policy designs are out of date. Dichotomous sets of policy alternatives – such as 'market versus state' – and metaphors – such as 'carrots versus sticks', for example – lend themselves to blunt thinking about instruments and their modalities. This is not helpful in conducting or thinking about policy design. Administrators and politicians involved in policy design have expanded the menu of government choice to include both substantive and procedural instruments and a wider range of options of each and scholars have begun to better understand the important context-based nature of instrument choices, in both cases improving or enhancing policy design theory and practice.

Beyond such obvious points, however, theorists and practitioners also need to move beyond simple notions of the pervasive impact of large-scale macro-developments, such as globalization and networkization, in affecting design choices. Understanding the precise nature of a policy space and its history of development over time is a prerequisite of successful design (Schön 1992). Innovative policy design, especially, requires that the parameters of instrument choice be well understood, both in order to reduce the risk of policy failure and to enhance the probability of policy success (Linder and Peters 1990a; Schneider and Ingram 1997).

Given the complexity of policy-making, it is not surprising many policies have failed. However, while not an optimal outcome, this has led to a greater appreciation of the difficulties encountered in designing public policies and the attempt to correct gaps in our understanding, a process which, albeit slowly, has improved our knowledge of the principles and elements of the nature of policy instruments and good policy design.

The challenge for a new generation of design studies is to continue to study instances of both success and failure in order to continue to develop not only the conceptual clarity and the methodological sophistication needed to identify design-relevant changes in policy contexts but also the techniques for understanding the interactions between these contexts and the elements of public policies arranged in specific kinds of policy designs (Eliadis et al. 2005; Yeung and Dixon-Woods 2010; del Rio et al. 2010; Hamelin 2010).

As the basis for the design and implementation of carefully calibrated policy measures, the templates developed by Doern, Hood, Linder, and Peters; Schneider and Ingram; and Salamon in the mid-1980s are still very useful in helping organize the literature on these subjects and to focus design discussions. But in spite of this work and the centrality and importance of design to public policy-making, the subject still remains, in many respects, a 'missing link' in policy studies (Hargrove 1975). Scholars need more empirical analysis in order to test their models and heuristics and provide better advice to governments about the processes of tool selection and how to better match tools to the job at hand. But while the design process is complex, often internally orchestrated between bureaucrats and target groups and usually much less accessible to public scrutiny than many other kinds of policy deliberations, this should not be allowed to stand in the way of its further elaboration and refinement (Kiviniemi 1986; Donovan 2001).

Readings

Balch, G. I. (1980). 'The Stick, the Carrot, and Other Strategies: A Theoretical Analysis of Governmental Intervention'. *Law and Policy Quarterly 2*, no. 1: 35–60.

Bason, C. (2014). *Design for Policy*. Farnham, UK and Burlington, VT: Gower.

Baxter-Moore, N. (1987). 'Policy Implementation and the Role of the State: A Revised Approach to the Study of Policy Instruments'. In R. J. Jackson, D. Jackson and N. Baxter-Moore (eds.), *Contemporary Canadian Politics: Readings and Notes*. Scarborough, ON: Prentice Hall, 336–355.

Coletti, P. (2015). 'Public Policy Design: How to Learn from Failures'. *World Political Science 11*, no. 2: 325–345.

Gunningham, N., P. Grabosky and D. Sinclair. (1998). *Smart Regulation: Designing Environmental Policy*. Oxford: Clarendon Press, 422–453.

Howlett, M. (2014). 'From the "Old" to the "New" Policy Design: Design Thinking beyond Markets and Collaborative Governance'. *Policy Sciences 47*, no. 3 (28 May): 187–207.

Howlett, M. (2017). 'The Criteria for Effective Policy Design: Character and Context in Policy Instrument Choice'. *Journal of Asian Public Policy 11*, no. 3 (6 December): 245–266.

Howlett, M. and I. Mukherjee. (2018). 'The Contribution of Comparative Policy Analysis to Policy Design: Articulating Principles of Effectiveness and Clarifying Design Spaces'. *Journal of Comparative Policy Analysis: Research and Practice* 20, no. *1* (1 January): 72–87.

Howlett, M., I. Mukherjee and J. J. Woo. (2015). 'From Tools to Toolkits in Policy Design Studies: The New Design Orientation towards Policy Formulation Research'. *Policy & Politics 43*, no. 2: 292–311.

Johnson, J. and M. Cook. (2014). 'Policy Design: A New Area of Design Research and Practice'. In M. Aiguier, F. Boulanger, D. Krob and C. Marchal (eds.), *Complex Systems Design & Management*. Cham, Germany: Springer, 51–62.

Justen, A., N. Fearnley, M. Givoni and J. Macmillen. (2014). 'A Process for Designing Policy Packaging: Ideals and Realities'. *Transportation Research Part A: Policy and Practice, Policy Packaging 60* (February): 9–18.

Lindquist, E. A. (1992). 'Public Managers and Policy Communities: Learning to Meet New Challenges'. *Canadian Public Administration 35*, no. 2: 127–159.

Mintrom, M. and J. Luetjens. (2016). 'Design Thinking in Policymaking Processes: Opportunities and Challenges'. *Australian Journal of Public Administration 75*, no. *3*: 391–402.

Mukherjee, I. and S. Giest. (2019). 'Designing Policies in Uncertain Contexts: Entrepreneurial Capacity and the Case of the European Emission Trading Scheme'. *Public Policy and Administration 34*, no. 3 (1 July): 262–286.

Öberg, P. O., M. Lundin and J. Thelander. (2015). 'Political Power and Policy Design: Why Are Policy Alternatives Constrained?' *Policy Studies Journal 43*, no. *1* (1 February): 93–114.

Peters, B. G., P. Ravinet, M. Howlett, G. Capano, I. Mukherjee and M. H. Chou. (2018). *Designing for Policy Effectiveness: Defining and Understanding a Concept*. Elements Series. Cambridge: Cambridge University Press.

Salamon, L. M. and B. G. Peters. (2002). 'The Politics of Tool Choice'. In L. M. Salamon (ed.), *The Tools of Government: A Guide to the New Governance*. New York: Oxford University Press, 552–564.

Turnbull, N. (2017). 'Policy Design: Its Enduring Appeal in a Complex World and How to Think It Differently'. *Public Policy and Administration 33*, no. 4: 357–364.

Wu, X., M. Ramesh and M. Howlett. (2015). 'Policy Capacity: A Conceptual Framework for Understanding Policy Competences and Capabilities'. *Policy and Society 34*, no. *3–4* (1 September): 165–171.

Bibliography

Abbott, K. W., D. Levi-Faur and D. Snidal. (2017). 'Introducing Regulatory Intermediaries'. *The Annals of the American Academy of Political and Social Science 670*, no. *1* (1 March): 6–13.

Abelson, D. E. (2002). *Do Think Tanks Matter? Assessing the Impact of Public Policy Institutes*. Kingston, ON: McGill-Queen's University Press.

Abelson, D. E. (2007). 'Any Ideas? Think Tanks and Policy Analysis in Canada'. In L. Dobuzinskis, M. Howlett and D. Laycock (eds), *Policy Analysis in Canada: The State of the Art*. Toronto, ON: University of Toronto Press, 298–310.

Abelson, J., P. G. Forest, J. Eyles, P. Smith, E. Martin and F. P. Gauvin. (2003). 'Deliberations About Deliberative Methods: Issues in the Design and Evaluation of Public Participation Processes'. *Social Science and Medicine 57*: 239–251.

Aberbach, J. D. and B. A. Rockman. (1989). 'On the Rise, Transformation and Decline of Analysis in the US Government'. *Governance 2*, no. *3*: 293–314.

Ackerman, B. (1981). *Clean Coal/Dirty Air: or How the Clean Air Act Became a Multibillion-Dollar Bail-Out for High-Sulfur Coal Producers*, vol. *23*. New Haven, CT: Yale University Press.

Adachi, Y. and S. Hosono (eds.). (2013). *Policy Analysis in Japan* (1st edn). Bristol, UK: Policy Press.

Adam, C., S. Hurka and C. Knill. (2015). 'Four Styles of Regulation and Their Implications for Comparative Policy Analysis'. *Journal of Comparative Policy Analysis: Research and Practice* (21 September): 1–18.

Adam, C., S. Hurka, C. Knill and Y. Steinebach. (2019). *Policy Accumulation and the Democratic Responsiveness Trap*. Cambridge: Cambridge University Press.

Adamowicz, W. (2007). 'Reflections on Environmental Policy in Canada'. *Canadian Journal of Agricultural Economics 55*: 1–13.

Adams, D. (2004). 'Usable Knowledge in Public Policy'. *Australian Journal of Public Administration 63*, no. *1*: 29–42.

Adcroft, A. and R. Willis. (2005). 'The (Un)Intended Outcome of Public Sector Performance Measurement'. *International Journal of Public Sector Management 18*, no. *5*: 386–400.

Adelle, C. and D. Russell. (2013). 'Climate Policy Integration: A Case of Déjà Vu?' *Environmental Policy and Governance 23*, no. *1*: 1–12.

Adger, W. N. and A. J. Jordan (eds.). (2009). *Governing Sustainability*. Cambridge: Cambridge University Press.

Adger, W. N., I. Lorenzoni and K. L. O'Brien (eds.). (2010). *Adapting to Climate Change: Thresholds, Values, Governance* (reissue). Cambridge: Cambridge University Press.

Adler, E. and P. M. Haas. (1992). 'Conclusion: Epistemic Communities, World Order, and the Creation of a Reflective Research Program'. *International Organization 46*: 367–390.

Adler, R. S. and R. D. Pittle. (1984). 'Cajolry or Command: Are Education Campaigns an Adequate Substitute for Regulation?' *Yale Journal on Regulation 1*, no. *2*: 159–193.

Advani, A. and S. Borins. (2001). 'Managing Airports: A Test of the New Public Management'. *International Public Management Journal 4*: 91–107.

Agranoff, R. (1998). 'Multinetwork Management: Collaboration and the Hollow State in Local Economic Policy'. *Journal of Public Administration Research and Theory 8*, no. *1*: 67–92.

Agranoff, R. and M. McGuire. (1999). 'Managing in Network Settings'. *Policy Studies Review 16*, no. *1*: 18–41.

Agranoff, R. and M. McGuire. (2001). 'Big Questions in Public Network Management Research'. *Journal of Public Administration Research and Theory 11*, no. *3*: 295–326.

Ajzen, I. (1991). 'The Theory of Planned Behavior'. *Organizational Behavior and Human Decision Processes 50*, no. *2*: 179–211.

Albrow, M. (1970). *Bureaucracy*. London: Pall Mall Press.

Aldrich, D. P. and M. A. Meyer. (2015). 'Social Capital and Community Resilience'. *American Behavioral Scientist 59*, no. 2 (1 February): 254–269.

Alexander, D., J. M. Lewis and M. Considine. (2014). 'How Governments Think: Skills, Expertise, and Experience in Public Policy Making'. In D. Alexander, J. M. Lewis and M. Considine (eds.), *Making Public Policy Decisions: Expertise, Skills and Experience*. London: Routledge, 44–65.

Alexander, E. (1982). 'Design in the Decision-Making Process'. *Policy Sciences 14*: 279–292.

Alford, J. (1998). 'A Public Management Road Less Travelled: Clients as Co-Producers of Public Services'. *Australian Journal of Public Administration 57*, no. *4*: 128–137.

Alford, J. (2002). 'Why Do Public-Sector Clients Coproduce? Toward a Contingency Theory'. *Administration & Society 34*, no. *1*: 32–56.

Alford, J. and B. W. Head. (2017). 'Wicked and Less Wicked Problems: A Typology and a Contingency Framework'. *Policy and Society 36*, no. *3* (3 July): 397–413.

Alford, R. (1972). 'The Political Economy of Health Care: Dynamics Without Change'. *Politics and Society 2*: 127–164.

Allcott, H. (2011). 'Social Norms and Energy Conservation'. *Journal of Public Economics 95*, no. *9–10*: 1082–1095.

Allcott, H. and T. Rogers. (2014). 'The Short-Run and Long-Run Effects of Behavioral Interventions: Experimental Evidence from Energy Conservation'. *American Economic Review 104*, no. *10*: 3003–3037.

Allison, G. T. and M. H. Halperin. (1972). 'Bureaucratic Politics: A Paradigm and Some Policy Implications'. *World Politics 24*, no. *Supplement*: 40–79.

Alonso, S., J. Keane and W. Merkel (eds.). (2011). *The Future of Representative Democracy*. Cambridge: Cambridge University Press.

Alshuwaikhat, H. M. and D. I. Nkwenti. (2002). 'Visualizing Decision-Making: Perspectives on Collaborative and Participative Approach to Sustainable Urban Planning and Management'. *Environment and Planning B: Planning and Design 29*: 513–531.

Althaus, C., L. Carson and K. Smith. (2021). 'Rethinking the Commissioning of Consultants for Enhancing Government Policy Capacity'. *Policy Sciences 54*, no. 4 (1 December): 867–889.

Altman, D. (2010). *Direct Democracy Worldwide*. Cambridge: Cambridge University Press.

Ambali, A. R. (2010). 'E-Government in Public Sector: Policy Implications and Recommendations for Policy-Makers'. *Research Journal of International Studies 17*: 133–145. www.eurojournals.com/RJIS_17_10.pdf.

Amenta, E. and B. G. Carruthers. (1988). 'The Formative Years of US Social Spending Policies: Theories of the Welfare State and the American States During the Great Depression'. *American Sociological Review 53*: 661–678.

Aminzade, R. (1992). 'Historical Sociology and Time'. *Sociological Methods and Research 20*, no. 4: 456–480.

Anderies, J. M. and M A. Janssen. (2013). 'Robustness of Social-Ecological Systems: Implications for Public Policy'. *Policy Studies Journal 41*, no. 3 (2013): 513–536.

Andersen, S. C. (2008). 'Private Schools and the Parents that Choose Them: Empirical Evidence from the Danish School Voucher System'. *Scandinavian Political Studies 31*, no. 1: 44–68.

Anderson, C. W. (1971). 'Comparative Policy Analysis: The Design of Measures'. *Comparative Politics 4*, no. 1: 117–131.

Anderson, C. W. (1977). *Statecraft: An Introduction to Political Choice and Judgement*. New York: John Wiley & Sons.

Anderson, G. (1996). 'The New Focus on the Policy Capacity of the Federal Government'. *Canadian Public Administration 39*, no. 4: 469–488.

Anderson, J. E. (1975). *Public Policymaking*. New York: Praeger.

Anderson, P. A. (1983). 'Decision Making by Objection and the Cuban Missile Crisis'. *Administrative Science Quarterly 28*: 201–222.

Andrews, R. (1998). 'Environmental Regulation and Business "Self-Regulation"'. *Policy Sciences 31*: 177–197.

Angelides, C. and G. Caiden. (1994). 'Adjusting Policy-thinking to Global Pragmatics and Future Problematics'. *Public Administration and Development 14*: 223–239.

Angus, W. H. (1974). 'Judicial Review: Do We Need It?' In D. J. Baum (ed.), *The Individual and the Bureaucracy*. Toronto, ON: Carswell, 101–135.

Anheier, H. K., S. Toepler and S. W. Sokolowski. (1997). 'The Implications of Government Funding for Non-Profit Organizations: Three Propositions'. *International Journal of Public Sector Management 10*, no. 3: 190–213.

Anker, H., V. Nellemann and S. Sverdrup-Jensen. (2004). 'Coastal Zone Management in Denmark: Ways and Means for Further Integration'. *Ocean and Coastal Management 47*: 495–513.

Ansell, C. and A. Gash. (2008). 'Collaborative Governance in Theory and Practice'. *Journal of Public Administration Research and Theory 18*, no. 4: 543–571.

Ansell, C. and A. Gash. (2017). 'Collaborative Platforms as a Governance Strategy'. *Journal of Public Administration Research and Theory 28*, no. 1 (13 December): 16–32.

Ansell, C., E. Sørensen and J. Torfing. (2017). 'Improving Policy Implementation Through Collaborative Policymaking'. *Policy & Politics 45*, no. 3 (7 July): 467–486.

Antonson, H. and A. Åkerskog. (2015). ' "This Is What We Did Last Time": Uncertainty Over Landscape Analysis and Its Procurement in the Swedish Road Planning Process'. *Land Use Policy 42* (January): 48–57.

Araña, J. E. and C. J. León. (2013). 'Can Defaults Save the Climate? Evidence from a Field Experiment on Carbon Offsetting Programs'. *Environmental and Resource Economics 54*, no. 4: 613–626.

Arellano-Gault, D. and G. Vera-Cortes. (2005). 'Institutional Design and Organisation of the Civil Protection National System in Mexico: The Case for a Decentralised and Participative Policy Network'. *Public Administration and Development 25*: 185–192.

Arestis, P. and Y. Kitromilides. (2010). 'What Economists Should Know About Public Policymaking?' *International Journal of Public Policy 6*, no. 1–2: 136–153.

Argote, L., S. L. Beckman and D. Epple. (1990). 'The Persistence and Transfer of Learning in Industrial Settings'. *Management Science 36*, no. 2: 140–154.

Ariely, D. (2010). *Predictably Irrational, Revised and Expanded Edition: The Hidden Forces That Shape Our Decisions* (expanded revised edn). New York: Harper Perennial.

Arkes, H. R. and C. Blumer. (1985). 'The Psychology of Sunk Cost'. *Organizational Behavior and Human Decision Processes 35*, no. 1: 124–140.

Armstrong, D. (1998). 'Globalization and the Social State'. *Review of International Studies 24*: 461–478.

Arrow, K. J. (1958). 'Tinbergen on Economic Policy'. *Journal of the American Statistical Association 53*, no. 281 (March): 89–97.

Arts, B., P. Leroy and J. van Tatenhove. (2006). 'Political Modernisation and Policy Arrangements: A Framework for Understanding Environmental Policy Change'. *Public Organization Review 6*, no. 2: 93–106.

Arts, B. and J. van Tatenhove. (2004). 'Policy and Power: A Conceptual Framework Between the "Old" and "New" Policy Idioms'. *Policy Sciences 37*: 339–356.

Arts, B., J. van Tatenhove and H. Goverde. (2000). 'Environmental Policy Arrangements: A New Concept'. In *Global and European Polity? Organizations, Policies, Contexts*. Aldershot: Ashgate, 223–237.

Ascher, K. (1987). *The Politics of Privatisation: Contracting Out Public Services*. London: Macmillan.

Asher, M. G. and A. S. Bali. (2015). 'Public Pension Programs in Southeast Asia: An Assessment'. *Asian Economic Policy Review 10*, no. 2: 225–245.

Asher, M. G. and A. Nandy. (2006). 'Health Financing in Singapore: A Case for Systemic Reforms'. *International Social Security Review 59*, no. 1: 75–92.

Atkinson, M. M. and W. Coleman. (1989a). *The State, Business and Industrial Change in Canada*. Toronto, ON: University of Toronto Press.

Atkinson, M. M. and W. Coleman. (1989b). 'Strong States and Weak States: Sectoral Policy Networks in Advanced Capitalist Economies'. *British Journal of Political Science 19*: 47–67.

Atkinson, M. M. and W. D. Coleman. (1992). 'Policy Networks, Policy Communities and the Problems of Governance'. *Governance 5*, no. 2: 154–180.

Atkinson, M. M. and R. A. Nigol. (1989). 'Selecting Policy Instruments: Neo-Institutional and Rational Choice Interpretations of Automobile Insurance in Ontario'. *Canadian Journal of Political Science 22*, no. 1: 107–135.

Attwell, K. and M. C. Navin. (2019). 'Childhood Vaccination Mandates: Scope, Sanctions, Severity, Selectivity, and Salience'. *The Milbank Quarterly 97, no. 4* (December): 978–1014.

AU Department of Finance. (2017). *Australian Government Assurance Reviews – Rescue Management Guide No. 106.* https://www.finance.gov.au/publications/resource-management-guides/guidance-assurance-reviews-process-rmg-106

AU Department of Finance. (2019). *Managing Commonwealth Resces Government.* www.finance.gov.au/government/managing-commonwealth-resces

AU Department of Finance. (2020). *Implementing the Commonwealth Risk Management Policy (RMG 211).* Managing Commonwealth Resces. www.finance.gov.au/government/managing-commonwealth-resces/implementing-commonwealth-risk-management-policy-rmg-211

Aucoin, P. (1990). 'Contribution of Commissions of Inquiry to Policy Analysis: An Evaluation'. In A. P. Pross, I. Christie and J. A. Yogis (eds.), *Commissions of Inquiry.* Toronto, ON: Carswell, 197–207.

Aucoin, P. (1995). *The New Public Management: Canada in Comparative Perspective.* Montreal, QC: Institute for Research on Public Policy.

Aucoin, P. (1997). 'The Design of Public Organizations for the 21st Century: Why Bureaucracy Will Survive in Public Management'. *Canadian Public Administration 40, no. 2:* 290–306.

Aucoin, P. (2006). 'Accountability and Coordination with Independent Foundations: A Canadian Case of Autonomization'. In T. Christensen and P. Lægreid (eds.), *Autonomy and Regulation: Coping with Agencies in the Modern State.* Cheltenham, UK: Edward Elgar, 110–133.

Aucoin, P. and H. Bakvis. (2005). 'Public Service Reform and Policy Capacity: Recruiting and Retaining the Best and the Brightest'. In M. Painter and J. Pierre (eds.), *Challenges to State Policy Capacity: Global Trends and Comparative Perspectives.* London: Palgrave Macmillan, pp. 185–204.

Auer, M. (1998). 'On Agency Reform as Decision Process'. *Policy Sciences 31:* 81–105.

Auld, G., B. Cashore, C. Balboa, L. Bozzi and S. Renckens. (2010). 'Can Technological Innovations Improve Private Regulation in the Global Economy?' *Business and Politics 12, no. 3:* 1–39.

Australian Public Service Commission. (2009). *Smarter Policy: Choosing Policy Instruments and Working with Others to Influence Behaviour.* Canberra, ACT: Australian Public Service Commission. http://trove.nla.gov.au/version/45613174

Aven, T. and O. Renn. (2010a). 'Risk Management'. In *Risk Management and Governance.* Berlin, Heidelberg: Springer, 121–158.

Averch, H. (1990). *Private Markets and Public Interventions: A Primer for Policy Designers.* Pittsburgh, PA: University of Pittsburgh Press.

Ayres, I. and J. Braithwaite. (1995). *Responsive Regulation: Transcending the Deregulation Debate.* Oxford: Oxford University Press.

Ayres, I., S. Raseman and A. Shih. (2013). 'Evidence from Two Large Field Experiments that Peer Comparison Feedback Can Reduce Residential Energy Usage'. *The Journal of Law, Economics, and Organization 29, no. 5:* 992–1022.

Azuela, G. E. and L. A. Barroso. (2012). *Design and Performance of Policy Instruments to Promote the Development of Renewable Energy: Emerging Experience in Selected Developing Countries.* Washington, DC: World Bank Publications.

Bacchi, C. (2014). *Analysing Policy.* New York: Pearson.

Bache, I. (2010). 'Partnership as an EU Policy Instrument: A Political History'. *West European Politics 33, no. 1:* 58–74.

335

Bachrach, P. and M. S. Baratz. (1970). *Power and Poverty: Theory and Practice*. New York: Oxford University Press.

Baetz, M. C. and A. B. Tanguay. (1998). ' "Damned if You Do, Damned if You Don't": Government and the Conundrum of Consultation in the Environmental Sector'. *Canadian Public Administration 41*, no. *3*: 395–418.

Bajari, P. and S. Tadelis. (2001). 'Incentives Versus Transaction Costs: A Theory of Procurement Contracts'. *RAND Journal of Economics 32*, no. *3*: 387–407.

Bakir, C. (2017). 'How Can Interactions Among Interdependent Structures, Institutions, and Agents Inform Financial Stability? What We Have Still to Learn from Global Financial Crisis'. *Policy Sciences 50*, no. *2* (1 June): 217–239.

Baksi, S. and P. Bose. (2007). 'Credence Goods, Efficient Labeling Policies and Regulatory Enforcement'. *Environmental and Resource Economics 37*: 411–430.

Bakvis, H. (1997). 'Advising the Executive: Think Tanks, Consultants, Political Staff and Kitchen Cabinets'. In P. Weller, H. Bakvis and R. A. W. Rhodes (eds.), *The Hollow Crown: Countervailing Trends in Core Executives*. New York: St Martin's Press.

Bakvis, H. (2000). 'Rebuilding Policy Capacity in the Era of the Fiscal Dividend: A Report from Canada'. *Governance 13*, no. *1*: 71–103.

Balch, G. I. (1980). 'The Stick, the Carrot, and Other Strategies: A Theoretical Analysis of Governmental Intervention'. *Law & Policy 2*, no. *1*: 35–60.

Baldwin, D. A. (1985). *Economic Statecraft*. Princeton, NJ: Princeton University Press.

Baldwin, R. and M. Cave. (1999). *Understanding Regulation: Theory, Strategy and Practice*. Oxford: Oxford University Press.

Bali, A. and D. Halpin. (2021). 'Agenda-Setting Instruments: Means and Strategies for the Management of Policy Demands'. *Policy and Society* (26 July): 1–12.

Bali, A. S., G. Capano and M. Ramesh. (2019). 'Anticipating and Designing for Policy Effectiveness'. *Policy & Society 38*, no. *1*: 1–13.

Bali, A. S., M. Howlett, J. M. Lewis and M. Ramesh. (2021). 'Procedural Policy Tools in Theory and Practice'. *Policy and Society 40*, no. *3* (3 July): 295–311.

Bali, A. S., M. Howlett and M. Ramesh. (2022). 'Unpacking Policy Portfolios: Primary and Secondary Aspects of Tool Use in Policy Mixes'. *Journal of Asian Public Policy*: 1–17.

Bali, A. S. and M. Ramesh. (2015). 'Health Care Reforms in India: Getting It Wrong'. *Public Policy and Administration 30*, no. *3–4*: 300–319.

Bali, A. S. and M. Ramesh. (2017). 'Designing Effective Healthcare: Matching Policy Tools to Problems in China'. *Public Administration and Development 37*, no. *1*: 40–50.

Bali, A. S. and M. Ramesh. (2019). 'Assessing Health Reform: Studying Tool Appropriateness & Critical Capacities'. *Policy and Society 38*, no. *1*: 148–166.

Bamberg, S. and G. Möser. (2007). 'Twenty Years After Hines, Hungerford, and Tomera: A New Meta-Analysis of Psycho-Social Determinants of pro-Environmental Behaviour'. *Journal of Environmental Psychology 27*, no. *1* (March): 14–25.

Bandsma, K., W. Rauws and G. de Roo. (2021). 'Optimising Nudges in Public Space: Identifying and Tackling Barriers to Design and Implementation'. *Planning Theory & Practice 22*, no. *4* (8 August): 556–571. https://doi.org/10.1080/1464935 7.2021.1962957

Banerjee, A. and E. Duflo. (2011). *Poor Economics: A Radical Rethinking of the Way to Fight Global Poverty* (reprinted). New York: Public Affairs.

Banfield, E. C. (1977). 'Policy Science as Metaphysical Madness'. In R. A. Goldwin (ed.), *Statesmanship and Bureaucracy*. Washington, DC: American Enterprise Institute for Public Policy, 1–35.

Bang, H. P. (2003). *Governance as Social and Political Communication*. Manchester, UK: Manchester University Press.

Banks, J. S. (1995). 'The Design of Institutions'. In D. L. Weimer (ed.), *Institutional Design*. Boston: Kluwer, 17–36.

Bannink, D. and M. Hoogenboom. (2007). 'Hidden Change: Disaggregation of Welfare Regimes for Greater Insight into Welfare State Change'. *Journal of European Social Policy 17*, no. 1: 19–32.

Banting, K. (1995). 'The Social Policy Review: Policy Making in a Semi-Sovereign Society'. *Canadian Public Administration 38*, no. 2: 283–290.

Barbazza, E. and J. E. Tello. (2014). 'A Review of Health Governance: Definitions, Dimensions and Tools to Govern'. *Health Policy 116*, no. 1: 1–11.

Bardach, E. (1977). *The Implementation Game: What Happens After a Bill Becomes a Law*. Cambridge, MA: MIT Press.

Bardach, E. (1980). 'Implementation Studies and the Study of Implements'. Paper presented to the American Political Science Association, University of California, Graduate School of Public Policy, Berkeley, CA.

Bardach, E. (1989a). 'Moral Suasion and Taxpayer Compliance'. *Law and Policy 11*, no. 1: 49–69.

Bardach, E. (1989b). 'Social Regulation as a Generic Policy Instrument'. In L. M. Salamon (ed.), *Beyond Privatization: The Tools of Government Action*. Washington, DC: Urban Institute, 197–229.

Barile, L., J. Cullis and P. Jones. (2015). 'Will One Size Fit All? Incentives Designed to Nurture Prosocial Behaviour'. *Journal of Behavioral and Experimental Economics 57* (August 1, 2015): 9–16 .

Barker, E. (1944). *The Development of Public Services in Western Europe 1660–1930*. Oxford: Oxford University Press.

Barnett, C. K. and B. Shore. (2009). 'Reinventing Program Design: Challenges in Leading Sustainable Institutional Change'. *Leadership & Organization*, 30, no. 1: 16–35.

Barnett, P., T. Tenbensel, J. Cuming, C. Alyden, T. Ashton, M. Pledger and M. Burnette. (2009). 'Implementing New Modes of Governance in the New Zealand Health System: An Empirical Study'. *Health Policy 93*: 118–127.

Barr, M. D. (2001). 'Medical Savings Accounts in Singapore: A Critical Inquiry'. *Journal of Health Politics, Policy and Law 26*, no. 4: 709–726.

Barr, M. S., S. Mullainathan and E. Shafir. (2009). 'The Case for Behaviorally Informed Regulation'. In *New Perspectives on Regulation*. Cambridge, MA: The Tobin Project, 25–62.

Barreiro-Hurlé, J., A. Gracia and T. de-Magistris. (2010). 'Does Nutrition Information on Food Products Lead to Healthier Food Choices?' *Food Policy 35*, no. 3 (June): 221–229.

Bartle, I. and P. Vass. (2007). 'Self-Regulation within the Regulatory State: Towards a New Regulatory Paradigm?' *Public Administration 85*, no. 4: 885–905.

Barzelay, M. and N. Fuchtner. (2003). 'Explaining Public Management Policy Change: Germany in Comparative Perspective'. *Journal of Comparative Policy Analysis 5*, no. 1: 7–28.

Barzelay, M. and F. Thompson. (2010). 'Back to the Future: Making Public Administration a Design Science'. *Public Administration Review 70*, no. Supplement 1: 295–297.

Bason, C. (2014). *Design for Policy*. Farnham, UK; Burlington, VT: Gower.

Bason, C. and A. Schneider. (2014). 'Public Design in Global Perspective; Empirical Trends'. In C. Bason (ed.), *Design for Policy*. London: Gower Pub Co., 23–40.

Batlle, C. and I. J. Perez-Arriaga. (2008). 'Design Criteria for Implementing a Capacity Mechanism in Deregulated Electricity Markets'. *Utilities Policy 16*: 184–193.

Bator, F. M. (1958). 'The Anatomy of Market Failure'. *Quarterly Journal of Economics 72*, no. 3: 351–379.

Bauer, J. (2006). *International Forest Sector Institutions and Policy Instruments for Europe: A Source Book*. Geneva, Switzerland: FAO/UNECE.

Bauer, M. W., A. Jordan, C. Green-Pedersen and A. Héritier (eds.). (2012). *Dismantling Public Policy: Preferences, Strategies, and Effects*. Oxford: Oxford University Press.

Baumgartner, F. R. and B. D. Jones. (1991). 'Agenda Dynamics and Policy Subsystems'. *The Journal of Politics 53*, no. 4: 1044–1074.

Baumgartner, F. R. and B. D. Jones. (1993). *Agendas and Instability in American Politics*. Chicago, IL: University of Chicago Press, 26, 239–241.

Baumgartner, F. R. and B. D. Jones. (2002a). *Policy Dynamics*. Chicago, IL: University of Chicago Press.

Baumgartner F. R. and B. D. Jones (2002b). 'Positive and Negative Feedback in Politics'. In F. R. Baumgartner and B. D. Jones (eds.), *Policy Dynamics*. Chicago: University of Chicago Press, 3–28.

Baumgartner, F. R., B. D. Jones and J. Wilkerson. (2011). 'Comparative Studies of Policy Dynamics'. *Comparative Political Studies 44*, no. 8: 947–972.

Baxter-Moore, N. (1987). 'Policy Implementation and the Role of the State: A Revised Approach to the Study of Policy Instruments'. In R. J. Jackson, D. Jackson and N. Baxter-Moore (eds.), *Contemporary Canadian Politics*. Scarborough, ON: Prentice Hall.

Bearce, D. H. (2008). 'Not Complements but Substitutes: Fixed Exchange Rate Commitments, Central Bank Independence and External Currency Stability'. *International Studies Quarterly 52*: 807–824.

Becker, G. S. (1983). 'A Theory of Competition Among Pressure Groups for Political Influence'. *Quarterly Journal of Economics 98* (August): 371–400.

Becker, S. W. and F. O. Brownson. (1964). 'What Price Ambiguity? Or the Role of Ambiguity in Decision-Making'. *Journal of Political Economy 72*, no. 1 (1 February): 62–73.

Beesley, M. E. (1992). *Privatization, Regulation and Deregulation*. New York: Routledge.

Beetham, D. (1987). *Bureaucracy*. Milton Keynes, UK: Open University Press.

Beetham, D. (1991). *The Legitimation of Power*. London: Macmillan.

Beh, E. H. Y., H. R. Maier and G. C. Dandy. (2015). 'Scenario Driven Optimal Sequencing Under Deep Uncertainty'. *Environmental Modelling & Software 68*, no. *Supplement C* (1 June): 181–195.

Behn, R. D. (1981). 'Policy Analysis and Policy Politics'. *Policy Analysis 7*, no. 2: 199–226.

Bekke, H. A. G. M. (1999). 'Studying the Development and Transformation of Civil Service Systems: Processes of De-Institutionalization'. *Research in Public Administration 5*: 1–18.

Bekke, H. A. G. M., J. L. Perry and T. A. J. Toonen. (1993). 'Comparing Civil Service Systems'. *Research in Public Administration 2*: 191–212.

Bekke, H. A. G. M., J. L. Perry and T. A. J. Toonen (eds.). (1996a). *Civil Service Systems in Comparative Perspective*. Bloomington, IN: Indiana University Press.

Bekke, H. A. G. M., J. L. Perry and T. A. J. Toonen. (1996b). 'Introduction: Conceptualizing Civil Service Systems'. In H. A. G. M. Bekke, J. L. Perry and T. A. J. Toonen (eds.), *Civil Service Systems in Comparative Perspective*. Bloomington, IN: Indiana University Press, 1–12.

Bekke, H. A. G. M. and F. M. van der Meer (eds.). (2000). *Civil Service Systems in Western Europe*. Cheltenham, UK: Edward Elgar.

Béland, D. (2007). 'Ideas and Institutional Change in Social Security: Conversion, Layering and Policy Drift'. *Social Science Quarterly 88*, no. *1*: 20–38.

Béland, D. and J. Hacker. (2004). 'Ideas, Private Institutions, and American Welfare State "Exceptionalism"'. *International Journal of Social Welfare 13*, no. *1*: 42–54.

Béland, D. and M. Howlett. (2016). 'How Solutions Chase Problems: Instrument Constituencies in the Policy Process'. *Governance 29*, no. *3*: 393–409.

Béland, D., M. Howlett, P. Rocco and A. Waddan. (2020). 'Designing Policy Resilience: Lessons from the Affordable Care Act'. *Policy Sciences 53*, no. *2* (June): 269–289.

Beland, D., P. Rocco and A. Waddan. (2016). *Obamacare Wars: Federalism, State Politics, and the Affordable Care Act* (1 edn). Lawrence, KS: University Press of Kansas.

Beland, D., P. Rocco and A. Waddan. (2019). 'Policy Feedback and the Politics of the Affordable Care Act'. *Policy Studies Journal 47*, no. *2*: 395–422.

Béland, D. and A. Waddan. (2012). 'The Obama Presidency and Health Insurance Reform: Assessing Continuity and Change'. *Social Policy and Society 11*, no. *3*: 319–330.

Bellehumeur, R. (1997). 'Review: An Instrument of Change'. *Optimum 27*, no. *1*: 37–42.

Bemelmans-Videc, M.-L. (1998). 'Introduction: Policy Instrument Choice and Evaluation'. In M. L. Bemelmans-Videc, R. C. Rist and E. Vedung (eds.), *Carrots, Sticks and Sermons: Policy Instruments and Their Evaluation*, New Brunswick, NJ: Transaction, 21–58.

Bemelmans-Videc, M.-L., R. C. Rist and E. Vedung (eds.). (1998). *Carrots, Sticks and Sermons: Policy Instruments and Their Evaluation*. New Brunswick, NJ: Transaction.

Bendor, J., S. Kumar and D. A. Siegel. (2009). 'Satisficing: A "Pretty Good" Heuristic'. *The B.E. Journal of Theoretical Economics 9*, no. *1*.

Ben-Gera, M. (2007). *The Role of Ministries in the Policy System: Policy Development, Monitoring and Evaluation*. Paris: OECD.

Benjamin, L. M. (2008). 'Bearing More Risk for Results: Performance Accountability and Nonprofit Relational Work'. *Administration and Society 39*, no. *8*: 959–983.

Bennett, C. J. (1988). 'Different Processes, One Result: The Convergence of Data Protection Policy in Europe and the United States'. *Governance 4*, no. *1*: 415–441.

Bennett, C. J. (1990). 'The Formation of a Canadian Privacy Policy: The Art and Craft of Lesson-Drawing'. *Canadian Public Administration 33*, no. *4*: 551–570.

Bennett, C. J. (1991a). 'How States Utilize Foreign Evidence'. *Journal of Public Policy 11*, no. *1*: 31–54.

Bennett, C. J. (1991b). 'Review Article: What Is Policy Convergence and What Causes It?' *British Journal of Political Science 21*, no. *2*: 215–233.

Bennett, C. J. (1992). *Regulating Privacy: Data Protection and Public Policy in Europe and the United States*. Ithaca, NY: Cornell University Press.

Bennett, C. J. (1997). 'Understanding Ripple Effects: The Cross-National Adoption of Policy Instruments for Bureaucratic Accountability'. *Governance 10*, no. 3: 213–233.

Bennett, C. J. and R. Bayley. (1999). 'The New Public Administration: Canadian Approaches to Access and Privacy'. In M. W. Westmacott and H. P. Mellon (eds.), *Public Administration and Policy: Governing in Challenging Times*. Scarborough, ON: Prentice Hall/Allyn & Bacon, 189–201.

Bennett, C. J. and M. Howlett. (1992). 'The Lessons of Learning: Reconciling Theories of Policy Learning and Policy Change'. *Policy Sciences 25*, no. 3: 275–294.

Bennett, C. J. and C. D. Raab. (2003). *The Governance of Privacy: Policy Instruments in Global Perspective*. Aldershot, UK: Ashgate.

Bennett, N. and G. James Lemoine. (2014a). 'What a Difference a Word Makes: Understanding Threats to Performance in a VUCA World'. *Business Horizons 57*, no. 3 (1 May): 311–317.

Bennett, N. and G. James Lemoine. (2014b). 'What VUCA Really Means for You'. *Harvard Business Review 92*, no. 1–2 (February).

Bennett, S. and M. McPhail. (1992). 'Policy Process Perceptions of Senior Canadian Federal Civil Servants: A View of the State and Its Environment'. *Canadian Public Administration 35*, no. 3: 299–316.

Bennion, E. A. and D. W. Nickerson. (2011). 'The Cost of Convenience: An Experiment Showing E-Mail Outreach Decreases Voter Registration'. *Political Research Quarterly 64*, no. 4 (1 December): 858–869.

Bentley, A. F. (1908). *The Process of Government*. Chicago, IL: University of Chicago Press.

Benyus, J. M. (1997). *Biomimicry: Innovation Inspired by Nature*. New York: Harper Perennial.

Berg, S. V. (2000). 'Sustainable Regulatory Systems: Laws, Resources and Values'. *Utilities Policy 9*: 159–170.

Berg, S. V., A. N. Memon and R. Skelton. (2000). *Designing an Independent Regulatory Commission*. London: IRC Research Paper.

Berger, S. (1981). *Organizing Interests in Western Europe: Pluralism, Corporatism and the Transformation of Politics*. Cambridge: Cambridge University Press.

Bernhagen, P. (2003). 'Is Globalization What States Make of It? Micro-Foundations of the State – Market Condominium in the Global Political Economy'. *Contemporary Politics 9*, no. 3: 257–276.

Bernier, L. (2011). 'The Future of Public Enterprises: Perspectives from the Canadian Experience'. *Annals of Public and Cooperative Economics 82*, no. 4 (1 December): 399–419.

Bernier, L., P. Bance and M. Florio (eds.). (2020). *The Routledge Handbook of State-Owned Enterprises*. Routledge International Handbooks. New York: Routledge.

Bernier, L., K. Brownsey and M. Howlett (eds.). (2005). *Executive Styles in Canada: Cabinet Structures and Leadership Practices in Canadian Government*. Toronto, ON: University of Toronto Press.

Bernstein, M. H. (1955). *Regulating Business by Independent Commission*. Princeton, NJ: Princeton University Press.

Bernstein, S. and B. Cashore. (2007). 'Can Non-State Global Governance Be Legitimate? An Analytical Framework'. *Regulation and Governance 1*: 347–371.

Berry, W. D., R. C. Fording and R. L. Hanson. (2003). 'Reassessing the "Race to the Bottom" in State Welfare Policy'. *The Journal of Politics 65*, no. 2: 327–349.

Bertelli, A. (2006). 'The Role of Political Ideology in the Structural Design of New Governance Agencies'. *Public Administration Review 66*, no. 4: 583–595.

Bertelli, A. M. and J. B. Wenger. (2009). 'Demanding Information: Think Tanks and the US Congress'. *British Journal of Political Science 39*, no. 2: 225–242.

BETA. (2016). *Behavioural Economics Team of the Australian Government | Department of the Prime Minister and Cabinet [Text]* (22 April). www.dpmc.gov.au/domestic-policy/behavioural-economics. Accessed 4 April 2017.

Bevir, M. (ed.). (2007). *Public Governance*, vol. 4. London: Sage.

Bevir, M. and R. A. W. Rhodes (2001). 'Decentering Tradition: Interpreting British Government'. *Administration and Society 33*, no. 2: 107–132.

Bevir, M., R. A. W. Rhodes and P. Weller. (2003). 'Traditions of Governance: Interpreting the Changing Role of the Public Sector'. *Public Administration 81*, no. 1: 1–17.

Bhatta, G. (2002). 'Evidence-Based Analysis and the Work of Policy Shops'. *Australian Journal of Public Administration 61*, no. 3: 98–105.

Biddle, J. C. and T. M. Koontz. (2014). 'Goal Specificity: A Proxy Measure for Improvements in Environmental Outcomes in Collaborative Governance'. *Journal of Environmental Management 145*: 268–276.

Binder, T. and E. Brandt. (2008). 'The Design Lab as Platform in Participatory Design Research'. *CoDesign 4*, no. 2: 115–129.

Binderkrantz, A. (2005). 'Interest Group Strategies: Navigating Between Privileged Access and Strategies of Pressure'. *Political Studies 53*: 694–715.

Bingham, L. B., T. Nabatchi and R. O'Leary. (2005). 'The New Governance: Practices and Processes for Stakeholder and Citizen Participation in the Work of Government'. *Public Administration Review 65*, no. 5: 547–558.

Birch, A. H. (1984). 'Overload, Ungovernability and Delegitimization: The Theories and the British Case'. *British Journal of Political Science 14*: 136–160.

Bird, R. M. (1970). *The Growth of Government Spending in Canada*. Toronto, ON: Canadian Tax Foundation.

Birkland, T. A. (1997). *After Disaster: Agenda Setting, Public Policy and Focusing Events*. Washington, DC: Georgetown University Press.

Birkland, T. A. (1998). 'Focusing Events, Mobilization, and Agenda Setting'. *Journal of Public Policy 18*, no. 1: 53–74.

Birkland, T. A. (2009). 'Disasters, Lessons Learned, and Fantasy Documents'. *Journal of Contingencies and Crisis Management 17*, no. 3: 146–156.

Birrell, D. (2008). 'Devolution and Quangos in the United Kingdom: The Implementation of Principles and Policies for Rationalisation and Democratisation'. *Policy Studies 29*, no. 1: 35–49.

Bishop, P. and G. Davis. (2002). 'Mapping Public Participation in Policy Choices'. *Australian Journal of Public Administration 61*, no. 1: 14–29.

Black, A. E., D. L. Koopman and D. K. Ryden. (2004). *Of Little Faith: The Politics of George W. Bush's Faith-Based Initiative*. Washington, DC: Georgetown University Press.

Blaikie, P. and H. Brookfield. (1987). *Land Degradation and Society*. London: Methuen.

Blair, R. (2002). 'Policy Tools Theory and Implementation Networks: Understanding State Enterprise Zone Partnerships'. *Journal of Public Administration Research and Theory 12*, no. 2: 161–190.

Blanc, F. (2018). *From Chasing Violations to Managing Risks: Origins, Challenges and Evolutions in Regulatory Inspections*. Cheltenham: Edward Elgar Publishing.

Blankart, C. (1985). 'Market and Non-Market Alternatives in the Supply of Public Goods: General Issues'. In F. Forte and A. Peacock (eds.), *Public Expenditure and Government Growth*. London: Basil Blackwell, 192–201.

Blind, P. K. (2006). *Building Trust in Government in the Twenty-First Century: Review of Literature and Emerging Issues*. New York: UNDESA.

Blomkamp, E. (2018). 'The Promise of Co-Design for Public Policy'. *Australian Journal of Public Administration 77*, no. 4: 729–743.

Blomqvist, A. (2011). 'Public Sector Health Care Financing'. In S. Glied and P. Smith (eds.), *The Oxford Handbook of Health Economics*. Chippenham: Oxford University Press, 257–284.

Blondel, J. (1987). *Political Leadership: Towards a General Analysis*. London; Beverly Hills, CA: Sage.

Blonz, J. A., S. P. Vajjhala and E. Safirova. (2008). *Growing Complexities: A Cross-Sector Review of US Biofuels Policies and Their Interactions*. Washington, DC: Resources for the Future.

Blum, S. and K. Schubert (eds.). (2013). *Policy Analysis in Germany*. Bristol, UK: Policy Press.

Blyth, M. M. (1997). ' "Any More Bright Ideas?" The Ideational Turn of Comparative Political Economy'. *Comparative Politics 29*: 229–250.

Boardman, A. E., D. H. Greenberg, A. R. Vining and D. L. Weimer. (2001). *Cost-Benefit Analysis: Concepts and Practice*. Upper Saddle River, NJ: Prentice Hall.

Boas, I., F. Biermann and N. Kanie. (2016). 'Cross-Sectoral Strategies in Global Sustainability Governance: Towards a Nexus Approach'. *International Environmental Agreements: Politics, Law and Economics 16*: 449–464.

Boase, J. P. (2000). 'Beyond Government: The Appeal of Public Private Partnerships'. *Canadian Public Administration 43*, no. 1: 75–91.

Boaz, A., L. Grayson, R. Levitt and W. Solesbury. (2008). 'Does Evidence-Based Policy Work? Learning from the UK Experience'. *Evidence & Policy 4*, no. 2: 233–253.

Bobrow, D. B. (1977). 'Beyond Markets and Lawyers'. *American Journal of Political Science 21*, no. 2: 415–433.

Bobrow, D. B. (2006). 'Policy Design: Ubiquitous, Necessary and Difficult'. In B. G. Peters and J. Pierre (eds.), *Handbook of Public Policy*. London: Sage, 75–96.

Bobrow, D. B. and J. S. Dryzek. (1987). *Policy Analysis by Design*. Pittsburgh, PA: University of Pittsburgh Press.

Bode, I. (2006). 'Disorganized Welfare Mixes: Voluntary Agencies and New Governance Regimes in Western Europe'. *Journal of European Social Policy 16*, no. 4: 346–359.

Boehmke, F. J. (2005). *The Indirect Effect of Direct Legislation*. Columbus, OH: Ohio State University Press.

Bogart, W. A. (2002). *Consequences: The Impact of Law and Its Complexity*. Toronto, ON: University of Toronto Press.

Boin, A., L. K. Comfort and C. C. Demchak. (2010). 'The Rise of Resilience'. In L. K. Comfort, A. Boin and C. C. Demchak (eds.), *Designing Resilience: Preparing for Extreme Events*. Pittsburgh, PA: University of Pittsburgh Press, 1–12.

Boin, A., L. A. Fahy and P. 't Hart. (2020). *Guardians of Public Value: How Public Organisations Become and Remain Institutions*. Cham: Springer Nature.

Boin, A., A. McConnell and P. 't Hart. (2021). *Governing the Pandemic: The Politics of Navigating a Mega-Crisis*. Cham: Springer International Publishing.

Boin, A. and P. 't Hart. (2010). 'Organising for Effective Emergency Management: Lessons from Research'. *Australian Journal of Public Administration 69*, no. 4: 357–371.

Boin, A. and P. 't Hart. (2022). 'From Crisis to Reform? Exploring Three Post-COVID Pathways'. *Policy and Society 41*, no. *1* (28 January): 13–24.

Boin, A., P. 't Hart, E. Stern and B. Sundelius. (2005). *The Politics of Crisis Management: Public Leadership Under Pressure*. Cambridge: Cambridge University Press.

Bolleyer, N. and T. A. Borzel. (2010). 'Non-Hierarchical Policy Coordination in Multi-level Systems'. *European Political Science Review 2*, no. 2: 157–185.

Bond, A., A. Morrison-Saunders, J. A. E. Gunn, J. Pope and F. Retief. (2015). 'Managing Uncertainty, Ambiguity and Ignorance in Impact Assessment by Embedding Evolutionary Resilience, Participatory Modeling and Adaptive Management'. *Journal of Environmental Management 151* (15 March): 97–104.

Boonekamp, P. G. M. (2006). 'Actual Interaction Effects Between Policy Measures for Energy Efficiency – A Qualitative Matrix Method and Quantitative Simulation Results for Households'. *Energy 31*, no. *14* (November): 2848–2873.

Boonstra, W. J. and F. W. de Boer. (2014). 'The Historical Dynamics of Social – Ecological Traps'. *AMBIO 43*, no. *3* (1 April): 260–274.

Borenstein, S. (2013). *A Microeconomic Framework for Evaluating Energy Efficiency Rebound and Some Implications*. Working Paper No. 19044. Washington, DC: National Bureau of Economic Research.

Borins, S. F. (1982). 'World War Two Crown Corporations: Their Wartime Role and Peacetime Privatization'. *Canadian Public Administration 25*, no. *3*: 380–404.

Borins, S. F. (2001). 'Public Management Innovation in Economically Advanced and Developing Countries'. *International Review of Administrative Sciences 67*: 715–731.

Borras, S. and C. Edquist. (2013). 'The Choice of Innovation Policy Instruments'. *Technological Forecasting & Social Change 80*: 1513–1522.

Borraz, O. (2007). 'Governing Standards: The Rise of Standardization Processes in France and in the EU'. *Governance 20*, no. *1*: 57–84.

Bos, D. (1991). *Privatization: A Theoretical Treatment*. Oxford: Clarendon Press.

Bos, J. J., R. R. Brown and M. A. Farrelly. (2013). 'A Design Framework for Creating Social Learning Situations'. *Global Environmental Change 23*, no. 2 (1 April): 398–412.

Boston, J. (1994). 'Purchasing Policy Advice: The Limits of Contracting Out'. *Governance 7*, no. *1*: 1–30.

Boston, J., J. Martin, J. Pallot and P. Walsh. (1996). *Public Management: The New Zealand Model*. Auckland, NZ: Oxford University Press.

Bostrom, A., R. E. O'Connor, G. Böhm, D. Hanss, O. Bodi, F. Ekström, P. Halder, S. Jeschke, B. Mack, M. Qu, L. Rosentrater, A. Sandve and I. Sælensminde. (2012). 'Causal Thinking and Support for Climate Change Policies: International Survey Findings'. *Global Environmental Change 22*, no. 1: 210–222.

Bougherara, D., G. Grolleau and N. Mzoughi. (2007). 'Is More Information Always Better? An Analysis Applied to Information-Based Policies for Environmental Protection'. *International Journal of Sustainable Development 10*, no. *3*: 197–213.

Bourgon, J. (1996). 'Strengthening Our Policy Capacity'. In Canadian Centre for Management Development (ed.), *Rethinking Policy: Strengthening Policy Capacity – Conference Proceedings*. Ottawa, ON: Ministry of Supply and Services, 22–30.

Bousquet, L., G. Poniatowski, C. Vellutini and G. Casamatta. (2019). *Estimating International Tax Evasion by Individuals*. Luxembourg: Publications Office of the European Union.

Bovaird, T. (2007). 'Beyond Engagement and Participation: User and Community Co-Production of Public Services'. *Public Administration Review 67*, no. 5: 846–860.

Bovaird, T., I. Briggs and M. Willis. (2014). 'Strategic Commissioning in the UK: Service Improvement Cycle or Just Going Round in Circles?' *Local Government Studies 40*, no. 4 (4 July): 533–559.

Bovens, L. (2009). 'The Ethics of Nudge'. In T. Grüne-Yanoff and S. O. Hansson (eds.), *Preference Change*. Dordrecht, Netherlands: Springer, 207–219.

Bovens, M. and P. 't Hart. (1995). 'Frame Multiplicity and Policy Fiascos: Limits to Explanation'. *Knowledge and Policy 8*, no. 4: 61–83.

Bovens, M. and P. 't Hart. (1996). *Understanding Policy Fiascoes*. New Brunswick, NJ: Transaction.

Bovens, M., P. 't Hart and B. G. Peters. (2001a). 'Analysing Governance Success and Failure in Six European States'. In M. Bovens, P. 't Hart and B. G. Peters (eds.), *Success and Failure in Public Governance: A Comparative Analysis*. Cheltenham, UK: Edward Elgar, 12–32.

Bovens, M., P. 't Hart and B. Guy Peters (eds.). (2001b). *Success and Failure in Public Governance: A Comparative Analysis*. Cheltenham: Edward Elgar Publishing Ltd.

Braathen, N. A. (2005). 'Environmental Agreements Used in Combination with Other Policy Instruments'. In E. Croci (ed.), *The Handbook of Environmental Voluntary Agreements*, vol. 43. Dordrecht: Springer, 335–364.

Braathen, N. A. (2007a). *Instrument Mixes Addressing Non-Point Sources of Water Pollution*. Paris: OECD.

Braathen, N. A. (2007b). 'Instrument Mixes for Environmental Policy: How Many Stones Should Be Used to Kill a Bird?' *International Review of Environmental and Resource Economics 1*, no. 2 (16 May): 185–235.

Braathen, N. A. and E. Croci. (2005). 'Environmental Agreements Used in Combination with Other Policy Instruments'. In *The Handbook of Environmental Voluntary Agreements*, vol. 43. Dordrecht, Netherlands: Springer, 335–364.

Brabham, D. C. (2008). 'Crowdsourcing as a Model for Problem Solving: An Introduction and Cases'. *Convergence 14*, no. 1 (1 February): 75–90.

Brabham, D. C., K. M. Ribisl, T. R. Kirchner and J. M. Bernhardt. (2014). 'Crowdsourcing Applications for Public Health'. *American Journal of Preventive Medicine 46*, no. 2 (February): 179–187.

Bradford, N. (1999). 'The Policy Influence of Economic Ideas: Interests, Institutions and Innovation in Canada'. *Studies in Political Economy 59*: 17–60.

Brady, M. (2011). 'Improvisation Versus Rigid Command and Control at Stalingrad'. *Journal of Management History 17*, no. 1 (11 January): 27–49.

Braithwaite, J. (2008). *Regulatory Capitalism: How It Works, Ideas for Making It Work Better*. Cheltenham, UK: Edward Elgar.

Braithwaite, J., J. Walker and P. Grabosky. (1987). 'An Enforcement Taxonomy of Regulatory Agencies'. *Law and Policy 9*, no. 3: 323–351.

Braithwaite, V. and M. Levi. (eds.). (2003). *Trust and Governance*. New York: Russell Sage Foundation Publications.

Braithwaite, V. A. (ed.). (2003). *Taxing Democracy: Understanding Tax Avoidance and Evasion*. Aldershot, Hants, England; Burlington, VT, USA: Ashgate Pub Ltd.

Brancati, D. (2014). 'Democratic Authoritarianism: Origins and Effects'. *Annual Review of Political Science 17*, no. 1: 313–326.

Brandl, J. (1988). 'On Politics and Policy Analysis as the Design and Assessment of Institutions'. *Journal of Policy Analysis and Management 7*, no. 3: 419–424.

Brandsen, T., M. Boogers and P. Tops. (2006). 'Soft Governance, Hard Consequences: The Ambiguous Status of Unofficial Guidelines'. *Public Administration Review* 66, no. 4: 546–553.

Brandsen, T. and M. Honingh. (2016). 'Distinguishing Different Types of Coproduction: A Conceptual Analysis Based on the Classical Definitions'. *Public Administration Review* 76, no. 3: 427–435.

Brandsen, T. and V. Pestoff. (2006). 'Co-Production, the Third Sector and the Delivery of Public Services'. *Public Management Review* 8: 493–501.

Brändström, A. and S. Kuipers. (2003). 'From "Normal Incidents" to Political Crisis: Understanding Selective Politicization of Policy Failures'. *Government and Opposition 38*, no. 3: 279–305.

Braun, B. (2013). 'Preparedness, Crisis Management and Policy Change: The Euro Area at the Critical Juncture of 2008–2013'. *The British Journal of Politics & International Relations 17*, no. 3: 419–441.

Braun, D. (1999). 'Interests or Ideas? An Overview of Ideational Concepts in Public Policy Research'. In D. Braun and A. Busch (eds.), *Public Policy and Political Ideas*. Cheltenham, UK: Edward Elgar, 11–29.

Bregha, F., J. Benidickson, D. Gamble, T. Shillington and E. Weick. (1990). *The Integration of Environmental Considerations into Government Policy*. Ottawa, ON: Canadian Environmental Assessment Research Council.

Bressers, H. T. A. (1998). 'The Choice of Policy Instruments in Policy Networks'. In B. G. Peters and F. K. M. Van Nispen (eds.), *Public Policy Instruments: Evaluating the Tools of Public Administration*. New York: Edward Elgar, 85–105.

Bressers, H. T. A., D. Fuchs and S. Kuks. (2004). 'Institutional Resource Regimes and Sustainability: Theoretical Backgrounds and Hypotheses'. *Environment and Policy 41*: 23–58.

Bressers, H. T. A. and M. Honigh. (1986). 'A Comparative Approach to the Explanation of Policy Effects'. *International Social Science Journal 108*: 267–288.

Bressers, H. T. A. and P.-J. Klok. (1988). 'Fundamentals for a Theory of Policy Instruments'. *International Journal of Social Economics 15*, no. 3–4: 22–41.

Bressers, H. T. A. and L. J. O'Toole. (1998). 'The Selection of Policy Instruments: A Network-Based Perspective'. *Journal of Public Policy 18*, no. 3: 213–239.

Bressers, H. T. A. and L. J. O'Toole. (2005). 'Instrument Selection and Implementation in a Networked Context'. In P. Eliadis, M. Hill and M. Howlett (eds.), *Designing Government: From Instruments to Governance*, Montreal, QC: McGill-Queen's University Press, 132–153.

Brewer, G. D. (1974). 'The Policy Sciences Emerge: To Nurture and Structure a Discipline'. *Policy Science 5*, no. 3: 239–244.

Brewer, G. D. and P. de Leon. (1983). *The Foundations of Policy Analysis*. Homewood, IL: Dorsey.

Breyer, S. (1979). 'Analyzing Regulatory Failure: Mismatches, Less Restrictive Alternatives and Reform'. *Harvard Law Review 92*, no. 3: 549–609.

Breyer, S. (1982). *Regulation and Its Reform*. Cambridge, MA: Harvard University Press.

Briassoulis, H. (2005a). 'Analysis of Policy Integration: Conceptual and Methodological Considerations'. In *Policy Integration for Complex Environmental Problems: The Example of Mediterranean Desertification*. Aldershot, UK: Ashgate, 50–80.

Briassoulis, H. (2005b). 'Complex Environment Problems and the Quest of Policy Integration'. In *Policy Integration for Complex Environmental Problems: The Example of Mediterranean Desertification*. Aldershot, UK: Ashgate, 1–49.

Briassoulis, H. (ed.). (2005c). *Policy Integration for Complex Environmental Problems: The Example of Mediterranean Desertification*. Aldershot, UK: Ashgate.

Bridge, L. and A. Salman. (2000). *Policy Instruments for ICZM in Nine Selected European Countries*. Leiden, Netherlands: EUCC.

Brinkerhoff, D. W. (2009). 'Developing Capacity in Fragile States'. *Public Administration and Development 30*, no. 1: 66–78.

Brinkerhoff, D. W. and B. L. Crosby. (2002). *Managing Policy Reform: Concepts and Tools for Decision-Makers in Developing and Transitional Countries*. Bloomfield, CT: Kumarian Press.

Brinkerhoff, D. W. and P. J. Morgan. (2010). 'Capacity and Capacity Development: Coping with Complexity'. *Public Administration and Development 30*, no. 1: 2–10.

Brint, S. (1990). 'Rethinking the Policy Influence of Experts: From General Characterizations to Analysis of Variation'. *Sociological Forum 5*, no. 3 (September): 361–385.

Brockman, J. (1998). ' "Fortunate Enough to Obtain and Keep the Title of Profession": Self-Regulating Organizations and the Enforcement of Professional Monopolies'. *Canadian Public Administration 41*, no. 4: 587–621.

Brooks, S. M. (1989). *Public Policy in Canada: An Introduction*. Toronto, ON: McClelland & Stewart.

Brooks, S. M. (2015). 'Social Protection for the Poorest: The Adoption of Antipoverty Cash Transfer Programs in the Global South'. *Politics & Society 43*, no. 4 (1 December): 551–582.

Brown, C. (1994). 'Politics and the Environment: Nonlinear Instabilities Dominate'. *American Political Science Review 88*, no. 2: 292–303.

Brown, C. L. and A. Krishna. (2004). 'The Skeptical Shopper: A Metacognitive Account for the Effects of Default Options on Choice'. *Journal of Consumer Research 31*, no. 3: 529–539.

Brown, D. and J. Eastman. (1981). *The Limits of Consultation*. Ottawa, ON: Science Council of Canada.

Brown, D. S. (1955). 'The Public Advisory Board as an Instrument of Government'. *Public Administration Review 15*: 196–201.

Brown, D. S. (1972). 'The Management of Advisory Committees; An Assignment for the 70's'. *Public Administration Review 32*: 334–342.

Brown, M. P. (1992). 'Organizational Design as a Policy Instrument'. In R. Boardman (ed.), *Canadian Environmental Policy: Ecosystems, Politics and Processes*. Toronto, ON: Oxford University Press, 24–42.

Brown, T. and J. Wyatt. (2009). 'Design Thinking for Social Innovation (SSIR)'. *Stanford Social Innovation Review 8* (Winter): 3135.

Brown, T. L. and M. Potoski. (2003). 'Transaction Costs and Institutional Explanations for Government Service Production Decisions'. *Journal of Public Administration Research and Theory 13*, no. 4: 441–468.

Brown, T. L., M. Potoski and D. M. Ven Syke. (2008). 'Changing Modes of Service Delivery: How Past Choices Structure future Choices'. *Environment and Planning C: Government and Policy 26*: 127–143.

Brown-John, C. L. (1979). 'Advisory Agencies in Canada: An Introduction'. *Canadian Public Administration 22*, no. 1: 72–91.

Brubaker, R. (1984). *The Limits of Rationality: An Essay on the Social and Moral Thought of Max Weber*. London: Allen & Unwin.

Brudney, J. L. (1987). 'Coproduction and Privatization: Exploring the Relationship and Its Implications'. *Nonprofit and Voluntary Sector Quarterly 16*, no. 3 (1 July): 11–21.

Brudney, J. L. and R. E. England. (1983). 'Toward a Definition of the Coproduction Concept'. *Public Administration Review 43*, no. 1: 59–65.

Brugnach, M. and H. Ingram. (2012). 'Ambiguity: The Challenge of Knowing and Deciding Together'. *Environmental Science & Policy 15*, no. 1 (January): 60–71.

Brunsson, N. (2006). *Mechanisms of Hope: Maintaining the Dream of the Rational Organizaton*. Copenhagen, Denmark: Copenhagen Business School Press.

Bryner, G. (2008). 'Failure and Opportunity. Environmental Groups in US Climate Change Policy'. *Environmental Politics 17*, no. 2: 319–336.

Bryson, J. M., B. C. Crosby and L. Bloomberg. (2014). 'Public Value Governance: Moving Beyond Traditional Public Administration and the New Public Management'. *Public Administration Review 74*, no. 4: 445–456.

Bryson, J. M., K. S. Quick, C. S. Slotterback and B. C. Crosby. (2013). 'Designing Public Participation Processes'. *Public Administration Review 73*, no. 1 (1 January): 23–34.

Brzezinski, Z. (2005). 'The Dilemma of the Last Sovereign'. *The American Interest 1*.

Bubak, O. (2021). 'The Structure-in-Evolution Approach: A Unified View of Evolutionary Change in Policy Systems'. *Policy Studies*. https://doi.org/10.1080/01442872.2021.1908534

Buchanan, J. M. (1980). 'Rent Seeking and Profit Seeking'. In J. M. Buchanan, R. D. Tollison and. G. Tullock (eds), *Toward a Theory of the Rent-Seeking Society*. College Station, TX: Texas A&M University Press.

Buchanan, J. M. and R. D. Tollison (eds.). (1984). *The Theory of Public Choice – II*. Ann Arbor, MI: University of Michigan Press.

Buchanan, J. M., R. D. Tollison and G. Tullock. (1980). *Toward a Theory of the Rent-Seeking Society*. College Station, TX: Texas A&M University Press.

Buckingham, H. (2009). 'Competition and Contracts in the Voluntary Sector: Exploring the Implications for Homelessness Service Providers in Southampton'. *Policy & Politics 37*, no. 2: 235–254.

Buckley, W. (1968). 'Society as a Complex Adaptive System'. In W. Buckley (ed.), *Modern System Research for the Behavioural Scientist*. Chicago, IL: Aldine.

Buckman, G. and M. Diesendorf. (2010). 'Design Limitations in Australian Renewable Electricity Policies'. *Energy Policy 38*, no. 7: 3365–3376.

Bulkley, H. (2000). 'Discourse Coalition and the Australian Climate Change Policy Network'. *Environment and Planning C: Government and Policy 18*: 727–748.

Bullock H., J. Mountford and R. Stanley. (2001). *Better Policy-Making*. London: Centre for Management and Policy Studies.

Bulmer, M. (1981). 'Applied Social Research? The Use and Non-Use of Empirical Social Inquiry by British and American Governmental Commissions'. *Journal of Public Policy 1*: 353–380.

Bulmer, S. J. (1993). 'The Governance of the European Union: A New Institutionalist Approach'. *Journal of Public Policy 13*, no. 4: 351–380.

Bunge, M. (1997). 'Mechanism and Explanation'. *Philosophy of the Social Sciences 27*, no. 4 (1 December): 410–465.

Bunge, M. (2004). 'How Does It Work? The Search for Explanatory Mechanisms'. *Philosophy of the Social Sciences 34*, no. 2 (1 June): 182–210.

Burke, F. G. (1969). 'Public Administration in Africa: The Legacy of Inherited Colonial Institutions'. *Journal of Comparative Administration 1*, no. 3: 345–378.

Burnaby, P. and S. Hass. (2009). 'Ten Steps to Enterprise-Wide Risk Management'. *Corporate Governance: The International Journal of Business in Society 9*, no. *5* (16 October): 539–550.

Burns, J. M. G. (2012). *Leadership*. New York: Open Road Media.

Burns, J. P. and B. Bowornwathana. (1993). *Civil Service Systems in Asia*. Cheltenham, UK: Edward Elgar.

Burris, S., P. Drahos and C. Shearing. (2005). 'Nodal Governance'. *Australian Journal of Legal Philosophy 30*: 30–58.

Burstein, P. (1991). 'Policy Domains: Organization, Culture and Policy Outcomes'. *Annual Review of Sociology 17*: 327–350.

Burt, S. (1990). 'Canadian Women's Groups in the 1980s: Organizational Development and Policy Influence'. *Canadian Public Policy 16*, no. *1*: 17–28.

Busch, A. (2002). *Divergence or Convergence? State Regulation of the Banking System in Western Europe and the United States*. Contribution to the Workshop on Theories of Regulation. Oxford: Nuffield College (25–26 May).

Busemeyer, M. R. (2009). 'From Myth of Reality: Globalisation and Public Spending in OECD Countries Revisited'. *European Journal of Political Research 48*: 455–482.

Bye, T. and A. Bruvoll. (2008). 'Multiple Instruments to Change Energy Behaviour: The Emperor's New Clothes?' *Energy Efficiency 1*, no. *4* (1 November): 373–386.

Cabinet Office Behavioural Insights Team. (2010). *Applying Behavioural Insight to Health*. London: Cabinet Office Behavioural Insights Team. www.gov.uk/govern ment/publications/applying-behavioural-insight-to-health-behavioural-insights-team-paper

Cabinet Office Behavioural Insights Team. (2011). *Behaviour Change and Energy Use*. Research and Analysis, Cabinet Office Behavioural Insights Team. www.gov.uk/ government/publications/behaviour-change-and-energy-use

Cabinet Office Behavioural Insights Team. (2014). *EAST: Four Simple Ways to Apply Behavioural Insights*. London: Cabinet Office Behavioural Insights Team. www. behaviouralinsights.co.uk/publications/east-four-simple-ways-to-apply-behavioural-insights/

Cahill, A. G. and E. S. Overman. (1990). 'The Evolution of Rationality in Policy Analysis'. In S. S. Nagel (ed.), *Policy Theory and Policy Evaluation: Concepts, Knowledge, Causes and Norms*. New York: Greenwood Press, 11–27.

Cairney, P. (2019). *Understanding Public Policy*. London: Red Globe Press.

Cairney, P. (2021). *The Politics of Policy Analysis*. London: Palgrave Macmillan.

Cairney, P. and M. D. Jones. (2016). 'Kingdon's Multiple Streams Approach: What is the Empirical Impact of this Universal Theory?' *Policy Studies Journal 44*, no. *1*: 37–58.

Cairney, P., S. Russell and E. St Denny. (2016). 'The "Scottish Approach" to Policy and Policymaking: What Issues Are Territorial and What Are Universal?' *Policy & Politics 44*, no. *3* (8 July): 333–350.

Cairns, A. C. (1990). 'Reflections on Commission Research'. In C. Innis, J. A. Yogis and A. P. Pross (eds.), *Commissions of Inquiry*. Toronto, ON: Carswell, 87–110.

Cairns, B., M. Harris and P. Young. (2005). 'Building the Capacity of the Voluntary Nonprofit Sector: Challenges of Theory and Practice'. *International Journal of Public Administration 28*: 869–885.

Cameron, D. R. (1978). 'The Expansion of the Public Economy: A Comparative Analysis'. *American Political Science Review 72*, no. *4*: 1243–1261.

Camilleri, A. R. and R. P. Larrick. (2013). 'Metric and Scale Design as Choice Architecture Tools'. *Journal of Public Policy & Marketing 33*, no. *1*: 108–125.

Campanella, M. L. (1993). 'The Effects of Globalization and Turbulence on Policy-Making Processes'. *Government and Opposition 28*, no. 2: 190–205.

Campbell, C. and G. J. Szablowski. (1979). *The Superbureaucrats: Structure and Behaviour in Central Agencies*. Toronto, ON: Macmillan.

Campbell, H. E., R. M. Johnson and E. H. Larson. (2004). 'Prices, Devices, People or Rules: The Relative Effectiveness of Policy Instruments in Water Conservation'. *Review of Policy Research 21*, no. 5: 637–662.

Campbell, J. L. (1998). 'Institutional Analysis and the Role of Ideas in Political Economy'. *Theory and Society 27*, no. 5: 377–409.

Campbell, J. L. (2002). 'Ideas, Politics and Public Policy'. *Annual Review of Sociology 28*, no. 1: 21–38.

Campbell-Smith, D. (2008). *Follow the Money: The Audit Commission, Public Money and the Management of Public Services, 1983–2008*. London: Allen Lane.

Canadian Government. (1996). *Strengthening Our Policy Capacity*. Report of the Task Force on Strengthening the Policy Capacity of the Federal Government. Ottawa, Canada: Ministry of Supply and Services.

Candel, J. and C. Daugbjerg. (2020). 'Overcoming the Dependent Variable Problem in Studying Food Policy'. *Food Security 12*, no. 1 (26 November): 169–178.

Cantor, R., S. Henry and S. Rayner. (1992). *Making Markets: An Interdisciplinary Perspective on Economic Exchange*. Westport, CT: Greenwood Press.

Capano, G. (2009). 'Understanding Policy Change as an Epistemological and Theoretical Problem'. *Journal of Comparative Policy Analysis: Research and Practice 11*, no. 1: 7–31.

Capano, G. (2011). 'Government Continues to Do Its Job. A Comparative Study of Governance Shifts in the Higher Education Sector'. *Public Administration 89*, no. 4: 1622–1642.

Capano, G. (2012). 'Policy Dynamics and Change: The Never-Ending Puzzle'. In E. Araral, S. Fritzen, M. Howlett, M. Ramesh and X. Wu (eds.), *Routledge Handbook of Public Policy*. New York: Routledge, 451–472.

Capano, G. and M. Howlett. (2020). 'The Knowns and Unknowns of Policy Instrument Analysis: Policy Tools and the Current Research Agenda on Policy Mixes'. *Sage Open 10*, no. 1.

Capano, G., M. Howlett, D. S. L. Jarvis and M. Ramesh. (2022). 'Long-Term Policy Impacts of the Coronavirus: Normalization, Adaptation, and Acceleration in the Post-COVID State'. *Policy and Society 41*, no. 1 (1 January): 1–12.

Capano, G., M. Howlett, D. S. L. Jarvis, M. Ramesh and N. Goyal. (2020). 'Mobilizing Policy (In)Capacity to Fight COVID-19: Understanding Variations in National Responses'. *Policy and Society 39*, no. 3: 285–308, 326–344.

Capano, G., M. Howlett and M. Ramesh (eds.). (2015). *Varieties of Governance: Studies in the Political Economy of Public Policy*. Basingstoke, UK; New York: Palgrave Macmillan.

Capano, G., M. Howlett and M. Ramesh. (2018). 'Designing for Robustness: Surprise, Agility and Improvisation in Policy Design'. *Policy & Society 37*, no. 4: 422–440.

Capano, G., M. Howlett, M. Ramesh and A. Virani (eds.). (2019). *Making Policies Work: First- and Second-Order Mechanisms in Policy Design*. Cheltenham: Edward Elgar.

Capano, G. and A. Lippi. (2017). 'How Policy Instruments Are Chosen: Patterns of Decision Makers' Choices'. *Policy Sciences 50*, no. 2: 269–293.

Capano, G. and J. J. Woo. (2017). 'Resilience and Robustness in Policy Design: A Critical Appraisal'. *Policy Sciences 50*, no. 3 (5 January): 1–28, 399–426.

Caplan, N. (1976). 'Factors Associated with Knowledge Use Among Federal Executives'. *Policy Studies Journal 4*, no. *3*: 229–234.

Cappella, J. N. and K. H. Jamieson. (1996). 'News Frames, Political Cynicism, and Media Cynicism'. *The Annals of the American Academy of Political and Social Science 546*: 71–84.

Cardozo, A. (1996). 'Lion Taming: Downsizing the Opponents of Downsizing'. In G. Swimmer (ed.), *How Ottawa Spends 1996–97: Life Under the Knife*. Ottawa, ON: Carleton University Press, 303–336.

Carley, S. and C. J. Miller. (2012). 'Regulatory Stringency and Policy Drivers: A Reassessment of Renewable Portfolio Standards'. *Policy Studies Journal 40*, no. *4*: 730–756.

Carlsson, L. (2000). 'Policy Networks as Collective Action'. *Policy Studies Journal 28*, no. *3*: 502–520.

Carmel, E. and J. Harlock. (2008). 'Instituting the "Third Sector" as a Governable Terrain: Partnership, Procurement and Performance in the UK'. *Policy and Politics 36*, no. *2*: 155–171.

Carmichael, C. M. (2010). 'Doing Good Better? The Differential Subsidization of Charitable Contributions'. *Policy and Society 29*, no. *3*: 201–217.

Carpenter, D. and D. A. Moss (eds.). (2013). *Preventing Regulatory Capture: Special Interest Influence and How to Limit It*. New York: Cambridge University Press.

Carroll, A. E. and A. Frakt. (2017). 'What Makes Singapore's Health Care So Cheap?' *The New York Times* (2 October).

Carstensen, M. B. (2010). 'The Nature of Ideas and Why Political Scientists Should Care: Analysing the Danish Jobcentre Reform from an Ideational Perspective'. *Political Studies 58*, no. *5*: 847–865.

Carstensen, M. B. (2011). 'Paradigm Man vs. the Bricoleur: Bricolage as an Alternative Vision of Agency in Ideational Change'. *European Political Science Review 3*, no. *1*: 147–167.

Carstensen, M. B. (2015). 'Bringing Ideational Power into the Paradigm Approach: Critical Perspectives on Policy Paradigms in Theory and Practice'. In J. Hogan and M. Howlett (eds.), *Policy Paradigms in Theory and Practice*. Basingstoke, UK: Palgrave Macmillan.

Carter, P. (2012). 'Policy as Palimpsest'. *Policy & Politics 40*, no. *3*: 423–443.

Cashore, B. (2002). 'Legitimacy and the Privatization of Environmental Governance: How Non-State Market-Driven (NSMD) Governance Systems Gain Rule-Making Authority'. *Governance 15*, no. *4*: 503–529.

Cashore, B., G. Auld and D. Newsom. (2003). 'Forest Certification (Eco-Labeling) Programs and their Policy-Making Authority: Explaining Divergence Among North American and European Case Studies'. *Forest Policy and Economics 5*: 225–247.

Cashore, B., G. Auld and D. Newsom. (2004). *Governing Through Markets: Forest Certification and the Emergence of Non-State Authority* (1st edn). New Haven, CT: Yale University Press.

Cashore, B. and M. Howlett. (2006). 'Behavioural Thresholds and Institutional Rigidities as Explanations of Punctuated Equilibrium Processes in Pacific Northwest Forest Policy Dynamics'. In R. Repetto (ed.), *Policy Dynamics*. New Haven, CT: Yale University Press, 137–161.

Cashore, B. and M. Howlett. (2007). 'Punctuating Which Equilibrium? Understanding Thermostatic Policy Dynamics in Pacific Northwest Forestry'. *American Journal of Political Science 51*, no. *3*: 532–551.

Castells, M. (1996). *The Information Age: Economy, Society and Culture, vol. I, the Rise of Network Society*. Malden, MA: Blackwell.

Castles, F. G. (1998). *Comparative Public Policy: Patterns of Post-War Transformation*. Cheltenham, UK: Edward Elgar.

Castles, F. G. (2001). 'On the Political Economy of Recent Public Sector Development'. *Journal of European Social Policy 11*, no. 3: 195–211.

Castree, N. (2008). 'Neoliberalising Nature: The Logics of Deregulation and Reregulation'. *Environment and Planning A 40*: 131–152.

Centre d'analyse stratégique. (2011). *Green Nudges: New Incentives for Ecological Behaviour*. Paris: Premier Ministre Republique Francaise. http://archives.strategie.gouv.fr/cas/system/files/2011-03-09-na-216-nudgesvertsgb_0.pdf

Centre for Sustainable Energy/Environmental Change Institute, University of Oxford. (2012). *Factors Influencing Energy Behaviours and Decision-Making in the Non-Domestic Sector: A Rapid Evidence Assessment*. Policy Paper. Department of Energy & Climate Change, UK. www.gov.uk/government/publications/factors-influencing-energy-behaviours-and-decision-making-in-the-non-domestic-sector-a-rapid-evidence-assessment

Cerny, P. G. (1990). *The Changing Architecture of Politics*. Beverly Hills, CA: Sage.

Cerny, P. G. (1993). 'Plurilateralism: Structural Differentiation and Functional Conflict in the Post-Cold War World Order'. *Millenium 22*, no. 1: 27–51.

Cerny, P. G. (1996). 'International Finance and the Erosion of State Policy Capacity'. In P. Gummett (ed.), *Globalization and Public Policy*, Cheltenham, UK: Edward Elgar, 83–104.

Cerny, P. G. (2010). 'The Competition State Today: From Raison d'État to Raison du Monde'. *Policy Studies 31*, no. 1: 5–21.

Chadwick, A. (2000). 'Studying Political Ideas: A Public Political Discourse Approach'. *Political Studies 48*: 283–301.

Chapman, B. (1971). *The Profession of Government*. London: Unwin.

Chapman, C. (1990). *Selling the Family Silver: Has Privatization Worked?* London: Hutchinson Business Books.

Chapman, R. A. (1973a). 'Commissions in Policy-Making'. In R. A. Chapman (ed.), *The Role of Commissions in Policy-Making*. London: George Allen & Unwin, 174–188.

Chapman, R. A. (ed.). (1973b). *The Role of Commissions in Policy-Making*. Sydney, NSW: Allen & Unwin.

Chapman, R. A. (2003). 'A Policy Mix for Environmentally Sustainable Development – Learning from the Dutch Experience'. *New Zealand Journal of Environmental Law 7*, no. 1: 29–51.

Chapman, T., J. Brown and R. Crow. (2008). 'Entering a Brave New World? An Assessment of Third Sector Readiness to Tender for the Delivery of Public Services in the United Kingdom'. *Policy Studies 29*, no. 1: 1–17.

Chari, R., G. Murphy and J. Hogan. (2007). 'Regulating Lobbyists: A Comparative Analysis of the United States, Canada, Germany and the European Union'. *The Political Quarterly 78*, no. 3: 422–438.

Charih, M. and A. Daniels (eds.). (1997). *New Public Management and Public Administration in Canada*. Toronto, ON: IPAC, 143–163.

Chatterton, T. and C. Wilson. (2014). 'The "Four Dimensions of Behaviour" Framework: A Tool for Characterising Behaviours to Help Design Better Interventions'. *Transportation Planning and Technology 37*, no. 1 (2 January): 38–61.

Chávez, C. A., M. G. Villena and K. Stranlund. (2009). 'The Choice of Policy Instruments to Control Pollution Under Costly Enforcement and Incomplete Information'. *Journal of Applied Economics 12* (November): 207–227.

Chelariu, C., W. J. Johnston and L. Young. (2002). 'Learning to Improvise, Improvising to Learn: A Process of Responding to Complex Environments'. *Journal of Business Research, Marketing Theory in the Next Millennium 55*, no. 2 (February): 141–147.

Cheng, H. Y. (1968). 'The Emergence and Spread of the Ombudsman Institution'. *The Annals of the American Academy of Political and Social Science 377*: 20–30.

Chenier, J. A. (1985). 'Ministers of State to Assist: Weighing the Costs and the Benefits'. *Canadian Public Administration 28*, no. 3: 397–412.

Cheung, A. B. L. (2005). 'The Politics of Administrative Reforms in Asia: Paradigms and Legacies, Paths and Diversities'. *Governance 18*, no. 2: 257–282.

Chiarini, A. (2012). *Lean Organization: From the Tools of the Toyota Production System to Lean Office* (2013 edn). Milan, Italy; New York: Springer.

Chindarkar, N., M. Howlett and M. Ramesh. (2007). 'Conceptualizing Effective Social Policy Design: Design Spaces and Capacity Challenges'. *Public Administration and Development 37*, no. 1 (1 February): 3–14.

Choi, D., F. Stokes Berry and A. Ghadimi. (2020). 'Policy Design and Achieving Social Outcomes: A Comparative Analysis of Social Enterprise Policy'. *Public Administration Review 80*, no. 3: 494–505.

Chow, C. C. and R. K. Sarin. (2002). 'Known, Unknown and Unknowable Uncertainties'. *Theory and Decision 52*, no. 2 (1 March): 127–138.

Christensen, J. G. and T. Pallesen. (2008). 'Public Employment Trends and the Organization of Public Sector Tasks'. In H.-U. Derlien and B. G. Peters (eds.), *The State at Work, vol. 2: Comparative Public Service Systems*. Cheltenham, UK: Edward Elgar.

Christensen, T. and P. Lægreid (eds.). (2001). *New Public Management: The Transformation of Ideas and Practice*. Aldershot, UK: Ashgate.

Christensen, T. and P. Lægreid. (2007). 'Regulatory Agencies – The Challenges of Balancing Agency Autonomy and Political Control'. *Governance 20*, no. 3: 499–520.

Christensen, T. and P. Lægreid. (2008). 'NPM and Beyond – Structure, Culture and Demography'. *International Review of Administrative Sciences 74*, no. 1 (1 March): 7–23.

Christensen, T. and P. Lægreid. (2012). 'Governance and Administrative Reforms'. In D. Levi-Faur (ed.), *The Oxford Handbook of Governance*. Oxford: Oxford University Press, 255–268.

Christensen, T., P. Lægreid and L. R. Wise. (2002). 'Transforming Administrative Policy'. *Public Administration 80*, no. 1: 153–179.

Christopoulos, D. and K. Ingold. (2011). 'Distinguishing Between Political Brokerage and Political Entrepreneurship'. *Procedia – Social and Behavioral Sciences 10*: 36–42.

Chu, A., S. Kwon and P. Cowley. (2019). 'Health Financing Reforms for Moving Towards Universal Health Coverage in the Western Pacific Region'. *Health Systems & Reform 5*, no. 1: 32–47.

Churchman, C. W. (1967). 'Wicked Problems'. *Management Science 14*, no. 4: B141–B142.

Cialdini, R. B. (2003). 'Crafting Normative Messages to Protect the Environment'. *Current Directions in Psychological Science 12*, no. 4: 105–109.

Cialdini, R. B. (2008). *Influence: Science and Practice* (5th edn). Boston, MA: Allyn & Bacon.

Cialdini, R. B., L. J. Demaine, B. J. Sagarin, D. W. Barrett, K. Rhoads and P. L. Winter. (2006). 'Managing Social Norms for Persuasive Impact'. *Social Influence 1*, no. *1* (1 March): 3–15.

Cialdini, R. B. and N. J. Goldstein. (2004). 'Social Influence: Compliance and Conformity'. *Annual Review of Psychology 55*, no. *1*: 591–621.

Cicin-Sain, B. and R. Knecht. (1998). *Integrated Coastal and Ocean Management: Concepts and Practices*. Washington, DC: Island Press.

Cismaru, M. and A. M. Lavack. (2007). 'Tobacco Warning Labels and the Protection Motivation Model: Implications for Canadian Tobacco Control Policy'. *Canadian Public Policy 33*, no. *4*: 477–486.

Citi, M. and A. M. Rhodes. (2007). *New Modes of Governance in the EU: Common Objectives Versus National Preferences*. European Governance Papers, No. N-07-01. www.connex-network.org/eurogov/pdf/egp-newgov-N-07-01.pdf. Accessed 29 February 2008.

Clark, C. D. and C. S. Russell. (2009). 'Ecological Conservation: The Problems of Targeting Policies and Designing Instruments'. *Journal of Natural Resources Policy Research 1*, no. *1*: 21–34.

Clark, I. (1998). 'Beyond the Great Divide: Globalization and the Theory of International Relations'. *Review of International Studies 24*: 479–498.

Clark, W. C. and G. Majone. (1985). 'The Critical Appraisal of Scientific Inquiries with Policy Implications'. *Science, Technology and Human Values 10*, no. *3*: 6–19.

Clarke, A. (2019). 'Digital Government Units: What Are They, and What Do They Mean for Digital Era Public Management Renewal?' *International Public Management Journal* (22 November): 1–31.

Clarke, A. and J. Craft. (2017). 'The Vestiges and Vanguards of Policy Design in a Digital Context'. *Canadian Public Administration 60*, no. *4* (1 December): 476–497.

Clarke, A. and J. Craft. (2019). 'The Twin Faces of Public Sector Design'. *Governance 32*, no. *5*: 5–21.

Clarke, A., E. A. Lindquist and J. Roy. (2017). 'Understanding Governance in the Digital Era: An Agenda for Public Administration Research in Canada'. *Canadian Public Administration 60*, no. *4* (1 December): 457–475.

Clarke, H. (2010). 'Formulating Policy Responses to Global Warming in the Face of Uncertainty'. *Agenda: A Journal of Policy Analysis and Reform 17*: 33–54.

Clayton, S. (2012). 'Will People Act to Mitigate Climate Change?' *Analyses of Social Issues and Public Policy 12*, no. *1*, 221–224.

Clemens, E. S. and J. M. Cook. (1999). 'Politics and Institutionalism: Explaining Durability and Change'. *Annual Review of Sociology 25*: 441–466.

Clokie, H. M. and J. W. Robinson. (1969). *Royal Commissions of Inquiry: The Significance of Investigations in British Politics*. New York: Octagon Books.

Cnossen, S. (2005). 'Economics and Politics of Excise Taxation'. In S. Cnossen (ed.), *Theory and Practice of Excise Taxation: Smoking, Drinking, Gambling, Polluting and Driving*. Oxford: Oxford University Press, 1–19.

Cobb, R. W. and C. D. Elder. (1972). *Participation in American Politics: The Dynamics of Agenda-Building*. Boston, MA: Allyn & Bacon.

Cochran, C. L. and E. F. Malone (1999). *Public Policy: Perspectives and Choices*. Boulder, CO: Lynne Rienner.

Codagnone, C., F. Bogliacino and G. Veltri. (2013). *Testing CO2/Car Labelling Options and Consumer Information*. Final Report. Brussels, Belgium: European Commission. http://ec.europa.eu/clima/policies/transport/vehicles/labelling/docs/report_car_labelling_en. pdf

Coglianese, C. (1997). 'Assessing Consensus: The Promise and Performance of Negotiated Rulemaking'. *Duke Law Journal 46*, no. 6: 1255–1349.

Cohen, M. A. and V. Santhakumar. (2007). 'Information Disclosure as Environmental Regulation: A Theoretical Analysis'. *Environmental and Resource Economics 37*: 599–620.

Cohen, M. D., J. G. March and J. P. Olsen. (1972). 'A Garbage Can Model of Organizational Choice'. *Administrative Science Quarterly 17*, no. 1: 1–25.

Cohen, M. D., J. G. March and J. P. Olsen. (1979). 'People, Problems, Solutions and the Ambiguity of Relevance'. In *Ambiguity and Choice in Organizations*. Bergen, Norway: Universitetsforlaget, 24–37.

Cohen, M. G. and S. McBride (eds.). (2003). *Global Turbulence: Social Activists' and State Responses to Globalization*. Aldershot, UK: Ashgate.

Cohen, W. M. and D. A. Levinthal. (1990). 'Absorptive Capacity: A New Perspective on Learning and Innovation'. *Administrative Sciences Quarterly 35*: 128–152.

Cohn, D. (2004). 'The Best of Intentions, Potentially Harmful Policies: A Comparative Study of Scholarly Complexity and Failure'. *Journal of Comparative Policy Analysis 6*, no. 1: 39–56.

Cole, D. H. and P. Z. Grossman. (1999). 'When Is Command-and-Control Efficient – Institutions, Technology, and the Comparative Efficiency of Alternative Regulatory Regimes for Environmental Protection'. *Wisconsin Law Review*: 887–937.

Colebatch, H. K. (1998). *Policy*. Minneapolis, MN: University of Minnesota Press.

Colebatch, H. K. (2005). 'Policy Analysis, Policy Practice and Political Science'. *Australian Journal of Public Administration 64*, no. 3: 14–23.

Colebatch, H. K. (2006a). 'What Work Makes Policy?' *Policy Sciences 39*, no. 4 (November): 309–321.

Colebatch, H. K. (ed.). (2006b). *The Work of Policy: An International Survey*. New York: Rowman & Littlefield.

Colebatch, H. K. (2018). 'The Idea of Policy Design: Intention, Process, Outcome, Meaning and Validity'. *Public Policy and Administration 33*, no. 4 (18 May): 365–383.

Colebatch, H. K., R. Hoppe and M. Noordegraaf (eds.). (2011). *Working for Policy*. Amsterdam, The Netherlands: Amsterdam University Press.

Colebatch, H. K. and B. A. Radin. (2006). 'Mapping the Work of Policy'. In H. K. Colebatch (ed.), *The Work of Policy: An International Survey*. New York: Rowman & Littlefield, 217–226.

Coleman, W. D. (1991). 'Monetary Policy, Accountability and Legitimacy: A Review of the Issues in Canada'. *Canadian Journal of Political Science 24*, no. 4: 711–734.

Coleman, W. D. (1996). *Financial Services, Globalization and Domestic Policy Change: A Comparison of North America and the European Union*. Basingstoke, UK: Macmillan.

Coletti, P. (2015). 'Public Policy Design: How to Learn from Failures'. *World Political Science 11*, no. 2: 325–345.

Collier, U. (1998). *Deregulation in the European Union: Environmental Perspectives*. London: Routledge.

Collins, A. E. (2013). 'Applications of the Disaster Risk Reduction Approach to Migration Influenced by Environmental Change'. *Environmental Science & Policy 27*, no. Supplement 1 (March): S112–S125.

Collins, A. E. and G. Judge. (2008). 'Client Participation in Paid Sex Markets under Alternative Regulatory Regimes'. *International Journal of Law and Economics 28*: 294–301.

Comfort, L. K. (2010). *Designing Resilience: Preparing for Extreme Events*. Pittsburgh, PA: University of Pittsburgh Press.

Comfort, L. K. (2012). 'Designing Disaster Resilience and Public Policy: Comparative Perspectives'. *Journal of Comparative Policy Analysis: Research and Practice 14*, no. 2 (1 April): 109–113.

Comfort, L. K., A. Boin and C. C. Demchak (eds.). (2010). *Designing Resilience: Preparing for Extreme Events*. Pittsburgh, PA: University of Pittsburgh Press.

CommGAP. (2009). *Communication for Good Governance*. Washington, DC: Communication for Governance and Accountability Program, World Bank. www.gsdrc.org/go/display&type=Document&id=3718

Compston, H. and I. Bailey. (2012). *Feeling the Heat: The Politics of Climate Change Policy in Rapidly Industrializing Countries*. Basingstoke, UK; New York: Palgrave Macmillan.

Compton, M. E., J. Luetjens and P. 't Hart. (2019). 'Designing for Policy Success'. *International Review of Public Policy 1*, no. *1–2* (10 October): 119–146.

Compton, M. E. and P. 't Hart. (2019). 'Looping to Success (and Failure): Second-Order Mechanisms and Policy Outcomes'. In G. Capano, M. Howlett, M. Ramesh and A. Virani (eds.), *Making Policies Work*. Cheltenham: Edward Elgar Publishing, 191–210.

Conn, W. D. (2009). 'Applying Environmental Policy Instruments to Used Oil'. *Journal of Environmental Planning and Management 52*, no. 4: 457–475.

Connaughton, B. (2010). 'Glorified Gofers, Policy Experts or Good Generalists: A Classification of the Roles of the Irish Ministerial Adviser'. *Irish Political Studies 25*, no. 3: 347–369.

Connaughton, B. (2015). 'Navigating the Borderlines of Politics and Administration: Reflections on the Role of Ministerial Advisers'. *International Journal of Public Administration 38*, no. *1* (2 January): 37–45.

Connolly, M. E. H. and A. W. Stark. (1992). 'Policy Making and the Demonstration Effect: Privatization in a Deprived Region'. *Public Administration 70*, no. 3: 369–385.

Connor, L. H. and N. Higginbotham. (2013). ' "Natural Cycles" in Lay Understanding of Climate Change'. *Global Environmental Change 23*, no. 6: 1852–1861.

Considine, M. (2001). *Enterprising States: The Public Management of Welfare-to-Work*. Cambridge: Cambridge University Press.

Considine, M. (2012). 'Thinking Outside the Box? Applying Design Theory to Public Policy'. *Politics & Policy 40*, no. 4: 704–724.

Considine, M., D. Alexander and J. M. Lewis. (2009). *Networks, Innovation and Public Policy: Politicians, Bureaucrats and Pathways to Change Inside Government*. Basingstoke, UK: Macmillan.

Considine, M., D. Alexander and J. M. Lewis. (2014). 'Policy Design as Craft: Design Expertise Using a Semi-Experimental Approach'. *Policy Sciences 47*, no. 3: 209–225.

Considine, M. and J. M. Lewis. (2003). 'Bureaucracy, Network, or Enterprise? Comparing Models of Governance in Australia, Britain, the Netherlands and New Zealand'. *Public Administration Review 63*, no. 2: 131–140.

Cook, D. (2002). 'Consultation, for a Change? Engaging Users and Communities in the Policy Process'. *Social Policy and Administration 36*, no. 5: 516–531.

Cook, P. and C. Kirpatrick. (1988). *Privatization in Less Developed Countries*. New York: St Martin's Press.

Cooke, P. (2007). 'Building a Partnership Model to Manage Irish Heritage: A Policy Tools Analysis'. *Irish Journal of Management 27*, no. 2: 75–97.

Coons, C. and M. Weber (eds.). (2014). *Manipulation: Theory and Practice*. Oxford; New York: Oxford University Press.

Corner, A. and A. Randall. (2011). 'Selling Climate Change? The Limitations of Social Marketing as a Strategy for Climate Change Public Engagement'. *Global Environmental Change 21*, no. 3 (August): 1005–1014.

COSO. (2004). *Enterprise Risk Management – Integrated Framework*. www.coso.org/Pages/erm-integratedframework.aspx

COSO. (2017). *Guidance on Enterprise Risk Management*. www.coso.org/Pages/erm.aspx

Cowan, L. G. (1990). *Privatization in the Developing World*. New York: Greenwood Press.

Cowles, M. G., J. Caporaso and T. Risse (eds.). (2001). *Transforming Europe: Europeanization and Domestic Change*. Ithaca, NY: Cornell University Press.

Cox, R. W. (1996). *Approaches to World Order*. Cambridge: Cambridge University Press, 296–313.

Craft, J. and J. Halligan. (2020). *Advising Governments in the Westminster Tradition: Policy Advisory Systems in Australia, Britain, Canada and New Zealand*. Cambridge Studies in Comparative Public Policy. Cambridge: Cambridge University Press.

Craft, J. and M. Howlett. (2012). 'Policy Formulation, Governance Shifts and Policy Influence: Location and Content in Policy Advisory Systems'. *Journal of Public Policy 32*, no. 2: 79–98.

Craft, J. and M. Howlett. (2013a). 'The Dual Dynamics of Policy Advisory Systems: The Impact of Externalization and Politicization on Policy Advice'. *Policy and Society 32*, no. 3: 187–197.

Craft, J. and M. Howlett. (2013b). 'Policy Advisory Systems and Evidence-Based Policy: The Location and Content of Evidentiary Policy Advice'. In S. Young (ed.), *Evidence-Based Policy-Making in Canada*. Toronto: University of Toronto Press, 27–44.

Craft, J., M. Howlett, M. Crawford and K. McNutt. (2013). 'Assessing Policy Capacity for Climate Change Adaptation: Governance Arrangements, Resource Deployments, and Analytical Skills in Canadian Infrastructure Policy Making'. *Review of Policy Research 30*, no. 1: 42–65.

Craft, J. and M. Wilder. (2017). 'Catching a Second Wave: Context and Compatibility in Advisory System Dynamics'. *Policy Studies Journal 45*, no. 1: 215–239.

Crew, M. A. and D. Parker (eds.). (2006). *International Handbook on Economic Regulation*. Cheltenham, UK: Edward Elgar.

Crew, M. A. and C. K. Rowley. (1986). 'Deregulation as an Instrument in Industrial Policy'. *Journal of Institutional and Theoretical Economics 142*: 52–70.

Croley, S. P. (2007). *Regulation and Public Interests: The Possibility of Good Regulatory Government*. Princeton, NJ: Princeton University Press.

Cronin, T. E. and N. C. Thomas. (1970). 'Educational Policy Advisors and the Great Society'. *Public Policy 18*, no. 5: 659–686.

Cross, M. K. D. (2015). 'The Limits of Epistemic Communities: EU Security Agencies'. *Politics and Governance 3*, no. 1: 90–100.

Cross, W. (2007). 'Policy Study and Development in Canada's Political Parties'. In L. Dobuzinskis, M. Howlett and D. Laycock (eds.), *Policy Analysis in Canada: The State of the Art*. Toronto, ON: University of Toronto Press, 233–242.

Crowley, K. (2009). 'Can Deliberative Democracy Be Practiced? A Subnational Policy Pathway'. *Politics and Policy 37*, no. 5: 995–1021.

Cubbage, F., P. Harou and E. Sills. (2007). 'Policy Instruments to Enhance Multifunctional Forest Management'. *Forest Policy and Economics 9*: 833–851.

Cunha, M. P. E., K. Kamoche and J. V. D. Cunha. (2002). *Organizational Improvisation*. London; New York: Routledge.

Cushman, R. E. (1941). *The Independent Regulatory Commissions*. London: Oxford University Press.

Cutler, A. C., V. Haufler and T. Porter. (1999). 'The Contours and Significance of Private Authority in International Affairs'. In A. C. Cutler, V. Haufler and T. Porter (eds.), *Private Authority and International Affairs*. Albany, NY: State University of New York, 333–376.

Cyert, R. M. and J. G. March. (1992). *Behavioral Theory of the Firm* (2nd edn). Cambridge, MA: Wiley-Blackwell.

Czarniavswka, B. (2009). 'Emerging Institutions: Pyramids or Anthills?' *Organization Studies 30*, no. 4: 423–441.

Dacey, R. and L. J. Carlson. (2004). 'Traditional Decision Analysis and the Poliheuristic Theory of Foreign Policy Decision Making'. *The Journal of Conflict Resolution 48*, no. 1: 38–55.

da Costa Canoquena, J. M. (2013). 'Reconceptualising Policy Integration in Road Safety Management'. *Transport Policy 25* (January): 61–80.

Dahl, R. A. and C. E. Lindblom. (1953). *Politics, Economics and Welfare: Planning and Politico-Economic Systems Resolved into Basic Social Processes*. New York: Harper & Row.

Dahlberg, L. (2005). 'Interaction Between Voluntary and Statutory Social Service Provision in Sweden: A Matter of Welfare Pluralism, Substitution or Complementarity?' *Social Policy and Administration 39*, no. 7: 740–763.

Dahlström, C., J. Lindvall and B. Rothstein. (2013). 'Corruption, Bureaucratic Failure and Social Policy Priorities'. *Political Studies 61*, no. 3 (1 October): 523–542.

Dahm, M. and Glazer, A. (2015). 'A Carrot and Stick Approach to Agenda-Setting'. *Journal of Economic Behavior & Organization 116*: 465–480.

Dalal-Clayton, B. and B. Sadler. (2005). *Strategic Environmental Assessment: A Sourcebook and Reference Guide to International Experience*. London: Earthscan.

Daneke, G. A. (1992). 'Back to the Future: Misplaced Elements of Political Inquiry and the Advanced Systems Agenda'. In W. N. Dunn and R. M. Kelly (eds.), *Advances in Policy Studies Since 1950*. New Brunswick, NJ: Transaction, 267–290.

Daniels, R. J. and M. J. Trebilcock. (1996). 'Private Provision of Public Infrastructure: An Organizational Analysis of the Next Privatization Frontier'. *University of Toronto Law Journal 46*: 375–426.

Darr, E. D., L. Argote and D. Epple. (1995). 'The Acquisition, Transfer, and Depreciation of Knowledge in Service Organizations: Productivity in Franchises'. *Management Science 41*, no. 11 (1 November): 1750–1762.

Datta, S., J. J. Miranda, L. Zorattoa, O. Calvo-González, M. Darling and K. Lorenzana. (2015). *A Behavioral Approach to Water Conservation: Evidence from Costa Rica*. Washington, DC: The World Bank.

Datta, S. and S. Mullainathan. (2014). 'Behavioral Design: A New Approach to Development Policy'. *Review of Income and Wealth 60*, no. 1: 7–35.

Daugbjerg, C. (1997). 'Policy Networks and Agricultural Policy Reforms: Explaining Deregulation in Sweden and Re-Regulation in the European Community'. *Governance 10*, no. 2: 123–142.

Daugbjerg, C. (1998). *Policy Networks Under Pressure: Pollution Control, Policy Reform and the Power of Farmers*. Aldershot, UK: Ashgate.

Daugbjerg, C. (2003). 'Policy Feedback and Paradigm Shift in EU Agricultural Policy: The Effects of the MacSharry Reform on Future Reform'. *Journal of European Public Policy 10*, no. 3: 421–437.

Daugbjerg, C. (2009). 'Sequencing in Public Policy: The Evolution of the CAP over a Decade'. *Journal of European Public Policy 16*, no. 2: 395–411.

Daugbjerg, C. (2012). 'Process Sequencing'. In E. Araral, S. Fritzen, M. Howlett, M. Ramesh and X. Wu (eds.), *Routledge Handbook of Public Policy*. London: Routledge, 473–479.

Daugbjerg, C. and G. Bazzan. (2022). 'Mixed Policy Feedback in Environmental Regulation: Instrument Recalibration and Layering in Danish Nitrogen Policy'. Paper Presented to the ECPR Joint Sessions of Workshops, Innsbruck, Austria.

Daugbjerg, C. and D. Marsh. (1998). 'Explaining Policy Outcomes: Integrating the Policy Network Approach with Macro-Level and Micro-Level Analysis'. In David Marsh (ed.), *Comparing Policy Networks*. Buckingham, UK: Open University Press, 52–71.

Daugbjerg, C. and A. McConnell. (2021). 'Rethinking Disproportionate Policy Making by Introducing Proportionate Politics'. *Policy Sciences 54*, no. 3 (1 September): 691–706.

Daugbjerg, C. and G. T. Svendsen. (2003). 'Designing Green Taxes in a Political Context: From Optimal to Feasible Environmental Regulation'. *Environmental Politics 12*, no. 4: 76–95.

Davies, H. T. O., S. M. Nutley and P. C. Smith (eds). (2000). *What Works? Evidence-based Policy and Practice in Public Services*. Bristol, UK: Policy Press.

Davies, P. (2004). *Is Evidence-Based Government Possible?* London: Polity Press.

Day, P. and R. Klein. (1989). 'Interpreting the Unexpected: The Case of AIDS Policy Making in Britain'. *Journal of Public Policy 9*, no. 3: 337–353.

Deber, R., M. J. Hollander and P. Jacobs. (2008). 'Models of Funding and Reimbursement in Health Care: A Conceptual Framework'. *Canadian Public Administration 51*, no. 3: 381–405.

de Bruijn, H. and A. L. Porter. (2004). 'The Education of a Technology Policy Analyst – to Process Management'. *Technology Analysis and Strategic Management 16*, no. 2: 261–274.

de Bruijn, J. A. and H. A. M. Hufen. (1998). 'The Traditional Approach to Policy Instruments'. In B. G. Peters and F. K. M. V. Nispen (eds), *Public Policy Instruments: Evaluating the Tools of Public Administration*. New York: Edward Elgar, 11–32.

de Bruijn, J. A. and E. F. ten Heuvelhof. (1991). 'Policy Instruments for Steering Autopoietic Actors'. In T. Veld, L. Schaap, C. J. A. M. Termeer and M. J. W. van Twist (eds.), *Autopoiesis and Configuration Theory: New Approaches to Societal Steering*. Dordrecht, The Netherlands: Kluwer, 161–170.

de Bruijn, J. A. and E. F. ten Heuvelhof. (1995). 'Policy Networks and Governance'. In D. L. Weimer (ed.), *Institutional Design*. Boston, MA: Kluwer Academic, 161–179.

de Bruijn, J. A. and E. F. ten Heuvelhof. (1997). 'Instruments for Network Management'. In W. J. M. Kickert, E.-H. Klijn and J. F. M. Koppenjan (eds.), *Managing Complex Networks: Strategies for the Public Sector*. London: Sage, 119–136.

Debus, M. and J. Müller. (2013). 'The Programmatic Development of CDU and CSU Since Reunification: Incentives and Constraints for Changing Policy Positions in the German Multi-Level System'. *German Politics 22*, no. 1–2: 151–171.

DECC/Behavioural Insights Team. (2014). *Evaluation of the DECC and John Lewis Energy Labelling Trial*. Research and Analysis No. 14D/320. Department of Energy & Climate Change, UK. www.gov.uk/government/publications/evaluation-of-the-decc-and-john-lewis-energy-labelling-trial

de Groot, J. I. M. and G. Schuitema. (2012). 'How to Make the Unpopular Popular? Policy Characteristics, Social Norms and the Acceptability of Environmental Policies'. *Environmental Science & Policy* 19–20 (May): 100–107. https://doi.org/10.1016/j.envsci.2012.03.004

Delacourt, S. and D. G. Lenihan (eds.). (2000). *Collaborative Government: Is There a Canadian Way?* Toronto, ON: Institute of Public Administration of Canada.

de la Mothe, J. (1996). 'One Small Step in an Uncertain Direction: The Science and Technology Review and Public Administration in Canada'. *Canadian Public Administration 39*, no. 3: 403–417.

de Lancer Julnes, P. and M. Holzer. (2001). 'Promoting the Utilization of Performance Measures in Public Organizations: An Empirical Study of Factors Affecting Adoption and Implementation'. *Public Administration Review 61*, no. 6: 693–708.

de la Rue du Can, S., G. Leventis, A. Phadke and A. Gopal. (2014). 'Design of Incentive Programs for Accelerating Penetration of Energy-Efficient Appliances'. *Energy Policy 72* (September): 56–66.

Delbosc, A. and G. Currie. (2016). 'Four Types of Fare Evasion: A Qualitative Study from Melbourne, Australia'. *Transportation Research Part F: Traffic Psychology and Behaviour 43*, no. 4 (1 November): 254–264.

DeLeon, P. (1979). *Development and Diffusion of the Nuclear Power Reactor: A Comparative Analysis*. Cambridge, MA: Ballinger.

DeLeon, P. (1988). 'The Contextual Burdens of Policy Design'. *Policy Studies Journal 17*, no. 2: 297–309.

DeLeon, P. (1992). 'Policy Formulation: Where Ignorant Armies Clash by Night'. *Review of Policy Research 11*, no. 3–4: 389–405.

DeLeon, P. (1999a). 'The Missing Link Revisited: Contemporary Implementation Research'. *Policy Studies Review 16*, no. 3: 311–338.

DeLeon, P. (1999b). 'The Stages Approach to the Policy Process: What Has It Done? Where Is It Going?' In P. A. Sabatier (ed.), *Theories of the Policy Process*. Boulder, CO: Westview, 19–34.

Delmas, M. A., M. Fischlein and O. I. Asensio. (2013). 'Information Strategies and Energy Conservation Behavior: A Meta-Analysis of Experimental Studies from 1975 to 2012'. *Energy Policy 61*: 729–739.

Delmas, M. A. and A. K. Terlaak. (2001). 'A Framework for Analyzing Environmental Voluntary Agreements'. *California Management Review 43*, no. 3: 44–63.

Deloitte. (2009). *Take the Right Steps – 9 Principles for Building the Risk Intelligent Enterprise*. www.in-gc-putting-risk-in-the-comfort-zone-nine-principles-for-risk-intelligent-enterprises-noexp.pdf

Del Río, P. (2007). 'The Interaction between Emissions Trading and Renewable Electricity Support Schemes. An Overview of the Literature'. *Mitigation and Adaptation Strategies for Global Change 12*, no. 8: 1363–1390.

Del Río, P. (2009). 'Interactions Between Climate and Energy Policies: The Case of Spain'. *Climate Policy 9*, no. 2: 119–138.

Del Río, P. (2010). 'Analysing the Interactions Between Renewable Energy Promotion and Energy Efficiency Support Schemes: The Impact of Different Instruments and Design Elements'. *Energy Policy 38*, no. 9 (September): 4978–4989.

Del Río, P. (2014). 'On Evaluating Success in Complex Policy Mixes: The Case of Renewable Energy Support Schemes'. *Policy Sciences 47*, no. *3*: 267–287.

Del Río, P. and M. P. Howlett. (2013). *Beyond the 'Tinbergen Rule' in Policy Design: Matching Tools and Goals in Policy Portfolios.* SSRN Scholarly Paper. Rochester, NY: Social Science Research Network (8 April). http://papers.ssrn.com/abstract=2247238

Del Río, P., A. C. Silvosa and G. I. Gómez. (2011). 'Policies and Design Elements for the Repowering of Wind Farms: A Qualitative Analysis of Different Options'. *Energy Policy 39*, no. *4* (April): 1897–1908.

Del Río, P., J. Carrillo-Hermosilla and T. Könnölä. (2010). 'Policy Strategies to Promote Eco-Innovation'. *Journal of Industrial Ecology 14*, no. *4*: 541–557.

Del Vicario, M., F. Zollo, G. Caldarelli, A. Scala and W. Quattrociocchi. (2017). 'Mapping Social Dynamics on Facebook: The Brexit Debate'. *Social Networks 50* (July): 6–16.

DeMenno, M. B. (2017). 'Technocracy, Democracy, and Public Policy: An Evaluation of Public Participation in Retrospective Regulatory Review'. *Regulation & Governance 13*, no. *3*: 362–383.

de Moor, A. P. G. (1997). *Perverse Incentives: Hundreds of Billions of Dollars in Subsidies now Harm the Economy, the Environment, Equity and Trade.* San Jose, CA: Earth Council.

Denzau, A. T. and D. C. North. (1994). 'Shared Mental Models: Ideologies and Institutions'. *Kyklos 47*, no. *1* (February): 3–31.

Derlien, H.-U. (2008). 'Conclusion'. In H.-U. Derlien and B. G. Peters (eds.), *The State at Work, vol. 1, Public Sector Employment in 10 Countries.* Cheltenham, UK: Edward Elgar, 283–291.

Derthick, M. and P. J. Quirk. (1985). *The Politics of Deregulation.* Washington, DC: Brookings Institution.

Dery, D. (1984). *Problem Definition in Policy Analysis.* Lawrence, KS: University of Kansas.

Dery, D. (1999). 'Policy by the Way: When Policy is Incidental to Making Other Policies'. *Journal of Public Policy 18*, no. *2*: 163–176.

de Saulles, M. (2007). 'When Public Meets Private: Conflicts in Information Policy'. *Info 9*, no. *6*: 10–16.

Desch, M. C. (2007/8). 'America's Liberal Illiberalism: The Ideological Origins of Overreaction in US Foreign Policy'. *International Security 32*, no. *3*: 7–43.

DeShazo, J. R., T. L. Sheldon and R. T. Carson. (2017). 'Designing Policy Incentives for Cleaner Technologies: Lessons from California's Plug-in Electric Vehicle Rebate Program'. *Journal of Environmental Economics and Management 84* (July): 18–43.

de Smith, S. A. (1973). *Judicial Review of Administrative Action.* London: Stevens & Son.

Deutsch, K. W. (1963). *The Nerves of Government: Models of Political Communication and Control.* New York: Free Press.

Deverell, E. (2009). 'Crises as Learning Triggers: Exploring a Conceptual Framework of Crisis-Induced Learning'. *Journal of Contingencies and Crisis Management 17*, no. *3*: 179–188.

de Vita, C. J. and E. C. Twombly. (2005). 'Who Gains from Charitable Tax Credit Programs? The Arizona Model'. *Public Administration Review 65*, no. *1*: 57–63.

de Vries, M. S. (1999). 'Developments in Europe: The Idea of Policy Generations'. *International Review of Administrative Sciences 65*, no. *4*: 491–510.

de Vries, M. S. (2002). 'The Changing Functions of Laws and its Implication for Government and Governance'. *International Review of Administrative Sciences 68*, no. 4: 599–618.

de Vries, M. S. (2005). 'Generations of Interactive Policy-Making in the Netherlands'. *International Review of Administrative Sciences 71*, no. 4: 577–591.

de Vries, M. S. (2010). *The Importance of Neglect in Policy-Making*. Basingstoke: Palgrave Macmillan.

Dewees, D. N. (1983). 'Instrument Choice in Environmental Policy'. *Economic Inquiry 31*: 53–71.

Diamond, L. J. (2002). 'Thinking About Hybrid Regimes'. *Journal of Democracy 13*, no. 2: 21–35.

Diamond, L. J. (2008). 'Capacity Building in the Voluntary and Community Sectors: Towards Relative Independence – Limits and Possibilities'. *Public Policy and Administration 23*, no. 2: 153–166.

Diani, M. (1992). 'Analysing Social Movement Networks'. In M. Diani and R. Eyerman (eds.), *Studying Collective Action*. London: Sage, 107–137.

Dietzenbacher, E. (2000). 'Spillovers of Innovation Effects'. *Journal of Policy Modeling 22*, no. 1: 27–42.

Dimaggio, P. J. and W. W. Powell. (1983). 'The Iron Cage Revisited: Institutional Isomorphism and Collective Rationality in Organizational Fields'. *American Sociological Review 48*, (April): 147–160.

DiMento, J. F. (1989). 'Can Social Science Explain Organizational Noncompliance with Environmental Law?' *Journal of Social Issues 45*, no. 1: 109–132.

Dimitrov, R. S. (2002). 'Confronting Nonregimes: Science and International Coral Reef Policy'. *The Journal of Environment Development 11*, no. 1 (March): 53–78.

Dimitrov, R. S. (2005). 'Hostage to Norms: States, Institutions and Global Forest Politics'. *Global Environmental Politics 5*, no. 4: 1–24.

Dimitrov, R. S., F. S. Detlef, G. M. DiGiusto and A. Kelle. (2007). 'International Nonregimes: A Research Agenda'. *The International Studies Review 9*: 230–258.

Dinner, I., E. J. Johnson, D. G. Goldstein and K. Liu. (2011). 'Partitioning Default Effects: Why People Choose not to Choose'. *Journal of Experimental Psychology. Applied 17*, no. 4: 332–341.

Dion, L. (1973). 'The Politics of Consultation'. *Government and Opposition 8*, no. 3: 332–353, 339.

Dittmar, M. (2014). 'Development Towards Sustainability: How to Judge Past and Proposed Policies?" *Science of the Total Environment 472* (15 February): 282–288.

Djanibekov, N. and V. Valentinov. (2015). 'Evolutionary Governance, Sustainability, and Systems Theory: The Case of Central Asia'. In K. Van Assche, R. Beunen and M. Duineveld (eds.), *Evolutionary Governance Theory*. New York: Springer, 119–134.

Dobbin, F., B. Simmons and G. Garrett. (2007). 'The Global Diffusion of Public Policies: Social Construction, Coercion, Competition, or Learning?' *Annual Review of Sociology 33*: 449–472.

Dobuzinskis, L. (1987). *The Self-Organizing Polity: An Epistemological Analysis of Political Life*. Boulder, CO: Westview.

Dobuzinskis, L., M. Howlett and D. Laycock (eds.). (2007). *Policy Analysis in Canada: The State of the Art*. Toronto, ON: University of Toronto Press.

Doern, G. B. (1967). 'The Role of Royal Commissions in the General Policy Process and in Federal – Provincial Relations'. *Canadian Public Administration 10*, no. 4: 417–433.

Doern, G. B. (1971). 'The Role of Central Advisory Councils: The Science Council of Canada'. In G. B. Doern and P. Aucoin (eds.), *The Structures of Policy-Making in Canada*. Toronto, ON: Macmillan, 246–266.

Doern, G. B. (1974). 'The Concept of Regulation and Regulatory Reform'. In G. B. Doern and V. S. Wilson (eds.), *Issues in Canadian Public Policy*. Toronto, ON: Macmillan, 8–35.

Doern, G. B. (1981). *The Nature of Scientific and Technological Controversy in Federal Policy Formation*. Ottawa, ON: Science Council of Canada.

Doern, G. B. (1983). 'The Mega-Project Episode and the Formulation of Canadian Economic Development Policy'. *Canadian Public Administration* 26, no. 2: 219–238.

Doern, G. B. and R. W. Phidd. (1983). *Canadian Public Policy: Ideas, Structure, Process* (1st edn). Toronto, ON: Methuen.

Doern, G. B. and R. W. Phidd. (1988). *Canadian Public Policy: Ideas, Structure, Process* (2nd edn). Toronto, ON: Nelson.

Doern, G. B. and S. Wilks. (1998). *Changing Regulatory Institutions in Britain and North America*. Toronto, ON: University of Toronto Press.

Doern, G. B. and V. S. Wilson. (1974). *Conclusions and Observations*. Issues in Canadian Public Policy 339. Toronto, ON: Methuen, 337–345.

Doerr, A. D. (1981). *The Machinery of Government in Canada*. Toronto, ON: Methuen.

Doerr, A. D. (1982). 'The Role of Coloured Papers'. *Canadian Public Administration* 25, no. 3: 366–379.

Doig, A. and S. Johnson. (2001). 'New Public Management, Old Populism and the Policing of Fraud'. *Public Policy and Administration* 16, no. 1: 91–111.

Dolan, P. and M. M. Galizzi. (2014). 'Getting Policy-Makers to Listen to Field Experiments'. *Oxford Review of Economic Policy* 30, no. 4: 725–752.

Dolan, P. and M. M. Galizzi. (2015). 'Like Ripples on a Pond: Behavioral Spillovers and Their Implications for Research and Policy'. *Journal of Economic Psychology* 47: 1–16.

Dolan, P., M. Hallsworth, D. Halpern, D. King and I. Vlaev. (2010). *Mindspace: Influencing Behaviour Through Public Policy*. London: Institute for Government. www.instituteforgovernment.org.uk/sites/default/files/publications/MIND-SPACE. pdf

Dolan, P. and R. Metcalfe. (2013). *Neighbors, Knowledge, and Nuggets: Two Natural Field Experiments on the Role of Incentives on Energy Conservation*. CEP Discussion Paper, No. CEPDP1222. London: Centre for Economic Performance, London School of Economics and Political Science. http://cep.lse.ac.uk/_new/publications/series.asp?prog=CEP

Dollery, B. and J. Wallis. (1999). *Market Failure, Government Failure, Leadership and Public Policy*. London: Macmillan.

Dollery, B. and J. Wallis. (2003). *The Political Economy of the Voluntary Sector: A Reappraisal of the Comparative Institutional Advantage of Voluntary Organizations*. Cheltenham, UK: Edward Elgar.

Dolowitz, D. P. and D. Marsh. (2000). 'Learning from Abroad: The Role of Policy Transfer in Contemporary Policy-Making'. *Governance* 13, no. 1: 5–23.

d'Ombrain, N. (1997). 'Public Inquiries in Canada'. *Canadian Public Administration* 40, no. 1: 86–107.

Donahue, J. D. (1989). *The Privatization Decision: Public Ends, Private Means*. New York: Basic Books.

Donovan, M. C. (2001). *Taking Aim: Target Populations and the Wars on Aids and Drugs*. Washington, DC: Georgetown University Press.

Doremus, H. (2003). 'A Policy Portfolio Approach to Biodiversity Protection on Private Lands'. *Environmental Science & Policy* 6: 217–232.

Douglas, S., T. Schillemans, P. 't Hart, C. Ansell, L. B. Andersen, M. Flinders, B. Head, D. Moynihan, T. Nabatchi, J. O'Flynn and B. G. Peters. (2021). 'Rising to Ostrom's Challenge: An Invitation to Walk on the Bright Side of Public Governance and Public Service'. *Policy Design and Practice* (3 September): 1–11.

Dowd, K. (1999). *Too Big to Fail? Long-Term Capital Management and the Federal Reserve*. Cato Institute Briefing Papers No. 52. www.cato.org/pubs/briefs/bp52.pdf

Downs, A. (1972). 'Up and Down with Ecology: The Issue-Attention Cycle'. *Public Interest* 28: 38–50.

Doz, Y. and M. Kosonen. (2014). *Governments for the Future: Building the Strategic and Agile State*. Helsinki, Finland: SITRA.

Drew, J. T. C., R. S. Applebaum, S. Atkinson, F. M. Clydesdale, E. Hentges, N. A. Higley and M. E. Westring. (2013). 'How Experts Are Chosen to Inform Public Policy: Can the Process Be Improved?' *Health Policy* 112, no. 3: 172–178.

Drezner, D. W. (2001a). 'Globalization and Policy Convergence'. *International Studies Review* 3, no. 1 (Spring): 53–78.

Drezner, D. W. (2001b). 'Reflection and Reappraisal: Globalization and Policy Convergence'. *International Studies Review* 3, no. 1: 53–78.

Drezner, D. W. (2005). 'Globalization, Harmonization and Competition: The Different Pathways to Policy Convergence'. *Journal of European Public Policy* 12, no. 5: 841–859.

Dror, Y. (1964). 'Muddling Through – "Science" or Inertia'. *Public Administration Review* 24, no. 3: 154–157.

Dryzek, J. S. (1983). 'Don't Toss Coins in Garbage Cans: A Prologue to Policy Design'. *Journal of Public Policy* 3, no. 4: 345–367.

Dryzek, J. S. and B. Ripley. (1988). 'The Ambitions of Policy Design'. *Policy Studies Review* 7, no. 4: 705–719.

Dryzek, J. S. and A. Tucker. (2008). 'Deliberative Innovation to Different Effect: Consensus Conferences in Denmark, France and the United States'. *Public Administration Review* 68, no. 5: 864–876.

Duesberg, S., Á. N. Dhubháin and D. O'Connor. (2014). 'Assessing Policy Tools for Encouraging Farm Afforestation in Ireland'. *Land Use Policy* 38 (May): 194–203.

Duit, A. (2016). 'Resilience Thinking: Lessons for Public Administration'. *Public Administration* 94, no. 2 (1 June): 364–380.

Dunleavy, P. (1986). 'Explaining the Privatization Boom: Public Choice Versus Radical Approaches'. *Public Administration* 64, no. 1: 13–34.

Dunleavy, P. and C. Hood. (1994). 'From Old Public Administration to New Public Management'. *Public Money and Management* 14, no. 3: 9–16.

Dunlop, C. A. (2009a). 'The Temporal Dimension of Knowledge and the Limits of Policy Appraisal: Biofuels Policy in the UK'. *Policy Sciences* 43, no. 4 (October): 343–363.

Dunlop, C. A. (2009b). 'Policy Transfer as Learning: Capturing Variation in What Decision-Makers Learn from Epistemic Communities'. *Policy Studies* 30, no. 3: 289–311.

Dunlop, C. A. (2017a). 'Policy Learning and Policy Failure: Definitions, Dimensions and Intersections'. *Policy & Politics* 45, no. 1 (17 January): 3–18.

Dunlop, C. A. (2017b). 'Pathologies of Policy Learning: What Are They and How Do They Contribute to Policy Failure?' *Policy & Politics 45*, no. *1* (January): 19–37.

Dunlop, C. A. and C. M. Radaelli. (2018a). "The Lessons of Policy Learning: Types, Triggers, Hindrances and Pathologies'. *Policy and Politics 46*, no. *2* (April): 255–272.

Dunlop, C. A. and C. M. Radaelli (eds.). (2018b). *Learning in Public Policy – Analysis, Modes and Outcomes*. London: Palgrave Macmillan.

Dunn, D. (1997). *Politics and Administration at the Top: Lessons from Down Under*. Pittsburgh: University of Pittsburgh Press.

Dunn, W. N. (1986). *Policy Analysis: Perspectives, Concepts and Methods*. New Brunswick, NJ: JAI Press.

Dunn, W. N. (2004). *Public Policy Analysis: An Introduction*. Upper Saddle River, NJ: Pearson/Prentice Hall.

Dunn, W. N. (2008). *Public Policy Analysis: An Introduction*. Upper Saddle River, NJ: Pearson/Prentice Hall.

Dunsire, A. (1978). *The Execution Process*. Oxford: Martin Robertson.

Dunsire, A. (1986). 'A Cybernetic View of Guidance, Control and Evaluation in the Public Sector'. In F.-X. Kaufman, G. Majone and V. Ostrom (eds.), *Guidance, Control and Evaluation in the Public Sector*. Berlin, Germany: Walter de Gruyter, 327–346.

Dunsire, A. (1993a). *Manipulating Social Tensions: Collibration as an Alternative Mode of Government Intervention*. Discussion Paper 93/7. Cologne, Germany: Max Planck Institute for the Study of Societies.

Dunsire, A. (1993b). 'Modes of Governance'. In J. Kooiman (ed.), *Modern Governance*. London: Sage, 21–34.

Dupuis, J. and R. Biesbroek. (2013). 'Comparing Apples and Oranges: The Dependent Variable Problem in Comparing and Evaluating Climate Change Adaptation Policies'. *Global Environmental Change 23*, no. *6* (1 December): 1476–1487.

Durant, R. F. (2008). 'Sharpening a Knife Cleverly: Organizational Change, Policy Paradox and the "Weaponizing" of Administrative Reform'. *Public Administration Review 68*, no. *2*: 282–294.

Durning, D. and W. Osama. (1994). 'Policy Analysts' Roles and Value Orientations: An Empirical Investigation Using Q Methodology'. *Journal of Policy Analysis and Management 13*, no. *4*: 629–657.

Durr, R. H. (1993). 'What Moves Policy Sentiment?' *American Political Science Review 87*: 158–172.

Dutil, P. and A. Migone. (2021). 'The Changing and Enduring Priorities of Deputy Ministers Through the IPAC Survey'. *Canadian Public Administration 64*, no. 122–142.

Dwivedi, O. P. (ed.). (1982). *The Administrative State in Canada: Essays in Honour of J.E. Hodgetts*. Toronto, ON: University of Toronto Press.

Dwivedi, O. P. and J. I. Gow. (1999). *From Bureaucracy to Public Management: The Administrative Culture of the Government of Canada*. Toronto, ON: IPAC.

Dyckman, C. S. (2018). 'Planning Without the Planners: South Carolina's Section 319 Local Watershed Planning Process'. *Environmental Science & Policy 89*: 126–141.

Dye, T. R. (1972). *Understanding Public Policy*. Englewood Cliffs, NJ: Prentice-Hall.

Dyerson, R. and F. Mueller. (1993). 'Intervention by Outsiders: A Strategic Perspective on Government Industrial Policy'. *Journal of Public Policy 13*, no. *1*: 69–88.

Easton, D. (1965). *A Systems Analysis of Political Life*. New York: Wiley.

Ebeling, F. and S. Lotz. (2015). 'Domestic Uptake of Green Energy Promoted by Opt-Out Tariffs'. *Nature Climate Change 5*, no. 9: 868–871.

Economic Council of Canada. (1979). *Responsible Regulation*. Ottawa, ON: Ministry of Supply and Services.

Edelenbos, J. and E.-H. Klijn. (2005). 'Managing Stakeholder Involvement in Decision-Making: A Comparative Analysis of Six Interactive Processes in the Netherlands'. *Journal of Public Administration Research and Theory 16*, no. 3: 2.

Edelenbos, J., A. van Buuren and N. van Schie. (2011). 'Co-Producing Knowledge: Joint Knowledge Production between Experts, Bureaucrats and Stakeholders in Dutch Water Management Projects'. *Environmental Science & Policy 14*, no. 6 (October): 675–684.

Edelenbos, J., N. van Schie and L. Gerrits. (2010). 'Organizing Interfaces Between Government Institutions and Interactive Governance'. *Policy Sciences 43*, no. 1: 73–94.

Edelman, M. (1964). *The Symbolic Uses of Politics*. Chicago, IL: University of Illinois Press.

Edelman, M. (1971). *Politics as Symbolic Action: Mass Arousal and Quiescence*. Chicago, IL: Markham Publishing.

Edelman, M. (1988). *Constructing the Political Spectacle*. Chicago, IL: University of Chicago Press.

Eden, S. (2009). 'The Work of Environmental Governance Networks: Traceability, Credibility and Certification by the Forest Stewardship Council'. *Geoforum 40*: 383–394.

Eden, S. and C. Bear. (2010). 'Third-Sector Global Environmental Governance, Space and Science: Comparing Fishery and Forestry Certification'. *Journal of Environmental Policy and Planning 12*, no. 1: 83–106.

Edley, C. F. J. (1990). *Administrative Law: Rethinking Judicial Control of Bureaucracy*. New Haven, CT: Yale University Press.

Edwards, L. (2009). 'Testing the Discourse of Declining Policy Capacity: Rail Policy and the Department of Transport'. *Australian Journal of Public Administration 68*, no. 3: 288–302.

EEA (European Environment Agency). (2001). *Environmental Signals 2001*. Brussels, Belgium: EEA. www.eea.europa.eu/publications/signals-2001

Egeberg, M. (1999). 'The Impact of Bureaucratic Structure on Policy Making'. *Public Administration*. 77, no. 1: 155–170.

Ehrenfel, T. (2018). 'Lessons the U.S. Can Learn from Singapore's Health System'. *Health Line* (24 January). www.healthline.com/health-news/us-can-learn-from-singapore-health-system#1

Eichbaum, C. and R. Shaw. (2007). 'Ministerial Advisers and the Politics of Policy-Making: Bureaucratic Permanence and Popular Control'. *The Australian Journal of Public Administration 66*, no. 4: 453–467.

Eichbaum, C. and R. Shaw. (2008). 'Revisiting Politicization: Political Advisers and Public Servants in Westminster Systems'. *Governance 21*, no. 3: 337–363.

Eijlander, P. (2005). 'Possibilities and Constraints in the Use of Self-Regulation and Co-Regulation in Legislative Policy: Experiences in the Netherlands – Lessons to Be Learned for the EU'. *Electronic Journal of Comparative Law 9*, no. 1: 1–8.

Eikenberry, A. M. (2007). 'Symposium-Theorizing Governance Beyond the State'. *Administrative Theory and Praxis 29*: 193–197.

Eisenstadt, S. E. (1963). *The Political Systems of Empires*. London: Collier.

365

Eisner, M. A. (1993). *Regulatory Politics in Transition*. Baltimore, MD: Johns Hopkins University Press.

Eisner, M. A. (1994a). 'Discovering Patterns in Regulatory History: Continuity, Change and Regulatory Regimes'. *Journal of Policy History 6*, no. 2: 157–187.

Eisner, M. A. (1994b). 'Economic Regulatory Policies: Regulation and Deregulation in Historical Context'. In D. H. Rosenbloom and R. D. Schwartz (eds.), *Handbook of Regulation and Administrative Law*. New York: Marcel Dekker, 91–116.

Elgie, R. (2006). 'Why Do Governments Delegate Authority to Quasi-Autonomous Agencies? The Case of Independent Administrative Authorities in France'. *Governance 19*, no. 2: 207–227.

Eliadis, P., M. Hill and M. Howlett (eds.). (2005). *Designing Government: From Instruments to Governance*. Montreal, QC: McGill-Queen's University Press.

Eliste, P. and P. G. Fredriksson. (1998). *Does Open Trade Result in a Race to the Bottom? Cross Country Evidence*. Washington, DC: World Bank.

Elkin, S. L. (1986). 'Regulation and Regime: A Comparative Analysis'. *Journal of Public Policy 6*, no. 1: 49–72.

Elkins, Z. and B. Simmons. (2005). 'On Clusters, Waves and Diffusion: A Conceptual Framework'. *Annals of the American Association of Political and Social Science 598*: 33–51.

Ellig, J. and D. Lavoie. (1995). 'The Principle-Agent Relationship in Organizations'. In P. Foss (ed.), *Economic Approaches to Organizations and Institutions: An Introduction*. Aldershot: Dartmouth, 267–295.

Elliott, C. and R. Schlaepfer. (2001). 'The Advocacy Coalition Framework: Application to the Policy Process for the Development of Forest Certification in Sweden'. *Journal of European Public Policy 8*, no. 4: 642–661.

Elliott, D. and M. McGuinness. (2001). 'Public Inquiry: Panacea or Placebo?' *Journal of Contingencies and Crisis Management 10*, no. 1: 14–25.

Elmore, R. F. (1978). 'Organizational Models of Social Program Implementation'. *Public Policy 26*, no. 2: 185–228.

Elmore, R. F. (1987). 'Instruments and Strategy in Public Policy'. *Policy Studies Review 7*, no. 1: 174–186.

Eloi, L. (2009). 'Carbon Tax: The French Connection'. *The Economists' Voice* (December): 1–4.

Elsen, M., R. Giesen and J. Leenheer. (2015). *Milan BExpo 2015 Behavioural Study on Food Choices and Eating Habits: Final Report*. Luxembourg: European Commission. http://bookshop.europa.eu/uri?target=EUB:NOTICE:DS0415694: EN:HTML

Elson, A. (2008). 'The Sovereign Wealth Funds of Singapore'. *World Economics 9*, no. 3: 73–96.

Elster, J. (1989). *The Cement of Society: A Study of Social Order*. Cambridge, UK; New York: Cambridge University Press.

Elster, J. (2009). *Reason and Rationality*. Princeton, NJ: Princeton University Press.

Enderlein, H., S. Wälti and M. Zürn. (2011). *Handbook on Multi-Level Governance*. Cheltenham, UK: Edward Elgar.

Engels, A., O. Hüther, M. Schäfer and H. Held. (2013). 'Public Climate-Change Skepticism, Energy Preferences and Political Participation'. *Global Environmental Change 23*, no. 5: 1018–1027.

English, L. M. and M. Skellern. (2005). 'Public – Private Partnerships and Public Sector Management Reform: A Comparative Analysis'. *International Journal of Public Policy 1*, no. 1–2: 1–21.

Enkler, J., S. Schmidt, S. Eckhard, C. Knill and S. Grohs. (2017). 'Administrative Styles in the OECD: Bureaucratic Policy-Making Beyond Formal Rules'. *International Journal of Public Administration 40*, no. 8: 637–648.

EPA (Environmental Protection Agency). (2001). *The United States Experience with Economic Incentives for Protecting the Environment.* No. EPA-240-R-01-001. National Center for Environmental Economics: Office of Policy, Economics, and Innovation Office of the Administrator US Environmental Protection Agency. https://www.epa.gov/environmental-economics/united-states-experience-economic-incentives-protecting-environment-2001

Ergas, H. (2010). 'New Policies Create a New Politics: Issues of Institutional Design in Climate Change Policy'. *Australian Journal of Agricultural and Resource Economics 54*, no. 2: 143–164.

Erwin C. (1975). *The Missing Link: The Study of the Implementation of Social Policy.* Washington, DC: Urban Institute.

Escribano, G. (2013). 'Ecuador's Energy Policy Mix: Development Versus Conservation and Nationalism with Chinese Loans'. *Energy Policy 57(c)*: 152–159.

Esmark, A. (2009). 'The Functional Differentiation of Governance: Public Governance beyond Hierarchy, Market and Networks'. *Public Administration 87*, no. 2: 351–370.

Esping-Andersen, G. (1990). *The Three Worlds of Welfare Capitalism.* Cambridge: Polity Press.

Esping-Andersen, G. (ed.). (1996). *Welfare States in Transition: National Adaptations in Global Economies.* London: Sage.

Esterling, K. M. (2004). *The Political Economy of Expertise: Information and Efficiency in American National Politics.* Ann Arbor: University of Michigan Press.

Europæiske, M. (2013). *Adaptation in Europe: Addressing Risks and Opportunities from Climate Change in the Context of Socio-Economic Developments.* Copenhagen, Denmark: European Environment Agency.

European Environment Agency (EEA). (2001). *Environmental Signals 2001.* Brussels: EEA. www.eea.europa.eu/publications/signals-2001

Evangelista, M. (1995). 'The Paradox of State Strength: Transnational Relations, Domestic Structures, and Security Policy in Russia and the Soviet Union'. *International Organization 49*, no. 1: 1–38.

Evans, B., T. Richmond and J. Shields. (2005). 'Structuring Neoliberal Governance: The Nonprofit Sector, Emerging New Modes of Control and the Marketisation of Service Delivery'. *Policy and Society 24*, no. 1: 73–97.

Evans, P. (1997). 'The Eclipse of the State? Reflections on Stateness in an Era of Globalization'. *World Politics 50*, no. 1: 62–87.

Everitt, J. and B. O'Neill (eds.). (2002). *Citizen Politics: Research and Theory in Canadian Political Behaviour.* Toronto, ON: Oxford University Press.

Evers, A. (2005). 'Mixed Welfare Systems and Hybrid Organizations: Changes in the Governance and Provision of Social Services'. *International Journal of Public Administration 28*: 737–748.

Evers, A. and H. Wintersberger (eds.). (1990). *Shifts in the Welfare Mix: Their Impact on Work, Social Services and Welfare Policies.* Frankfurt, Germany; Boulder, CO: Campus/Westview.

Executive Research Group. (1999). *Investing in Policy: Report on Other Jurisdictions and Organizations.* Toronto, ON: Ministry of the Environment.

Falco, G. (2017). *Constraint Tree Analysis: A Method to Evaluate Threats to Technology Policy Goals.* SSRN Scholarly Paper. Rochester, NY: Social Science Research Network (19 February).

Falk, R. A. (1997). 'State of Siege: Will Globalization Win Out?' *International Affairs* 73, no. *1*: 123–136.

Falkenmark, M. (2004). 'Towards Integrated Catchment Management: Opening the Paradigm Locks Between Hydrology, Ecology and Policy-Making'. *Water Resources Development 20*, no. *3*: 275–282.

Falkner, G. (2000). 'Policy Networks in a Multi-Level System: Convergence Towards Moderate Diversity?' *West European Politics 2*, no. *4*: 94–120.

Falleti, T. G. and J. F. Lynch. (2009). 'Context and Causal Mechanisms in Political Analysis'. *Comparative Political Studies 42*, no. *9*: 1143–1166.

Farazmand, A. (1999). 'Globalization and Public Administration'. *Public Administration Review 59*, no. *6*: 509–522.

FATF. (2021). *Guidance on Proliferation Financing Risk Assessment and Mitigation.* www.fatf-gafi.org/publications/financingofproliferation/documents/proliferation-financing-risk-assessment-mitigation.html

Feeley, M. (1970). 'Coercion and Compliance: A New Look at an Old Problem'. *Law & Society Review 4*, no. *4* (1 May): 505–519.

Fehr, E. and K. M. Schmidt. (2003). 'Theories of Fairness and Reciprocity: Evidence and Economic Applications'. In M. Dewatripont, L. P. Hansen and S. J. Turnovsky (eds.), *Advances in Economics and Econometrics*. Cambridge, UK: Cambridge University Press, 208–257.

Feindt, P. H. (2012). 'The Politics of Biopatents in Food and Agriculture, 1950–2010: Value Conflict, Competing Paradigms and Contested Institutionalisation in Multilevel Governance'. *Policy and Society 31*, no. *4* (November): 281–293.

Feindt, P. H. and A. Flynn. (2009). 'Policy Stretching and Institutional Layering: British Food Policy Between Security, Safety, Quality, Health and Climate Change'. *British Politics 4*, no. *3*: 386–414.

Feiock, R. C., A. F. Tavares and M. Lubell. (2008). 'Policy Instrument Choices for Growth Management and Land Use Regulation'. *Policy Studies Journal 36*, no. *3*: 461–480.

Feitsma, J. (2018). ' "Rationalized Incrementalism": How Behavior Experts in Government Negotiate Institutional Logics'. *Critical Policy Studies 14* (20 December): 1–18.

Feldman, D. (2019). *Chaos and Dynamical Systems*. Princeton: Princeton University Press.

Feldman, M. (1989). *Order Without Design: Information Production and Policy Making* (1st edn). Stanford: Stanford University Press.

Feldman, M. S. and A. M. Khademian. (2007). 'The Role of the Public Manager in Inclusion: Creating Communities of Participation'. *Governance 20*, no. *2*: 305–324.

Feldman, Y. (2018). *The Law of Good People: Challenging States' Ability to Regulate Human Behavior*. Cambridge, UK: Cambridge University Press.

Fellegi, I. (1996). *Strengthening Our Policy Capacity*. Ottawa, ON: Deputy Ministers Task Force.

Felsen, G., N. Castelo and P. B. Reiner. (2013). 'Decisional Enhancement and Autonomy: Public Attitudes Towards Overt and Covert Nudges'. *Judgment and Decision Making 8*, no. *3*: 202–213.

Ferlie, E., A. Pettigrew, L. Ashburner and L. Fitzgerald. (1996). *The New Public Management in Action*. New York: Oxford University Press.

Ferraro, P. J., J. J. Miranda and M. K. Price. (2011). 'The Persistence of Treatment Effects with Norm-Based Policy Instruments: Evidence from a Randomized

Environmental Policy Experiment'. *American Economic Review 101*, no. *3*: 318–322.

Ferraro, P. J. and M. K. Price. (2013). 'Using Nonpecuniary Strategies to Influence Behavior: Evidence from a Large-Scale Field Experiment'. *The Review of Economics and Statistics 95*, no. *1*: 64–73.

Ferreira, A. and D. Otley. (2009). 'The Design and Use of Performance Management Systems: An Extended Framework for Analysis'. *Management Accounting Research 20*, online.

Festinger, L. (1962). *A Theory of Cognitive Dissonance*. Stanford, CA: Stanford University Press.

Finer, D., P. Tillgren, K. Berensson, K. Guldbrandsson and B. Hagland. (2005). 'Implementation of a Health Impact Assessment (HIA) Tool in a Regional Health Organization in Sweden – A Feasibility Study'. *Health Promotion International 20*, no. *3*: 277–284.

Finer, S. E. (1997). *The History of Government from the Earliest Times, vol. III: Empires, Monarchies and the Modern State*. Oxford: Oxford University Press; especially Chapter 7. 'The Transplantation of European State-Models, 1500–1715'.

Finkle, P., K. Webb, W. Stanbury and P. Pross. (1994). *Federal Government Relations with Interest Groups: A Reconsideration*. Ottawa, ON: Privy Council Office.

Finley, L. K. (ed.). (1989). *Public Sector Privatization: Alternative Approaches to Service Delivery*. New York: Quorum Books.

Firestone, O. J. (1970). *The Public Persuader: Government Advertising*. Toronto, ON: Methuen.

Fischer, C. (2010). 'Combining Policies for Renewable Energy: Is the Whole Less Than the Sum of Its Parts?' *International Review of Environmental and Resource Economics 4*, no. *1* (30 June): 51–92.

Fischer, F. (ed.). (1987). *Confronting Values in Policy Analysis: The Politics of Criteria*. Beverly Hills, CA: Sage.

Fischer, F. (1990). *Technocracy and the Politics of Expertise*. Beverley Hills: Sage.

Fischer, F. (2019). *Politics, Values, and Public Policy: The Problem of Methodology*. New York: Routledge.

Fischer, F. and J. Forester. (1987). *Confronting Values in Policy Analysis: The Politics of Criteria*. Beverly Hills, CA: Sage.

Fischer, F. and J. Forester. (1993). *The Argumentative Turn in Policy Analysis and Planning*. Durham, NC: Duke University Press.

Fischhoff, B. (2010). 'Judgment and Decision Making'. *Wiley Interdisciplinary Reviews: Cognitive Science 1*, no. *3*: 724–738.

Flanagan, K., E. Uyarra and M. Laranja. (2011). 'Reconceptualising the "Policy Mix" for Innovation'. *Research Policy 40*, no. *5* (June): 702–713.

Fleischer, J. (2009). 'Power Resources of Parliamentary Executives: Policy Advice in the UK and Germany'. *West European Politics 32*, no. *1*: 196–214.

Fleischer, J., P. Bezes, O. James and K. Yesilkagit. (2023). 'The Politics of Government Reorganization in Western Europe'. *Governance 36*, no. *1*: 255–274.

Fligstein, N. (1996). 'Markets as Politics: A Political-Cultural Approach to Market Institutions'. *American Sociological Review 61* (August): 656–673.

Flinders, M. V. and H. McConnel. (1999). 'Diversity and Complexity: The Quango-Continuum'. In M. V. Flinders and M. J. Smith (eds.), *Quangos, Accountability and Reform: The Politics of Quasi-Government*. Sheffield, UK: Political Economy Research Centre, 17–39.

Flitner, D. (1986). *The Politics of Presidential Commissions*. New York: Transnational.

Flora, P. and A. J. Heidenheimer (eds.). (1981). *The Development of Welfare States in Europe and America*. New Brunswick, NJ: Transaction.

Flumian, M., A. Coe and K. Kernaghan. (2007). 'Transforming Service to Canadians: The Service Canada Model'. *International Review of Administrative Sciences 73*, no. 4: 557–568.

Folke, C. (2006). 'Resilience: The Emergence of a Perspective for Social-Ecological Systems Analyses'. *Global Environmental Change 16*, no. 3 (August): 253–267.

Ford, R. and D. Zussman. (1997). *Alternative Service Delivery: Sharing Governance in Canada*. Toronto, ON: KPMG/IPAC.

Forester, J. (1983). 'What Analysts Do'. In W. N. Dunn (ed.), *Values, Ethics and the Practice of Policy Analysis*. Lexington, KY: Lexington Books, 47–62.

Forester, J. (1984). 'Bounded Rationality and the Politics of Muddling Through'. *Public Administration Review 44*, no. 1: 23–31.

Forester, J. (1989). *Planning in the Face of Power*. Berkeley, CA: University of California Press.

Forsyth, A., C. S. Slotterback and K. J. Krizek. (2010). 'Health Impact Assessment Review'. *Environmental Impact Assessment Review 30*: 42–51.

Foster, C. D. and F. J. Plowden. (1996). *The State under Stress: Can the Hollow State Be Good Government?* Buckingham, UK; Philadelphia, PA: Open University Press.

Foster, E., M. Haward and S. Coffen-Smout. (2005). 'Implementing Integrated Oceans Management: Australia's South East Regional Marine Plan (SERMP) and Canada's Eastern Scotian Shelf Integrated Management (ESSIM) Initiative'. *Marine Policy 29*: 391–405.

Foucault, M. (1979). 'On Governmentality'. *Ideology and Consciousness 6*: 5–21.

Franchino, F. and B. Hoyland. (2009). 'Legislative Involvement in Parliamentary Systems: Opportunities, Conflict and Institutional Constraints'. *American Political Science Review 103*, no. 4: 607–621.

Franz, J. S. and C. Kirkpatrick. (2008). 'Improving the Quality of Integrated Policy Analysis: Impact Assessment for Sustainable Development in the European Commission'. *Evidence & Policy 4*, no. 2: 171–185.

Fraussen, B. and D. Halpin. (2017). 'Think Tanks and Strategic Policy-Making: The Contribution of Think Tanks to Policy Advisory Systems'. *Policy Sciences 50*, no. 1 (1 March): 105–124.

Fraussen, B., A. Albareda and C. Braun. (2020). 'Conceptualizing Consultation Approaches: Identifying Combinations of Consultation Tools and Analyzing Their Implications for Stakeholder Diversity'. *Policy Sciences 53*, no. 3 (25 April): 473–493.

Frederick, S., G. Loewenstein and T. O'Donoghue. (2002). 'Time Discounting and Time Preference: A Critical Review'. *Journal of Economic Literature 40*, no. 2: 351–401.

Frederiks, E. R., K. Stenner and E. V. Hobman. (2015). 'Household Energy Use: Applying Behavioural Economics to Understand Consumer Decision-Making and Behaviour'. *Renewable and Sustainable Energy Reviews 41*: 1385–1394.

Freiberg, A. (2018). 'Authority Tools: Pervasive, Persistent and Powerful'. In M. Howlett and I. Mukherjee (eds.), *Routledge Handbook of Policy Design*. New York: Routledge, 261–273.

Freeman, G. P. (1985). 'National Styles and Policy Sectors: Explaining Structured Variation'. *Journal of Public Policy 5*, no. 4: 467–496.

Freeman, J. (1997). 'Collaborative Governance in the Administrative State'. *UCLA Law Review 45*, no. 1: 77–177.

Freeman, J. L. and J. P. Stevens. (1987). 'A Theoretical and Conceptual Reexamination of Subsystem Politics'. *Public Policy and Administration 2*, no. 1: 9–24.

Freeman, J. R. (1989). *Democracy and Markets: The Politics of Mixed Economies*. Ithaca, NY: Cornell University Press.

French, R. (1980). *How Ottawa Decides: Planning and Industrial Policy-Making 1968–1980*. Toronto, ON: Lorimer.

Friedman, T. L. (1999). *The Lexus and the Olive Tree*. New York: HarperCollins.

Frischtak, C. R. (1995). 'The Changed Role of the State: Regulatory Policies and Reform in a Comparative Perspective'. In C. R. Frischtak (ed.), *Regulatory Policies and Reform: A Comparative Perspective*. New York: World Bank, 1–15.

Frye, T., O. J. Reuter and D. Szakonyi. (2012). *Political Machines at Work: Voter Mobilization and Electoral Subversion in the Workplace*. SSRN Scholarly Paper. Rochester, NY: Social Science Research Network. http://papers.ssrn.com/abstract=2110201

Fukuyama, F. (2013). 'What Is Governance?' *Governance 26*, no. 3: 347–368.

Fung, A. (2003). 'Survey Article: Recipes for Public Spheres: Eight Institutional Design Choices and Their Consequences'. *Journal of Political Philosophy 11*, no. 3 (1 September): 338–367.

Furlong, S. R. and C. M. Kerwin. (2004). 'Interest Group Participation in Rule Making: A Decade of Change'. *Journal of Public Administration Research and Theory 15*, no. 3: 353–370.

Gabrielian, V. and F. Fischer. (1996). 'Reforming Eastern European Bureaucracy: Does the American Experience Apply?' In H. K. Asmerom and E. P. Reis (eds), *Democratization and Bureaucratic Neutrality*. London: Macmillan, 109–126.

Gadamer, H. (1989). *Truth and Method*. New York: Cross Road.

Gage, R. W. and M. P. Mandell (eds.). (1990). *Strategies for Managing Intergovernmental Policies and Networks*. New York: Praeger.

Gailmard, S. and J. W. Patty. (2007). 'Slackers and Zealots: Civil Service, Policy Discretion, and Bureaucratic Expertise'. *American Journal of Political Science 51*, no. 4: 873–889.

Gains, F. and G. Stoker. (2011). 'Special Advisers and the Transmission of Ideas from the Policy Primeval Soup'. *Policy & Politics 39*, no. 4: 485–498.

Galanter, M. (1980). 'Legality and Its Discontents: A Preliminary Assessment of Current Theories of Legalization and Delegalization'. In E. Blankenburg, E. Klausa and H. Rottleuthner (eds.), *Alternative Rechtsforen und Alternativen Zum Recht*. Bonn, Germany: Westdeutscher Verlag, 11–26.

Galizzi, M. M. (2014). 'What Is Really Behavioral in Behavioral Health Policy? And Does It Work?' *Applied Economic Perspectives and Policy 36*, no. 1 (3 January): 25–60.

Gall, G. L. (1983). *The Canadian Legal System*. Toronto, ON: Carswell.

Gall, T., F. Vallet and B. Yannou. (2022). 'How to Visualise Futures Studies Concepts: Revision of the Futures Cone'. *Futures 143* (October): 103024.

Gandrud, C. and C. Grafström. (2015). 'Inflated Expectations: How Government Partisanship Shapes Monetary Policy Bureaucrats' Inflation Forecasts'. *Political Science Research and Methods 3*, no. 2: 353–380.

Gandy, O. H. (1982). *Beyond Agenda Setting: Information Subsidies and Public Policy*. Norwood, NJ: Ablex.

Ganghof, S. (2006). 'Tax Mixes and the Size of the Welfare State: Causal Mechanisms and Policy Implications'. *Journal of European Social Policy 16*, no. 4: 360–373.

Gans-Morse, J., S. Mazzuca and S. Nichter. (2014). 'Varieties of Clientelism: Machine Politics during Elections'. *American Journal of Political Science 58*, no. 2 (1 April): 415–432.

Ganuza, E. and F. Francés. (2012). 'The Deliberative Turn in Participation: The Problem of Inclusion and Deliberative Opportunities in Participatory Budgeting'. *European Political Science Review 2*, no. 2: 283–302.

GAO. (2014). *Standards for Internal Control in the Federal Government.* GAO-14-704G. www.gao.gov/assets/gao-14-704g.pdf

Garcia Martinez, M. (2015). 'Solver Engagement in Knowledge Sharing in Crowdsourcing Communities: Exploring the Link to Creativity'. *Research Policy 44*, no. 8 (October): 1419–1430.

Garcia-Murillo, M. (2005). 'Regulatory Responses to Convergence; Experience from Four Countries'. *Info – The Journal of Policy, Regulation and Strategy for Telecommunications 7*, no. 1: 20–40.

Garson, G. D. (1986). 'From Policy Science to Policy Analysis: A Quarter Century of Progress'. In W. N. Dunn (ed.), *Policy Analysis: Perspectives, Concepts and Methods.* Greenwich, CT: JAI Press, 3–22.

Gayle, D. J. and J. N. Goodrich (eds.). (1990). *Privatization and Deregulation in Global Perspective.* Westport, CT: Quorum Books.

Gehring, T. and S. Oberthur. (2009). 'The Causal Mechanisms of Interaction Between International Institutions'. *European Journal of International Relations 15*, no. 1: 125–156.

Gelders, D. and O. Ihlen. (2009). 'Minding the Gap: Applying a Service Marketing Model into Government Policy Communications'. *Government Information Quarterly 27*, no. 1: 34–40.

Gelders, D. and O. Ihlen. (2010). 'Government Communication about Potential Policies: Public Relations, Propaganda or Both?' *Public Relations Review 36*, no. 1: 59–62.

George, A. L. (1969). 'The "Operational Code": A Neglected Approach to the Study of Political Leaders and Decision-Making'. *International Studies Quarterly 13*: 190–222.

Gerard, D. and L. Lave. (2007). 'Experiments in Technology Forcing: Comparing the Regulatory Processes of US Automobile Safety and Emissions Regulations'. *International Journal of Technology, Policy and Management 7*, no. 1: 1.

Gero, J. S. (1990). 'Design Prototypes: A Knowledge Representation Schema for Design'. *Text Serial Journal 11*, no. 4 (15 December): 26–36.

Geva-May, I. and A. M. Maslove. (2006). 'Canadian Public Policy Analysis and Public Policy Programs: A Comparative Perspective'. *Journal of Public Affairs Education 12*, no. 4: 413–438.

Geva-May, I. and A. M. Maslove. (2007). 'In Between Trends: Developments of Public Policy Analysis and Policy Analysis Instruction in Canada, the United States and the European Union'. In L. Dobuzinskis, M. Howlett and D. Laycock (eds.), *Policy Analysis in Canada: The State of the Art.* Toronto, ON: University of Toronto Press, 186–216.

Gibson, R. B. (1999). *Voluntary Initiatives and the New Politics of Corporate Greening.* Toronto, ON: University of Toronto Press.

Giebels, D., A. van Buuren and J. Edelenbos. (2015). 'Using Knowledge in a Complex Decision-Making Process – Evidence and Principles from the Danish Houting

Project's Ecosystem-Based Management Approach'. *Environmental Science & Policy 47* (March): 53–67.

Gifford, R. and L. A. Comeau. (2011). 'Message Framing Influences Perceived Climate Change Competence, Engagement, and Behavioral Intentions'. *Global Environmental Change 21*, no. 4: 1301–1307.

Gilabert, P. and H. Lawford-Smith. (2012). 'Political Feasibility: A Conceptual Exploration'. *Political Studies 60*, no. 4: 809–825.

Gilardi, F. (2002). 'Policy Credibility and Delegation to Independent Regulatory Agencies: A Comparative Empirical Analysis'. *Journal of European Public Policy 9*, no. 6: 873–893.

Gilardi, F. (2005a). 'Evaluating Independent Regulators'. In OECD Working Party on Regulatory Management and Reform (ed.), *Designing Independent and Accountable Regulatory Authorities for High Quality Regulation – Proceedings of an Expert Meeting in London, United Kingdom 10–11 January 2005*. Paris: OECD, 101–125.

Gilardi, F. (2005b). 'The Formal Independence of Regulators: A Comparison of 17 Countries and 7 Sectors'. *Swiss Political Science Review 11*, no. 4: 139–167.

Gilardi, F. (2005c). 'The Institutional Foundations of Regulatory Capitalism: The Diffusion of Regulatory Agencies in Western Europe'. *Annals of the American Academy of Political and Social Science 595*, no. 1: 84–101.

Gill, N. N. (1940). 'Permanent Advisory Committees in the Federal Government'. *Journal of Politics 2*: 411–425.

Gilmore, T. N. and J. Krantz. (1991). 'Innovation in the Public Sector: Dilemmas in the Use of Ad Hoc Processes'. *Journal of Policy Analysis and Management 10*, no. 3: 455–468.

Gipperth, L. (2008). 'The Legal Design of the International and European Union Ban on Tributyltin Antifouling Paint: Direct and Indirect Effects'. *Journal of Environmental Management 90*, no. Supplement: S86–S95.

Givoni, M. (2014). 'Addressing Transport Policy Challenges through Policy-Packaging'. *Transportation Research Part A: Policy and Practice 60* (February): 1–8.

Givoni, M., J. Macmillen, D. Banister and E. Feitelson. (2012). 'From Policy Measures to Policy Packages'. *Transport Reviews 33*, no. 1: 1–20.

Gleeson, D. H., D. G. Legge and D. O'Neill. (2009). 'Evaluating Health Policy Capacity: Learning from International and Australian Experience'. *Australia and New Zealand Health Policy 6*, no. 1 (26 February).

Gleeson, D. H., D. Legge, D. O'Neill and M. Pfeffer. (2011). 'Negotiating Tensions in Developing Organizational Policy Capacity: Comparative Lessons to Be Drawn'. *Journal of Comparative Policy Analysis: Research and Practice 13*, no. 3 (June): 237–263.

Gleirscher, N. (2008). 'Policy Instruments in Support of Organic Farming in Austria'. *International Journal of Agricultural Resources, Governance and Ecology 7*, no. 1–2: 51–62.

Glennan, S. (2002). 'Rethinking Mechanistic Explanation'. *Proceedings of the Philosophy of Science Association*, no. 3: 342–353.

Glennerster, R. and K. Takavarasha. (2013). *Running Randomized Evaluations: A Practical Guide*. http://public.eblib.com/choice/publicfullrecord.aspx?p=1458376

Glicken, J. (2000). 'Getting Stakeholder Participation "Right": A Discussion of Participatory Processes and Possible Pitfalls'. *Environmental Science and Policy 3*: 305–310.

Goetz, A. M. (2007). 'Manouevring Past Clientelism: Institutions and Incentives to Generate Constituencies in Support of Governance Reforms'. *Commonwealth and Comparative Politics 45*, no. 4: 403–424.

Goffman, E. (1974). *Frame Analysis: An Essay on the Organization of Experience*. Cambridge, MA: Harvard University Press.

Goggin, M. L. (1987). *Policy Design and the Politics of Implementation: The Case of Child Health Care in the American States*. Knoxville, TN: University of Tennessee Press.

Goggin, M. L., A. O. M. Bowman, J. P. Lester and L. J. O'Toole. (1990). *Implementation Theory and Practice: Toward a Third Generation*. Glenview, IL: Scott, Foresman/Little, Brown.

Goldhamer, H. (1978). *The Adviser*. New York: Elsevier.

Goldmann, K. (2005). 'Appropriateness and Consequences: The Logic of Neo-Institutionalism'. *Governance 18*, no. 1: 35–52.

Goldsmith, S. and W. D. Eggers. (2004). *Governing by Network: The New Shape of the Public Sector*. Washington, DC: Brookings Institution.

Goldstein, J. and R. O. Keohane (eds.). *Ideas and Foreign Policy: Beliefs, Institutions and Political Change*. Ithaca, NY: Cornell University Press.

Goldstein, N. J., R. B. Cialdini, V. Griskevicius and J. D. Article. (2008). 'A Room with a Viewpoint: Using Social Norms to Motivate Environmental Conservation in Hotels'. *Journal of Consumer Research 35*, no. 3: 472–482.

González-Eguino, M. (2011). 'The Importance of the Design of Market-Based Instruments for CO_2 Mitigation: An Age Analysis for Spain'. *Ecological Economics 70*, no. 12 (October): 2292–2302.

Goodin, R. E. (1980). *Manipulatory Politics*. New Haven, CT: Yale University Press.

Goodin, R. E. and M. Rein. (2001). 'Regimes on Pillars: Alternative Welfare State Logics and Dynamics'. *Public Administration 79*, no. 4: 769–801.

Goodwin, T. (2012). 'Why We Should Reject "Nudge"'. *Politics 32*, no. 2: 85–92.

Gormley, W. T. (1989). *Taming the Bureaucracy: Muscles, Prayers and Other Strategies*. Princeton, NJ: Princeton University Press.

Gormley, W. T. (1998). 'Regulatory Enforcement'. *Political Research Quarterly 51*, no. 2: 363–383.

Gormley, W. T. (2007). 'Public Policy Analysis: Ideas and Impact'. *Annual Review of Political Science 10*: 297–313.

Gossum, P., B. Arts and K. Verheyen. (2010). 'From "Smart Regulation" to "Regulatory Arrangements"'. *Policy Sciences 43*, no. 3: 245–261.

Gough, C. and S. Shackley. (2001). 'The Respectable Politics of Climate Change: The Epistemic Communities and NGOs'. *International Affairs 77*: 329–346.

Goulder, L. H. and A. R. Schein. (2013). 'Carbon Taxes Versus Cap and Trade: A Critical Review'. *Climate Change Economics 4*, no. 3: 1–28.

Gourdet, C., K. C. Giombi, K. Kosa, J. Wiley and S. Cates. (2017). 'How Four U.S. States Are Regulating Recreational Marijuana Edibles'. *International Journal of Drug Policy 43* (May): 83–90.

Gourevitch, P. (2004). 'Corporate Governance: Global Markets, National Politics'. In M. Kahler and D. Lake (eds.), *Governance in a Global Economy*. Princeton, NJ: Princeton University Press, 305–331.

Government Communication Service. (2018). *Emergency Planning Framework*. https://3x7ip91ron4ju9ehf2unqrm1-wpengine.netdna-ssl.com/wp-content/uploads/2020/04/Emergency-planning-framework-1.pdf

Gow, J. I. and S. L. Sutherland. (2004). 'Comparison of Canadian Masters Programs in Public Administration, Public Management and Public Policy'. *Canadian Public Administration*. 47, no. 3: 379–405.

Goyal, N. and M. Howlett. (2019). 'Framework or Metaphor? Analysing the Status of Policy Learning in the Policy Sciences'. *Journal of Asian Public Policy 12*, no. *3* (2 September): 257–273.

Grabosky, P. N. (1994). 'Green Markets: Environmental Regulation by the Private Sector'. *Law and Policy 16*, no. *4*: 419–448.

Grabosky, P. N. (1995). 'Counterproductive Regulation'. *International Journal of the Sociology of Law 23*: 347–369.

Graham, K. A. and S. D. Phillips. (1997). 'Citizen Engagement: Beyond the Customer Revolution'. *Canadian Public Administration 40*, no. *2*: 225–273.

Grant, W. (2009). 'Intractable Policy Failure: The Case of Bovine TB and Badgers'. *British Journal of Politics and International Relations 11*: 557–573.

Grant, W. (2010). 'Policy Instruments in the Common Agricultural Policy'. *West European Politics 33*, no. *1*: 22–38.

Grant, W. and A. MacNamara. (1995). 'When Policy Communities Intersect: The Cases of Agriculture and Banking'. *Political Studies 43*: 509–515.

Grantham, A. (2001). 'How Networks Explain Unintended Policy Implementation Outcomes: The Case of UK Rail Privatization'. *Public Administration 79*, no. *4*: 851–870.

Grasmick, H. G., R. J. Bursik and K. A. Kinsey. (1991). 'Shame and Embarrassment as Deterrents to Noncompliance with the Law: The Case of an Antilittering Campaign'. *Environment and Behavior 23*, no. *2* (3 January): 233–251.

Graycar, A. (2015). 'Corruption: Classification and Analysis'. *Policy and Society 34*, no. *2* (1 June): 87–96.

Graycar, A. and T. Prenzler. (2013). *Understanding and Preventing Corruption* (2013 edn). London: Palgrave Pivot.

Greener, I. (2002). 'Understanding NHS Reform: The Policy-Transfer, Social Learning and Path Dependency Perspectives'. *Governance 15*, no. *2*: 161–183.

Greener, I. (2006). 'Markets in the Public Sector: When Do They Work and What Do We Do When They Don't'. *Policy and Politics 36*, no. *1*: 93–108.

Green-Pedersen, C. (2004). 'The Dependent Variable Problem within the Study of Welfare State Retrenchment: Defining the Problem and Looking for Solutions'. *Journal of Comparative Policy Analysis 6*, no. *1*: 3–14.

Greenstone, M. (2001). *The Impacts of Environmental Regulations on Industrial Activity: Evidence from the 1970 & 1977 Clean Air Act Amendments and the Census of Manufactures.* No. w8484. Washington, DC: National Bureau of Economic Research.

Greenwood, D. J. J. (2005). 'Democracy and Delaware: The Mysterious Race to the Bottom/Top'. *Yale Law and Policy Review 23*, no. *2*: 402–425.

Griffin, R. (2013). 'Auction Designs for Allocating Wind Energy Leases on the US Outer Continental Shelf'. *Energy Policy 56* (May): 603–611.

Grima, A. (1985). 'Participatory Rites: Integrating Public Involvement in Environmental Impact Assessment'. In J. B. R. Whitney and V. W. Maclaren (eds.), *Environmental Impact Assessment: The Canadian Experience.* Toronto, ON: University of Toronto Institute for Environmental Studies, 33–51.

Grimsey, D. and M. K. Lewis. (2004). *Public Private Partnerships: The Worldwide Revolution in Infrastructure Provision and Project Finance.* Cheltenham, UK: Edward Elgar.

Grimshaw, D., S. Vincent and H. Willmott. (2001). 'New Control Modes and Emergent Organizational Forms: Private – Public Contracting in Public Administration'. *Administrative Theory and Practice 23*, no. *3*: 407–430.

Grimshaw, J. M., M. P. Eccles, J. N. Lavis, S. J. Hill and J. E. Squires. (2012). 'Knowledge Translation of Research Findings'. *Implementation Science 7*, no. *1* (31 May): 50.

Grin, J. and H. V. De Graaf. (1996). 'Implementation as Communicative Action: An Interpretative Understanding of Interactions between Policy Actors and Target Groups'. *Policy Sciences 29*: 291–319.

Grohmann, P. and P. H. Feindt. (2023). 'The Importance of Calibration in Policy Mixes: Environmental Policy Integration in the Implementation of the European Union's Common Agricultural Policy in Germany (2014–2022)'. *Environmental Policy and Governance*. https://doi.org/10.1002/eet.2052

Gromet, D. M., H. Kunreuther and R. P. Larrick. (2013). 'Political Ideology Affects Energy-Efficiency Attitudes and Choices'. *Proceedings of the National Academy of Sciences 110*, no. 23: 9314–9319.

Gronn, P. (2009). 'Leadership Configurations'. *Leadership 5*, no. 3 (1 August): 381–394.

Gross, M. (2010). *Ignorance and Surprise: Science, Society, and Ecological Design*. Cambridge, MA: MIT Press.

Grossback, L. J., S. Nicholson-Crotty and D. A. Peterson. (2004). 'Ideology and Learning in Policy Diffusion'. *American Politics Research 32*, no. 5: 521–545.

Grüne-Yanoff, T. and R. Hertwig. (2016). 'Nudge Versus Boost: How Coherent are Policy and Theory?' *Minds and Machines 26*, no. 1–2: 149–183.

Gulbrandsen, L. H. (2010). *Transnational Environmental Governance: The Emergence and Effects of the Certification of Forests and Fisheries*. Cheltenham, UK: Edward Elgar.

Gullberg, A. T. and T. Skodvin. (2011). 'Cost Effectiveness and Target Group Influence in Norwegian Climate Policy'. *Scandinavian Political Studies 34*, no. 2 (1 June): 123–142.

Gunningham, N., P. Grabosky and D. Sinclair. (1998). *Smart Regulation: Designing Environmental Policy*. Oxford: Clarendon Press.

Gunningham, N. and J. Rees. (1997). 'Industry Self-Regulation: An Institutional Perspective'. *Law and Policy 19*, no. 4: 363–414.

Gunningham, N. and D. Sinclair. (1999a). 'New Generation Environmental Policy: Environmental Management Systems and Regulatory Reform'. *Melbourne University Law Review 22*, no. 3: 592–616.

Gunningham, N. and D. Sinclair. (1999b). 'Regulatory Pluralism: Designing Policy Mixes for Environmental Protection'. *Law and Policy 21*, no. 1: 49–76.

Gunningham, N. and D. Sinclair. (2002). *Leaders and Laggards: Next Generation Environmental Regulation*. Sheffield, UK: Greenleaf.

Gunningham, N. and M. D. Young. (1997). 'Toward Optimal Environmental Policy: The Case of Biodiversity Conservation'. *Ecology Law Quarterly 24*: 243–298.

Guo, C. (2007). 'When Government Becomes the Principal Philanthropist: The Effects of Public Funding on Patterns of Nonprofit Governance'. *Public Administration Review 67*, no. 3: 458–473.

Gupta, J., C. Termeer, J. Klostermann, S. Meijerink, M. van den Brink, P. Jong, S. Nooteboom and E. Bergsma. (2010). 'The Adaptive Capacity Wheel: A Method to Assess the Inherent Characteristics of Institutions to Enable the Adaptive Capacity of Society'. *Environmental Science & Policy 13*, no. 6 (October): 459–471.

Haas, E. B. (1958). *The Uniting of Europe: Political, Social and Economical Forces 1950–1957*. London: Stevens & Sons.

Haas, P. M. (1992). 'Introduction: Epistemic Communities and International Policy Coordination'. *International Organisation 46*: 1–36.

Haas, P. M. (2001). 'Policy Knowledge: Epistemic Communities'. In *International Encyclopedia of the Social and Behavioral Sciences*. Oxford: Pergamon, 11578–11586.

Haas, P. M. (2004). 'When Does Power Listen to Truth? A Constructivist Approach to the Policy Process'. *Journal of European Public Policy 11*, no. 4: 569–592.

Haasnoot, M., J. H. Kwakkel, W. E. Walker and J. ter Maat. (2013). 'Dynamic Adaptive Policy Pathways: A Method for Crafting Robust Decisions for a Deeply Uncertain World'. *Global Environmental Change 23*, no. 2: 485–498.

Haber, H. (2011). 'Regulating-for-Welfare: A Comparative Study of "Regulatory Welfare Regimes" in the Israeli, British, and Swedish Electricity Sectors'. *Law & Policy 33*, no. 1: 116–148.

Habermas, J. (1973). 'What Does a Legitimation Crisis Mean Today? Legitimation Problems in Late Capitalism'. *Social Research 40*, no. 4: 643–667.

Habermas, J. (1974). *Knowledge and Human Interests*. Boston, MA: Beacon Press.

Habermas, J. (1975). *Legitimation Crisis*. Boston, MA: Beacon Press.

Hacker, J. S. (2004a). 'Privatizing Risk without Privatizing the Welfare State: The Hidden Politics of Social Policy Retrenchment in the United States'. *American Political Science Review 98*: 243–260.

Hacker, J. S. (2004b). 'Reform Without Change, Change without Reform: The Politics of US Health Policy Reform in Comparative Perspective'. In M. A. Levin and M. Shapiro (eds.), *Transatlantic Policymaking in an Age of Austerity: Diversity and Drift*. Washington, DC: Georgetown University Press, 13–63.

Hacker, J. S. (2004c). 'Review Article: Dismantling the Health Care State? Political Institutions, Public Policies and the Comparative Politics of Health Reform'. *British Journal of Political Science*. 34: 693–724.

Hacker, J. S. (2005). 'Policy Drift: The Hidden Politics of US Welfare State Retrenchment'. In W. Streek and K. Thelen (eds.), *Beyond Continuity: Institutional Change in Advanced Political Economies*. Oxford: Oxford University Press, 40–82.

Hagman, W., D. Andersson, D. Västfjäll and G. Tinghög. (2015). 'Public Views on Policies Involving Nudges'. *Review of Philosophy and Psychology 6*, no. 3: 439–453.

Hahn, R. W. (2008). *Greenhouse Gas Auctions and Taxes: Some Practical Considerations*. Working Paper 8–12. Washington, DC: AEI Centre for Regulatory and Market Studies.

Hahn, R. W. and P. M. Dudley. (2007). 'How Well Does the U.S. Government Do Benefit-Cost Analysis?'. *Review of Environmental Economics and Policy 1*, no. 2 (1 July): 192–211.

Haider, D. (1989). 'Grants as a Tool of Public Policy'. In L. M. Salamon (ed.), *Beyond Privatization: The Tools of Government Action*. Washington, DC: Urban Institute, 93–124.

Haider, H., C. Mcloughlin and Z. Scott. (2011). *Communication and Governance*. Washington, DC: The World Bank.

Hajer, M. A. (1997). *The Politics of Environmental Discourse: Ecological Modernization and the Policy Process*. Oxford: Oxford University Press.

Hajer, M. A. (2005). 'Setting the Stage: A Dramaturgy of Policy Deliberation'. *Administration and Society 36*, no. 6: 624–647.

Halffman, W. and R. Hoppe. (2005). 'Science/Policy Boundaries: A Changing Division of Labour in Dutch Expert Policy Advice'. In S. Maasen and P. Weingart (eds.), *Democratization of Expertise?* Dordrecht, Netherlands: Springer, 135–151.

Hall, M. and K. Banting. (2000). 'The Nonprofit Sector in Canada: An Introduction'. In Keith Banting (ed.), *The NonProfit Sector in Canada: Roles and Relationships*. Montreal, QC: McGill-Queen's University Press, 1–28.

Hall, P. A. (1986). *Governing the Economy: The Politics of State Intervention in Britain and France*. Cambridge: Polity Press.

Hall, P. A. (1989a). 'Conclusion: The Political Power of Economic Ideas'. In P. A. Hall (ed.), *The Political Power of Economic Ideas: Keynesianism Across Nations*. Princeton, NJ: Princeton University Press, 361–392.

Hall, P. A. (1989b). *The Political Power of Economic Ideas: Keynesianism Across Nations*. Princeton, NJ: Princeton University Press.

Hall, P. A. (1990). 'Policy Paradigms, Experts, and the State: The Case of Macroeconomic Policy-Making in Britain'. In S. Brooks and A. G. Gagnon (eds.), *Social Scientists, Policy and the State*. New York: Praeger, 53–78.

Hall, P. A. (1992). 'The Change from Keynesianism to Monetarism: Institutional Analysis and British Economic Policy in the 1970s'. In S. Steinmo, K. Thelen and F. Longstreth (eds.), *Structuring Politics: Historical Institutionalism in Comparative Analysis*. Cambridge: Cambridge University Press, 90–114.

Hall, P. A. (1993). 'Policy Paradigms, Social Learning and the State: The Case of Economic Policy-Making in Britain'. *Comparative Politics 25*, no. 3: 275–296.

Hall, P. A. and D. Soskice. (2001). 'Varieties of Capitalism: The Institutional Foundations of Comparative Advantage'. In P. A. Hall and David Soskice (eds.), *An Introduction to Varieties of Capitalism*. New York: Oxford University Press, 1–70.

Hall, P. A. and R. C. R. Taylor. (1996). 'Political Science and the Three New Institutionalisms'. *Political Studies 44*: 936–957.

Hall, T. E. (2008). 'Steering Agencies with Short-Term Authorizations'. *Public Administration Review 68*, no. 2: 366–379.

Hall, T. E. and L. J. O'Toole. (2000). 'Structures for Policy Implementation: An Analysis of National Legislation, 1965–66 and 1993–94'. *Administration and Society 31*, no. 6: 667–686.

Hall, T. E. and L. J. O'Toole. (2004). 'Shaping Formal Networks through the Regulatory Process'. *Administration and Society 36*, no. 2: 186–207.

Halligan, J. (1995). 'Policy Advice and the Public Sector'. In B. G. Peters and D. T. Savoie (eds.), *Governance in a Changing Environment*. Montreal, QC: McGill-Queen's University Press, 138–172.

Halligan, J. and J. Power. (1992). *Political Management in the 1990's*. Melbourne: OUP Australia and New Zealand.

Hallsworth, M. (2016). *Behavioural Insights: The Road to "Better" Policies?* www.hertie-school.org/the-governance-post/2016/08/behavioural-insights-road-better-policies. Accessed 1 August.

Halpern, C. (2010). 'Governing Despite Its Instruments? Instrumentation in EU Environmental Policy'. *West European Politics 33*, no. 1: 39–57.

Halpern, D. (2015). *Inside the Nudge Unit: How Small Changes Can Make a Big Difference*. London: W. H. Allen.

Halpin, D. (2011). 'Explaining Policy Bandwagons: Organized Interest Mobilization and Cascades of Attention'. *Governance 24*, no. 2 (April): 205–230.

Halpin, D. and A. Binderkrantz. (2011). 'Explaining Breadth of Policy Engagement: Patterns of Interest Group Mobilization in Public Policy'. *Journal of European Public Policy 18*, no. 2 (March): 201–219.

Halpin, D. R., B. Fraussen and A. J. Nownes. (2018). 'The Balancing Act of Establishing a Policy Agenda: Conceptualizing and Measuring Drivers of Issue Prioritization Within Interest Groups'. *Governance 31*, no. 2 (1 April): 215–237.

Hamalainen, T., M. Kosonen and Y. L. Doz. (2012). *Strategic Agility in Public Management*. SSRN Scholarly Paper. Rochester, NY: Social Science Research Network (12 March). http://papers.ssrn.com/abstract=2020436.

Hamdouch, A. and M.-H. Depret. (2010). 'Policy Integration Strategy and the Development of the "Green Economy": Foundations and Implementation Patterns'. *Journal of Environmental Planning and Management 53*, no. 4: 473.

Hamelin, F. (2010). 'Renewal of Public Policy via Instrumental Innovation: Implementing Automated Speed Enforcement in France'. *Governance 23*, no. 3: 509–530.

Hammersley, M. (2005). 'Is the Evidence-Based Practice Movement Doing More Good Than Harm? Reflections on Iain Chalmers' Case for Research-Based Policy Making and Practice'. *Evidence & Policy 1*, no. 1: 85–100.

Hammond, T. H. (1986). 'Agenda Control, Organizational Structure, and Bureaucratic Politics'. *American Journal of Political Science 30*, no. 2: 379–420.

Hammond, T. H. and J. H. Knott. (1988). 'The Deregulatory Snowball: Explaining Deregulation in the Financial Industry'. *Journal of Politics 50*, no. 1: 3–30.

Hammond, T. H. and J. H. Knott. (1999). 'Political Institutions, Public Management, and Policy Choice'. *Journal of Public Administration Research and Theory 9*, no. 1: 33–85.

Hanberger, A. (2003). 'Public Policy and Legitimacy: A Historical Policy Analysis of the Interplay of Public Policy and Legitimacy'. *Policy Sciences 36*: 257–258.

Hancock, T. and C. Bezold. (1994). 'Possible Futures, Preferable Futures'. *The Healthcare Forum Journal 37*, no. 2: 23–29.

Hanke, S. H. and S. J. K. Walters. (1990). 'Privatization and Public Choice: Lessons for the LDCs'. In D. J. Gayle and J. N. Goodrich (eds.), *Privatization and Deregulation in Global Perspective*. New York: Quorum Books, 97–108.

Hansen, R., N. Fruntzeskaki, T. McPhearson, E. Roll, N. Kabisch, A. Kaczorowska, J.-H. Kain, M. Artmann and S. Pauleil. (2015). 'The Uptake of the Ecosystem Services Concept in Planning Discourses of European and American Cities'. *Ecosystem Services 12* (April): 228–246.

Hanson, M. (1974). 'Organizational Bureaucracy in Latin America and the Legacy of Spanish Colonialism'. *Journal of Inter-American Studies and World Affairs 16*, no. 2: 199–219.

Hansson, S. O. (1996). 'Decision Making Under Great Uncertainty'. *Philosophy of the Social Sciences 26*, no. 3 (9 January): 369–386.

Hansson, S. O. (2018). 'Defensive Semiotic Strategies in Government: A Multimodal Study of Blame Avoidance'. *Social Semiotics 28*, no. 4 (8 August): 472–493.

Hardiman, N. and C. Scott. (2010). 'Governance as Polity: An Institutional Approach to the Evolution of State Functions in Ireland'. *Public Administration 88*, no. 1: 170–189.

Hardin, G. (1968). 'The Tragedy of the Commons'. *Science 162*: 1243–1248.

Hardin, R. (1982). *Collective Action*. Baltimore, MD: Johns Hopkins University Press.

Hardisty, D. J., E. J. Johnson and E. U. Weber. (2010). 'A Dirty Word or a Dirty World? Attribute Framing, Political Affiliation, and Query Theory'. *Psychological Science 21*, no. 1: 86–92.

Hardy, K. (2010). *Managing Risk in Government: An Introduction to Enterprise Risk Management*. IBM Center for the Business of Government. http://enterrasolutions.com/media/docs/2013/09/RiskinGovernment.pdf

Hargadon, A. B. and Y. Douglas. (2001). 'When Innovations Meet Institutions: Edison and the Design of the Electric Light'. *Administrative Science Quarterly 46*, no. 3: 476.

Hargrove, E. L. (1975). *The Missing Link: The Study of the Implementation of Social Policy*. Washington, DC: Urban Institute.

Harring, N. (2016). 'Reward or Punish? Understanding Preferences toward Economic or Regulatory Instruments in a Cross-National Perspective'. *Political Studies 64*, no. 3 (1 October): 573–592.

Harrington, W., R. D. Morgenstern and T. Sterner. (2004). 'Comparing Instrument Choices'. In W. Harrington, R. D. Morgenstern and T. Sterner (eds.), *Choosing Environmental Policy: Comparing Instruments and Outcomes in the United States and Europe*. Washington, DC: RFF Press, 1–22.

Harris, P. (2007). 'Collective Action on Climate Change: The Logic of Regime Failure'. *Natural Resources 47*, no. 1: 195–224.

Harris, R. and S. Milkis. (1989). *The Politics of Regulatory Change*. New York: Oxford University Press.

Harris, S. L. (2004). 'Financial Sector Reform in Canada: Interests and the Policy Process'. *Canadian Journal of Political Science 37*, no. 1: 161–184.

Harrison, D., A. Foss, P. Klevnas and D. Radov. (2011). *Economic Policy Instruments for Reducing Greenhouse Gas Emissions*. www.oxfordhandbooks.com/view/10.1093/oxfordhb/9780199566600.001.0001/oxfordhb-9780199566600-e-35

Harrison, K. (1999). 'Retreat from Regulation: The Evolution of the Canadian Environmental Regulatory Regime'. In G. B. Doern, R. J. Schultz and M. M. Hill (eds.), *Changing the Rules: Canadian Regulatory Regimes and Institutions*. Toronto, ON: University of Toronto Press, 122–142.

Harrison, K. and L. M. Sundstrom (eds.). (2010). *Global Commons, Domestic Decisions: The Comparative Politics of Climate Change*. Cambridge, MA; London: The MIT Press.

Harrop, M. (1992). *Power and Policy in Liberal Democracies*. Cambridge: Cambridge University Press.

Hart, O. (2017). 'Incomplete Contracts and Control'. *American Economic Review 107*, no. 7: 1731–1752.

Harter, P. J. and G. C. Eads. (1985). 'Policy Instruments, Institutions and Objectives: An Analytical Framework for Assessing "Alternatives" to Regulation'. *Administrative Law Review 37*: 221–258.

Hartle, D. G. (1978). *The Expenditure Budget Process in the Government of Canada*. Toronto, ON: Canadian Tax Foundation.

Hartley, K. and Howlett, M. (2021). 'Policy Assemblages and Policy Resilience: Lessons for Non-Design from Evolutionary Governance Theory'. *Politics and Governance 9*, no. 2: 451–459.

Hartley, K. and G. Kuecker. (2021). *The Epistemics of Public Policy in an Age of Disruption*. Cambridge: Cambridge University Press.

Hartley, K., G. Kuecker and J. J. Woo. (2019). 'Practicing Public Policy in an Age of Disruption'. *Policy Design and Practice 2*, no. 2: 163–181.

Harvey, G. E. (2012). 'The Process of Risk Management: Important Steps to Take'. *Petroleum Accounting and Financial Management Journal 31*, no. 1: 77.

Hasan, S. and J. Onyx (eds.). (2008). *Comparative Third Sector Governance in Asia*. Dordrecht, The Netherlands: Springer.

Haseltine, W. A. (2013). *Affordable Excellence: The Singapore Healthcare Story: How to Create and Manage Sustainable Healthcare Systems*. Washington, DC: Brookings Institution Press.

Hastak, M., M. B. Mazes and L. A. Morris. (2001). 'The Role of Consumer Surveys in Public Policy Decision Making'. *Journal of Public Policy and Marketing 20*, no. 2: 170–185.

Hatvani, E. N. C. (2015). 'Risk Analysis and Risk Management in the Public Sector and in Public Auditing'. *Public Finance Quarterly 1*, no. 7: 7–28.

Haufler, V. (2000). 'Private Sector International Regimes'. In R. A. Higgott, G. R. D. Underhill and A. Bieler (eds.), *Non-State Actors and Authority in the Global System*. London: Routledge, 121–137.

Haufler, V. (2001). *A Public Role for the Private Sector: Industry Self-Regulation in a Global Economy*. Washington, DC: Carnegie Endowment for International Peace.

Hausman, D. M. and B. Welch. (2010). 'Debate: To Nudge or Not to Nudge'. *Journal of Political Philosophy 18*, no. 1: 123–136.

Hawke, G. R. (1993). *Improving Policy Advice*. Wellington, NZ: Victoria University Institute of Policy Studies.

Hawkesworth, M. (1992). 'Epistemology and Policy Analysis'. In W. Dunn and R. M. Kelly (eds), *Advances in Policy Studies*. New Brunswick, NJ: Transaction, 291–329.

Hawkins, K. and J. M. Thomas. (1989). 'Making Policy in Regulatory Bureaucracies'. In K. Hawkins and J. M. Thomas (eds.), *Making Regulatory Policy*. Pittsburgh, PA: University of Pittsburgh Press, 3–30.

Hay, C. (2006). 'Globalization and Public Policy'. In M. Moran, M. Rein and R. E. Goodin (eds.), *The Oxford Handbook of Public Policy*. Oxford: Oxford University Press, 587–604.

Hay, C. and N. J.-A. Smith. (2010). 'How Policy-Makers (Really) Understand Globalization: The Internal Architecture of Anglophone Globalization Discourse in Europe'. *Public Administration 88*, no. 4: 903–927.

Haydu, J. (1998). 'Making Use of the Past: Time Periods as Cases to Compare and as Sequences of Problem Solving'. *American Journal of Sociology 104*, no. 2: 339–371.

Haydu, J. (2010). 'Reversals of Fortune: Path Dependency, Problem Solving, and Temporal Cases'. *Theory and Society 39*, no. 1: Article 25.

Hayes, M. T. (1992). *Incrementalism and Public Policy*. New York: Longmans.

Hayes, M. T. (2007). 'Policy Making Through Disjointed Incrementalism'. In G. Morcol (ed.), *Handbook of Decision Making*. New York: CRC/Taylor & Francis, 39–59.

Haynes, K. E. and Q. Li. (1993). 'Policy Analysis and Uncertainty: Lessons from the IVHS Transportation Development Process'. *Computers, Environment and Urban Systems 17*, no. 1 (January): 1–14.

Hayoz, N. (2015). 'Cultures of Informality and Networks of Power in POST-SOVIET NON-Democracies'. In K. Van Assche, R. Beunen and M. Duineveld (eds.), *Evolutionary Governance Theory*. Cham: Springer, 73–85.

Head, B. W. (2008). 'Three Lenses of Evidence-Based Policy'. *Australian Journal of Public Administration 67*, no. 1: 1–11.

Head, B. W. (2010). 'Reconsidering Evidence-Based Policy: Key Issues and Challenges'. *Policy and Society 29*, no. 2: 77–94.

Head, B. W. (2019). 'Forty Years of Wicked Problems Literature: Forging Closer Links to Policy Studies'. *Policy and Society 38*, no. 2: 180–197.

Head, B. W. and J. Alford. (2015). 'Wicked Problems: Implications for Public Policy and Management'. *Administration & Society 47*, no. 6: 711–739.

Head, B. W. and K. Crowley (eds.). (2015). *Policy Analysis in Australia*. International Library of Policy Analysis. Bristol: Policy Press.

Heady, F. (1996). 'Configurations of Civil Service Systems'. In H. A. G. M. Bekke, J. L. Perry and T. A. J. Toonen (eds.), *Civil Service Systems in Comparative Perspective*. Bloomington, IN: Indiana University Press, 207–226.

Heald, D. (1990). 'The Relevance of Privatization to Developing Economies'. *Public Administration and Development 10*, no. 1.

Heclo, H. (1974). *Modern Social Politics in Britain and Sweden: From Relief to Income Maintenance*. New Haven, CT: Yale University Press.

Hedström, P. and R. Swedberg. (1996). 'Social Mechanisms'. *Acta Sociologica 39*, no. 3 (1 July): 281–308.

Hedström, P. and R. Swedberg (eds.). (1998). *Social Mechanisms: An Analytical Approach to Social Theory*. Cambridge; New York: Cambridge University Press.

Hedström, P. and P. Ylikoski. (2010). 'Causal Mechanisms in the Social Sciences'. *Annual Review of Sociology 36*, no. 1: 49–67.

Heggers, D., M. Lamers, A. van Zeijl-Rozema and C. Dieperink. (2012). 'Conceptualising Joint Knowledge Production in Regional Climate Change Adaptation Projects: Success Conditions and Levers for Action'. *Environmental Science & Policy 18* (April): 52–65.

Heidbreder, E. (2011). 'Structuring the European Administrative Space: Policy Instruments of Multi-Level Administration'. *Journal of European Public Policy 18*, no. 4: 709–727.

Heilman, J. G. and R. W. Walsh. (1992). 'Introduction: Energy Program Evaluation and Policy Design'. *Policy Studies Journal 20*, no. 1: 42–47.

Heinmiller, B. T. (2007). 'The Politics of "Cap and Trade" Policies'. *Natural Resources Journal 47*, no. 2: 445–467.

Heinmiller, B. T., M. A. Hennigar and S. Kopec. (2017). 'Degenerative Politics and Youth Criminal Justice Policy in Canada'. *Politics & Policy 45*, no. 3 (June): 405–431.

Heinrichs, H. (2005). 'Advisory Systems in Pluralistic Knowledge Societies: A Criteria-Based Typology to Assess and Optimize Environmental Policy Advice'. In S. Maasen and P. Weingart (eds.), *Democratization of Expertise? Exploring Novel Forms of Scientific Advice in Political Decision-Making*. Dordrecht, The Netherlands: Springer, 41–61.

Heinz, J. P., E. O. Laumann, R. H. Salisbury and R. L. Nelson. (1990). 'Inner Circles or Hollow Cores'. *Journal of Politics 52*, no. 2: 356–390.

Held, D., A. McGrew, D. Goldblatt and J. Perraton. (1999). *Global Transformations: Politics, Economics and Culture*. Cambridge: Polity Press.

Helleiner, E. (1994). *States and the Reemergence of Global Finance*. Ithaca, NY: Cornell University Press.

Helms, L. B., S. B. Kurtt and A. B. Henkin. (1993). 'Assuring Failure: Implementation Design and Policy Environment of a Federal Program Provision'. *The American Review of Public Administration 23*, no. 3 (1 September): 263–277.

Hendrick, R. (1994). 'A Heuristic Approach to Policy Analysis and the Use of Sensitivity Analysis'. *Public Productivity & Management Review 18*, no. 1: 37–55.

Hendriks, C. (2009a). 'Deliberative Governance in the Context of Power'. *Policy and Society 28*, no. 3: 173–184.

Hendriks, C. (2009b). 'Policy Design Without Democracy? Making Democratic Sense of Transition Management'. *Policy Sciences 42*, no. 4: 341–368.

Hendriks, C. and L. Carson. (2008). 'Can the Market Help the Forum? Negotiating the Commercialization of Deliberative Democracy'. *Policy Sciences 41*, no. 4: 293–313.

Hennicke, P. (2004). 'Scenarios for a Robust Policy Mix: The Final Report of the German Study Commission on Sustainable Energy Supply'. *Energy Policy 32*, no. *15* (October): 1673–1678.

Henriques, I. and P. Sadorsky. (2008). 'Voluntary Environmental Programs: A Canadian Perspective'. *Policy Studies Journal 36*, no. *1*: 143–166.

Heritier, A. (2001). 'Market Integration and Social Cohesion: The Politics of Public Services in European Regulation'. *Journal of European Public Policy 8*, no. *5*: 825–852.

Heritier, A. and D. Lehmkuhl. (2008). 'Introduction: The Shadow of Hierarchy and New Modes of Governance'. *Journal of Public Policy 28*, no. *1*: 1–17.

Heritier, A. and S. Eckert. (2008). 'New Modes of Governance in the Shadow of Hierarchy: Self-Regulation by Industry in Europe'. *Journal of Public Policy 28*, no. *1*: 113–138.

Heritier, A., C. Knill and S. Mingers. (1996). *Ringing the Changes in Europe: Regulatory Competition and the Transformation of the State. Britain, France, Germany.* Berlin, Germany: Walter de Gruyter.

Hermann, C. F. (1982). 'Instruments of Foreign Policy'. In P. Callahan, L. P. Brady and M. G. Hermann (eds.), *Describing Foreign Policy Behaviour*. Beverly Hills, CA: Sage, 153–174.

Hernes, G. (1976). 'Structural Change in Social Processes'. *American Journal of Sociology 82*, no. *3*: 513–547.

Herranz, J. (2007). 'The Multisectoral Trilemma of Network Management'. *Journal of Public Administration Research and Theory 18*, no. *1*: 1–31.

Herrick, C. (2004). 'Objectivity Versus Narrative Coherence: Science, Environmental Policy and the US Data Quality Act'. *Environmental Science and Policy 7*, no. *5*: 419–433.

Hesse, J. J. (1997). 'Rebuilding the State: Public Sector Reform in Central and Eastern Europe'. In J.-E. Lane (ed.), *Public Sector Reform: Rationale, Trends and Problems*. London: Sage, 114–145.

Hessing, M., M. Howlett and T. Summerville. (2005). *Canadian Natural Resource and Environmental Policy: Political Economy and Public Policy*. Vancouver, BC: University of British Columbia Press.

Hickle, G. T. (2014). 'Moving Beyond the "Patchwork": A Review of Strategies to Promote Consistency for Extended Producer Responsibility Policy in the US'. *Journal of Cleaner Production 64*, no. *1*: 266–276.

Hicklin, A. and E. Godwin. (2009). 'Agents of Change: The Role of Policy Managers in Public Policy'. *Policy Studies Journal 37*, no. *1*: 13–20.

Hicks, R. and P. Watson. (2007). *Policy Capacity: Strengthening the Public Service's Support to Elected Officials*. Edmonton, AB: Government of Alberta.

Hilgartner, S. and C. L. Bosk. (1988). 'The Rise and Fall of Social Problems: A Public Arenas Model'. *American Journal of Sociology 94*, no. *1*: 53–78.

Hill, C. J. and L. E. Lynn. (2004). 'Is Hierarchical Governance in Decline? Evidence from Empirical Research'. *Journal of Public Administration Research and Theory 15*, no. *2*: 173–195.

Hill, M. and P. L. Hupe. (2006). 'Analysing Policy Processes as Multiple Governance: Accountability in Social Policy'. *Policy and Politics 34*, no. *3*: 557–573.

Hill, M. and P. L. Hupe. (2014). *Implementing Public Policy: An Introduction to the Study of Operational Governance* (3rd edn). London: Sage.

Hillier, B. and A. Leaman. (1974). 'How is Design Possible: A Sketch for a Theory'. *DMG-DRS Journal: Design Research and Methods 8*, no. *1*: 40–50.

Hillier, B., J. Musgrave and P. O'Sullivan. (1972). 'Knowledge and Design'. In W. J. Mitchell (ed.), *Environmental Design: Research and Practice*. Los Angeles, CA: University of California, 29.3.1–29.3.14.

Hills, J. and M. Michalis. (2000). 'Restructuring Regulation: Technological Convergence and European Telecommunications and Broadcasting Markets'. *Review of International Political Economy 7*, no. *3*: 434–464.

Hinterleitner, M. (2018). 'Policy Failures, Blame Games and Changes to Policy Practice'. *Journal of Public Policy 38*, no. 2 (June): 221–242.

Hinterleitner, M. (2020). *Policy Controversies and Political Blame Games*. Cambridge Studies in Comparative Public Policy. Cambridge: Cambridge University Press.

Hippes, G. (1988). 'New Instruments for Environmental Policy: A Perspective'. *International Journal of Social Economics 15*, no. *3–4*: 42–51.

Hira, A., D. Huxtable and A. Leger. (2005). 'Deregulation and Participation: An International Survey of Participation in Electricity Regulation'. *Governance 18*, no. *1*: 53–88.

Hird, J. A. (2005a). 'Policy Analysis for What? The Effectiveness of Nonpartisan Policy Research Organizations'. *Policy Studies Journal 33*, no. *1*: 83–105.

Hird, J. A. (2005b). *Power, Knowledge and Politics: Policy Analysis in the States*. Washington, DC: Georgetown University Press.

Hird, J. A. (ed.). (2018). *Policy Analysis in the United States*. Bristol: Policy Press.

HM Government. (2020). *The Orange Book – Management of Risk – Principles and Concepts*. London: HM Government. https://assets.publishing.service.gov.uk/government/uploads/system/uploads/attachment_data/file/866117/6.6266_HMT_Orange_Book_Update_v6_WEB.PDF

HM Treasury. (2016). *Audit and Risk Assurance Committee Handbook*. London: HM Treasury. https://assets.publishing.service.gov.uk/government/uploads/system/uploads/attachment_data/file/512760/PU1934_Audit_committee_handbook.pdf. Accessed 9 October 2020.

HM Treasury. (2017). *Corporate Governance in Central Government Departments: Code of Good Practice*. London: HM Treasury. https://assets.publishing.service.gov.uk/government/uploads/system/uploads/attachment_data/file/609903/PU2077_code_of_practice_2017.pdf

HM Treasury. (2019). *Guidance Code of Conduct for Board Members of Public Bodies*. Gov.UK (June). www.gov.uk/government/publications/code-of-conduct-for-board-members-of-public-bodies/code-of-conduct-for-board-members-of-public-bodies-june-2019. Accessed 9 October 2020.

Hoberg, G. (1996). 'Putting Ideas in Their Place: A Response to "Learning and Change in the British Columbia Forest Policy Sector"'. *Canadian Journal of Political Science 29*, no. *1*: 135–144.

Hoberg, G. and E. Morawaski. (1997). 'Policy Change Through Sector Intersection: Forest and Aboriginal Policy in Clayoquot Sound'. *Canadian Public Administration 40*, no. *3*: 387–414.

Hobson, J. and M. Ramesh. (2002). 'Globalisation Makes of States What States Make of It: Between Agency and Structure in the State/Globalisation Debate'. *New Political Economy 7*, no. *1*: 5–22.

Hobson, K. and S. Niemeyer. (2013). '"What Sceptics Believe": The Effects of Information and Deliberation on Climate Change Scepticism'. *Public Understanding of Science 22*, no. *4*: 396–412.

Hodge, G. A. and C. Greve. (2007). 'Public – Private Partnerships: An International Performance Review'. *Public Administration Review* (May–June): 545–558.

Hodgetts, J. E. (1955). *Pioneer Public Service: An Administrative History of the United Canadas, 1841–1867*. Toronto, ON: University of Toronto Press.

Hodgetts, J. E. (1964). 'Challenge and Response: A Retrospective View of the Public Service of Canada'. *Canadian Public Administration 7*, no. 4: 409–421.

Hodgetts, J. E. (1973). *The Canadian Public Service: A Physiology of Government 1867–1970*. Toronto, ON: University of Toronto Press.

Hodgetts, J. E., G. B. Doern, V. S. Wilson and R. Whitaker. (1972). *The Biography of an Institution: The Civil Service Commission of Canada, 1908–1967*. Kingston, ON: McGill-Queen's University Press.

Hoek, J. and B. King. (2008). 'Food Advertising and Self-Regulation: A View from the Trenches'. *Australian and New Zealand Journal of Public Health 32*, no. 3: 261–265.

Hofferbert, R. I. (1974). *The Study of Public Policy*. Indianapolis: Bobbs-Merrill.

Hoffmann, M. J. (2011). *Climate Governance at the Crossroads: Experimenting with a Global Response After Kyoto*. Oxford: Oxford University Press.

Hofstede, G. (1980). *Culture's Consequences: International Differences in Work-Related Values*. Beverly Hills, CA: Sage.

Hogan, J. and M. Howlett (eds.). (2015). *Policy Paradigms in Theory and Practice*. Cheltenham, UK: Palgrave.

Hogan, J. and M. Howlett. (2015). 'Reflections on Our Understanding of Policy Paradigms and Policy Change'. In J. Hogan and M. Howlett (eds.), *Policy Paradigms in Theory and Practice. Studies in the Political Economy of Public Policy*. Basingstoke, UK: Palgrave Macmillan, 3–18.

Hogan, J., M. Howlett and M. Murphy. (2022). 'Re-Thinking the Coronavirus Pandemic as a Policy Punctuation: COVID-19 as a Path-Clearing Policy Accelerator'. *Policy and Society 41*, no. 1 (1 March): 40–52.

Hogwood, B. W. and B. G. Peters. (1982). 'The Dynamics of Policy Change: Policy Succession'. *Policy Sciences 14*, no. 3: 225–245.

Holland, S. P. and M. R. Moore. (2013). 'Market Design in Cap and Trade Programs: Permit Validity and Compliance Timing'. *Journal of Environmental Economics and Management 66*, no. 3 (November): 671–687.

Hollander, M. J. and M. J. Prince. (1993). 'Analytical Units in Federal and Provincial Governments: Origins, Functions and Suggestions for Effectiveness'. *Canadian Public Administration 36*, no. 2: 190–224.

Holling, C. S. (1973). 'Resilience and Stability of Ecological Systems'. *Annual Review of Ecology and Systematics 4*, no. 1: 1–23.

Ho Kyeong Jang. (2018). 'Mooncare: South Korea's Proposed Health Insurance Reform in Full'. *Korea Expose* (31 May). www.koreaexpose.com/mooncare-south-korea-proposed-health-insurance-reform/

Holmberg, S. and B. Rothstein. (2012). *Good Government: The Relevance of Political Science*. Cheltenham, UK; Northampton, MA: Edward Elgar.

Holmström, B. and P. Milgrom. (1991). 'Multitask Principal-Agent Analyses: Incentive Contracts, Asset Ownership, and Job Design'. *Journal of Law, Economics, and Organization 7*: 24–52.

Holt, D. and R. Barkemeyer. (2012). 'Media Coverage of Sustainable Development Issues – Attention Cycles or Punctuated Equilibrium?' *Sustainable Development 20*, no. 1: 1–17.

Holtmann, A. G. and D. L. Weimer. (1991). 'Beyond Efficiency: Economics and Distributional Analysis'. In *Policy Analysis and Economics: Developments, Tensions, Prospects*. Boston: Kluwer, 45–64.

Holzinger, K. (2005). 'Tax Competition and Tax Co-Operation in the EU: The Case of Savings Taxation'. *Rationality and Society 17*: 475–510.

Hondeghem, A. (2011). 'Changing Public Service Bargains for Top Officials'. *Public Policy and Administration 26*, no. 2 (5 April): 159–165.

Hood, C. (1983). 'Using Bureaucracy Sparingly'. *Public Administration 61*, no. 2: 197–208.

Hood, C. (1986a). *Administrative Analysis: An Introduction to Rules, Enforcement and Organizations*. Brighton, UK: Wheatsheaf.

Hood, C. (1986b). 'The Hidden Public Sector: The "Quangocratization" of the World?' In F.-X. Kaufman, G. Majone and V. Ostrom (eds.), *Guidance, Control and Evaluation in the Public Sector*. Berlin, Germany: Walter de Gruyter, 183–207.

Hood, C. (1986c). *The Tools of Government*. London: Chatham House.

Hood, C. (1991). 'A Public Management for All Seasons?' *Public Administration 69* (Spring): 3–19.

Hood, C. (1993). 'The Hidden Side of the American Welfare States'. *Political Science Quarterly 108*, no. 3: 403–436.

Hood, C. (1995). 'Contemporary Public Management: A New Global Paradigm?' *Public Policy and Administration 10*, no. 2: 104–117.

Hood, C. (2002a). 'Control, Bargains and Cheating: The Politics of Public Service Reform'. *Journal of Public Administration Research and Theory 12*, no. 3: 309–332.

Hood, C. (2002b). 'The Risk Game and the Blame Game'. *Government and Opposition 37*, no. 1: 15–54.

Hood, C. (2002c). 'Tax Expenditures'. In L. M. Salamon (ed.), *The Tools of Government: A Guide to the New Governance*. New York: Oxford University Press, 410–444.

Hood, C. (2004). 'Controlling Public Services and Government: Towards a Cross-National Perspective'. In C. Hood, O. James, B. G. Peter and C. Scott (eds.), *Controlling Modern Government; Variety, Commonality and Change*. Cheltenham, UK: Edward Elgar, 3–21.

Hood, C. (2006). 'The Tools of Government in the Information Age'. In M. Moran, M. Rein and R. E. Goodin (eds.), *The Oxford Handbook of Public Policy*. New York: Oxford University Press, 469–481.

Hood, C. (2007a). 'Intellectual Obsolescence and Intellectual Makeovers: Reflections on the Tools of Government After Two Decades'. *Governance 20*, no. 1: 127–144.

Hood, C. (2007b). 'What Happens When Transparency Meets Blame-Avoidance?' *Public Management Review 9*, no. 2: 191–210.

Hood, C. (2010). *The Blame Game: Spin, Bureaucracy, and Self-Preservation in Government*. Princeton, NJ: Princeton University Press.

Hood, C. and H. Z. Margetts. (2007). *The Tools of Government in the Digital Age*. Basingstoke, UK: Palgrave Macmillan.

Hood, C., C. Scott, O. James, G. Jones and T. Travers. (1999). *Regulation Inside Government: Waste-Watchers, Quality Police and Sleazebusters*. Oxford: Oxford University Press.

Hooghe, L. and G. Marks. (2003). 'Unraveling the Central State, But How? Types of Multi-Level Governance'. *American Political Science Review 97*, no. 2: 233–243.

Hoogvelt, A. (1997). *Globalisation and the Postcolonial World*. Basingstoke, UK: Macmillan, 134–139.

Hopkin, P. (2018). *Fundamentals of Risk Management: Understanding, Evaluating and Implementing Effective Risk Management*. London: Kogan Page Publishers.

Hoppe, R. (1999). 'Policy Analysis, Science and Politics: From "Speaking Truth to Power" to "Making Sense Together"'. *Science and Public Policy 26*, no. 3: 201–210.

Hoppe, R. (2017). 'Heuristics for Practitioners of Policy Design: Rules-of-Thumb for Structuring Unstructured Problems'. *Public Policy and Administration 33*, no. 4 (1 October): 384–408.

Hoppe, R. and M. Jeliazkova. (2006). 'How Policy Workers Define Their Job: A Netherlands Case Study'. In H. K. Colebatch (ed.), *The Work of Policy: An International Survey*. New York: Rowman & Littlefield, 35–60.

Hornik, R. (1989). 'The Knowledge-Behavior Gap in Public Information Campaigns'. In C. Salmon (ed.), *Information Campaigns: Managing the Process of Social Change*. Newbury Park, CA: Sage.

Hosseus, D. and L. A. Pal. (1997). 'Anatomy of a Policy Area: The Case of Shipping'. *Canadian Public Policy 23*, no. 4: 399–416.

Hou, Y. and G. Brewer. (2010). 'Substitution and Supplementation Between Co-Functional Policy Instruments: Evidence from State Budget Stabilization Practices'. *Public Administration Review 70*, no. 6: 914–924.

Hovik, S. and K. B. Stokke. (2007). 'Network Governance and Policy Integration – The Case of Regional Coastal Zone Planning in Norway'. *European Planning Studies 15*, no. 7: 927–944.

Howard, C. (1995). 'Testing the Tools Approach: Tax Expenditures Versus Direct Expenditures'. *Public Administration Review 55*, no. 5: 439–447.

Howard, C. (1997). *The Hidden Welfare State: Tax Expenditures and Social Policy in the United States*. Princeton, NJ: Princeton University Press.

Howard, C. (2002). 'Tax Expenditures'. In L. M. Salamon (ed.), *The Tools of Government: A Guide to the New Governance*. New York: Oxford University Press, 410–444.

Howard, J. L. and W. T. Stanbury. (1984). 'Measuring Leviathan: The Size, Scope and Growth of Governments in Canada'. In G. Lermer (ed.), *Probing Leviathan: An Investigation of Government in the Economy*. Vancouver, BC: Fraser Institute.

Howe, R. B. and D. Johnson. (2000). *Restraining Equality: Human Rights Commissions in Canada*. Toronto, ON: University of Toronto Press.

Howell, W. G. and S. P. Jackman. (2013). 'Interbranch Negotiations over Policies with Multiple Outcomes'. *American Journal of Political Science 57*, no. 4 (1 October): 956–970.

Howells, G. (2005). 'The Potential and Limits of Consumer Empowerment by Information'. *Journal of Law and Society 32*, no. 3: 349–370.

Howlett, M. (1990). 'The Round Table Experience: Representation and Legitimacy in Canadian Environmental Policy Making'. *Queen's Quarterly 97*, no. 4: 580–601.

Howlett, M. (1991). 'Policy Instruments, Policy Styles and Policy Implementation: National Approaches to Theories of Instrument Choice'. *Policy Studies Journal 19*, no. 2: 1–21.

Howlett, M. (1994). 'Policy Paradigms and Policy Change: Lessons from the Old and New Canadian Policies Towards Aboriginal Peoples'. *Policy Studies Journal 22*, no. 4: 631–649.

Howlett, M. (1996). 'Legitimacy and Governance: Re-Discovering Procedural Policy Instruments'. Paper presented to the Annual Meeting of the British Columbia Political Studies Association, Vancouver, BC.

Howlett, M. (1997). 'Issue-Attention Cycles and Punctuated Equilibrium Models Re-Considered: An Empirical Examination of Agenda-Setting in Canada'. *Canadian Journal of Political Science 30*: 5–29.

Howlett, M. (1998). 'Predictable and Unpredictable Policy Windows: Issue, Institutional and Exogenous Correlates of Canadian Federal Agenda-Setting'. *Canadian Journal of Political Science 31*, no. 3: 495–524.

Howlett, M. (1999). 'Federalism and Public Policy'. In J. Bickerton and A. Gagnon (eds.), *Canadian Politics* (3rd edn). Peterborough, ON: Broadview Press.

Howlett, M. (2000a). 'Beyond Legalism? Policy Ideas, Implementation Styles and Emulation-Based Convergence in Canadian and US Environmental Policy'. *Journal of Public Policy 20*, no. 3: 305–329.

Howlett, M. (2000b). 'Complex Network Management and the Governance of the Environment: Prospects for Policy Change and Policy Stability'. In E. Parsons (ed.), *Governing the Environment: Persistent Challenges, Uncertain Innovations*. Montreal, Canada: McGill-Queens University Press, 303–344.

Howlett, M. (2000c). 'Managing the "Hollow State": Procedural Policy Instruments and Modern Governance'. *Canadian Public Administration 43*, no. 4: 412–431.

Howlett, M. (2001). 'Policy Venues, Policy Spillovers and Policy Change: The Courts, Aboriginal Rights and British Columbia Forest Policy'. In B. Cashore, G. Hoberg, M. Howlett, J. Rayner and J. Wilson (eds.), *In Search of Sustainability: British Columbia Forest Policy in the 1990s*. Vancouver, BC: University of British Columbia Press, 120–140.

Howlett, M. (2002a). 'Policy Development'. In C. Dunn (ed.), *The Oxford Handbook of Canadian Public Administration*. Toronto, ON: Oxford University Press.

Howlett, M. (2002b). 'Policy Instruments and Implementation Styles: The Evolution of Instrument Choice in Canadian Environmental Policy'. In L. Debora Van Nijnatten and R. Boardman (eds.), *Canadian Environmental Policy: Context and Cases*. Toronto, ON: Oxford University Press, 25–45.

Howlett, M. (2002c). 'Understanding National Administrative Cultures and Their Impact Upon Administrative Reform: A Neo-Institutional Model and Analysis'. *Policy, Organization & Society. 21*, no. 1: 1–24.

Howlett, M. (2004a). 'Administrative Styles and the Limits of Administrative Reform: A Neo-Institutional Analysis of Administrative Culture'. *Canadian Public Administration 46*, no. 4: 471–494.

Howlett, M. (2004b). 'Beyond Good and Evil in Policy Implementation: Instrument Mixes, Implementation Styles and Second Generation Theories of Policy Instrument Choice'. *Policy and Society 23*, no. 2: 1–17.

Howlett, M. (2005). 'What Is a Policy Instrument? Policy Tools, Policy Mixes and Policy Implementation Styles'. In P. Eliadis, M. Hill and M. Howlett (eds.), *Designing Government: From Instruments to Governance*. Montreal, QC: McGill-Queen's University Press, 31–50.

Howlett, M. (2007). 'Analyzing Multi-Actor, Multi-Round Public Policy Decision-Making Processes in Government: Findings from Five Canadian Cases'. *Canadian Journal of Political Science 40*, no. 3: 659–684.

Howlett, M. (2009a). 'Governance Modes, Policy Regimes and Operational Plans: A Multi-Level Nested Model of Policy Instrument Choice and Policy Design'. *Policy Sciences 42*: 73–89.

Howlett, M. (2009b). 'Government Communication as a Policy Tool: A Framework for Analysis'. *Canadian Political Science Review 3*, no. 2: 23–37.

Howlett, M. (2009c). 'Policy Advice in Multi-Level Governance Systems: Sub-National Policy Analysts and Analysis'. *International Review of Public Administration 13*, no. *3*: 1–16.

Howlett, M. (2009d). 'Policy Analytical Capacity and Evidence-Based Policy-Making: Lessons from Canada'. *Canadian Public Administration 52*, no. 2: 153–175.

Howlett, M. (2011). *Designing Public Policies: Principles and Instruments*. New York: Routledge.

Howlett, M. (2012). 'The Lessons of Failure: Learning and Blame Avoidance in Public Policy-Making'. *International Political Science Review 33*, no. *5* (24 October): 539–555.

Howlett, M. (2013). 'Policy Work, Policy Advisory Systems and Politicization'. *Central European Journal of Public Policy 7*, no. *1* (June): 4–7.

Howlett, M. (2014a). 'From the "Old" to the "New" Policy Design: Design Thinking Beyond Markets and Collaborative Governance'. *Policy Sciences 47*, no. *3*: 187–207.

Howlett, M. (2014b). 'Policy Design: What, Who, How and Why?' In C. Halpern, L. Pierre and P. L. Gales (eds.), *L'instrumentation et ses effets*. Paris: Presses de Sciences Po.

Howlett, M. (2014c). 'Why Are Policy Innovations Rare and So Often Negative? Blame Avoidance and Problem Denial in Climate Change Policy-Making'. *Global Environmental Change 29*, no. 2 (November): 395–403.

Howlett, M. (2015). 'Policy Analytical Capacity: The Supply and Demand for Policy Analysis in Government'. *Policy & Society 34*, no. 3: 173–182.

Howlett, M. (2016). *Policy Tools & Their Targets: Beyond Nudges and Utility Maximization in Policy Compliance*. Workshop No. 2. Pisa, Italy: Behavioural Change and Public Policy.

Howlett, M. (2017). 'The Criteria for Effective Policy Design: Character and Context in Policy Instrument Choice'. *Journal of Asian Public Policy 11*, no. 3: 245–266.

Howlett, M. (2018a). 'The Criteria for Effective Policy Design: Character and Context in Policy Instrument Choice'. *Journal of Asian Public Policy 11*, no. 3 (2 September–6 December): 245–266.

Howlett, M. (2018b). 'Matching Policy Tools and Their Targets: Beyond Nudges and Utility Maximisation in Policy Design'. *Policy & Politics 46*, no. 1 (18 January): 101–124.

Howlett, M. (2019a). *Designing Public Policies: Principles and Instruments* (2nd edn). London: Routledge.

Howlett, M. (2019b). 'The Temporal Dimension(s) of Policy Designs: Resilience, Robustness and the Sequencing of Tools in Policy Mixes'. *International Review of Public Policy 1*, no. 1: 27–45.

Howlett, M. (2019c). 'Comparing Policy Advisory Systems Beyond the OECD: Models, Dynamics and the Second-Generation Research Agenda'. *Policy Studies 40*, no. 3–4 (4 July): 241–259.

Howlett, M. (2020a). 'Dealing with the Dark Side of Policy-Making: Managing Behavioural Risk and Volatility in Policy Designs'. *Journal of Comparative Policy Analysis: Research and Practice 22*, no. 6: 612–625.

Howlett, M. (2020b). 'Challenges in Applying Design Thinking to Public Policy: Dealing with the Varieties of Policy Formulation and Their Vicissitudes'. *Policy & Politics 48*, no. 1: 49–65.

Howlett, M. (2021a). 'Avoiding a Panglossian Policy Science: The Need to Deal with the Darkside of Policy-Maker and Policy-Taker Behaviour'. *Public Integrity, 2021*: 1–13.

Howlett, M. (2021b). 'From National Lockdowns to Herd Immunity: Understanding the Spectrum of Government Responses to COVID-19 (2019–2021)'. *Bestuurskunde 30*, no. *3* (October): 8–23.

Howlett, M. (2022). 'Avoiding a Panglossian Policy Science: The Need to Deal with the Darkside of Policy-Maker and Policy-Taker Behaviour'. *Public Integrity 24*, no. *3* (4 May): 306–318.

Howlett, Michael, and Ching Leong. (2022). "The 'Inherent Vices' of Policy Design: Uncertainty, Maliciousness, and Noncompliance." *Risk Analysis 42*, no. *5*: 920–930.

Howlett, Michael, ed. (2022a). The Routledge Handbook of Policy Tools. New York: Routledge, 2022a.

Howlett, M., G. Capano and M. Ramesh. (2018). 'Designing for Robustness: Surprise, Agility and Improvisation in Policy Design'. *Policy and Society 37*, no. *4*: 422–440.

Howlett, M. and B. Cashore. (2007). 'Re-Visiting the New Orthodoxy of Policy Dynamics: The Dependent Variable and Re-Aggregation Problems in the Study of Policy Change'. *Canadian Political Science Review 1*, no. *2*: 50–62.

Howlett, M. and B. Cashore. (2009). 'The Dependent Variable Problem in the Study of Policy Change: Understanding Policy Change as a Methodological Problem'. *Journal of Comparative Policy Analysis: Research and Practice 11*, no. *1*: 33–46.

Howlett, M., J. Craft and L. Zibrik. (2010). 'Government Communication and Democratic Governance: Electoral and Policy-Related Information Campaigns in Canada'. *Policy and Society 29*, no. *1* (January): 13–22.

Howlett, M. and P. del Rio. (2015). 'The Parameters of Policy Portfolios: Verticality and Horizontality in Design Spaces and Their Consequences for Policy Mix Formulation'. *Environment and Planning C 33*, no. *5*: 1233–1245.

Howlett, M. and K. H. Goetz. (2014). 'Time, Temporality and Timescapes in Administration and Policy'. *International Review of Administrative Sciences 80*, no. *3* (1 September): 477–492.

Howlett, M. and D. Jarvis. (2021). 'Policy Science Beyond Self-Congratulatory Virtue Signalling: Matching Supply and Demand in the Scholarship, Pedagogy and Purpose of the Policy Enterprise'. In A. Brik and L. Pal (eds.), *The Future of the Policy Sciences*. Cheltenham: Edward Elgar Publishing, 51–69.

Howlett, M., A. Kekez and O. Poocharoen. (2017). 'Understanding Co-Production as a Policy Tool Integrating New Public Governance and Comparative Policy Theory'. *Journal of Comparative Policy Analysis 19*, no. *5*: 487–501.

Howlett, M. and A. Kemmerling. (2017). 'Calibrating Climate Change Policies: The Causes and Consequences of Sustained Under-Reaction'. *Journal of Environmental Policy & Planning 19*, no. *6* (2 November): 625–637.

Howlett, M., J. Kim and P. Weaver. (2006). 'Assessing Instrument Mixes Through Program- and Agency-Level Data: Methodological Issues in Contemporary Implementation Research'. *Review of Policy Research 23*, no. *1*: 129–151.

Howlett, M. and R. P. Lejano. (2013). 'Tales from the Crypt: The Rise and Fall (and Rebirth?) of Policy Design'. *Administration & Society 45*, no. *3* (1 April): 357–381.

Howlett, M. and C. Leong. (2022a). 'What Is Behavioral in Policy Studies?: How Far Has the Discipline Moved Beyond Traditional Utilitarianism?' *Journal of Behavioral Public Administration 5*, no. *1* (14 April).

Howlett, M. and C. Leong. (2022b). 'The "Inherent Vices" of Policy Design: Uncertainty, Maliciousness, and Noncompliance'. *Risk Analysis 42*, no. *5*: 920–930.

Howlett, M. and E. Lindquist. (2004). 'Policy Analysis and Governance: Analytical and Policy Styles in Canada'. *Journal of Comparative Policy Analysis 6*, no. *3*: 225–249.

Howlett, M., A. McConnell and A. Perl. (2014). 'Streams and Stages: Reconciling Kingdon and Policy Process Theory'. *European Journal of Political Research 54*, no. 3: 419–434.

Howlett, M. and A. Migone. (2011). 'Charles Lindblom is Alive and Well and Living in Punctuated Equilibrium Land'. *Policy and Society 30*, no. 1, 53–62.

Howlett, M. and A. Migone. (2013). 'Policy Advice Through the Market: The Role of External Consultants in Contemporary Policy Advisory Systems'. *Policy & Society 32*, no. 3: 241–254.

Howlett, M. and I. Mukherjee. (2014). 'Policy Design and Non-Design: Towards a Spectrum of Policy Formulation Types'. *Politics and Governance 2*, no. 2 (13 November): 57–71.

Howlett, M. and I. Mukherjee (eds.). (2017a). *Handbook of Policy Formulation.* Cheltenham: Edward Elgar.

Howlett, M. and I. Mukherjee. (2017b). 'Design and Non-Design in Policy Formulation: Where Knowledge Meets Power in the Policy Process'. In I. Muhkerjee (ed.), *Handbook of Policy Formulation.* Cheltenham: Edward Elgar Publishing, 3–22.

Howlett, M. and I. Mukherjee. (2017c). 'Policy Design: From Tools to Patches'. *Canadian Public Administration 60*, no. 1: Article 140.

Howlett, M. and I. Mukherjee. (2018). 'The Contribution of Comparative Policy Analysis to Policy Design: Articulating Principles of Effectiveness and Clarifying Design Spaces'. *Journal of Comparative Policy Analysis: Research and Practice 20*, no. 1 (1 January): 72–87.

Howlett, M., I. Mukherjee and J. Rayner. (2014). 'The Elements of Effective Program Design: A Two-Level Analysis'. *Politics and Governance 2*, no. 2 (June 9): 1–12.

Howlett, M., I. Muhkerjee and J. Rayner. (2017). 'The Elements of Effective Program Design: A Two-Level Analysis'. In I. Muhkerjee (ed.), *Handbook of Policy Formulation.* Cheltenham: Edward Elgar Publishing, 129–144.

Howlett, M., I. Mukherjee and J. J. Woo. (2015). 'From Tools to Toolkits in Policy Design Studies: The New Design Orientation Towards Policy Formulation Research'. *Policy & Politics 43*, no. 2: 291–311.

Howlett, M., I. Mukherjee and J. J. Woo. (2014). 'The New Policy Design Orientation: From Tools to Toolkits in Policy Instrument Studies'. *Policy & Politics 43*, no. 2: 292–311.

Howlett, M. and S. Nair. (2017a). 'The Central Conundrums of Policy Formulation: Ill-Structured Problems and Uncertainty'. In M. Howlett and I. Mukherjee (eds.), *Handbook of Policy Formulation.* New York: Routledge, 23–38.

Howlett, M. and S. Nair. (2017b). 'From Robustness to Resilience: Avoiding Policy Traps in the Long-Term'. *Sustainability Science 11*, no. 6 (1 November): 909–917.

Howlett, M. and J. Newman. (2010). 'Policy Analysts and Policy Work in Federal Systems: Policy Advice and Its Contribution to Evidence-Based Policy-Making in Multi-Level Governance Systems'. *Policy and Society 29*, no. 2: 1–14.

Howlett, M. and J. Newman. (2013). 'After "the Regulatory Moment" in Comparative Regulatory Studies: Modeling the Early Stages of Regulatory Life Cycles'. *Journal of Comparative Policy Analysis: Research and Practice 15*, no. 2: 107–121.

Howlett, M. and M. Ramesh. (1993). 'Patterns of Policy Instrument Choice: Policy Styles, Policy Learning and the Privatization Experience'. *Policy Studies Review 12*, no. 1: 3–24.

Howlett, M. and M. Ramesh. (1998). 'Policy Subsystem Configurations and Policy Change: Operationalizing the Postpositivist Analysis of the Politics of the Policy Process'. *Policy Studies Journal 26*, no. 3: 466–482.

Howlett, M. and M. Ramesh. (2002). 'The Policy Effects of Internationalization: A Subsystem Adjustment Analysis of Policy Change'. *Journal of Comparative Policy Analysis 4*, no. *1*: 31–50.

Howlett, M. and M. Ramesh. (2003). *Studying Public Policy: Policy Cycles and Policy Subsystems*. Toronto, ON: Oxford University Press.

Howlett, M. and M. Ramesh. (2006). 'Globalization and the Choice of Governing Instruments: The Direct, Indirect and Opportunity Effects of Internationalization'. *International Public Management Journal 9*, no. *2*: 175–194.

Howlett, M. and M. Ramesh. (2014). 'The Two Orders of Governance Failure: Design Mismatches and Policy Capacity Issues in Modern Governance'. *Policy and Society 33*, no. *4*.

Howlett, M. and M. Ramesh. (2016a). 'Achilles' Heels of Governance: Critical Capacity Deficits and Their Role in Governance Failures'. *Regulation & Governance 10*, no. *4* (1 December): 301–313.

Howlett, M. and M. Ramesh. (2016b). 'Understanding the Role of Policy Capacity in Policy Success and Failure: Government Competencies and Capabilities in Public Policy and Administration'. In T. R. Klassen, D. Cepiku and T. J. Lah (eds.), *Global Public Policy and Administration*. London: Routledge.

Howlett, M., M. Ramesh and G. Capano. (2020). 'Policy-Makers, Policy-Takers and Policy Tools: Dealing with Behaviourial Issues in Policy Design'. *Journal of Comparative Policy Analysis: Research and Practice 22*, no. *6* (1 November): 487–497.

Howlett, M., M. Ramesh and G. Capano. (2023, Forthcoming). 'The Role of Tool Calibrations and Policy Specifications in Policy Change: Evidence from Healthcare Reform Efforts in South Korea 1988–2021'. *Journal of Asian Public Policy*.

Howlett, M., M. Ramesh and A. Perl. (2009). *Studying Public Policy*. Toronto, ON: Oxford University Press.

Howlett, M., M. Ramesh and A. Perl. (2020). *Studying Public Policy: Principles and Processes* (4th edn). Don Mills: Oxford University Press.

Howlett, M., M. Ramesh and X. Wu. (2015). 'Understanding the Persistence of Policy Failures: The Role of Politics, Governance and Uncertainty'. *Public Policy and Administration 30*, no. *3–4* (1 July): 209–220.

Howlett, M., M. Ramesh, X. Wu and S. Fritzen. (2017). *The Public Policy Primer*. London: Taylor & Francis.

Howlett, M. and J. Rayner. (1995). 'Do Ideas Matter? Policy Subsystem Configurations and the Continuing Conflict Over Canadian Forest Policy'. *Canadian Public Administration 38*, no. *3*: 382–410.

Howlett, M. and J. Rayner. (2004). '(Not So) "Smart Regulation"? Canadian Shellfish Aquaculture Policy and the Evolution of Instrument Choice for Industrial Development'. *Marine Policy 28*, no. *2*: 171–184.

Howlett, M. and J. Rayner. (2006a). 'Convergence and Divergence in "New Governance", Arrangements: Evidence from European Integrated Natural Resource Strategies'. *Journal of Public Policy 26*, no. *2*: 167–189.

Howlett, M. and J. Rayner. (2006b). 'Globalization and Governance Capacity: Explaining Divergence in National Forest Programmes as Instances of "Next-Generation" Regulation in Canada and Europe'. *Governance 19*, no. *2*: 251–275.

Howlett, M. and J. Rayner. (2006c). 'Policy Divergence as a Response to Weak International Regimes: The Formulation and Implementation of Natural Resource New Governance Arrangements in Europe and Canada'. *Policy and Society 24*, no. *2*: 16–45.

Howlett, M. and J. Rayner. (2007). 'Design Principles for Policy Mixes: Cohesion and Coherence in "New Governance Arrangements"'. *Policy and Society 26*, no. *4*: 1–18.

Howlett, M. and J. Rayner. (2013). 'Patching Vs Packaging in Policy Formulation: Assessing Policy Portfolio Design'. *Politics and Governance 1*, no. 2: 170–182.

Howlett, M. and J. Rayner. (2017a). 'Patching vs packaging in policy formulation'. In I. Muhkerjee (ed.), *Handbook of Policy Formulation*. Cheltenham: Edward Elgar Publishing, 112–128.

Howlett, M. and J. Rayner. (2017b). 'Program Design: A Two Level Analysis of Formulation Practices'. In I. Muhkerjee (ed.), *Handbook of Policy Formulation*. Cheltenham: Edward Elgar Publishing.

Howlett, M. and J. Rayner. (2020). 'Administrative Clientelism and Policy Reform Failure: The Western Canada Integrated Land Management Experience 1990–2015'. *Acta Politica 56*, no. 4 (16 April): 622–638.

Howlett, M., J. Rayner and C. Tollefson. (2009). 'From Government to Governance in Forest Planning? Lesson from the Case of the British Columbia Great Bear Rainforest Initiative'. *Forest Policy and Economics 11*: 383–391.

Howlett, M., S. L. Tan, A. Migone, A. Wellstead and B. Evans. (2014). 'The Distribution of Analytical Techniques in Policy Advisory Systems: Policy Formulation and the Tools of Policy Appraisal'. *Public Policy and Administration 29*, no. 4 (24 March): 271–291.

Howlett, M. and J. Tosun (eds.). (2019). *Policy Styles and Policy-Making: Exploring the National Dimension*. New York: Routledge.

Howlett, M. and J. Tosun. (2021a). 'National Policy Styles in Theory and Practice'. In M. Howlett and J. Tosun (eds.), *The Routledge Handbook of Policy Styles*. New York: Routledge, 15–24.

Howlett, M. and J. Tosun. (eds.). (2021b). *The Routledge Handbook of Policy Styles*. London: Routledge.

Howlett, M., J. Vince and P. del Río. (2017). 'Policy Integration and Multi-Level Governance: Dealing with the Vertical Dimension of Policy Mix Designs'. *Politics and Governance 5*, no. 2 (5 May): 69–78.

Howlett, M. and R. M. Walker. (2012). 'Public Managers in the Policy Process: More Evidence on the Missing Variable?' *Policy Studies Journal 40*, no. 2 (1 May): 211–233.

Howlett, M. and A. Wellstead. (2009). 'Re-Visiting Meltsner: Policy Advice Systems and the Multi-Dimensional Nature of Professional Policy Analysis'. *SSRN eLibrary*. http://papers.ssrn.com/sol3/papers.cfm?abstract_id=1546251. Accessed 30 December 2009.

Howlett, M. and A. Wellstead. (2011). 'Policy Analysts in the Bureaucracy Revisited: The Nature of Professional Policy Work in Contemporary Government'. *Politics & Policy 39*, no. 4 (1 August): 613–633.

Howlett, M. and I. Mukherjee. (2017). 'Design and Non-Design in Policy Formulation: Where Knowledge Meets Power in the Policy Process'. In *Handbook of Policy Formulation*. Cheltenham: Edward Elgar.

Howlett, M. and J. Tosun. (2018). 'Policy Styles: A New Approach'. In M. Howlett and J. Tosun (eds.), *Policy Styles and Policy-Making*. London: Routledge.

Howlett, M. and M. Ramesh. (2023). 'Designing for Adaptation: Static and Dynamic Robustness in Policy-Making'. *Public Administration 101*, no. 1: 23–35.

Howlett, M. and S. Nair. (2017). 'The Central Conundrums of Policy Formulation: Ill-Structured Problems and Uncertainty'. In I. Mukherjee (ed.), *Handbook of Policy Formulation*. New York: Routledge, 23–38.

Howlett, M. and J. Tosun. (2018). 'Empirical Insights on National Policy Styles and Political Regimes'. In M. Howlett and J. Tosun (eds.), *Policy Styles and Policy-Making*. New York: Routledge, 377–396.

Howlett, M., J. Vince and P. del Río. (2017). 'Policy Integration and Multi-Level Governance: Dealing with the Vertical Dimension of Policy Mix Designs'. *Politics and Governance 5*, no. 2 (5 May): 69–78.

Howse, R., J. R. S. Prichard and M. J. Trebilcock. (1990). 'Smaller or Smarter Government?' *University of Toronto Law Journal 40*: 498–541.

Hsiao, W. C. (2001). 'Commentary: Behind the Ideology and Theory: What Is the Empirical Evidence for Medical Savings Accounts?' *Journal of Health Politics, Policy and Law 26*, no. 4: 733–737.

Hsiao, W. C. and Shaw, R. P. (eds.). (2007). *Social Health Insurance for Developing Nations*. Washington, DC: The World Bank.

Huber, G. P. (1991). 'Organization Learning: The Contributing Processes and the Literatures'. *Organization Science 2*: 88–115.

Hudson, J., S. Lowe, N. Oscroft and C. Snell. (2007). 'Activating Policy Networks: A Case Study of Local Environmental Policy-Making in the United Kingdom'. *Policy Studies 28*, no. 1: 55–70.

Huestis, L. (1993). 'Enforcement of Environmental Law in Canada'. In M. L. McConnell and L. Huestis (eds.), *Environmental Law and Business in Canada*. Aurora, ON: Thompson/Canada Law Book, 240–255.

Huitt, R. K. (1968). 'Political Feasibility'. In A. Rannay (ed.), *Political Science and Public Policy*. Chicago, IL: Markham, 263–276.

Hula, R. C. (1988). 'Using Markets to Implement Public Policy'. In R. C. Hula (ed.), *Market-Based Public Policy*. London: Macmillan, 3–20.

Hula, R. C., C. Jackson-Elmoore and L. Reese. (2007). 'Mixing God's Work and the Public Business: A Framework for the Analysis of Faith-Based Service Delivery'. *Review of Policy Research 24*, no. 1: 67–89.

Hull, A. (2008). 'Policy Integration: What Will It Take to Achieve More Sustainable Transport Solutions in Cities?' *Transport Policy 15*, no. 2 (March): 94–103.

Human Rights Watch. (2021). *World Report 2021*. Human Rights Watch. www.hrw.org/world-report/2021

Huntington, S. P. (1952). 'The Marasmus of the ICC: The Commissions, the Railroads and the Public Interest'. *Yale Law Review 61*, no. 4: 467–509.

Hupe, P. L. and M. J. Hill. (2016). 'And the Rest Is Implementation. Comparing Approaches to What Happens in Policy Processes Beyond Great Expectations'. *Public Policy and Administration 31*, no. 2 (1 April): 103–121.

Hussain, K. (2018). *Job Safety Analysis and Risk Assessment: A Case Study of Frontier Ceramics Ltd.* www.researchgate.net/profile/Zahid-Hussain-5/publication/328723240_Job_Safety_Analysis_and_Risk_Assessment_A_case_study_of_Frontier_Ceramics_Ltd/links/5bddb05da6fdcc3a8dbb3e67/Job-Safety-Analysis-and-Risk-Assessment-A-case-study-of-Frontier-Ceramics-Ltd.pdf

Hustedt, T. and S. Veit. (2017). 'Policy Advisory Systems: Change Dynamics and Sources of Variation'. *Policy Sciences 50*, no. 1 (1 March): 41–46.

Hutter, B. M. (1989). 'Variations in Regulatory Enforcement Styles'. *Law and Policy 11*, no. 2: 153–174.

Hutter, B. M. and P. K. Manning. (1990). 'The Contexts of Regulation: The Impact upon Health and Safety Inspectorates in Britain'. *Law and Policy 12*, no. 2: 103–136.

Hysing, E. (2009). 'From Government to Governance? A Comparison of Environmental Governing in Swedish Forestry and Transport'. *Governance 22*: 547–672.

Iacobucci, E., M. Trebilcock and R. A. Winter. (2006). 'The Canadian Experience with Deregulation'. *University of Toronto Law Journal 56*, no. 1: 1–63.

Iannuzzi, A. (2001). *Industry Self-Regulation and Voluntary Environmental Compliance*. Boca Raton, FL: Lewis Publishers.

ICT Export Cluster. (2017). *Utilities-e-Estonia*. https://e-estonia.com/the-story/digital-society/utilities. Accessed 8 April 2017.

Igielska, B. (2008). 'Climate Change Mitigation: Overview of the Environmental Policy Instruments'. *International Journal of Green Economics 2*, no. 2: 210–225.

Ikenberry, G. J. (1990). 'The International Spread of Privatization Policies: Inducements, Learning and "Policy Bandwagoning" '. In E. N. Suleiman and J. Waterbury (eds.), *The Political Economy of Public Sector Reform and Privatization*. Boulder, CO: Westview, 88–110.

Ingraham, P. (1987). 'Toward More Systematic Considerations of Policy Design'. *Policy Studies Journal 15*, no. 4: 611–628.

Ingram, H. M. and D. E. Mann. (1980). 'Policy Failure: An Issue Deserving Analysis'. In H. M. Ingram and D. E. Mann (eds.), *Why Policies Succeed or Fail*. Beverly Hills, CA: Sage, 11–32.

Ingram, H. M. and A. Schneider. (1990). 'Improving Implementation Through Framing Smarter Statutes'. *Journal of Public Policy, 10*, no. 1, 67–88.

Innes, J. E. (1990). *Knowledge and Public Policy: The Search for Meaningful Indicators*. New Brunswick, NJ: Transaction Publishers.

Innvaer, S., G. Vist, M. Trommald and A. Oxman. (2002). 'Health Policy-Makers' Perceptions of Their Use of Evidence: A Systematic Review'. *Journal of Health Services Research and Policy 7*, no. 4: 239–245.

Inwood, G. J. and C. M. Johns. (2016). 'Commissions of Inquiry and Policy Change: Comparative Analysis and Future Research Frontiers'. *Canadian Public Administration 59*, no. 3 (1 September): 382–404.

IPCC. (2014a). 'Annex II: Glossary, edited by K. J. Mach, S. Planton and C. von Stechow'. In R. K. Pachauri, L. Mayer and IPCC (eds.), *Climate Change 2014: Synthesis Report. Contribution of Working Groups I, II and III to the Fifth Assessment Report of the Intergovernmental Panel on Climate Change*. Geneva, Switzerland: IPCC, 117–130.

IPCC. (2014b). *Climate Change 2014: Mitigation of Climate Change. Contribution of Working Group III to the Fifth Assessment Report of the Intergovernmental Panel on Climate Change*. O. Edenhofer, R. Pichs-Madruga, Y. Sokona, E. Farahani, S. Kadner, K. Seyboth, A. Adler, I. Baum, S. Brunner, P. Eickemeier, B. Kriemann, J. Savolainen, S. Schlömer, C. von Stechow, T. Zwickel and J. C. Minx (eds.). New York: Cambridge University Press.

IPCC (Intergovernmental Panel on Climate Change). (2001). 'Working Group III: "Mitigation" '. In R. T. Watson and Core Writing Team (eds.), *Climate Change 2001 – IPCC Third Assessment Report*. Cambridge; New York: Cambridge University Press.

Irwin, L. G. (2003). *The Policy Analysts Handbook: Rational Problem Solving in a Political World*. Armonk: M.E. Sharpe.

ISO. (2018). *ISO 31000:2018 Risk Management Guidelines*. www.iso.org/obp/ui#iso:std:iso:31000:ed-2:v1:en

Issalys, P. (2005). 'Choosing Among Forms of Public Action: A Question of Legitimacy'. In P. Eliadis, M. Hill and M. Howlett (eds.), *Designing Government: From Instruments to Governance*. Montreal: McGill-Queen's University Press, 154–181.

Ito, T. and A. O. Kreuger (eds.). (2004). *Governance, Regulation and Privatization in the Asia-Pacific Region*. Chicago, IL: University of Chicago Press.

Jackson, A. and B. Baldwin. (2007). 'Policy Analysis by the Labour Movement in a Hostile Environment'. In L. Dobuzinskis, M. Howlett and D. Laycock (eds.), *Policy Analysis in Canada: The State of the Art*. Toronto, ON: University of Toronto Press, 260–272.

Jackson, P. M. (2007). 'Making Sense of Policy Advice'. *Public Money & Management* 27, no. 4: 257–264.

Jacobs, A. M. (2011). *Governing for the Long Term: Democracy and the Politics of Investment* (1st edn). Cambridge: Cambridge University Press.

Jacobs, A. M. and K. Weaver. (2010). *Policy Feedback and Policy Change*. SSRN Scholarly Paper. Rochester, NY: Social Science Research Network (19 July). http://papers.ssrn.com/abstract=1642636.

Jacobs, A. M. and K. Weaver. (2014). 'When Policies Undo Themselves: Self-Undermining Feedback as a Source of Policy Change'. *Governance: An International Journal of Policy, Administration, and Institutions 28*, no. 4: 441–457.

Jacobs, A. S. (2008). 'The Politics of When: Redistribution, Investment and Policy Making for the Long Term'. *British Journal of Political Science 38*, no. 2: 193–220.

Jacobs, A. S. and R. Weaver. (2010). *Policy Feedback and Policy Change*. SSRN Scholarly Paper. Rochester, NY: Social Science Research Network (10 January).

Jacobsen, J. K. (1995). 'Much Ado About Ideas: The Cognitive Factor in Economic Policy'. *World Politics* no. 47: 283–310.

Jacobzone, S. (2005). 'Independent Regulatory Authorities in OECD Countries: An Overview'. In *Designing Independent and Accountable Regulatory Authorities for High Quality Regulation – Proceedings of an Expert Meeting in London, United Kingdom 10–11 January 2005*. Paris: OECD Working Party on Regulatory Management and Reform, 72–100.

Jaffe, L. L. (1965). *Judicial Control of Administrative Action*. Boston, MA: Little, Brown.

Jahn, G., M. Schramm and A. Spiller. (2005). 'The Reliability of Certification: Quality Labels as a Consumer Policy Tool'. *Journal of Consumer Policy 28*: 53–73.

James, T. E. and P. D. Jorgensen. (2009). 'Policy Knowledge, Policy Formulation, and Change: Revisiting a Foundational Question'. *Policy Studies Journal 37*, no. 1: 141–162.

Jann, W. (1991). 'From Policy Analysis to Political Management? An Outside Look at Public Policy Training in the United States'. In C. H. W. Peter Wagner (ed.), *Social Sciences and Modern States: National Experiences and Theoretical Crossroads*. Cambridge: Cambridge University Press, 110–130.

Jann, W. and K. Wegrich. (2007). 'Theories of the Policy Cycle'. In F. Fischer, G. J. Miller and M. S. Sidney (eds.), *Handbook of Public Policy Analysis: Theory, Politics and Methods*. Boca Raton, FL: CRC Press, 43–62.

Jarvis, D. S. L. (2011a). *Infrastructure Regulation What Works, Why and How Do We Know? Lessons from Asia and Beyond*. Singapore: World Scientific.

Jarvis, D. S. L. (2011b). 'Theorising Risk and Uncertainty in International Relations: The Contributions of Frank Knight'. *International Relations 25*, no. 3 (1 September): 296–312.

Jarvis, D. S. L. (2014). 'Policy Transfer, Neo-Liberalism or Coercive Institutional Isomorphism? Explaining the Emergence of a Regulatory Regime for Quality Assurance in the Hong Kong Higher Education Sector'. *Policy and Society 33*, no. 3: 237–252.

Jasanoff, S. (1998). *The Fifth Branch: Science Advisers as Policymakers*. Cambridge, MA: Harvard University Press.

Jayasuriya, K. (2001). 'Globalization and the Changing Architecture of the State: The Regulatory State and the Politics of Negative Co-ordination'. *Journal of European Public Policy 8*, no. 1: 101–123.

Jayasuriya, K. (2004). 'The New Regulatory State and Relational Capacity'. *Policy and Politics 32*, no. 4: 487–501.

Jensen, O. (2017). 'Public – Private Partnerships for Water in Asia: A Review of Two Decades of Experience'. *International Journal of Water Resources Development* 33, no. *1* (2 January): 4–30.

Jenson, J. (1994). 'Commissioning Ideas: Representation and Royal Commissions'. In S. D. Phillips (ed.), *How Ottawa Spends, 1994–95: Making Change.* Ottawa, ON: Carleton University Press, 39–69.

Jentoft, S. (2000). 'Legitimacy and Disappointment in Fisheries Management'. *Marine Policy 24*: 141–148.

Jochim, A. E. and P. J. May. (2010). 'Beyond Subsystems: Policy Regimes and Governance'. *Policy Studies Journal 38*, no. 2: 303–327.

Johannesen, A. B. (2006). 'Designing Integrated Conservation and Development Projects (ICDPs): Illegal Hunting, Wildlife Conservation and the Welfare of the Local People'. *Environment and Development Economics 11*, no. *1*: 247–267.

Johansson, R. and K. Borell. (1999). 'Central Steering and Local Networks: Old-Age Care in Sweden'. *Public Administration 77*, no. *3*: 585–598.

John, P. (2013). 'All Tools Are Informational Now: How Information and Persuasion Define the Tools of Government'. *Policy & Politics 41*, no. 4 (1 October): 605–620.

John, P., G. Smith and G. Stoker. (2009). 'Nudge Nudge, Think Think: Two Strategies for Changing Civic Behaviour'. *The Political Quarterly 80*, no. 3 (1 July): 361–370.

Johnsen, A. (2005). 'What Does 25 Years of Experience Tell Us about the State of Performance Measurement in Public Policy and Management?' *Public Money and Management 25*, no. *1*: 9–17.

Johnson, C. (2012). 'Bricoleur and Bricolage: From Metaphor to Universal Concept'. *Paragraph 35*, no. *3*: 355–372.

Johnson, E. J. and D. Goldstein. (2003). 'Do Defaults Save Lives?' *Science 302*, 5649: 1338–1339.

Johnson, E. J. and D. G. Goldstein. (2013). 'Decisions by Default'. In E. Shafir (ed.), *The Behavioral Foundations of Public Policy.* Princeton, NJ: Princeton University Press, 417–427.

Johnson, E. J., S. B. Shu, B. G. C. Dellaert, C. Fox, D. G. Goldstein, G. Häubl, R. P. Larrick, J. W. Payne, E. Peters, D. Schkade and B. Wansink. (2012). 'Beyond Nudges: Tools of a Choice Architecture'. *Marketing Letters 23*, no. 2 (June): 487–504.

Johnson, J. and M. Cook. (2014). 'Policy Design: A New Area of Design Research and Practice'. In M. Arguierc, F. Bonlanger, D. Krub and C. Marchal (eds.), *Complex Systems Design & Management.* Cham, Germany: Springer, 51–62.

Jones, B. D. (2002). 'Bounded Rationality and Public Policy: Herbert A. Simon and the Decisional Foundation of Collective Choice'. *Policy Sciences 35*: 269–284.

Jones, B. D. (2001). *Politics and the Architecture of Choice: Bounded Rationality and Governance.* Chicago: University of Chicago Press.

Jones, B. D., G. Boushey and S. Workman. (2006). 'Behavioral Rationality and the Policy Processes: Toward a New Model of Organizational Information Processing'. In B. G. Peters and J. Pierre (eds.), *Handbook of Public Policy.* London: Sage, 49–74.

Jones, B. D., H. F. Thomas III and M. Wolfe. (2014). 'Policy Bubbles'. *Policy Studies Journal 42*, no. *1*: 146–171.

Jones, C. O. (1984). *An Introduction to the Study of Public Policy.* Monterey, CA: Brooks/Cole.

Jones, R., J. Pykett and M. Whitehead. (2011). 'Governing Temptation: Changing Behaviour in an Age of Libertarian Paternalism'. *Progress in Human Geography 35*, no. 4 (8 January): 483–501.

Jonsson, G. and I. Zakrisson. (2005). 'Organizational Dilemmas in Voluntary Associations'. *International Journal of Public Administration 28*: 849–856.

Jordan, A. (2003). 'The Europeanization of National Government and Policy: A Departmental Perspective'. *British Journal of Political Science 33*, no. 1: 261–282.

Jordan, A., D. Benson, R. Wurzel and A. Zito. (2011). 'Policy Instruments in Practice'. In J. S. Dryzek, R. B. Norgaard and D. Schlosberg (eds), *Oxford Handbook of Climate Change and Society*. Oxford: Oxford University Press, 536–549.

Jordan, A., D. Benson, A. Zito and Wurzel, R. (2012). 'Environmental Policy: Governing by Multiple Policy Instruments?' In J. J. Richardson (ed.), *Constructing a Policy State? Policy Dynamics in the EU*. Oxford: Oxford University Press.

Jordan, A. and E. Matt. (2014). 'Designing Policies That Intentionally Stick: Policy Feedback in a Changing Climate'. *Policy Sciences* (11 June): 1–21.

Jordan, A., R. Wurzel and A. Zito. (2003). 'New Instruments of Environmental Governance'. *Environmental Politics 12*, no. 3: 1–24.

Jordan, A., R. Wurzel and A. Zito. (2005). 'The Rise of "New" Policy Instruments in Comparative Perspective: Has Governance Eclipsed Government?' *Political Studies 53*: 477–496.

Jordan, A., R. Wurzel and A. Zito. (2013). 'Still the Century of "New" Environmental Policy Instruments? Exploring Patterns of Innovation and Continuity'. *Environmental Politics 22*, no. 1: 155–173.

Jordan, A. G. (1981). 'Iron Triangles, Woolly Corporatism and Elastic Nets: Images of the Policy Process'. *Journal of Public Policy 1*, no. 1: 95–123.

Jordan, A. G. (2008). 'The Governance of Sustainable Development: Taking Stock and Looking Forwards'. *Environment and Planning C: Government and Policy 26*: 17–33.

Jordan, A. J. and D. Huitema. (2014). 'Innovations in Climate Policy: The Politics of Invention, Diffusion and Evaluation Environmental Politics'. *Environmental Politics 23* (Special Issue), no. 5: 715–734.

Jordan, A. J., D. Huistema, M. Hilden, H. van Assett, T. Rayner, J. Schoenfeld, J. Tosun, J. Forster and E. Bousson. (2015). 'Emergence of Polycentric Climate Governance and Its Future Prospects'. *Nature Climate Change 5*: 977–982.

Jordan, G. and J. Richardson. (1982). 'The British Policy Style or the Logic of Negotiation?' In J. Richardson (ed.), *Policy Styles in Western Europe*. London: Allen & Unwin, 80–110.

Jordana, J. and D. Levi-Faur. (2004a). 'The Politics of Regulation in the Age of Governance'. In J. Jacint and D. Levi-Faur (eds.), *Politics of Regulation*. Cheltenham, UK: Edward Elgar, 1–28.

Jordana, J. and D. Levi-Faur (eds.). (2004b). *The Politics of Regulation: Institutions and Regulatory Reforms for the Age of Governance*. Cheltenham, UK: Edward Elgar.

Jordan-Zachery, J. S. (2007). 'Policy Interaction: The Mixing of Fatherhood, Crime and Urban Policies'. *Journal of Social Policy 27*, no. 1: 81–102.

Jorgensen, H. and F. Larsen. (1997). *The Blessings of Network Steering? Theoretical and Empirical Arguments for Coordination Concepts as Alternatives to Policy Design*. Working Paper. Aalborg, Denmark: Aalborg University.

Jorgensen, P. (2017). 'The Politics of Policy Formulation: Overcoming Subsystem Dynamics'. In M. Howlett and I. Mukherjee (eds.), *Handbook of Policy Formulation*. Cheltenham, UK: Edward Elgar, 449–462.

Junginger, S. (2013). 'Design and Innovation in the Public Sector: Matters of Design in Policy-Making and Policy Implementation'. *Annual Review of Policy Design 1*, no. *1* (13 September): 1–11.

Justen, A., N. Fearnley, M. Givoni and J. Macmillen. (2014). 'A Process for Designing Policy Packaging: Ideals and Realities'. *Transportation Research Part A: Policy and Practice 60* (February): 9–18.

Justen, A., J. Schippl, B. Lenz and T. Fleischer. (2013). 'Assessment of Policies and Detection of Unintended Effects: Guiding Principles for the Consideration of Methods and Tools in Policy-Packaging'. *Transportation Research Part A: Policy and Practice 60* (February): 19–30.

Kagan, R. A. (1991). 'Adversarial Legalism and American Government'. *Journal of Policy Analysis and Management 10*, no. *3*: 369–406.

Kagan, R. A. (1994). 'Regulatory Enforcement'. In D. H. Rosenbloom and R. D. Schwartz (eds.), *Handbook of Regulation and Administrative Law*. New York: Marcel Dekker, 383–422.

Kagan, R. A. (1996). 'The Political Construction of American Adversarial Legalism'. In A. Ranney (ed.), *Courts and the Political Process*. Berkeley, CA: Institute of Governmental Studies Press, 19–39.

Kagan, R. A. (1997). 'Should Europe Worry About Adversarial Legalism?' *Oxford Journal of Legal Studies 17*, no. *2*: 165–183.

Kagan, R. A. (2001). *Adversarial Legalism: The American Way of Law*. Cambridge, MA: Harvard University Press.

Kagan, R. A. and L. Axelrad. (1997). 'Adversarial Legalism: An International Perspective'. In P. S. Nivola (ed.), *Comparative Disadvantages? Social Regulations and the Global Economy*. Washington, DC: Brookings Institution, 146–202.

Kagan, R. A. and J. H. Skolnick. (1993). 'Banning Smoking: Compliance Without Enforcement'. *Smoking Policy: Law, Politics, and Culture 69*: 78–80.

Kahler, M. (2004). *Modeling Races to the Bottom*. Unpublished Paper. http://irp-shome.ucsd.edu/faculty/mkahler/RaceBott.pdf

Kahler, M. and D. Lake (eds.). (2004). *Governance in a Global Economy*. Princeton, NJ: Princeton University Press.

Kahn, A. E. (1970). *The Economic of Regulation: Principles and Institutions, vol. 1: Economic Principles*. New York: John Wiley.

Kahneman, D. (1994). 'New Challenges to the Rationality Assumption'. *Journal of Institutional and Theoretical Economics (JITE)/Zeitschrift Für Die Gesamte Staatswissenschaft 150*, no. *1* (1 March): 18–36.

Kahneman, D. (2003). 'Maps of Bounded Rationality: Psychology for Behavioral Economics'. *American Economic Review 93*, no. *5*: 1449–1475.

Kahneman, D. (2013a). Foreword. In E. Shafir (ed.), *The Behavioral Foundations of Public Policy*. Princeton, NJ: Princeton University Press.

Kahneman, D. (2013b). *Thinking, Fast and Slow* (1st edn). New York: Farrar, Straus & Giroux.

Kahneman, D. and A. Tversky. (1979). 'Prospect Theory: An Analysis of Decision Under Risk'. *Econometrica*, 47, no. *2*: 263–291.

Kahneman, D. and A. Tversky (eds). (2000). *Choices, Values, and Frames* (1st edn). New York; Cambridge: Cambridge University Press.

Kaine, G., H. Murdoch, R. Lourey and D. Bewsell. (2010). 'A Framework for Understanding Individual Response to Regulation'. *Food Policy 35*, no. *6* (December): 531–537.

Kaiser, A., A. Kaiser and J. Biela. (2012). *Policy Making in Multilevel Systems: Federalism, Decentralisation, and Performance in the OECD Countries*. Exeter, UK: European Consortium for Political Research Press.

Kallbekken, S., H. Sælen and E. A. T. Hermansen. (2013). 'Bridging the Energy Efficiency Gap: A Field Experiment on Lifetime Energy Costs and Household Appliances'. *Journal of Consumer Policy*, 36, no. 1: 1–16.

Kallgren, C. A., R. R. Reno and R. B. Cialdini. (2000). 'A Focus Theory of Normative Conduct: When Norms Do and Do Not Affect Behavior'. *Personality and Social Psychology Bulletin 26*, no. 8 (10 January): 1002–1012.

Kamerman, S. B. and A. J. Kahn (eds.). (1989). *Privatization and the Welfare State*. Princeton, NJ: Princeton University Press.

Kang, M. M. (2022). 'Whistleblowing in the Public Sector: A Systematic Literature Review'. *Review of Public Personnel Administration 43*, no. 2 (1 June): 381–406.

Kapstein, E. B. (1994). *Governing the Global Economy*. Cambridge, MA: Harvard University Press.

Karamanos, P. (2001). 'Voluntary Environmental Agreements: Evolution and Definition of a New Environmental Policy Approach'. *Journal of Environmental Planning and Management 44*, no. 1: 67–84.

Karlan, D. S. and J. Appel. (2011). *More Than Good Intentions: How a New Economics Is Helping to Solve Global Poverty*. New York: Dutton.

Karty, K. D. (2002). 'Closure and Capture in Federal Advisory Committees'. *Business and Politics 4*, no. 2: 213–238.

Kash, J. P. (2008). 'Enemies to Allies: The Role of Policy-Design Adaptation in Facilitating a Farmer-Environmentalist Alliance'. *Policy Studies Journal 36*, no. 1: 39–60.

Kassim, H. and P. Le Galès. (2010). 'Exploring Governance in a Multi-Level Polity: A Policy Instruments Approach'. *West European Politics 33*, no. 1: 1–21.

Kato, J. (1996). 'Review Article: Institutions and Rationality in Politics – Three Varieties of Neo-Institutionalists'. *British Journal of Political Science 26*: 553–582.

Katzenstein, P. J. (1977). 'Conclusion: Domestic Structures and Strategies of Foreign Economic Policy'. *International Organization 31*, no. 4: 879–920.

Katzenstein, P. J. (1985). *Small States in World Markets: Industrial Policy in Europe*. Ithaca, NY: Cornell University Press.

Katzman, M. T. (1988). 'Societal Risk Management through the Insurance Market'. In R. C. Hula (ed.), *Market-Based Public Policy*. London: Macmillan, 21–42.

Kautto, P. and J. Simila. (2005). 'Recently Introduced Policy Instruments and Intervention Theories'. *Evaluation 11*, no. 1: 55–68.

Kay, A. (2007). 'Tense Layering and Synthetic Policy Paradigms: The Politics of Health Insurance in Australia'. *Australian Journal of Political Science 42*, no. 4: 579–591.

Kay, A. (2011). 'Evidence-Based Policy-Making: The Elusive Search for Rational Public Administration'. *Australian Journal of Public Administration 70*, no. 3 (1 September): 236–245.

Kay, A. and P. Baker. (2015). 'What Can Causal Process Tracing Offer to Policy Studies? A Review of the Literature'. *Policy Studies Journal 43*, no. 1: 1–21.

Keast, R., K. Brown and M. Mandell. (2007). 'Getting the Right Mix: Unpacking Integration Meanings and Strategies'. *International Public Management Journal 10*, no. 1 (1 January): 9–33.

Keast, R., M. Mandell and K. Brown. (2006). 'Mixing State, Market and Network Governance Modes: The Role of Government in "Crowded" Policy Domains'. *International Journal of Organization Theory and Behavior 9*, no. 1: 27–50.

Kehinde, B. (2014). 'Applicability of Risk Transfer Tools to Manage Loss and Damage from Slow-Onset Climatic Risks'. *Procedia Economics and Finance*, 4th International Conference on Building Resilience, Incorporating the 3rd Annual Conference of the ANDROID Disaster Resilience Network, 8th–11th September, Salford Quays, UK, 710–717.

Kekez, A., M. Howlett and M. Ramesh (eds.). (2020). *Collaboration in Public Service Delivery: Promise and Pitfalls*. Cheltenham: Edward Elgar.

Kemp, R. L. (1991). *Privatization: The Provision of Public Services by the Private Sector*. Jefferson, NC: McFarland & Co.

Kemp, R. and D. Loorbach. (2006). 'Transition Management: A Reflexive Governance Approach'. In J.-P. Voss and D. Bauknecht (eds.), *Reflexive Governance for Sustainable Development*. Cheltenham: Edward Elgar, 103–130.

Kempf, R. J. (2015). 'Crafting Accountability Policy: Designing Offices of Inspector General'. *Policy and Society* 34: 147–149.

Keohane, N. O., R. L. Revesz and R. N. Stavins. (1998). 'The Choice of Regulatory Instruments in Environmental Policy'. *Harvard Environmental Law Review* 22: 313–367.

Keohane, R. O. (1989). *International Institutions and State Power: Essays in International Relations Theory*. Boulder, CO: Westview, 163.

Keohane, R. O. and S. Hoffman. (1991). 'Institutional Change in Europe in the 1980s'. In R. O. Keohane and S. Hoffman (eds.), *The New European Community: Decision-Making and Institutional Change*. Boulder, CO: Westview, 1–40.

Keohane, R. O. and D. G. Victor. (2011). 'The Regime Complex for Climate Change'. *Perspectives on Politics 9*, no. 1 (March): 7–23.

Kern, F. and M. Howlett. (2009). 'Implementing Transition Management as Policy Reforms: A Case Study of the Dutch Energy Sector'. *Policy Sciences 42*, no. 4: 391–408.

Kernaghan, K. (1985). 'Judicial Review of Administration Action'. In K. Kernaghan (ed.), *Public Administration in Canada: Selected Readings*. Toronto, ON: Methuen, 358–373.

Kernaghan, K. (1993). 'Partnership and Public Administration: Conceptual and Practical Considerations'. *Canadian Public Administration 36*, no. 1: 57–76.

Kernaghan, K., B. Marson and S. Borins. (2000). *The New Public Organization*. Toronto, ON: Institute of Public Administration of Canada.

Kerr, D. H. (1976). 'The Logic of "Policy" and Successful Policies'. *Policy Sciences 7*, no. 3: 351–363.

Kersh, R. (2015). 'Of Nannies and Nudges: The Current State of US Obesity Policymaking'. *Public Health 129*, no. 8 (August): 1083–1091.

Kerwin, C. M. (1994). 'The Elements of Rule-Making'. In D. H. Rosenbloom and R. D. Schwartz (eds), *Handbook of Regulation and Administrative Law*. New York: Marcel Dekker, 345–381.

Kerwin, C. M. (1999). *Rulemaking: How Government Agencies Write Law and Make Policy*. Washington, DC: CQ Press.

Kettl, D. F. (2000). *The Global Public Management Revolution: A Report on the Transformation of Governance*. Washington, DC: Brookings Institution.

Keyes, J. M. (1996). 'Power Tools: The Form and Function of Legal Instruments for Government Action'. *Canadian Journal of Administrative Law and Practice 10*: 133–174.

Keysar, E. (2005). 'Procedural Integration in Support of Environmental Policy Objectives: Implementing Sustainability'. *Journal of Environmental Planning and Management 48*, no. 4: 549–569.

Kickert, W. J. M. (2001). 'Public Management of Hybrid Organizations: Governance of Quasi-Autnomous Executive Agencies'. *International Public Management Journal 4*: 135–150.

Kickert, W. J. M., E.-H. Klijn and J. F. M. Koppenjan. (1997). 'Managing Networks in the Public Sector: Findings and Reflections'. In W. J. M. Kickert, E.-H. Klijn and J. F. M. Koppenjan (eds), *Managing Complex Networks: Strategies for the Public Sector*. London: Sage, 166–191.

Kickert, W. J. M. and J. F. M. Koppenjan. (1997). 'Public Management and Network Management: An Overview'. In W. J. M. Kickert, E.-H. Klijn and J. F. M. Koppenjan (eds), *Managing Complex Networks: Strategies for the Public Sector*. London: Sage, 35–61.

Kiel, L. D. and Elliott, E. W. (1996). *Chaos theory in the Social Sciences: Foundations and Applications*. Ann Arbor: University of Michigan Press.

Kiesling, L. (2001). 'Flimsy Excuse for More Regulation'. *Houston Chronicle* (2 December).

Kiliç, B. İ., Ö. Kuvat and E. Boztepe. (2021). *Measurement of the Effectiveness of Internal Audits in Public Sector: In Contemporary Issues in Public Sector Accounting and Auditing*. New York: Emerald Publishing Limited.

King, D. C. and J. L. Walker. (1991). 'The Origins and Maintenance of Groups'. In J. L. Walker (ed.), *Mobilizing Interest Groups in America: Patrons, Professions and Social Movements*. Ann Arbor, MI: University of Michigan Press, 75–102.

King, G. (2003). 'The Role of Participation in the European Demonstration Projects in ICZM'. *Coastal Management 31*, no. 2: 137–143.

Kingdon, J. W. (1984). *Agendas, Alternatives and Public Policies*. Boston, MA: Little, Brown.

Kingdon, J. W. (2001). 'A Model of Agenda-Setting, with Applications'. *Law Review of Michigan State University Detroit College of Law 2001*: 331.

Kirschen, E. S., J. Benard, H. Besters, F. Blackaby, O. Eckstein, J. Faaland, F. Hartog, L. Morissens and E. Tosco (eds). (1964). *Economic Policy in Our Time. I – General Theory*. Chicago, IL: Rand McNally.

Kiss, B., C. González Manchón and L. Neij. (2012). 'The Role of Policy Instruments in Supporting the Development of Mineral Wool Insulation in Germany, Sweden and the United Kingdom'. *Journal of Cleaner Production 48*, no. 2: 187–199.

Kissane, R. J. (2007). 'How Do Faith-Based Organizations Compare to Secular Providers? Nonprofit Directors' and Poor Women's Assessments of FBOs'. *Journal of Poverty 11*, no. 4: 91–115.

Kiviniemi, M. (1986). 'Public Policies and Their Targets: A Typology of the Concept of Implementation'. *International Social Science Journal 38*, no. 108: 251–266.

Kjær, A. M. (2004). *Governance*. Cambridge: Polity Press.

Kleiman, M. A. R. and S. M. Teles. (2006). 'Market and Non-Market Failures'. In M. Moran, M. Rein and R. E. Goodin (eds), *The Oxford Handbook of Public Policy*. Oxford: Oxford University Press, 624–650.

Klein, L., C. Biesenthal and E. Dehlin. (2015). 'Improvisation in Project Management: A Praxeology'. *International Journal of Project Management 33*, no. 2 (February): 267–277.

Klijn, E.-H. (1996). 'Analyzing and Managing Policy Processes in Complex Networks: A Theoretical Examination of the Concept Policy Network and Its Problems'. *Administration and Society 28*, no. 1: 90–119.

Klijn, E.-H. (2002). 'Governing Networks in the Hollow State: Contracting Out, Process Management, or a Combination of the Two?' *Public Management Review 4*, no. 2: 149–165.

Klijn, E. H. (2010). 'Trust in Governance Networks: Looking for Conditions for Innovative Solutions and Outcome' In S. P. Osborne (ed.), *The New Public Governance: Emerging Perspectives on the Theory and Practice of Public Governance*. London: Routledge, 303–322.

Klijn, E.-H., S. Bram and J. Edelenbos. (2010). 'The Impact of Network Management on Outcomes in Governance Network'. *Public Administration 88*, no. 4: 1063–1082.

Klijn, E.-H. and K. Joop. (2012). 'Governance Network Theory: Past, Present and Future'. *Policy & Politics 40*, no. 4: 587–606.

Klijn, E. H. and J. F. Koppenjan. (2000a). 'Interactive Decision Making and Representative Democracy: Institutional Collisions and Solutions'. In O. van Heffen, W. Kickert and J. Thomassen (eds.), *Governance in Modern Society: Effects, Change and Formation of Government Institutions*. Dordrecht, Netherlands: Kluwer, 109–134.

Klijn, E. H. and J. F. Koppenjan. (2000b). 'Politicians and Interactive Decision Making: Institutional Spoilsports or Playmakers'. *Public Administration 78*, no. 2: 365–387.

Klijn, E. H. and J. F. Koppenjan. (2000c). 'Public Management and Policy Networks: Foundations of a Network Approach to Governance'. *Public Management: An International Journal of Research and Theory*, 2, no. 2, 135–158.

Klijn, E. H. and J. F. Koppenjan. (2006). 'Institutional Design: Changing Institutional Features of Networks'. *Public Management Review 8*, no. 1: 141–160.

Klijn, E. H. and J. F. Koppenjan. (2007). 'Governing Policy Networks'. In G. Morcol (ed.), *Handbook of Decision Making*. New York: CRC/Taylor & Francis, 169–187.

Klijn, E. H., J. F. Koppenjan and K. Termeer. (1995). 'Managing Networks in the Public Sector: A Theoretical Study of Management Strategies in Policy Networks'. *Public Administration 73*, no. 3: 437–454.

Klijn, E.-H. and C. Skelcher. (2007). 'Democracy and Governance Networks: Compatible or Not?' *Public Administration 85*, no. 3: 587–608.

Klijn, E. H. and G. R. Teisman. (1991). 'Effective Policymaking in a Multi-Actor Setting: Networks and Steering'. In R. T. Veld, L. Schaap, C. J. A. M. Termeer and M. J. W. Van Twist (eds), *Autopoiesis and Configuration Theory: New Approaches to Societal Steering*. Dordrecht, Netherlands: Kluwer, 99–111.

Klitgaard, M. B. (2008). 'School Vouchers and the New Politics of the Welfare State'. *Governance 21*, no. 4: 479–498.

Klüver, H. (2013). *Lobbying in the European Union: Interest Groups, Lobbying Coalitions, and Policy Change*. Oxford University Press.

Knaggård, Å. (2015). 'The Multiple Streams Framework and the Problem Broker'. *European Journal of Political Research 54*, no 3: 450–465.

Knetsch, J. (2011). 'Behavioural Economics, Policy Analysis and the Design of Regulatory Reform'. In D. Low (ed.), *Behavioural Economics and Policy Design*. Singapore: Civil Service College, 161–182.

Knight, F. H. (2014 [1921]). *Risk Uncertainty and Profit* (illustrated edn). New York: Martino Fine Books.

Knill, C. (1998). 'European Policies: The Impact of National Administrative Traditions'. *Journal of Public Policy 18*, no. 1: 1–28.

Knill, C. (1999). 'Explaining Cross-National Variance in Administrative Reform: Autonomous Versus Instrumental Bureaucracies'. *Journal of Public Policy 19*, no. 2: 113–139.

Knill, C. (2001a). *The Europeanization of National Administrations: Patterns of Institutional Change and Persistence*. Cambridge: Cambridge University Press.

Knill, C. (2001b). 'Private Governance across Multiple Arenas: European Interest Associations as Interface Actors'. *Journal of European Public Policy 8*, no. 2: 227–246.

Knill, C. and A. Lenschow. (2005). 'Compliance, Communication and Competition: Patterns of EU Environmental Policy Making and Their Impact on Policy Convergence'. *European Environment 15*: 114–128.

Knill, C. and D. Lehmkuhl. (2002). 'Private Actors and the State: Internationalization and Changing Patterns of Governance'. *Governance 15*, no. 1: 41–63.

Knill, C., K. Schulze and J. Tosun. (2012). 'Regulatory Policy Outputs and Impacts: Exploring a Complex Relationship'. *Regulation & Governance 6*, no. 4: 427–444.

Knoepfel, P. and I. Kissling-Naf. (1998). 'Social Learning in Policy Networks'. *Policy and Politics 26*, no. 3: 343–367.

Knoke, D. (1987). *Political Networks: The Structural Perspective*. Cambridge: Cambridge University Press.

Knoke, D. (1993). 'Networks as Political Glue: Explaining Public Policy-Making'. In W. J. Wilson (ed.), *Sociology and the Public Agenda*. London: Sage, 164–184.

Knoke, D. (2004). 'The Sociopolitical Construction of National Policy Domains'. In C. H. C. A. Henning and C. Melbeck (eds), *Interdisziplinäre Sozialforschung: Theorie und empirische Anwendungen*. Frankfurt, Germany: Campus Verlag, 81–96.

Knoke, D. and J. H. Kuklinski. (1991). 'Network Analysis: Basic Concepts'. In G. Thompson, J. Frances, R. Levacic and J. Mitchell (eds.), *Markets, Hierarchies and Networks: The Coordination of Social Life*. London: Sage, 173–182.

Knott, J. H. and D. McCarthy. (2007). 'Policy Venture Capital: Foundations, Government Partnerships and Child Care Programs'. *Administration and Society 39*, no. 3: 319–353.

Knudson, W. (2009). 'The Environment, Energy, and the Tinbergen Rule'. *Bulletin of Science, Technology & Society 29*, no. 4 (1 August): 308–312.

Koch, P. (2013). 'Overestimating the Shift from Government to Governance: Evidence from Swiss Metropolitan Areas'. *Governance 26*, no. 3: 397–423.

Koen, V., P. G. Roness, B. Verschuere, K. Rubecksen and M. MacCarthaigh. (2010). *Autonomy and Control of State Agencies: Comparing States and Agencies*. London: Palgrave Macmillan.

Koffijberg, J., H. De Bruijn and H. Priemus. (2012). 'Combining Hierarchical and Network Strategies. Successful Changes in Dutch Social Housing'. *Public Administration 90*, no. 1: 262–275.

Kogan, V. (2010). 'Lessons from Recent State Constitutional Conventions'. *California Journal of Politics and Policy 2*, no. 2: Article 3.

Koh, T. Y. (2011). 'Key Ideas in Behavioural Economics—And What They Mean for Policy Design'. In D. Low (ed.), *Behavioural Economics and Policy Design*. Singapore: Civil Service College, 17–34.

Kohler-Koch, B. (1996). 'Catching Up with Change: The Transformation of Governance in the European Union'. *Journal of European Public Policy 3*, no. 3: 359–380.

Koliba, C., J. W. Meek and A. Zia. (2010). *Governance Networks in Public Administration and Public Policy* (1st edn). Boca Raton, FL: CRC Press.

Könnölä, T., J. E. Smith and A. Eerola. (2009). 'Future-Oriented Technology Analysis (FTA): Impacts and Implications for Policy and Decision Making'. *The 2008 FTA International Seville Conference 76*, no. 9 (November): 1135–1137.

Kooiman, J. (ed.). (1993). 'Governance and Governability: Using Complexity, Dynamics and Diversity'. In *Modern Governance*. London: Sage, 35–50.

Kooiman, J. (2000). 'Societal Governance: Levels, Models and Orders of Social – Political Interaction'. In J. Pierre (ed.), *Debating Governance*. Oxford: Oxford University Press, 138–166.

Kooiman, J. (2008). 'Exploring the Concept of Governability'. *Journal of Comparative Policy Analysis 10*, no. *2*: 171–190.

Koppell, J. G. S. (2003). *The Politics of Quasi-Government: Hybrid Organizations and the Dynamics of Bureaucratic Control*. Cambridge: Cambridge University Press.

Koppenjan, J., M. Kars and H. van der Voort. (2009). 'Vertical Politics in Horizontal Policy Networks: Framework Settings as Coupling Arrangement'. *Policy Studies Journal 37*, no. *4*: 769–792.

Koppenjan, J. and E.-H. Klijn. (2004). *Managing Uncertainties in Networks: A Network Approach to Problem Solving and Decision Making*. London: Routledge.

Korpi, W. (1980). 'Social Policy and Distributional Conflict in Capitalist Democracies'. *West European Politics 3*: 296–316.

Krause, R. M. (2011). 'Policy Innovation, Intergovernmental Relations, and the Adoption of Climate Protection Initiatives by US Cities'. *Journal of Urban Affairs 33*, no. *1*: 45–60.

Kritzinger, S. and H. Pulzl. (2008). 'Governance Modes and Interests: Higher Education and Innovation Policy in Austria'. *Journal of Public Policy 28*, no. *3*: 289–307.

Krosnick, J. A., A. L. Holbrook, L. Lowe and P. S. Visser. (2006). 'The Origins and Consequences of Democratic Citizens' Policy Agendas: A Study of Popular Concern About Global Warming'. *Climatic Change*, 77, no. *1–2*: 7–43.

Krysiak, F. C. and P. Schweitzer. (2010). 'The Optimal Size of a Permit Market'. *Journal of Environmental Economics and Management 60*, no. *2*: 133–143.

Kuhfuss, L., R. Préget, S. Thoyer and N. Hanley. (2016). 'Nudging Farmers to Enrol Land into Agri-Environmental Schemes: The Role of a Collective Bonus'. *European Review of Agricultural Economics 43*, no. *4*: 609–636.

Kuhlmann, E. and J. Allsop. (2008). 'Professional Self-Regulation in a Changing Architecture of Governance: Comparing Health Policy in the UK and Germany'. *Policy and Politics 36*, no. *2*: 173–189.

Kuhn, M. and L. Siciliani. (2013). 'Manipulation and Auditing of Public Sector Contracts'. *European Journal of Political Economy 32* (1 December): 251–267.

Kuhn, T. S. (1962). *The Structure of Scientific Revolutions*. Chicago, IL: University of Chicago Press.

Kuhn, T. S. (1974). 'Second Thoughts on Paradigms'. In F. Suppe (ed.), *The Structure of Scientific Theories*. Urbana, IL: University of Illinois Press, 459–482.

Kuhner, S. (2007). 'Country-Level Comparisons of Welfare State Change Measures: Another Facet of the Dependent Variable Problem Within the Comparative Analysis of the Welfare State'. *Journal of European Social Policy 17*, no. *1*: 5–18.

Kuipers, B., H., Malcolm, K., Walter, T. G. Lars, G. Jolien and V. V. Joris. (2013). *The Management of Change in Public Organisations: A Literature Review*. Public Administration. SSRN. http://ssrn.com/abstract=2226612

Kuks, S. (2004). 'Comparative Review and Analysis of Regime Changes in Europe'. *Environmental Politics 40*, no. *2*: 329–368.

Kulesher, R. and E. Forrestal. (2014). 'International Models of Health Systems Financing'. *Journal of Hospital Administration 3*, no. *4*: 127–139.

Kulick, J., J. Prieger and M. A. R. Kleiman. (2016). 'Unintended Consequences of Cigarette Prohibition, Regulation, and Taxation'. *International Journal of Law, Crime and Justice 46* (1 September): 69–85.

Kwakkel, J. H., W. E. Walker and V. A. W. J. Marchau. (2010). 'Classifying and Communicating Uncertainties in Model-Based Policy Analysis'. *International Journal of Technology, Policy and Management 10*, no. 4 (1 January): 299–315.

Kwaterski, J. (2010). *Opportunities for Rationalizing the Capacity Development Knowledge Architecture.* Washington, DC: The World Bank Institute and Learning Network for Capacity Development.

Kwon, S. (2018). *Advancing Universal Health Coverage: What Developing Countries Can Learn from the Korean Experience?* Universal Health Coverage Study Series No. 33. Washington, DC: The World Bank.

La Porte, T. (ed.). (1975). *Organized Social Complexity Challenge to Politics and Policy.* Princeton, NJ: Princeton University Press.

Lackey, R. T. (2007). 'Science, Scientists, and Policy Advocacy'. *Conservation Biology 21*: 12–17.

Ladi, S. (2000). 'Globalization, Think-Tanks and Policy Transfer'. In D. Stone (ed.), *Banking on Knowledge: The Genesis of the GDN.* London: Routledge, 203–220.

Lægreid, P., P. G. Roness and K. Rubecksen. (2008). 'Controlling Regulatory Agencies'. *Scandinavian Political Studies 31*, no. 1: 1–26.

Lafferty, W. M. and E. Hovden. (2003). 'Environmental Policy Integration: Towards an Analytical Framework'. *Environmental Politics 12*, no. 3: 1–22.

Laffont, J. J. and J. Tirole. (1991). 'The Politics of Government Decision-Making: A Theory of Regulatory Capture'. *The Quarterly Journal of Economics 106*, no. 4: 1089–1127.

Laforest, R. and M. Orsini. (2005). 'Evidence-Based Engagement in the Voluntary Sector: Lessons from Canada'. *Social Policy and Administration 39*, no. 5: 481–497.

Lai, A. Y. (2012). 'Organizational Collaborative Capacity in Fighting Pandemic Crises: A Literature Review from the Public Management Perspective'. *Asia-Pacific Journal of Public Health 24*, no. 1 (1 January): 7–20.

Landes, W. M. and R. A. Posner. (1975). 'The Independent Judiciary in an Interest Group Perspective'. *Journal of Law and Economics 18* (December): 875–901.

Landry, R. (1991). 'Party Competition in Quebec: Direct Confrontation or Selective Emphasis?' In H. G. Thorburn (ed.), *Party Politics in Canada.* Scarborough, ON: Prentice-Hall, 401–413.

Landry, R., M. Lamari and N. Amara. (2003). 'The Extent and Determinants of the Utilization of University Research in Government Agencies'. *Public Administration Review 63*, no. 2: 192–205.

Landry, R., F. Varone and M. L. Goggin. (1998). 'The Determinants of Policy Design: The State of the Theoretical Literature'. Paper presented to the Midwest Political Science Association, Chicago, IL.

Landuyt, Dries, Steven Broekx, Guy Engelen, Inge Uljee, Maarten Van der Meulen and Peter L. M. Goethals. (2016). 'The Importance of Uncertainties in Scenario Analyses – A Study on Future Ecosystem Service Delivery in Flanders'. *Science of The Total Environment 553* (15 May): 504–518.

Lane, J. E. (2000). *New Public Management.* London: Routledge.

Lang, A. (2019). 'Collaborative Governance in Health and Technology Policy: The Use and Effects of Procedural Policy Instruments'. *Administration & Society 51*, no. 2 (1 February): 272–298.

Lang, A. (2022). 'The Need to Understand and Integrate Procedural and Substantive Tools'. In M. Howlett (ed.), *The Routledge Handbook of Policy Tools*. London: Routledge.

Lange, P., P. Driessen, A. Scuerc, B. Bornemann and P. Burgen. (2013). 'Governing towards Sustainability – Conceptualizing Modes of Governance'. *Journal of Environmental Policy & Planning 15*, no. 3: 403–425.

Langenbrunner, J. C., S. O'Duagherty and C. S. Cashin (eds.). (2009). *Designing and Implementing Health Care Provider Payment Systems: "How-to" Manuals*. Washington, DC: The World Bank.

Lanzalaco, L. (2011). 'Bringing the Olympic Rationality Back In? Coherence, Integration and Effectiveness of Public Policies'. *World Political Science Review 7*, no. 1 (25 May): 1098.

Larsen, T. P., P. Taylor-Gooby and J. Kananen. (2006). 'New Labour's Policy Style: A Mix of Policy Approaches'. *International Social Policy 35*, no. 4: 629–649.

Larson, J. S. (1980). *Why Government Programs Fail: Improving Policy Implementations*. New York: Praeger.

Lascoumes, P. and P. Le Galès. (2007). 'Introduction: Understanding Public Policy through Its Instruments – From the Nature of Instruments to the Sociology of Public Policy Instrumentation'. *Governance 20*, no. 1: 1–21.

Lasswell, H. (1956). *The Decision Process: Seven Categories of Functional Analysis*. College Park, MD: University of Maryland Press.

Lasswell, H. (1958). *Politics: Who Gets What, When, How*. New York: Meridian.

Lasswell, H. (1971). *A Pre-View of Policy Sciences*. New York: Elsevier.

Lasswell, H. D. (1951). 'The Policy Orientation'. In D. Lerner and H. D. Lasswell (eds.), *The Policy Sciences: Recent Developments in Scope and Method*. Palo Alto, CA: Stanford University Press, 3–15.

Lasswell, H. D. (1954). 'Key Symbols, Signs and Icons'. In L. Bryson, L. Finkelstein, R. M. MacIver and R. McKean (eds.), *Symbols and Values: An Initial Study*. New York: Harper, 77–94.

Lasswell, H. D. (1970). 'The Emerging Conception of the Policy Sciences'. *Policy Sciences 1*: 3–14.

Latin, H. A. (2012). *Climate Change Policy Failures*. Hackensack, NJ: World Scientific Publishing.

Laux, J. (1993). 'How Private is Privatization'. *Canadian Public Policy 19*, no. 4: 398–411.

Laux, J. K. and M. A. Molot. (1988). *State Capitalism: Public Enterprise in Canada*. Ithaca, NY: Cornell University Press.

Lawrence, D. P. (2001). 'Choices for EIA Process Design and Management'. *Journal of Environmental Assessment Policy and Management 3*, no. 4: 437–464.

Lawrence, M., T. Homer-Dixon, S. Janzwood, J. Rockstrom, O. Renn and J. F. Donges. (2023). 'Global Polycrisis: The Causal Mechanisms of Crisis Entanglement'. SSRN Scholarly Paper, Rochester, NY, 18 June. https://doi.org/10.2139/ssrn.4483556

Lazarus, R. J. (2009). 'Super Wicked Problems and Climate Change: Restraining the Present to Liberate the Future'. *Cornell Law Review 94*: 1153–1234.

Lazer, D. and V. Mayer-Schonberger. (2002). 'Governing Networks: Telecommunication Deregulation in Europe and the United States'. *Brooklyn Journal of International Law* no. 3: 820–851.

Le Grand, J. (ed.). (1984). *Privatization and the Welfare State*. London: Allen & Unwin.

407

Le Grand, J. (1991). 'The Theory of Government Failure'. *British Journal of Political Science 21*, no. 4: 423–442.

Le Grand, J. (2007). *The Other Invisible Hand: Delivering Public Services through Choice and Competition*. Princeton, NJ: Princeton University Press.

Le Grand, J. (2009). 'Choice and Competition in Publicly Funded Health Care'. *Health Economics, Policy and Law 4*, no. 3: 479–488.

Lecuyer, O. and R. Bibas. (2012). *Combining Climate and Energy Policies: Synergies or Antagonism? Modeling Interactions with Energy Efficiency Instruments*. SSRN Scholarly Paper. Rochester, NY: Social Science Research Network. http://papers. ssrn.com/abstract=1992324. Accessed 26 January.

Lecuyer, O. and P. Quirion. (2013). 'Can Uncertainty Justify Overlapping Policy Instruments to Mitigate Emissions?' *Ecological Economics 93* (September): 177–191.

Ledingham, J. A. (2003). 'Explicating Relationship Management as a General Theory of Public Relations'. *Journal of Public Relations Research 15*, no. 2: 181–198.

Lee, N. (2006). 'Bridging the Gap Between Theory and Practice in Integrated Assessment'. *Environmental Impact Assessment Review 26*: 57–78.

Lee, Y. (2008). 'Design Participation Tactics: The Challenges and New Roles for Designers in the Co-Design Process'. *CoDesign 4*, no. 1: 31–50.

Leech, B. L., F. R. Baumgartner, T. La Pira and N. A. Semanko. (2005). 'Drawing Lobbyists to Washington: Government Activity and the Demand for Advocacy'. *Political Research Quarterly 58*, no. 1: 19–30.

Leenheer, J., M. Elsen, N. Mikola, M. Wagt, L. L. van der, European Commission and GFK. (2014). *Study on the Effects on Consumer Behaviour of Online Sustainability Information Displays: Final Report*. Luxembourg: Publications Office of the European Union. http://bookshop.europa.eu/uri?target=EUB:NOTICE:KK0214676:EN:HTML.

Leeuw, F. L. (1991). 'Policy Theories, Knowledge Utilization, and Evaluation'. *Knowledge and Policy 4*, no. 3: 73–91.

Leeuw, F. L. (1998). 'The Carrot: Subsidies as a Tool of Government'. In M.-L. Bemelmans-Videc, R. C. Rist and E. Vedung (eds.), *Carrots, Sticks and Sermons: Policy Instruments and Their Evaluation*. New Brunswick, NJ: Transaction, 77–102.

Leggett, J. A. (2011). *Climate Change: Conceptual Approaches and Policy Tools* (CRS Report for Congress No. 7–5700). Washington, DC: Congressional Research Service. http://biotech.law.lsu.edu/blog/R41973.pdf.

LeGrand, J. (1984). *Privatization and the Welfare State*. London: Unwin Hyman.

Legrand, T. (2018). 'Structure, Agency and Policy Learning: Australia's Multinational Corporations Dilemma'. In C. A. Dunlop, C. M. Radaelli and P. Trein (eds.), *Learning in Public Policy: Analysis, Modes and Outcomes*. International Series on Public Policy. Cham: Springer International Publishing, 215–241.

Legrand, T. (2022). 'The Malign System in Policy Studies: Strategies of Structural and Agential Political Exclusion'. *International Journal of Public Policy 16*, no. 2–4 (January): 88–105.

Legrand, T. and L. Jarvis. (2014). 'Enemies of the State: Proscription Powers and Their Use in the United Kingdom'. *British Politics 9*, no. 4 (1 December): 450–471.

Lehmbruch, G. (1979). 'Consociational Democracy, Class Conflict and the New Corporatism'. In P. C. Schmitter and G. Lehmbruch (eds.), *Trends Towards Corporatist Intermediation*. Beverley Hills, CA: Sage, 53–61.

Lehmbruch, G. (1991). 'The Organization of Society, Administrative Strategies and Policy Networks'. In R. M. Czada and A. Windhoff-Heritier (eds.), *Political*

Choice: Institutions, Rules and the Limits of Rationality. Boulder, CO: Westview, 121–155.

Lehmbruch, G. and P. Schmitter. (1982). *Patterns of Corporatist Policy-Making.* London: Sage.

Lehmkuhl, D. (2008). 'On Government, Governance and Judicial Review: The Case of European Competition Policy'. *Journal of Public Policy 28*, no. 1: 139–159.

Lehner, M., O. Mont and E. Heiskanen. (2015). 'Nudging – a Promising Tool for Sustainable Consumption Behaviour?' *Journal of Cleaner Production,* Special Volume: Transitions to Sustainable Consumption and Production in Cities, 134 (October 15, 2016): 166–177.

Lehoux, P., J.-L. Denis, S. Tailliez and M. Hivon. (2005). 'Dissemination of Health Technology Assessments: Identifying the Visions Guiding and Evolving Policy Innovation in Canada'. *Journal of Health Politics, Policy and Law 30*, no. 4: 603–641.

Lehtonen, M. (2017). 'Operationalizing Information: Measures and Indicators in Policy Formulation'. In M. Howlett and I. Mukherjee (eds.), *Handbook of Policy Formulation.* Cheltenham: Edward Elgar, 161–181.

Lehtonen, M. (2022). 'Indicators and Measures as Policy Tools'. In M. Howlett (ed.), *Handbook of Policy Tools.* Cheltenham: Edward Elgar, 185–196.

Leik, R. K. (1992). 'New Directions for Network Exchange Theory: Strategic Manipulation of Network Linkages'. *Social Networks 14*: 309–323.

Leiss, W. and D. A. Powell. (2004). *Mad Cows and Mother's Milk: The Perils of Poor Risk Communication* (2nd edn). Montreal, QC: McGill-Queen's University Press.

Leiter, Andrea and Marie Petersmann. (2022). 'Tech-Based Prototypes in Climate Governance: On Scalability, Replicability, and Representation'. *Law and Critique 33*, no. 3 (31 July): 319–333.

Lejano, R. P. and H. Ingram. (2009). 'Collaborative Networks and New Ways of Knowing'. *Environmental Science and Policy 12*, no. 6: 653–662.

Lejano, R. P. and C. Leong. (2012). 'A Hermeneutic Approach to Explaining and Understanding Public Controversies'. *Journal of Public Administration Research and Theory 22*: 793–814.

Lejano, R. P. and S. Shankar. (2013). 'The Contextualist Turn and Schematics of Institutional Fit: Theory and a Case Study from Southern India'. *Policy Sciences 46*, no. 1 (1 March): 83–102.

Leland, S. and O. Smirnova. (2009). 'Reassessing Privatization Strategies 25 Years Later: Revisting Perry and Babitsky's Comparative Performance Study of Urban Bus Transit Services'. *Public Administration Review 69*, no. 5: 855–867.

Leman, C. K. (1989). 'The Forgotten Fundamental: Successes and Excesses of Direct Government'. In L. M. Salamon (ed.), *Beyond Privatization: The Tools of Government Action.* Washington, DC: Urban Institute, 51–92.

Leman, C. K. (2002). 'Direct Government'. In L. M. Salamon (ed.), *The Tools of Government: A Guide to the New Governance.* New York: Oxford University Press, 48–79.

Lemke, Thomas. (2002). 'Foucault, Governmentality, and Critique'. *Rethinking Marxism 14*, no. 3 (1 September): 49–64.

Lempert, R., S. Popper and S. Bankes. (2002). 'Confronting Surprise'. *Social Science Computer Review 20*, no. 4: 420–440.

Lenihan, D. G. and R. Alcock. (2000). *Collaborative Government in the Post-Industrial Age: Five Discussion Pieces – Changing Government* (Vol. I). Ottawa, ON: Centre for Collaborative Government.

Leone, L. (2010). *Opening Up Innovation: Strategy, Organization and Technology.* London: Imperial College Business School.

Leong, Ching and Michael Howlett. (2022a). 'Policy Learning, Policy Failure, and the Mitigation of Policy Risks: Re-Thinking the Lessons of Policy Success and Failure'. *Administration & Society 54*, no. 7: 1379–1401.

Leong, Ching and Michael Howlett. (2022b). 'Theorizing the Behavioral State: Resolving the Theory-Practice Paradox of Policy Sciences'. *Public Policy and Administration 37*, no. 2 (1 April): 203–225.

Leong, Ching and Michael Howlett. (2022c). 'Soft OR as a Response to Inherent Vices: Problem Structuring to Offset Policy Volatility'. *EURO Journal on Decision Processes 10* (1 January): 100019.

Leplay, S. and S. Thoyer. (2011). *Synergy Effects of International Policy Instruments to Reduce Deforestation: A Cross-country Panel Data Analysis* (Working Paper). Montpellier, France: LAMETA, University of Montpellier. http://ideas.repec. org/p/lam/wpaper/11-01.html.

Lerner, D. and H. D. Lasswell (eds.). (1951). *The Policy Sciences: Recent Developments in Scope and Method.* Stanford: Stanford University Press.

Leroux, T., M. Hirtle and L.-N. Fortin. (1998). 'An Overview of Public Consultation Mechanisms Developed to Address the Ethical and Social Issues Raised by Biotechnology'. *Journal of Consumer Policy 21*, no. 4: 445–481.

Lester, J. P. and M. L. Goggin. (1998). 'Back to the Future: The Rediscovery of Implementation Studies'. *Policy Currents 8*, no. 3: 1–9.

Leung, W., B. Noble, J. Gunn and J. A. G. Jaeger. (2015). 'A Review of Uncertainty Research in Impact Assessment'. *Environmental Impact Assessment Review 50* (January): 116–123.

Leutz, W. N. (1999). 'Five Laws for Integrating Medical and Social Services: Lessons from the United States and the United Kingdom'. *The Milbank Quarterly 77*, no. *1* (1 January): 77–110.

Levi-Faur, D. (2003). 'The Politics of Liberalisation: Privatisation and Regulation-For-Competition in Europe's and Latin America's Telecoms and Electricity Industries'. *European Journal of Political Research 42*, no. *5*: 705–723.

Levi-Faur, D. (2009). 'Regulatory Capitalism and the Reassertion of the Public Interest'. *Policy and Society 27*, no. *3*: 181–191.

Levi-Faur, D. (2012). 'From "Big Government" to "Big Governance"?' In D. Levi-Faur (ed.), *The Oxford Handbook of Governance.* Oxford: Oxford University Press, 3–18.

Levi-Faur, D. (2014). 'The Welfare State: A Regulatory Perspective'. *Public Administration 92*, no. *3*: 599–614.

Levi-Faur, D. and S. Gilad. (2005). 'The Rise of the British Regulatory State – Transcending the Privatization Debate'. *Comparative Politics 37*, no. *1*: 105–124.

Levi-Strauss, C. (1966). *The Savage Mind.* Chicago: The University of Chicago Press.

Levin, K., B. Cashore, S. Bernstein and G. Auld. (2012). 'Overcoming the Tragedy of Super Wicked Problems: Constraining our Future Selves to Ameliorate Global Climate Change'. *Policy Sciences. 45*, no. 2: 123–152.

Levin, Lia. (2023). 'Contracting out Public Participation to External Consultants: Observations on Epistemic Justice'. *Public Administration Review 83*, no. 1: 92–102.

Levine, M. E. and J. L. Forrence. (1990). 'Regulatory Capture, Public Interest and the Public Agenda: Towards Synthesis'. *Journal of Law, Economics and Organization 6*: 167–198.

Levitsky, S. and L. A. Way. (2010). *Competitive Authoritarianism: Hybrid Regimes after the Cold War.* Cambridge: Cambridge University Press.

Levitt, B. and J. G. March. (1988). 'Organizational Learning'. *Annual Review of Sociology 14*: 319–340.

Levy, B. and P. T. Spiller. (1994). 'The Institutional Foundations of Regulatory Commitment: A Comparative Analysis of Telecommunications Regulation'. *Journal of Law, Economics and Organization* 10, no. 2: 201–246.

Levy, D. and M. Scully. (2007). 'The Institutional Entrepreneur as Modern Prince: The Strategic Face of Power in Contested Fields'. *Organization Studies 28*, no. 7 (1 July): 971–991.

Lewis, M. (2007). *States of Reason: Freedom, Responsibility and the Governing of Behaviour Change*. London: Institute for Public Policy Research.

Li, C., X. Yu, J. R. G. Butler, V. Yiengprugsawan and M. Yu. (2011). 'Moving Towards Universal Health Insurance in China: Performance, Issues and Lessons from Thailand'. *Social Science & Medicine 73*, no. 3 (August): 359–366.

Li, Y., E. J. Johnson and L. Zaval. (2011). 'Local Warming: Daily Temperature Change Influences Belief in Global Warming'. *Psychological Science 22*, no. 4: 454–459.

Libecap, G. D. (1986). 'Deregulation as an Instrument in Industrial Policy: Comment'. *Journal of Institutional and Theoretical Economics 142*: 70–74.

Libecap, G. D. (2005). 'State Regulations of Open-Access, Common-Pool Resources'. In C. Menard and M. M. Shirley (eds.), *Handbook of New Institutional Economics*. Dordrecht, Netherlands: Springer, 545–572.

Lichtenstein, S. and P. Slovic. (2006). *The Construction of Preference*. Cambridge and New York: Cambridge University Press.

Lidskog, R. and I. Flander. (2010). 'Addressing Climate Change Democratically. Multilevel Governance, Transnational Networks and Governmental Structures'. *Sustainable Development 18*: 32–41.

Liefferink, D. (2006). 'The Dynamics of Policy Arrangements: Turning Round the Tetrahedron'. In B. Arts and P. Leroy (eds.), *Institutional Dynamics in Environmental Governance*. Dordrecht, Netherlands: Springer, 45–68.

Liefferink, D., B. Arts, J. Kamstra and J. Ooijevaar. (2009). 'Leaders and Laggards in Environmental Policy: A Quantitative Analysis of Domestic Policy Outputs'. *Journal of European Public Policy 16*, no. 5: 677–700.

Lierse, H. (2010). 'European Economic Governance: The OMC as a Road to Integration?' *International Journal of Public Policy 6*, no. 1/2: 35–49.

Lijphart, A. (1969). 'Consociational Democracy'. *World Politics 21*, no. 2: 207–225.

Lindblom, C. E. (1955). *Bargaining: The Hidden Hand in Government*. Los Angeles, CA: Rand Corporation.

Lindblom, C. E. (1958a). 'Policy Analysis'. *American Economic Review 48*, no. 3: 298–312.

Lindblom, C. E. (1958b). 'Tinbergen on Policy-Making'. *The Journal of Political Economy 66*, no. 6 (December): 531–538.

Lindblom, C. E. (1959). 'The Science of Muddling Through'. *Public Administration Review 19*, no. 2: 79–88.

Lindblom, C. E. and D. K. Cohen. (1979). *Usable Knowledge: Social Science and Social Problem Solving*. New Haven: Yale University Press.

Linder, S. H. (1999). 'Coming to Terms with Public – Private Partnership'. *American Behavioural Scientist 43*, no. 1: 35–51.

Linder, S. H. and B. G. Peters. (1984). 'From Social Theory to Policy Design'. *Journal of Public Policy 4*, no. 3: 237–259.

Linder, S. H. and B. G. Peters. (1987). 'A Design Perspective on Policy Implementation: The Fallacy of Misplaced Precision'. *Review of Policy Research 6*: 459–475.

Linder, S. H. and B. G. Peters. (1988). 'The Analysis of Design or the Design of Analysis?' *Policy Studies Review 7*, no. 4: 738–750.

Linder, S. H. and B. G. Peters. (1989). 'Instruments of Government: Perception and Contexts'. *Journal of Public Policy 9*, no. 1: 35–58.

Linder, S. H. and B. G. Peters. (1990a). 'The Design of Instruments for Public Policy'. In S. S. Nagel (ed.), *Policy Theory and Policy Evaluation: Concepts, Knowledge, Causes and Norms*. New York: Greenwood Press, 103–119.

Linder, S. H. and B. G. Peters. (1990b). 'An Institutional Approach to the Theory of Policy-Making: The Role of Guidance Mechanisms in Policy Formulation'. *Journal of Theoretical Politics 2*, no. 1 (1 January): 59–83.

Linder, S. H. and B. G. Peters. (1990c). 'Policy Formulation and the Challenge of Conscious Design'. *Evaluation and Program Planning 13*: 303–311.

Linder, S. H. and B. G. Peters. (1990d). 'Research Perspectives on the Design of Public Policy: Implementation, Formulation and Design'. In D. J. Palumbo and D. J. Calista (eds.), *Implementation and the Policy Process: Opening up the Black Box*. New York: Greenwood Press.

Linder, S. H. and B. G. Peters. (1991). 'The Logic of Public Policy Design: Linking Policy Actors and Plausible Instruments'. *Knowledge, Technology & Policy 4*, no. 1: 125–151.

Linder, S. H. and B. G. Peters. (1992). 'A Metatheoretic Analysis of Policy Design'. In W. N. Dunn and R. M. Kelly (eds.), *Advances in Policy Studies Since 1950*. New Brunswick, NJ: Transaction, 201–238.

Linder, S. H. and B. G. Peters. (1988). 'The Analysis of Design or the Design of Analysis?' *Policy Studies Review 7*, no. 4: 738–750.

Linders, D. (2012). 'From E-Government to We-Government: Defining a Typology for Citizen Coproduction in the Age of Social Media'. *Government Information Quarterly* (Social Media in Government – Selections from the 12th Annual International Conference on Digital Government Research) dg.o2011 29, no. 4 (October): 446–454.

Lindquist, E. (2006). 'Organizing for Policy Implementation: The Emergence and Role of Implementation Units in Policy Design and Oversight'. *Journal of Comparative Policy Anlaysis: Research and Practice 8*, no. 4: 311–324.

Lindquist, E. and J. Desveaux. (1998). *Recruitment and Policy Capacity in Government*. Ottawa, ON: Public Policy Forum.

Lindquist, E. A. (1992 (2000)). 'Public Managers and Policy Communities: Learning to Meet New Challenges'. *Canadian Public Administration 35*, no. 2: 127–159.

Lindquist, E. A. (1998). 'A Quarter Century of Canadian Think Tanks: Evolving Institutions, Conditions and Strategies'. In D. Stone, A. Denham and M. Garnett (eds.), *Think Tanks Across Nations: A Comparative Approach*. Manchester, UK: Manchester University Press, 127–144.

Lindquist, E. A. (ed.). (2000). *Government Restructuring and Career Public Service in Canada*. Toronto, ON: Institute of Public Administration of Canada.

Lindquist, E. A. (2006). 'Organizing for Policy Implementation: The Emergence and Role of Implementation Units in Policy Design and Oversight'. *Journal of Comparative Policy Analysis: Research and Practice 8*, no. 4: 311–324.

Lindquist, E. A. and J. Desveaux. (2007). 'Policy Analysis and Bureaucratic Capacity: Context, Competencies, and Strategies'. In L. Dobuzinskis, M. Howlett and D. Laycock (eds.), *Policy Analysis in Canada*. Toronto: University of Toronto Press, 116–142.

Lindqvist, K. (2016). 'Dilemmas and Paradoxes of Regional Cultural Policy Implementation: Governance Modes, Discretion, and Policy Outcome'. *Administration & Society 51*, no. 1 (20 January): 63–90.

Lindvall, J. (2009). 'The Real but Limited Influence of Expert Ideas'. *World Politics* 61, no. 4: 703–730.

Ling, T. (2002). 'Delivering Joined Up Government in the UK: Dimensions, Issues and Problems'. *Public Administration 80*, no. 4: 615–642.

Liu, J., V. Hull, H. C. J. Godfray, D. Tilman, P. Gleick, H. Hoff and S. Li. (2018). 'Nexus Approaches to Global Sustainable Development'. *Nature Sustainability 1*, no. 9: 466–476.

Liu, S., L. Yang, C. Zhang, Y. T. Xiang, Z. Liu, S. Hu and B. Zhang. (2020). 'Online Mental Health Services in China during the Covid-19 Outbreak'. *The Lancet Psychiatry 7*, no. 4: 17–18.

Liu, X. (2003). *Policy Tools for Allocative Efficiency of Health Services*. Geneva: World Health Organization.

Locke, W. (2009). 'Reconnecting the Research – Policy – Practice Nexus in Higher Education: 'Evidence-Based Policy" in Practice in National and International Contexts'. *Higher Education Policy 22*: 119–140.

Lockton, D., D. Harrison and N. A. Stanton. (2016). 'Design for Sustainable Behaviour: Investigating Design Methods for Influencing User Behaviour'. *Annual Review of Policy Design 4*, no. 1 (28 October): 1–10.

Lockwood, M. (2013). 'The Political Sustainability of Climate Policy: The Case of the UK Climate Change Act'. *Global Environmental Change 23*: 1339–1348.

Lodge, M. (2003). 'Institutional Choice and Policy Transfer: Reforming British and German Railway Regulation'. *Governance 16*, no. 2: 159–178.

Lodge, M. (2008). 'Regulation, the Regulatory State and European Politics'. *West European Politics 31*, no. 1–2: 280–301.

Loewenstein, G. (2008). *Exotic Preferences: Behavioral Economics and Human Motivation*. Oxford and New York: Oxford University Press.

Loewenstein, G., C. Bryce, D. Hagmann and S. Rajpal. (2015). 'Warning: You Are About to Be Nudged'. *Behavioral Science & Policy 1*, no. 1 (1 April): 35–42.

Logan, D. C. (2009). 'Known Knowns, Known Unknowns, Unknown Unknowns and the Propagation of Scientific Enquiry'. *Journal of Experimental Botany 60*, no. 3 (1 March): 712–714.

Lombardo, E. (2005). 'Integrating or Setting the Agenda? Gender Mainstreaming in the European Constitution-Making Process'. *Social Politics 12*, no. 3: 412–432.

Lombe, M. and M. Sherraden. (2008). 'Inclusion in the Policy Process: An Agenda for Participation of the Marginalized'. *Journal of Policy Practice 7*, no. 2–3: 199–213.

Lorenzoni, I., S. Nicholson-Cole and L. Whitmarsh. (2007). 'Barriers Perceived to Engaging with Climate Change Among the UK Public and Their Policy Implications'. *Global Environmental Change 18*, no. 3–4: 445–459.

Lorenzoni, I. and N. F. Pidgeon. (2006). 'Public Views on Climate Change. European and USA Perspectives'. *Climate Change 77*: 73–95.

Lourenço, J. S., E. Ciriolo, S. R. Almeida and X. Troussard. (2016). *Behavioural Insights Applied to Policy: European Report 2016*. Brussels, Belgium: European Commission.

Lovan, W. R., M. Murray and R. Shaffer. (2004). 'Participatory Governance in a Changing World'. In W. R. Lovan, M. Murray and R. Shaffer (eds.), *Participatory Governance: Planning, Conflict Mediation and Public Decision-Making in Civil Society*. Aldershot, UK: Ashgate, 1–20.

Lovink, J. A. A. (1999). 'Choosing the Right Autonomy for Operators of Privatized Government Services: The Case of Nav Canada'. *Canadian Public Administration 42*, no. 3: 371–386.

Low, D. (2012). *Behavioural Economics and Policy Design: Examples from Singapore*. Singapore and Hackensack, NJ: World Scientific.

Lowi, T. J. (1966). 'Distribution, Regulation, Redistribution: The Functions of Government'. In R. B. Ripley (ed.), *Public Policies and Their Politics: Techniques of Government Control*. New York: W. W. Norton, 27–40.

Lowi, T. J. (1969). *The End of Liberalism: Ideology, Policy and the Crisis of Public Authority*. New York: Norton.

Lowi, T. J. (1972). 'Four Systems of Policy, Politics and Choice'. *Public Administration Review 32*, no. 4: 298–310.

Lowi, T. J. (1985). 'The State in Politics: The Relation between Policy and Administration'. In R. G. Noll (ed.), *Regulatory Policy and the Social Sciences*. Berkeley, CA: University of California Press, 67–105.

Lowndes, V. and C. Skelcher. (1998). 'The Dynamics of Multi-Organizational Partnerships: An Analysis of Changing Modes of Governance'. *Public Administration 76*: 313–333.

Lowry, R. C. (1999). 'Foundation Patronage toward Citizen Groups and Think Tanks: Who Gets Grants?' *The Journal of Politics 81*, no. 3: 758–776.

Lunn, P. D. (2013). 'Behavioural Economics and Policymaking: Learning from the Early Adopters'. *The Economic and Social Review 43*, no. 3 (Autumn): 423–449.

Lunn, P. D. (2014). *Regulatory Policy and Behavioural Economics*. Paris, France: Organisation for Economic Co-operation and Development. www.oecdilibrary.org/content/book/9789264207851-en.

Lutz, S. (2003). *Convergence within National Diversity: A Comparative Perspective on the Regulatory State in Finance* (Discussion Paper 03/7). Cologne, Germany: Max Planck Institute for the Study of Societies.

Lybecker, K. M. and R. A. Freeman. (2007). 'Funding Pharmaceutical Innovation Through Direct Tax Credits'. *Health Economics, Politics and Law 2*, no. 3: 267–284.

Lyden, F. J., G. A. Shipman and R. W. Wilkinson. (1968). 'Decision-Flow Analysis: A Methodology for Studying the Public Policy-Making Process'. In P. P. Le Breton (ed.), *Comparative Administrative Theory*. Seattle, WA: University of Washington Press, 155–168.

Lynn Jr, L. E. (1978). *Knowledge and Policy: The Uncertain Connection*. Washington, DC: National Academy of Sciences.

Lynn Jr, L. E. (1980). *Designing Public Policy: A Casebook on the Role of Policy Analysis*. Tucson, AZ: Goodyear Publishing.

Lynn Jr, L. E. (1986). 'The Behavioral Foundations of Public Policy-Making'. *The Journal of Business 59*, no. 4: S379–S384.

Lynn Jr, L. E. (2001). 'Globalization and Administrative Reform: What is Happening in Theory?' *Public Management Review 3*, no. 2: 191–208.

Lynn Jr, L. E. (2012). 'The Many Faces of Governance: Adaptation? Transformation? Both? Neither?' In D. Levi-Faur (ed.), *The Oxford Handbook of Governance*. Oxford: Oxford University Press, 49–64.

MacAvoy, P., W. T. Stanbury, G. Yarrow and R. Zeckhauser. (1989). *Privatization and State-Owned Enterprises: Lessons from the United States, Great Britain and Canada*. Boston, MA: Kluwer Academic Publishers.

Machiavelli, Niccolo, Quentin Skinner and Russell Price. (1988). 'The Prince/Machiavelli'. In Quentin Skinner and Russell Price (eds.), *Cambridge Texts in the History of Political Thought*. Cambridge and New York: Cambridge University Press.

Macmillan, R. (2010). *The Third Sector Delivering Public Services: An Evidence Review* (Working Paper 20). Birmingham: Third Sector Research Centre.

MacRae, D. (1985). *Policy Indicators: Links Between Social Science and Public Debate*. Chapel Hill: The University of North Carolina Press.

MacRae, D. (1991). 'Policy Analysis and Knowledge Use'. *Knowledge and Policy 4*, no. 3: 27–40.

MacRae Jr, D. and A. James. (1985). *Wilde. Policy Analysis for Public Decisions*. Lanham, MD: University Press of America.

MacRae, D. and D. Whittington. (1997). *Expert Advice for Policy Choice: Analysis and Discourse*. Washington, DC: Georgetown University Press.

MacRae Jr, D. and J. A. Wilde. (1976). *Policy Analysis for Public Decisions*. North Scituate, MA: Duxbury Press.

Maddison, S. (2005). 'Democratic Constraint and Embrace: Implications for Progressive Non-Government Advocacy Organisations in Australia'. *Australian Journal of Political Science 40*, no. 3: 373–389.

Madrian, B. C. (2014). 'Applying Insights from Behavioral Economics to Policy Design'. *Annual Review of Economics 6*, no. 1: 663–688.

Mahoney, C. and M. J. Beckstrand. (2009). 'Following the Money: EU Funding of Civil Society Organizations'. Paper presented to the ECPR Joint Sessions of Workshops, Potsdam, Germany.

Mahoney, J. (2000). 'Path Dependence in Historical Sociology'. *Theory and Society 29*, no. 4: 507–548.

Mahoney, J. and Thelen, K. (2010). *A Theory of Gradual Institutional Change. Explaining Institutional Change: Ambiguity, Agency, and Power, 1*. Cambridge: Cambridge University Press.

Majone, G. (1975). 'On the Notion of Political Feasibility'. *European Journal of Political Research 3*: 259–274.

Majone, G. (1976). 'Choice among Policy Instruments for Pollution Control'. *Policy Analysis 2*, no. 4: 589–613.

Majone, G. (1989). *Evidence, Argument, and Persuasion in the Policy Process*. New Haven, CT: Yale University Press.

Majone, G. (1997). 'From the Positive to the Regulatory State: Causes and Consequences of Changes in the Mode of Governance'. *Journal of Public Policy 17* no. 2: 139–167.

Majone, G. (2005). 'Strategy and Structure: The Political Economy of Agency Independence and Accountability'. In *Designing Independent and Accountable Regulatory Authorities for High Quality Regulation – Proceedings of an Expert Meeting in London, United Kingdom, 10–11 January 2005*. Paris: OECD Working Party on Regulatory Management and Reform, 126–155.

Maley, M. (2000). 'Conceptualising Advisers' Policy Work: The Distinctive Policy Roles of Ministerial Advisers in the Keating Government, 1991–96'. *Australian Journal of Political Science 35*, no. 3: 449.

Maley, M. (2011). 'Strategic Links in a Cut-Throat World: Rethinking the Role and Relatgionships of Australian Ministerial Staff'. *Public Administration 89*, no. 4 (April): 1469–1488.

Malloy, J. (1999). 'What Makes a State Advocacy Structure Effective? Conflicts Between Bureaucratic and Social Movements Criteria'. *Governance 12*, no. 3: 267–288.

Malloy, J. (2003). *Colliding Worlds: The Inherent Ambiguity of Government Agencies for Aboriginal and Women's Policy*. Toronto, ON: University of Toronto Press: IPAC Series in Public Management and Governance.

Mandell, M. P. (1994). 'Managing Interdependencies through Program Structures: A Revised Paradigm'. *American Review of Public Administration 25*, no. 1: 99–121.

Mandell, M. P. (2000). 'A Revised Look at Management in Network Structures'. *International Journal of Organizational Theory and Behavior 3*, no. 1/2: 185–210.

Mandell, S. (2008). 'Optimal Mix of Emissions Taxes and Cap-and-Trade'. *Journal of Environmental Economics and Management 56*: 131–140.

Manitoba Office of the Provincial Auditor. (2001). *A Review of the Policy Development Capacity within Government Departments*. Winnipeg, Canada: Queen's Printer.

Mann, C. and A. Simons. (2014). 'Local Emergence and International Developments of Conservation Trading Systems: Innovation Dynamics and Related Problems'. *Environmental Conservation 42*, no. 4: 1–10.

Mann, S. and H. Wustemann. (2010). 'Public Goverance of Information Asymmetries: The Gap between Reality and Economic Theory'. *The Journal of Socio-Economics 39*, no. 2: 278–285.

Manor, J. (2013). 'Post-Clientelist Initiatives'. In *Democratization in the Global South. International Political Economy*. London: Palgrave Macmillan, 243–253.

Manski, C. F. (2011). 'Policy Analysis with Incredible Certitude'. *The Economic Journal 121*, no. 554 (1 August): F261–F289.

Manski, Charles F. (2013). *Public Policy in an Uncertain World: Analysis and Decisions*. Cambridge: Harvard University Press.

Manwaring, R. (2018). 'Understanding Impact in Policy Advisory Systems: The Australian Case of the 'Thinker in Residence''. *International Journal of Public Administration 41*, no. 11: 868–879.

Maor, M. (2012a). 'Policy Overreaction'. *Journal of Public Policy 32*, no. 3: 231–259.

Maor, M. (2012b). *Risk and Policy Underreaction*. Unpublished paper.

Maor, M. (2014a). 'Policy Bubbles: Policy Overreaction and Positive Feedback'. *Governance 27*, no. 3: 469–487.

Maor, M. (2014b). 'Policy Persistence, Risk Estimation and Policy Underreaction'. *Policy Sciences 47*, no. 4: 425–443.

Maor, M. (2015). 'Emotion-Driven Negative Policy Bubbles'. *Policy Sciences 49*, no. 2 (1 September): 191–210.

Maor, M. (2017). 'The Implications of the Emerging Disproportionate Policy Perspective for the New Policy Design Studies'. *Policy Sciences 50*, no. 3 (19 July): 1–16.

Maor, M. (2020). 'Policy Over-and Under-Design: An Information Quality Perspective'. *Policy Sciences 53*: 395–411.

Maor, Moshe, Jale Tosun and Andrew Jordan. (2017). 'Proportionate and Disproportionate Policy Responses to Climate Change: Core Concepts and Empirical Applications'. *Journal of Environmental Policy & Planning* (24 January): 1–13.

March, J. G. (1978). 'Bounded Rationality, Ambiguity, and the Engineering of Choice'. *Bell Journal of Economics 9*, no. 2: 587–608.

March, J. G. (1981). 'Decision Making Perspective: Decisions in Organizations and Theories of Choice'. In A. H. van de Ven and W. F. Joyce (eds.), *Perspectives on Organization Design and Behaviour*. New York: Wiley.

March, J. G. (1994). *A Primer on Decision-Making: How Decisions Happen*. New York: Free Press.

March, J. G. and J. P. Olsen. (1979). *Ambiguity and Choice in Organizations*. Bergen, Norway: Universitetsforlaget.

March, J. G. and J. P. Olsen. (1983). 'Organizing Political Life: What Administrative Reorganization Tells Us about Government'. *American Political Science Review* 77, no. 2: 281–296.

March, J. G. and J. P. Olsen. (1984). 'The New Institutionalism: Organizational Factors in Political Life'. *American Political Science Review* 78: 734–749.

March, J. G. and J. P. Olsen. (1989). *Rediscovering Institutions*. New York: Free Press.

March, J. G. and J. P. Olsen. (1994). *Institutional Perspectives on Political Institutions*. Berlin, Germany: International Political Science Association, 5.

March, J. G. and J. P. Olsen. (1996). 'Institutional Perspectives on Political Institutions'. *Governance* 9, no. 3: 247–264.

March, J. G. and J. P. Olsen. (2004a). 'The Logic of Appropriateness'. In M. Rein, M. Moran and R. E. Goodin (eds.), *Handbook of Public Policy*. Oxford: Oxford University Press.

March, J. G. and J. P. Olsen. (2004b). *The Logic of Appropriateness*. Oslo: ARENA Working Paper.

Marchildon, G. F. (2007). 'Royal Commissions and the Policy Cycle in Canada: The Case of Health Care'. In J. Hans, M. Donald, C. Story and J. S. Steeves (eds.), *Political Leadership and Representation in Canada*. Toronto, ON: University of Toronto Press.

Marciano, Reut. (2023). 'Beyond Consultocracy and Servants of Power: Explaining the Role of Consultants in Policy Formulation'. *Governance*.

Margerum, R. D. (2008). 'A Typology of Collaboration Efforts in Environmental Management'. *Environmental Management* 41: 487–500.

Margetts, H. and P. John. (2023). 'How Rediscovering Nodality Can Improve Democratic Governance in a Digital World'. *Public Administration*.

Marier, P. (2008). 'Empowering Epistemic Communities: Specialized Politicians, Policy Experts and Policy Reform'. *West European Politics* 31, no. 3: 513–533.

Marier, P. (2009). 'The Power of Institutionalized Learning: The Uses and Practices of Commissions to Generate Policy Change'. *Journal of European Public Policy* 16, no. 8: 1204–1223.

Marin, B. and R. Mayntz (eds.). (1991). *Policy Networks: Empirical Evidence and Theoretical Considerations*. Boulder, CO: Westview Press.

Marion, Justin and Erich Muehlegger. (2007). *Measuring Illegal Activity and the Effects of Regulatory Innovation: A Study of Diesel Fuel Tax Evasion*. Cambridge: John F. Kennedy School of Government Faculty Research Working Paper Series RWP07–026.

Marion, R. (1999). *The Edge of Organization: Chaos and Complexity Theories of Formal Social Systems*. London: Sage.

Markoff, J. and V. Montecinos. (1993). 'The Ubiquitous Rise of Economists'. *Journal of Public Policy* 13, no. 1: 37–68.

Marriott, L. (2010). 'Power and Ideas: The Development of Retirement Savings Taxation in Australasia'. *Critical Perspectives on Accounting* 21, no. 7: 597–610.

Marsh, D. (1991). 'Privatization under Mrs Thatcher: A Review of the Literature'. *Public Administration* 69, no. 4: 459–480.

Marsh, D. and A. McConnell. (2010). 'Towards a Framework for Establishing Policy Success'. *Public Administration* 88, no. 2: 564–583.

Martikke, S. and C. Moxham. (2010). 'Public Sector Commissioning: Experiences of Voluntary Organizations Delivering Health and Social Services'. *International Journal of Public Administration* 33: 790–799.

Martin, S. and I. Sanderson. (1999). 'Evaluating Public Policy Experiments Measuring Outcomes, Monitoring Processes or Managing Pilots?' *Evaluation 5*, no. 3 (7 January): 245–258.

Marx, S. M. and E. U. Weber. (2011). 'Decision Making Under Climate Uncertainty: The Power of Understanding Judgment and Decision Processes'. In T. Dietz and D. Bidwell (eds.), *Climate Change in the Great Lakes Region: Navigating an Uncertain Future*. East Lansing, MI: MSU Press.

Maslove, A. M. (1978). 'The Other Side of Public Spending: Tax Expenditures in Canada'. In G. B. Doern and A. M. Maslove (eds.), *The Public Evaluation of Government Spending*. Montreal, QC: Institute for Research on Public Policy, 149–168.

Maslove, A. M. (1983). 'Loans and Loan Guarantees: Business as Usual Versus the Politics of Risk'. In G. B. Doern (ed.), *How Ottawa Spends: The Liberals, the Opposition and Federal Priorities*. Toronto, ON: James Lorimer, 121–132.

Massey, E. and D. Huitema. (2013). 'The Emergence of Climate Change Adaptation as a Policy Field: The Case of England'. *Regional Environmental Change 13*, no. 2: 341–352.

Mathauer, Inke and Ke Xu. (2009). *An Analysis of the Health Financing System of the Republic of Korea and Options to Strengthen Health Financing Performance*. Geneva: World Health Organization. www.who.int/health_financing/documents/hsfr_e_09-korea.pdf

Matheson, C. (2000). 'Policy Formulation in Australian Government: Vertical and Horizontal Axes'. *Australian Journal of Public Administration 59*, no. 2 (1 June): 44–55.

Mathijssen, J., A. Petersen, P. Besseling, A. Rahman and H. Don (eds.). (2007). *Dealing with Uncertainty in Policy Making*. CPB/PBL/Rand Europe, Final Report of the Conference Dealing with Uncertainty in Policy Making, The Hague, Netherlands, 16–17 May.

Mathur, N. and C. Skelcher. (2007). 'Evaluating Democratic Performance Methodologies for Assessing the Relationship between Network Governance and Citizens'. *Public Administration Review 67*, no. 2: 228–237.

Matland, R. E. (1995). 'Synthesizing the Implementation Literature: The Ambiguity-Conflict Model of Policy Implementation'. *Journal of Public Administration Research and Theory 5*, no. 2: 145–174.

Matthies, B. D., T. Kalliokoski, K. Eyvindson, N. Honkela, J. I. Hukkinen, N. J. Kuusinen, P. Räisänen and L. T. Valsta. (2016). 'Nudging Service Providers and Assessing Service Trade-Offs to Reduce the Social Inefficiencies of Payments for Ecosystem Services Schemes'. *Environmental Science & Policy 55* (January): 228–237.

Maxim, L. and J. P. van der Sluijs. (2011). 'Quality in Environmental Science for Policy: Assessing Uncertainty as a Component of Policy Analysis'. *Environmental Science & Policy 14*, no. 4 (June): 482–492.

May, P. J. (1981). 'Hints for Crafting Alternative Policies'. *Policy Analysis 7*, no. 2: 227–244.

May, P. J. (1991). 'Reconsidering Policy Design: Policies and Publics'. *Journal of Public Policy 11*, no. 2: 187–206.

May, P. J. (1992). 'Policy Learning and Failure'. *Journal of Public Policy 12*: 331–354.

May, P. J. (1993). 'Mandate Design and Implementation: Enhancing Implementation Efforts and Shaping Regulatory Styles'. *Journal of Policy Analysis and Management 12*, no. 4: 634–663.

May, P. J. (1996). 'Coercive Versus Cooperative Policies: Comparing Intergovernmental Mandate Performance'. *Journal of Policy Analysis and Management 15*, no. 2: 171–206.

May, P. J. (1999). 'Fostering Policy Learning: A Challenge for Public Administration'. *International Review of Public Administration 4*, no. 1: 21–31.

May, P. J. (2002). 'Social Regulation'. In L. M. Salamon (ed.), *The Tools of Government: A Guide to the New Governance*. New York: Oxford University Press, 156–185.

May, P. J. (2003). 'Policy Design and Implementation'. In B. G. Peters and J. Pierre (eds.), *Handbook of Public Administration*. Beverly Hills, CA: Sage, 223–233.

May, P. J. (2004). 'Compliance Motivations: Affirmative and Negative Bases'. *Law & Society Review 38*, no. 1: 41–68.

May, P. J. (2005a). 'Policy Maps and Political Feasibility'. In I. Geva-May (ed.), *Thinking Like a Policy Analyst: Policy Analysis as a Clinical Profession*. London: Palgrave Macmillan, 127–151.

May, P. J. (2005b). 'Regulation and Compliance Motivations: Examining Different Approaches'. *Public Administration Review 65*, no. 1: 31–44.

May, P. J. (2007). 'Regulatory Regimes and Accountability'. *Regulation and Governance 1*, no. 1: 8–26.

May, P. J. and J. W. Handmer. (1992). 'Regulatory Policy Design: Co-operative versus Deterrent Mandates'. *Australian Journal of Public Administration 51*, no. 1: 45–53.

May, P. J. and A. E. Jochim. (2013). 'Policy Regime Perspective: Policies, Politics and Governing'. *Policy Studies Journal 39*: 285–305.

May, P. J., B. D. Jones, B. E. Beem, E. A. Neff-Sharum and M. K. Poague. (2005). 'Policy Coherence and Component-Driven Policymaking: Arctic Policy in Canada and the United States'. *Policy Studies Journal 33*, no. 1: 37–63.

May, P. J., J. Saptichne and S. Workman. (2005). 'Policy Coherence and Policy Design'. In *Annual Research Meeting of the Association for Public Analysis and Management*. Washington, DC.

May, P. J., J. Sapotichne and S. Workman. (2009). 'Widespread Policy Disruption: Terrorism, Public Risks, and Homeland Security'. *The Policy Studies Journal 37*, no. 2: 171–194.

May, P. J. and S. Winter. (1999). 'Regulatory Enforcement and Compliance: Examining Danish Agro-Environmental Policy'. *Journal of Policy Analysis and Management 18*, no. 4: 625–651.

Mayer, I., P. Bots and E. van Daalen. (2004). 'Perspectives on Policy Analysis: A Framework for Understanding and Design'. *International Journal of Technology, Policy and Management 4*, no. 1: 169–191.

Mayntz, R. (1975). 'Legitimacy and the Directive Capacity of the Political System'. In Leon N. Lindberg, Robert Alford, Colin Crouch and Claus Offe (eds.), *Stress and Contradiction in Modern Capitalism*. Lexington, MA: Lexington Books, 261–274.

Mayntz, R. (1979). 'Public Bureaucracies and Policy Implementation'. *International Social Science Journal 31*, no 4: 633–645.

Mayntz, R. (1983). 'The Conditions of Effective Public Policy: A New Challenge for Policy Analysis'. *Policy & Politics 11* (April): 123–143.

Mayntz, R. (1993). 'Modernization and the Logic of Interorganizational Networks'. In J. C. M. Crozier and R. Mayntz (eds.), *Societal Change between Market and Organization*. Aldershot, UK: Avebury, 3–18.

Mazmanian, D. M. and P. A. Sabatier. (1983). *Implementation and Public Policy.* Glenview, IL: Scott, Foresman, 21–25.

McAllister, L. K. (2009). 'Dimensions of Enforcement Style: Factoring in Autonomy and Capacity'. *Law and Policy 32*, no. *1*: 61–78.

McAllister, L. K., B. V. Rooij and R. A. Kagan. (2010). 'Reorienting Regulation: Pollution Enforcement in Industrializing Countries'. *Law and Policy 32*, no. *1*: 1–13.

McArthur, D. (2007). 'Policy Analysis in Provincial Governments in Canada: From PPBS to Network Management'. In L. Dobuzinskis, M. Howlett and D. Laycock (eds.), *Policy Analysis in Canada: The State of the Art.* Toronto, ON: University of Toronto Press, 132–145.

McCalley, T., F. Kaiser, C. Midden, M. Keser and M. Teunissen. (2006). 'Persuasive Appliances: Goal Priming and Behavioral Response to Product-Integrated Energy Feedback'. In W. A. IJsselsteijn, Y. A. W. de Kort, C. Midden, B. Eggen and E. van den Hoven (eds.), *Persuasive Technology, Lecture Notes in Computer Science 3962.* Berlin, Heidelberg, Germany: Springer, 45–49.

McConnell, A. (2010a). 'Policy Success, Policy Failure and Grey Areas In-Between'. *Journal of Public Policy 30*, no. *03*: 345–362.

McConnell, A. (2010b). *Understanding Policy Success: Rethinking Public Policy.* Basingstoke, UK: Palgrave Macmillan.

McConnell, A. (2015). 'What Is Policy Failure? A Primer to Help Navigate the Maze'. *Public Policy and Administration 30*, no. *3–4* (1 July): 221–242.

McConnell, A. (2017). 'Hidden Agendas: Shining a Light on the Dark Side of Public Policy'. *Journal of European Public Policy 25*, no. *12* (3 October): 1739–1758.

McConnell, A. (2020). 'The Use of Placebo Policies to Escape from Policy Traps'. *Journal of European Public Policy 27*, no. *7* (2 July): 957–976.

McConnell, Allan and Lynn Drennan. (2006). 'Mission Impossible? Planning and Preparing for Crisis1'. *Journal of Contingencies and Crisis Management 14*, no. 2 (June): 59–70.

McConnell, Allan, Liam Grealy and Tess Lea. (2020). 'Policy Success for Whom? A Framework for Analysis'. *Policy Sciences 53*, no. *4* (1 December): 589–608.

McConnell, A. and P. 't Hart. (2019). 'Inaction and Public Policy: Understanding Why Policymakers 'Do Nothing''. *Policy Sciences 52*, no. *4* (1 December): 645–661.

McCool, D. (1998). 'The Subsystem Family of Concepts: A Critique and a Proposal'. *Political Research Quarterly 51*, no. 2: 551–570.

McCourt, W. and M. Minogue (eds.). (2001). *The Internationalization of Public Management: Reinventing the Third World State.* Cheltenham, UK: Edward Elgar.

McCrudden, C. (2004). 'Using Public Procurement to Achieve Social Outcomes'. *Natural Resources Journal 28*: 257–267.

McCubbins, M. D. and A. Lupia. (1994). 'Learning from Oversight: Fire Alarms and Policy Patrols Reconstructed'. *Journal of Law, Economics and Organization 10*, no. *1*: 96–125.

McCubbins, M. D., R. G. Noll and B. R. Weingast. (1987). 'Administrative Procedures as Instruments of Political Control'. *Journal of Law, Economics and Organization 3*, no. 2: 243–277.

McCubbins, M. D. and T. Schwartz. (1984). 'Congressional Oversight Overlooked: Policy Patrols versus Fire Alarms'. *American Journal of Political Science 28*, no. *1*: 165–179.

McDavid, J. C. and E. G. Clemens. (1995). 'Contracting Out Local Government Services: The BC Experience'. *Canadian Public Administration 38*, no. 2: 177–193.

McDermott, C. L., B. Cashore and P. Kanowski. (2009). 'Setting the Bar: An International Comparison of Public and Private Forest Policy Specifications and Implications for Explaining Policy Trends'. *Environmental Sciences 6*, no. *3*: 217–237.

McDermott, C. L., B. Cashore and P. Kanowski. (2010). *Global Environmental Forest Policies. An International Comparison.* London: Earthscan.

McDermott, R. (1992). 'Prospect Theory in International Relations: The Iranian Hostage Rescue Mission'. *Political Psychology 13*, no. *2*: 237–263.

McDonnell, L. M. and R. F. Elmore. (1987). *Alternative Policy Instruments.* Santa Monica, CA: Center for Policy Research in Education.

McFadgen, B. (2019). 'Connecting Policy Change, Experimentation, and Entrepreneurs: Advancing Conceptual and Empirical Insights'. *Ecology and Society 24*, no. *1* (19 March).

McFarland, A. S. (1991). 'Interest Groups and Political Time: Cycles in America'. *British Journal of Political Science 21*, no. *3*: 257–284.

McGann, J. and R. Sabatini (eds.). (2013). *Global Think Tanks: Policy Networks and Governance.* New York: Routledge.

McGann, J. G. and E. C. Johnson. (2005). *Comparative Think Tanks, Politics and Public Policy.* Cheltenham, UK: Edward Elgar.

McGann, J. G., A. Viden and J. Rafferty. (2014). *How Think Tanks Shape Social Development Policies.* Philadelphia, PA: University of Pennsylvania Press.

McGann, M., E. Bomkamp and J. M. Lewis. (2018). 'The Rise of Public Sector Innovation Labs: Experiments in Design Thinking for Policy'. *Policy Sciences 9*: 1–19.

McGarity, T. O. (1991). *Reinventing Rationality: The Role of Regulatory Analysis in the Federal Bureaucracy.* New York: Cambridge University Press.

McGoldrick, D. E. and A. V. Boonn. (2010). 'Public Policy to Maximize Tobacco Cessation'. *American Journal of Preventive Medicine 38*, no. *3*, Supplement 1 (March): S327–S332.

McGuire, M. (2002). 'Managing Networks: Propositions on What Managers Do and Why They Do It'. *Public Administration Review 62*, no. *5*: 599–609.

McIlroy-Young, Bronwyn, Daniel Henstra and Jason Thistlethwaite. (2022). 'Treasure Tools: Using Public Funds to Achieve Policy Objectives'. In M. Howlett (ed.), *The Routledge Handbook of Policy Tools.* New York: Routledge, 332–344.

McInerney, D., R. Lempert and K. Keller. (2012). 'What Are Robust Strategies in the Face of Uncertain Climate Threshold Responses?' *Climatic Change 112*, no. *3–4* (3 January): 547–568.

McKee, M. and R. Busse. (2013). 'Medical Savings Accounts: Singapore's Non-Solution to Healthcare Costs'. *BMJ 347*: f4797. https://doi.org/10.1136/bmj.f4797

McKelvey, B. (1978). 'Organizational Systematics: Taxonomic Lessons from Biology'. *Management Science 24*, no. *13*: 1428–1440.

McKelvey, B. (1982). *Organizational Systematics: Taxonomy, Evolution, Classification.* Berkeley, CA: University of California Press.

McKenna, J. and A. Cooper. (2006). 'Sacred Cows in Coastal Management: The Need for a 'Cheap and Transitory" Model'. *Area 38*, no. *4*: 421–431.

McKenzie, C. R. M., M. J. Liersch and S. R. Finkelstein. (2006). 'Recommendations Implicit in Policy Defaults'. *Psychological Science 17*, no. *5*: 414–420.

McKirnan, D. J. (1980). 'The Identification of Deviance: A Conceptualization and Initial Test of a Model of Social Norms'. *European Journal of Social Psychology 10*, no. *1*: 75–93.

McLeod, L. J., D. W. Hine, P. M. Please and A. B. Driver. (2015). 'Applying Behavioral Theories to Invasive Animal Management: Towards an Integrated Framework'. *Journal of Environmental Management 161* (15 September): 63–71.

McMillin, W. D. and J. S. Fackler. (1984). 'Monetary vs Credit Aggregates: An Evaluation of Monetary Policy Targets'. *Southern Economic Journal 50*, no. 3: 711–723.

McNees, S. K. (1990). 'The Role of Judgment in Macroeconomic Forecasting Accuracy'. *International Journal of Forecasting 6*, no. 3: 287–299.

McWilliams, W. C. (1971). 'On Political Illegitimacy'. *Public Policy 19*, no. 3: 444–454.

Medzini, Rotem and David Levi-Faur. (2023). 'Self-Governance via Intermediaries: Credibility in Three Different Modes of Governance'. *Journal of Comparative Policy Analysis: Research and Practice* (20 January): 1–23.

Mees, H. L. P., J. Dijk, D. van Soest, P. P. J. Driessen, M. H. F. M. W. van Rijswick and H. Runhaar. (2014). 'A Method for the Deliberate and Deliberative Selection of Policy Instrument Mixes for Climate Change Adaptation'. *Ecology and Society 19*, no. 2.

Mees, P. (2005). 'Privatization of Rail and Tram Services in Melbourne: What Went Wrong?' *Transport Reviews 25*, no. 4: 433–449.

Meier, K. J. and D. R. Morgan. (1982). 'Citizen Compliance with Public Policy: The National Maximum Speed Law'. *The Western Political Quarterly 35*, no. 2 (1 June): 258–273.

Meijers, E. (2004). 'Policy Integration: A Literature Review'. In D. Stead, H. Geerlings and E. Meijers (eds.), *Policy Integration in Practice: The Integration of Land Use Planning, Transport and Environmental Policy-Making in Denmark, England and Germany*. Delft, Netherlands: Delft University Press, 9–24.

Meijers, E. and D. Stead. (2004). 'Policy Integration: What Does It Mean and How Can It Be Achieved? A Multi-Disciplinary Review'. In *2004 Berlin Conference on the Human Dimensions of Global Environmental Change: Greening of Policies – Interlinkages and Policy Integration*, Berlin, Germany, 1–15.

Meltsner, A. J. (1972). 'Political Feasibility and Policy Analysis'. *Public Administration Review 32*: 859–867.

Meltsner, A. J. (1975). 'Bureaucratic Policy Analysts'. *Policy Analysis 1*, no. 1: 115–131.

Meltsner, A. J. (1976). *Policy Analysts in the Bureaucracy*. Berkeley, CA: University of California Press.

Meltsner, A. J. (1979). 'Creating a Policy Analysis Profession'. *Society 16*, no. 6: 45–51.

Meltsner, A. J. (1980). 'Creating a Policy Analysis Profession'. In S. S. Nagel (ed.), *Improving Policy Analysis*. Beverley Hills: Sage, 235–249.

Menahem, G. and R. Stein. (2013). 'High-Capacity and Low-Capacity Governance Networks in Welfare Services Delivery: A Typology and Empirical Examination of the Case of Israeli Municipalities'. *Public Administration 91*, no. 1: 211–231.

Menard, C. and M. Ghertman. (2009). *Regulation, Deregulation, Reregulation: Institutional Perspectives*. Cheltenham, UK: Edward Elgar.

Mendes, L. M. Z. and G. Santos. (2008). 'Using Economic Instruments to Address Emissions from Air Transport in the European Union'. *Environment and Planning A 40*: 189–209.

Merelman, R. M. (1966). 'Learning and Legitimacy'. *American Political Science Review 60*, no. 3: 548–561.

Mergel, Ines, Yiwei Gong and John Bertot. (2018). 'Agile Government: Systematic Literature Review and Future Research'. *Government Information Quarterly 35*, no. 2 (April): 291–298.

Merton, R. K. (1936). 'The Unanticipated Consequences of Purposive Social Action'. *American Sociology Review* 6: 1894–1904.

Merton, R. K. (1948a). 'The Role of Applied Social Science in the Formation of Policy: A Research Memorandum'. *Philosophy of Science* 16, no. 3: 161–181.

Merton, R. K. (1948b). 'The Self-Fulfilling Prophecy'. *The Antioch Review* 8, no. 2: 193–210.

Meseguer, C. (2003). 'The Diffusion of Privatization in OECD and Latin America Countries: What Role for Learning?' Paper presented at the Conference on The Internationalization of Regulatory Reforms, Berkeley, CA, 25–26 April.

Meseguer, C. (2005). 'Policy Learning, Policy Diffusion and the Making of a New Order'. *Annals of the American Academy of Political and Social Science* 598, no. 1: 67–82.

Meseguer, C. (2006). 'Rational Learning and Bounded Learning in the Diffusion of Policy Innovations'. *Rationality and Society* 18, no. 1: 35–66.

Metcalfe, L. (2000). 'Reforming the Commission: Will Organizational Efficiency Produce Effective Governance?' *Journal of Common Market Studies* 38, no. 5: 817–841.

Meuleman, L. (2009). 'Metagoverning Governance Styles: Increasing the Public Manager's Toolbox'. Paper presented at The ECPR General Conference, Potsdam.

Meuleman, L. (2010a). 'The Cultural Dimension of Metagovernance: Why Governance Doctrines May Fail'. *Public Organization Review* 10, no. 1: 49–70.

Meuleman, L. (2010b). *Public Management and the Metagovernance of Hierarchies, Networks and Markets: The Feasibility of Designing and Managing Governance Style Combinations.* Heidelberg, Germany: Physica-Verlag.

Meyer, A. D. (1982). 'Adapting to Environmental Jolts'. *Administrative Science Quarterly* 27: 515–537.

Meyer, J. L., P. C. Frumhoff, S. P. Hamburg and C. de la Rosa. (2010). 'Above the Din but in the Fray: Environmental Scientists as Effective Advocates'. *Frontiers in Ecology and the Environment* 8: 299–305.

Mickwitz, P. (2003). 'A Framework for Evaluating Environmental Policy Instruments: Context and Key Concepts'. *Evaluation* 9, no. 4: 415–436.

Mickwitz, P. H. H. and P. Kivimaa. (2008). 'The Role of Policy Instruments in the Innovation and Diffusion of Environmentally Friendlier Technologies: Popular Claims versus Case Study Experiences'. *Journal of Cleaner Production* 16, no. 1 (January): S162–S170.

Middleton, P. (2007). *A Brief Guide to the End of Oil.* London: Robinson.

Migone, Andrea and Michael Howlett. (2022). 'Policy Shops, Hired Guns, and Gatekeepers: The Organization and Distribution of Policy Analysts in Ontario'. *Canadian Public Administration* 65, no. 4: 690–718.

Migone, Andrea and Michael Howlett. (2023). 'Assessing the "Forgotten Fundamental" in Policy Advisory Systems Research: Policy Shops and the Role(s) of Core Policy Professionals'. *Australian Journal of Public Administration.*

Mikenberg, M. (2001). 'The Radical Right in Public Office: Agenda-Setting and Policy Effects'. *West European Politics* 24, no. 4: 1–21.

Milkman, K. L., M. C. Mazza, L. L. Shu, C. Tsay and M. H. Bazerman. (2012). 'Policy Bundling to Overcome Loss Aversion: A Method for Improving Legislative Outcomes'. *Organizational Behavior and Human Decision Processes* 117, no. 1: 158–167.

Miller, D. B. and L. Rudnick. (2011). 'Trying It on for Size: Design and International Public Policy'. *Design Issues* 27, no. 2 (1 April): 6–16.

Miller, R. W. (1978). 'Methodological Individualism and Social Explanation'. *Philosophy of Science 45*, no. 3: 387–414.

Miller, S. E. and B. F. Mannix. (2016). 'One Standard to Rule Them All: The Disparate Impact of Energy Efficiency Regulations'. In S. Abdukadirov (ed.), *Nudge Theory in Action*. Cham, Germany: Springer, 251–287.

Miller, S. M. (1990). 'The Evolving Welfare State Mixes'. In A. Evers and H. Winterberger (eds.), *Shifts in the Welfare Mix: Their Impact on Work, Social Services and Welfare Policies*. Frankfurt: Campus Verlag, 371–388.

Miller, S. M., A. Evers and H. Winterberger. (1990). 'The Evolving Welfare State Mixes'. In *Shifts in the Welfare Mix: Their Impact on Work, Social Services and Welfare Policies*. Frankfurt, Germany: Campus Verlag, 371–388.

Mills, A., R. Meek and D. Gojkovic. (2011). 'Exploring the Relationship Between the Voluntary Sector and the State in Criminal Justice'. *Voluntary Sector Review 2*, no. 2: 195–213.

Mills, C. (2013). 'Why Nudges Matter: A Reply to Goodwin'. *Politics 33*, no. 1: 28–36.

Milner, H. V. and R. O. Keohane. (1996). 'Internationalization and Domestic Politics: A Conclusion'. In R. O. Keohane and H. V. Milner (eds.), *Internationalization and Domestic Politics*. Cambridge: Cambridge University Press, 243–258.

Milward, H. B. and K. G. Provan. (2000). 'Governing the Hollow State'. *Journal of Public Administration Research and Theory 10*, no. 2: 359–380.

Milward, H. B., K. G. Provan and B. A. Else. (1993). 'What Does the "Hollow State" Look Like?' In B. Bozeman (ed.), *Public Management: The State of the Art*. San Francisco, CA: Jossey-Bass, 309–323.

Minogue, M. (2002). 'Governance-Based Analysis of Regulation'. *Annals of Public and Cooperative Economics 73*, no. 4: 649–666.

Mintrom, M. (1997). 'Policy Entrepreneurs and the Diffusion of Innovation'. *American Journal of Political Science 41*, no. 3: 738–770.

Mintrom, M. (2007). 'The Policy Analysis Movement'. In D. M. Howlett and D. Laycock (eds.), *Policy Analysis in Canada: The State of the Art*. Toronto, ON: University of Toronto Press, 71–84.

Mintrom, M. and J. Luetjens. (2016). 'Design Thinking in Policymaking Processes: Opportunities and Challenges'. *Australian Journal of Public Administration 75*, no. 3 (1 July): 391–402.

Mintrom, Michael and Joannah Luetjens. (2018). 'The Investment Approach to Public Service Provision'. *Australian Journal of Public Administration 77*, no. 1: 136–144.

Mintrom, M. and P. Norman. (2009). 'Policy Entrepreneurship and Policy Change'. *Policy Studies Journal 37*, no. 4: 649–667.

Mintz, A. (1993). 'The Decision to Attack Iraq: A Noncompensatory Theory of Decision Making'. *The Journal of Conflict Resolution 37*, no. 4: 595–618.

Mintz, A. (2004). 'How Do Leaders Make Decisions? A Poliheuristic Perspective'. *The Journal of Conflict Resolution 48*, no. 1: 3–13.

Mintz, A., N. Geva, S. B. Redd and A. Carnes. (1997). 'The Effect of Dynamic and Static Choice Sets on Political Decision Making: An Analysis Using the Decision Board Platform'. *The American Political Science Review 91*, no. 3: 553–566.

Mitnick, B. M. (1978). 'The Concept of Regulation'. *Bulletin of Business Research 53*, no. 5: 1–20.

Mitnick, B. M. (1980). *The Political Economy of Regulation: Creating, Designing and Removing Regulatory Forms*. New York: Columbia University Press, 401–404.

Mittenzwei, K., T. Persson, M. Höglind and S. Kværnø. (2017). 'Combined Effects of Climate Change and Policy Uncertainty on the Agricultural Sector in Norway'. *Agricultural Systems 153* (May): 118–126.

Mizrahi, S. (2012). 'Self-Provision of Public Services: Its Evolution and Impact'. *Public Administration Review 72*, no. 2: 285–291.

Moffet, J. and F. Bregha. (1999). 'Non-Regulatory Environmental Measures'. In R. B. Gibson (ed.), *Voluntary Initiatives: The New Politics of Corporate Greening*. Peterborough, ON: Broadview Press, 15–31.

Mols, F., S. A. Haslam, J. Jetten and N. K. Steffens. (2015). 'Why a Nudge Is Not Enough: A Social Identity Critique of Governance by Stealth'. *European Journal of Political Research 54*, no. 1: 81–98.

Momsen, K. and S. Thomas. (2014). 'From Intention to Action: Can Nudges Help Consumers to Choose Renewable Energy?' *Energy Policy 74* (November): 376–382.

Mondou, M. and É. Montpetit. (2010). 'Policy Styles and Degenerative Politics: Poverty Policy Designs in Newfoundland and Quebec'. *Policy Studies Journal 38*, no. 4 (November): 703–722.

Monios, Jason. (2016). 'Policy Transfer or Policy Churn? Institutional Isomorphism and Neoliberal Convergence in the Transport Sector'. *Environment and Planning A 49*, no. 2 (1 February): 351–371.

Montgomery, J. D. (2000). 'Social Capital as a Policy Resource'. *Policy Sciences 33*: 227–243.

Montpetit, É. (2002). 'Policy Networks, Federal Arrangements, and the Development of Environmental Regulations: A Comparison of the Canadian and American Agricultural Sectors'. *Governance 15*, no. 1: 1–20.

Montpetit, É. (2003a). 'Biotechnology, Life Sciences and Policy Networks in the European Union'. *Swiss Political Science Review 9*, no. 2: 127–134.

Montpetit, É. (2003b). *Misplaced Distrust: Policy Networks and the Environment in France, the United States, and Canada*. Vancouver, BC: University of British Columbia Press.

Montpetit, É. (2003c). 'Public Consultations in Policy Network Environments'. *Canadian Public Policy 29*, no. 1: 95–110.

Montpetit, É. (2008). 'Policy Design for Legitimacy: Expert Knowledge, Citizens, Time and Inclusion in the United Kingdom's Biotechnology Sector'. *Public Administration 86*, no. 1: 259–277.

Moon, M. J., J. Lee and C. Roh. (2014). 'The Evolution of Internal IT Applications and E-Government Studies in Public Administration Research Themes and Methods'. *Administration & Society 46*, no. 1 (1 January): 3–36.

Moon, M. Jae and Sabinne Lee. (2022). 'The Future of Informational Tools with Big Data Informatics: Opportunities and Challenges for Evidence-Based Policymaking'. In Michael Howlett (ed.), *The Routledge Handbook of Policy Tools*. London: Routledge, 559–569.

Moore, D. A. and P. J. Healy. (2008). 'The Trouble with Overconfidence'. *Psychological Review 115*, no. 2: 502–517.

Moore, M. H. (1988). 'What Sort of Ideas Become Public Ideas?' In R. B. Reich (ed.), *The Power of Public Ideas*. Cambridge, MA: Ballinger, 55–83.

Moore, M. H. (1994). 'Public Value as the Focus of Strategy'. *Australian Journal of Public Administration 53*, no. 3: 296–303.

Moore, M. H. (1995). *Creating Public Value: Strategic Management in Government*. Cambridge: Harvard University Press.

Moran, M. (2000). 'Understanding the Welfare State: The Case of Health Care'. *The British Journal of Politics and International Relations 2*, no. 2: 135–160.

Moran, M. (2002). 'Review Article: Understanding the Regulatory State'. *British Journal of Political Science 32*, no. 2: 391–413.

Morgan, M. G. and M. Henrion. (1990). *Uncertainty: A Guide to Dealing with Uncertainty in Quantitative Risk and Policy Analysis*. Cambridge: Cambridge University Press.

Moseley, A. and G. Stoker. (2015). 'Putting Public Policy Defaults to the Test: The Case of Organ Donor Registration'. *International Public Management Journal 18*, no. 2 (3 April): 246–264.

Moseley, A. and S. Tierney. (2004). 'Evidence-Based Practice in the Real World'. *Evidence & Policy 1*, no. 1: 113–119.

Mosley, L. (2003). *Global Capital and National Governments*. New York: Cambridge University Press.

Moss, D. A. (2002). *When All Else Fails: Government as the Ultimate Risk Manager*. Cambridge, MA: Harvard University Press.

Moxey, A., B. White and A. Ozanne. (1999). 'Efficient Contract Design for Agri-Environment Policy'. *Journal of Agricultural Economics 50*, no. 2: 187–202.

Moynihan, D. P. (2008). 'Combining Structural Forms in the Search for Policy Tools: Incident Command Systems in US Crisis Management'. *Governance 21*, no. 2: 205–229.

Moynihan, D. P. (2009a). 'From Intercrisis to Intracrisis Learning'. *Journal of Contingencies and Crisis Management 17*, no. 3: 189–198.

Moynihan, D. P. (2009b). 'The Network Governance of Crisis Response: Case Studies of Incident Command Systems'. *Journal of Public Adminstration Research and Theory 19*, no. 4 (1 October): 895–915.

Moyson, S., P. Scholten and C. M. Weible. (2017). 'Policy Learning and Policy Change: Theorizing Their Relations from Different Perspectives'. *Policy and Society 36*, no. 2 (3 April): 161–177.

Mucciaroni, G. (1992). 'The Garbage Can Model and the Study of Policymaking: A Critique'. *Polity 24*, no. 3: 460–482.

Mueller, C. (1973). *The Politics of Communication: A Study in the Political Sociology of Language, Socialization and Legitimation*. New York: Oxford University Press.

Mueller, D. (2011). 'Antecedents and Determinants of Improvisation in Firms'. *Problems and Perspectives in Management 9*, no. 4: 117–130.

Mueller, J. (2005). 'Simplicity and Spook: Terrorism and the Dynamics of Threat Exaggeration'. *International Studies Perspectives 6*, no. 2: 208–234.

Mukherjee, I. and A. S. Bali. (2019). 'Policy Effectiveness and Capacity: Two Sides of the Design Coin'. *Policy Design and Practice 2*, no. 2 (3 April): 103–114.

Mukherjee, I. and S. Giest. (2017). 'Designing Policies in Uncertain Contexts: Entrepreneurial Capacity and the Case of the European Emission Trading Scheme'. *Public Policy and Administration 34*, no. 3 (1 July): 262–286.

Mukherjee, I. and M. Howlett. (2015). 'Who Is a Stream? Epistemic Communities, Instrument Constituencies and Advocacy Coalitions in Public Policy-Making'. *Politics and Governance 3*, no. 2: 65–75.

Mukherjee, Ishani, M. Kerem Coban and Azad Singh Bali. (2021). 'Policy Capacities and Effective Policy Design: A Review'. *Policy Sciences 54*, no. 2 (June): 243–268.

Mukherjee, I., B. G. Peters, M. Chou, P. Ravinet, M. Howlett and G. Capano. (2018). *Designing for Policy Effectiveness: Defining and Understanding a Concept*. Elements Series. Cambridge: Cambridge University Press.

Mulder, K. F. (2007). 'Innovation for Sustainable Development: From Environmental Design to Transition Management'. *Sustainability Science 2*, no. 2: 253–263.

Mulford, C. L. and A. Etzioni. (1978). 'Why They Don't Even When They Ought to: Implications of Compliance Theory for Policymakers'. In *Policy Research*. Leiden: E. J. Brill, 47–62.

Mulgan, G. (2008). *The Art of Public Strategy: Mobilizing Power and Knowledge for the Common Good*. Oxford and New York: Oxford University Press.

Mullainathan, S. and E. Shafir. (2013). 'Decision Making and Policy in Contexts of Poverty'. In E. Shafir (ed.), *The Behavioral Foundations of Public Policy*. Princeton, NJ: Princeton University Press.

Mullainathan, S. and E. Shafir. (2014). *Scarcity: The New Science of Having Less and How It Defines Our Lives* (reprint edn). New York: Picador.

Murphy, J. J., A. Dinar, R. E. Howitt, S. J. Rassenti, V. L. Smith and M. Weinberg. (2009). 'The Design of Water Markets When Instream Flows Have Value'. *Journal of Environmental Management 90*: 1089–1096.

Murray, C. (2007). 'The Media'. In L. Dobuzinskis, M. Howlett and D. Laycock (eds.), *Policy Analysis in Canada: The State of the Art*. Toronto, ON: University of Toronto Press, 286–297.

Murray, F. (2013). 'The Changing Winds of Atmospheric Environment Policy'. *Environmental Science & Policy 29* (May): 115–123.

Myers, N. and J. Kent. (2001). *Perverse Subsidies: How Tax Dollars Can Undercut the Environment and the Economy*. Washington, DC: Island Press.

Myles, J. (1989). *Old Age in the Welfare State: The Political Economy of Public Pensions*. Lawrence, KS: University Press of Kansas.

Nair, S. and M. Howlett. (2015). 'Scaling up of Policy Experiments and Pilots: A Qualitative Comparative Analysis and Lessons for the Water Sector'. *Water Resources Management 29*, no. 14: 4945–4961.

Nair, S. and M. Howlett. (2016). 'From Robustness to Resilience: Avoiding Policy Traps in the Long Term'. *Sustainability Science 11*, no. 6 (1 November): 909–917.

Nair, S. and M. Howlett. (2017). 'Policy Myopia as a Source of Policy Failure: Adaptation and Policy Learning under Deep Uncertainty'. *Policy & Politics 45*, no. 1: 103–118.

Natural Resources Canada. (2003). *Corporate Social Responsibility: Lessons Learned*. Ottawa, ON: Natural Resources Canada.

Nelson, M. and J. A. Vucetich. (2009). 'On Advocacy by Environmental Scientists: What, Whether, Why, and How'. *Conservation Biology 23*: 1090–1101.

Nelson, R. (1977). *The Moon and the Ghetto: An Assay on Public Policy Analysis*. Chicago, IL: W. W. Norton.

Nemetz, P. (1986). 'The Fisheries Act and Federal – Provincial Environmental Regulation: Duplication or Complementarity?' *Canadian Public Administration 29*: 401–424.

Nesta. (2011). *Prototyping in Public Services*. London, UK: NESTA.

Newbery, D. M. (2003). 'Network Capacity Auctions: Promise and Problems'. *Utilities Policy 11*: 27–32.

Newig, Jens, Elisa Kochskämper, Edward Challies and Nicolas W. Jager. (2015). 'Exploring Governance Learning: How Policymakers Draw on Evidence,

Experience and Intuition in Designing Participatory Flood Risk Planning'. *Environmental Science & Policy 55* (1 January): 353–360.

Newman, J. (2001). *Modernising Governance: New Labour Policy and Society*. London and Newbury Park, CA: Sage.

Newman, J. (2014). 'Measuring Policy Success: Case Studies from Canada and Australia'. *Australian Journal of Public Administration 73*, no. 2 (1 June): 192–205.

Newman, J. and B. W. Head. (2015). 'Categories of Failure in Climate Change Mitigation Policy in Australia'. *Public Policy and Administration 30*, no. 3–4: 342–358.

Newman, J. and M. Howlett. (2014). 'Regulation and Time: Temporal Patterns in Regulatory Development'. *International Review of Administrative Sciences 80*, no. 3: 493–511.

Newman, Joshua and Brian W. Head. (2017). 'Wicked Tendencies in Policy Problems: Rethinking the Distinction between Social and Technical Problems'. *Policy and Society 36*, no. 3 (3 July): 414–429.

Nickerson, R. S. (1998). 'Confirmation Bias: A Ubiquitous Phenomenon in Many Guises'. *Review of General Psychology 2*, no. 2: 175.

Nielsen, A. S. E., A. Sand, P. Sørensen, M. Knutsson, P. Martinsson., E. Persson and C. Wollbrant. (2017). *Nudging and Pro-environmental Behaviour*. Copenhagen, Denmark: Nordic Council of Ministers.

Nielsen, V. L. and C. Parker. (2012). 'Mixed Motives: Economic, Social, and Normative Motivations in Business Compliance'. *Law & Policy 34*, no. 4: 428–462.

Nilsson, M., A. Jordan, J. Turnpenny, J. Hertin, B. Nykvist and D. Russel. (2008). 'The Use and Non-Use of Policy Appraisal Tools in Public Policy Making: An Analysis of Three European Countries and the European Union'. *Policy Sciences 41*: 335–355.

NIST, (2018). *Risk Management Framework for Information Systems and Organizations: A System Life Cycle Approach for Security and Privacy*. SP 800–37 Rev. 2. https://csrc.nist.gov/publications/detail/sp/800-37/rev-2/final. Accessed 23 January 2022

Nohrstedt, D. (2016). 'Collaborative Governance Regimes'. *Public Administration 94*, no. 4: 1157–1159.

Noordegraaf, Mirko. (2011). 'Academic Accounts of Policy Experience'. In Hal Colebatch, Robert Hoppe and Mirko Noordegraaf (eds.), *Working for Policy*. Amsterdam: University of Amsterdam Press, 45–67.

Nordhaus, W. D. (2015). *The Climate Casino: Risk, Uncertainty, and Economics for a Warming World*. New Haven, CT; London: Yale University Press.

Nowlan, D. M. (1994). 'Local Taxation as an Instrument of Policy'. In F. Frisken (ed.), *The Changing Canadian Metropolis: A Public Policy Perspective*. Berkeley, CA: Institute of Governmental Studies, 799–841.

Nownes, A. J. (2000). 'Policy Conflict and the Structure of Interest Communities'. *American Politics Quarterly 28*, no. 3: 309–327.

Nownes, A. J. (2004). 'The Population Ecology of Interest Group Formation: Mobilizing for Gay and Lesbian Rights in the United States, 1950–98'. *British Journal of Political Science 34*, no. 1: 49–67.

Nownes, A. J. and G. Neeley. (1996). 'Toward an Explanation for Public Interest Group Formation and Proliferation: "Seed Money". Disturbances, Entrepreneurship and Patronage'. *Policy Studies Journal 24*, no. 1: 74–92.

Nutley, S. M., I. Walter and H. T. O. Davies. (2007). *Using Evidence: How Research Can Inform Public Services*. Bristol, UK: Policy Press.

O'Brien, K., M. Pelling, A. Patwardhan, S. Hallegatte, A. Maskrey, T. Oki, Ú. Oswald-Spring et al. (2012). 'Toward a Sustainable and Resilient Future'. In C. B. Field, V. Barros, T. F. Stocker and Q. Dahe (eds.), *Managing the Risks of Extreme Events and Disasters to Advance Climate Change Adaptation* (1st edn). Cambridge: Cambridge University Press, 437–486.

O'Connor, A., G. Roos and T. Vickers-Willis. (2007). 'Evaluating an Australian Public Policy Organization's Innovation Capacity'. *European Journal of Innovation Management 10*, no. *4*: 532–558.

O'Donoghue, T. and M. Rabin. (1999). 'Doing It Now or Later'. *The American Economic Review 89*, no. *1*: 103–124.

O'Faircheallaigh, C. (2010). 'Public Participation and Environmental Impact Assessment: Purposes, Implications and Lessons for Public Policy Making'. *Environmental Impact Assessment Review 30*: 19–27.

O'Flynn, J. (2007). 'From New Public Management to Public Value: Paradigmatic Change and Managerial Implications'. *Australian Journal of Public Administration 66*, no. *3*: 353–366.

O'Toole, L. J. (2000). 'Research on Policy Implementation: Assessment and Prospects'. *Journal of Public Administration Research and Theory 10*, no. *2*: 263–288.

O'Toole, L. J. and K. J. Meier. (2010). 'In Defense of Bureaucracy – Public Managerial Capacity, Slack and the Dampening of Environmental Shocks'. *Public Management Review 12*, no. *3*: 341.

Öberg, P., M. Lundin and J. Thelander. (2015). 'Political Power and Policy Design: Why Are Policy Alternatives Constrained?' *Policy Studies Journal 43*, no. *1* (1 February): 93–114.

Obinger, H. and U. Wagschal. (2001). 'Families of Nations and Public Policy'. *West European Politics 24*, no. *1*: 99–114.

OECD (Organisation for Economic Co-operation and Development). (1995). *Recommendation of the Council of the OECD on Improving the Quality of Government Regulation.* Paris: OECD.

OECD. (1996). *Building Policy Coherence: Tools and Tensions.* Public Management Occasional Papers No. 12. Paris: OECD.

OECD. (1996–7). *Issues and Developments in Public Management: Survey.* Paris: OECD.

OECD. (2017). *Behavioural Insights and Public Policy.* Paris: OECD.

OECD. (2011). 'Strategic Agility for Strong Societies and Economies. Summary and Issues for Further Debate'. International Workshop, 10 November, OECD Conference Centre, Paris.

OECD. (2021). *OECD Health Statistics.* Paris: OECD. www.oecd.org/els/health-systems/health-data.htm

Offe, C. (2006). 'Political Institutions and Social Power: Conceptual Explorations'. In I. Shapiro, S. Skowronek and D. Galvin (eds.), *Rethinking Political Institutions: The Art of the State.* New York: New York University Press, 9–31.

OFGEM (Office of Gas and Electricity Markets). (2011). *Energy Demand Research Project Final Analysis.* Reports and Plans. www.ofgem.gov.uk/publications-and-updates/energy-demand-research-project-final-analysis.

Oh, C. H. (1997). 'Explaining the Impact of Policy Information on Policy-Making'. *Knowledge and Policy 10*, no. *3*: 22–55.

Ohmae, K. (1990). *The Borderless World.* London: Collins.

Oikonomou, V., A. Flamos and S. Grafakos. (2010). 'Is Blending of Energy and Climate Policy Instruments Always Desirable?' *Energy Policy 38*, no. *8*: 4186–4195.

Oikonomou, V., A. Flamos, M. Gargiulo, G. Giannakidis, A. Kanudia, E. Spijker and S. Grafakos. (2011b). 'Linking Least-Cost Energy System Costs Models with MCA: An Assessment of the EU Renewable Energy Targets and Supporting Policies'. *Energy Policy 39*, no 5: 2786–2799.

Oikonomou, V., A. Flamos, D. Zeugolis and S. Grafakos. (2011a). 'A Qualitative Assessment of EU Energy Policy Interactions'. *Energy Sources, Part B: Economics, Planning, and Policy 7*, no. 2: 177–187.

Oikonomou, V. and C. J. Jepma. (2007). 'A Framework on Interactions of Climate and Energy Policy Instruments'. *Mitigation and Adaptation Strategies for Global Change 13*, no. 2 (15 February): 131–156.

Olejniczak, Karol, Sylwia Borkowska-Waszak, Anna Domaradzka-Widła and Yaerin Park. (2020). 'Policy Labs: The Next Frontier of Policy Design and Evaluation?' *Policy & Politics 48*, no. 1 (1 January): 89–110.

Olejniczak, K., E. Raimondo and T. Kupiec. (2016). 'Evaluation Units as Knowledge Brokers: Testing and Calibrating an Innovative Framework'. *Evaluation 22*, no. 2 (1 April): 168–189.

Olejniczak, Karol, Paweł Śliwowski and Frans Leeuw. (2020). 'Comparing Behavioral Assumptions of Policy Tools: Framework for Policy Designers'. *Journal of Comparative Policy Analysis: Research and Practice 22*, no. 6 (1 November): 498–520.

Olejniczak, Karol, Paweł Śliwowski and Magdalena Roszczyńska-Kurasińska. (2019). 'Behaviour Architects: A Framework for Employing Behavioural Insights in Public Policy Practice'. *Public Governance/Zarządzanie Publiczne 47*, no. 1 (27 June): 18–32.

Olejniczak, Karol, Paweł Śliwowski and Rafał Trzciński. (2018). 'The Role of Analysts in Public Agencies: Toward an Empirically Grounded Typology'. In Xun Wu and Michael Howlett (eds.), *Policy Capacity and Governance*. Cham: Palgrave Macmillan, 151–178.

Oliphant, S. and M. Howlett. (2010). 'Assessing Policy Analytical Capacity: Comparative Insights from a Study of the Canadian Environmental Policy Advice System'. *Journal of Comparative Policy Analysis: Research and Practice 12*, no. 4: 439.

Oliver, A. (2013). 'From Nudging to Budging: Using Behavioural Economics to Inform Public Sector Policy'. *Journal of Social Policy 42*, no. 4: 685–700.

Oliver, A. (2015). 'Nudging, Shoving, and Budging: Behavioural Economic-Informed Policy'. *Public Administration 93*, no. 3: 700–714.

Oliver, A. (2017). 'Nudges, Shoves and Budges: Behavioural Economic Policy Frameworks'. *The International Journal of Health Planning and Management 33*, no. 1: 272–275.

Oliver, J. Eric and Thomas J. Wood. (2014). 'Conspiracy Theories and the Paranoid Style(s) of Mass Opinion'. *American Journal of Political Science 58*, no. 4: 952–966.

Oliver, K. and W. Pearce. (2017). 'Three Lessons from Evidence-Based Medicine and Policy: Increase Transparency, Balance Inputs and Understand Power'. *Palgrave Communications 3*, no. 1 (12 December): 43.

Oliver, Michael J. and Hugh Pemberton. (2004). 'Learning and Change in 20th-Century British Economic Policy'. *Governance 17*, no. 3: 415–441.

Oliver, P. E. (1993). 'Formal Models of Collective Action'. *Annual Review of Sociology 19*: 271–300.

Olsen, J. P. (2005). 'Maybe It Is Time to Rediscover Bureaucracy'. *Journal of Public Administration Research and Theory 16*, no. 1: 1–24.

Olsen, J. P. and B. G. Peters (eds.). (1996). *Lessons from Experience: Experiential Learning in Administrative Reforms in Eight Democracies*. Oslo, Norway: Scandinavian University Press.

Olson, M. (1965). *The Logic of Collective Action: Public Goods and the Theory of Groups*. Cambridge, MA: Harvard University Press.

Oosterveer, P. (2002). 'Reinventing Risk Politics: Reflexive Modernity and the European BSE Crisis'. *Journal of Environmental Policy and Planning 4*: 215–229.

Optic Optimal Policies for Transportation in Combination. (2014). 'Best Practices and Recommendations on Policy Packaging'. *Annual Review of Policy Design 2*, no. 1 (8 November): 1–10.

Oreskes, Naomi and Erik M. Conway. (2011). *Merchants of Doubt: How a Handful of Scientists Obscured the Truth on Issues from Tobacco Smoke to Global Warming* (Export edn). New York, NY: Bloomsbury Press.

Orren, K. and S. Skowronek. (1998). 'Regimes and Regime Building in American Government: A Review of Literature on the 1940s'. *Political Science Quarterly 113*, no. 4: 689–702.

Osborne, D. and E. Gaebler. (1992). *Reinventing Government*. Reading, MA: Addison-Wesley.

Osborne, K., C. Bacchi and C. Mackenzie. (2008). 'Gender Analysis and Community Consultation: The Role of Women's Policy Units'. *Australian Journal of Public Administration 67*, no. 2: 149–160.

Osborne, S. P. (2006). 'The New Public Governance?' *Public Management Review 8*, no. 3: 377–387.

Osborne, S. P. (2010). *The New Public Governance: Emerging Perspectives on the Theory and Practice of Public Governance*. London: Routledge.

Osborne, Stephen P., Greta Nasi and Madeline Powell. (2021). 'Beyond Co-Production: Value Creation and Public Services'. *Public Administration 99*, no. 4: 641–657.

Ostrom, E. (1986). 'A Method of Institutional Analysis'. In F. X. Kaufman, G. Majone and V. Ostrom (eds.), *Guidance, Control and Evaluation in the Public Sector*. Berlin, Germany: de Gruyter, 459–475.

Ostrom, E. (1996). 'Crossing the Great Divide: Co-Production, Synergy, and Development'. *World Development 24*, no. 6: 1037–1087.

Ostrom, E. (1999). 'Institutional Rational Choice: As Assessment of the Institutional Analysis and Development Framework'. In P. A. Sabatier (ed.), *Theories of the Policy Process*. Boulder, CO: Westview, 35–71.

Ostrom, E. (2003). 'How Types of Goods and Property Rights Jointly Affect Collective Action'. *Journal of Theoretical Politics 15*, no. 3: 239–270.

Ostrom, E. (2009). 'Beyond Markets and States: Polycentric Governance of Complex Economic Systems'. *Nobel Prize Lecture*. http://dlc.dlib.indiana.edu/dlc/bitstream/handle/10535/7707/ostrom.pdf?sequence=1

Ostrom, E. (2011). 'Background on the Institutional Analysis and Development Framework'. *Policy Studies Journal 39*, no. 1 (February): 7–27.

Ostrom, E., J. Burger, C. B. Field, R. B. Norgaard and D. Policansky. (1999). 'Revisiting the Commons: Local Lessons, Global Challenges'. *Science 284*, no. 5412 (9 April): 278–282.

Ostrom, E. and R. B. Parks. (1973). 'Suburban Police Departments: Too Many and Too Small?' In B. P. Roger, L. H. Masotti and J. K. Hadden (eds.), *The Urbanization of the Suburbs*. Urban Affairs Annual Reviews 7. Beverly Hills, CA: Sage, 367–402.

Ouimet, M., P. Bédard, J. Turgeon, J. N. Lavis, F. Gélineau, F. Gagnon and C. Dallaire. (2010). 'Correlates of Consulting Research Evidence Among Policy Analysts in Government Ministries: A Cross-Sectional Survey'. *Evidence & Policy: A Journal of Research, Debate and Practice* 6, no. 4 (22 November): 433–460.

Overbye, E. (1994). 'Convergence in Policy Outcomes: Social Security Systems in Perspectives'. *Journal of Public Policy* 14, no. 2: 147–174.

Owens, S. and T. Rayner. (1999). ' "When Knowledge Matters": The Role and Influence of the Royal Commission on Environmental Pollution'. *Journal of Environmental Policy and Planning* 1: 7–24.

Packwood, A. (2002). 'Evidence-Based Policy: Rhetoric and Reality'. *Social Policy & Society* 1, no. 3: 267–272.

Padberg, D. I. (1992). 'Nutritional Labeling as a Policy Instrument'. *American Journal of Agricultural Economics* 74, no. 5: 1208–1213.

Paehlke, R. (1990). 'Regulatory and Non-Regulatory Approaches to Environmental Protection'. *Canadian Public Administration* 33, no. 1: 17–36.

Page, E. C. (2001). *Governing by Numbers: Delegated Legislation and Everyday Policy-Making.* Portland, OR: Hart Publishing.

Page, E. C. (2006). *The Roles of Public Opinion Research in Canadian Government.* Toronto, ON: University of Toronto Press.

Page, E. C. (2010). 'Bureaucrats and Expertise: Elucidating a Problematic Relationship in Three Tableaux and Six Jurisdictions'. *Sociologie du Travail* 52, no. 2: 255–273.

Page, E. C. and B. Jenkins. (2005). *Policy Bureaucracy: Governing with a Cast of Thousands.* Oxford: Oxford University Press.

Painter, M. and B. G. Peters (eds.). (2010). *Tradition and Public Administration.* London: Palgrave Macmillan.

Painter, M. and J. Pierre (eds.). (2005). *Challenges to State Policy Capacity: Global Trends and Comparative Perspectives.* London: Palgrave Macmillan.

Pal, L. A. (1987). *Public Policy Analysis: An Introduction.* Toronto, ON: Methuen.

Pal, L. A. (1993). *Interests of State: The Politics of Language, Multiculturalism and Feminism in Canada.* Montreal, QC and Kingston, ON: McGill-Queen's University Press.

Pal, L. A. (1997). *Beyond Policy Analysis: Public Issue Management in Turbulent Times.* Toronto, ON: ITP Nelson.

Palan, R. and J. Abbott. (1996). *State Strategies in the Global Political Economy.* London: Pinter.

Palumbo, D. J. and D. J. Calista. (1990). 'Opening Up the Black Box: Implementation and the Policy Process'. In D. J. Palumbo and D. J. Calista (eds.), *Implementation and the Policy Process.* New York: Greenwood Press.

Pandemic Prevention Institute. (2021). 'Ending the Current Covid-19 Pandemic and Preventing Future Global Disease Outbreaks Requires Fast, Accurate Data'. *The Rockefeller Foundation* (blog). www.rockefellerfoundation.org/pandemicpreventioninstitute/.

Papaioannou, H. R. and J. Bassant. (2006). 'Performance Management: Benchmarking as a Policy-Making Tool: From the Private to the Public Sector'. *Science and Public Policy* 33, no. 2: 91–102.

Parks, R. B., P. C. Baker, L. Kiser, R. Oakerson, E. Ostrom, V. Ostrom, S. L. Percy, M. B. Vandivort, G. P. Whitaker and R. Wilson. (1981). 'Consumers as Coproducers of Public Services: Some Economic and Institutional Considerations'. *Policy Studies Journal* 9, no. 7 (1 June): 1001–1011.

Parson, E. A. and K. Fisher-Vanden. (1999). 'Joint Implementation of Greenhouse Gas Abatement under the Kyoto Protocol's "Clean Development Mechanism": Its Scope and Limits'. *Policy Sciences 3*: 207–224.

Parsons, M., K. Fisher and J. Nalau. (2016). 'Alternative Approaches to Co-Design: Insights from Indigenous/Academic Research Collab- Orations'. *Current Opinion in Environmental Sustainability 20*: 99–105.

Parsons, W. (1995). *Public Policy: An Introduction to the Theory and Practice of Policy Analysis*. Aldershot, UK and Cheltenham, UK: Edward Elgar.

Parsons, W. (2001). 'Modernising Policy-Making for the Twenty First Century: The Professional Model'. *Public Policy and Administration 16*, no. 3: 93–110.

Parsons, W. (2004). 'Not Just Steering but Weaving: Relevant Knowledge and the Craft of Building Policy Capacity and Coherence'. *Australian Journal of Public Administration 63*, no. 1: 43–57.

Pasek, Josh, Tobias H. Stark, Jon A. Krosnick and Trevor Tompson. (2015). 'What Motivates a Conspiracy Theory? Birther Beliefs, Partisanship, Liberal-Conservative Ideology, and Anti-Black Attitudes'. *Electoral Studies 40*: 482–489.

Pasquier, M. and J. Villeneuve. (2007). 'Organizational Barriers to Transparency: A Typology and Analysis of Organizational Behaviour Tending to Prevent or Restrict Access to Information'. *International Review of Administrative Sciences 73*, no. 1: 147–162.

Patashnik, E. (2003). 'After the Public Interest Prevails: The Political Sustainability of Reforms'. *Governance 16*, no. 2: 203–234.

Patchen, M. (2010). 'What Shapes Public Reactions to Climate Change? Overview of Research and Policy Implications'. *Analyses of Social Issues and Public Policy 10*, no. 1: 47–68.

Patt, A. G. and D. Schröter. (2008). 'Perceptions of Climate Risk in Mozambique: Implications for the Success of Adaptation Strategies'. *Global Environmental Change 18*, no. 3: 458–467.

Patton, C. V. and D. S. Sawicki. (1993). '*Basic Methods of Policy Analysis and Planning*'. Englewood Cliffs, NJ: Prentice Hall.

Pattyn, V., A. Gouglas and J. De Leeuwe. (2020). 'The Knowledge Behind Brexit. A Bibliographic Analysis of Ex-Ante Policy Appraisals on Brexit in the United Kingdom and the European Union'. *Journal of European Public Policy* (2 June): 1–19.

Pauly, L. W. and S. Reich. (1997). 'National Structures and Multinational Corporate Behaviour: Enduring Differences in the Age of Globalisation'. *International Organization 51*, no. 1: 1–30.

Pautz, M. C. (2009). 'Perceptions of the Regulated Community in Environmental Policy: The View from Below'. *Review of Policy Research 26*, no. 5: 533–550.

Pawson, R. (2002). 'Evidence-Based Policy: In Search of a Method?' *Evaluation 8*, no. 2: 157–181.

Pawson, R. (2006). *Evidence-Based Policy: A Realist Perspective*. London: Sage.

Pawson, R., T. Greenhalgh, G. Harvey and K. Walshe. (2005). 'Realist Review – A New Method of Systematic Review Designed for Complex Policy Interventions'. *Journal of Health Services Research Policy 10*, Supplement 1: S1:21–S1:34.

Pearse, P. H. (1980). 'Property Rights and the Regulation of Commercial Fisheries'. In P. N. Nemetz (ed.), *Resource Policy: International Perspectives*. Montreal, QC: Institute for Research on Public Policy, 185–210.

Pedersen, L. H. (2007). 'Ideas Are Transformed as They Transfer: A Comparative Study of Eco-Taxation in Scandinavia'. *Journal of European Public Policy 14*, no. 1: 59–77.

Peled, A. (2002). 'Why Style Matters: A Comparison of Two Administrative Reform Initiatives in the Israeli Public Sector, 1989–98'. *Journal of Public Administration Research and Theory 12*, no. 2: 217–240.

Pellikaan, H. and R. J. van der Veen. (2002). *Environmental Dilemmas and Policy Design*. Cambridge: Cambridge University Press.

Peltzman, S. (1976). 'Toward a More General Theory of Regulation'. *Journal of Law and Economics 19* (August): 211–240.

Pentland, B. and M. Feldman. (2008). 'Designing Routines: On the Folly of Designing Artifacts, While Hoping for Patterns of Action'. *Information and Organization 18*, no. 4 (October): 235–250.

Perez-Batres, L. A., V. V. Miller and M. J. Pisani. (2011). 'Institutionalizing Sustainability: An Empirical Study of Corporate Registration and Commitment to the United Nations Global Compact Guidelines'. *Journal of Cleaner Production 19*, no. 8: 843–851.

Pérez-Ramírez, M., G. Ponce-Díaz and S. Lluch-Cota. (2012). 'The Role of MSC Certification in the Empowerment of Fishing Cooperatives in Mexico: The Case of Red Rock Lobster Co-Managed Fishery'. *Ocean & Coastal Management 63* (July): 24–29.

Perl, Anthony, Michael Howlett and M. Ramesh. (2018). 'Policy-Making and Truthiness: Can Existing Policy Models Cope with Politicized Evidence and Willful Ignorance in a 'Post-Fact' World?" *Policy Sciences 51*, no. 4 (December): 581–600.

Perl, A. and D. J. White. (2002). 'The Changing Role of Consultants in Canadian Policy Analysis'. *Policy and Society 21*, no. 1: 49–73.

Perrow, C. (1984). *Normal Accidents: Living with High-Risk Technologies*. New York: Basic Books.

Perry, J. L. and H. G. Rainey. (1988). 'The Public – Private Distinction in Organization Theory: A Critique and Research Strategy'. *Academy of Management Review 13*, no. 2: 182–201.

Persson, J. and L. Mathiassen. (2009). 'A Process for Managing Risks in Distributed Teams'. *IEEE Software 27*, no. 1: 20–29.

Pestoff, V. (2006). 'Citizens and Co-Production of Welfare Services'. *Public Management Review 8* (December): 503–519.

Pestoff, V. and T. Brandsen. (2009). *Co-Production: The Third Sector and the Delivery of Public Services*. New York: CRC Press.

Pestoff, V. and T. Brandsen. (2010). 'Public Governance and the Third Sector: Opportunities for Co-Production and Innovation?' In S. P. Osborne (ed.), *The New Public Governance: Emerging Perspectives on the Theory and Practice of Public Governance*. London: Routledge, 223–237.

Pestoff, V., T. Brandsen and B. Verschuere. (2012). *New Public Governance, the Third Sector and Co-Production*. New York: Routledge.

Pestoff, V., S. P. Osborne and T. Brandsen. (2006). 'Patterns of Co-Production in Public Services'. *Public Management Review 8* (December): 591–595.

Petek, A. (2011). 'Transformacija politike prema osobama s invaliditetom: analiza ciljeva' (Transformation of Policy for Persons with Disability in Croatia: Analysis of Goals). *Anali Hrvatskog politološkog društva* no. 8: 101–123.

Petek, Ana, Nikola Baketa, Anka Kekez, Marko Kovačić, Mario Munta, Krešimir Petković, Marjeta Šinko and Borna Zgurić. (2021). 'Unboxing the Vague Notion of Policy Goals: Comparison of Croatian Public Policies'. *European Policy Analysis 7*, no. 2: 451–469.

Petek, Ana, Borna Zgurić, Marjeta Šinko, Krešimir Petković, Mario Munta, Marko Kovačić, Anka Kekez and Nikola Baketa. (2022). 'From Hierarchy to Continuum: Classifying the Technical Dimension of Policy Goals'. *Policy Sciences* (March).

Peters, B. G. (ed.). (1988). *Comparing Public Bureaucracies: Problems of Theory and Method*. Tuscaloosa, AL: University of Alabama Press, 8.

Peters, B. G. (1990). 'Administrative Culture and Analysis of Public Organizations'. *Indian Journal of Public Administration 36*: 420–428.

Peters, B. G. (1992a). 'Government Reorganization: A Theoretical Analysis'. *International Political Science Review 13*, no. 2: 199–218.

Peters, B. G. (1992b). 'The Policy Process: An Institutionalist Perspective'. *Canadian Public Administration 35*, no. 2: 160–180.

Peters, B. G. (1996a). *The Future of Governing: Four Emerging Models*. Lawrence, KS: University Press of Kansas.

Peters, B. G. (1996b). *The Policy Capacity of Government*. Ottawa, ON: Canadian Centre for Management Development.

Peters, B. G. (1996c). 'Theory and Methodology'. In H. A. G. M. Bekke, J. L. Perry and T. A. J. Toonen (eds.), *Civil Service Systems in Comparative Perspective*. Bloomington, IN: Indiana University Press. 13–41.

Peters, B. G. (1998). *Managing Horizontal Government: The Politics of Coordination*. Ottawa, ON: Canadian Centre for Management Development.

Peters, B. G. (2000a). 'Policy Instruments and Public Management: Bridging the Gaps'. *Journal of Public Administration Research and Theory 10*, no. 1: 35–48.

Peters, B. G. (2000b). 'Public-Service Reform: Comparative Perspectives'. In E. Lindquist (ed.), *Government Restructuring and Career Public Services*. Toronto, ON: Institute of Public Administration of Canada, 27–40.

Peters, B. G. (2001). *The Politics of Bureaucracy*. London and New York: Routledge.

Peters, B. G. (2002). 'Governing in a Market Era: Alternative Models of Governing'. *Public Administration and Public Policy 99*: 85–97.

Peters, B. G. (2004). *The Search for Coordination and Coherence in Public Policy: Return to the Center?* Unpublished Paper. Pittsburgh, PA: University of Pittsburgh.

Peters, B. G. (2005a). 'Conclusion: The Future of Instruments Research'. In P. Eliadis, M. Hill and M. Howlett (eds.), *Designing Government: From Instruments to Governance*. Montreal, QC: McGill-Queen's University Press, 353–363.

Peters, B. G. (2005b). 'The Problem of Policy Problems'. In P. Eliadis, M. Hill and M. Howlett, (eds.), *Designing Government: From Instruments to Governance*. Montreal, QC: McGill-Queen's University Press, 77–105.

Peters, B. G. (2010). 'Meta-Governance and Public Management' In S. P. Osborne (ed.), *The New Public Governance: Emerging Perspectives on the Theory and Practice of Public Governance*. London: Routledge, 36–52.

Peters, B. G. (2017). 'Is Governance for Everybody?' *Policy and Society 33*, no. 4 (December): 317–327.

Peters, B. G. (2018). *Policy Problems and Policy Design*. Cheltenham: Edward Elgar Publishing.

Peters, B. G. (2021). *Administrative Traditions: Understanding the Roots of Contemporary Administrative Behavior*. Oxford University Press.

Peters, B. G. and A. Barker. (1993). *Advising West European Governments: Inquiries, Expertise and Public Policy*. Edinburgh, UK: Edinburgh University Press.

Peters, B. G., J. C. Doughtie and M. K. McCulloch. (1978). 'Do Public Policies Vary in Different Types of Democratic System?' In P. G. Lewis, D. C. Potter and F. G.

Castles (eds.), *The Practice of Comparative Politics: A Reader*. London: Longman, 70–100.

Peters, B. G., P. Eliadis, M. Hill and M. Howlett. (2005). 'Conclusion: The Future of Instruments Research'. In *Designing Government: From Instruments to Governance*. Montreal, QC: McGill-Queen's University Press, 353–363.

Peters, B. G. and J. A. Hoornbeek. (2005). 'The Problem of Policy Problems'. In P. Eliadis, M. Hill and M. Howlett (eds.), *Designing Government: From Instruments to Governance*. Montreal, QC: McGill-Queen's University Press, 77–105.

Peters, B. G. and M. L. Nagel. (2020). *Zombie Ideas: Why Failed Policy Ideas Persist. Elements in Public Policy*. Cambridge: Cambridge University Press, November.

Peters, B. G. and J. Pierre. (1998). 'Governance Without Government? Rethinking Public Administration'. *Journal of Public Administration Research and Theory 8*, no. 2: 223–244.

Peters, B. G. and J. Pierre. (2000). 'Citizens versus the New Public Manager: The Problem of Mutual Empowerment'. *Administration and Society 32*, no. 1: 9–28.

Peters, B. G. and J. Pierre. (2003). *Handbook of Public Administration*. Beverley Hills: Sage Publications Ltd.

Peters, B. G., P. Ravinet, M. Howlett, G. Capano, I. Mukherjee and M. H. Chou. (2018). *Designing for Policy Effectiveness: Defining and Understanding a Concept*. Elements Series. Cambridge: Cambridge University Press.

Peters, B. G. and M. Tarpey. (2019). 'Are Wicked Problems Really So Wicked? Perceptions of Policy Problems'. *Policy and Society 38*, no. 2: 218–236.

Peters, B. G. and F. K. M. Van Nispen (eds.) (1998). *Public Policy Instruments: Evaluating the Tools of Public Administration*. New York: Edward Elgar.

Pew Research Center. (2009). *Modest Support for 'Cap and Trade' Policy: Fewer Americans See Solid Evidence of Global Warming*. Washington, DC: Pew Research Center.

Pfeffer, J. (1977). 'The Ambiguity of Leadership'. *Academy of Management Review 2*, no. *1* (1 January): 104–112.

Phidd, R. W. (1975). 'The Economic Council of Canada: Its Establishment, Structure and Role in the Canadian Policy-Making System 1963–74'. *Canadian Public Administration 18*, no. *3*: 428–473.

Phidd, R. W. and G. B. Doern. (1983). *Canadian Public Policy: Ideas, Structures, Process*. Toronto, ON: Methuen.

Philibert, C. (2011). *Interactions of Policies for Renewable Energy and Climate*. IEA Energy Paper. OECD. http://econpapers.repec.org/paper/oecieaaaa/2011_2f6-en.htm.

Phillips, S. D. (1991). 'How Ottawa Blends: Shifting Government Relationships with Interest Groups'. In F. Abele (ed.), *How Ottawa Spends 1991–92: The Politics of Fragmentation*. Ottawa, ON: Carleton University Press, 183–228.

Phillips, S. D. (2001). 'From Charity to Clarity: Reinventing Federal Government – Voluntary Sector Relationships'. In L. A. Pal (ed.), *How Ottawa Spends 2001–2: Power in Transition*. Toronto, ON: Oxford University Press, 145–176.

Phillips, S. D. (2007). 'Policy Analysis and the Voluntary Sector: Evolving Policy Styles'. In L. Dobuzinskis, M. Howlett and D. Laycock (eds.), *Policy Analysis in Canada: The State of the Art*. Toronto, ON: University of Toronto Press, 272–284.

Phillips, S. D., R. Laforest and A. Graham. (2010). 'From Shopping to Social Innovation: Getting Public Financing Right in Canada'. *Policy and Society 29*, no. *3*: 189–199.

Phillips, S. D. and K. Levasseur. (2004). 'The Snakes and Ladders of Accountability: Contradictions between Contracting and Collaboration for Canada's Voluntary Sector'. *Canadian Public Administration 47*, no. 4: 451–474.

Phillips, S. D. and M. Orsini. (2002). *Mapping the Links: Citizen Involvement in Policy Processes*. Ottawa, ON: Canadian Policy Research Networks.

Pichert, D. and K. V. Katsikopoulos. (2008). 'Green Defaults: Information Presentation and Pro-Environmental Behaviour'. *Journal of Environmental Psychology 28*, no. 1: 63–73.

Pielke Jr, R. (2010). *The Climate Fix. What Scientists and Politicians Won't Tell You About Global Warming*. New York: Basic Books.

Pierre, J. (1995). 'Conclusions: A Framework of Comparative Public Administration'. In J. Pierre (ed.), *Bureaucracy in the Modern State: An Introduction to Comparative Public Administration*. Aldershot, UK: Edward Elgar, 205–218.

Pierre, J. (1998). 'Public Consultation and Citizen Participation: Dilemmas of Policy Advice'. In B. G. Peters and D. J. Savoie (eds.), *Taking Stock: Assessing Public Sector Reforms*. Montreal, QC: McGill-Queen's Press, 137–163.

Pierre, J. (2012). 'Governance and Institutional Flexibility'. In D. Levi-Faur (ed.), *The Oxford Handbook of Governance*. Oxford: Oxford University Press, 187–201.

Pierre, J. and B. G. Peters. (2005). *Governing Complex Societies: Trajectories and Scenarios*. London: Palgrave Macmillan.

Pierson, P. (1992). ' "Policy Feedbacks" and Political Change: Contrasting Reagan and Thatcher's Pension Reform Initiatives'. *Studies in American Political Development 6*: 359–390.

Pierson, P. (1993). 'When Effect Becomes Cause: Policy Feedback and Political Change'. *World Politics 45*: 595–628.

Pierson, P. (2000). 'Increasing Returns, Path Dependence, and the Study of Politics'. *American Political Science Review 94*, no. 2: 251–267.

Pierson, P. (2004). *Politics in Time: History, Institutions and Social Analysis*. Princeton, NJ: Princeton University Press.

Pigou, A. C. (1932). *The Economics of Welfare*. London: Macmillan.

Pina e Cunha, M., J. V. da Cunha and K. Kamoche. (1999). 'Organizational Improvisation: What, When, How and Why'. *International Journal of Management Reviews 1*, no. 3: 299–341.

Pittel, K. and D. T. G. Rubbelke. (2006). 'Private Provision of Public Goods: Incentives for Donations'. *Journal of Economic Studies 33*, no. 6: 497–519.

Plaček, Michal, Milan Půček and František Ochrana. (2018). 'Identifying Corruption Risk: A Comparison of Bulgaria and the Czech Republic'. *Journal of Comparative Policy Analysis: Research and Practice* (3 September): 1–19.

Pluchinotta, Irene, Raffaele Giordano, Dimitrios Zikos, Tobias Krueger and Alexis Tsoukiàs. (2020). 'Integrating Problem Structuring Methods and Concept-Knowledge Theory for An Advanced Policy Design: Lessons from a Case Study in Cyprus'. *Journal of Comparative Policy Analysis: Research and Practice 22*, no. 6 (1 November): 626–647.

Pollack, M. A. (2003). 'Control Mechanism or Deliberative Democracy? Two Images of Comitology'. *Comparative Political Studies 36*, no. 1/2: 125–155.

Pollitt, C. (2001a). 'Clarifying Convergence: Striking Similarities and Durable Differences in Public Management Reform'. *Public Management Review 4*, no. 1: 471–492.

Pollitt, C. (2001b). 'Convergence: The Useful Myth?' *Public Administration 79*, no. 4: 933–947.

Pollitt, C. and G. Bouckaert. (2011). *Public Management Reform: A Comparative Analysis – New Public Management, Governance, and the Neo-Weberian State* (3rd edn). Oxford: Oxford University Press.

Pollitt, M. G. and I. Shaorshadze. (2011). *The Role of Behavioural Economics in Energy and Climate Policy*. Cambridge Working Paper in Economics (CWPE). Cambridge: University of Cambridge.

Pontusson, J. (1995). 'From Comparative Public Policy to Political Economy: Putting Institutions in their Place and Taking Interests Seriously'. *Comparative Political Studies 28*, no. 1: 117–147.

Poocharoen, O. and B. Ting. (2015). 'Collaboration, Co-Production, Networks: Convergence of Theories'. *Public Management Review 17*, no. 4: 587–614.

Poortinga, W., A. Spence, L. Whitmarsh, S. Capstick and N. F. Pidgeon. (2011). 'Uncertain Climate: An Investigation into Public Scepticism about Anthropogenic Climate Change'. *Global Environmental Change 21*, no. 3: 1015–1024.

Pope, J. and J. M. Lewis. (2008). 'Improving Partnership Governance: Using a Network Approach to Evaluate Partnerships in Victoria'. *Australian Journal of Public Administration 67*, no. 4: 443–456.

Pope, J. and A. D. Owen. (2009). 'Emission Trading Schemes: Potential Revenue Effects, Compliance Costs and Overall Tax Policy Issues'. *Energy Policy 37*: 4595–4603.

Porter, T. and K. Ronit. (2006). 'Self-Regulation as Policy Process: The Multiple and Crisscrossing Stages of Private Rule-Making'. *Policy Sciences 39*: 41–72.

Porumbescu, G. A., M. I. H. Lindeman, E. Ceka and M. Cucciniello. (2017). 'Can Transparency Foster More Understanding and Compliant Citizens?' *Public Administration Review 77*, no. 6: 840–850.

Posner, R. A. (1974). 'Theories of Economic Regulation'. *Bell Journal of Economics and Management Science 5*: 335–358.

Post, L. A., T. Salmon and A. Raile. (2008). 'Using Public Will to Secure Political Will'. In S. Odugbemi and T. Jacobson (eds.), *Governance Reform Under Real World Conditions. Communication for Governance and Accountability Program.* Washington, DC: World Bank, Chapter 7. www.gsdrc.org/go/display&type=Document&id=3710.

Potoski, M. (2002). 'Designing Bureaucratic Responsiveness: Administrative Procedures and Agency Choice in State Environmental Policy'. *State Politics and Policy Quarterly 2*, no. 1: 1–23.

Potoski, M. and A. Prakash (eds.). (2009). *Voluntary Programs: A Club Theory Perspective*. Cambridge, MA: MIT Press.

Power, M. and L. S. McCarty. (2002). 'Trends in the Development of Ecological Risk Assessment and Management Frameworks'. *Human and Ecological Risk Assessment 8*, no. 1: 7–18.

Prasser, S. (2006). 'Royal Commissions in Australia: When Should Governments Appoint Them?' *Australian Journal of Public Administration 65*, no. 3: 28–47.

Pratt, J. W. and R. J. Zeckhauser. (1991). *Principals and Agents: The Structure of Business*. Cambridge, MA: Harvard Business School Press.

Prentice, S. (2006). 'Childcare, Co-Production and the Third Sector in Canada'. *Public Management Review 8*, no. 4: 521–536.

Preskill, H. and S. Boyle. (2008). 'A Multidisciplinary Model of Evaluation Capacity Building'. *American Journal of Evaluation 29*, no. 4: 443–459.

Pressman, J. L. and A. B. Wildavsky. (1973). *Implementation: How Great Expectations in Washington Are Dashed in Oakland*. Berkeley, CA: University of California Press.

Prichard, J. R. S. (1983). *Crown Corporations in Canada: The Calculus of Instrument Choice*. Toronto, ON: Butterworths.

Prince, M. J. (1979). 'Policy Advisory Groups in Government Departments'. In G. B. Doern and P. Aucoin (eds.), *Public Policy in Canada: Organization, Process, Management*. Toronto, ON: Gage, 275–300.

Prince, M. J. (1983). *Policy Advice and Organizational Survival*. Aldershot, UK: Gower.

Prince, M. J. (2007). 'Soft Craft, Hard Choices, Altered Context: Reflections on 25 Years of Policy Advice in Canada'. In L. Dobuzinskis, M. Howlett and D. Laycock (eds.), *Policy Analysis in Canada: The State of the Art*. Toronto, ON: University of Toronto Press, 95–106.

Prince, M. J. (2008). *Reviewing the Literature on Policy Instruments*. Ottawa, ON: Human Resources and Social Development Canada.

Prince, M. J. and J. Chenier. (1980). 'The Rise and Fall of Policy Planning and Research Units'. *Canadian Public Administration 22*, no. 4: 536–550.

Proag, S. and V. Proag. (2014). 'The Cost Benefit Analysis of Providing Resilience'. Procedia Economics and Finance, 4th International Conference on Building Resilience, Incorporating the 3rd Annual Conference of the ANDROID Disaster Resilience Network, 8–11 September 2014, Salford Quays, UK 18: 361–368.

Proctor, Robert and Londa Schiebinger (eds.). (2008). *Agnotology: The Making and Unmaking of Ignorance*. Stanford, CA: Stanford University Press.

Pross, A. P. (1992). *Group Politics and Public Policy*. Toronto, ON: Oxford University Press.

Pross, A. P. and I. S. Stewart. (1993). 'Lobbying, the Voluntary Sector and the Public Purse'. In S. D. Phillips (ed.), *How Ottawa Spends 1993–94: A More Democratic Canada?* Ottawa, ON: Carleton University Press, 109–142.

Provan, K. G. and P. Kenis. (2008). 'Modes of Network Governance: Structure, Management and Effectiveness'. *Journal of Public Administration Research and Theory 18*, no. 2: 229–252.

Prpic, J., A. Taeihagh and J. Melton. (2015). 'The Fundamentals of Policy Crowdsourcing'. *Policy & Internet 1* August.

Przeworski, A. (1990). *The State and the Economy under Capitalism*. Chur, Switzerland: Harwood.

PwC (PricewaterhouseCoopers). (2014). *Agility: The Future of Government*. www.pwc.com/ca/en/public-sector-government/agility.jhtml. Accessed 13 September.

Pwc. (n.d.). *Risk Management and Compliance. Risk Assurance. Services*. www.pwc.com/me/en/services/risk-assurance/risk-management-and-compliance.html.

Pykett, J., R. Jones, M. Welsh and M. Whitehead. (2014). 'The Art of Choosing and the Politics of Social Marketing'. *Policy Studies 35*, no. 2 (4 March): 97–114.

Qualter, T. H. (1985). *Opinion Control in the Democracies*. London: Macmillan.

Quirk, Paul J. (1988). 'In Defense of the Politics of Ideas'. *The Journal of Politics 50*: 31–45.

Qureshi, H. (2004). 'Evidence in Policy and Practice: What Kinds of Research Designs?' *Journal of Social Work 4*, no. 1: 7–23.

Raadschelders, J. C. N. (1998). *Handbook of Administrative History*. New Brunswick, NJ: Transaction.

Raadschelders, J. C. N. (2000). 'Administrative History of the United States: Development and State of the Art'. *Administration and Society 32*, no. 5: 499–528.

Raadschelders, J. C. N. and M. R. Rutgers. (1996). 'The Evolution of Civil Service Systems'. In H. A. G. M. Bekke, J. L. Perry and T. A. J. Toonen (eds.), *Civil Service*

Systems in Comparative Perspective. Bloomington, IN: Indiana University Press, 67–99.

Rabe, B., C. Borick and E. Lachapelle. (2011). *Climate Compared: Public Opinion on Climate Change in the United States and Canada*. Brookings Institution. www.brookings.edu/research/papers/2011/04/climate-change-opinion.

Radaelli, C. M. (1995). 'The Role of Knowledge in the Policy Process'. *Journal of European Public Policy* 2, no. 2: 159–183.

Radaelli, C. M. (2005). 'Diffusion without Convergence: How Political Context Shapes the Adoption of Regulatory Impact Assessment'. *Journal of European Public Policy* 12, no. 5: 924–943.

Radaelli, C. M. (2009). 'Measuring Policy Learning: Regulatory Impact Assessment in Europe'. *Journal of European Public Policy* 16, no. 8: 1145–1164.

Radaelli, C. M. and C. A. Dunlop. (2013). 'Learning in the European Union: Theoretical Lenses and Meta-Theory'. *Journal of European Public Policy* 20, no. 6: 923–940.

Radaelli, C. M. and A. C. M. Meuwese. (2009). 'Better Regulation in Europe: Between Public Management and Regulatory Reform'. *Public Administration* 87, no. 3: 639–654.

Radin, B. A. (1992). 'Policy Analysis in the Office of the Assistant Secretary for Planning and Evaluation in the HEW/HHS: Institutionalization and the Second Generation'. In C. H. Weiss (ed.), *Organizations for Policy Analysis: Helping Government Think*. Sage, 144–160.

Radin, B. A. (1997). 'Presidential Address: The Evolution of the Policy Analysis Field: From Con- Versation to Conversations'. *Journal of Policy Analysis and Management* 16, no. 2: 204–218.

Radin, B. A. (2000). *Beyond Machiavelli: Policy Analysis Comes of Age*. Washington, DC: Georgetown University Press.

Radin, B. A. and J. P. Boase. (2000). 'Federalism, Political Structure, and Public Policy in the United States and Canada'. *Journal of Comparative Policy Analysis* 2, no. 1: 65–90.

Radnor, Z. J. and R. Boaden. (2004). 'Developing an Understanding of Corporate Anorexia'. *International Journal of Operations & Production Management* 24, no. 4 (1 April): 424–440.

Raghunandan, A. (2018). *Government Subsidies and Corporate Fraud*. SSRN Scholarly Paper. Rochester, NY: Social Science Research Network, 20 November.

Rajan, S. C. (1992). 'Legitimacy in Environmental Policy: The Regulation of Automobile Pollution in California'. *International Journal of Environmental Studies* 42: 243–258.

Ramesh, M. (1995). 'Economic Globalization and Policy Choices: Singapore'. *Governance* 8, no. 2: 243–260.

Ramesh, M. (2008). 'Autonomy and Control in Public Hospital Reforms in Singapore'. *The American Review of Public Administration* 38, no. 1: 62–79.

Ramesh, M. (2009). 'Healthcare Reforms in Thailand: Rethinking Conventional Wisdom'. In M. Ramesh and S. Fritzen (eds.), *Transforming Asian Governance: Rethinking Assumptions, Challenging Practices*. London: Routledge.

Ramesh, M. and A. S. Bali. (2019). 'Healthcare in Singapore'. In Mallory Compton and Paul t'Hart (eds.), *Great Policy Successes: How Governments Get It Right in a Big Way at Least Some of the Time*. Oxford: Oxford University Press.

Ramesh, M. and A. S. Bali. (2021). *Health Policy in Asia: A Policy Design Approach*. Cambridge: Cambridge University Press.

Ramesh, M. and S. Fritzen (eds.). (2009). *Transforming Asian Governance: Rethinking Assumptions, Challenging Practices*. New York: Routledge.

Ramesh, M. and M. Howlett (eds.). (2006). *Deregulation and Its Discontents: Rewriting the Rules in Asia*. Aldershot, UK: Edward Elgar.

Ramesh, M., X. Wu and M. Howlett. (2015). 'Second Best Governance? Governments and Governance in the Imperfect World of Health Care Delivery in China, India and Thailand in Comparative Perspective'. *Journal of Comparative Policy Analysis: Research and Practice 21* (January): 1–17.

Rasmussen, K. (1999). 'Policy Capacity in Saskatchewan: Strengthening the Equilibrium'. *Canadian Public Administration 42*, no. 3: 331–348.

Rathi, S. S. and A. Chunekar. (2015). 'Not to Buy or Can Be 'Nudged' to Buy? Exploring Behavioral Interventions for Energy Policy in India'. *Energy Research & Social Science 7* (May): 78–83.

Rayner, J. (2013). 'On Smart Layering as Policy Design: Tackling the Biofuels Policy Mess in Canada and the United Kingdom'. *Policy Sciences* (Special Issue on Policy Design).

Rayner, J., B. Cashore, M. Howlett and J. Wilson. (2001). 'Privileging the Sub-Sector: Critical Sub-Sectors and Sectoral Relationships in Forest Policy-Making'. *Forest Policy and Economics 2*, no. 3–4: 319–332.

Rayner, J. and M. Howlett. (2009). 'Conclusion: Governance Arrangements and Policy Capacity for Policy Integration'. *Policy and Society 28*, no. 2 (July): 165–172.

Rayner, J., M. Howlett and A. Wellstead. (2017). 'Policy Mixes and Their Alignment Over Time: Patching and Stretching in the Oil Sands Reclamation Regime in Alberta, Canada: Alberta Oil Sands'. *Environmental Policy and Governance 27*, no. 5: 472–483.

Rayner, J., K. McNutt and A. Wellstead. (2013). 'Dispersed Capacity and Weak Coordination: The Challenge of Climate Change Adaptation in Canada's Forest Policy Sector'. *Review of Policy Research 30*, no. 1: 66–90.

Reagan, M. D. (1987). *Regulation: The Politics of Policy*. Boston, MA: Little, Brown.

Redström, J. (2006). 'Persuasive Design: Fringes and Foundations'. In A. I. Wijnand, Y. A. W. de Kort, C. Midden, B. Eggen and E. van den Hoven (eds.), *Persuasive Technology. Lecture Notes in Computer Science 3962*. Berlin/Heidelberg: Springer, 112–122.

Regens, J. L. and R. W. Rycroft. (1988). *The Acid Rain Controversy*. Pittsburgh, PA and London: University of Pittsburgh Press.

Reich, R. B. (1991). *The Work of Nations*. New York: Alfred Knopf.

Reichardt, Kristin and Karoline Rogge. (2016). 'How the Policy Mix Impacts Innovation: Findings from Company Case Studies on Offshore Wind in Germany'. *Environmental Innovation and Societal Transitions 18* (1 March): 62–81.

Rein, M., G. Esping-Andersen and L. Rainwater. (1987). *Stagnation and Renewal in Social Policy: The Rise and Fall of Policy Regimes*. Armonk: M.E. Sharpe.

Rein, M. and D. Scholl (1991). 'Frame-Reflective Policy Discourse'. In P. Wagner, C. H. Weiss, B. Wittrock and H. Wollman (eds.), *Social Sciences and Modern States: National Experiences and Theoretical Crossroads*. Cambridge: Cambridge University Press, 262–289.

Rein, M. and S. H. White. (1977a). 'Can Policy Research Help Policy?' *The Public Interest 49*: 119–136.

Rein, M. and S. H. White. (1977b). 'Policy Research: Belief and Doubt'. *Policy Analysis 3*, no. 2: 239–270.

Reinicke, W. H. (1998). *Global Public Policy: Governing Without Government?* Washington, DC: Brookings Institution.

Reisch, L. A. and C. R. Sunstein. (2016). 'Do Europeans Like Nudges?' *Judgement and Decision Making 11*, no. 4: 310–325.

Relyea, H. C. (1977). 'The Provision of Government Information: The Freedom of Information Act Experience'. *Canadian Public Administration 20*, no. 2: 317–341.

Renn, O. (1995). 'Style of Using Scientific Expertise: A Comparative Framework'. *Science and Public Policy 22*, no. 3: 147–156.

Resodihardjo, S. L. (2006). 'Wielding a Double-Edged Sword: The Use of Inquiries at Times of Crisis'. *Journal of Contingencies and Crisis Management 14*, no. 4: 199–206.

Rhodes, R. A. W. (1994). 'The Hollowing Out of the State: The Changing Nature of the Public Service in Britain'. *The Political Quarterly 65*, no. 2: 138–151.

Rhodes, R. A. W. (1996). 'The New Governance: Governing Without Government'. *Political Studies 44*: 652–667.

Rhodes, R. A. W. (1997). 'From Marketisation to Diplomacy: It's the Mix that Matters'. *Australian Journal of Public Administration 56*, no. 2: 40–54.

Rhodes, R. A. W. (2007). 'Understanding Governance: Ten Years On'. *Organization Studies 28*: 1243–1264.

Rhodes, R. A. W. (2012). 'Waves of Governance'. In D. Levi-Faur (ed.), *The Oxford Handbook of Governance*. Oxford: Oxford University Press, 33–48.

Rhodes, R. A. W. and P. Weller. (2001). *The Changing World of Top Officials*. Buckingham, UK: Open University Press.

Rhue, L. and A. Sundararajan. (2014). 'Digital Access, Political Networks and the Diffusion of Democracy'. *Social Networks 36* (January): 40–53.

Riccucci, N. M. and M. K. Meyers. (2008). 'Comparing Welfare Service Delivery Among Public, Nonprofit and For-Profit Work Agencies'. *International Journal of Public Administration 31*: 1441–1454.

Rich, A. (2004). *Think Tanks, Public Policy, and the Politics of Expertise*. New York: Cambridge University Press.

Rich, R. F. (1981). *Social Science Information and Public Policy Making*. Jossey-Bass Social and Behavioral Science Series, The NORC Series in Social Research. San Francisco: Jossey-Bass.

Rich, R. F. (1997). 'Measuring Knowledge Utilization: Processes and Outcomes'. *Knowledge and Policy 10*, no. 3: 11–24.

Richardson, J. (2000). 'Government, Interest Groups and Policy Change'. *Political Studies 48*, no. 5 (December): 1006–1025.

Richardson, J., G. Gustafsson and G. Jordan. (1982). 'The Concept of Policy Style'. In J. J. Richardson (ed.), *Policy Styles in Western Europe*. London: George Allen & Unwin, 1–16.

Richardson, J. J. (ed.). (1990). *Privatisation and Deregulation in Canada and Britain*. Aldershot, UK: Dartmouth Publishing.

Richardson, J. J. and A. G. Jordan. (1979). *Governing Under Pressure: The Policy Process in a Post-Parliamentary Democracy*. Oxford: Martin Robertson.

Richardson, J. J., A. G. Jordan and R. H. Kimber. (1978). 'Lobbying, Administrative Reform and Policy Styles: The Case of Land Drainage'. *Political Studies 26*, no. 1: 47–64.

Ricoeur, P. and J. B. Thompson. (1981). *Hermeneutics and the Human Sciences: Essays on Language, Action and Interpretation*. Cambridge: Cambridge University Press.

Riddell, N. (1998). *Policy Research Capacity in the Federal Government*. Ottawa, ON: Policy Research Initiative.

Riedel, J. A. (1972). 'Citizen Participation: Myths and Realities'. *Public Administration Review* (May–June): 211–220.

Riker, W. H. (1982). *Liberalism Against Populism: A Confrontation Between the Theory of Democracy and the Theory of Social Choice*. San Francisco, CA: Freeman.

Riker, W. H. (1983). 'Political Theory and the Art of Heresthetics'. In W. Finifter (ed.), *Political Science: The State of the Discipline*. Washington, DC: American Political Science Association, 47–67.

Riker, W. H. (1986). *The Art of Political Manipulation*. New Haven, CT: Yale University Press.

Rimkutė, D. and M. Haverland. (2015). 'How Does the European Commission Use Scientific Expertise? Results from a Survey of Scientific Members of the Commission's Expert Committees'. *Comparative European Politics 13*, no. 4: 430–494.

Rimlinger, G. V. (1971). *Welfare Policy and Industrialization in Europe, America and Russia*. New York: Wiley.

Ring, I., M. Drechsler, A. J. A. van Teeffelen, S. Irawan and O. Venter. (2010). 'Biodiversity Conservation and Climate Mitigation: What Role Can Economic Instruments Play?' *Current Opinion in Environmental Sustainability 2*, no. 1–2: 50–58.

Ring, I. and C. Schroter-Schlaack. (2011). *Instrument Mixes for Biodiversity Policies*. Leipzig, Germany: Helmholtz Centre for Environmental Research.

Ringquist, E. J., J. Worsham and M. A. Eisner. (2003). 'Salience, Complexity and the Legislative Direction of Regulatory Bureaucracies'. *Journal of Public Administration Research and Theory 13*, no. 2: 141–165.

Rittel, H. W. J. and M. M. Webber. (1973). 'Dilemmas in a General Theory of Planning'. *Policy Sciences 4*: 155–169.

Roberts, A. (1999). 'Retrenchment and Freedom of Information: Recent Experience under Federal, Ontario and British Columbia Law'. *Canadian Public Administration 42*, no. 4: 422–451.

Roberts, A. and J. Rose. (1995). 'Selling the Goods and Services Tax: Government Advertising and Public Discourse in Canada'. *Canadian Journal of Political Science 28*, no. 2: 311–330.

Roberts, R. and L. E. R. Dean. (1994). 'An Inquiry into Lowi's Policy Typology: The Conservation Coalition and the 1985 and 1990 Farm Bill'. *Environment and Planning C, Government and Policy 12*, no. 1: 71–86.

Robins, L. (2008). 'Perspectives on Capacity Building to Guide Policy and Program Development and Delivery'. *Environmental Science and Policy 11*: 687–701.

Roch, C., D. Pitts and I. Navarro. (2010). 'Representative Bureaucracy and Policy Tools: Ethnicity, Student Discipline, and Representation in Public Schools'. *Administration & Society 42*, no. 1: 38–65.

Rochefort, D. A. and R. W. Cobb (eds.). (1994). *The Politics of Problem Definition: Shaping the Policy Agenda*. Lawrence, KS: University Press of Kansas.

Rochet, C. (2004). 'Rethinking the Management of Information in the Strategic Monitoring of Public Policies by Agencies'. *Industrial Management and Data Systems 104*, no. 3: 201–208.

Rodrik, D. (1997). *Has Globalization Gone Too Far?* Washington, DC: Institute for International Economics.

Rodrik, D. (1998). 'Why Do Open Economies Have Bigger Governments?' *Journal of Political Economy 106*, no. 5: 997–1032.

Roe, E. (2016). 'Policy Messes and Their Management'. *Policy Sciences 49*, no. 4: 351–372.

Roehrich, J. K., M. A. Lewis and G. George. (2014). 'Are Public – Private Partnerships a Healthy Option? A Systematic Literature Review of "Constructive" Partnerships between Public and Private Actors'. *Social Science & Medicine 113* (July): 110–119.

Rogge, K. S. and K. Reichardt. (2016). 'Policy Mixes for Sustainability Transitions: An Extended Concept and Framework for Analysis'. *Research Policy 45*, no. 8: 1620–1635.

Rolfstam, M. (2009). 'Public Procurement as an Innovation Policy Tool: The Role of Institutions'. *Science and Public Policy 36*, no. 5: 349–360.

Roman, A. J. and K. Hooey. (1993). 'The Regulatory Framework'. In G. Thompson, M. L. McConnell and L. B. Huestis (eds.), *Environmental Law and Business in Canada*. Aurora, ON: Canada Law Books, 55–75.

Romans, J. T. (1966). 'Moral Suasion as an Instrument of Economic Policy'. *American Economic Review 56*, no. 5: 1220–1226.

Ronal, G.-C., R. Guinza-Carmenates, J. Carlos Attamirans-Cabrera, P. Thalmann and L. Dronet. (2010). 'Trade-offs and Performances of a Range of Alternative Global Climate Architectures for Post-2012'. *Environmental Science & Policy 13*, no. 1 (February): 63–71.

Rondinelli, D. A. (1983). *Development Projects as Policy Experiments: An Adaptive Approach to Development Administration*. London: Methuen.

Ronit, K. (2001). 'Institutions of Private Authority in Global Governance: Linking Territorial Forms of Self-regulation'. *Administration and Society 33*, no. 5: 555–578.

Room, G. (2013a). *Agile Policy on Complex Terrains: Nudge or Nuzzle?* 2 October. www.horizons.gc.ca/eng/content/agile-policy-complex-terrains-%E2%80%93-nudge-or-nuzzle.

Room, G. (2013b). 'Evidence for Agile Policy Makers: The Contribution of Transformative Realism'. *Evidence & Policy: A Journal of Research, Debate and Practice 9*, no. 2 (24 May): 225–244.

Roots, R. I. (2004). 'When Laws Backfire: Unintended Consequences of Public Policy'. *American Behavioural Scientist 47*, no. 11: 1376–1394.

Rose, J. (1993). 'Government Advertising in a Crisis: The Quebec Referendum Precedent'. *Canadian Journal of Communication 18*: 173–196.

Rose, R. (1976). *The Dynamics of Public Policy: A Comparative Analysis*. London: Sage.

Rose, R. (1988a). 'Comparative Policy Analysis: The Program Approach'. In M. Dogan (ed.), *Comparing Pluralist Democracies: Strains on Legitimacy*. Boulder, CO: Westview, 219–241.

Rose, R. (1988b). 'The Growth of Government Organization: Do We Count the Number or Weigh the Programs?' In C. Campbell and B. G. Peters (eds.), *Organizing Governance/Governing Organizations*. Pittsburgh, PA: University of Pittsburgh Press, 99–128.

Rose, R. (1991). 'What is Lesson-Drawing?' *Journal of Public Policy 11*, no. 1: 3–30.

Rose, R. (1993). *Lesson-Drawing in Public Policy: A Guide to Learning Across Time and Space*. London: Chatham House.

Rose, R. (2005). *Learning from Comparative Public Policy*. London: Routledge.

Rosenau, J. N. (1980). *The Study of Global Interdependence*. London: Pinter.

Rosenau, P. V. (1999). 'The Strengths and Weaknesses of Public – Private Policy Partnerships'. *American Behavioral Scientist 43*, no. 1: 10–34.

Rosenbloom, D. H. (2007). 'Administrative Law and Regulation'. In J. Rabin, W. B. Hildreth and G. J. Miller (eds.), *Handbook of Public Administration*. London: CRC and Taylor & Francis, 635–696.

Ross, H., M. Buchy and W. Proctor. (2002). 'Laying Down the Ladder: A Typology of Public Participation in Australian Natural Resource Management'. *Australian Journal of Environmental Management 9*, no. 4: 205–217.

Rotberg, R. I. (2014). 'Good Governance Means Performance and Results'. *Governance 27*, no. 3: 511–518.

Rothmayr, C. and S. Hardmeier. (2002). 'Government and Polling: Use and Impact of Polls in the Policy-Making Process in Switzerland'. *International Journal of Public Opinion Research 14*, no. 2: 123–140.

Rotmans, J., R. Kemp and M. van Asselt. (2001). 'More Evolution Than Revolution: Transition Management in Public Policy'. *Foresight 3*, no. 1: 15–31.

Rouban, L. (1999). 'Introduction Citizens and the New Governance'. In L. Rouban (ed.), *Citizens and the New Governance: Beyond New Public Management*. Amsterdam, Netherlands: IOS Press, 1–5.

Rourke, F. E. (1957). 'The Politics of Administrative Organization: A Case History'. *The Journal of Politics 19*, no. 1: 461–478.

Rowe, G. and L. J. Frewer. (2005). 'A Typology of Public Engagement Mechanisms'. *Science, Technology & Human Values 30*, no. 2: 251–290.

Rowe, M. and L. McAllister. (2006). 'The Roles of Commissions of Inquiry in the Policy Process'. *Public Policy and Administration 21*, no. 4: 99–115.

Rowe, S., N. Alexander, C. M. Weaver, J. T. Dwyer, C. Drew, R. S. Applebaum, S. Atkinson, F. M. Clydesdale, E. Hentges, N. A. Higley and M. E. Westring (2013). 'How Experts Are Chosen to Inform Public Policy: Can the Process Be Improved?' *Health Policy 112*, no. 3: 172–178.

Royer, A. (2008). 'The Emergence of Agricultural Marketing Boards Revisited: A Case Study in Canada'. *Canadian Journal of Agricultural Economics 56*: 509–522.

Rubsamen, V. (1989). 'Deregulation and the State in Comparative Perspective: The Case of Telecommunications'. *Comparative Politics 22*, no. 1: 105–120.

Rudd, M. (2014). 'A Scientist's Perspectives on Global Ocean Research Priorities'. *Frontiers in Marine Science 1*: 36.

Rudd, M. (2015). 'Scientists' Framing of the Ocean Science – Policy Interface'. *Global Environmental Change 33*: 44–60.

Ruderman, A. P. (1988). 'Health Planning in Singapore: Limits to Privatization'. *Journal of Public Health Policy 9*, no. 1: 121–131.

Rudolph, L. and S. Rudolph. (1979). 'Authority and Power in Bureaucratic and Patrimonial Bureaucracy'. *World Politics 31*, no. 2: 195–227.

Ruijer, Erna, Francoise Détienne, Michael Baker, Jonathan Groff and Albert J. Meijer. (2020). 'The Politics of Open Government Data: Understanding Organizational Responses to Pressure for More Transparency'. *The American Review of Public Administration 50*, no. 3 (1 April): 260–274.

Rutgers, M. R. (2001). 'Traditional Flavors? The Different Sentiments in European and American Administrative Thought'. *Administration and Society 33*, no. 2: 220–244 (at p. 239).

Ryan, P. (1995). 'Miniature Mila and Flying Geese: Government Advertising and Canadian Democracy'. In S. D. Phillips (ed.), *How Ottawa Spends 1995–96: Mid-Life Crises*. Ottawa, ON: Carleton University Press, 263–286.

Sabatier, P. A. (1987). 'Knowledge, Policy-Oriented Learning, and Policy Change'. *Knowledge: Creation, Diffusion, Utilization 8*, no. 4: 649–692.

Sabatier, P. A. (1988). 'An Advocacy Coalition Framework of Policy Change and the Role of Policy-Oriented Learning Therein'. *Policy Sciences 21*, no. 2/3: 129–168.

Sabatier, P. A. (1991). 'Toward Better Theories of the Policy Process'. *PS: Political Science and Politics 24*, no. 2: 144–156.

Sabatier, P. A. (1998). 'The Advocacy Coalition Framework: Revisions and Relevance for Europe'. *Journal of European Public Policy 5*, no. 1: 98–130.

Sabatier, P. A. (1999). *Theories of the Policy Process*, Boulder, CO: Westview Press.

Sabatier, P. A. and H. Jenkins-Smith. (1993a). 'The Advocacy Coalition Framework: Assessment, Revisions, and Implications for Scholars and Practitioners'. In P. Sabatier and H. Jenkins-Smith (eds.), *Policy Change and Learning: An Advocacy Coalition Approach*. Boulder, CO: Westview, 211–236.

Sabatier, P. A. and H. Jenkins-Smith (eds.). (1993b). *Policy Change and Learning. An Advocacy Coalition Approach*. Boulder, CO: Westview Press.

Sabatier, P. A. and D. A. Mazmanian. (1981). *Effective Policy Implementation*. Lexington, MA: Lexington Books.

Sabatier, P. A. and N. Pelkey. (1987). 'Incorporating Multiple Actors and Guidance Instruments into Models of Regulatory Policymaking: An Advocacy Coalition Framework'. *Administration and Society 19*, no. 2: 236–263.

Sabatier, P. A. and C. M. Weible. (2007). *Theories of the Policy Process*. Boulder, CO: Westview Press.

Sadler, Barry. (2005). *Strategic Environmental Assessment at the Policy Level: Recent Progress, Current Status and Future Prospects*. Prague: Ministry of the Environment.

Sager, F. and Y. Rielle. (2013). 'Sorting through the Garbage Can: Under What Conditions Do Governments Adopt Policy Programs?' *Policy Sciences 46*, no. 1 (1 March): 1–21.

Saguin, K. (2020). 'Policy Completeness of new Governance Arrangements'. Paper presented at the University of Melbourne-NUS Workshop on Policy Tools, 23–24 January. University of Melbourne

Saint-Martin, D. (1998). 'Management Consultants, the State, and the Politics of Administrative Reform in Britain and Canada'. *Administration Society 30*, no. 5 (1 November): 533–568.

Saint-Martin, D. (2013). 'Making Government More "Business-Like": Management Consultants as Agents of Isomorphism in Modern Political Economies'. In J. Mikler (ed.), *The Handbook of Global Companies*. New York: John Wiley, 173–192.

Salamon, L. M. (1981). 'Rethinking Public Management: Third-Party Government and the Changing Forms of Government Action'. *Public Policy 29*, no. 3: 255–275.

Salamon, L. M. (1987). 'Of Market Failure, Voluntary Failure, and Third-Party Government: Toward a Theory of Government – Nonprofit Relations in the Modern Welfare State'. *Journal of Voluntary Action Research 16*, no. 1/2: 29–49.

Salamon, L. M. (1989a). 'The Changing Tools of Government Action: An Overview'. In *Beyond Privatization: The Tools of Government Action*. Washington, DC: Urban Institute, 1–22.

Salamon, L. M. (1989b). 'The Tools Approach: Basic Analytics'. In L. S. Salamon and M. S. Lund (eds.), *Beyond Privatization: The Tools of Government Action*. Washington, DC: Urban Institute, 23–50.

Salamon, L. M. (2001). 'New Governance and the Tools of Public Action: An Introduction'. *Fordham Urban Law Journal 28*: 1611.

Salamon, L. M. (2002a). 'Economic Regulation'. In L. M. Salamon (ed.), *The Tools of Government: A Guide to the New Governance*. New York: Oxford University Press, 117–155.

Salamon, L. M. (2002b). 'The New Governance and the Tools of Public Action'. In L. M. Salamon (ed.), *The Tools of Government: A Guide to the New Governance*. New York: Oxford University Press, 1–47.

Salamon, L. M. (2002c). *The Tools of Government: A Guide to the New Governance*. New York: Oxford University Press.

Salamon, L. M. and M. S. Lund. (1989). 'The Tools Approach: Basic Analytics'. In L. M. Salamon (ed.), *Beyond Privatization: The Tools of Government Action*. Washington, DC: Urban Institute, 23–50.

Salisbury, R. H. (1969). 'An Exchange Theory of Interest Groups'. *Midwest Journal of Political Science 13*, no. *1*: 1–32.

Salmon, C. (1989a). 'Campaigns for Social Improvement: An Overview of Values, Rationales and Impacts'. In C. Salmon (ed.), *Information Campaigns: Managing the Process of Social Change*. Newbury Park, CA: Sage, 1–32.

Salmon, C. (ed.). (1989b). *Information Campaigns: Managing the Process of Social Change*. Newbury Park, CA: Sage.

Salomonsen, H. H. and T. Knudsen. (2011). 'Changes in Public Service Bargains: Ministers and Civil Servants in Denmark'. *Public Administration 89*, no. *3* (1 September): 1015–1035.

Salter, L. (1990). 'The Two Contradictions in Public Inquiries'. In A. P. Pross, I. Christie and J. A. Yogis (eds.), *Commissions of Inquiry*. Toronto, ON: Carswell, 175–195.

Salter, L. (2003). 'The Complex Relationship between Inquiries and Public Controversy'. In A. Manson and D. Mullan (eds.), *Commissions of Inquiry: Praise or Reappraise?* Toronto, ON: Irwin Law, 185–209.

Salter, L. and D. Slaco. (1981). *Public Inquiries in Canada*. Ottawa, ON: Science Council of Canada.

Sanders, Elizabeth B.-N. and Pieter Jan Stappers. (2014). 'Probes, Toolkits and Prototypes: Three Approaches to Making in Codesigning'. *CoDesign 10*, no. *1* (2 January): 5–14.

Sanderson, I. (2002a). 'Evaluation, Policy Learning and Evidence-Based Policy Making'. *Public Administration 80*, no. *1*: 1–22.

Sanderson, I. (2002b). 'Making Sense of What Works: Evidence Based Policymaking as Instrumental Rationality?' *Public Policy and Administration 17*, no. *3*: 61–75.

Sanderson, I. (2006). 'Complexity, "Practical Rationality" and Evidence-Based Policy Making'. *Policy & Politics 34*, no. *1*: 115–132.

Santos, G., H. Behrendt and A. Teytelboym. (2010). 'Part II: Policy Instruments for Sustainable Road Transport'. *Research in Transportation Economics 28*, no. *1*: 46–91.

Sappington, D. E. M. (1994). 'Designing Incentive Regulation'. *Review of Industrial Organization 9*, no. *3*: 245–272.

Sassen, S. (1998). *Globalization and Its Discontents*. New York: New Press.

Savas, E. S. (1977). *Alternatives for Delivering Public Services: Toward Improved Performance*. Boulder, CO: Westview.

Savas, E. S. (1987). *Privatization: The Key to Better Government*. London: Chatham House.

Savas, E. S. (1989). 'A Taxonomy of Privatization Strategies'. *Policy Studies Journal 18*: 343–355.

Savoie, D. J. (1999). *Governing from the Centre: The Concentration of Power in Canadian Politics*. Toronto, ON: University of Toronto Press.

Saward, M. (1990). 'Cooption and Power: Who Gets What from Formal Incorporation'. *Political Studies 38*: 588–602.

Saward, M. (1992). *Co-Optive Politics and State Legitimacy*. Aldershot, UK: Dartmouth.

Saxonhouse, A. W. (2015). 'Aristotle on the Corruption of Regimes: Resentment and Justice'. In Thornton Lockwood and Thanassis Samaras (eds.), *Aristotle's Politics: A Critical Guide*. Cambridge: Cambridge University Press, 184–203.

Schaar, John H. (1981). *Legitimacy in the Modern State*. New Brunswick, NJ: Transaction.

Schaffrin, A., S. Sewerin and S. Seubert. (2014). 'The Innovativeness of National Policy Portfolios – Climate Policy Change in Austria, Germany, and the UK'. *Environmental Politics 23*, no. 5: 860–883.

Schaffrin, A., S. Sewerin and S. Seubert. (2015). 'Toward a Comparative Measure of Climate Policy Output'. *Policy Studies Journal 43*, no. 2: 257–282.

Scharpf, F. W. (1986). 'Policy Failure and Institutional Reform: Why Should Form Follow Function?' *International Social Science Journal 108*: 179–190.

Scharpf, F. W. (1990). 'Games Real Actors Could Play: The Problem of Mutual Predictability'. *Rationality and Society 2*: 471–494.

Scharpf, F. W. (1991). 'Political Institutions, Decision Styles and Policy Choices'. In R. M. Czada and A. Windhoff-Heritier (eds.), *Political Choice: Institutions, Rules and the Limits of Rationality*. Frankfurt, Germany: Campus Verlag, 53–86.

Scharpf, F. W. (1998). 'Globalization: The Limitations on State Capacity'. *Swiss Political Science Review 4*, no. 1: 2–8.

Scharpf, F. W. (2000). 'Institutions in Comparative Policy Research'. *Comparative Political Studies 33*, no. 6/7: 762–790.

Schattschneider, E. E. (1960). *The Semisovereign People: A Realist's View of Democracy in America*. New York: Holt, Rinehart & Winston.

Scheb, J. M. and J. M. Scheb II. (2005). *Law and the Administrative Process*. Toronto, ON: Thomson Wadsworth.

Scheraga, J. D. and J. Furlow. (2001). 'From Assessment to Policy: Lessons Learned from the US National Assessment'. *Human and Ecological Risk Assessment 7*, no. 5: 1227–1246.

Scherer, F. M. (2008). 'The Historical Foundations of Communications Regulation'. In *Kennedy School Faculty Working Papers Series RWP08–050*. Boston, MA: Harvard University.

Schlager, E. (1999). 'A Comparison of Frameworks, Theories and Models of Policy Processes'. In P. A. Sabatier (ed.), *Theories of the Policy Process*. Boulder, CO: Westview, 233–260.

Schlager, E. and Blomquist W. (1996). 'Emerging Political Theories of the Policy Process: Institutional Rational Choice, the Politics of Structural Choice, and Advocacy Coalitions'. *Political Research Quarterly 49*: 651–672.

Schmalensee, R., P. L. Joskow, A. D. Ellerman, J. P. Montero and E. M. Bailey. (1998). 'An Interim Evaluation of Sulfur Dioxide Emissions Trading'. *The Journal of Economic Perspectives 12*, no. 3 (Summer): 53–68.

Schmidt, A., A. Ivanova and M. S. Schäfer. (2013). 'Media Attention for Climate Change around the World: A Comparative Analysis of Newspaper Coverage in 27 Countries'. *Global Environmental Change 23*, no. 5: 1233–1248.

Schmidt, M. G. (1996). 'When Parties Matter: A Review of the Possibilities and Limits of Partisan Influence on Public Policy'. *European Journal of Political Research 30*: 155–183.

Schmidt, Tobias S. and Sebastian Sewerin. (2019). 'Measuring the Temporal Dynamics of Policy Mixes – An Empirical Analysis of Renewable Energy Policy Mixes' Balance and Design Features in Nine Countries'. *Research Policy 48*, no. *10* (1 December).

Schmidt, V. A. (2008). 'Discursive Institutionalism: The Explanatory Power of Ideas and Discourse'. *Annual Review of Political Science* 11: 303–326.

Schmitter, P. C. (1977). 'Modes of Interest Intermediation and Models of Societal Change in Western Europe'. *Comparative Political Studies 10*, no. *1*: 7–38.

Schmitter, P. C. (1985). 'Neo-Corporatism and the State'. In W. Grant (ed.), *The Political Economy of Corporatism*. London: Macmillan, 32–62.

Schneider, A. and H. Ingram. (1988). 'Systematically Pinching Ideas: A Comparative Approach to Policy Design'. *Journal of Public Policy 8*, no. *1*: 61–80.

Schneider, A. and H. Ingram. (1990a). 'Behavioral Assumptions of Policy Tools'. *The Journal of Politics 52*, no. *2*: 510–529.

Schneider, A. and H. Ingram. (1990b). 'Policy Design: Elements, Premises and Strategies'. In S. S. Nagel (ed.), *Policy Theory and Policy Evaluation: Concepts, Knowledge, Causes and Norms*. New York: Greenwood Press, 77–102.

Schneider, A. and H. Ingram. (1993). 'Social Construction of Target Populations: Implications for Politics and Policy'. *The American Political Science Review 87*, no. *2*: 334–347.

Schneider, A. and H. Ingram. (1994). 'Social Constructions and Policy Design: Implications for Public Administration'. *Research in Public Administration 3*: 137–173.

Schneider, A. and H. Ingram. (1997). *Policy Design for Democracy*. Lawrence, KS: University Press of Kansas.

Schneider, A. and H. Ingram. (2005). *Deserving and Entitled: Social Constructions and Public Policy*. SUNY Series in Public Policy. Albany, NY: State University of New York.

Schneider, A. and M. Sidney. (2009). 'What Is Next for Policy Design and Social Construction Theory?' *Policy Studies Journal 37*, no. *1*: 103–119.

Schneider, A. L. and Helen M. Ingram (eds.). (2005). *Deserving and Entitled: Social Constructions and Public Policy*. SUNY Series in Public Policy. Albany: State University of New York.

Schneider, J. W. (1985). 'Social Problems Theory: The Constructionist View'. *Annual Review of Sociology 11*: 209–229.

Schneider, M. and P. Teske. (1995). *Public Entrepreneurs: Agents for Change in American Government*. Princeton, NJ: Princeton University Press.

Scholte, J. A. (1997). 'Global Capitalism and the State'. *International Affairs 73*: 440–451.

Scholz, J. T. (1984). 'Cooperation, Deterrence, and the Ecology of Regulatory Enforcement'. *Law Society Review 18*, no. *2*: 179–224.

Scholz, J. T. (1991). 'Cooperative Regulatory Enforcement and the Politics of Administrative Effectiveness'. *American Political Science Review 85*, no. *1*: 115–136.

Schön, D. A. (1988). 'Designing: Rules, Types and Words'. *Design Studies 9*, no. *3*: 181–190.

Schön, D. A. (1992). 'Designing as Reflective Conversation with the Materials of a Design Situation'. *Knowledge-Based Systems 5*, no. *1* (March): 3–14.

Schön, D. A. and M. Rein. (1994). *Frame Reflection: Solving Intractable Policy Disputes*. New York: Basic Books.

Schout, A., A. Jordan and M. Twena. (2010). 'From "Old" to "New" Governance in the EU: Explaining a Diagnostic Deficit'. *West European Politics 33*, no. *1*: 154–170.

Schrader, S., W. M. Riggs and R. P. Smith. (1993). 'Choice Over Uncertainty and Ambiguity in Technical Problem Solving'. *Journal of Engineering and Technology Management 10*, no. 1–2 (June): 73–99.

Schreffler, L. (2013). *The Use of Expertise by Independent Regulatory Agencies: The Case of Economic Knowledge*. Exeter: ECPR Press.

Schubert, C. (2007). 'Green Nudges: Do They Work? Are They Ethical?' *Ecological Economics 132*, Supplement C (February): 329–342.

Schudson, M. (2006). 'The Trouble with Experts – and Why Democracies Need Them'. *Theory & Society 35*: 491–506.

Schultz, D. (2007). 'Stupid Public Policy Ideas and Other Political Myths'. Paper presented to the American Political Science Association, Chicago, IL.

Schultz, David. (2017). 'Alternative Facts and Public Affairs'. *Journal of Public Affairs Education 23*, no. 3: 775–778.

Schultze, C. L. (1977). *The Public Use of Private Interests*. Washington: Brookings Institute.

Schwartz, B. (1997). 'Public Inquiries'. *Canadian Public Administration 40*, no. 1: 72–85.

Scott, C. (2001). 'Analysing Regulatory Space: Fragmented Resources and Institutional Design'. *Public Law* (Summer): 329–353.

Scott, C., J. Jordana and D. Levi-Faur. (2004). 'Regulation in the Age of Governance: The Rise of the Post-Regulatory State'. In J. Jordane and D. Levi-Faur (eds.), *The Politics of Regulation: Institutions and Regulatory Reforms for the Age of Governance*. Cheltenham, UK: Edward Elgar, 145–174.

Scott, J. C. (1969a). 'Corruption, Machine Politics, and Political Change'. *American Political Science Review 63*, no. 4: 1142–1158.

Scott, J. C. (1969b). 'The Analysis of Corruption in Developing Nations'. *Comparative Studies in Society and History 11*, no. 03: 315–341.

Scott, Robert E. and George G. Triantis. (2005). 'Incomplete Contracts and the Theory of Contract Design'. *Case Western Reserve Law Review 56*: 187–201.

Scrase, J. I. and W. R. Sheate. (2002). 'Integration and Integrated Approaches to Assessment: What Do They Mean for the Environment'. *Journal of Environmental Policy and Planning 4*, no. 1: 275–294.

Scruggs, L. and S. Benegal. (2012). 'Declining Concern about Climate Change: Can We Blame the Great Recession?' *Global Environmental Change 22*, no. 2: 505–515.

Seeliger, R. (1996). 'Conceptualizing and Researching Policy Convergence'. *Policy Studies Journal 24*, no. 2: 287–310.

Selling, Niels and Stefan Svallfors. (2019). 'The Lure of Power: Career Paths and Considerations among Policy Professionals in Sweden'. *Politics & Policy 47*, no. 5: 984–1012.

Selmier II, W. Travis. (2016). 'Design Rules for More Resilient Banking Systems'. *Policy and Society, Institutional and Policy Design for the Financial Sector 35*, no. 3 (September): 253–267.

Selznick, P. (1984). *Leadership in Administration: A Sociological Interpretation*. Berkeley, CA: University of California Press.

Sethi-Iyengar, S., G. Huberman and G. Jiang. (2004). 'How Much Choice Is Too Much? Contributions to 401(k) Retirement Plans'. In O. S. Mitchell and S. P. Utkus (eds.), *Pension Design and Structure: New Lessons from Behavioural Finance*. Oxford: Oxford University Press.

Sewerin, Sebastian, Benjamin Cashore and Michael Howlett. (2022). 'New Pathways to Paradigm Change in Public Policy: Combining Insights from Policy Design, Mix and Feedback'. *Policy & Politics 50*, no. *3* (July): 442–459.

Shafir, E., (ed.). (2013). *The Behavioral Foundations of Public Policy*. Princeton, NJ: Princeton University Press.

Shafir, E., I. Simonson and A. Tversky. (1993). 'Reason-Based Choice'. *Cognition 49*, no. *1–2* (November): 11–36.

Shah, A. K. and D. M. Oppenheimer. (2008). 'Heuristics Made Easy: An Effort-Reduction Framework'. *Psychological Bulletin 134*, no. *2*: 207–222.

Shalev, M. (1983). 'The Social Democratic Model and Beyond: Two Generations of Comparative Research on the Welfare State'. *Comparative Social Research 6*: 315–351.

Shapiro, S. A. and C. H. Schroeder. (2008). 'Beyond Cost – Benefit Analysis: A Pragmatic Reorientation'. *Harvard Environmental Law Review 32*: 433–501.

Sharkansky, I. (1971). 'Constraints on Innovation in Policy Making: Economic Development and Political Routines'. In F. Marini (ed.), *Toward a New Public Administration: The Minnowbrook Perspective*. Scranton, PA: Chandler, 261–279.

Sharkansky, I. and Y. Zalmanovitch. (2000). 'Improvisation in Public Administration and Policy Making in Israel'. *Public Administration Review 60*, no. *4* (1 July): 321–329.

Sharma, B. and J. Wanna. (2005). 'Performance Measures, Measurement and Reporting in Government Organisations'. *International Journal of Business Performance Management 7*, no. *3*: 320–333.

Sharpe, D. (2001). 'The Canadian Charitable Sector: An Overview'. In J. Phillips, B. Chapman and D. Stevens (eds.), *Between State and Market: Essays on Charities Law and Policy in Canada*. Toronto, ON: University of Toronto Press, 1–30.

Shaw, S. E., J. Russell, W. Parsons and T. Greenhalgh. (2015). 'The View from Nowhere? How Think Tanks Work to Shape Health Policy'. *Critical Policy Studies 9*, no. *1*: 58–77.

Shaxson, L. (2004). 'Is Your Evidence Robust Enough? Questions for Policy Makers and Practitioners'. *Evidence & Policy 1*, no. *1*: 101–111.

Sheriff, P. E. (1983). 'State Theory, Social Science and Governmental Commissions'. *American Behavioural Scientist 26*, no. *5*: 669–680.

Shore, Cris, Susan Wright and Davide Pero (eds.). (2011). *Policy Worlds: Anthropology and Analysis of Contemporary Power*. London: Berghahn Books.

Shroff, Monal R., Sonya J. Jones, Edward A. Frongillo and Michael Howlett. (2012). 'Policy Instruments Used by States Seeking to Improve School Food Environments'. *American Journal of Public Health 102*, no. *2* (February): 222–229.

Shulock, N. (1999). 'The Paradox of Policy Analysis: If It Is Not Used, Why Do We Produce So Much of It?' *Journal of Policy Analysis and Management 18*, no. *2*: 226–244.

Siddiki, Saba. (2020). *Understanding and Analyzing Public Policy Design*. Cambridge: Cambridge University Press.

Sidney, M. S. (2007). 'Policy Formulation: Design and Tools'. In F. Fischer, G. J. Miller and M. S. Sidney (eds.), *Handbook of Public Policy Analysis: Theory, Politics and Methods*. New Brunswick, NJ: CRC/Taylor & Francis, 79–87.

Simmons, A. B. and K. Keohane. (1992). 'Canadian Immigration Policy: State Strategies and the Quest for Legitimacy'. *Canadian Review of Sociology and Anthropology 29*, no. *4*: 421–452.

Simmons, B. A. and Z. Elkins. (2004). 'Globalization and Policy Diffusion: Explaining Three Decades of Liberalization'. In M. Kahler and D. Lake (eds.), *Governance in a Global Economy*. Princeton, NJ: Princeton University Press, 275–304.

Simmons, R. and J. Birchall. (2005). 'A Joined-Up Approach to User Participation in Public Services: Strengthening the "Participation Chain"'. *Social Policy and Administration 39*, no. 3: 260–283.

Simmons, R. H., B. W. Davis, R. J. K. Chapman and D. D. Sager. (1974). 'Policy Flow Analysis: A Conceptual Model for Comparative Public Policy Research'. *Western Political Quarterly 27*, no. 3: 457–468.

Simon, H. A. (1955). 'A Behavioral Model of Rational Choice'. *The Quarterly Journal of Economics 69*, no. 1: 99–118.

Simon, H. A. (1957). *Models of Man: Social and Rational: Mathematical Essays on Rational Human Behavior in a Social Setting*. New York: Wiley.

Simon, H. A. (1967). 'The Logic of Heuristic Decision Making'. In Nicholas Rescher (ed.), *The Logic of Decision and Action*. Pittsburgh: University of Pittsburgh Press, 1–35.

Simon, H. A. (1969). *The Sciences of the Artificial*. Boston: MIT Press.

Simon, H. A. (1971). 'Style in Design'. In *Proceedings of the 2nd Annual Conference of the Environmental Design Research Association*. Pittsburgh: Carnegie Mellon University Press, 1–10.

Simon, H. A. (1973). 'The Structure of Ill Structured Problems'. *Artificial Intelligence 4*, no. 3–4 (Winter): 181–201.

Simon, H. A. (1976). *Administrative Behavior: A Study of Decision Making Processes in Administrative Organization* (3rd edn). New York: Free Press.

Simon, Herbert A. (1978). 'Rationality as Process and as Product of Thought'. *The American Economic Review 68*, no. 2 (1 May): 1–16.

Simons, A. and J.-P. Voss. (2017). 'Policy Instrument Constituencies'. In M. Howlett and I. Mukherjee (eds.), *Handbook of Policy Formulation*. Cheltenham, UK: Edward Elgar, 355–372.

Simons, A. and J.-P. Voss. (2018). 'The Concept of Instrument Constituencies: Accounting for Dynamics and Practices of Knowing Governance'. *Policy and Society 37*, no. 1: 14–35.

Sinclair, D. (1997). 'Self-Regulation versus Command and Control? Beyond False Dichotomies'. *Law and Policy 19*, no. 4: 529–559.

Singleton, J. (2001). *A Review of the Policy Capacity Between Departments*. Winnipeg, MB: Office of the Auditor-General.

Skeete, J.-P. (2017). 'Examining the Role of Policy Design and Policy Interaction in EU Automotive Emissions Performance Gaps'. *Energy Policy 104* (May): 373–381.

Skelly, J. M. and J. L. Innes. (1994). 'Waldsterben in the Forests of Central Europe and Eastern North America: Fantasy or Reality?' *Plant Disease 78*, no. 11: 1021–1032.

Skodvin, T., A. T. Gullberg and S. Aakre. (2010). 'Target-Group Influence and Political Feasibility: The Case of Climate Policy Design in Europe'. *Journal of European Public Policy 17*, no. 6: 854.

Skowronek, S. (1982). *Building a New American State: The Expansion of National Administrative Capacities 1877–1920*. Cambridge: Cambridge University Press.

Slovic, P. (1992). 'Perception of Risk: Reflections on the Psychometric Paradigm'. In S. Krimsky and D. Golding (eds.), *Social Theories of Risk*. Westport, CT and London: Praeger.

Smismans, S. (2008). 'New Modes of Governance and the Participatory Myth'. *West European Politics 31*, no. 5: 874–895.

Smith, A. (2000). 'Policy Networks and Advocacy Coalitions: Explaining Policy Change and Stability in UK Industrial Pollution Policy'. *Environment and Planning C: Government and Policy 18*: 95–114.

Smith, B. L. R. (1977). 'The Non-Governmental Policy Analysis Organization'. *Public Administration Review 37*, no. 3: 253–258.

Smith, M. (2005a). *A Civil Society? Collective Actors in Canadian Political Life*. Peterborough, ON: Broadview Press.

Smith, M. (2005b). 'Diversity and Identity in the Non-Profit Sector: Lessons from LGBT Organizing in Toronto'. *Social Policy and Administration 39*, no. 5: 463–480.

Smith, M. J. (1994). 'Policy Networks and State Autonomy'. In S. Brooks and A.-G. Gagnon (eds.), *The Political Influence of Ideas: Policy Communities and the Social Sciences*. New York: Praeger.

Smith, M. J. (2004). 'Mad Cows and Mad Money: Problems of Risk in the Making and Understanding of Policy'. *The British Journal of Politics and International Relations 6*, no. 3: 312–332.

Smith, M. J., D. Marsh and D. Richards. (1993). 'Central Government Departments and the Policy Process'. *Public Administration 71*: 567–594 (at p. 580).

Smith, M. P. (2008). 'All Access Points Are Not Created Equal: Explaining the Fate of Diffuse Interests in the EU'. *British Journal of Politics and International Relations 10*: 64–83.

Smith, T. B. (1977). 'Advisory Committees in the Public Policy Process'. *International Review of Administrative Sciences 43*, no. 2: 153–166.

Sorensen, E. (2012). 'From Governance and Innovation in the Public Sector'. In D. Levi-Faur (ed.), *The Oxford Handbook of Governance*. Oxford: Oxford University Press, 215–228.

Sorensen, E. and J. Torfing. (2005). 'Democratic Anchorage of Governance Networks'. *Scandinavian Political Studies 28*: 195–218.

Sørensen, Eva and Christopher Ansell. (2021). 'Towards a Concept of Political Robustness'. *Political Studies 71*, no. 1 (8 April): 69–88.

Sorrell, S. and J. Sijm. (2003). 'Carbon Trading in the Policy Mix'. *Oxford Review of Economic Policy 19*, no. 3 (1 September): 420–437.

Sorrentino, M., C. Guglielmetti, S. Gilardi and M. Marsilio (2015). 'Health Care Services and the Coproduction Puzzle: Filling in the Blanks'. *Administration & Society 49*, no. 10 (1 November): 1424–1449.

Sousa, D. and C. Klyza. (2007). 'New Directions in Environmental Policy Making: An Emerging Collaborative Regime or Reinventing Interest Group Liberalism'. *Natural Resources Journal 47*, no. 2: 377–444.

Sousa, L. J., E. Ciriolo, A. S. Rafael, X. Troussard, European Commission and Joint Research Centre. (2016). *Behavioural Insights Applied to Policy: European Report 2016*. Luxembourg: European Commission and Joint Research Centre. http://bookshop.europa.eu/uri?target=EUB:NOTICE:KJNA27726:EN:HTML.

Sovacool, B. K. (2011). 'The Policy Challenges of Tradable Credits: A Critical Review of Eight Markets'. *Energy Policy 39*, no. 2: 575–585.

Speers, K. (2007). 'The Invisible Public Service: Consultants and Public Policy in Canada'. In L. Dobuzinskis, M. Howlett and D. Laycock (eds.), *Policy Analysis in Canada: The State of the Art*. Toronto, ON: University of Toronto Press, 220–231.

Spence, A., W. Poortinga, C. Butler and N. F. Pidgeon. (2011). 'Perceptions of Climate Change and Willingness to Save Energy Related to Flood Experience'. *Nature Climate Change 1*, no. 1: 46–49.

Spicker, P. (2005). 'Targeting, Residual Welfare and Related Concepts: Modes of Operation in Public Policy'. *Public Administration 83*, no. 2: 345–365.

Sproule-Jones, M. (1983). 'Institutions, Constitutions and Public Policies: A Public-Choice Overview'. In M. Atkinson and M. Chandler (eds.), *The Politics of Canadian Public Policy*. Toronto, ON: University of Toronto Press, 127–150.

Stanbury, W. T. (1986). *Business – Government Relations in Canada: Grappling with Leviathan*. Toronto, ON: Methuen.

Stanbury, W. T. (1993). 'A Sceptic's Guide to the Claims of So-Called Public Interest Groups'. *Canadian Public Administration 36*, no. 4: 580–605.

Stanbury, W. T., G. J. Gorn and C. B. Weinberg. (1983). 'Federal Advertising Expenditures'. In G. B. Doern (ed.), *How Ottawa Spends: The Liberals, the Opposition and Federal Priorities*. Toronto, ON: James Lorimer and Company, 133–172.

Stanbury, W. T. and J. Fulton. (1984). 'Suasion as a Governing Instrument'. In A. Maslove (ed.), *How Ottawa Spends 1984: The New Agenda*. Toronto, ON: Lorimer, 282–324.

Stanton, T. H. (2002). 'Loans and Loan Guarantees'. In L. M. Salamon (ed.), *The Tools of Government: A Guide to the New Governance*. New York: Oxford University Press, 381–409.

Stanton, Thomas H. (2007). 'The Life Cycle of the Government-Sponsored Enterprise: Lessons for Design and Accountability'. *Public Administration Review 67*, no. 5: 837–845.

Stark, Alastair. (2014). 'Bureaucratic Values and Resilience: An Exploration of Crisis Management Adaptation'. *Public Administration 92*, no. 3: 692–706.

Stark, Alastair and Sophie Yates. (2021). 'Public Inquiries as Procedural Policy Tools'. *Policy and Society*: 1–17.

Starr, P. (1989). 'The Meaning of Privatization'. In S. B. Kamerman and A. J. Kahn (eds.), *Privatization and the Welfare State*. Princeton, NJ: Princeton University Press, 15–48.

Starr, P. (1990a). 'The Limits of Privatization'. In D. J. Gayle and J. N. Goodrich (eds.), *Privatization and Deregulation in Global Perspective*. New York: Quorum Books, 109–125.

Starr, P. (1990b). 'The New Life of the Liberal State: Privatization and the Restructuring of State – Society Relations'. In E. N. Suleiman and J. Waterbury (eds.), *The Political Economy of Public Sector Reform and Privatization*. Boulder, CO: Westview, 22–54.

Stasiulis, D. K. (1988). 'The Symbolic Mosaic Reaffirmed: Multiculturalism Policy'. In K. A. Graham (ed.), *How Ottawa Spends 1988/89: The Conservatives Heading into the Stretch*. Ottawa, ON: Carleton University Press, 81–111.

State Services Commission. (1999a). *Essential Ingredients: Improving the Quality of Policy Advice*. Wellington, New Zealand: State Services Commission.

State Services Commission. (1999b). *High Fliers: Developing High Performing Policy Units*. Occasional Paper No. 22. Wellington, New Zealand: State Services Commission.

Statistics Canada. (2004). *Cornerstones of Community: Highlights of the National Survey of Nonprofit and Voluntary Organizations*. Ottawa, ON: Ministry of Industry.

Staub, E. (1972). 'Instigation to Goodness: The Role of Social Norms and Interpersonal Influence'. *Journal of Social Issues 28*, no. 3: 131–150.

Staupe-Delgado, Reidar. (2019). 'Progress, Traditions and Future Directions in Research on Disasters Involving Slow-Onset Hazards'. *Disaster Prevention and Management: An International Journal 28*, no. 5 (7 October): 623–635.

Stavins, R. N. (1996). 'Correlated Uncertainty and Policy Instrument Choice'. *Journal of Environmental Economics and Management 30*, no. 2 (March): 218–232.

Stavins, R. N. (1998). 'What Can We Learn from the Grand Policy Experiment? Lessons from SO2 Allowance Trading'. *Journal of Economic Perspectives 12*, no. 3: 69–88.

Stavins, R. N. (2001). *Lessons from the American Experiment with Market-Based Environmental Policies*. Washington, DC: Resources for the Future.

Stavins, R. N. (2008). 'A Meaningful US Cap-and-Trade System to Address Climate Change'. *Harvard Environmental Law Review 32*: 293–364.

Stead, D. (2017). 'Policy Preferences and the Diversity of Instrument Choice for Mitigating Climate Change Impacts in the Transport Sector'. *Journal of Environmental Planning and Management 61*, no. 14: 2445–2467.

Stead, D., H. Geerlings and E. Meijers (eds.). (2004). *Policy Integration in Practice: The Integration of Land Use Planning, Transport and Environmental Policy-Making in Denmark, England and Germany*. Delft, Netherlands: Delft University Press.

Stead, D. and E. Meijers. (2004). 'Policy Integration in Practice: Some Experiences of Integrating Transport, Land-Use Planning and Environmental Politics in Local Government'. In *2004 Berlin Conference on the Human Dimensions of Global Environmental Change: Greening of Policies – Interlinkages and Policy Integration*, Berlin, Germany, 1–13.

Stead, D. and E. Meijers. (2009). 'Spatial Planning and Policy Integration: Concepts, Facilitators and Inhibitors'. *Planning Theory & Practice 10*, no. 3 (September): 317–332.

Steen, M. A. van der and M. J. W. van Twist. (2013). 'Foresight and Long-Term Policy-Making: An Analysis of Anticipatory Boundary Work in Policy Organizations in The Netherlands'. *Futures 54*, no. Supplement C (1 November): 33–42.

Steenblik, Ronald. (2018). 'Treasure Tools: A Primer on Subsidies'. In Michael Howlett and Ishani Mukherjee (eds.), *Routledge Handbook of Policy Design*. New York: Routledge, 261–273.

Steg, L., J. W. Bolderdijk, K. Keizer and G. Perlaviciute. (2014). 'An Integrated Framework for Encouraging Pro-Environmental Behaviour: The Role of Values, Situational Factors and Goals'. *Journal of Environmental Psychology 38* (June 1, 2014): 104–115.

Stein, C. and L. J. Jaspersen. (2019). 'A Relational Framework for Investigating Nexus Governance'. *The Geographical Journal 185*, no. 4: 377–390.

Stein, J. G., D. Cameron and R. Simeon. (1999). 'Citizen Engagement in Conflict Resolution: Lessons for Canada in International Experience'. In D. Cameron (ed.), *The Referendum Papers: Essays on Secession and National Unity*. Toronto, ON: University of Toronto Press, 144–198.

Stern, J. (1997). 'What Makes and Independent Regulator Independent?' *Business Strategy Review 8*, no. 2: 67–74.

Stern, J. and S. Holder. (1999). 'Regulatory Governance: Criteria for Assessing the Performance of Regulatory Systems – An Application to Infrastrucrure Industries in the Developing Countries of Asia'. *Utilities Policy 8*: 33–50.

Stern, N. H. (2007). *The Economics of Climate Change: The Stern Review*. Cambridge: Cambridge University Press.

455

Sterner, T. (2003). *Policy Instruments for Environmental and Natural Resource Management.* Washington, DC: Resources for the Future.

Steurer, R. (2009). 'The Role of Governments in Corporate Social Responsibility: Characterising Public Policies on CSR in Europe'. *Policy Sciences 43*, no. 1: 49–72.

Steurer, R. (2013). 'Disentangling Governance: A Synoptic View of Regulation by Government, Business and Civil Society'. *Policy Sciences 46*, no. 4 (1 December): 387–410.

Steurle, C. E. and E. C. Twombly. (2002). 'Vouchers'. In L. M. Salamon (ed.), *The Tools of Government: A Guide to the New Governance.* New York: Oxford University Press, 445–465.

Stevens, P. F. (1994). *The Development of Biological Systematics.* New York: Columbia University Press.

Stewart, J. (1993). 'Rational Choice Theory, Public Policy and the Liberal State'. *Policy Sciences 26*, no. 4: 317–330.

Stewart, J. and R. Ayres. (2001). 'Systems Theory and Policy Practice: An Exploration'. *Policy Sciences 34*: 79–94.

Stewart, J. and A. J. Sinclair. (2007). 'Meaningful Public Participation in Environmental Assessment: Perspectives from Canadian Participants, Proponents and Government'. *Journal of Environmental Assessment Policy and Management 9*, no. 2: 161–183.

Stewart, K. and P. J. Smith. (2007). 'Immature Policy Analysis: Building Capacity in Eight Major Canadian Cities'. In L. Dobuzinskis, M. Howlett and D. Laycock (eds.), *Policy Analysis in Canada: The State of the Art.* Toronto, ON: University of Toronto Press, 146–158.

Stigler, G. J. (1975a). *The Citizen and the State: Essays on Regulation.* Chicago, IL: University of Chicago Press.

Stigler, G. J. (1975b). 'The Theory of Economic Regulation'. In G. Stigler (ed.), *The Citizen and the State.* Chicago, IL: University of Chicago Press, 114–141.

Stiglitz, J. (1998). 'The Private Uses of Public Interests: Incentives and Institutions'. *Journal of Economic Perspectives 12*, no. 2: 3–22.

Stiller, S. (2010). *Ideational Leadership in German Welfare State Reform: How Politicians and Policy Ideas Transform Resilient Institutions.* Amsterdam: Amsterdam University Press.

Stillman, P. G. (1974). 'The Concept of Legitimacy'. *Polity 7*, no. 1: 32–56.

Stimson, J. A. (1991). *Public Opinion in America: Moods Cycles and Swings.* Boulder, CO: Westview Press.

Stimson, J. A., M. B. Mackuen and R. S. Erikson. (1995). 'Dynamic Representation'. *American Political Science Review 89*: 543–565.

Stirling, A. (2010). 'Keep It Complex'. *Nature 468*, no. 7327 (23 December): 1029–1031.

Stokey, E. and R. Zeckhauser. (1978). *A Primer for Policy Analysis.* New York: W. W. Norton.

Stone, D. (1999). 'Learning Lessons and Transferring Policy across Time, Space and Disciplines'. *Politics 19*, no. 1: 51–59.

Stone, D. (2000). 'Non-Governmental Policy Transfer: The Strategies of Independent Policy Institutes'. *Governance 13*, no. 1: 45–62.

Stone, D. (2008). 'Global Public Policy, Transnational Policy Communities, and Their Networks'. *Policy Studies Journal 36*, no. 1: 19–38.

Stone, D. A. (1988). *Policy Paradox and Political Reason.* Glenview, IL: Scott, Foresman.

Stone, D. A. (1989). 'Causal Stories and the Formation of Policy Agendas'. *Political Science Quarterly 104*, no. 2: 281–300.

Stone, D. A. (2001). *Learning Lessons, Policy Transfer and the International Diffusion of Policy Ideas* (Working Paper 69/01). Coventry, UK: Centre for the Study of Globalization and Regionalization, University of Warwick.

Stone, D. A. and A. Denham (eds.). (2004). *Think Tank Traditions: Policy Research and the Politics of Ideas*. Manchester, UK: Manchester University Press.

Stouten, H., A. Heene, X. Gellynck and H. Polet. (2011). 'Policy Instruments to Meet Fisheries Management Objectives in Belgian Fisheries'. *Fisheries Research* (in press, accepted manuscript) *111*, no. *1–2*: 8–23.

Stover, R. V. and D. W. Brown. (1975). 'Understanding Compliance and Noncompliance with Law: The Contributions of Utility Theory'. *Social Science Quarterly 56*, no. *3* (1 December): 363–375.

Strange, S. (1996). *The Retreat of the State*. Cambridge: Cambridge University Press.

Strassheim, H. (2021). 'Who Are Behavioural Public Policy Experts and How Are They Organised Globally?" *Policy & Politics 49*, no. *1* (1 January): 69–86.

Strassheim, H. and R.-L. Korinek. (2015). 'Behavioural Governance in Europe'. In *Future Directions for Scientific Advice in Europe*. London: University of Cambridge/University of Sussex, 155–162.

Strassheim, H. and R.-L. Korinek. (2016). 'Cultivating "Nudge": Behavioural Governance in the UK'. In J.-P. Voß and R. Freeman (eds.), *Knowing Governance*. Basingstoke: Palgrave Macmillan, 107–126.

Streeck, W. and Thelen, K. A. (2005). 'Introduction: Institutional Change in Advanced Political Economies'. In *Beyond Continuity*. Oxford: Oxford University Press, 1–39.

Stritch, A. (2007). 'Business Associations and Policy Analysis in Canada'. In L. Dobuzinskis, M. Howlett and D. Laycock (eds.), *Policy Analysis in Canada: The State of the Art*. Toronto, ON: University of Toronto Press, 242–259.

Strolovitch, D. Z. (2006). 'Do Interest Groups Represent the Disadvantaged? Advocacy at the Intersections of Race, Class and Gender'. *The Journal of Politics 68*, no. *4*: 894–910.

Stromsdorfer, E. W. (1985). 'Social Science Analysis and the Formulation of Public Policy: Illustrations of What the President "Knows"'. In *Social Experimentation*. Chicago: University of Chicago Press, 257–282.

Stubbs, P. and S. Zrinšcak. (2007). 'Croatia'. In B. Deacon and P. Stubbs (eds.), *Social Policy and International Interventions in South East Europe*. Cheltenham, UK: Edward Elgar, 103–129.

Studlar, D. T. (2002). *Tobacco Control: Comparative Politics in the United States and Canada*. Peterborough: Broadview Press.

Stutz, J. R. (2008). 'What Gets Done and Why: Implementing the Recommendations of Public Inquiries'. *Canadian Public Administration 51*, no. *3*: 502–521.

Subramaniam, V. (1977). *Transplanted Indo-British Administration*. New Delhi, India: Ashish Publishing House.

Suchman, M. C. (1995). 'Managing Legitimacy: Strategic and Institutional Approaches'. *Academy of Management Review 20*, no. *3*: 571–610.

Suleiman, E. N. and J. Waterbury (eds.). (1990). *The Political Economy of Public Sector Reform and Privatization*. Boulder, CO: Westview Press.

Sulitzeanu-Kenan, R. (2007). 'Scything the Grass: Agenda-Setting Consequences of Appointing Public Inquiries in the UK, a Longitudinal Analysis'. *Policy and Politics 35*, no. *4*: 629–650.

Sulitzeanu-Kenan, R. (2010). 'Reflection in the Shadow of Blame: When Do Politicians Appoint Commissions of Inquiry?' *British Journal of Political Science 40*, no. 3: 613–634.

Sulitzeanu-Kenan, R. and C. Hood. (2005). 'Blame Avoidance with Adjectives? Motivation, Opportunity, Activity and Outcome'. Paper for ECPR Joint Sessions, Blame Avoidance and Blame Management Workshop, Granada, Spain, 14–20 April.

Sunnevag, K. J. (2000). 'Designing Auctions for Offshore Petroleum Lease Allocation'. *Resources Policy 26*, no. 1: 3–16.

Sunstein, C. R. (1996). 'Social Norms and Social Roles'. *Columbia Law Review 96*, no. 4: 903–968.

Sunstein, C. R. (2006). 'The Availability Heuristic, Intuitive Cost-Benefit Analysis, and Climate Change'. *Climatic Change 77*, no. 1–2: 195–210.

Sunstein, C. R. (2013). *Simpler: The Future of Government* (reprint edn). New York: Simon & Schuster.

Sunstein, C. R. (2014). 'Nudging: A Very Short Guide'. *Journal of Consumer Policy 37*, no. 4: 583–588.

Sunstein, C. R. (2015a). *Why Nudge? The Politics of Libertarian Paternalism* (reprint edn). New Haven, CT: Yale University Press.

Sunstein, C. R. (2015b). *Fifty Shades of Manipulation*. SSRN Scholarly Paper. Rochester, NY, 18 February.

Sunstein, C. R. (2016a). *The Ethics of Influence: Government in the Age of Behavioral Science*. Cambridge: Cambridge University Press.

Sunstein, C. R. (2016b). 'People Prefer System 2 Nudges (Kind Of)'. *Duke Law Journal 66*, no. 1 (1 October): 121–168.

Sunstein, C. R., D. Kahneman, D. Schkade and I. Ritov. (2001). *Predictably Incoherent Judgments*. SSRN Scholarly Paper. Rochester, NY: Social Science Research Network, 1 July. http://papers.ssrn.com/abstract=279181.

Sunstein, C. R. and L. A. Reisch. (2013). 'Green by Default'. *Kyklos 66*, no. 3: 398–402.

Sunstein, C. R. and L. A. Reisch. (2016). *Climate-Friendly Default Rules* (Discussion Paper No. 878). Cambridge, MA: Harvard Law School. www.law.harvard.edu/programs/olin_center/papers/pdf/Sunstein_878.pdf.

Sunstein, C. R. and R. H. Thaler. (2003), 'Libertarian Paternalism Is not an Oxymoron'. *The University of Chicago Law Review*: 1159–1202.

Surel, Y. (2000). 'The Role of Cognitive and Normative Frames in Policy-Making'. *Journal of European Public Policy 7*, no. 4: 495–512.

Surrey, S. S. (1979). 'Tax Expenditure Analysis: The Concept and Its Uses'. *Canadian Taxation 1*, no. 2: 3–14.

Suzuki, M. (1992). 'Political Business Cycles in the Public Mind'. *American Political Science Review 86*: 989–996.

Svallfors, Stefan. (2017). 'Knowing the Game: Motivations and Skills among Partisan Policy Professionals'. *Journal of Professions and Organization 4*, no. 1 (1 March): 55–69.

Svallfors, Stefan. (2020). *Politics for Hire: The World and Work of Policy Professionals*. Northampton: Edward Elgar Pub.

Svara, J. H. (1994). *Facilitative Leadership in Local Government: Lessons from Successful Mayors and Chairpersons*. San Francisco, CA: Jossey-Bass.

Swank, D. (2000). *Diminished Democracy? Global Capital, Political Institutions and Policy Change in Developed Welfare States*. New York: Cambridge University Press.

Swank, D. (2002). *Global Capital, Political Institutions and Policy Change in Developed Welfare States*. New York: Cambridge University Press.

Swann, D. (1988). *The Retreat of the State: Deregulation and Privatisation in the UK and US.* Hemel Hempstead, UK: Harvester Wheatsheaf.

Swanson, D., S. Barg, S. Tyler, H. Venema, S. Tomar, S. Bhadwal, S. Nair, D. Roy and J. Drexhage. (2010). 'Seven Tools for Creating Adaptive Policies'. *Technological Forecasting and Social Change 77*, no. 6 (July): 924–939.

Swanson, D. and S. Bhadwal (eds.). (2009). *Creating Adaptive Policies: A Guide for Policy-Making in an Uncertain World.* Winnipeg, MB: IISD. www.iisd.org/publications/creating-adaptive-policies-guide-policy-making-uncertain-world.

Swedlow, B. (2011). 'Cultural Surprises as Sources of Sudden, Big Policy Change'. *PS: Political Science & Politics 44*, no. 4: 736–739.

Székely, M. (2011). *Toward Results-Based Social Policy Design and Implementation* (CGD Working Paper 249). Washington, DC: Center for Global Development. www.cgdev.org/content/publications/detail/1425010.

t'Hart, P., L. Heyse and A. Boin. (2001). 'New Trends in Crisis Management Practice and Crisis Management Research: Setting the Agenda'. *Journal of Contingencies and Crisis Management 9*, no. 4: 181–188.

Taeihagh, A. (2017). 'Crowdsourcing: A New Tool for Policy-Making?' *Policy Sciences 50*, no. 4 (1 December): 629–647.

Taeihagh, A., R. Bañares-Alcántara and M. Givoni. (2014). 'A Virtual Environment for the Formulation of Policy Packages'. *Transportation Research Part A: Policy and Practice 60*, no. 1: 53–68.

Taeihagh, A., R. Bañares-Alcántara and Z. Wang. (2009). 'A Novel Approach to Policy Design Using Process Design Principles'. In C. A. O. do Nascimento and E. C. B. R. M. de Brito Alves (eds.), *Computer Aided Chemical Engineering* (Vol. 27). London: Elsevier, 2049–2054.

Taeihagh, A., M. Givoni and R. Bañares-Alcántara. (2013). 'Which Policy First? A Network-Centric Approach for the Analysis and Ranking of Policy Measures'. *Environment and Planning B: Planning and Design 40*, no. 4: 595–616.

Tallontire, A. (2007). 'CSR and Regulation: Towards a Framework for Understanding Private Standards Initiatives in the Agri-Food Chain'. *Third World Quarterly 28*, no. 4: 775–791.

Tanner, S. (2007). *Common Themes on Commissioning the VCS in Selected Local Authorities in Greater London.* London: London Councils.

Taylor, C., S. Pollard, S. Rocks and A. Angus. (2012). 'Selecting Policy Instruments for Better Environmental Regulation: A Critique and Future Research Agenda'. *Environmental Policy and Governance 22*, no. 4 (2012): 268–292.

Taylor, C. M., Elaine A. Gallagher, Simon J. T. Pollard, Sophie A. Rocks, Heather M. Smith, Paul Leinster and Andrew J. Angus. (2019). 'Environmental Regulation in Transition: Policy Officials' Views of Regulatory Instruments and Their Mapping to Environmental Risks'. *Science of the Total Environment 646*: 811–820.

Taylor, C. M., S. J. T. Pollard, A. J. Angus and S. A. Rocks. (2013). 'Better by Design: Rethinking Interventions for Better Environmental Regulation'. *Science of The Total Environment 447* (1 March): 488–499.

Taylor, C. W. (1988). *Alternative World Scenarios for Strategic Planning.* Washington DC: US Army War College.

Taylor, J. (2021). 'Public Officials' Gaming of Performance Measures and Targets: The Nexus between Motivation and Opportunity'. *Public Performance & Management Review 44*, no. 2 (4 March): 272–293.

Taylor, M. (2008). 'Beyond Technology-Push and Demand-Pull: Lessons from California's Solar Policy'. *Energy Economics 30*: 2829–2854.

Taylor, R. and A. Migone. (2017). 'From Procurement to the Commissioning of Public Services'. Paper presented at the IPAC, Charlottetown, PE.

459

Teghtsoonian, K. and L. Chappell. (2008). 'The Rise and Decline of Women's Policy Machinery in British Columbia and New South Wales: A Cautionary Tale'. *International Political Science Review 29*, no. *1*: 29–51.

Teghtsoonian, K. and J. Grace. (2001). ' "Something More Is Necessary": The Mixed Achievements of Women's Policy Agencies in Canada'. In A. G. Mazur (ed.), *State Feminism, Women's Movements and Job Training: Making Democracies Work in a Global Economy*. New York: Routledge, 235–269.

Teisman, G. R. (2000). 'Models for Research into Decision-Making Processes: On Phases, Streams and Decision-Making Rounds'. *Public Administration 78*, no. *4*: 937–956.

Tenbensel, T. (2004). 'Does More Evidence Lead to Better Policy? The Implications of Explicit Priority-Setting in New Zealand's Health Policy for Evidence-Based Policy'. *Policy Studies 25*, no. *3*: 190–207.

Tenbensel, T. (2005). 'Multiple Modes of Governance: Disentangling the Alternatives to Hierarchies and Markets'. *Public Management Review 7*, no. *2*: 267–288.

Tenbensel, T. (2008). 'The Role of Evidence in Policy: How the Mix Matters'. Paper presented at the International Research Society for Public Management, Queensland University of Technology, Brisbane, QLD, Australia, 26–8 March.

Termeer, C. J. A. M. and J. F. M. Koppenjan. (1997). 'Managing Perceptions in Networks'. In W. J. M. Kickert, E.-H. Klijn and J. F. M. Koppenjan (eds.), *Managing Complex Networks: Strategies for the Public Sector*. London: Sage, 79–97.

Thadani, K. B. (2014). 'Public Private Partnership in the Health Sector: Boon or Bane'. *Procedia: Social and Behavioral Sciences*. International Relations Conference on India and Development Partnerships in Asia and Africa: Towards a New Paradigm, *157* (27 November): 307–316.

Thaler, R. H. (2015). *Misbehaving: The Making of Behavioral Economics*. New York: W. W. Norton.

Thaler, R. H. and S. Mullainathan. (2008). 'Behavioral Economics'. In *The Concise Encyclopedia of Economics* (2nd edn). www.econlib.org/library/Enc/Behavioral Economics.html.

Thaler, R. H. and C. R. Sunstein. (2009). *Nudge: Improving Decisions about Health, Wealth, and Happiness* (expanded and revised edn). New York: Penguin Books.

Thaler, R. H., C. R. Sunstein and J. P. Balz. (2010). *Choice Architecture*. SSRN Scholarly Paper. Rochester, NY: Social Science Research Network, 2 April. http://papers.ssrn.com/abstract=1583509.

Thatcher, M. (2002). 'Analyzing Regulatory Reform in Europe'. *Journal of European Public Policy 9*, no. *6*: 859–872.

Thatcher, M. and A. Stone-Sweet (eds.). (2003). *The Politics of Delegation*. London: Frank Cass.

Thelen, K. (2003). 'How Institutions Evolve: Insights from Comparative Historical Analysis'. In J. Mahoney and D. Rueschemeyer (eds.), *Comparative Historical Analysis in the Social Sciences*. Cambridge: Cambridge University Press, 208–240.

Thelen, K. (2004). *How Institutions Evolve: The Political Economy of Skills in Germany, Britain, the United States and Japan*. Cambridge: Cambridge University Press.

Tholoniat, L. (2010). 'The Career of the Open Method of Coordination: Lessons from a "Soft" EU-Instrument'. *West European Politics 33*, no. *1*: 93.

Thomann, E. (2018). 'Donate Your Organs, Donate Life!" Explicitness in Policy Instruments'. *Policy Sciences 51*, no. *4*: 433–456.

Thomas, Alyssa S., Taciano L. Milfont and Michael C. Gavin. (2016). 'A New Approach to Identifying the Drivers of Regulation Compliance Using Multivariate

Behavioural Models'. Edited by Petr Heneberg. *PLoS One 11*, no. *10* (11 October): e0163868.

Thomas, E. V. (2003). 'Sustainable Development, Market Paradigms and Policy Integration'. *Journal of Environmental Policy and Planning 5*, no. *2*: 201–216.

Thomas, H. G. (2001). 'Towards a New Higher Education Law in Lithuania: Reflections on the Process of Policy Formulation'. *Higher Education Policy 14*, no. *3*: 213–223.

Thomas, J. S., S. E. Ong, K. S. Chia and H. P. Lee. (2016). 'A Brief History of Public Health in Singapore'. In C. Y. Lee and K Saktu (eds.), *Singapore's Health Care System: What 50 Years Have Achieved*. Singapore: World Scientific, 33–56.

Thompson, C. R. (1994). 'The Cabinet Member as Policy Entrepreneur'. *Administration Society 25*, no. *4*: 395–409.

Thompson, G. F. (2003). *Between Hierarchies and Markets: The Logic and Limits of Network Forms of Organization*. Oxford: Oxford University Press.

Thomson, J. E. and S. D. Krasner. (1989). 'Global Transactions and the Consolidation of Sovereignty'. In E. O. Czempiel and J. N. Rosenau (eds.), *Global Changes and Theoretical Challenges*. Lexington, CT: Lexington Books, 195–219.

Thorelli, H. B. (1986). 'Networks: Between Markets and Hierarchies'. *Strategic Management Journal 7*: 37–51.

Tiernan, A. (2011). 'Advising Australian Federal Governments: Assessing the Evolving Capacity and Role of the Australian Public Service'. *Australian Journal of Public Administration 70*, no. *4* (1 December): 335–346.

Tiernan, A. and J. Wanna. (2006). 'Competence, Capacity, Capability: Towards Conceptual Clarity in the Discourse of Declining Policy Skills'. Paper presented at the Govnet International Conference, Australian National University, Canberra, ACT, Australia.

Timmermans, A., C. Rothmayr, U. Serduelt and F. Varone. (1998). 'The Design of Policy Instruments: Perspectives and Concepts'. Paper presented to the Midwest Political Science Association, Chicago, IL.

Tinbergen, J. (1952). *On the Theory of Economic Policy*. Dordrecht, Netherlands: North-Holland.

Tinbergen, J. (1958). *The Design of Development*. Baltimore, MD: Johns Hopkins University Press.

Tinbergen, J. (1967). *Economic Policy: Principles and Design*. Chicago, IL: Rand McNally.

Toke, D. (2008). 'Trading Schemes, Risks, and Costs: The Cases of the European Union Emissions Trading Scheme and the Renewables Obligation'. *Environment and Planning C: Government and Policy 26*: 938–953.

Tollefson, C. (2004). 'Indigenous Rights and Forest Certification in British Columbia'. In J. Kirton and M. Trebilcock (eds.), *Hard Choices, Soft Law: Voluntary Standards in Global Trade, Environment and Social Governance*. Aldershot, UK: Ashgate.

Tollefson, C., A. R. Zito and F. Gale. (2012). 'Symposium Overview: Conceptualizing New Governance Arrangements'. *Public Administration 90*, no. *1*: 3–18.

Tollefson, C. G. F. and D. Haley. (2008). *Setting the Standard: Certification, Governance and the Forest Stewardship Council*. Vancouver, BC: University of British Columbia Press.

Tollison, R. D. (1991). 'Regulation and Interest Groups'. In J. High (ed.), *Regulation: Economic Theory and History*. Ann Arbor, MI: University of Michigan Press, 59–76.

Torenvlied, R. and A. Akkerman. (2004). 'Theory of "Soft" Policy Implementation in Multilevel Systems with an Application to Social Partnership in the Netherlands'. *Acta Politica 39*: 31–58.

Torgerson, D. (1985). 'Contextual Orientation in Policy Analysis: The Contribution of Harold D. Lasswell'. *Policy Sciences 18*: 240–252.

Torgerson, D. (1986). 'Between Knowledge and Politics: Three Faces of Policy Analysis'. *Policy Sciences 19*, no. 1: 33–59.

Torgerson, D. (1990). 'Origins of the Policy Orientation: The Aesthetic Dimension in Lasswell's Political Vision'. *History of Political Thought 11* (Summer): 340–344.

Torgler, B. (2004). 'Moral Suasion: An Alternative Tax Policy Strategy? Evidence from a Controlled Field Experiment in Switzerland'. *Economics of Governance 5*, no. 1: 235–253.

Torres, L. (2004). 'Trajectories in Public Administration Reforms in European Continental Countries'. *Australian Journal of Public Administration 63*, no. 3: 99–112.

Tosun, J. (2013). 'How the EU Handles Uncertain Risks: Understanding the Role of the Precautionary Principle'. *Journal of European Public Policy 20*, no. 10: 1517–1528.

Tosun, Jale, Maria Tullia Galanti and Michael Howlett. (2022). 'The Significance of Leadership in the Evolution of Policy Styles: Reconciling Policy-Making in the Short and Long Term'. *Politische Vierteljahresschrift 63*, no. 2 (2 May): 337–358.

Tosun, Jale and Michael Howlett. (2021). 'Managing Slow Onset Events Related to Climate Change: The Role of Public Bureaucracy'. *Current Opinion in Environmental Sustainability*, Slow Onset Events related to Climate Change *50* (1 June): 43–53.

Tosun, Jale and Michael Howlett. (2022). 'Analyzing National Policy Styles Empirically Using the Sustainable Governance Indicators (SGI): Insights into Long-Term Patterns of Policy-Making'. *European Policy Analysis 8*, no. 2: 160–177.

Tosun, Jale and Achim Lang. (2017). 'Policy Integration: Mapping the Different Concepts'. *Policy Studies 38*, no. 6 (2 November): 553–570.

Tosun, J. and K. Marcinkiewicz. (2015). 'Contesting Climate Change: Mapping the Political Debate in Poland'. *East European Politics 31*, no. 2: 187–207.

Townsend, R. E., J. McColl and M. D. Young. (2006). 'Design Principles for Individual Transferable Quotas'. *Marine Policy 30*: 131–141.

Treasury Board of Canada Secretariat. (2007). *Assessing, Selecting and Implementing Instruments for Government Action*. Ottawa, ON: Treasury Board.

Trebilcock, M. J. (1983). 'Regulating Service Quality in Professional Markets'. In D. N. Dewees (ed.), *The Regulation of Quality: Products, Services, Workplaces and the Environment*. Toronto, ON: Butterworths, 83–108.

Trebilcock, M. J. (2008). 'Regulating the Market for Legal Services'. *Alberta Law Review 45*: 215–232.

Trebilcock, M. J., D. Dewees and D. G. Hartle. (1982). *The Choice of Governing Instrument*. Ottawa, ON: Economic Council of Canada.

Trebilcock, M. J. and D. G. Hartle. (1982). 'The Choice of Governing Instrument'. *International Review of Law and Economics 2*: 29–46.

Trebilcock, M. J. and J. R. S. Prichard. (1983). 'Crown Corporations: The Calculus of Instrument Choice'. In J. R. S. Prichard (ed.), *Crown Corporations in Canada: The Calculus of Instrument Choice*. Toronto, ON: Butterworths, 1–50.

Trebilcock, M. J., C. J. Tuohy and A. D. Wolfson. (1979). *Professional Regulation: A Staff Study of Accountancy, Architecture, Engineering, and Law in Ontario*

Prepared for the Professional Organizations Committee. Toronto, ON: Ontario Ministry of the Attorney General.

Treib, O., H. Bahr and G. Falkner. (2007). 'Modes of Governance: Towards a Conceptual Clarification'. *Journal of European Public Policy 14*: 1–20.

Trein, Philipp, Manuel Fischer, Martino Maggetti and Francesco Sarti. (2023). 'Empirical Research on Policy Integration: A Review and New Directions'. *Policy Sciences 56*, no. 1 (9 January): 29–48.

Trein, Philipp, Martino Maggetti and Iris Meyer. (2020). 'Necessary Conditions for Policy Integration and Administrative Coordination Reforms: An Exploratory Analysis'. *Journal of European Public Policy*: 1–22.

Treisman, D. (2007). 'What Have We Learned about the Causes of Corruption from Ten Years of Cross-National Empirical Research?' *Annual Review of Political Science 10*: 211–244.

Tribe, L. H. (1972). 'Policy Science: Analysis or Ideology?' *Philosophy and Public Affairs 2*, no. 1: 66–110.

Trondal, J. and L. Jeppesen. (2008). 'Images of Agency Governance in the European Union'. *West European Politics 31*, no. 3: 417–441.

True, J. and M. Mintrom. (2001). 'Transnational Networks and Policy Diffusion: The Case of Gender Mainstreaming'. *International Studies Quarterly 45*: 27–57.

Truman, D. R. (1964). *The Governmental Process: Political Interests and Public Opinion*. New York: Knopf.

Tsao, K. K. (2009). 'Building Administrative Capacity: Lessons Learned from China'. *Public Administration Review 69*, no. 6: 1021–1024.

Tsasis, P. (2008). 'The Politics of Governance: Government – Voluntary Sector Relationships'. *Canadian Public Administration 51*, no. 2: 265–290.

Tschakert, P. and K. A. Dietrich. (2010). 'Anticipatory Learning for Climate Change Adaptation and Resilience'. *Ecology and Society 15*, no. 2: 11.

Tsebelis, G. (2002). *Veto Players. How Political Institutions Work*. Princeton, NJ: Princeton University Press.

Tunzelmann, N. von. (2010). 'Technology and Technology Policy in the Postwar UK: Market Failure or Network Failure?' *Revue d'économie industrielle*, no. 129–30: 237–258.

Tuohy, C. (1992). *Policy and Politics in Canada: Institutionalized Ambivalence*. Philadelphia, PA: Temple University Press.

Tuohy, C. (1999). *Accidental Logics: The Dynamics of Change in the Health Care Arena in the United States, Britain and Canada*. New York: Oxford University Press.

Tuohy, C. J. and A. D. Wolfson. (1978). 'Self-Regulation: Who Qualifies?' In P. Slayton and M. J. Trebilcock (eds.), *The Professions and Public Policy*. Toronto, ON: University of Toronto Press, 111–122.

Tupper, A. (1979). 'The State in Business'. *Canadian Public Administration 22*, no. 1: 124–150.

Tupper, A. and G. B. Doern. (1981). 'Public Corporations and Public Policy in Canada'. In A. Tupper and G. B. Doern (eds.), *Public Corporations and Public Policy in Canada*. Montreal, QC: Institute for Research on Public Policy, 1–50.

Turnbull, Nick. (2018). 'Policy Design: Its Enduring Appeal in a Complex World and How to Think It Differently'. *Public Policy and Administration 33*, no. 4: 357–364.

Turnpenny, J., M. Nilsson, D. Russel, A. Jordan, J. Hertin and B. Nykvist. (2008). 'Why is Integrating Policy Assessment So Hard? A Comparative Analysis of the

Institutional Capacity and Constraints'. *Journal of Environmental Planning and Management 51*, no. 6: 759–775.

Turnpenny, J., C. M. Radaelli, A. Jordan and K. Jacob. (2009). 'The Policy and Politics of Policy Appraisal: Emerging Trends and New Directions'. *Journal of European Public Policy 16*, no. 4: 640–653.

Tversky, A. and D. Kahneman. (1973). 'Availability: A Heuristic for Judging Frequency and Probability'. *Cognitive Psychology 5*, no. 2: 207–232.

Tversky, A. and D. Kahneman. (1974). 'Judgment under Uncertainty: Heuristics and Biases'. *Science 185*, no. *4157*: 1124–1131.

Tversky, A. and D. Kahneman. (1981). 'The Framing of Decisions and the Psychology of Choice'. *Science 211*, no. *4481*: 453–458.

Tyler, T. R. (1990). *Why People Obey the Law*. New Haven: Yale University Press.

Tyler, T. R. (2013). *Why People Cooperate: The Role of Social Motivations* (reprint edn). Princeton: Princeton University Press.

Uhr, J. (1996). 'Testing the Policy Capacities of Budgetary Agencies: Lessons from Finance'. *Australian Journal of Public Administration 55*, no. 4: 124–134.

Uhr, J. and K. Mackay (eds.). (1996). *Evaluating Policy Advice: Learning from Commonwealth Experience*. Canberra, ACT: Australian National University, Federalism Research Centre.

UK Cabinet Office. (1999). *Professional Policy Making for the Twenty-First Century*. London: Cabinet Office, Strategic Policy Making Team.

Ulrich, B. (1995). 'The History and Possible Causes of Forest Decline in Central Europe, with Particular Attention to the German Situation'. *Environmental Reviews 3*: 262–276.

Underdal, A. (1980). 'Integrated Marine Policy: What/Why/How?' *Marine Policy 4*, no. *3*: 159–169.

UNFCC. (1992). 'United Nations Framework Convention on Climate Change' (Treaty). http://unfccc.int/files/essential_background/background_publications_htmlpdf/appl ication/pdf/conveng.pdf.

Ungar, S. (1992). 'The Rise and (Relative) Decline of Global Warming as a Social Problem'. *The Sociological Quarterly 33*, no. 4: 483–501.

Unger, B. and F. van Waarden. (1995). 'Introduction: An Interdisciplinary Approach to Convergence'. In B. Unger and F. van Waarden (eds.), *Convergence or Diversity? Internationalization and Economic Policy Response*. Aldershot, UK: Avebury, 1–35.

Unsworth, K. L. and K. S. Fielding. (2014). 'It's Political: How the Salience of One's Political Identity Changes Climate Change Beliefs and Policy Support'. *Global Environmental Change 27* (July): 131–137.

Uribe, C. A. (2014). 'The *Dark Side* of Social Capital Re-Examined from a Policy Analysis Perspective: Networks of Trust and Corruption'. *Journal of Comparative Policy Analysis: Research and Practice 16*, no. 2: 175–189.

Utton, M. A. (1986). *The Economics of Regulating Industry*. London: Basil Blackwell.

Vaitsman, Jeni, Jose M. Ribeiro and Lenaura Lobato. (2013). *Policy Analysis in Brazil*. Bristol: Policy Press.

Valkama, P. and S. J. Bailey. (2001). 'Vouchers as an Alternative Public Sector Funding System'. *Public Policy and Administration 16*, no. 1: 32–58.

Van Assche, K., R. Beunen and M. Duineveld. (2014). *Evolutionary Governance Theory: An Introduction*. New York: Springer Science & Business Media.

Van Assche, K., R. Beunen and M. Duineveld. (2017). 'Co-evolutionary Planning Theory'. In Michael Gunder, Ali Mandanipour and Vanessa Watson (eds.), *The Routledge Handbook of Planning Theory*. New York: Routledge, 221–243.

Van Assche, K., R. Beunen, M. Gruezmacher and M. Duineveld. (2020). 'Rethinking Strategy in Environmental Governance'. *Journal of Environmental Policy & Planning* 22, no. 5: 695–708.

van Bavel, R., B. Herrmann, G. Esposito and A. Proestakis. (2013). 'Applying Behavioural Sciences to EU Policy-Making'. In *Institute for Prospective Technological Studies*. Luxembourg: Publications Office of the European Union.

Van Beers, C. and A. De Moor. (2001). *Public Subsidies and Policy Failures. How Subsidies Distort the Natural Environment, Equity and Trade and How to Reform Them*. Cheltenham, UK and Northampton, MA: Edward Elgar.

van Buuren, A. and E.-H. Klijn. (2006). 'Trajectories of Institutional Design in Policy Networks: European Interventions in the Dutch Fishery Network as an Example'. *International Review of Administrative Sciences* 72, no. 3: 395–415.

van Buuren, A., J. M. Lewis, B. G. Peters and W. Voorberg. (2020). 'Improving Public Policy and Administration: Exploring the Potential of Design'. *Policy & Politics* 48, no. 1: 3–19.

van Buuren, A. and D. Loorbach. (2009). 'Policy Innovation in Isolation? Conditions for Policy Renewal by Transition Arenas and Pilot Projects'. *Public Management Review* 11, no. 3: 375–392.

Van de Walle, S. (2014). 'Building Resilience in Public Organizations: The Role of Waste and Bricolage'. *The Innovation Journal: The Public Sector Innovation Journal* 19, no. 2: 1–18.

Van den Berg, C. F. (2017). 'Dynamics in the Dutch Policy Advisory System: Externalization, Politicization and the Legacy of Pillarization'. *Policy Sciences* 50, no. 1 (1 March): 63–84.

Van den Bosch, S. and J. Rotmans. (2008). *Deepening, Broadening and Scaling Up: A Framework for Steering Transition Experiments*. https://repub.eur.nl/pub/15812. Accessed 1 January 2008.

Van der Heijden, J. (2011). 'Institutional Layering: A Review of the Use of the Concept'. *Politics 31*, no. 1 (10 January): 9–18.

van der Linden, S. (2015). 'Exploring Beliefs about Bottled Water and Intentions to Reduce Consumption: The Dual-Effect of Social Norm Activation and Persuasive Information'. *Environment and Behavior 47*, no. 5: 526–550.

van der Sluijs, J. (2005). 'Uncertainty as a Monster in the Science-Policy Interface: Four Coping Strategies'. *Water Science and Technology: A Journal of the International Association on Water Pollution Research 52*, no. 6: 87–92.

Van Detten, R. (ed.). (2013). *Das Waldsterben. Rückblick auf einen Ausnahmezustand*. Munich, Germany: Oekom Verlag.

van Dooren, W. (2004). 'Supply and Demand of Policy Indicators: A Cross-Sectoral Comparison'. *Public Management Review 6*, no. 4: 511–530.

Van Gossum, P., B. Arts and K. Verheyen. (2009). '"Smart Regulation": Can Policy Instrument Design Solve Forest Policy Aims of Expansion and Sustainability in Flanders and the Netherlands?' *Forest Policy and Economics 11*: 616–627.

Van Heffen, O., W. J. M. Kickert and J. A. A. Thomassen. (2000a). *Governance in Modern Society: Effects, Change and Formation of Government Institutions*. Dordrecht, Netherlands: Kluwer.

Van Heffen, O., W. J. M. Kickert and J. J. A. Thomassen. (2000b). 'Introduction: Multi-Level and Multi-Actor Governance'. In O. Van Heffen, W. J. M. Kickert and J. J. A. Thomassen (eds.), *Governance in Modern Society: Effects, Change and Formation of Government Institutions*. Dordrecht, Netherlands: Kluwer, 3–12.

Van Kersbergen, K. and F. Van Waarden. (2004). ' "Governance" as a Bridge between Disciplines: Cross-Disciplinary Inspiration Regarding Shifts in Governance and Problems of Governability, Accountability and Legitimacy'. *European Journal of Political Research 43*, no. 2: 143–172.

van Meter, D. and C. van Horn. (1975). 'The Policy Implementation Process: A Conceptual Framework'. *Administration and Society 6*: 445–488.

van Nispen, F. K. M. and A. B. Ringeling. (1998). 'On Instruments and Instrumentality: A Critical Assessment'. In B. G. Peters and F. K. M. V. Nispen (eds.), *Public Policy Instruments: Evaluating the Tools of Public Administration*. New York: Edward Elgar, 204–217.

van Thiel, S. (2008). 'The "Empty Nest" Syndrome: Dutch Ministries after the Separation of Policy and Administration'. Paper presented to the IRSPM Conference, Brisbane, QLD, Australia.

van Waarden, F. (1995). 'Persistence of National Policy Styles: A Study of Their Institutional Foundations'. In B. Unger and F. van Waarden (eds.), *Convergence or Diversity? Internationalization and Economic Policy Response*. Aldershot, UK: Avebury, 333–372.

Vancoppenolle, D., H. Sætren and P. Hupe. (2015). 'The Politics of Policy Design and Implementation: A Comparative Study of Two Belgian Service Voucher Programs'. *Journal of Comparative Policy Analysis: Research and Practice 17*, no. 2 (21 April): 157–173.

Varone, F. (1998). 'Policy Design: Le choix des instruments des politiques publiques'. *Evaluation 2*: 5–14.

Varone, F. (2000). 'Le choix des instruments de l'action publique analyse comparée des politiques energetiques en Europe at en Amerique du Nord'. *Revue Internationale de Politique Comparee 7*, no 1: 167–201.

Varone, F. (2001). 'Les instruments de la politique energetique: Analyse comparée du Canada et des Etats Unis'. *Canadian Journal of Political Science 34*, no. 1: 3–28.

Varone, F. and B. Aebischer. (2001). 'Energy Efficiency: The Challenges of Policy Design'. *Energy Policy 29*, no. 8: 615–629.

Vedung, E. (1997a). 'Policy Instruments: Typologies and Theories'. In M. L. Bemelmans-Videc, R. C. Rist and E. Vedung (eds.), *Carrots, Sticks and Sermons: Policy Instruments and Their Evaluation*. New Brunswick, NJ: Transaction, 21–58.

Vedung, E. (1997b). 'Public Policy and Program Evaluation. Transaction Publishers of Political Feasibility'. *Futures 1*, no. 4: 282–288.

Vedung, E. and F. C. J. van der Doelen. (1998). 'The Sermon: Information Programs in the Public Policy Process – Choice, Effects and Evaluation'. In M.-L. Bemelmans-Videc, R. C. Rist and E. Vedung (eds.), *Carrots, Sticks and Sermons: Policy Instruments and Their Evaluation*. New Brunswick, NJ: Transaction Publishers, 103–128.

Veggeland, N. (2008). 'Path Dependence and Public Sector Innovation in Regulatory Regimes'. *Scandinavian Political Studies 31*, no. 3: 268–290.

Veld, R. J. in't (1998). 'The Dynamics of Instruments'. In B. G. Peters and F. K. M. Van Nispen (eds.), *Public Policy Instruments: Evaluating the Tools of Public Administration*. New York: Edward Elgar, 153–162.

Veljanovski, C. (1988). *Selling the State: Privatisation in Britain*. London: Weidenfeld & Nicolson.

Verbruggen, Aviel and Volkmar Lauber. (2012). 'Assessing the Performance of Renewable Electricity Support Instruments'. *Energy Policy 45* (1 June): 635–644.

Verheijen, T. (1999). *Civil Service Systems in Central and Eastern Europe*. Cheltenham, UK: Edward Elgar.

Verhoest, K., P. G. Roness, B. Verschuere, K. Rubecksen and M. MacCarthaigh. (2010). *Autonomy and Control of State Agencies: Comparing States and Agencies*. London: Palgrave Macmillan.

Verhoest, K., B. Verschuere and G. Bouckaert. (2007). 'Pressure, Legitimacy and Innovative Behavior by Public Organizations'. *Governance 20*, no. 3: 469–497.

Verschuere, B. (2009). 'The Role of Public Agencies in the Policy Making Process'. *Public Policy and Administration 24*, no. 1: 23–46.

Verweij, M., R. Ellis, F. Hendriks, S. Ney, M. Thompson et al. (2006). 'Clumsy Solutions for a Complex World. The Case of Climate Change'. *Public Administration 84*, no. 4: 817–843.

Veselý, A. (2014). 'The Profile and Work of Officials in Central and Regional Administration Compared: The Case of the Czech Republic'. *NISPAcee Journal of Public Administration and Policy 7*, no. 1: 107–128.

Veselý, A. and I. Petrúšek. (2021). 'Decision Makers' Preferences of Policy Instruments'. *European Policy Analysis 7*, no. 1: 165–184.

Veselý, A., A. Wellstead and B. Evans. (2014). 'Comparing Sub-National Policy Workers in Canada and the Czech Republic: Who Are They, What They Do, and Why It Matters?' *Policy and Society 33*, no. 2 (June 1, 2014): 103–115.

Vigoda, E. (2002). 'From Responsiveness to Collaboration: Governance, Citizens and the Next Generation of Public Administration'. *Public Administration Review 62*, no. 5: 527–540.

Vigoda, E. and E. Gilboa. (2002). 'The Quest for Collaboration: Toward a Comprehensive Strategy for Public Administration'. *Public Administration and Public Policy 99*: 99–117.

Vijayakumar, A. N. and N. Nagaraja. (2012). 'Internal Control Systems: Effectiveness of Internal Audit in Risk Management at Public Sector Enterprises'. *BVIMR Management Edge 5*, no. 1.

Villa Alvarez, Diana Pamela, Valentina Auricchio and Marzia Mortati. (2020). 'Design Prototyping for Policymaking'. *DRS Conference Papers* (11 August). https://dl.designresearchsociety.org/drs-conference-papers/drs2020/researchpapers/79.

Villa Alvarez, Diana Pamela, Valentina Auricchio and Marzia Mortati. (2022). 'Mapping Design Activities and Methods of Public Sector Innovation Units through the Policy Cycle Model'. *Policy Sciences 55*, no. 1 (1 March): 89–136.

Vimpani, G. (2005). 'Getting the Mix Right: Family, Community and Social Policy Interventions to Improve Outcomes for Young People at Risk of Substance Misuse'. *Drug and Alcohol Review 24*: 111–125.

Vincent-Jones, P. (2006). *The New Public Contracting: Regulation, Responsiveness, Relationality*. Oxford: Oxford University Press.

Vine, Edward and Jayant Sathaye. (1999). 'The Monitoring, Evaluation, Reporting and Verification of Climate Change Projects'. *Mitigation and Adaptation Strategies for Global Change 4*, no. 1 (1 March): 43–60.

Vining, A. R. and A. C. Boardman. (2007). 'The Choice of Formal Policy Analysis Methods in Canada'. In Laurent Dobuzinskis, Michael Howlett and David Laycock (eds.), *Policy Analysis in Canada: The State of the Art*. Toronto: University of Toronto Press, 48–85.

Vining, A. R. and A. E. Boardman. (2008). 'Public – Private Partnerships: Eight Rules for Governments'. *Public Works Management & Policy 13*, no. 2 (1 October): 149–161.

Vining, A. R., A. E. Boardman and F. Poschmann. (2005). 'Public – Private Partnerships in the US and Canada: 'There Are No Free Lunches'''. *Journal of Comparative Policy Analysis* 7, no. 3: 199–220.

Vining, A. R. and R. Botterell. (1983). 'An Overview of the Origins, Growth, Size and Functions of Provincial Crown Corporations'. In J. R. S. Pritchard (ed.), *Crown Corporations: The Calculus of Instrument Choice.* Toronto, ON: Butterworths, 303–368.

Viscusi, W. K. and T. Gayer. (2015). 'Behavioral Public Choice: The Behavioral Paradox of Government Policy'. *Harvard Journal of Law & Public Policy* 38: 973.

Vogel, D. (1986). *National Styles of Regulation: Environmental Policy in Great Britain and the United States.* Ithaca, NY: Cornell University Press.

Vogel, D. (2001). 'Is There a Race to the Bottom? The Impact of Globalization on National Regulatory Policies'. *The Tocqueville Review/La Revue Tocqueville* 22: 1.

Vogel, D. (2005). *The Market for Virtue: The Potential and Limits of Corporate Social Responsibility.* Washington, DC: Brookings Institution.

Vogel, D. and R. A. Kagan (eds.). (2002). *Dynamics of Regulatory Change: How Globalization Affects National Regulatory Policies.* Berkeley, CA: University of California Press.

Vogel, S. K. (1996). *Freer Markets, More Rules: Regulatory Reform in Advanced Industrial Countries.* Ithaca, NY: Cornell University Press.

Volkery, A. and T. Ribeiro. (2009). 'Scenario Planning in Public Policy: Understanding Use, Impacts and the Role of Institutional Context Factors'. *Technological Forecasting and Social Change* 76, no. 9: 1198–1207.

von Homeyer, I., S. Oberthür and A. J. Jordan. (2021). 'EU Climate and Energy Governance in Times of Crisis: Towards a New Agenda'. *Journal of European Public Policy* 28, no. 7 (3 July): 959–979.

Voorberg, W. H., V. J. J. M. Bekkers and L. G. Tummers. (2015). 'A Systematic Review of Co-Creation and Co-Production: Embarking on the Social Innovation Journey'. *Public Management Review* 17, no. 9 (21 October): 1333–1357.

Voros, Joseph. (2017). 'Big History and Anticipation'. In Roberto Poli (ed.), *Handbook of Anticipation: Theoretical and Applied Aspects of the Use of Future in Decision Making.* Cham: Springer International Publishing, 1–40.

Voss, J.-P. (2007). 'Innovation Process in Governance: The Development of "Emissions Trading" as a New Policy Instrument'. *Science and Public Policy* 34, no. 5: 329–343.

Voss, J.-P., D. Bauknecht and R. Kemp (eds.). (2006). *Reflexive Governance for Sustainable Development.* Cheltenham, UK: Edward Elgar.

Voss, J.-P. and B. Bornemann. (2011). 'The Politics of Reflexive Governance: Challenges for Designing Adaptive Management and Transition Management'. *Ecology and Society* 16, no. 2: 9.

Voss, J.-P. and A. Simons. (2014). 'Instrument Constituencies and the Supply Side of Policy Innovation: The Social Life of Emissions Trading'. *Environmental Politics* 23, no. 5: 735–754.

Voss, J.-P., A. Smith and J. Grin. (2009). 'Designing Long-term Policy: Rethinking Transition Management'. *Policy Sciences* 42, no. 4: 275–302.

Voyer, J.-P. (2007). 'Policy Analysis in the Federal Government: Building the Forward-Looking Policy Research Capacity'. In. L. Dobuzinskis, M. Howlett and D. Laycock (eds.), *Policy Analysis in Canada: The State of the Art.* Toronto, ON: University of Toronto Press, 123–131.

Vreugdenhil, H. and S. Nair. (2015). 'Policy Making: Pilot Projects as Predictive Methods'. In *Encyclopedia of Public Administration and Public Policy – 5 Volume Set* (3rd edn). New York: Routledge.

Vreugdenhil, H. and P. K. Rault. (2010). 'Pilot Projects for Evidence-Based Policy-Making: Three Pilot Projects in the Rhine Basin'. *German Policy Studies 6*, no. 2 (22 June): 115–151.

Vreugdenhil, Heleen, Jill Slinger, Wil Thissen and Philippe Ker Rault. (2010). 'Pilot Projects in Water Management'. *Ecology and Society 15*, no. 3.

Vreugdenhil, H., S. Taljaard and J. H. Slinger. (2012). 'Pilot Projects and Their Diffusion: A Case Study of Integrated Coastal Management in South Africa'. *International Journal of Sustainable Development 15*, no. 1/2: 148.

Wagenaar, H. and S. D. N. Cook. (2003). 'Understanding Policy Practices: Action, Dialectic and Deliberation in Policy Analysis'. In M. A. Hajer and H. Wagenaar (eds.), *Deliberative Policy Analysis: Understanding Governance in the Network Society*. London: Cambridge University Press, 139–171.

Waldo, D. (1948). *The Administrative State: A Study of the Political Theory of American Public Administration*. New York: Ronald Press.

Walker, A. (1984). 'The Political Economy of Privatisation'. In J. Le Grand and R. Robinson (eds.), *Privatisation and the Welfare State*. London: George Allen & Unwin, 19–44.

Walker, Brian, C. S. Hollings, Stephen R. Carpenter and Ann Kinzig. (2004). 'Resilience, Adaptability and Transformability in Social-Ecological Systems'. *Ecology and Society 9*, no. 2: article 5.

Walker, J. L. (1969). 'The Diffusion of Innovations Among the States'. *American Political Science Review 63*, no. 3: 880–899.

Walker, J. L. (1977). 'Setting the Agenda in the US Senate: A Theory of Problem Selection'. *British Journal of Political Science 7*: 423–445.

Walker, J. L. (1983). 'The Origins and Maintenance of Interest Groups in America'. *American Political Science Review 77*, no. 2: 390–406.

Walker, J. L. (1991). *Mobilizing Interest Groups in America: Patrons, Professions and Social Movements*. Ann Arbor, MI: University of Michigan Press.

Walker, W. E. (2000). 'Policy Analysis: A Systematic Approach to Supporting Policymaking in the Public Sector'. *Journal of Multi-Criteria Decision Analysis 9*, no. 1: 11–27.

Walker, W. E., R. J. Lempert and J. H. Kwakkel. (2013). 'Deep Uncertainty'. In S. I. Goss and M. C. Fu (eds.), *Encyclopaedia of Operations Research and Management Science*. New York: Springer, 395–402.

Walker, W. E., S. A. Rahman and J. Cave. (2001). 'Adaptive Policies, Policy Analysis, and Policy-Making'. *European Journal of Operational Research 128*, no. 2 (16 January): 282–289.

Walker, W. E., V. A. W. J. Marchau and J. H. Kwakkel. (2013). 'Uncertainty in the Framework of Policy Analysis'. In W. A. H. Thissen and W. E. Walker (eds.), *Public Policy Analysis: New Developments*. Dordrecht: Springer, 215–260.

Walker, W. E., V. A. W. J. Marchau and D. Swanson. (2010). 'Addressing Deep Uncertainty Using Adaptive Policies: Introduction to Section 2'. *Technological Forecasting and Social Change 77*, no. 6: 917–923.

Waller, M. (1992). 'Evaluating Policy Advice'. *Australian Journal of Public Administration 51*, no. 4: 440–449.

Walls, C. E. S. (1969). 'Royal Commissions: Their Influence on Public Policy'. *Canadian Public Administration 12*, no. 3: 365–371.

469

Walsh, C. (1988). 'Individual Irrationality and Public Policy: In Search of Merit/ Demerit Policies'. *Journal of Public Policy 7*, no. 2: 103–134.

Walsh, C. (1990). 'Individual Irrationality and Public Policy: In Search of Merit/ Demerit Policies'. In G. Brennan and C. Walsh (eds.), *Rationality, Individualism and Public Policy*. Canberra, ACT: Australian National University, Centre for Research on Federal Financial Relations, 145–177.

Walsh, J. I. (1994). 'Institutional Constraints and Domestic Choices: Economic Convergence and Exchange Rate Policy in France and Italy'. *Political Studies 42*, no. 2: 243–258.

Walsh, P., M. McGregor-Lowndes and C. J. Newton. (2008). 'Shared Services: Lessons from the Public and Private Sectors for the Nonprofit Sector'. *Australian Journal of Public Administration 67*, no. 2: 200–212.

Walters, L. C., J. Aydelotte and J. Miller. (2000). 'Putting More Public in Policy Analysis'. *Public Administration Review 60*, no. 4: 349–359.

Walters, W. (2004). 'Some Critical Notes on "Governance"'. *Studies in Political Economy 73*: 27–46.

Wan, C., G. Q. Shen and A. Yu. (2014). 'The Role of Perceived Effectiveness of Policy Measures in Predicting Recycling Behaviour in Hong Kong'. *Resources, Conservation and Recycling 83* (February): 141–151.

Wan, C., G. Q. Shen and A. Yu. (2015). 'Key Determinants of Willingness to Support Policy Measures on Recycling: A Case Study in Hong Kong'. *Environmental Science & Policy 54* (December): 409–418.

Warburton, R. N. and W. P. Warburton. (2004). 'Canada Needs Better Data for Evidence-Based Policy: Inconsistencies between Administrative and Survey Data on Welfare Dependence and Education'. *Canadian Public Policy 30*, no. 3: 241–255.

Wardekker, J. A., A. de Jong, J. M. Knoop and J. P. van der Sluijs. (2010). 'Operationalising a Resilience Approach to Adapting an Urban Delta to Uncertain Climate Changes'. *Technological Forecasting and Social Change 77*, no. 6 (July): 987–998.

Warren, R. (1987). 'Coproduction, Volunteerism, Privatization, and the Public Interest'. *Nonprofit and Voluntary Sector Quarterly 16*, no. 3 (1 January): 5–10.

Warren, R., K. S. Harlow and M. S. Rosentraub. (1982). 'Citizen Participation of Services: Methodological and Policy Issues in Coproduction Research'. *Southwest Review of Management and Economics 2*: 41–55.

Warwick, P. V. (2000). 'Policy Horizons in West European Parliamentary Systems'. *European Journal of Political Research 38*, no. 1: 37–61.

Wazny, K. (2017). '"Crowdsourcing" Ten Years in: A Review'. *Journal of Global Health 7*, no. 2: 020602.

Weatherford, M. S. (1989). 'Political Economy and Political Legitimacy: The Link Between Economic Policy and Political Trust'. In H. D. Clarke, M. C. Stewart and G. Zuk (eds.), *Economic Decline and Political Change: Canada, Great Britain, the United States*. Pittsburgh, PA: University of Pittsburgh Press, 225–251.

Weaver, R. K. (1986). 'The Politics of Blame Avoidance'. *Journal of Public Policy 6*, no. 4: 371–398.

Weaver, R. K. (2009a). 'If You Build It, Will They Come? Overcoming Unforeseen Obstacles to Program Effectiveness'. In *The Tansley Lecture*. Saskatoon, SK: University of Saskatchewan.

Weaver, R. K. (2009b). *Target Compliance: The Final Frontier of Policy Implementation*. Washington, DC: Brookings Institution. www.brookings.edu/research/papers/2009/09/30-compliance-weaver.

Weaver, R. K. (2010a). *But Will It Work? Implementation Analysis to Improve Government Performance*. Washington, DC: Brookings Institution. www.brookings. edu/research/papers/2010/02/implementation-analysis-weaver.

Weaver, R. K. (2010b). 'Paths and Forks or Chutes and Ladders? Negative Feedbacks and Policy Regime Change'. *Journal of Public Policy 30*, no. 2: 137–162.

Weaver, R. K. (2014). 'Compliance Regimes and Barriers to Behavioral Change'. *Governance 27*, no. 2: 243–265.

Weaver, R. K. (2015). 'Getting People to Behave: Research Lessons for Policy Makers'. *Public Administration Review 75*, no. 6: 806–816.

Weaver, R. K. (2016). 'Privileging Policy Change? Sustaining Automatic Stabilizing Mechanisms in Public Pensions'. *Social Policy & Administration 50*, no. 2 (1 March): 148–164.

Weaver, R. K. and B. A. Rockman. (1993a). 'Assessing the Effects of Institutions'. In R. K. Weaver and B. A. Rockman (eds.), *Do Institutions Matter? Government Capabilities in the United States and Abroad*. Washington, DC: Brookings Institution, 1–41.

Weaver, R. K. and B. A. Rockman. (1993b). 'When and How Do Institutions Matter?' In R. K. Weaver and B. A. Rockman (eds.), *Do Institutions Matter? Government Capabilities in the United States and Abroad*. Washington, DC: Brookings Institution, 445–463.

Webb, K. (1987). 'Between the Rocks and Hard Places: Bureaucrats, the Law and Pollution Control'. *Alternatives 14*, no. 2: 4–13.

Webb, K. (1990). 'On the Periphery: The Limited Role for Criminal Offences in Environmental Protection'. In D. Tingley (ed.), *Into the Future: Environmental Law and Policy for the 1990s*. Edmonton, AB: Environmental Law Centre, 58–69.

Webb, K. (2000). *Cinderella's Slippers? The Role of Charitable Tax Status in Financing Canadian Interest Groups*. Vancouver, BC: SFU-UBC Centre for the Study of Government and Business.

Webb, K. (2005). 'Sustainable Governance in the Twenty-First Century: Moving Beyond Instrument Choice'. In P. Eliadis, M. Hill and M. Howlett (eds.), *Designing Government: From Instruments to Governance*. Montreal, QC: McGill-Queen's University Press, 242–280.

Webb, K. and J. C. Clifford. (1988). *Pollution Control in Canada: The Regulatory Approach in the 1980s*. Ottawa, ON: Law Reform Commission of Canada.

Webber, D. J. (1986). 'Analyzing Political Feasibility: Political Scientists' Unique Contribution to Policy Analysis'. *Policy Studies Journal 14*, no. 4: 545–554.

Weber, E. P. and A. M. Khademian. (2008). 'Wicked Problems, Knowledge Challenges and Collaborative Capacity Builders in Network Settings'. *Public Administration Review 68*, no. 2: 334–349.

Weber, E. U. (2016). 'What Shapes Perceptions of Climate Change? New Research Since 2010: What Shapes Perceptions of Climate Change'. *Wiley Interdisciplinary Reviews: Climate Change 7*, no. 1: 125–134.

Weber, E. U. and P. C. Stern. (2011). 'Public Understanding of Climate Change in the United States'. *American Psychologist 66*, no. 4: 315.

Weber, M. (1978). *Economy and Society: An Outline of Interpretive Sociology*. Berkeley, CA: University of California Press.

Weber, M., P. P. J. Driessen and H. A. C. Runhaar. (2011). 'Environmental Noise Policy in the Netherlands: Drivers of and Barriers to Shifts from Government to Governance'. *Journal of Environmental Policy and Planning 13*: 119–137.

Webler, T. and S. Tuler. (2000). 'Fairness and Competence in Citizen Participation'. *Administration and Society 32*, no. 5: 566–595.

WEF (World Economic Forum). (Various years). *Global Competitiveness Report.* Geneva, Switzerland: WEF.

Weible, C. M. (2008). 'Expert-Based Information and Policy Subsystems: A Review and Synthesis'. *Policy Studies Journal 36*, no. 4: 615–635.

Weible, C. M. (2018). 'Instrument Constituencies and the Advocacy Coalition Framework: An Essay on the Comparisons, Opportunities, and Intersections'. *Policy and Society 37*, no. 1 (2 January): 59–73.

Weible, C. M., Paul Cairney and Jill Yordy. (2022). 'A Diamond in the Rough: Digging up and Polishing Harold D. Lasswell's Decision Functions'. *Policy Sciences 55*, no. 1 (1 March): 209–222.

Weible, C. M. and P. A. Sabatier. (2009). 'Coalitions, Science, and Belief Change: Comparing Adversarial and Collaborative Policy Subsystems'. *Policy Studies Journal 37*, no. 2: 195–212.

Weible, C. M., P. A. Sabatier, H. C. Jenkins-Smith, D. Nohrstedt, A. D. Henry and P. deLeon. (2011). 'A Quarter Century of the Advocacy Coalition Framework: An Introduction to the Special Issue'. *Policy Studies Journal 39*, no. 3: 349–360.

Weible, C. M., P. A. Sabatier and K. McQueen. (2009). 'Themes and Variations: Taking Stock of the Advocacy Coalition Framework'. *Policy Studies Journal 37*, no. 1: 121–140.

Weick, Karl E. and Kathleen M. Sutcliffe. (2001). *Managing the Unexpected: Assuring High Performance in an Age of Complexity* (1st edn). San Francisco: Jossey-Bass.

Weimer, D. L. (1992a). 'Claiming Races, Broiler Contracts, Heresthetics and Habits: Ten Concepts for Policy Design'. *Policy Sciences 25*: 135–159.

Weimer, D. L. (1992b). 'The Craft of Policy Design: Can It Be More Than Art?' *Policy Studies Review 11*, no. 3/4: 370–388.

Weimer, D. L. (1993). 'The Current State of Design Craft: Borrowing, Tinkering and Problem Solving'. *Public Administration Review 53*, no. 2 (April): 110–120.

Weimer, D. L. (2007). 'Public and Private Regulation of Organ Transplantation: Liver Allocation and the Final Rule'. *Journal of Health Politics, Policy and Law 32*, no. 1: 9–49.

Weimer, D. L. (2020). 'When Are Nudges Desirable? Benefit Validity When Preferences Are Not Consistently Revealed'. *Public Administration Review 80*, no. 1: 118–126.

Weimer, D. L. and A. R. Vining. (1989). *Policy Analysis: Concepts and Practice* (1st edn). Englewood Cliffs, NJ: Prentice Hall.

Weimer, D. L. and A. R. Vining. (1999). *Policy Analysis: Concepts and Practice* (3rd edn). Englewood Cliffs, NJ: Prentice Hall.

Weimer, D. L. and A. R. Vining. (2004). *Policy Analysis: Concepts and Practice* (4th edn). Englewood Cliffs, NJ: Prentice Hall.

Weimer, D. L. and A. R. Vining. (2011). *Policy Analysis: Concepts and Practice* (5th edn). Upper Saddle River, NJ: Pearson/Prentice Hall.

Weiner, N., Y. Bhosale, M. Gazzola and H. King. (2020). 'Mechanics of Randomly Packed Filaments: The "Bird Nest" as Meta-Material'. *Journal of Applied Physics 127*, no. 5: Article 050902.

Weir, M. (1992). 'Ideas and the Politics of Bounded Innovation'. In S. Steinmo, K. Thelen and F. Longstreth (eds.), *Structuring Politics: Historical Institutionalism in Comparative Analysis*. Cambridge: Cambridge University Press, 188–216.

Weir, M. (2010). 'Collaborative Governance and Civic Empowerment: A Discussion of Investing in Democracy: Engaging Citizens in Collaborative Governance'. *Perspectives on Politics 8*, no. 2: 595–598.

Weirich, P. (2004). *Realistic Decision Theory: Rules for Nonideal Agents in Nonideal Circumstances*. Oxford: Oxford University Press.

Weishaar, H., A. Amos and J. Collin. (2015). 'Best of Enemies: Using Social Network Analysis to Explore a Policy Network in European Smoke-Free Policy'. *Social Science & Medicine 133*: 85–92.

Weiss, C. H. (1977). 'Research for Policy's Sake: The Enlightenment Function of Social Research'. *Policy Analysis 3*: 531–545.

Weiss, C. H. (1980). 'Knowledge Creep and Decision Accretion'. *Knowledge 1*, no. 3: 381–404.

Weiss, C. H. (1992). 'Helping Government Think; Functions and Consequences of Policy Analysis Organizations'. In *Organizations for Policy Analysis: Helping Government Think*, 1–18. London: Sage Publications.

Weiss, C. H. and M. J Bucuvalas. (1980). *Social Science Research and Decision-Making*. New York: Columbia University Press.

Weiss, J., Elisa Dunkelberg and Thomas Vogelpohl. (2012). 'Improving Policy Instruments to Better Tap into Homeowner Refurbishment Potential: Lessons Learned from a Case Study in Germany'. *Energy Policy 44* (1 May): 406–415.

Weiss, J. A. (1976). 'Using Social Science for Social Policy'. *Policy Studies Journal 4*, no. 3: 234–238.

Weiss, J. A. and J. E. Gruber. (1984). 'Using Knowledge for Control in Fragmented Policy Arenas'. *Journal of Policy Analysis and Management 3*, no. 2: 225–247.

Weiss, J. A. and M. Tschirhart. (1994). 'Public Information Campaigns as Policy Instruments'. *Journal of Policy Analysis and Management 13*, no. 1: 82–119.

Weiss, L. (1998). *The Myth of the Powerless State: Governing the Economy in a Global Era*. Cambridge: Polity Press.

Weiss, L. (1999). 'Globalization and National Governance: Antinomy or Interdependence?' *Review of International Studies 25*, no. 5: 1–30.

Weiss, L. (2005). 'The State-Augmenting Effects of Globalisation'. *New Political Economy 10*, no. 3: 345–353.

Weiss, L. (ed.). (2003). *States in the Global Economy: Bringing Domestic Institutions Back In*. Cambridge: Cambridge University Press.

Welch, E. W. and W. Wong. (2001). 'Effects of Global Pressures on Public Bureaucracy: Modeling a New Theoretical Framework'. *Administration and Society 33*, no. 4: 371–402.

Weller, P. and B. Stevens. (1998). 'Evaluating Policy Advice: The Australian Experience'. *Public Administration 76* (Autumn): 579–589.

Wellstead, Adam. (2020). *The Rise of Policy Innovation Labs: A Catalog of Policy Innovation in the United States*. SSRN Scholarly Paper. Rochester, NY: Social Science Research Network, 3 January.

Wellstead, A., J. Rayner and M. Howlett. (2016). 'Alberta's Oil Sands Reclamation Policy Trajectory: The Role of Tense Layering, Policy Stretching, and Policy Patching in Long-Term Policy Dynamics'. *Journal of Environmental Planning and Management 59*, no. 10: 1873–1890.

Wellstead, A., R. Stedman and E. Lindquist. (2007). 'Beyond the National Capital Region: Federal Regional Policy Capacity'. In *Report Prepared for the Treasury Board Secretariat of Canada*. Ottawa, ON: Treasury Board.

Wellstead, A. M., Anat Gofen and Angie Carter. (2021). 'Policy Innovation Lab Scholarship: Past, Present, and the Future – Introduction to the Special Issue on Policy Innovation Labs'. *Policy Design and Practice 4*, no. 2 (3 April): 193–211.

Wellstead, A. M. and Michael Howlett. (2022). '(Re)Thinking Think Tanks in the Age of Policy Labs: The Rise of Knowledge-Based Policy Influence Organisations'. *Australian Journal of Public Administration 81*, no. *1*: 224–232.

Wenig, M. M. and P. Sutherland. (2004). 'Considering the Upstream/Downstream Effects of the Mackenzie Pipeline: Rough Paddling for the National Energy Board'. *Resources 86*: 1–8.

Wescott, G. (2002). 'Integrated Natural Resource Management in Australia'. *Australian Journal of Environmental Management 9*, no. *3*: 138–140.

Wesley, Jared J. and Geoff Salomons. (2019). 'Cannabis Legalization and the Machinery of Government'. *Canadian Public Administration 62*, no. *4*: 573–592.

West, W. (2005). 'Administrative Rulemaking: An Old and Emerging Literature'. *Public Administration Review 65*, no. *6*: 655–668.

Weyland, K. (2005). 'Theories of Policy Diffusion: Lessons from Latin American Pension Reform'. *World Politics 57*, no. *2*: 262–295.

Wheeler, D. (2001). 'Racing to the Bottom? Foreign Investment and Air Pollution in Developing Countries'. *Journal of Environment and Development 10*, no. *3*: 225–245.

Whitaker, G. P. (1980). 'Coproduction: Citizen Participation in Service Delivery'. *Public Administration Review 40*, no. *3*: 240–246.

White, M. D. (2016). 'Overview of Behavioral Economics and Policy'. In S. Abdukadirov (ed.), *Nudge Theory in Action*. Cham, Germany: Springer International Publishing, 15–36.

Whiteman, D. (1985). 'The Fate of Policy Analysis in Congressional Decision Making: Three Types of Use in Committees'. *Western Political Quarterly 38*, no. *2*: 294–311.

Whiteman, D. (1995). *Communication in Congress: Members, Staff and the Search for Information*. Lawrence, KS: University Press of Kansas.

Whitmarsh, L. (2009). 'What's in a Name? Commonalities and Differences in Public Understanding of "Climate Change" and "Global Warming"'. *Public Understanding of Science 18*, no. *4*: 401–420.

Whitten, S. M. (2017). 'Designing and Implementing Conservation Tender Metrics: Twelve Core Considerations'. *Land Use Policy 63* (April): 561–571.

WHO. (2021). 'WHO National Health Accounts'. https://apps.who.int/nha/database/Select/Indicators/en

Whyte, G. and Levi, A. S. (1994). 'The Origins and Function of the Reference Point in Risky Group Decision Making the Case of the Cuban Missile Crisis'. *Journal of Behavioral Decision Making 7*, no. *4*: 243–260.

Wijen, F. and S. Ansari. (2007). 'Overcoming Inaction Through Collective Institutional Entrepreneurship: Insights from Regime Theory'. *Organization Studies 28*, no. 7 (1 July): 1079–1100.

Wildavsky, A. B. (1969). 'Rescuing Policy Analysis from PPBS'. *Public Administration Review* (March–April): 189–202.

Wildavsky, A. B. (1979). *Speaking Truth to Power: The Art and Craft of Policy Analysis*. Boston, MA: Little, Brown.

Wildavsky, A. B. (1988). *Searching for Safety*. New Brunswick, NJ: London: Transaction.

Wilder, M. (2017). 'Comparative Public Policy: Origins, Themes, New Directions'. *Policy Studies Journal 45*(S1), S47–S66.

Wilder, M. and M. Howlett. (2014). 'The Politics of Policy Anomalies: Bricolage and the Hermeneutics of Paradigms'. *Critical Policy Studies 8*, no. *2*: 183–202.

Wilder, Matt and Michael Howlett. (2015). 'Paradigm Construction and the Politics of Policy Anomalies'. In John Hogan and Michael Howlett (eds.), *Policy Paradigms in Theory and Practice*. New York: Palgrave Macmillan, 101–115.

Wilensky, H. L. (1975). *The Welfare State and Equality: Structural and Ideological Roots of Public Expenditures*. Berkeley, CA: University of California Press.

Wilensky, H. L. and L. Turner. (1987). *Democratic Corporatism and Policy Linkages: The Interdependence of Industrial, Labor-Market, Incomes, and Social Policies in Eight Countries*. Berkeley, CA: Institute of International Studies.

Wilkinson, T. M. (2013). 'Nudging and Manipulation'. *Political Studies 61*, no. 2: 341–355.

Wilks, S. and I. Battle. (2003). 'The Unanticipated Consequences of Creating Independent Competition Agencies'. In M. Thatcher and A. S. Sweet (eds.), *The Politics of Delegation*. London: Frank Cass, 148–172.

Williams, A. M. and V. Balaz. (1999). 'Privatisation in Central Europe: Different Legacies, Methods and Outcomes'. *Environment and Planning C: Government and Policy 17*: 731–751.

Williams, J. A. (2000). 'The Delegation Dilemma: Negotiated Rulemaking in Perspective'. *Policy Studies Review 17*, no. 1: 125–146.

Williams, M., E. B. Comartin and R. D. Lytle. (2020). 'The Politics of Symbolic Laws: State Resistance to the Allure of Sex Offender Residence Restrictions'. *Law & Policy 42*, no. 3: 209–235.

Williams, R. A. (2012). 'The Limits of Policy Analytical Capacity: Canadian Financial Regulatory Reform'. *International Journal of Public Sector Management 25*, no. 6/7: 455–463.

Williamson, O. E. (1975). *Markets and Hierarchies*. New York: Free Press.

Williamson, O. E. (1996a). *The Mechanisms of Governance*. Oxford: Oxford University Press.

Williamson, O. E. (1996b). 'Transaction Cost Economics and Organization Theory'. In O. E. Williamson (ed.), *The Mechanisms of Governance*. New York: Oxford University Press, 219–249.

Wilsford, D. (1994). 'Path Dependency, or Why History Makes It Difficult but Not Impossible to Reform Health Care Systems in a Big Way'. *Journal of Public Policy 14*, no. 3: 251–284.

Wilson, G. K. (2003). 'Changing Regulatory Systems'. Paper for the Annual Convention of the American Political Science Association, Philadelphia, August. www.lafollette.wisc.edu/facultystaff/wilson/ChangingRegulatorySystems.pdf.

Wilson, J. Q. (1974). 'The Politics of Regulation'. In J. W. McKie (ed.), *Social Responsibility and the Business Predicament*. Washington, DC: Brookings Institution, 135–168.

Wilson, V. S. (1971). 'The Role of Royal Commissions and Task Forces'. In G. B. Doern and P. Aucoin (eds.), *The Structures of Policy-Making in Canada*. Toronto, ON: Macmillan, 113–129.

Wilson, W. (1887). 'The Study of Administration'. *Political Science Quarterly 2*, no. 2: 197–222.

Wilts, H. and M. O'Brien. (2018). 'A Policy Mix for Resource Efficiency in the EU: Key Instruments, Challenges and Research Needs'. *Ecological Economics 33*, no. 4: 357–364.

Windholz, Eric. (2018). *Governing Through Regulation: Public Policy, Regulation and the Law*. New York: Taylor & Francis.

Winter, S. C. and P. J. May. (2001). 'Motivation for Compliance with Environmental Regulations'. *Journal of Policy Analysis and Management 20*, no. 4: 675–698.

Wintges, R. (2007). *Monitoring and Analysis of Policies and Public Financing Instruments Conducive to Higher Levels of R&D Investments: The 'Policy Mix' Project: Case Study: The Netherlands*. Maastricht, Netherlands: UNU-MERIT.

Wissel, S. and F. Watzold. (2010). 'A Conceptual Analysis of the Application of Tradable Permits to Biodiversity Conservation'. *Conservation Biology 24*, no. 2: 404–411.

Wolf Jr, C. (1979). 'A Theory of Nonmarket Failure: Framework for Implementation Analysis'. *Journal of Law and Economics 22*, no. 1: 107–139.

Wolf Jr, C. (1987). 'Markets and Non-Market Failures: Comparison and Assessment'. *Journal of Public Policy 7*: 43–70.

Wolf Jr, C. (1988). *Markets or Governments: Choosing Between Imperfect Alternatives*. Cambridge, MA: MIT Press.

Wollmann, H. (1989). 'Policy Analysis in West Germany's Federal Government: A Case of Unfinished Governmental and Administrative Modernization?' *Governance 2*, no. 3: 233–266.

Wolman, H. (1981). 'The Determinants of Program Success and Failure'. *Journal of Public Policy 1*, no. 4: 433–464.

Wolman, H. (1992). 'Understanding Cross National Policy Transfers'. *Governance 5*, no. 1: 27–45.

Wonka, A. and B. Rittberger. (2010). 'Credibility, Complexity and Uncertainty: Explaining the Institutional Independence of 29 EU – Agencies'. *West European Politics 33*, no. 4: 730.

Woo, J. J., M. Ramesh and M. Howlett. (2015). 'Legitimation Capacity: System-Level Resources and Political Skills in Public Policy'. *Policy and Society 34*, no. 3–4: 271–283.

Wood, B. D. and J. Bohte. (2004). 'Political Transaction Costs and the Politics of Administrative Design'. *Journal of Politics 66*, no. 1: 176–202.

Wood, D. and L. Hagerman. (2010). 'Mission Investing and the Philanthropic Toolbox'. *Policy and Society 29*, no. 3: 257–268.

Wood, R. S. (2006). 'The Dynamics of Incrementalism: Subsystems, Politics, and Public Lands'. *Policy Studies Journal 34*, no. 1: 1–16.

Woodley, A. (2008). 'Legitimating Public Policy'. *University of Toronto Law Journal 58*: 153–184.

Woodside, K. (1979). 'Tax Incentives vs. Subsidies: Political Considerations in Governmental Choice'. *Canadian Public Policy 5*, no. 2: 248–256.

Woodside, K. (1983). 'The Political Economy of Policy Instruments: Tax Expenditures and Subsidies in Canada'. In M. Atkinson and M. Chandler (eds.), *The Politics of Canadian Public Policy*. Toronto, ON: University of Toronto Press, 173–197.

Woodside, K. (1986). 'Policy Instruments and the Study of Public Policy'. *Canadian Journal of Political Science 19*, no. 4: 775–793.

Woolley, A. (2008). 'Legitimating Public Policy'. *University of Toronto Law Journal 58*: 153–184.

World Bank. (1994). *Averting the Old Age Crisis*. Washington, DC: World Bank Group.

World Bank. (2010). *World Development Report 2010: Development and Climate Change*. Washington, DC. https://openknowledge.worldbank.org/handle/10986/4387.

World Bank. (2011). 'The Contribution of Government Communication Capacity to Achieving Good Governance Outcomes'. In *Brief for Policymakers: Communication for Governance & Accountability Program*. Washington, DC: World Bank.

World Bank. (2015). *World Development Report 2015: Mind Society and Behaviour*. Washington, DC: World Bank. https://openknowledge.worldbank.org/handle/10986/20597.

World Bank. (2018). *World Development Indicators*. Washington DC: World Bank.

Wraith, R. E. and G. B. Lamb. (1971). *Public Inquiries as an Instrument of Government*. London: George Allen & Unwin.

Wu, I. (2008). 'Who Regulates Phones, Television and the Internet? What Makes a Communications Regulator Independent and Why It Matters'. *Perspectives on Politics 6*, no. 4: 769–783.

Wu, X. and M. Ramesh. (2014a). 'Market Imperfections, Government Imperfections, and Policy Mixes: Policy Innovations in Singapore'. *Policy Sciences*: 1–16.

Wu, X. and M. Ramesh. (2014b). 'Market Imperfections, Government Imperfections, and Policy Mixes: Policy Innovations in Singapore'. *Policy Sciences 47*, no. 3: 305–320.

Wu, X., M. Ramesh and M. Howlett. (2015a). 'Blending Skill and Resources Across Multiple Levels of Activity: Competences, Capabilities and the Policy Capacities of Government'. *Policy and Society 34*, no. 3–4: 271–283.

Wu, X., M. Ramesh and M. Howlett. (2015b). 'Policy Capacity: A Conceptual Framework for Understanding Policy Competences and Capabilities'. *Policy and Society* (Special Issue on The Dynamics of Policy Capacity) *34*, no. 3–4 (September): 165–171.

Wu, X., M. Ramesh, M. Howlett and S. Fritzen. (2010). *The Public Policy Primer: Managing Public Policy*. London: Routledge.

Wunder, B. (1995). 'Le Modele Napoleonien d'Administration: Apercu Comparatif'. In B. Wunder (ed.), *The Influences of the Napoleonic 'Model' of Administration on the Administrative Organization of Other Countries*. Brussels, Belgium: International Institute of Administrative Sciences.

Wyborn, C. (2015). 'Co-Productive Governance: A Relational Framework for Adaptive Governance'. *Global Environmental Change 30* (January): 56–67.

Xu, H. Daniel and Rashmita Basu. (2020). 'How the United States Flunked the COVID-19 Test: Some Observations and Several Lessons'. *The American Review of Public Administration 50*, no. 6–7 (August): 568–576.

Yackee, J. W. and S. W. Yackee. (2010). 'Administrative Procedures and Bureaucratic Performance: Is Federal Rule-Making "Ossified"?' *Journal of Public Administration Research and Theory 20*, no. 2 (1 April): 261–282.

Yee, A. S. (1996). 'The Causal Effects of Ideas on Policies'. *International Organization 50*, no. 1: 69–108.

Yeung, K. and M. Dixon-Woods. (2010). 'Design-Based Regulation and Patient Safety: A Regulatory Studies Perspective'. *Social Science & Medicine 71*, no. 3: 502–509.

Yi, H. and R. C. Feiock. (2012). 'Policy Tool Interactions and the Adoption of State Renewable Portfolio Standards'. *Review of Policy Research 29*, no. 2 (1 March): 193–206.

Yi, I. (2015). *New Challenges for and New Directions in Social Policy*. New York: United Nations Research Institute for Social Development (UNRISD).

Young, K., D. Ashby, A. Boaz and L. Grayson. (2002). 'Social Science and the Evidence-Based Policy Movement'. *Social Policy and Society 1*, no. 3: 215–224.

Young, L. and J. Everitt. (2004). *Advocacy Groups*. Vancouver, BC: University of British Columbia Press.

Young, S. (2007). 'The Regulation of Government Advertising in Australia: The Politicisation of a Public Policy Issue'. *Australian Journal of Public Administration 66*, no. 4: 438–452.

Young, T. R. (1991). 'Chaos and Social Change: Metaphysics of the Postmodern'. *The Social Science Journal 28*, no. *3*: 289–305.

Zahariadis, N. (2007). 'The Multiple Streams Framework: Structure, Limitations, Prospects'. In P. Sabatier (ed.), *Theories of the Policy Process* (2nd edn). Boulder, CO: Westview, 65–92.

Zarco-Jasso, H. (2005). 'Public – Private Partnerships: A Multidimensional Model for Contracting'. *International Journal of Public Policy 1*, no. *1/2*: 22–40.

Zaval, L. and J. F. M. Cornwell. (2016). 'Cognitive Biases, Non-Rational Judgments, and Public Perceptions of Climate Change'. In M. C. Weibet, M. Schafe, E. Markowitz, S. Ho, S. O'Neill and J. Thaker (eds.), *Oxford Research Encyclopaedia of Climate Science*. Oxford: Oxford University Press.

Zaval, L., E. A. Keenan, E. J. Johnson and E. U. Weber. (2014). 'How Warm Days Increase Belief in Global Warming'. *Nature Climate Change 4*, no. 2: 143–147.

Zeckhauser, R. (1981). 'Preferred Policies When There Is a Concern for Probability of Adoption'. *Journal of Environmental Economics and Management 8*: 215–237.

Zeckhauser, R. and E. Schaefer. (1968). 'Public Policy and Normative Economic Theory'. In R. A. Bauer and K. J. Gergen (eds.), *The Study of Policy Formation*. New York: Free Press, 27–102.

Zehavi, A. (2008). 'The Faith-Based Initiative in Comparative Perspective: Making Use of Religious Providers in Britain and the United States'. *Comparative Politics 40*, no. *3*: 331–351.

Zelli, F., I. Möller and H. van Asselt. (2017). 'Institutional Complexity and Private Authority in Global Climate Governance: The Cases of Climate Engineering, REDD+ and Short-Lived Climate Pollutants'. *Environmental Politics 26*, no. 4 (5 May): 669–693.

Zerbe, R. O. and H. E. McCurdy. (1999). 'The Failure of Market Failure'. *Journal of Policy Analysis and Management 18*, no. 4: 558–578.

Zhang, Y., R. Lee and K. Yang. (2012). 'Knowledge and Skills for Policy-Making: Stories from Local Public Managers in Florida'. *Journal of Public Affairs Education 18*, no. *1*: 183–208.

Zielonka, J. (2007). 'Plurilateral Governance in the Enlarged European Union'. *Journal of Common Market Studies 45*, no. *1*: 187–209.

Ziller, J. (2005). 'Public Law: A Tool for Modern Management, Not an Impediment to Reform'. *International Review of Administrative Sciences 71*, no. 2: 267–277.

Zito, A. R. (2001). 'Epistemic Communities, Collective Entrepreneurship and European Integration'. *Journal of European Public Policy 8*, no. 4: 585–603.

Zito, A. R., A. Jordan, R. Wurzel and L. Brueckner. (2003). 'Instrument Innovation in an Environmental Lead State: "New" Environmental Policy Instruments in the Netherlands'. *Environmental Politics 12*, no. *1*: 157–178.

Zittoun, P. (2009). 'Understanding Policy Change as a Discursive Problem'. *Journal of Comparative Policy Analysis 11*, no. *1*: 65–82.

Zuckerman, E. W. (2012). 'Construction, Concentration, and (Dis)Continuities in Social Valuations'. *Annual Review of Sociology 38*, no. *1* (11 August): 223–245.

Zysman, J. (1994). 'How Institutions Create Historically Rooted Trajectories of Growth'. *Industrial and Corporate Change 3*, no. *1*: 243–283.

Index

301–302, 305, 307–309, 315, 324, 325–326, 328–330; *see also* cost-benefit analysis; data analysis; evidence-informed analysis; interval analysis; institutional analysis; policy analysis; scenario analysis; social scientific analysis; statistical analysis
analysts 22, 40, 65, 67–68, 89, 107, 120, 131, 134–135, 139, 141–142, 149–150, 215, 286, 293, 325; *see also* actors
analytical capacity 90, 136, 322, 324; *see also* capacity
analytical competences 155, 293, 324
analytical units 200
anarchistic (non)design 70; *see also* garbage can decision-making
anthills 65
Artificial Intelligence (AI) 24, 78; *see also* information
auction 30
auditing 41, 83–84, 178, 213, 218–219, 229, 311, 315
authoritarianism 70
authoritative instrumentalism 68, 71–72, 74–75
authoritative tools 108, 209, 222–223, 231, 267; *see also* policy tools; Tools
authority 30, 59–60, 62, 99, 105, 107–108, 111, 121, 148, 169–170, 175–178, 190, 193, 200, 209–210, 213–214, 216–218, 220, 222–223, 225, 228–229, 231, 233, 262–263, 265, 283, 304, 311–312
authority-based tools 108, 209, 231, 265; *see also* policy tools; tools
auto-adaptation 298
automatic and less reflective motivations and cognitive strategies 107; *see also* strategy
automaticity 84, 192, 211, 224, 233, 243
automatic or semi-automatic adjustment 310
automobiles 261; *see also* infrastructure
avoidability 280–281

balance sheets 192–193, 280
bans 30, 63, 109, 256
bargaining 6, 11–12, 15, 54, 65, 71, 75, 88, 144, 179–180, 282; *see also* bargaining; intra- or intergovernmental bargaining; legislative bargaining; political bargaining
barriers 105–106, 119, 137, 215, 253, 291, 302, 313–314
bason 4, 23, 36, 38, 43, 69, 75, 300, 327, 329
behaviour 3, 6–7, 9–12, 13–14, 16, 28–29, 36–43, 48, 53, 56, 58, 60, 62–64, 68–70, 88, 95–110, 112–115, 121, 129, 134–135, 152, 161–162, 169, 172, 174–175, 177, 180–181, 189, 192, 198–200, 209–212, 214–215, 217–220, 225, 228, 231–232, 239, 241, 247–253, 254, 258–259, 269–270, 282, 286–292, 302–305, 307–308, 310–315, 326; *see also* policy behaviour; producer behaviour; public or consumer behaviour; satisficing behaviour
behavioural assumptions 175
behavioural change 97, 103, 105–106, 115, 292, 302; *see also* policy change
behavioural characteristics 36, 112
behavioural economics 37, 97, 100, 112, 251; *see also* economics
behavioural mechanisms 95; *see also* policy mechanisms
behavioural needs for resource effectiveness 108; *see also* effectiveness
behavioural psychology and economics 103; *see also* economics
behavioural responses 107, 112, 270
behavioural spillover 252
benefaction 168
best practices 21, 75, 126, 217, 273–274, 279, 302, 320; *see also* practice
big data 259; *see also* data; information
binding rules 209

INDEX